MANUAL OF PERIOPERATIVE CARE IN CARDIAC SURGERY

Third Edition

D1636447

MANUAL OF PERIOPERATIVE CARE IN CARDIAC SURGERY

Third Edition

by

Robert M. Bojar, M.D.
Associate Professor of Surgery
Tufts University School of Medicine
Senior Surgeon and Chief
Division of Cardiothoracic Surgery
New England Medical Center, Boston

with

Kenneth G. Warner, M.D.
Assistant Professor of Surgery
Tufts University School of Medicine
Assistant Surgeon
Division of Cardiothoracic Surgery
New England Medical Center, Boston

Blackwell
Publishing

© 1999 by Robert M. Bojar
 Blackwell Science
a Blackwell Publishing company

Blackwell Publishing, Inc., 350 Main Street, Malden, Massachusetts 02148-5018, USA
Blackwell Science Ltd, Osney Mead, Oxford OX2 0EL, UK
Blackwell Science Asia Pty Ltd, 550 Swanston Street, Carlton, Victoria 3053, Australia
Blackwell Verlag GmbH, Kurfürstendamm 57, 10707 Berlin, Germany

02 03 04 05 6

ISBN: 0-632-04365-2

Library of Congress Cataloging-in-Publication Data

Bojar, Robert M., 1951-
      Manual of perioperative care in cardiac surgery/ by Robert M. Bojar
  With Kenneth G. Warner. –3rd ed.
     p. cm.
  Rev. ed. of: Manual of perioperative care in cardiac and thoracic surgery/ by
  Robert M. Bojar, with contributions from Douglas J. Mathisen, Kenneth G.
  Warner. 2nd ed. c1994.
  Includes bibliographical references and index.
  ISBN 0-632-04365-2 (alk. Paper)
 1. Heart--Surgery--Handbooks, manuals, etc. 2. Therapeutics, Surgical--
Handbooks, manuals, etc. I. Warner, Kenneth G. II. Bojar, Robert M., 1951--
Manual of perioperative care in cardiac and thoracic surgery. III Title.
RD598.B64   1998
617.4'12--ddc21
                       98-33471
                        CIP

A catalogue record for this title is available from the British Library

Typesetter: Best-Set Typesetter Ltd. in Hong Kong
Printed and bound by Edwards Brothers, Inc. in North Carolina, USA.

For further information on Blackwell Publishing, visit our website:
www.blackwellscience.com

Table of Contents

Preface

As we approach the new millennium, cardiac surgeons are faced with ever increasing challenges. Some arise from the changing patient profile of surgical patients, as older and sicker patients with more advanced disease are undergoing surgical procedures. Others are derived from the extrinsic forces that have influenced the manner in which pre- and postoperative care are delivered, primarily by mandating a reduction in the cost of delivering care and decreasing the duration of hospital stay. Furthermore, the advent of minimally invasive surgery has altered patient selection and the intensity of postoperative care. All of these factors challenge the judgment and ingenuity of the practicing cardiac surgeon and those involved in providing care to the cardiac surgical patient.

Once the decision to proceed with surgery has been made, everyone participating in a patient's care assumes the responsibility of ensuring an optimal surgical outcome. This results not only from a complete and expeditious operation, but, almost as importantly, from astute perioperative care. Assessment of preoperative problems that can impact recovery, knowledge of the pathophysiology of the organ systems affected by surgery, and prevention or identification of postoperative complications at an early stage are critical to ensuring the best possible result.

Although the general principles of postoperative care have not changed significantly during the past 10 years, there has been a trend toward "fast-tracking," with implementation of critical pathways and modification of anesthetic and ICU protocols to accomplish early extubation. There has also been a refocusing on "leveling of the playing field" by adjusting mortality rates by severity of illness. Thus, a new chapter to discuss means of risk assessment seemed timely.

As stated in the preface to the first edition, this manual has been written to assist individuals on the firing line, those who "must have the practical knowledge, judgment, and flexibility to incorporate newer concepts, use new and better medications, experiment when one treatment modality has failed, and make critical decisions in extremely ill patients—often without all the facts." I am gratified that both the first and second editions of this postoperative manual have been so well received by those for whom it is intended: physician assistants, junior and senior members of the house staff, cardiac surgeons-in-training, junior practicing cardiothoracic surgeons, cardiologists, as well as critical care nurses and medical students.

Although I have retained the outline format to provide instant access to important information, it appeared that the book was becoming unwieldy in terms of its size. Therefore, the management of the patient with noncardiac thoracic disease has been eliminated, hence the change in the manual's title.

I hope that the third edition will provide a timely update on perioperative care and will continue to prove of great value to those individuals involved in the care of adult and pediatric cardiac surgical patients. My major intent remains to provide a manual that will enable its readers to deliver the best possible care to their patients.

Robert M. Bojar, M.D.

Acknowledgments

Achievement of excellence in patient management evolves from a healthy interaction among professional colleagues, residents, physician assistants, and nurses. I would like to acknowledge the assistance of Drs. Kamal Khabbaz, Mark Link, William Panza, and Ajay Singh, who set aside valuable time to review material in their areas of expertise. I am also grateful to Richard E. Murphy, PAC, for his contributions on postoperative pediatric care in the first edition of this manual (much of which has been retained) and to Philip Carpino, PAC, who reviewed sections of the manuscript to corroborate that what is written is what we do. I would particularly like to thank Dr. Maureen Strafford for her critical review of the second edition of the pediatric cardiac section, much of which has been retained.

I am grateful to the Educational Media Center of New England Medical Center for their excellent assistance with illustrations. I am indebted to the staff of Blackwell Science with whom I have worked on four book projects during the past 10 years for their ongoing support of this book.

Special gratitude is extended to the nurses of the adult Cardiothoracic Unit and pediatric ICU of New England Medical Center who personally deliver the excellent care upon which this book is based.

Notice

The indications and dosage of all drugs in this book have been recommended in the medical literature and conform to the practices of the general medical community. The medications described do not necessarily have specific approval by the Food and Drug Administration for use in the diseases and dosages for which they are recommended. The package insert for each drug should be consulted for use and dosage as approved by the FDA. Because standards of usage change, it is advisable to keep abreast of revised recommendations, particularly those concerning new drugs.

Part I
Adult Cardiac Surgery

1 Synopsis of Adult Cardiac Surgical Disease

Coronary Artery Disease

Left Ventricular Aneurysm

Ventricular Septal Defect

Aortic Stenosis

Aortic Regurgitation

Mitral Stenosis

Mitral Regurgitation

Tricuspid Valve Disease

Endocarditis

Hypertrophic Cardiomyopathy

Aortic Dissections

Thoracic Aortic Aneurysms

Ventricular Arrhythmias

Partial Left Ventriculectomy (Batista Procedure)

Pericardial Disease

1 Synopsis of Adult Cardiac Surgical Disease

An understanding of the nature of cardiac disease and of surgical decision-making is invaluable when preparing a patient for surgery and analyzing complex postoperative problems. This chapter presents the spectrum of adult cardiac surgical disease that is encountered in most cardiac surgical practices and includes the pathophysiology, indications for surgery, specific preoperative and prebypass anesthetic considerations, and surgical techniques for various diseases. Additional preoperative considerations involving noncardiac issues for all patients undergoing cardiac surgery are presented in Chapter 3. Postoperative concerns specific to each type of surgical procedure are discussed in Chapter 7.

I. Coronary Artery Disease

A. **Pathophysiology.** Coronary artery disease (CAD) results from progressive blockage of the coronary arteries by atherosclerosis. Clinical syndromes result from an imbalance of oxygen supply and demand resulting in inadequate myocardial perfusion to meet metabolic demand (ischemia). Plaque hemorrhage and rupture and superimposed thrombosis are responsible for most ischemic syndromes.

B. **Indications for surgery**[1]

1. Symptomatic coronary disease is initially treated pharmacologically with nitrates, β-adrenergic blockers, and/or calcium-channel blockers. An assessment of the patient's clinical presentation, coronary anatomy, degree of inducible ischemia on stress testing, and status of ventricular function is used to determine whether the patient is an appropriate candidate for surgery.

2. The primary objective of surgery is the relief of ischemia. Therefore, surgery is indicated for any patient with the appropriate coronary anatomy for bypass in whom refractory angina is present or in whom the degree of ischemia, symptomatic or not, threatens to lead to myocardial infarction.

   a. Class III–IV chronic stable angina refractory to medical therapy (table 1.1)

   b. Unstable angina refractory to medical therapy

   c. Acute ischemia or hemodynamic instability following attempted percutaneous transluminal coronary angioplasty (PTCA) or stenting

   d. Acute evolving infarction within 4 to 6 hours of the onset of chest pain or later if evidence of ongoing ischemia (early postinfarction ischemia)

   e. Markedly positive stress test prior to major intraabdominal or vascular surgery

   f. Ischemic pulmonary edema, a common angina equivalent in elderly women

3. A second group of patients includes those without disabling angina or refractory ischemia in whom the extent of coronary disease, the

Table 1.1 *New York Heart Association Functional Classification*

Class

I   No limitation of physical activity.

II Slight limitation of physical activity. Ordinary activity results in fatigue, palpitation, dyspnea, or anginal pain.

III Marked limitation of physical activity. Less than ordinary activity causes fatigue, palpitation, dyspnea, or anginal pain.

IV Inability to carry out any physical activity without discomfort. Symptoms may be present even at rest.

status of ventricular function, and the degree of inducible ischemia on stress testing are such that surgery may improve long-term survival. This is presumed to occur by preventing infarction and preserving ventricular function. Surgery is especially beneficial for patients with markedly impaired ventricular function and inducible ischemia, in whom the medical prognosis is unfavorable.

    a. Left main stenosis >50%

    b. Three-vessel disease with ejection fraction <50%

    c. Three-vessel disease with ejection fraction >50% and significant inducible ischemia

    d. One- and two-vessel disease with extensive myocardium in jeopardy but lesions not amenable to PTCA

4. A third group of patients should undergo bypass surgery when other open-heart procedures are indicated:

    a. Valvular operations, septal myectomy, and so on, with associated CAD

    b. Concomitant surgery for postinfarction mechanical defects (left ventricular aneurysm, ventricular septal rupture, acute mitral regurgitation)

    c. Coronary artery anomalies with risk of sudden death (vessel passing between the aorta and pulmonary artery)

5. When the indications for an intervention are present, selection of the appropriate procedure depends on the extent and nature of the coronary disease.

    a. Percutaneous transluminal coronary angioplasty is best applied to single-vessel and uncomplicated multivessel disease. Studies comparing PTCA and coronary artery bypass graft (CABG) surgery for patients with multivessel disease have shown comparable end points (angina, infarction rate, survival, costs) at 5 years, although patients undergoing PTCA commonly require additional interventions.[2]

    b. Coronary stents may improve the long-term results when used to supplement PTCA by producing a larger luminal diameter.[3] The most common indications for stents are ostial lesions, large native vessels, threatened closure after PTCA, and stenotic bypass grafts. Acute closure is minimized by the use of aspirin with ticlopidine or clopidogrel.[4,5]

   c. Minimally invasive direct coronary artery bypass (MIDCAB) is usually performed through a short left and/or right anterior thoracotomy incision (see below under surgical procedures).[6] The indications for standard MIDCAB include the following:

      i. Isolated left anterior descending (LAD) and/or right coronary artery (RCA) disease

      ii. LAD disease with occluded circumflex (Cx) or RCA that is well collateralized

      iii. Critical stenosis in the LAD with moderate disease in other vessels that can be approached by PTCA

      iv. Critical stenosis in the LAD in a very high risk patient in whom the other vessels are not critically narrowed

      v. Redo grafting to the LAD

   d. Standard coronary bypass grafting performed through a median sternotomy using cardiopulmonary bypass is preferred for most patients who require multivessel bypass. It is occasionally possible to bypass several arteries through this incision without using cardiopulmonary bypass. Other "minimally invasive" procedures can be considered in patients with multivessel disease (see below).

C. Preoperative considerations

   1. Preoperative autologous blood donation is feasible in patients with chronic stable angina to reduce the requirement for homologous transfusion. It should be avoided in patients with unstable ischemic syndromes and left main coronary disease. With the use of antifibrinolytic drugs in the operating room, more than 50% of patients undergoing CABG do not receive any blood products. Therefore, there is little benefit to autologous blood donation in the healthy, elective patient.

   2. All antianginal medications should be continued up to and including the morning of surgery. Patients being admitted the morning of surgery should be reminded to take their medication before coming to the hospital. Aggressive management of ischemia is indicated in unstable patients to reduce the risk of surgery. This may include adequate sedation, additional or higher doses of anti-ischemic medications (IV nitrates and β-blockers), and/or placement of an intraaortic balloon pump (IABP).

   3. Intravenous heparin is often used in patients with unstable angina, left main coronary disease, or a preoperative IABP. The heparin should generally be continued up to the time of surgery to avoid the potential problem of precipitating ischemia in the prebypass period when the anticoagulant effect of heparin dissipates. Central lines can usually be placed safely while the patient is heparinized. Patients receiving heparin should have their platelet count rechecked daily to detect the development of heparin-induced thrombocytopenia, particularly within 24 hours of surgery.

4. Preoperative blood transfusions should be considered in patients with unstable angina and a hematocrit <26%. This may not only improve the ischemic syndrome but will minimize hemodilution during surgery. Patients with profound anemia commonly require several units of blood during surgery and frequently require blood component therapy (fresh frozen plasma, platelets) to achieve hemostasis.

5. Aspirin should be stopped 1 week before surgery in elective patients and as soon as possible in patients requiring urgent surgery. Aspirin usage has been associated with increased intraoperative bleeding in some, but not all, studies. Bleeding times are of little value because they are usually not altered by the use of aspirin; furthermore, little correlation has been shown between elevated bleeding times and the degree of intraoperative bleeding. Nonetheless, there are a few patients with the so-called "intermediate syndrome of platelet dysfunction" in whom the bleeding time is significantly elevated by aspirin before surgery, and these patients do seem more susceptible to intraoperative bleeding. If a bleeding time has been obtained and is well over 10 minutes, surgery should probably be deferred, if possible, for several days.

D. **Anesthetic considerations**

1. Factors that increase myocardial oxygen demand, such as tachycardia and hypertension, must be prevented in the prebypass period, especially during the induction of anesthesia. Hypotension—often resulting from the use of narcotics and anxiolytics, such as midazolam or propofol—should be counteracted with fluids and α-agents, because hypotension is even more likely than hypertension to produce ischemia.

2. Detection and treatment of ischemia is critical in the prebypass period. Transesophageal echocardiography is the most sensitive means of detecting ischemic regional wall motion abnormalities but is usually not used in routine cases. Ischemia may also be manifested by an elevation in the pulmonary capillary wedge pressure (PCWP), indicating diastolic dysfunction, and by ST segment elevation in the ECG tracing. Aggressive management with nitroglycerin, β-blockers (esmolol), and narcotics can usually control prebypass ischemia.

3. Narcotic/sedative regimens are popular for coronary surgery, especially in patients with left ventricular dysfunction. Use of low-dose fentanyl or shorter-acting narcotics, such as sufentanil or alfentanil, along with judicious use of midazolam and propofol may allow for earlier postoperative extubation. Use of inhalational anesthetics reduces the total dosage of medications required during surgery and also contributes to earlier awakening from surgery.

4. Anesthetic techniques for minimally invasive procedures continue to evolve. Uni-Vent or double-lumen tubes are commonly used to decompress the left lung to improve visualization during mammary artery harvest. A pacing Swan-Ganz catheter is helpful in the event that severe bradycardia or heart block occurs during pharmaco-

logic slowing of the heart. The latter may be accomplished with esmolol, diltiazem or verapamil, or neostigmine. Some centers use repeated boluses of adenosine to produce transient cardiac standstill. R2 pads should be placed for potential external defibrillation.

E. **Surgical procedures**

1. Standard coronary bypass surgery is performed during cardiopulmonary bypass (CPB). Myocardial preservation is usually provided by cardioplegic arrest, although some surgeons use alternative techniques such as intermittent ischemic arrest and hypothermic fibrillatory arrest. The procedure involves bypassing the coronary blockages with a variety of conduits. The left internal mammary (or thoracic) artery (IMA) is usually used as a pedicled graft to the left anterior descending artery and is supplemented by saphenous vein grafts interposed between the aorta and the coronary arteries (figure 1.1). Since improved event-free survival has been documented with use of arterial conduits, expanded use of the IMA (bilateral IMAs and sequential grafts) and use of the radial artery have become commonplace.[7] Intravenous diltiazem is given during surgery at a rate of 0.1 mg/kg/hour (usually 5–10 mg/h) to minimize spasm in radial artery conduits.

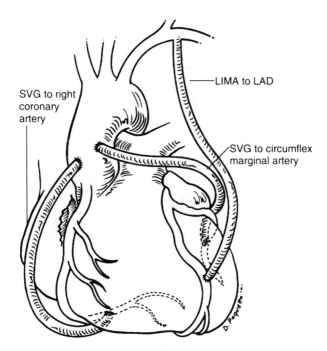

Figure 1.1 *Coronary artery bypass grafting. The internal mammary artery has been placed to the left anterior descending artery. Aortocoronary saphenous vein grafts have been sewn to the right and circumflex marginal arteries.*

2. Minimally invasive bypass surgery can be performed in a variety of ways.

    a. The least invasive technique is termed a "minimally invasive direct coronary artery bypass" or MIDCAB. It is performed through a short left anterior thoracotomy with anastomosis of the left internal mammary artery (LIMA) to the left anterior descending artery (figure 1.2). Grafting of the RCA with the RIMA can be accomplished through a right thoracotomy incision.

    b. Single or multivessel bypasses performed through a median sternotomy incision may be termed minimally invasive by virtue of avoidance of CPB.

    c. The Heartport™ system involves CPB established through the femoral vessels with intraluminal balloon occlusion of the aorta and administration of cardioplegia. Single or multivessel bypasses are then performed through a small left thoracotomy incision. This is minimally invasive by virtue of the smaller incision, but not the avoidance of cardiopulmonary bypass.[6]

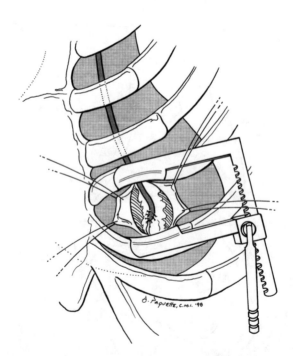

Figure 1.2 *MIDCAB procedure. A left anterior thoracotomy incision is made in the 4th intercostal space. The internal mammary artery, located at the medial aspect of the incision, is mobilized to the first intercostal space. The pericardium is opened and the IMA is sewn to the left anterior descending artery on a beating heart. Stabilization devices improve the precision of the anastomosis.*

II. Left Ventricular Aneurysm

A. Pathophysiology

1. A left ventricular aneurysm (LVA) results from the occlusion of a major coronary artery that produces an extensive transmural infarction. The damaged myocardium is converted to thin scar tissue which exhibits dyskinesia during ventricular systole.[8]

2. The two most common presentations are ischemic syndromes and congestive heart failure (CHF). Angina results from the presence of multivessel disease associated with the increased systolic wall stress of a dilated ventricle. CHF results from poor ventricular function and the reduction of stroke volume caused by the dyskinetic segment of the left ventricle.

3. Systemic thromboembolism may result from thrombus formation within the dyskinetic segment.

4. Malignant ventricular arrhythmias or sudden death may result from the development of a macroreentry circuit at the border zone between scar tissue and viable myocardium.

B. Indications for surgery.
Surgery is usually not indicated for the patient with an asymptomatic aneurysm because of its favorable natural history. This is in contrast to the unpredictable prognosis and absolute indication for surgery in a patient with a false aneurysm, caused by a contained rupture of the ventricular muscle. Surgery may be beneficial in the asymptomatic patient with an extremely large aneurysm or when extensive clot formation is present within the aneurysm. Surgery is most commonly indicated to improve symptoms and prolong survival when one of the four clinical syndromes noted above is present: 1) angina, 2) congestive heart failure, 3) systemic thromboembolism, or 4) malignant arrhythmias. In the past, the latter was treated by a map-guided endocardial resection, but the expensive equipment for intraoperative mapping is no longer manufactured. Therefore, it is treated by a nonguided endocardial resection through the aneurysm with/without cryosurgery along with subsequent placement of a transvenous implantable cardioverter-defibrillator (ICD) (see Chapter 1, Section XIII).

C. Preoperative considerations

1. Patients should be maintained on heparin if left ventricular thrombus is present.

2. If equipment is available for intraoperative mapping, a preoperative electrophysiologic study should also be performed. Antiarrhythmic medications should be stopped several days before surgery if an endocardial resection is planned. This will improve the accuracy of intraoperative mapping and allow for a more precise assessment of the success of the procedure in ablating the arrhythmogenic focus.

3. A biplane left ventriculogram is the gold standard for differentiating aneurysms from areas of akinesis and for evaluating the function of the nonaneurysmal ventricle.

D. **Anesthetic considerations**

1. Avoidance of myocardial depression is important because of the association of LVAs with significant left ventricular dysfunction. Swan-Ganz monitoring is helpful in optimizing preload and contractility before and after bypass.

2. A transesophageal echocardiogram is the most sensitive means of detecting the presence of LV thrombus.

E. **Surgical procedures**[9]

1. Standard aneurysmectomy entails a ventriculotomy through the

Figure 1.3 *Endoaneurysmorrhaphy technique for repair of a left ventricular aneurysm. (A) The aneurysm is opened. (B,C) A Dacron or pericardial patch is sewn to the edges of endocardial scar. (D) The aneurysm wall is closed over the repair primarily or over felt strips. (Reproduced with permission from Cooley DA. Ventricular endoaneurysmorrhaphy. Results of an improved method of repair. Texas Heart Inst J 1989;16:72–5.)*

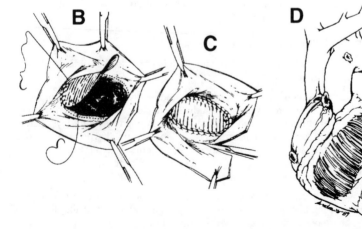

aneurysm, resection of the aneurysm wall, and linear closure over felt strips.

2. The "endoaneurysmorrhaphy" technique is used for large aneurysms. A pericardial or Dacron patch is sewn to the edges of viable myocardium at the base of the aneurysm and the aneurysm wall is reapproximated over the patch (figure 1.3). This preserves left ventricular geometry and improves ventricular function to a greater degree than the linear closure method. Other fairly comparable methods of repair that involve tailoring of the residual muscle before patch closure are the Jatene operation and the endoventricular circular patch plasty technique of Dor.[9]

3. Coronary bypass grafting of critically diseased vessels should be performed. Bypass of the LAD and diagonal arteries should be considered if septal reperfusion can be accomplished.

III. Ventricular Septal Defect

A. **Pathophysiology.** Extensive myocardial damage subsequent to occlusion of a major coronary vessel may result in septal necrosis and rupture. This usually occurs within the first week of an infarction, more commonly in the anteroapical region (from occlusion of the left anterior descending artery) and less commonly in the inferior wall (usually from occlusion of the right coronary artery). The presence of a ventricular septal defect (VSD) is suggested by the presence of a loud holosystolic murmur that reflects the left-to-right shunting across the ruptured septum. The patient usually develops acute pulmonary edema and cardiogenic shock from the left-to-right shunt.

B. **Indications for surgery.** Surgery is indicated on an emergency basis for nearly all postinfarction VSDs to prevent the development of progressive multisystem organ failure. Occasionally, a small VSD with a shunt of <2:1 can be managed medically, but it usually should be repaired after 6 weeks to prevent future hemodynamic problems.

C. **Preoperative considerations**

1. Prompt diagnosis can be made using a Swan-Ganz catheter, which detects a step-up of oxygen saturation in the right ventricle. Two-dimensional echocardiography can confirm the diagnosis of a VSD and differentiate it from acute mitral regurgitation, which can produce a similar clinical scenario.

2. Inotropic support and reduction of afterload, usually with an IABP, are indicated in all patients with compromised ventricular function in anticipation of urgent cardiac catheterization and surgery.

3. Cardiac catheterization with coronary angiography should be performed to confirm the severity of the shunt and to identify associated coronary artery disease. Bypass grafting of associated CAD improves long-term survival after surgery.[10]

D. **Anesthetic considerations.** Narcotic-based anesthesia is used to avoid myocardial depression. Systemic hypertension may increase the shunt and should be prevented.

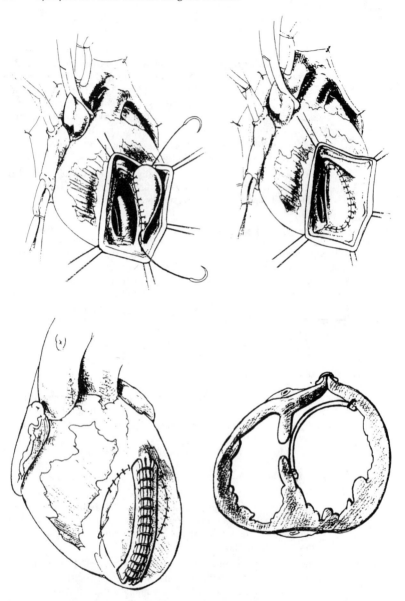

Figure 1.4 *Repair of an anterior VSD using the infarct exclusion technique. An incision is made through the infarct zone and the septal defect is visualized. A 4–6 cm pericardial patch is sewn to the lower part of the noninfarcted septal endocardium and then to the noninfarcted portion of the anterolateral wall. The ventriculotomy is then closed over felt strips. (Reproduced with permission from David TE, Dale L, Sun Z. Postinfarction ventricular septal rupture: repair by endocardial patch with infarct exclusion. J Thorac Cardiovasc Surg 1995;110:1315–22.)*

E. **Surgical procedures**

   1. The traditional surgical treatment has been the performance of a ventriculotomy through the infarcted zone, resection of the area of septal necrosis, and Teflon felt or pericardial patching of the septum and free wall. This technique requires transmural suturing and is prone to recurrence.[11]

   2. Circumferential pericardial patching around the border of the infarcted ventricular muscle that excludes the infarcted septum can eliminate the shunt and reduce recurrence rates because suturing is performed to viable myocardium away from the area of necrosis (figure 1.4).[12]

   3. Coronary bypass grafting of critically diseased vessels should be performed.[10]

IV. Aortic Stenosis

A. **Pathophysiology.** Aortic stenosis (AS) results from thickening, calcification, and/or fusion of the aortic valve leaflets, which produce an obstruction to left ventricular emptying. This leads to pressure overload, compensatory left ventricular hypertrophy, and reduced ventricular compliance. Cardiac output is relatively fixed across the valve orifice and can lead to syncope. Angina may result from subendocardial ischemia, even in the absence of coronary artery disease. Symptoms of CHF result from elevation of filling pressures due to diastolic dysfunction and eventually by progressive decline in left ventricular systolic function. The degree of valve stenosis is determined by measuring the cardiac output and the peak or mean pressure gradient across the valve (pressures obtained from the left ventricle and aorta). A valve area is calculated from the ratio of the cardiac output to the square root of the valve gradient.

$$AVA = \frac{CO/(SEP \times HR)}{44.5\sqrt{\text{mean gradient}}}$$

where:

SEP = systolic ejection period/beat
CO = cardiac output in mL/min
HR = heart rate
AVA = aortic valve area in cm^2 (normal = 2.5–3.5 cm^2)

The severity of AS can be readily diagnosed by either cardiac catheterization or echocardiography (if the valve cannot be crossed by the catheter).[13]

B. **Indications for surgery.** Surgery is generally not indicated in the asymptomatic patient, no matter how severe the degree of stenosis. However, the majority of patients with critical AS (aortic valve area <0.75 cm^2) will become symptomatic in a short period of time and are at an increased risk of sudden death.[14] The Doppler flow velocity and its rate of increase during serial studies can predict the rate of hemodynamic progression of the AS and the clinical outcome.[15] The indications for surgery are the presence of angina, congestive heart failure, syncope, or resuscitation from an episode of sudden death. Symptoms are usually associated with an AVA <0.8 cm^2 and a transvalvular peak gradient >50 mm Hg.

C. **Preoperative considerations**

1. Coronary angiography should be performed in any patient over the age of 40 years or a younger patient with angina or a positive stress test.

2. Ischemic syndromes in patients with AS require judicious management. Medications that can reduce preload (nitroglycerin), afterload (calcium-channel blockers), or heart rate (β-blockers) should be avoided because they may lower cardiac output and precipitate cardiac arrest in patients with critical AS. The ventricular response to atrial fibrillation must be controlled, and cardioversion should be performed if this rhythm is poorly tolerated.

3. Dental work should be performed before surgery to minimize the risk of prosthetic valve endocarditis unless it is felt to be a prohibitive risk.

4. Selection of the appropriate procedure (Ross procedure, homograft, bioprosthetic or mechanical valve replacement) depends on a number of factors, including the patient's age, contraindications to long-term anticoagulation, and the patient's desire to avoid anticoagulation.

D. **Anesthetic considerations.** The induction of anesthesia is a critical period for patients with AS. Narcotic-based anesthesia is used to minimize hemodynamic alterations such as myocardial depression, vasodilation, tachycardia, or dysrhythmias, all of which can lower cardiac output precipitously. Alpha agents, such as phenylephrine or norepinephrine, are particularly valuable in supporting systemic resistance.

E. **Surgical procedures**

1. Traditionally, aortic valve procedures have been performed through a full median sternotomy incision. Minimally invasive incisions have become more routine, most commonly using an upper sternotomy with a "J" or "T" incision into the third or fourth intercostal space. Cannulation for CPB can be performed either through the incision or through the femoral vessels.

2. Reparative procedures, such as commissurotomy or débridement have little role in the management of critical aortic stenosis. However, débridement is valuable in the patient with moderate AS in whom the valve disease is not severe enough to warrant valve replacement, but in whom decalcification may delay surgery for a number of years.

3. The standard treatment is aortic valve replacement with either a tissue (stented or stentless) or mechanical valve (figure 1.5). Homografts should be considered in younger patients, especially when anticoagulation is contraindicated (potential for pregnancy) or not desired, or when endocarditis is present. The Ross procedure, in which the patient's own pulmonary valve is used to replace the aortic root (with the pulmonary valve replaced with a homograft), is also a valuable but more complicated procedure generally reserved for younger patients (< age 50).[16]

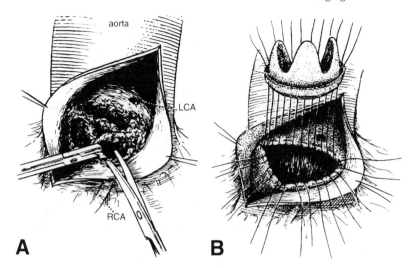

Figure 1.5 *Aortic valve replacement. (A) An aortotomy incision has been made, the valve is removed with scissors, and the annulus is débrided. (B) Horizontal mattress sutures (often with pledgets) are placed through the annulus and the sewing ring of the valve. The valve is seated, the sutures tied, and the aortotomy incision is closed. (Reproduced with permission from Cohn LH, Aortic valve replacement. In: Cohn LH, ed. Modern technics in surgery: cardiac/thoracic surgery. Mt. Kisco, NY: Futura Publishing, 1979:8-1–8-7.)*

V.   Aortic Regurgitation

A. **Pathophysiology.** Aortic regurgitation (AR) results from abnormalities in the aortic valve leaflets (postinflammatory deformity, destruction from endo-carditis, cusp prolapse from aortic dissection) or from aortic root dilata-tion. Chronic AR produces pressure and volume overload of the left ventricle, resulting in progressive left ventricular dilatation and symptoms of left-sided failure. Angina may occur on occasion. Acute AR from endo-carditis or a type A dissection produces acute left ventricular failure and pulmonary edema because the ventricle is unable to dilate acutely to handle the volume overload.

B. **Indications for surgery**

1. Acute congestive heart failure

2. Endocarditis with hemodynamic compromise, persistent bac-teremia or sepsis, conduction abnormalities, recurrent systemic embolization from vegetations, annular abscess formation, or new conduction abnormalities

3. Symptoms of congestive heart failure or angina. Surgery is usually reserved for the patient with class III–IV symptoms. However, ven-tricular decompensation may occur during the asymptomatic

phase, following which operation will not normalize ventricular function. Thus, surgery should often be considered for patients with severe AR and class II symptoms.[17,18]

4. Evidence of left ventricular decompensation in the asymptomatic patient:

   a. Ejection fraction <55%

   b. End-diastolic dimension approaching 70 mm by echo-cardiography

   c. End-systolic dimension approaching 55 mm by echo-cardiography

C. **Preoperative considerations**

1. Systemic hypertension should be controlled with vasodilators to reduce the degree of regurgitation. However, excessive afterload reduction may reduce diastolic coronary perfusion pressure and exacerbate ischemia.

2. β-blockers for control of ischemia should be avoided because a slow heart rate increases the amount of regurgitation.

3. Placement of an intraaortic balloon for control of anginal symptoms is contraindicated.

4. As for all valve patients, dental work should be completed before surgery.

5. Contraindications to warfarin should be identified so that the appropriate valve can be chosen.

D. **Anesthetic considerations.** The hemodynamic goals in the prebypass period are to maintain satisfactory preload and avoid bradycardia and hypertension. Narcotic-based anesthesia is generally selected, especially when there is evidence of compromised ventricular function. Vasodilatation may be beneficial, but myocardial depression must be avoided.

E. **Surgical procedures**

1. Aortic valve replacement has traditionally been the procedure of choice for adults with aortic regurgitation. This may involve use of a tissue or mechanical valve, or a cryopreserved homograft. The Ross procedure, as noted above, should be considered in younger patients.

2. Aortic valve repair, involving resection of portions of the valve leaflets and reapproximation to improve leaflet coaptation (especially for bicuspid valves), often with a suture annuloplasty, has been used successfully. This is valuable in the younger patient in whom a valve-sparing procedure is preferable to valve replacement.[19]

3. A valved conduit (Bentall procedure) is placed if an ascending aortic aneurysm (annuloaortic ectasia) is also present (figure 1.6).

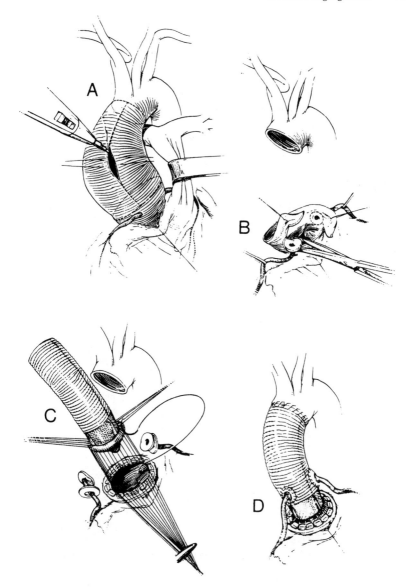

Figure 1.6   *Bentall procedure. (A) The aorta is opened longitudinally and then divided proximally and distally. (B) Coronary ostial buttons are mobilized. (C) A valved conduit is sewn to the aortic annulus proximally. (D) The coronary ostial buttons have been sewn to the graft and the distal anastomosis is completed. (Reproduced with permission from Svensson FG, Crawford ES. Aortic dissection and aortic aneurysm surgery: clinical observations, experimental investigations, and statistical analyses. Part III. Curr Probl Surg 1993;30:75.)*

VI.   Mitral Stenosis

A. **Pathophysiology.** Mitral stenosis (MS) occurs nearly exclusively as a consequence of rheumatic fever. Thickening of the valve leaflets with commissural fusion, and thickening and shortening of the chordae tendineae gradually reduce the size of the mitral valve orifice and the efficiency of left ventricular filling. These changes decrease the forward output and increase the left atrial and pulmonary venous pressures, leading to congestive heart failure. The development of atrial fibrillation may further decrease ventricular filling and precipitate symptoms of CHF. The development of pulmonary hypertension may eventually lead to right-sided heart failure and functional tricuspid regurgitation (TR). The severity of MS is determined by measuring a transvalvular gradient (pulmonary capillary wedge pressure minus the mean left ventricular diastolic pressure) and calculating a mitral valve area (MVA) which relates the cardiac output to the gradient.

$$MVA = \frac{CO/(DFP \times HR)}{37.7\sqrt{mean\ gradient}}$$

where

DFP = diastolic filling period/beat
Mean gradient = PCWP minus the left ventricular mean diastolic pressure
MVA = mitral valve area in cm^2 (normal = 4–6 cm^2)

B. **Indications for surgery**

1. An interventional procedure is indicated for:

   a. New York Heart Association (NYHA) classes III–IV

   b. NYHA class II when critical mitral stenosis (MVA < 1 cm^2) is present

   c. History of systemic thromboembolism from a left atrial thrombus

2. Percutaneous balloon mitral valvuloplasty (PBMV) is the procedure of choice.[13,20] An echocardiographic assessment (echo score) is performed to assess the degree of valve thickness, leaflet motion, commissural calcification, or subvalvular fusion. The echo score, in addition to other factors, such as the presence of atrial clot, atrial fibrillation, and mitral regurgitation, can determine whether this is an appropriate procedure.

3. Surgery is indicated when PBMV is contraindicated or not feasible.

C. **Preoperative considerations**

1. Many patients with long-standing MS are cachectic and at increased risk of respiratory failure. Aggressive preoperative diuresis and nutritional supplementation may reduce morbidity in the early postoperative period.

2. Warfarin may be used for atrial fibrillation or the presence of left atrial thrombus. It should be stopped 4 days before surgery and the patient placed on heparin until the morning of surgery if the INR is subtherapeutic.

3. Digoxin should be used as necessary to control the ventricular response to atrial fibrillation. It is usually given the morning of surgery.

D. **Anesthetic considerations.** Narcotic-based anesthesia is recommended to maintain hemodynamic stability. Attention should be paid to maintaining preload, reducing heart rate, and preventing an increase in pulmonary vascular resistance (PVR).

1. Preload must be adjusted judiciously to ensure adequate left ventricular filling across the stenotic valve, while simultaneously avoiding excessive fluid administration that could lead to pulmonary edema. A volumetric Swan-Ganz catheter is valuable in the assessment of right ventricular volumes and ejection fractions (RVEF). The pulmonary artery diastolic pressure may overestimate the left atrial pressure and may require placement of a left atrial line for postbypass monitoring. Balloon inflation (wedging) of a pulmonary artery (PA) catheter should be avoided or performed with a minimal amount of balloon inflation in patients with pulmonary hypertension because of the increased risk of PA rupture.

2. The heart rate should be reduced to prolong the diastolic filling period. For patients in atrial fibrillation, small doses of esmolol can be used to control a rapid ventricular response. Atropine should be avoided as a premedication.

3. Factors that can increase PVR must be avoided. Preoperative sedation should be light to prevent hypercarbia. Hypoxemia, hypercarbia, acidosis, and nitrous (not nitric) oxide should be avoided in the operating room. The PVR can be reduced with pulmonary vasodilators before bypass (usually nitroglycerin), and with inotropic agents after bypass that can produce pulmonary vasodilatation (amrinone or isoproterenol). Prostaglandin E_1 or nitric oxide can be used to reduce PVR after bypass if there is evidence of significant RV failure.

E. **Surgical procedures**

1. Closed mitral commissurotomy has been supplanted by PBMV which produces similar results. Either should be considered in the pregnant patient with critical MS in whom cardiopulmonary bypass should be avoided.

2. Traditional mitral valve operations have been performed through a median sternotomy incision. Other approaches, such as an upper sternotomy with superior approach to the valve (between the aorta and superior vena cava), a right parasternal incision (biatrial transseptal approach), or a right anterolateral thoracotomy (posterior approach behind the interatrial septum) have become popular and are termed "minimally invasive" because of the smaller skin incision. CPB can be established either through the chest or through the femoral vessels.

3. Open mitral commissurotomy is performed if PBMV is not felt to be feasible or there is evidence of left atrial thrombus (figure 1.7).[21]

4. Mitral valve replacement (MVR) is indicated if the valve leaflets or subvalvular apparatus are severely scarred and not amenable to an open mitral commissurotomy (figure 1.8).

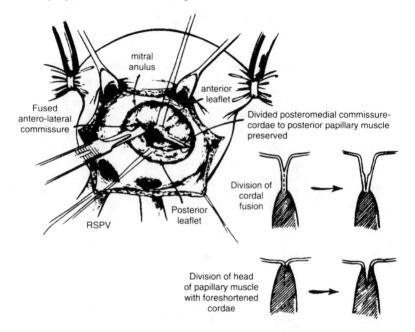

Figure 1.7   *Open mitral commissurotomy. The commissures are incised to within 2 mm of the annulus. Areas of fusion of the subvalvular apparatus are incised. (Reproduced with permission from Olinger GN, Bonchek LI. Cardiac surgical techniques and intraoperative complications. In: Bonchek LI, Brooks HL, eds. Office management of medical and surgical heart disease: a concise guide for physicians. Boston: Little, Brown, 1981:285–304.)*

5. A tricuspid valve ring should be considered for patients with 3–4+ TR, especially when the PVR is elevated. Although functional TR usually improves after left-sided surgery, a better clinical result will usually ensue if a tricuspid annuloplasty is performed for significant TR.

VII.   Mitral Regurgitation

A. **Pathophysiology.** Mitral regurgitation may result from abnormalities of the annulus (dilatation), valve leaflets (myxomatous change with redundancy and prolapse, leaflet defect from endocarditis, leaflet shrinkage from rheumatic disease), chordae tendineae (rupture, elongation), or papillary muscles (rupture, ischemic dysfunction).

1. Acute MR usually results from myocardial ischemia or infarction, endocarditis, or idiopathic chordal rupture. The regurgitant jet into a small noncompliant left atrium results in acute pulmonary edema.

2. Chronic MR is characterized by a progressive increase in compliance of the left atrium and ventricle, followed by progressive dilatation of the left ventricle. Ventricular function may be impaired despite a normal ejection fraction because of ventricular unloading into the left atrium, which reduces left ventricular systolic wall

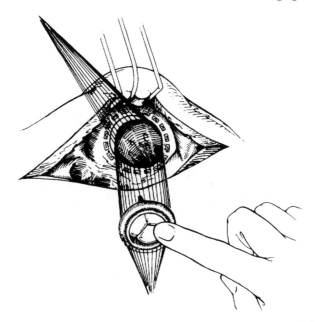

Figure 1.8 *Mitral valve replacement. Exposure has been obtained by making a left atriotomy incision behind the interatrial groove. Pledgetted sutures are placed above the annulus and through the valve sewing ring. The valve is then seated in place and the sutures are tied. (Reproduced with permission from Cooley DA. How to do it: implantation of an Ionescu-Shiley valve. Cardiovasc Dis 1981;8:216–20.)*

stress. Patients may remain asymptomatic well after ventricular decompensation has occurred.

B. **Indications for surgery**

1. Acute MR associated with congestive heart failure or cardiogenic shock

2. Acute endocarditis with hemodynamic compromise, persistent bacteremia or sepsis, recurrent systemic embolization from vegetations, or threatened embolization from large vegetations

3. NYHA class III–IV symptoms

4. Class I–II symptoms with evidence of deteriorating LV function:

    a. Ejection fraction <55%

    b. End-diastolic dimension approaching 75 mm by echocardiography

    c. End-systolic dimension approaching 45 mm by echocardiography

5. Earlier operation has been recommended for asymptomatic or class I–II patients with 3–4+ MR and normal ventricular function to minimize the risk of developing atrial fibrillation (and the need for anticoagulation) and the development of pulmonary hypertension.[13]

C. **Preoperative considerations**

1. Patients with acute MR are susceptible to pulmonary edema and multisystem organ failure from a reduced forward cardiac output. Use of inotropes, vasodilators, and the intraaortic balloon can transiently improve myocardial function and forward flow in anticipation of urgent cardiac catheterization and surgery. Intubation and mechanical ventilation are frequently required for progressive hypoxia or hypercarbia. Some patients with chordal rupture who present with acute pulmonary edema may stabilize and develop chronic MR that can be treated electively.

2. Patients with chronic MR are managed with digoxin, diuretics, and oral unloading agents, such as the angiotensin-converting enzyme (ACE) inhibitors. The progression of MR and changes in left ventricular dimensions and function should be followed by serial echocardiograms. When surgery is required, digoxin should be continued up until the time of surgery for rate control if the patient is in atrial fibrillation. Diuretics and ACE inhibitors should also be continued up to the time of surgery.

D. **Anesthetic considerations**

1. In the prebypass period, adequate preload must be maintained to ensure forward output. Bradycardia and systemic hypertension should be avoided because they increase the amount of regurgitation. Systemic vasodilators may improve forward flow. The IABP is very beneficial for patients with ischemic MR.

2. Narcotic-based anesthesia is usually used to avoid myocardial depression that can reduce forward output.

3. Measures that can increase pulmonary artery pressure, such as hypoxemia, hypercarbia, acidosis, and nitrous oxide should be avoided. Preoperative sedation should be light.

4. Transesophageal echocardiography is invaluable in identifying the precise anatomic cause for mitral regurgitation and in evaluating the surgical result. This is usually performed once the patient is anesthetized. Elevation of the blood pressure with α-agents can be performed to assess the amount of regurgitation in patients with moderate ischemic MR in whom a decision must be made about repairing the valve during bypass surgery.

E. **Surgical procedures**

1. Mitral valve reconstruction is applicable to more than 90% of patients with degenerative MR. Techniques include annuloplasty rings, leaflet repairs, and chordal transfers, shortening, or replacement (figure 1.9).[22] These techniques can also be applied to patients with mitral valve endocarditis.[23]

2. Mitral valve replacement (MVR) is indicated only when satisfactory repair cannot be accomplished. Acute MR from papillary muscle rupture usually requires MVR. Chordal preservation to at least the posterior leaflet should be considered for all MVRs performed for MR. This improves ventricular function and will minimize the risk of LV rupture.

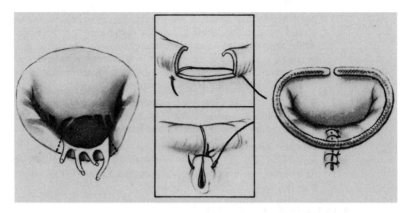

Figure 1.9 *Mitral valve repair for mitral regurgitation produced by ruptured chordae to the posterior leaflet. This is repaired by a quadrangular resection of the posterior leaflet with reapproximation of the leaflet tissue and placement of an annuloplasty ring. (Reproduced with permission from Carpentier A. Cardiac valve surgery—"the French correction." J Thorac Cardiovasc Surg 1983;86:323–37.)*

VIII.   Tricuspid Valve Disease

A. **Pathophysiology.** Isolated tricuspid stenosis (TS) is very rare, but tricuspid regurgitation (TR) is commonly seen on a functional basis secondary to mitral valve disease, which leads to pulmonary hypertension and right ventricular dilatation. Progressive TR produces signs of right heart failure with fatigue, peripheral edema, and a low output state.

B. **Indications for surgery**

1. Repair of TS is indicated for class III–IV symptoms, including hepatic congestion, ascites, and peripheral edema that are refractory to salt restriction and diuretics.

2. Repair of TR is indicated for severe symptoms or when moderate-to-severe functional TR is present at the time of left-sided valve surgery. Repair is especially important if the PVR is elevated.

C. **Preoperative considerations**

1. Passive congestion of the liver frequently leads to coagulation abnormalities, which should be treated aggressively before and during surgery. Aprotinin should be considered to minimize blood loss during surgery, but blood component therapy should also be available. Frequently, these patients have uncorrectable prothrombin times before surgery.

2. Salt restriction, digoxin, and diuretics may improve hepatic function, but significant improvement in liver function tests may not be possible until after surgery.

D. **Anesthetic considerations**

1. Maintenance of an elevated central venous pressure (CVP) is essential to achieve satisfactory forward flow. A Swan-Ganz catheter can

be placed for monitoring of left-sided pressures in patients with tricuspid regurgitation, although cardiac output determinations are of little value. A Swan-Ganz catheter can be used after valve repair or tissue valve replacement, but not after mechanical valve replacement. Alternatively, an LA line and PA thermistor can be placed for cardiac output determinations.

2. A normal sinus mechanism provides better hemodynamics than atrial fibrillation, although the latter is frequently present. Slower heart rates are preferable for TS and faster heart rates for TR.

3. Narcotic-based anesthesia should be used to avoid myocardial depression. This is especially important in patients with TR and right ventricular dysfunction. Measures that lower the PVR are also beneficial.

E. **Surgical procedures**

1. Tricuspid commissurotomy can be performed for rheumatic TS.

2. Tricuspid annuloplasty with a ring (Carpentier) or suture technique (DeVega or bicuspidization) is feasible for the majority of patients with annular dilatation (figure 1.10).[24]

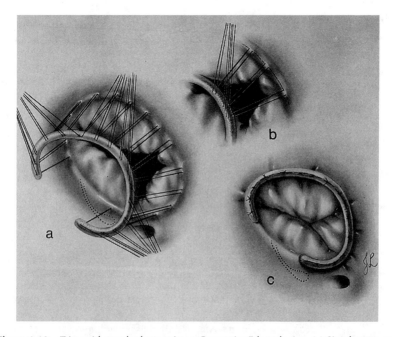

Figure 1.10 *Tricuspid annuloplasty using a Carpentier-Edwards ring. (a) Simple sutures are placed through the annulus except in the region of the septal leaflet to avoid the conduction system. Reduction of annular dilatation occurs at the base of the anterior and posterior leaflets. (b) The sutures are more widely spaced on the annulus than in the ring. (c) The completed annuloplasty. (Reproduced with permission from Sabiston DC Jr, Spencer FC, eds. Gibbon's surgery of the chest. 4th ed. Philadelphia: WB Saunders, 1983:1218.)*

3. Tricuspid valve replacement is necessary when leaflet shrinkage and poor coaptation prevent an annuloplasty technique from eliminating the TR.[25]

IX. Endocarditis

A. **Pathophysiology.** Endocarditis can result in destruction of valve leaflets, invasion of surrounding myocardial tissue, systemic embolization of valve vegetations, and persistent systemic sepsis. Tricuspid valve endocarditis is usually caused by intravenous drug abuse.[26]

B. **Indications for surgery in native valve endocarditis**

1. Presence of moderate-to-severe congestive heart failure
2. Persistent sepsis
3. Evidence of local extension producing annular or myocardial abscesses, conduction disturbances, or intracardiac fistulas
4. Systemic embolization
5. Enlarging vegetations with threatened embolization

C. **Indications for surgery in prosthetic valve endocarditis (PVE)**[27,28]

1. All of the above
2. Fungal etiology
3. Valve obstruction
4. Unstable prosthesis
5. New onset of heart block
6. Relative indications: nonstreptococcal organism, perivalvular leak, relapse following completion of therapy, early onset PVE, culture-negative PVE with persistent fever

D. **Preoperative considerations**

1. A 6-week course of antibiotics should ideally be completed before surgery to reduce the risk of PVE. However, surgery is frequently indicated at an earlier phase, following which antibiotics should be continued for a total course of 6 weeks. The risk of prosthetic valve endocarditis is significantly greater, however, if performed during the active phase (about 10%).
2. Attempts should be made to optimize hemodynamic and renal status before operation, but surgery should not be delayed if there is evidence of progressive organ system deterioration.
3. If the patient has developed a neurologic deficit from a cerebral embolism, surgery can be performed safely as long as a computed tomographic (CT) scan does not demonstrate a hemorrhagic infarction.

E. **Anesthetic considerations**

1. Anesthetic management is dictated by the hemodynamic derangements associated with the particular valve involved.

2. Patients with aortic valve endocarditis may have evidence of heart block from involvement of the conduction system by periannular infection. This may require preoperative placement of a transvenous pacing wire.

F. **Surgical procedures**

1. Surgery entails excision of all infected valve tissue, drainage and débridement of abscess cavities, and repair or replacement of the damaged valves. The homograft is the valve of choice for aortic valve endocarditis because of its increased resistance to infection, although homograft root replacement is a more complex procedure than tissue or mechanical valve replacement. The latter have fairly comparable risks of developing prosthetic valve endocarditis.

2. Mitral endocarditis can frequently be repaired, especially if leaflet perforation is the primary pathology. More advanced stages of endocarditis usually require valve replacement.

3. If tricuspid valve repair cannot be accomplished, tricuspid valvulectomy can be performed in patients without pulmonary hypertension with few adverse hemodynamic sequelae.[29] Otherwise, a tricuspid valve should be placed. A valve is best avoided in the IV drug abuser because of the significant risk of prosthetic valve endocarditis.

X. Hypertrophic Cardiomyopathy

A. **Pathophysiology.** Asymmetric septal hypertrophy and mitral septal-apposition that produce dynamic left ventricular outflow tract obstruction are present to varying degrees in patients with hypertrophic cardiomyopathy (HCM). Diastolic dysfunction is also commonly present. These changes can produce the clinical picture of myocardial ischemia, mitral regurgitation, CHF, and the potential for sudden death.[30]

B. **Indications for surgery**

1. Peak gradient >50 mm Hg and persistent symptoms despite medical therapy with β-blockers, calcium-channel blockers, or DDD pacing. Surgery can alleviate symptoms, although it has little impact on the natural history of the disease and the risk of sudden death.

2. Peak gradient >80 mm Hg in an asymptomatic patient who is considered at high risk for sudden death (family history, age <40 years).

C. **Preoperative and anesthetic considerations**

1. Measures that produce hypovolemia or vasodilatation must be avoided because they increase the outflow tract gradient. Volume infusions should be used to maintain preload with the use of α-agents to maintain systemic resistance.

2. Use of β-blockers and calcium-channel blockers to reduce heart rate and contractility are beneficial in the immediate preoperative and prebypass periods. Inotropic drugs with predominantly β-adrenergic effects should be avoided.

D. **Surgical procedures**[31]

   1. Left ventricular myotomy-myectomy (LVMM) is the procedure of choice. A $1.5 \times 4\,cm$ wedge of septum is resected below the right coronary aortic leaflet through an aortotomy incision (figure 1.11).

   2. Mitral valve replacement is indicated if the septal thickness is less than 18 mm, if there is atypical septal morphology, significant mitral regurgitation, or failure of a LVMM procedure to relieve the subaortic gradient.

XI.   Aortic Dissections

A. **Pathophysiology.** An aortic dissection results from an intimal tear that allows passage of blood into the media, creating a false channel. This channel is contained externally by the outer medial and adventitial layers of the aorta. With each cardiac contraction, the dissected channel can extend proximally or distally, potentially leading to cardiac tamponade from hemopericardium, or to aortic regurgitation, aortic rupture, or branch artery compromise. Dissections involving the ascending aorta are classified as Stanford type A (DeBakey type I–II), whereas those not involving the ascending aorta are called Stanford type B (DeBakey type III) dissections.[32,33]

B. **Indications for surgery**

   1. **Type A dissection:** surgery is indicated for all patients unless it is felt to carry a prohibitive risk because of medical debility, extensive renal, myocardial, or bowel infarction, or massive stroke.

   2. **Type B dissections:** patients with uncomplicated type B dissections are usually treated medically, with surgery reserved for complicated dissections (i.e., patients with persistent pain, uncontrollable hypertension, evidence of aneurysmal expansion or rupture, or visceral, renal, or lower extremity vascular compromise).[34] Centers with extensive experience in thoracic aortic surgery are more routinely operating upon good-risk candidates with acute type B dissections with low mortality and excellent long-term results.

C. **Preoperative considerations**

   1. Upon suspicion of the diagnosis, all patients should be treated pharmacologically to reduce the blood pressure (to about 100 mm Hg systolic), the heart rate (to 60–70/min), and the force of cardiac ejection (dp/dt). Monitoring lines, including an arterial line and Swan-Ganz catheter, should be inserted and the patient observed in the ICU. The appropriate diagnostic tests can be performed subsequently.

   2. Recommended antihypertensive regimens include sodium nitroprusside with a β-blocker (esmolol or propranolol), esmolol alone, or labetalol (see Table 10.7 for doses).

   3. A careful pulse examination may indicate the extent of the dissection. Particular attention should be paid to the carotid, radial, and femoral pulses. Differential upper extremity blood pressures in a young patient with chest pain is a strong clue to the presence of a dissection.

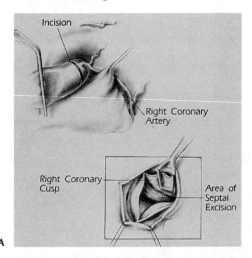

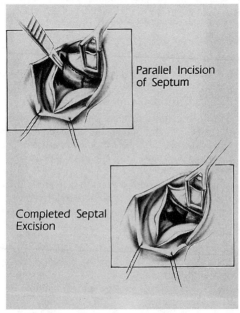

Figure 1.11 *Left ventricular myotomy-myectomy. (A) A transverse aortotomy incision is made and the right coronary valve leaflet is retracted. (B) Parallel incisions are made perpendicular to the septum and the septal muscle is excised. (Reproduced with permission from Doty DB. Cardiac surgery. A looseleaf workbook and update service. Chicago: Year Book Medical, 1985.)*

4. A detailed preoperative neurologic examination is required because a deficit recognized postoperatively may have been present at the time of presentation. A change in neurologic status may indicate progressive compromise of brachiocephalic perfusion that necessitates emergency surgery. Evidence of renal dysfunction (rising BUN or creatinine, oliguria) or evidence of bowel ischemia (abdominal pain, acidosis) may modify the surgical approach. Recurrent chest or back pain may indicate extension and potential rupture of the dissection.

5. Dissections can be diagnosed by numerous methods. The most precise and expeditious is echocardiography, which has become the gold standard for identifying intimal flaps in the ascending aorta. Other studies, such as a computed tomographic (CT) scan, aortography, or magnetic resonance imaging (MRI) scan should only be performed when expert echocardiography is not available or results are equivocal. When a dissection is considered in the differential diagnosis of chest pain in smaller hospitals, a CT scan is usually performed and then the patient is transferred to an open-heart center.

6. Because of the urgency of an operative procedure, coronary arteriography is rarely done. Furthermore, catheter manipulation in the proximal ascending aorta is fraught with danger.

D. **Anesthetic considerations**

1. Maintenance of hemodynamic stability is critical to prevent aortic rupture. Use of a Swan-Ganz catheter is essential because many patients will have concomitant coronary artery disease and require sophisticated monitoring at the conclusion of bypass. However, its insertion can be delayed until after intubation to minimize the stress response.

2. Most patients require emergency surgery and should be considered to have a full stomach. A modified rapid sequence induction should be performed to minimize the risk of aspiration while ensuring hemodynamic stability.

3. Transesophageal echocardiography is valuable in localizing the site and often the extent of the dissection. This should **never** be done in the awake patient with a suspected dissection for fear of precipitating hypertension, rupture, and then tamponade.

4. Repair of type A dissections may require a period of circulatory arrest. See discussion below under ascending aortic aneurysms.

5. Repair of type B dissections requires a period of descending aortic cross-clamping. Because less collateral flow is present with dissections than with atherosclerotic aneurysms, the risk of paraplegia is greater. Consideration should be given to measures to reduce spinal cord ischemia. These techniques and other means of controlling proximal hypertension and maintaining distal perfusion are discussed below under descending thoracic aneurysms.

E. **Surgical procedures**

1. **Type A dissection.** Repair involves resuspension or replacement of the aortic valve (if aortic regurgitation is present), resection of the

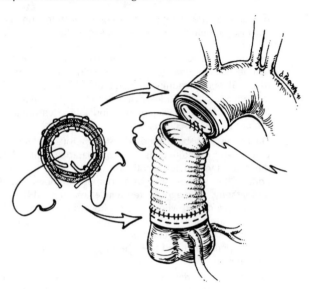

Figure 1.12   *Repair of a type A aortic dissection. The aortic wall is reinforced proximally and distally by Teflon felt rings placed inside the intima and outside the adventitia. An interposition graft is then sewn to the reinforced wall. (Modified with permission from Cachera JP, Vouhe PR, Loisance DY, et al. Surgical management of acute aortic dissections involving the ascending aorta. Early and late results in 38 patients. J Thoracic Cardiovasc Surg 1981;82:576–84; and from Crawford ES, Crawford JL. Diseases of the aorta including an atlas of angiographic pathology and surgical techniques. Baltimore: Williams & Wilkins, 1984:183. 1984, the Williams & Wilkins Co., Baltimore.)*

intimal tear, and interposition graft replacement to reapproximate the aortic wall (figure 1.12). Some groups have used biologic glue either for primary repair or to improve tissue integrity for grafting.

2. **Type B dissection.** Repair involves resection of the intimal tear and interposition graft replacement to reapproximate the aortic wall. If there is evidence of visceral artery compromise without rupture, aortic fenestration can be performed without grafting.[35]

XII.   Thoracic Aortic Aneurysms

A. **Pathophysiology.** Ascending aortic (AAo) aneurysms usually result from medial degeneration, whereas those in the distal arch, descending thoracic, and thoracoabdominal aorta are generally atherosclerotic in nature. Aneurysms in any location may result from expansion of chronic dissections. Although progressive enlargement may result in compression of adjacent structures, most deaths result from aneurysmal rupture.

B. **Indications for surgery**[36–38]

1. **Ascending aortic (AAo) aneurysms**

   a. Symptomatic, expanding, >5.5 cm in diameter (Marfan's syndrome or not), or greater than twice the size of the normal aorta

   b. Aneurysms >4.5 cm if operation is indicated for aortic regurgitation (annuloaortic ectasia)
   c. All acute type A dissections (as noted above)
   d. Mycotic aneurysms

2. **Transverse arch aneurysms**

   a. AAo aneurysms that require replacement that also extend into the arch
   b. Acute arch dissections with intimal tear in the arch or evidence of arch expansion or rupture
   c. Aneurysms >6 cm in diameter

3. **Descending thoracic (DAo) aneurysms**

   a. Symptomatic aneurysms
   b. Aneurysms >6 cm in diameter
   c. Complicated type B dissections (uncomplicated if low-risk patient)

C. Preoperative considerations

1. Coronary angiography is required before surgery for ascending aortic and proximal arch aneurysms (not acute dissections). If significant coronary disease is present, it is bypassed at the time of the aneurysm resection.

2. Stress imaging (dipyridamole-thallium or sestamibi) is indicated in patients with descending thoracic aneurysms because of the high incidence of coexistent coronary artery disease. If the scan is positive, coronary angiography should be performed. The presence of significant coronary disease usually warrants preliminary coronary bypass grafting before aneurysm resection to reduce the risk of cardiac complications associated with repair of the aneurysm.

3. A careful preoperative neurologic evaluation is important because of the risks associated with circulatory arrest (stroke, seizures) and aortic crossclamping (paraplegia).

4. Renal function must be monitored carefully after angiography, especially in diabetic patients. The creatinine should be allowed to return to baseline before surgery to reduce the risk of renal dysfunction associated with aortic crossclamping.

D. Anesthetic considerations

1. **Ascending aortic aneurysms**

   a. CPB is required for repair of AAo aneurysms. When the aneurysm extends to involve the arch, repair is usually accomplished during a period of circulatory arrest.
   b. Adjuncts that can improve cerebral protection during a period of circulatory arrest include pentobarbital 5–10 mg/kg, methylprednisolone 30 mg/kg, packing the head in ice, and continuous retrograde perfusion of the superior vena cava (SVC). An alternative to complete circulatory arrest is selective brachiocephalic perfusion.
   c. Profound hypothermia and warming are associated with a coagulopathy. Platelets, fresh frozen plasma, and cryoprecipitate are helpful in achieving hemostasis.

d. Aprotinin is helpful in reducing intraoperative bleeding in patients undergoing surgery with deep hypothermia, but adverse neurologic sequelae have been described with its use.[39] However, this can be avoided by ensuring adequate heparinization and stopping the aprotinin infusion during the period of circulatory arrest, or alternatively, starting the aprotinin after the period of circulatory arrest.[40]

3. **Descending aortic aneurysms**

a. Arterial monitoring lines are inserted in the right radial and occasionally the femoral artery to monitor proximal and distal pressures during the period of aortic crossclamping. The femoral line is valuable when shunting or left-heart bypass techniques are used.

b. A Swan-Ganz catheter is important to monitor filling pressures during the period of crossclamping. Transesophageal echocardiography is helpful in evaluating myocardial function and often demonstrates a hypovolemic left ventricular chamber despite elevated pulmonary artery pressures when the crossclamp is removed. Ensuring adequate intravascular volume will reduce the risk of "declamping shock" upon release of the aortic crossclamp.

c. One-lung anesthesia using a double-lumen or Uni-Vent tube improves operative exposure.

d. Mannitol should be given during the period of aortic crossclamping to improve renal perfusion.

e. Control of proximal hypertension is essential during the crossclamp period. Nitroprusside is commonly used, but it can reduce renal and spinal cord perfusion and increase cerebrospinal fluid (CSF) pressure. CSF drainage may reduce the incidence of spinal ischemia. Other pharmacologic adjuncts to reduce this risk include intrathecal local anesthetics, and systemic oxygen free-radical scavengers, steroids, or calcium-channel blockers. Use of distal shunting procedures listed under surgical techniques may minimize, but not completely eliminate, the risk of paraplegia.

E. **Surgical procedures**

1. **Ascending aortic aneurysms**

a. Supracoronary interposition graft placement is performed if the aneurysm does not involve the sinuses.

b. A valved conduit (Bentall procedure) is placed in the patient with Marfan's syndrome, if the sinuses are involved, or for annuloaortic ectasia (see figure 1.6). Extensive aortic resection with preservation of the aortic valve can also be performed.[41]

2. **Transverse arch aneurysms**

a. Hemiarch repair is performed if the ascending aorta and proximal arch are involved. A graft is sewn to the undersurface of the arch leaving the brachiocephalic vessels attached to the native aorta.

   b. Extended arch repair involves placement of an interposition graft and reimplantation of a brachiocephalic island during a period of circulatory arrest. Retrograde SVC perfusion or selective brachiocephalic perfusion can be used to minimize the risk of cerebral complications.

   c. Distal arch repair can be performed via a left thoracotomy without cardiopulmonary bypass. Use of CPB and a period of circulatory arrest (through either a sternotomy or thoracotomy incision) may be useful when additional exposure is required for the proximal anastomosis or when a difficult dissection is anticipated (reoperations).

   d. If it is anticipated that a descending aortic repair may be necessary in the future, a piece of graft material is left dangling from the distal anastomosis and can be retrieved at a subsequent operation through the left chest (the "elephant trunk" procedure).

3. **Descending thoracic aorta**

   a. Interposition graft placement

   b. Consideration should be given to use of adjuncts (medications, CSF drainage, shunting) to prevent spinal cord ischemia. Shunting can be accomplished by draining blood from a site proximal to the aortic crossclamp (left atrium/proximal aorta) and returning it distally (distal aorta/femoral artery) to perfuse the spinal cord and kidneys. A Bio-Medicus centrifugal pump, which actively returns blood to the patient at a designated rate, is commonly used. Alternatively, partial femoro-femoral bypass can be used.

XIII. Ventricular Arrhythmias

A. **Pathophysiology**

1. Late (>48 hours) postinfarction ventricular tachycardia (VT) results from heterogeneous myocardial damage that produces the electrophysiologic substrate for the development of a reentrant rhythm. This commonly occurs at the border zone of a left ventricular aneurysm between dense subendocardial scar tissue and normal myocardium. Premature stimuli may initiate an impulse that triggers the reentrant circuit of monomorphic VT. These stimuli may occur spontaneously or may be delivered in the electrophysiology (EP) laboratory to induce the reentrant rhythm (inducible VT).

2. Nonischemic ventricular tachycardia may be the result of reentrant circuits or the result of abnormal or triggered automaticity. It may be associated with cardiomyopathies, arrhythmogenic right ventricular dysplasia, or it may be idiopathic. In many of these conditions, the arrhythmogenic focus cannot be localized well enough to be ablated.

3. Out-of-hospital cardiac arrest is frequently not associated with a myocardial infarction, although it usually occurs in patients with coronary artery disease.[42] Many patients do not have inducible arrhythmias, and coronary revascularization may not provide ade-

quate protection against recurrent sudden death. Placement of an implantable cardioverter-defibrillator (ICD) cannot prevent the recurrence of the arrhythmia, but it can treat a malignant rhythm when it occurs.

B. **Indications for surgery**

1. Map-guided endocardial resection was performed in the past when antiarrhythmic drug therapy or ablative techniques in the EP lab failed to control the arrhythmia. Because the equipment for intraoperative mapping is no longer commercially available, only "blind" endocardial resections and cryosurgery can be performed, usually during operations on a left ventricular aneurysm. Therefore, the primary surgical procedure for patients with recurrent malignant arrhythmias is placement of an ICD device.

2. Thus, indications for placement of an ICD device include:[43]

   a. Ventricular tachycardia, inducible or not, that recurs despite medical, ablative, and/or surgical therapy.

   b. Resuscitation from an out-of-hospital cardiac arrest without a Q wave myocardial infarction.

   c. Patients with VT undergoing CABG or endocardial resection in whom it is felt there is a high likelihood of recurrence.

C. **Preoperative considerations**

1. Endocardial resection (map-guided)

   a. If technology is available for intraoperative mapping, preoperative mapping in the EP lab is essential to localize the site of origin of the arrhythmia and improve the success rate of arrhythmia ablation.

   b. Heparin may be used in patients with large left ventricular aneurysms.

   c. Antiarrhythmic medications should be stopped before surgery so that intraoperative testing can accurately determine whether the arrhythmia has been ablated successfully.

   d. Patients receiving high doses of amiodarone (>400 mg/day) are susceptible to respiratory failure after surgery. Preoperative pulmonary function testing is warranted to assess whether the patient can tolerate an extensive procedure on bypass. If not, placement of an ICD may be preferable.

2. ICD implantation

   a. A thorough preoperative evaluation should be performed to determine whether other surgical procedures (CABG, endocardial resection) might offer a cure for the arrhythmia. These studies include a signal-averaged ECG, coronary angiography, ventriculography, EP study, and stress testing. The latter can determine the upper rate limit above which the device should be set.

   b. Patients should be evaluated for severe comorbid conditions that may limit their life span. Generally, ICD implantation is not indicated in a patient with an anticipated life span of less than 1 year.

D. **Anesthetic considerations**

1. Endocardial resections: antiarrhythmic medications should not be administered to avoid interference with intraoperative electrophysiologic testing.

2. ICD implantation

   a. ICD implantation in the EP lab can be performed under moderate sedation, allowing patients to breath spontaneously. When ventricular fibrillation (VF) is induced, deepening of the level of sedation with propofol and assisted ventilation usually suffice.

   b. When a thoracotomy incision is used for patch implantation, short-acting narcotics or hypnotic agents are used to avoid myocardial depression and allow for early extubation. A double-lumen tube, R2 external defibrillator pads, and epidural narcotics for postoperative analgesia should be used.

E. **Surgical procedures**

1. Bypass surgery alone is unlikely to prevent the recurrence of ventricular tachycardia, and ICD implantation will usually be necessary. Some patients with ventricular fibrillation may be cured of their arrhythmias by bypass surgery, but at the current time, no technology is available that can predict which patients will be cured.

2. Endocardial resection

   a. Map-guided surgery requires intraoperative mapping to confirm the site of origin of the arrhythmia and direct the endocardial resection or adjunctive cryoablation. The aneurysm is usually closed with the endoaneurysmorrhaphy technique (see figure 1.3, and Chapter 1, Section II). Coronary bypass grafting is performed subsequently during a period of cardioplegic arrest. Postoperatively, an EP study is performed. If VT is still inducible, an ICD device is placed in the EP lab.

   b. Blind subendocardial resection was performed before map-guided surgery became possible. Although successful in many cases, it was not as efficacious as map-guided procedures. For this reason, most patients today undergo ICD implantation rather than a surgical procedure.

3. ICD implantation

   a. Most ICD implantations take place in the EP lab and involve transvenous leads and infrequently a subcutaneous array to improve defibrillation thresholds. The device is implanted in a prepectoral pocket. Testing of the leads for sensing and defibrillation thresholds (DFTs) is performed. The generator is then connected to the leads and the system retested.

   b. Prior to the widespread usage of transvenous systems, ICD implantation was performed through left thoracotomy, median sternotomy, subcostal, or subxiphoid approaches. Although these approaches are rarely used today, device replacement and removal of infected lead systems mandate an understanding of their implantation methods. These systems usually involved two rate-sensing electrodes placed into the right or left ventricular epicardium and two titanium mesh patches for defibrillation placed over the ventricles, either intra- or extrapericardially.

XIV.   Partial Left Ventriculectomy (Batista Procedure)

A. Pathophysiology

1. End-stage heart failure is characterized by progressive dilatation and remodeling of the left ventricle. Dilatation results in progressive deterioration of ventricular function and, according to Laplace's law, increased wall stress. Theoretically, reducing the size of the ventricle should allow the heart to contract more efficiently at a lower workload. Eventually, it is theorized that the patient's clinical status will improve along with recovery of hemodynamic function.[44,45]

2. The prognosis for the patient with end-stage heart failure is dismal. Some improvement has been noted with use of ACE inhibitors and medications such as carvedilol, an α and β blocker. Cardiac transplantation has become the standard treatment for these patients, but limited donor availability remains a problem.

B. Indications for surgery.
Patients who might benefit from this operation are still being defined. They usually include those with end-stage heart failure associated with viral or idiopathic dilated cardiomyopathy. Patients with ischemic cardiomyopathy probably derive little benefit. Some centers select only potential transplant candidates, whereas other centers select only nontransplant candidates. At the Cleveland Clinic, the best candidates have a dilated cardiomyopathy with a left ventricular internal diameter exceeding 7 cm, a severely decreased ejection fraction, and no specific regional wall motion abnormalities.[45,46]

C. Preoperative and anesthetic considerations

1. All patients undergoing this procedure have severe left ventricular dysfunction. Standard narcotic-based anesthesia is used along with Swan-Ganz catheter monitoring.

2. At the termination of bypass, moderate hypotension (systolic pressure of 90) with use of sodium nitroprusside has been recommended to minimize bleeding from the left ventricular suture line. Although inotropes are not recommended by Batista, use of milrinone can be considered to improve biventricular function without producing hypertension.

D. Surgical procedure

1. The procedure may be performed at normothermia in the beating heart or using standard cold cardioplegic arrest.

2. A large segment of left ventricle is resected between the two papillary muscles (figure 1.13). Mitral valve repair or replacement is performed through the ventriculotomy, but can be performed transatrially. If the heart is very large, the papillary muscles may be

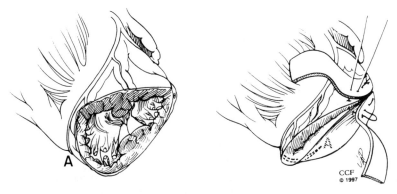

Figure 1.13 *Left ventricular reduction surgery (Batista operation). Starting at the apex, a wedge of the lateral wall including the marginal arteries is excised between the two papillary muscles. The ventricle is then closed. The left anterior descending (A) wraps around the reconstructed apex. (Reproduced with permission from McCarthy PM, Starling RC, Wong J, et al. Early results with partial left ventriculectomy. J Thorac Cardiovasc Surg 1997;114:755–65.)*

resected and the mitral valve replaced. The ventricle is then closed in two layers.

E. **Outcome**

1. Results of this operation have been variable. Hemodynamic studies have shown a decrease in left ventricular end-diastolic and systolic dimensions, an increase in ejection fraction, and a modest increase in stroke volume. Many patients are improved clinically out of proportion to the hemodynamic improvement. To some extent, symptomatic improvement may be attributable to a reduction in mitral regurgitation.[47]

2. Although the quoted mortality for the procedure is about 10–20%, a substantial percentage of patients will survive only with the use of assist devices and/or subsequent transplantation. Long-term results are also compromised by heart failure progression and sudden death from ventricular arrhythmias.[45–48] Use of amiodarone and placement of an ICD may reduce this risk.

XV. Pericardial Disease

A. **Pathophysiology.** The pericardium may become involved in a variety of systemic disease processes that produce either pericardial effusions or constriction. The most common causes of effusions are idiopathic (probably viral), malignant, uremic, pyogenic, and tuberculous. The most common causes of constriction are idiopathic, radiation, and tuberculous.[49]

1. Large effusions result in tamponade physiology with progressive low output states. They are best documented by two-dimensional echocardiography, which delineates their size and provides evidence of tamponade. Equilibration of intracardiac pressures will be detected by cardiac catheterization.

2. Constriction can also produce a low output state. Cardiac catheterization will demonstrate a "square-root sign" in the right ventricular tracing, indicating rapid early filling and a diastolic plateau caused by severe restriction to right ventricular filling. CT scanning can assess the thickness of the pericardium.

B. **Indications for surgery**

1. Large effusions that fail to respond to other measures (dialysis for uremia, antibiotics for infection, radiation or chemotherapy for malignancy) or recur after repeat pericardiocenteses should be treated by either a subxiphoid pericardial window or a pericardiectomy.

2. Constriction that produces a refractory low output state, hepatomegaly, or peripheral edema should be treated by a pericardiectomy.

C. **Preoperative considerations**

1. Low-grade tamponade frequently leads to renal dysfunction and hepatic congestion, but neither problem will improve until the operation is performed.

2. Preliminary pericardiocentesis for very large effusions improves the safety of anesthetic induction, which can produce vasodilatation, a fall in filling pressures, and profound hypotension.

D. **Anesthetic considerations**

1. Cardiac output and blood pressure depend on adequate preload, increased sympathetic tone, and increased heart rate. Therefore, agents that produce vasodilatation or bradycardia must be avoided. Volume infusions and α-agents are beneficial in maintaining hemodynamic stability. Because loss of sympathetic tone can be catastrophic in a patient with tamponade physiology, prepping and draping of the patient before the induction of anesthesia should be strongly considered.

2. Swan-Ganz monitoring is helpful in maintaining adequate preload and in assessing the hemodynamic response to the procedure.

E. **Surgical procedures**

1. A pericardiocentesis should be the initial procedure for a large pericardial effusion. If it recurs, consideration may be given to use of a sclerosing agent instilled into the pericardium to prevent reaccumulation of fluid (doxycycline, bleomycin, thiotepa).[50,51] This should probably be considered only in patients with malignant pericardial effusions.

2. A subxiphoid pericardial window is used to drain the pericardial space, obtain a small biopsy specimen, and obliterate the pericardial space by the formation of adhesions. Although recurrence rates have been reported to be low, this procedure is best reserved for patients with end-stage malignancy.

3. Pericardiectomy via either a left anterolateral thoracotomy or median sternotomy approach is very effective in preventing the

recurrence of effusions. Constrictive pericarditis is best approached through a median sternotomy with pump standby. The pericardium is removed from between the phrenic nerves on either side, or at least as far as exposure allows. Decortication of the left ventricle should be performed first to prevent pulmonary edema that could occur if the right ventricle is freed up while the left ventricle remains constricted.

References

1. Favaloro RG. Critical analysis of coronary artery bypass graft surgery: a 30-year journey. J Am Coll Cardiol 1998;31(suppl B):1B–63B.

2. King SB III. The development of interventional cardiology. J Am Coll Cardiol 1998;31(suppl B):64B–88B.

3. Pepine CJ, Holmes DR Jr. Coronary artery stents. J Am Coll Cardiol 1996;28:782–94.

4. Hall P, Nakamura S, Maiello L, et al. A randomized comparison of combined ticlopidine and aspirin therapy versus aspirin therapy alone after successful intravascular ultrasound-guided stent implantation. Circulation 1996;93:215–22.

5. Rupprecht HJ, Darius H, Borkowski U, et al. Comparison of antiplatelet effects of aspirin, ticlopidine, or their combination after stent implantation. Circulation 1998;97:1046–52.

6. Calafiore AM, Angelini GD, Bergsland J, Salerno TA. Minimally invasive coronary artery bypass grafting. Ann Thorac Surg 1996;62:1545–8.

7. Dietl CA, Benoit CH. Radial artery graft for coronary revascularization: technical considerations. Ann Thorac Surg 1995;60:102–10.

8. Ba'albaki HA, Clements SD Jr. Left ventricular aneurysm: a review. Clin Cardiol 1989;12:5–13.

9. Dor V, ed. Ventricular aneurysm surgery. Sem Thorac Cardiovasc Surg 1997;9:112–55.

10. Muehrcke DD, Daggett WM Jr, Buckley MJ, Akins CW, Hilgenberg AD, Austen WG. Postinfarct ventricular septal defect repair: effect of coronary artery bypass grafting. Ann Thorac Surg 1992;54:876–83.

11. Heitmiller R, Jacobs ML, Daggett WM. Surgical management of postinfarction ventricular septal rupture. Ann Thorac Surg 1986;41:683–91.

12. David TE, Dale L, Sun Z. Postinfarction ventricular septal rupture: repair by endocardial patch with infarct exclusion. J Thorac Cardiovasc Surg 1995;110:1315–22.

13. Carabello BA, Crawford FA Jr. Valvular heart disease. N Engl J Med 1997;337:32–41.

14. Lester SJ, Heilbron B, Gin K, Dodek A, Jue J. The natural history and rate of progression of aortic stenosis. Chest 1998;113:1109–14.

15. Otto CM, Burwash IG, Legget ME, et al. Prospective study of asymptomatic valvular aortic stenosis. Clinical, echocardiographic, and exercise predictors of outcome. Circulation 1997;95:2262–70.

16. Ross D. Replacement of the aortic valve with a pulmonary autograft: the "switch" operation. Ann Thorac Surg 1991;52:1346–50.

17. Gaasch WH, Sundaram M, Meyer TE. Managing asymptomatic patients with chronic aortic regurgitation. Chest 1997;111:1702–9.

18. Klodas E, Enriquez-Sarano M, Tajik AJ, Mullany CJ, Bailey KR, Seward JB. Optimizing timing of surgical correction in patients with severe aortic regurgitation: role of symptoms. J Am Coll Cardiol 1997;30:746–52.

19. Fraser CD, Cosgrove DM III. Surgical techniques for aortic valvuloplasty. Texas Heart Inst J 1994;21:305–9.

20. Turi ZG, Reyes VP, Raju BS, et al. Percutaneous balloon versus surgical closed commissurotomy for mitral stenosis. A prospective, randomized trial. Circulation 1991;83:1179–85.

21. Farhet MB, Boussadia H, Gandjbakhch I, et al. Closed versus open mitral commissurotomy in pure noncalcific mitral stenosis: hemodynamic studies before and after operation. J Thorac Cardiovasc Surg 1990;99:639–44.

22. Cosgrove DM, ed. Mitral valve repair. Sem Thorac Cardiovasc Surg 1989;1:105–212.

23. Dreyfus G, Serraf A, Jebara VA, et al. Valve repair in acute endocarditis. Ann Thorac Surg 1990;49:706–13.

24. Rivera R, Duran E, Ajuria M. Carpentier's flexible ring versus De Vega's annuloplasty. A prospective randomized study. J Thorac Cardiovasc Surg 1985;89:196–203.
25. McGrath LB, Gonzalez-Lavin L, Bailey BM, Grunkemeier GL, Fernandez J, Laub GW. Tricuspid valve operations in 530 patients. Twenty-five-year assessment of early and late phase events. J Thorac Cardiovasc Surg 1990;99:124–33.
26. MacGregor JS, Cheitlin MD. Diagnosis and management of infective endocarditis. Texas Heart Inst J 1989;16:230–8.
27. Cowgill LD, Addonizio VP, Hopeman AR, Harken AH. A practical approach to prosthetic valve endocarditis. Ann Thorac Surg 1987;43:450–7.
28. Vlessis AA, Khaki A, Grunkemeier GL, Li HH, Starr A. Risk, diagnosis, and management of prosthetic valve endocarditis: a review. J Heart Valve Dis 1997;6:443–65.
29. Arbulu A, Holmes RJ, Asfaw I. Tricuspid valvulectomy without replacement. Twenty years' experience. J Thorac Cardiovasc Surg 1991;102:917–22.
30. Spirito P, Seidman CE, McKenna WJ, Maron BJ. The management of hypertrophic cardiomyopathy. N Engl J Med 1997;336:775–85.
31. McIntosh CL, Maron BJ. Current operative treatment of obstructive hypertrophic cardiomoyopathy. Circulation 1988;78:487–95.
32. Crawford ES. The diagnosis and management of aortic dissection. JAMA 1990;264:2537–41.
33. Fann JI, Smith JA, Miller DC, et al. Surgical management of aortic dissection during a 30-year period. Circulation 1995;92(suppl 2):II-113–21.
34. Elefteriades JA, Hartleroad J, Gusberg RJ, et al. Long-term experience with descending aortic dissection: the complication-specific approach. Ann Thorac Surg 1992;53:11–21.
35. Elefteriades JA, Hammond GL, Gusberg KJ, Kopf FS, Baldwin JC. Fenestration revisited. A safe and effective procedure for descending aortic dissection. Arch Surg 1990;125:786–90.
36. Kouchoukos NT, Dougenis D. Surgery of the thoracic aorta. N Engl J Med 1997;336:1876–88.
37. Pitt MPI, Bonser RS. The natural history of thoracic aortic aneurysm disease: an overview. J Cardiac Surg 1997;12:270–8.
38. Coady MA, Rizzo JA, Hammond GL, et al. What is the appropriate size criterion for resection of thoracic aortic aneurysms? J Thorac Cardiovasc Surg 1997;113:476–91.
39. Sundt TM, Kouchoukos NT, Saffitz JE, Murphy SF, Wareing TH, Stahl DJ. Renal dysfunction and intravascular coagulation after use of aprotinin in thoracic aortic operations employing hypothermic cardiopulmonary bypass and circulatory arrest. Ann Thorac Surg 1993;55:1418–24.
40. Royston D. A case for aprotinin in patients having deep hypothermic circulatory arrest. J Card Surg 1997;12(suppl):215–21.
41. David TE, Feindel CM. An aortic-sparing operation for patients with aortic incompetence and aneurysms of the ascending aorta. J Thorac Cardiovasc Surg 1992;103:617–22.
42. Brooks R, McGovern BA, Garan H, Ruskin JN. Current treatment of patients surviving out-of-hospital cardiac arrest. JAMA 1991;265:762–8.
43. Gregoratos G, Cheitlin MD, Conill A, et al. ACC/AHA guidelines for implantation of cardiac pacemakers and antiarrhythmia devices: executive summary. A report of the American College of Cardiology/American Heart Association Task Force on Practice Guidelines (Committee on pacemaker implantation). Circulation 1998;97:1325–30.
44. Batista RJV, Verde J, Nery P, et al. Partial left ventriculectomy to treat end-stage heart disease. Ann Thorac Surg 1997;64:634–8.

45. McCarthy PM, Starling TC, Wong J, et al. Early results with partial left ventriculectomy. J Thorac Cardiovasc Surg 1997;114:755–65.

46. Cadeville M, Insler S, Scalia GM, et al. Anesthetic considerations for the patient undergoing partial left ventriculectomy (Batista procedure). J Cardiothorac Vasc Anesthesia 1998;12:101–10.

47. Moreira LFP, Stolf NAG, Bocchi EA, et al. Partial left ventriculectomy with mitral valve preservation in the treatment of patients with dilated cardiomyopathy. J Thorac Cardiovasc Surg 1998;115:800–7.

48. Bocchi EA, Bellotti GM, de Moraes AV, et al. Clinical outcome after left ventricular surgical remodeling in patients with idiopathic dilated cardiomyopathy referred for heart transplantation. Short-term results. Circulation 1997;96(suppl II):165–72.

49. DeValeria PA, Baumgartner WA, Casale AS, et al. Current indications, risks, and outcome after pericardiectomy. Ann Thorac Surg 1991;52:219–24.

50. Maher EA, Shepherd FA, Todd TJR. Pericardial sclerosis as the primary management of malignant pericardial effusion and cardiac tamponade. J Thorac Cardiovasc Surg 1996;112:637–43.

51. Girardi LN, Ginsberg RJ, Burt ME. Pericardiocentesis and intrapericardial sclerosis: effective therapy for malignant pericardial effusions. Ann Thorac Surg 1997;64:1422–8.

2 Diagnostic Techniques in Cardiac Surgery

Chest X-ray

Myocardial Perfusion Imaging

Cardiac Catheterization

Coronary Angiography

Echocardiography

Computerized Tomography (CT Scanning)

Magnetic Resonance Imaging (MRI Scanning)

Aortography

2 Diagnostic Techniques in Cardiac Surgery

Although the general nature of a patient's cardiac disease can usually be ascertained from a thorough history and physical examination, diagnostic tests are essential to define the precise nature and extent of cardiac disease. Both noninvasive and invasive modalities are available to obtain this information and should be chosen selectively. Some techniques provide unique and complementary information, whereas others may provide comparable information and need not be performed. This chapter will briefly review the basic types of diagnostic modalities available to the clinician and define their role in preoperative evaluation.

I. Chest X-ray

A. A PA and lateral chest x-ray should be obtained on all patients before surgery. It should be consistent with the patient's cardiac diagnosis and can provide a wealth of potential information to the surgeon.

1. Compatibility with the diagnosis: left ventricular (LV) enlargement in patients with volume overload (aortic or mitral regurgitation), left ventricular hypertrophy (LVH) in aortic stenosis, large left atrium in mitral disease, calcified mitral valve or annulus, cardiomegaly in dilated cardiomyopathy, enlarged cardiac silhouette with large pericardial effusions.

2. Identify complications of cardiac disease: congestive heart failure or pulmonary vascular redistribution (mitral stenosis, mitral regurgitation, ischemic pulmonary edema).

3. Identify other potentially relevant abnormalities.

a. Pulmonary: pneumonia, interstitial disease, emphysema, previous pulmonary resection

b. Pleural: effusions, fibrothorax

c. Mediastinal: tumors or widened mediastinum consistent with aortic disease

d. Osseous: pectus, rib resection from a previous thoracotomy

e. Foreign bodies: sternal wires from a previous sternotomy, pacemaker wires, central venous catheters

B. The chest x-ray also provides specific information of importance to the surgeon during an operative procedure.

1. Calcification of the ascending aorta or arch may influence the techniques of cannulation, clamping, and myocardial protection to reduce the risk of stroke. Calcification of the aortic knob is fairly common but of little significance. In contrast, suspicion of ascending aortic calcification is very important and may be further defined by CT scanning.

2. An elevated hemidiaphragm on one side might deter the surgeon from using the contralateral internal mammary artery (IMA), espe-

cially in diabetic patients who are more prone to phrenic nerve paresis.[1]

3. Mitral annular calcification in patients with mitral regurgitation makes mitral valve repair, as well as replacement, much more difficult and may necessitate alternative surgical techniques.

4. For patients undergoing reoperation, the PA film will identify the proximity of the IMA pedicle to the midline. The lateral film will determine the proximity of the cardiac structures and the IMA pedicle clips to the posterior sternal table.

5. For patients with ascending aortic aneurysms, close proximity of the aneurysm to the posterior sternal table may necessitate groin cannulation for bypass before performing the sternotomy.

6. The location and orientation of the heart should be considered when selecting the appropriate incision for minimally invasive surgery. For example, in thin patients and those with emphysema, the heart has a vertical orientation and lies quite caudad in the chest. Thus, a partial upper sternotomy incision for aortic valve surgery may require a transverse incision in the 4th rather than the 3rd interspace. For minimally invasive direct coronary artery bypass (MIDCAB), an anterior thoracotomy incision may be more appropriate in the 5th interspace rather than the 4th. In obese women with horizontal hearts and high diaphragms, the x-ray may indicate that an inframammary incision would be at the level of the diaphragm and well below the intended anastomotic site on the heart.

7. The patient in profound congestive heart failure may benefit from aggressive diuresis and hemofiltration during bypass.

II. Myocardial Perfusion Imaging

A. Resting and stress imaging play a major role in the assessment of the patient with coronary disease. Their primary role is to identify viable and ischemic myocardium that will benefit from an interventional procedure. The technology of stress imaging and radionuclide testing has become very sophisticated; only the salient features are presented here.[2]

B. **Types of stress testing**

1. In its simplest form, an exercise tolerance test (ETT) is performed with a graded protocol on a treadmill. The development of symptoms, ECG changes (>2 mm ST elevation), or a decreased or blunted blood pressure response is indicative of ischemia.

2. More commonly, **myocardial perfusion imaging** is performed with planar images using thallium-201 or technetium-99m sestamibi (Cardiolite) as the tracer. At peak exercise, the tracer is injected and scintigraphy is performed. These agents are taken up by viable myocardium and "light up"; they are not taken up by irreversibly infarcted muscle which appears as a "cold spot." Ischemic muscle will light up on a delayed basis due to redistribution or with rein-jection. If the patient cannot exercise, use of adenosine or dipyri-damole (Persantine) can mimic the effect of exercise on the distribution of blood flow and will give comparable results to

exercise-induced ischemia. If a stress radionuclide angiogram is performed, a fall in ejection fraction is suggestive of ischemia.[3]

3. **Exercise echocardiography** is based on the principle that stress-induced ischemia caused by coronary artery stenoses will result in regional wall motion abnormalities. These tests may be performed using bicycle or treadmill exercise. An alternative to exercise is the use of dobutamine to increase myocardial oxygen demand. If this cannot be met by an increase in blood flow, regional wall motion abnormalities in the distribution of the stenotic coronary artery will be noted. These tests have provided fairly comparable results to those of thallium imaging.[4,5]

C. **Viability studies.** Myocardial viability studies are useful in patients with severe left ventricular dysfunction to identify "hibernating myocardium" that may recover function after revascularization. Rest imaging with thallium is the most basic form, using either planar imaging or single photon emission computed tomography (SPECT). Ischemic zones will perfuse at rest (c.f., during stress imaging, they light up from redistribution on delayed imaging). More sophisticated testing involves measurement of ^{18}F-deoxyglucose uptake by positron emission tomography (PET) or SPECT scanning. These tests may identify evidence of preserved metabolic activity in zones of reduced perfusion and may detect zones considered non-viable by thallium imaging.[6-8] A biphasic response during dobutamine echocardiography (improvement in function at low dose and worsening of function at peak stress from high doses of dobutamine) is also highly predictive of recovery of regional contractile function in patients with LV dysfunction.[9]

III. Cardiac Catheterization

A. The gold standard for the diagnosis of most forms of cardiac disease remains cardiac catheterization.[10] It is indicated in most patients for whom an interventional procedure is contemplated based on review of the history, examination, and stress test results. The exceptions are acute type A aortic dissections and patients with aortic valve endocarditis with vegetations, in whom the risk of catheter manipulation in the root is significant.

B. **Techniques** (See table 2.1 and figures 2.1 and 2.2.)

1. **Right heart catheterization** (RHC) is performed in patients with valve disease and those with coronary disease and left ventricular dysfunction. It involves placement of a Swan-Ganz catheter through the venous system into the pulmonary artery. Intracardiac pressure measurements and pressure waves are obtained. In addition, oxygen saturations are obtained from each chamber and can detect intracardiac shunts (atrial or ventricular septal defects). Measurement of a mixed venous oxygen saturation from the pulmonary artery (PA) port indirectly reflects the cardiac output. A thermodilution cardiac output is obtained and can be used along with pressure gradients obtained from right and left heart catheterization to calculate valve areas using the Gorlin formula (see Chapter 1).

Table 2.1 *Information Obtained from Right and Left Heart Catheterization*

Elevated RA pressures	Tricuspid stenosis (large a wave)
	Tricuspid regurgitation (large v wave)
	Right ventricular dysfunction (pulmonary hypertension, RV infarction)
	Constrictive pericarditis/tamponade
Elevated RV pressures	RV dysfunction (pulmonary hypertension, RV infarction)
	Constrictive pericarditis (square root sign)
	Cardiac tamponade
Elevated PA pressures	Mitral stenosis/regurgitation
	LV systolic or diastolic dysfunction (ischemic, dilated cardiomyopathy, aortic stenosis/regurgitation)
	Pulmonary hypertension of other etiologies
	Constrictive pericarditis/tamponade
Elevated PCWP	LV systolic or diastolic dysfunction (ischemic, dilated cardiomyopathy, aortic stenosis/regurgitation)
	Constrictive pericarditis/tamponade
Elevated LVEDP	LV systolic or diastolic dysfunction (ischemic, dilated cardiomyopathy, aortic stenosis/regurgitation)
	Constrictive pericarditis/tamponade

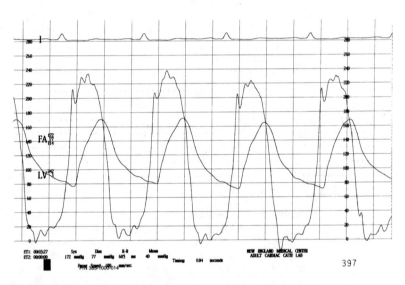

Figure 2.1 *Left heart catheterization of aortic stenosis. Comparison of the simultaneous peak left ventricular and femoral artery pressures demonstrates a peak gradient of 60 mm Hg. If there is a discrepancy between the central aortic and femoral artery pressures, the pullback gradient is calculated as the catheter is withdrawn from the left ventricle into the aorta. (Courtesy of Dr. John J. Smith, Division of Cardiology, New England Medical Center.)*

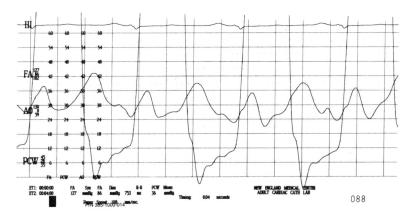

Figure 2.2 *Left and right heart catheterization of mitral stenosis. There is a pressure difference (gradient) of approximately 20 mm Hg between the pulmonary capillary wedge pressure and the mean left ventricular end-diastolic pressure. (Courtesy of Dr. John J. Smith, Division of Cardiology, New England Medical Center.)*

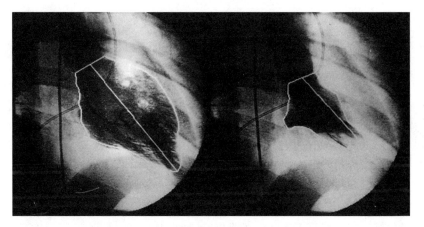

Figure 2.3 *Digital left ventriculogram. The ejection fraction is calculated from the end-diastolic volume (left) minus the end-systolic volume (right).*

2. **Left heart catheterization** involves placing a catheter from the aorta through the aortic valve into the left ventricle. This allows for measurement of the left ventricular end-diastolic pressure, assessment of ejection fraction by a **left ventriculogram** (end-diastolic volume minus end-systolic volume) (figure 2.3), and measurement of the gradient across the aortic valve during pullback of the catheter. A Fick cardiac output can be calculated.

3. An **aortogram** ("root shot") is usually performed in patients with aortic valve disease to assess the degree of aortic regurgitation. It will also give an estimate of aortic size that might necessitate replacement of the ascending aorta. A rough evaluation of aortic

size can be obtained after a left ventriculogram when dye is ejected into the aorta. Excessive whip of an angiographic catheter may suggest the presence of a dilated aortic root. A CT scan or echocardiogram may be indicated to further assess the size of the aorta.

IV. Coronary Angiography

A. Coronary angiography is performed as part of the cardiac catheterization by placing special preformed catheters directly into the coronary ostia and injecting dye into the coronary arteries. It provides the road map that the surgeon memorizes in planning a revascularization procedure (figure 2.4). Calcification of the ascending aorta can be identified during fluoroscopy.

B. **Important indications**

1. Any patient with suspected coronary artery disease (CAD) in whom an interventional procedure might be indicated on a clinical basis (unstable or progressive symptoms, postinfarction angina, or positive stress test).

2. Patients older than age 40 who require open-heart surgery for other reasons. It should also be considered in younger patients if there are other reasons to suspect premature CAD.

3. Annual follow-up of the cardiac transplant patient to detect the development of silent allograft CAD.

C. Angiography will define whether the circulation is right or left dominant (*i.e.*, whether the posterior descending artery arises from the right or left system), and it will define the location, extent, and nature of coronary stenoses. It will also identify the quality and bypassability of the target vessels based on their size and the extent of distal disease. Based on the clinical picture, the results of the stress test and angiogram, and an assessment of left ventricular function, an informed decision can be made as to whether an interventional procedure (PTCA, stent, or surgery) is indicated.

V. Echocardiography

A. Echocardiography provides real-time two-dimensional imaging of the cardiac structures. It is an invaluable noninvasive means of evaluating ventricular and valvular function before, during, and after surgery.[11–15] Although a transthoracic study is usually performed initially in the preoperative patient, biplanar or multiplanar transesophageal imaging (TEE) provides superior imaging because of the proximity of the probe to the heart. Sophisticated echocardiographic analysis involves use of color-flow Doppler and contrast studies.

B. Examples of information that can be derived from transesophageal echocardiography in the pre-, intra-, and postoperative periods are noted in tables 2.2 through 2.4.

Figure 2.4 *Left coronary angiograms. (A) The left main artery divides into the left anterior descending (LAD) and circumflex (CX) arteries. The circumflex gives rise to obtuse marginal branches. (B) This angiogram demonstrates tight left main stenosis. (Courtesy of Dr. John J. Smith, Division of Cardiology, New England Medical Center.)*

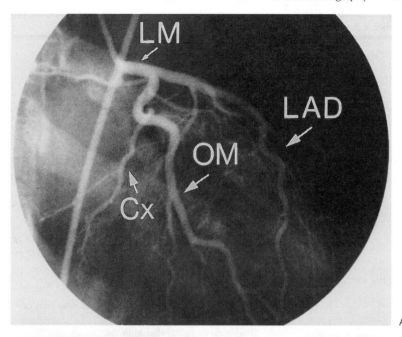

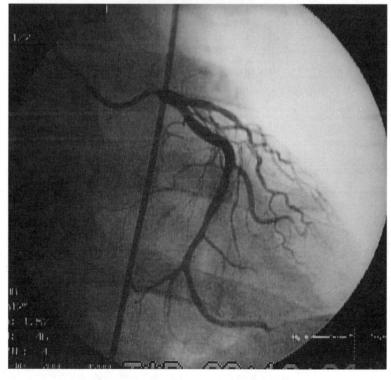

Table 2.2 *Information Obtained from Preoperative Echocardiography*

All patients	Global and regional wall motion abnormalities
	Valve function
	Aortic atherosclerosis
	Pericardial fluid and thickening
Coronary artery disease	Global and regional wall motion abnormalities
	LV mural thrombus
	Presence of mitral regurgitation
	Stress imaging for ischemic zones
Mitral stenosis	Size of left atrium
	Diastolic gradient
	Planimetry of valve area
	Presence of left atrial thrombus
Mitral regurgitation	Size of left atrium
	Degree of regurgitation
	Nature of pathology (annular dilatation, anterior or posterior leaflet prolapse, elongated or torn chords, papillary muscle rupture)
Aortic stenosis	Gradient calculation from flow velocity
	Planimetry of valve area
	Annular diameter (root enlargement, selection of homograft size)
	Presence of mitral regurgitation
Aortic regurgitation	Degree of regurgitation
	Annular diameter (selection of homograft size)
Tricuspid valve disease	Calculation of pulmonary artery pressure from TR jet velocity ($4V^2$)
	Gradient (TS) or degree of regurgitation (TR)
Endocarditis	Vegetations
	Annular abscesses
	Valvular regurgitation
Aortic dissection	Location of intimal flap
	Detection of aortic regurgitation
Cardiac masses	Location and relationship to cardiac structures of tumors, thrombus, vegetations
Pericardial tamponade	Diastolic collapse of ventricular chambers
	Location of fluid around heart

VI.   Computerized Tomography (CT Scanning)

A. CT scanning is indicated primarily for the evaluation of thoracic aortic disease and has few applications in the assessment of cardiac disease.[16] Most commonly, it is obtained in a patient with chest pain in whom an aortic dissection cannot be ruled out, especially when echocardiographic capabilities are not available.

B. Specific indications for obtaining a CT scan in a cardiac surgical patient include:

   1. Identification of an aortic dissection in a patient with unexplained chest pain (if echocardiography is not available or not interpretable)

Table 2.3 *Specific Uses of Intraoperative Echocardiography*

All patients	Epiaortic imaging for aortic atherosclerosis
	Evaluation of poor cardiac performance (regional/global dysfunction)
	Evaluation of iatrogenic aortic dissections
Coronary disease	Regional dysfunction (incomplete/inadequate revascularization)
Valve surgery	Valve regurgitation from paravalvular leak or inadequate repair
	Outflow tract obstruction after mitral valve repair
	Residual stenosis after commissurotomy
	Presence of intracardiac air
Intraaortic balloon pump (IABP)	Location of device relative to the aortic arch
Ventricular septal defect closure	Residual VSD

Table 2.4 *Indications for Postoperative Echocardiography*

Low output states	Left ventricular systolic or diastolic dysfunction
	Cardiac tamponade
	Hypovolemia
	Right ventricular dysfunction
New/persistent murmur (recurrent CHF)	Paravalvular leak
	Inadequate valve repair
	Outflow tract gradient from small valve or systolic anterior motion of mitral valve (SAM)
	Recurrent ventricular septal defect
Evaluation of ventricular recovery after assist device insertion	Left or right ventricular systolic function

2. Assessment of aortic size

    a. When the standard angiogram (left ventriculogram, root shot, or unusual passage of an angiogram catheter) suggests ascending aortic enlargement. One should not be deceived when a transverse coursing structure (such as a tortuous or ectatic segment of aorta) appears enlarged on a transverse section because this does not represent the true diameter.

    b. Descending thoracic aneurysms (figure 2.5A)

3. Evaluation of ascending aortic calcification suggested by chest x-ray or angiogram (figure 2.6). This may require alternative techniques of cannulation and clamping.

4. Identification of the thickness of the pericardium in cases of constrictive pericarditis.

5. Identification of pulmonary or mediastinal abnormalities on preoperative chest x-ray. Obtaining a baseline CT scan prior to cardiac surgery eliminates the potential distortion of pulmonary pathology by postoperative changes.

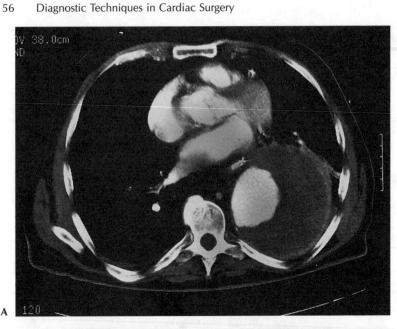

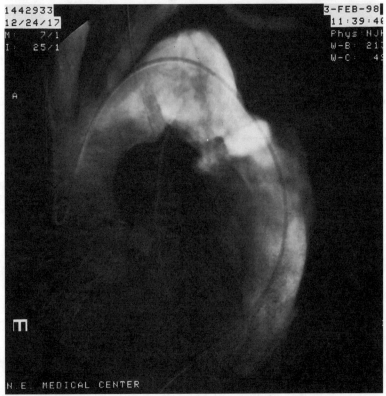

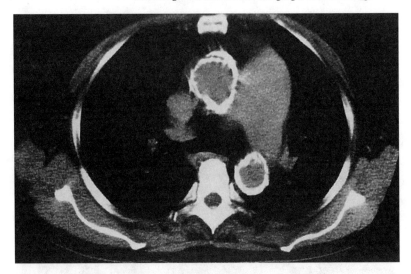

Figure 2.6 *A CT scan demonstrating severe calcification of the ascending and descending aorta ("porcelain aorta"). (Reproduced with permission from the Society of Thoracic Surgeons from The Annals of Thoracic Surgery 1997;64:1179–81.)*

6. Follow-up evaluation of patients undergoing repair of aortic dissection.

VII. Magnetic Resonance Imaging (MRI Scanning)

A. MRI provides excellent images of the cardiac structures and aorta in multiple planes. It can assess blood flow (MR angiography) and does not use radiation. Although the technology is sophisticated and can be used to assess saphenous graft patency and function using phase velocity imaging, its primary indication is for the evaluation of aortic disease.[17]

  1. MRI is very sensitive in the detection of aortic dissection, but generally cannot be performed in the unstable patient (figure 2.7).

  2. Follow-up of patients who have had aortic surgery. It is very sensitive in identifying fluid collections around aortic grafts when infection is suspected.

  3. Evaluation of inflammatory aneurysms

B. MRI scanning cannot be performed in patients with pacemakers, implantable defibrillators, and early generation (Starr-Edwards) valves. However, it can be performed safely in patients with other valve replacements or retained epicardial pacing wires.[18] It cannot be performed feasibly in patients requiring acute physiologic monitoring.

◄───

Figure 2.5 *(A) CT scan of a large descending thoracic aortic aneurysm. Notice the large amount of thrombus surrounding the vascular channel. (B) A digital aortogram of the same patient. Although this gives a better appreciation of the proximal and distal extent of the aneurysm and its relationship to side branches, it significantly underestimates the overall size of the aneurysm.*

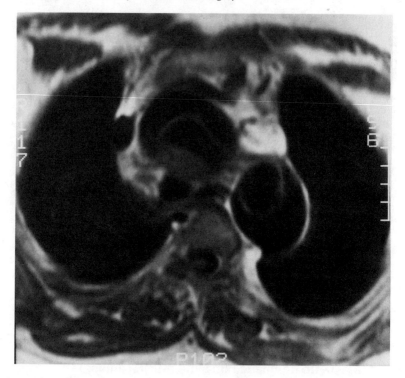

Figure 2.7 *MRI scan demonstrating the intimal flap separating the true and false lumens in a patient with an extensive aortic dissection.*

VIII.   Aortography

A. Once considered the gold standard for the diagnosis of aortic dissections, aortography is now reserved for the evaluation of aortic aneurysms, traumatic aortic tears, and chronic dissections. It images only the vascular lumen and can underestimate the size of an aneurysm (see figure 2.5B). However, it gives a better appreciation of the extent of an aneurysm and its relationship to the aortic branches than other modalities.[19]

B. Advances in angiographic imaging have reduced some of the complications of angiography. One of the major drawbacks was dye-induced renal dysfunction, noted in a study from the 1980s to have an incidence of 10% overall but of nearly 50% in patients with preexisting renal insufficiency.[20] Current technology uses digital acquisition, allowing for use of more dilute contrast in smaller amounts. Embolization of atheromatous material, aortic dissection, and puncture site complications (bleeding, false aneurysms) can still occur with intraarterial injections.

C. Limited aortic-iliofemoral angiography is essential for patients undergoing minimally invasive surgery using the Heartport™ system. This can usually be performed during routine coronary angiography as the catheter is advanced into the lower abdominal aorta.

References

1. Yamazaki K, Kato H, Tsujimoto S, Kitamura R. Diabetes mellitus, internal thoracic artery grafting, and the risk of an elevated hemidiaphragm after coronary artery bypass surgery. J Cardiothorac Vasc Anesthesia 1994;8:437–40.
2. Gibbons RJ, Balady GJ, Beasley JW, et al. ACC/AHA guidelines for exercise testing. J Am Coll Cardiol 1997;30:260–315.
3. Ritchie JL, Bateman TM, Bonow RO, et al. ACC/AHA guidelines for clinical use of cardiac radionuclide imaging. J Am Coll Cardiol 1995;25:521–47.
4. Roger VL, Pellikka PA, Oh JK, Miller FA, Seward JB, Tajik AJ. Stress echocardiography. Part I. Exercise echocardiography: techniques, implementation, clinical applications, and correlations. Mayo Clin Proc 1995;70:5–15.
5. Pellikka PA, Roger VL, Oh JK, Miller FA, Seward JB, Tajik AJ. Part II. Dobutamine stress echocardiography: techniques, implementation, clinical applications, and correlations. Mayo Clin Proc 1995;70:16–27.
6. Ragosta M, Beller GA. The noninvasive assessment of myocardial viability. Clin Cardiol 1993;16:531–8.
7. Rahimtoola SH. Importance of diagnosing hibernating myocardium: how and in whom? J Am Coll Cardiol 1997;30:1701–6.
8. Srinivasan G, Kitsiou AN, Bacharach SL, Bartlett ML, Miller-Davis C, Dilsizian V. 18-Fluorodeoxyglucose single photon emission computed tomography. Can it replace PET and thallium SPECT for the assessment of myocardial viability? Circulation 1998;97:843–50.
9. Cornel JH, Bax JJ, Elhendy A, et al. Biphasic response to dobutamine predicts improvement of global left ventricular function after surgical revascularization in patients with stable coronary artery disease. Implications of time course of recovery on diagnostic accuracy. J Am Coll Cardiol 1998;31:1002–10.
10. Baim DS, Grossman W. Cardiac catheterization, angiography, and intervention, 5th ed. Baltimore: Williams & Wilkins, 1996.
11. Daniel WG, Mügge A. Transesophageal echocardiography. N Engl J Med 1995; 332:1268–79.
12. Seward JB, Khandheria BK, Freeman WK, et al. Multiplane transesophageal echocardiography: image orientation, examination technique, anatomic correlations, and clinical applications. Mayo Clin Proc 1993;68:523–51.
13. Lazar HL, Plehn J. Intraoperative echocardiography. Ann Thorac Surg 1990;50: 1010–18.
14. Cicek S, Dermirkilic U, Kuralay E, Tatar H, Ozturk O. Transesophageal echocardiography in cardiac surgical emergencies. J Cardiac Surg 1995;10:236–44.
15. Reichert CLA, Visser CA, Koolen JJ, et al. Transesophageal echocardiography in hypotensive patients after cardiac operations. Comparison with hemodynamic parameters. J Thorac Cardiovasc Surg 1992;104:321–6.
16. Bateman TM. X-ray computed tomography of the cardiovascular system. Curr Probl Cardiol 1991;16:765–829.
17. Barron DJ, Livesey SA, Brown IW, Delaney DJ, Lamb RK, Monro JL. Twenty-year follow-up of acute type A dissection: the incidence and extent of distal aortic disease using magnetic resonance imaging. J Cardiac Surg 1997;12:147–59.
18. Hartnell GG, Spence L, Hughes LA, Cohen MC, Saouaf R, Buff B. Safety of MR imaging in patients who have retained metallic materials after cardiac surgery. Am J Roentgenol 1997;168:1157–9.
19. Crawford ES, Crawford JL. Diseases of the aorta including an atlas of angiographic pathology and surgical technique. Baltimore: Williams & Wilkins, 1984.
20. Martin-Paredero V, Dixon SM, Baker JD, et al. Risk of renal failure after major angiography. Arch Surg 1983;118:1417–20.

3 General Preoperative Considerations and Preparation of the Patient for Surgery

3   General Preoperative Considerations and Preparation of the Patient for Surgery

I.   General Comments

A.   Once a patient is considered a candidate for cardiac surgery, a multidisciplinary approach should be used to prepare the patient for surgery. Patients requiring urgent surgery are usually evaluated in the inpatient setting, whereas the vast majority of patients undergoing elective procedures will be admitted to the hospital the morning of surgery and must therefore be evaluated on an outpatient basis.

B.   An appropriate evaluation includes a detailed history and physical examination, paying attention to findings that confirm the patient's cardiac diagnosis and noncardiac problems that might need to be addressed before surgery to minimize postoperative morbidity (table 3.1). Attention should also be paid to identifying new cardiac abnormalities that may have arisen since the initial cardiac catheterization that may warrant further work-up. Baseline laboratory tests, if not recently performed, are also obtained. Analysis of demographic factors, cardiac disease, and noncardiac comorbidity can afford the surgeon and patient an insight into the risk of surgery (see Chapter 4).

C.   A cardiac anesthesiologist should interview the patient and discuss issues related to sedation, monitoring lines, awakening from anesthesia, and mechanical ventilation.

D.   Nurses who will be involved with postoperative care should discuss a simplified critical pathway so that the patient has a realistic expectation of what will transpire during the hospital stay. Informing the patient of what procedures will take place and when, what is expected of him or her on each day, when discharge should be anticipated, and what the options are for post-hospital discharge care (rehabilitation facility, skilled nursing facility, home health care) are extremely beneficial in promoting prompt recovery from surgery and early hospital discharge.

II.   History

A.   Recent **aspirin** use may be associated with increased perioperative blood loss by superimposing impaired platelet function on the numerous derangements in the clotting mechanism caused by cardiopulmonary bypass.[1] Aspirin irreversibly acetylates platelet cyclooxygenase, impairing thromboxane A_2 formation and inhibiting platelet aggregation for up to 7 days. Therefore, in elective situations, it is best to stop aspirin for 5–7 days before surgery to allow for replenishment of functional platelets.

1.   In most patients, aspirin usage is not associated with an elevation in the bleeding time. These patients may be considered "aspirin

Table 3.1 *Preoperative Evaluation for Open-Heart Surgery*

History
1. Bleeding issues: aspirin, warfarin, bleeding history
2. Smoking (COPD, bronchospasm)
3. Alcohol (cirrhosis, delirium tremens)
4. Diabetes (protamine reactions, wound infections)
5. Neurologic symptoms (TIAs, remote stroke, previous carotid endarterectomy)
6. Vein stripping (alternative conduits)
7. Ulcer disease/gastrointestinal bleeding (stress prophylaxis)
8. Active infections (urinary tract)
9. Current medications
10. Drug allergies

Physical Examination
1. Skin infections/rash
2. Dental caries (valve surgery)
3. Vascular examination—carotid bruits (stroke) and peripheral pulses (IABP placement)
4. Heart/lungs (congestive heart failure, new murmur)
5. Differential arm blood pressures (pedicled IMA graft)
6. Varicose veins (alternative conduits)

Laboratory Data
1. Hematology: CBC, PT, PTT, platelet count
2. Chemistry: electrolytes, BUN, creatinine, blood sugar, liver function tests
3. Urinalysis
4. Chest x-ray (PA and lateral)
5. Electrocardiogram

nonresponders" and bleeding is rarely an issue during surgery. However, some "aspirin responders" develop what has been termed the "intermediate syndrome of platelet dysfunction." These patients will have an elevated bleeding time and frequently seem to have increased perioperative bleeding. Nonetheless, most studies suggest that an elevated bleeding time is a relatively insensitive predictor of bleeding. Consequently, bleeding times are usually not indicated before surgery, even in patients on aspirin.[2]

2. Aspirin is commonly used in the treatment of unstable angina and in potential candidates for angioplasty; thus, the vast majority of patients will undergo surgery soon after aspirin usage. Fortunately, antifibrinolytic agents and desmopressin are effective in reducing perioperative bleeding in these patients.[3,4]

B. Patients taking **warfarin,** usually for atrial fibrillation, a previous mechanical valve replacement, or a previous stroke, should stop their warfarin 4 days before surgery. Consideration may be given to using IV heparin when the international normalized ratio (INR) falls below the therapeutic range, although the risk of thromboembolism is considered to be very low during the brief period of subtherapeutic anticoagulation.[5]

1. If there are concerns about an increased risk of thromboembolism, patients are usually admitted the day before surgery and given IV heparin. It may be feasible to use low-molecular-weight heparin (3000 units or 30 mg SC bid) as an alternative to avoid hospitalization, but this has not been well studied.[6]

2. Heparin is also used in many patients with unstable angina and should be continued up to the time of surgery. It should usually be continued up to the time of systemic heparinization for cardiopulmonary bypass (CPB), especially in reoperative cases. Cessation of heparin can cause reactivation of unstable angina and may increase coagulation within highly stenotic grafts. This could precipitate thrombosis, resulting in perioperative ischemia and infarction.[7] When heparin is used preoperatively, the platelet count should be checked on a daily basis.

C. Any patient with a known clinical **bleeding disorder** or coagulopathy requires further preoperative evaluation. Even if the abnormality cannot be corrected before surgery, identification of the specific problem will direct postoperative management in the event of persistent mediastinal bleeding. If a patient requires emergent surgery after receiving **thrombolytic therapy** or **antiplatelet medications** (ticlopidine, clopidogrel, or one of the glycoprotein IIb/IIIa inhibitors, such as abciximab (ReoPro), tirofiban (Aggrastat), or eptifibatide (Integrilin)), specific measures may be necessary (see page 152). **Nonsteroidal antiinflammatory drugs** have a reversible effect on platelet function and need to be stopped only a few days before surgery.

D. **Chronic obstructive pulmonary disease** (COPD) is associated with an increased incidence of pulmonary complications, longer ICU stays, and increased operative mortality.[8–12] Pulmonary complications are more common in patients with advanced age, obesity, lower respiratory tract colonization,[13] and a current **smoking** history (fourfold increase in complications in one study, but not in another).[14–16] A patient who is actively smoking should be advised to terminate smoking at least 2 weeks (and preferably 2 months) before surgery to decrease the volume of airway secretions and improve mucociliary transport. Stopping smoking within days of surgery is probably of little benefit and may increase airway secretions.[16]

1. An active pulmonary or bronchitic process (evidenced by a productive cough) should be resolved before surgery using antibiotics. Bronchospastic disease should be treated with bronchodilators and, if severe, with steroids.

2. Pulmonary function tests (PFTs) should be obtained to assess the patient's pulmonary risk when the patient has severe exercise limitation on the basis of suspected poor pulmonary function. Severe reduction in expiratory flow parameters (FEV_1, FVC, or $MMEF_{50-75}$ less than 50% of predicted) is associated with the need for prolonged intubation and a longer ICU stay. This may be associated with an increased risk of pulmonary complications.[17] However, it is often difficult to assess the contribution of a cardiac problem (congestive heart failure, reversible pulmonary hypertension) to abnormal PFTs. Therefore, surgery should not be withheld on the

basis of poor PFTs unless advanced, irreversible pulmonary disease is suspected.

3. Baseline arterial blood gases are frequently valuable for comparison with postoperative values when weaning the patient from the ventilator. An elevated PCO_2 has been found to be the most significant marker for postoperative pulmonary morbidity and mortality.[18]

4. Of particular concern is evidence that patients receiving amiodarone (usually >400 mg/day) for the treatment of malignant ventricular arrhythmias may develop pulmonary toxicity manifested by dyspnea, hypoxia, radiographic infiltrates, and a decrease in diffusion capacity. Evidence of preoperative pulmonary toxicity, even with apparent resolution, has been found to predispose to the development of the adult respiratory distress syndrome (ARDS) following surgery. Avoidance of contributing causes, such as a long duration of bypass, oxygen toxicity, pneumonia, and fluid overload, is critical to avoid life-threatening complications. Advanced pulmonary toxicity may contraindicate a cardiac surgical procedure.[19]

E. A history of heavy **alcohol** abuse identifies potential problems with intraoperative bleeding and postoperative hepatic dysfunction and delirium. Prevention of postoperative delirium tremens with benzodiazepines should be considered. Bioprosthetic valves should be selected to avoid postoperative anticoagulation.

1. Mildly elevated liver function tests are often of unclear significance and usually do not require further evaluation. However, in a patient with a drinking history, they may suggest the presence of alcoholic hepatitis or cirrhosis, and a further evaluation is indicated.

2. A history of GI bleeding, an elevated prothrombin time or low serum albumin, indicating impaired synthetic function or malnutrition, or a low platelet count may suggest the presence of severe cirrhosis with portal hypertension and/or hypersplenism. A liver biopsy may be indicated to evaluate the risk of surgery and the potential for postoperative hepatic failure. The mortality rate of patients with cirrhosis undergoing open-heart surgery is significant.[20]

3. Patients with advanced alcoholic cirrhosis (Child-Turcotte-Pugh class B or C) are generally not candidates for cardiac surgery. However, patients in class A with a bilirubin <2 mg/dL and albumin >3.5 g/dL will usually tolerate cardiopulmonary bypass without adverse effect.

F. **Diabetes mellitus** is a relative contraindication to bilateral internal mammary artery (IMA) bypass grafting because of the significantly increased risk of developing a mediastinal wound infection.[21] Diabetics are also more prone to phrenic nerve dysfunction after IMA harvesting and to a higher incidence of stroke and renal dysfunction.[22,23] Patients taking NPH insulin are at increased risk of experiencing a protamine reaction.[24]

G. **Neurologic symptoms,** whether active (transient ischemic attack) or remote (history of a stroke), increase the risk of perioperative stroke and warrant evaluation.[25] Generally, a carotid noninvasive study should be performed in patients with neurologic symptoms or asymptomatic carotid bruits to assess for significant stenoses or flow-limiting lesions. It should also be considered in patients who have undergone a previous carotid endarterectomy. Further evaluation by carotid arteriography is often performed if noninvasive studies are inconclusive or more precise visualization of the carotid vessels is desired.

1. Actively symptomatic carotid disease always warrants carotid endarterectomy (CE) either prior to or at the time of cardiac surgery. Concomitant coronary artery bypass grafting (CABG) and CE should be performed in the patient with unstable angina or significant myocardium at risk if neurologic symptoms are present.[26,27]

2. The management of asymptomatic lesions is noted below in the discussion of carotid bruits.

H. A history of **saphenous vein strippings and/or ligation** alerts the surgeon to potential problems obtaining satisfactory conduits for bypass grafting. Noninvasive venous mapping of the lower extremities may identify satisfactory greater or lesser saphenous veins for use. Doppler assessment of the palmar arch (Allen's test) should be performed, because the radial artery can be used as a conduit only if ulnar dominance is demonstrated. Venipunctures and IV catheters should be avoided in the arm from which the radial artery will be harvested. The anesthesiologist should also be alerted to avoid placing a radial artery line or IV catheter in that arm in the operating room!

I. **Urologic symptoms** in women suggest the presence of an active urinary tract infection that must be treated before surgery. In men, a history of prostatic cancer treated by irradiation, a prior transurethral resection, or other urinary symptoms consistent with prostatic hypertrophy identify the potential need for a Coudé catheter or suprapubic tube in the operating room and the need for prolonged postoperative urinary drainage.

J. A history of significant **ulcer disease** or **gastrointestinal bleeding** may necessitate further evaluation by endoscopy, especially if the patient will require postoperative anticoagulation. Further evaluation in patients with significant coronary disease may need to be deferred until after surgery. Use of postoperative H_2 blockers, omeprazole, or sucralfate should be considered in these patients.[28]

K. The risk of **infection** is increased if another infectious source is present in the body (commonly a urinary tract or skin infection). Concurrent infections must be identified and treated before surgery. An upper respiratory infection may increase the risk of pulmonary complications,[13] and bacterial infections may increase the risk of a hematogenous sternal wound infection.

L. **Other medical problems** that may require further evaluation or perioperative treatment should be sought. These include hypothyroidism, psychiatric illnesses, including anxiety and depression, and hyperlipidemia.

M. The patient's **medications and allergies** should be reviewed. Cardiac medications should be continued up to the time of surgery; others must be stopped in advance (warfarin, antiplatelet drugs, metformin); and others may require specific attention during anesthesia and the early postoperative course (steroids, insulin, MAO inhibitors, alternative antibiotics for antibiotic allergies, etc.).

III.   Physical Examination

A. An active **skin infection or rash** that might be secondarily infected must be treated before surgery to minimize the risk of sternal wound infection.

B. **Dental caries** must be treated before operations during which prosthetic material (valves, grafts) will be placed.[29] Dental extractions, however, should be recommended cautiously to patients with severe ischemic heart disease or critical aortic stenosis. Cardiac complications may occur even if dental procedures are performed under local anesthesia.

C. **Carotid bruits** are a marker, although an insensitive one, of significant carotid disease. Carotid noninvasive studies are warranted in most patients with bruits to assess for high-grade unilateral or bilateral disease.

1. The management of an asymptomatic carotid lesion in a patient requiring bypass surgery is controversial. The risk of stroke with high-grade unilateral stenotic lesions during an isolated CABG is considered to be higher than normal.[30] Thus, many surgeons would perform a combined CABG-CE for unilateral stenosis >90%. The risk of stroke in a combined operation for unilateral asymptomatic disease is very low, and this approach reduces the subsequent risk of stroke and is more cost-effective.[26,27,31]

2. The risk of stroke with bilateral disease (>75% bilaterally) is significant during isolated CABG (10–15%), especially in patients with unilateral stenosis with contralateral occlusion.[32] However, it remains quite significant even with a combined operation. Thus, the operations should be staged with the carotid endarterectomy performed first if cardiac disease permits. If this is not possible because of unstable angina, left main or severe three-vessel disease with a large amount of "myocardium in jeopardy," a combined operation must be accepted with an increased risk of stroke.

D. **Differential arm blood pressures** identify possible subclavian artery stenosis, a contraindication to use of a pedicled IMA graft. This finding is also noted in some patients presenting with an acute aortic dissection.

E. The presence of a **heart murmur** may warrant a pre- or intraoperative echocardiogram if no valvular abnormality had been identified at the time of catheterization. Occasionally, new-onset ischemic mitral regurgitation or unsuspected aortic valve disease will be detected.

F. An **abdominal aortic aneurysm** detected upon palpation should be evaluated by ultrasound. Intraaortic balloon placement through the femoral artery should be avoided to prevent atheroembolism.

G. Severe **peripheral vascular disease** (PVD) must be assessed by a careful pulse examination.

1. Poor pulses may indicate the unsuitability of the femoral arteries for cannulation or placement of an intraaortic balloon. Careful vascular evaluation, often with an angiogram, is essential for patients

undergoing minimally invasive valve surgery during which femoral artery cannulation is used for arterial access and passage of an intravascular occlusion "Endoclamp" (Heartport™ system).

2. PVD may contribute to poor wound healing. Generally, the saphenous vein should be harvested from the leg with the best circulation to improve wound healing. This will also leave venous conduit for future peripheral vascular reconstruction. "Minimally invasive" vein harvesting through short "skip incisions" under direct vision or with endoscopic equipment may be preferable to one long incision in the leg.

H. The presence of **varicose veins** identifies potential problems with conduits for CABG. The distribution of varicosities may indicate whether or not the greater saphenous vein is involved. Noninvasive venous mapping may identify a normal greater saphenous vein despite significant varicosities. The lesser saphenous vein distribution should be inspected to determine whether it might serve as a potential conduit. Assessment of the radial artery, as noted above, should be considered.

IV. Laboratory Assessment

A. Complete blood count (CBC), prothrombin time (PT), partial thromboplastin time (PTT), and platelet count. It is especially important to check a daily platelet count during heparinization, because heparin-induced thrombocytopenia is fairly common. A bleeding time (as noted in Section IIA) is rarely of value.

B. Electrolytes, BUN, creatinine, blood sugar. Patients with an elevated creatinine, especially those with diabetes mellitus, should have their serum creatinine rechecked after cardiac catheterization. Surgery should be deferred until renal function has returned to baseline because of the increased risk of postoperative renal failure, which is associated with significant operative mortality.[11] Measures should be taken to optimize renal function before surgery, paying particular attention to hydration and optimizing hemodynamic status (see also Chapter 11).

C. Liver function tests (bilirubin, alkaline phosphatase, ALT, AST, albumin) and serum amylase. Abnormalities suggestive of hepatitis or cirrhosis may warrant further evaluation. Those associated with chronic passive congestion may not improve until after surgery has been performed.

D. Urinalysis. A catheter specimen should be obtained in women if the initial urinalysis suggests contamination.

E. Chest x-ray (PA and lateral). The x-ray should be consistent with the patient's cardiac diagnosis. A lateral film should always be obtained before reoperation through a median sternotomy incision. This gives an assessment of the proximity of the cardiac structures and the IMA pedicle clips to the posterior sternal table. It also allows for optimal planning of minimally invasive incisions.

F. Electrocardiogram (ECG). A baseline study should be obtained for comparison with postoperative ECGs. Evidence of an interval infarction or new ischemia since the time of catheterization may warrant reevaluation of ventricular function and, occasionally, a repeat coronary angiogram.

Patients being evaluated for elective surgery with active ischemia on ECG should be hospitalized and undergo urgent procedures. If atrial fibrillation (AF) is present, it should be rate-controlled and its duration should be ascertained. The likelihood of conversion to sinus rhythm after surgery is nearly 80% for patients in AF less than 6 months, but unlikely if of longer duration. Thus, the duration of AF would influence the aggressiveness of postoperative treatment. The presence of a left bundle branch block (LBBB) raises the risk of heart block during the insertion of a Swan-Ganz catheter.

G. Most test results are acceptable when performed within 1 month of surgery. However, it is beneficial to have a CBC, electrolytes, BUN, and creatinine within a few days of surgery.

V. Preoperative Blood Donation

A. The use of antifibrinolytic drugs, such as epsilon-aminocaproic acid, aprotinin and tranexamic acid, has significantly reduced the amount of perioperative blood loss.[33,34] In addition, the use of intraoperative plasmapheresis, intraoperative cell-saving or ultrafiltration devices, and postoperative autotransfusion systems have also been helpful in reducing transfusion requirements.[35]

1. The percentage of patients requiring blood transfusions after coronary surgery is less than 50% and the average number of units transfused is only about 1.5 units/patient. In addition to the measures mentioned above, a lower threshold for transfusions has evolved with the recognition that postoperative hematocrits as low as 22% to 24% are safe.[36,37]

2. Refinement in testing for hepatitis C (0.03% risk) and human immunodeficiency virus (0.004% risk) has lowered their risks and the morbid fear of many patients of receiving transfusions.[38,39] Nonetheless, blood transfusions may still cause febrile, allergic, or transfusion reactions.

B. Preoperative autologous blood donation still remains a feasible objective in patients with stable angina or valvular heart disease. However, its limited use can be ascribed to the urgency of surgery in most cases, concerns about precipitating angina in patients with severe coronary disease, questions about its cost-effectiveness with the availability of other measures to reduce blood loss, and logistic considerations.[40]

1. One unit of blood may be donated every week as long as the hematocrit exceeds 33%, allowing an additional 2 to 3 weeks before surgery for the hematocrit to return to normal.

2. The use of recombinant erythropoietin (100 U/kg intravenously or subcutaneously every day for 1 to 2 weeks; or 600 U/kg subcutaneously 7 and 14 days before surgery) with iron supplementation may also improve the preoperative hematocrit in anemic patients and those who donate their own blood.[41,42] This is primarily beneficial in patients who are Jehovah's Witnesses.

VI. Preoperative Medications

A. All antianginal and antihypertensive medications should be continued up to and including the morning of surgery. This prevents rebound hypertension and recurrence of ischemia, and provides for a more stable anesthetic course. The substitution of a shorter-acting β-blocker or calcium-channel blocker for a longer-acting one (propranolol or metoprolol for nadolol; diltiazem for Cardizem CD) should be considered.

B. Digoxin should be given the morning of surgery if used for rate control.

C. Diuretics are continued up to the morning of surgery. Hypokalemia from diuretics is usually not a problem intraoperatively because of the high doses of potassium present in the cardioplegia solutions used for myocardial protection.

D. Warfarin should be stopped 4 days before surgery to allow for normalization of the INR. Intravenous heparin may be given when the prothrombin time becomes subtherapeutic (INR < 2), although this practice has been questioned.[5] Heparin given for unstable angina is generally continued up to the time of surgery, especially in patients with critical coronary disease or in reoperative procedures with tight saphenous vein graft stenoses in order to maintain patency and coronary blood flow. It rarely causes problems with insertion of central lines.

E. Insulin-dependent (type I) diabetics should refrain from taking their usual morning insulin dose. A blood sugar should be checked in the operating room and insulin given as necessary. Patients taking metformin should not take this for several days before surgery because it may contribute to lactic acidosis during periods of depressed renal function associated with surgery.

F. Antiarrhythmic therapy should be continued until the time of surgery unless ablative arrhythmia surgery is planned, during which it may interfere with intraoperative mapping and evaluation of the efficacy of the procedure. It should be continued in patients undergoing placement of an implantable cardioverter-defibrillator (ICD) device.

G. Preoperative prophylactic antibiotics must be administered before surgical incision. A first-generation cephalosporin, such as cefazolin, is commonly chosen because of its effectiveness against gram-positive organisms. There is some evidence that overall infection rates may be lower with use of second-generation cephalosporins, such as cefamandole or cefuroxime.[43,44] Vancomycin is used if there is a severe allergy to penicillin or the cephalosporins. It is more expensive than the cephalosporins, but because of its increased efficacy against gram-positive organisms, it should probably be selected for all patients undergoing valvular surgery.[44-46] It should not be used indiscriminately, however, to minimize the emergence of strains of vancomycin-resistant enterococci (VRE), a growing concern in intensive care units.

H. Preoperative medications are ordered by the anesthesia service. These usually include sedation with narcotics (morphine) and scopolamine. Additional sedation with IV midazolam may be given in the operating room. The selection of preoperative medications usually depends on the nature of the patient's cardiac disease, as discussed in Chapter 1.

VII. Preoperative Checklist

The evening before surgery, the covering physician/physician assistant/nurse practitioner should write a brief preoperative note summarizing essential information that should be reviewed before proceeding with the operation. Writing this note prevents important details from being overlooked. For patients undergoing elective surgery, the surgeon's office must confirm the night before admission that all of the requisite information is present in the patient's office chart and is available to the operating room when the patient arrives in the morning. The following should be noted:

A. The planned operative procedure

B. Brief summary of the cardiac catheterization

C. Results of the laboratory data listed above

D. Surgical note and consent in chart

E. Anesthesia note and consent in chart

F. Confirmation of blood bank cross-match and blood set-up

    1. The major determinants of the need for transfusion are the patient's blood volume (which correlates with body size and usually with gender), and the preoperative hemoglobin level.[47,48] Other risk factors for transfusion include older age, urgent or emergency operations, reoperations, and the presence of comorbidities (insulin-dependent diabetes, peripheral vascular disease, elevated creatinine, albumin <4 g/dL consistent with poor nutrition).

    2. Guidelines for blood set-up are as follows:

Procedure	PRBC Set-Up
Minimally invasive CABG without pump	Type and Screen
Weight >70 kg and hematocrit >35%	One unit
Weight <70 kg or hematocrit <35%	Two units
Reoperations	Three units
Ascending aortic surgery	Three units
Descending aortic surgery	Six units

G. Preoperative orders are written:

    1. Antibiotics: (always check for allergy)

       • Cefazolin, 1 g IV to be given in the operating room

        or

       • Vancomycin, 1 g IV (about 15 mg/kg) to be given in operating room (given over 30 minutes to avoid hypotension and the "red-neck syndrome")[45,46,49]

    2. Antiseptic scrub (chlorhexidine) with which to shower the night before surgery[50]

    3. Skin preparation. This is best performed the morning of surgery as it has been well documented that the closer the prep to the time

of surgery, the lower the wound infection rate.[51] Use of a depilatory or clippers is preferable to shaving with a razor, which increases the risk of infection.

4. Nothing by mouth (NPO) after midnight
5. Preoperative medications per anesthesia service

References

1. Sethi GK, Copeland JG, Goldman S, Moritz T, Zadina K, Henderson WG. Implications of preoperative administration of aspirin in patients undergoing coronary artery bypass grafting. J Am Coll Cardiol 1990;15:15–20.
2. Lind SE. The bleeding time does not predict surgical bleeding. Blood 1991;77:2747–52.
3. Murkin JM, Lux J, Shannon NA, et al. Aprotinin significantly decreases bleeding and transfusion requirements in patients receiving aspirin and undergoing cardiac operations. J Thorac Cardiovasc Surg 1994;107:554–61.
4. Gratz I, Koehler J, Olsen D, et al. The effect of desmopressin acetate on postoperative hemorrhage in patients receiving aspirin therapy before coronary artery bypass operations. J Thorac Cardiovasc Surg 1992;104:1417–22.
5. Kearon C, Hirsh J. Management of anticoagulation before and after elective surgery. N Engl J Med 1997;336:1506–11.
6. Cohen M, Demers C, Gurfinkel EP, et al. A comparison of low-molecular weight heparin with unfractionated heparin for unstable coronary artery disease. N Engl J Med 1997;337:447–52.
7. Theroux P, Waters D, Lam J, Juneau M, McCans J. Reactivation of unstable angina after the discontinuation of heparin. N Engl J Med 1992;327:141–5.
8. Higgins TL, Estafanous FG, Loop FD, Beck GJ, Blum JM, Paranandi L. Stratification of morbidity and mortality by preoperative risk factors in coronary artery bypass patients. A clinical severity score. JAMA 1992;267:2344–8.
9. Geraci JM, Rosen AK, Ash AS, McNiff KJ, Moskowitz MA. Predicting the occurrence of adverse events after coronary artery bypass surgery. Ann Intern Med 1993;118:18–24.
10. Kurki TSO, Kataja M. Preoperative prediction of postoperative morbidity in coronary artery bypass grafting. Ann Thorac Surg 1996;61:1740–5.
11. The Society of Thoracic Surgeons. Data analyses of The Society of Thoracic Surgeons National Cardiac Surgery Database, January 1996. Summit Medical Systems, 1996.
12. Cohen A, Katz M, Katz R, Hauptman E, Schachner A. Chronic obstructive pulmonary disease in patients undergoing coronary artery bypass grafting. J Thorac Cardiovasc Surg 1995;109:574–81.
13. Zickmann B, Sablotzki A, Fussle R, Gorlach G, Hempelmann G. Perioperative microbiologic monitoring of tracheal aspirates as a predictor of pulmonary complications after cardiac operations. J Thorac Cardiovasc Surg 1996;111:1213–8.
14. Warner MA, Offord KP, Warner ME, Lennon RL, Conover MA, Jansson-Schumacher U. Role of preoperative cessation of smoking and other factors in postoperative pulmonary complications: a blinded prospective study of coronary artery bypass patients. Mayo Clin Proc 1989;64:609–16.
15. Utley JR, Leyland SA, Fogarty CM, et al. Current smoking is not a predictor of mortality and morbidity following coronary artery bypass grafting. J Cardiac Surg 1996;11:377–84.
16. Pearce AC, Jones RM. Smoking and anesthesia: preoperative abstinence and postoperative morbidity. Anesthesiology 1984;61:576–84.
17. Bevelaqua F, Garritan S, Hass F, Salazar-Schicchi J, Axen K, Reggiani JL. Complications after cardiac operations in patients with severe pulmonary impairment. Ann Thorac Surg 1990;50:602–6.
18. Cain HD, Stevens PM, Adaniya R. Preoperative pulmonary function and complications after cardiovascular surgery. Chest 1979;76:130–5.
19. Mickleborough LL, Maruyama H, Mohamed S, et al. Are patients receiving amiodarone at increased risk for cardiac operations? Ann Thorac Surg 1994;58:622–9.
20. Ziser A, Plevak DJ, Offord KP. Morbidity and mortality in cirrhotic patients undergo-

ing major cardiac, thoracic or vascular surgery. J Cardiothorac Vasc Anesthesia 1994;8(suppl 3):72.

21. Grossi EA, Esposito R, Harris LJ, et al. Sternal wound infections and use of internal mammary artery grafts. J Thorac Cardiovasc Surg 1991;102:342–7.

22. Yamazaki K, Kato H, Tsujimoto S, Kitamura R. Diabetes mellitus, internal thoracic artery grafting, and the risk of an elevated hemidiaphragm after coronary artery bypass surgery. J Cardiothorac Vasc Anesthesia 1994;8:437–40.

23. Clement R, Rousou JA, Engleman RM, Breyer RH. Perioperative morbidity in diabetics requiring coronary artery bypass surgery. Ann Thorac Surg 1988;46:321–3.

24. Weiler JM, Gellhaus MA, Carter JG, et al. A prospective study of the risk of an immediate adverse reaction to protamine sulfate during cardiopulmonary bypass surgery. J Allergy Clin Immunol 1990;85:713–9.

25. Redmond JM, Greene PS, Goldsborough MA, et al. Neurologic injury in cardiac surgical patients with a history of stroke. Ann Thorac Surg 1996;61:42–7.

26. Rizzo RJ, Whittemore AD, Couper GS, et al. Combined carotid and coronary revascularization: the preferred approach to the severe vasculopath. Ann Thorac Surg 1992;54:1099–109.

27. Akins CW, Moncure AC, Daggett WM, et al. Safety and efficacy of concomitant carotid and coronary operations. Ann Thorac Surg 1995;60:311–8.

28. Tryba M. Sucralfate versus antacids or H_2-antagonists for stress ulcer prophylaxis: a meta-analysis on efficacy and pneumonia rate. Crit Care Med 1991;19:942–9.

29. Terezhalmy GT, Safadi TJ, Longworth DL, Muehrcke DD. Oral disease burden in patients undergoing prosthetic heart valve implantation. Ann Thorac Surg 1997;63:402–4.

30. Hertzer NR, Loop FD, Beven EG, O'Hara PJ, Krajewski LP. Surgical staging for simultaneous coronary and carotid disease: a study including prospective randomization. J Vasc Surg 1989;9:455–63.

31. Chang BB, Darling RC III, Shah DM, Paty PSK, Leather RP. Carotid endarterectomy can be safely performed with acceptable mortality and morbidity in patients requiring coronary artery bypass grafts. Am J Surg 1994;168:94–6.

32. D'Agostino RS, Svensson LG, Neumann DJ, Balkhy HH, Williamson WA, Shahian DM. Screening carotid ultrasonography and risk factors for stroke in coronary artery surgery patients. Ann Thorac Surg 1996;62:1714–23.

33. Fremes SE, Wong BI, Lee E, et al. Metaanalysis of prophylactic drug treatment in the prevention of postoperative bleeding. Ann Thorac Surg 1994;58:1580–8.

34. Chen RH, Frazier OH, Cooley DA. Antifibrinolytic therapy in cardiac surgery. Texas Heart Inst J 1995;22:211–5.

35. Scott WJ, Kessler R, Wernly JA. Blood conservation in cardiac surgery. Ann Thorac Surg 1990;50:843–51.

36. Johnson RG, Thurer RL, Kruskall MS, et al. Comparison of two transfusion strategies after elective operations for myocardial revascularization. J Thorac Cardiovasc Surg 1992;104:307–14.

37. Doak GJ, Hall RI. Does hemoglobin concentration affect perioperative myocardial lactate flux in patients undergoing coronary artery bypass surgery? Anesth Analg 1995;80:910–6.

38. Donahue JG, Munoz A, Ness PM, et al. The declining risk of post-transfusion hepatitis C virus infection. N Engl J Med 1992;327:369–73.

39. Nelson KE, Donahue JG, Munoz A, et al. Transmission of retroviruses from seronegative donors by transfusion during cardiac surgery. A multicenter study of HIV-1 and HTLV-I/II infections. Ann Intern Med 1992;117:554–9.

40. Birkmeyer JD, AuBuchon JP, Littenberg B, et al. Cost-effectiveness of preoperative autologous donation in coronary artery bypass grafting. Ann Thorac Surg 1994;57:161–9.

41. Watanabe Y, Fuse K, Konishi T, et al. Autologous blood transfusion with recombinant human erythropoietin in heart operations. Ann Thorac Surg 1991;51:767–72.

42. Watanabe Y, Fuse K, Naruse Y, et al. Subcutaneous use of erythropoietin in heart surgery. Ann Thorac Surg 1992;54:479–84.

43. Kreter B, Woods M. Antibiotic prophylaxis for cardiothoracic operations. Metaanalysis of thirty years of clinical trials. J Thorac Cardiovasc Surg 1992;104:590–9.

44. Maki DG, Bohn MJ, Stolz SM, Kroncke GM, Acher CW, Myerowitz PD. Comparative study of cefazolin, cefamandole, and vancomycin for surgical prophylaxis in cardiac and vascular operations. J Thorac Cardiovasc Surg 1992;104:1423–34.

45. Southorn PA, Plevak DJ, Wright AJ, Wilson WR. Adverse effects of vancomycin administered in the perioperative period. Mayo Clin Proc 1986;61:721–4.

46. Farber BF, Karchmer AW, Buckley MJ, Moellering RC Jr. Vancomycin prophylaxis in cardiac operations: determination of the optimal dosage regimen. J Thorac Cardiovasc Surg 1983;85:933–5.

47. Magovern JA, Sakert T, Benckart DH, et al. A model for predicting transfusion after coronary artery bypass grafting. Ann Thorac Surg 1996;61:27–32.

48. Cosgrove DM, Loop FD, Lytle BW, et al. Determinants of blood utilization during myocardial revascularization. Ann Thorac Surg 1995;40:380–4.

49. Rosenberg JM, Wahr JA, Smith KA. Effect of vancomycin infusion on cardiac function in patients scheduled for cardiac operation. J Thorac Cardiovasc Surg 1995;109:561–4.

50. Kaiser AB, Kernodle DS, Barg NL, Petracek MR. Influence of preoperative showers on staphylococcal skin colonization: a comparative trial of antiseptic skin cleansers. Ann Thorac Surg 1988;45:35–8.

51. Ko W, Lazenby WD, Zelano JA, Isom OW, Krieger KH. Effects of shaving methods and intraoperative irrigation on suppurative mediastinitis after bypass operations. Ann Thorac Surg 1992;53:301–5.

4 Risk Assessment in Cardiac Surgery

General Concepts

Univariate Models

Multivariate Regression Models

Bayesian Analysis and Neural Networks (Artificial Intelligence)

Morbidity Analysis

4 Risk Assessment in Cardiac Surgery

An important element of preoperative preparation for cardiac surgery is an assessment of the patient's surgical risk. Risk stratification can afford patients and their families insight into the real risk of complications and mortality. It can also increase the awareness of the health care team to the high-risk patient for whom more aggressive therapy in the pre-, intra- or postoperative period may be beneficial. Although an understanding of sophisticated statistical models for risk assessment can seem overwhelming, the essential elements of the basic models are rather straightforward.

I. General Concepts

A. Although outcome analysis using risk-adjusted mortality rates should be used to assess and improve the delivery of medical care, it is being increasingly utilized as a means of comparing surgical results among hospitals. Risk stratification "levels the playing field" by accommodating differences in the severity of illness when predicting patient outcomes. It has thus become an important element in managed care contracting and will have a profound impact on the business and practice of medicine in the future.

B. Risk assessment has been used to predict not only morbidity and mortality rates, but also length of stay (LOS) and the consumption of resources. This might theoretically lead to increased prospective reimbursement for patients at higher risk for whom hospital costs are significantly greater. However, in the absence of increased reimbursement, patients at higher "economic risk" might be rejected as candidates for surgery in some centers because of the financial drain they impose.

C. Many studies have examined the relationship between risk factors and mortality.[1-9] However, the overall mortality for coronary bypass surgery is about 3% nationwide, whereas the incidence of complications after surgery is probably between 25 and 40%. Thus, the ability to predict and hopefully prevent postoperative morbidity has even greater impact on improving the quality of care and reducing hospital costs. Several studies have identified risk factors that are associated with morbidity, ICU stay, and hospital costs.[3,10-14]

D. Risk stratification is based on an assessment of three important categories of risk factors (table 4.1):

1. **Patient demographics.** These refer to patient-related factors, independent of disease, such as age, gender, and body surface area (BSA).

2. **Comorbidities.** These refer to coexisting diseases that are not directly related to the cardiac disease but can have significant impact on the patient's ability to recover from surgery. In the vast majority of patients, surgical complications and death are related to preexisting comorbidities, such as renal dysfunction, cerebrovascular disease, chronic obstructive pulmonary disease, and

Table 4.1   *Essential Data Entered in the Society of Thoracic Surgeons (STS) Database*

Demographics	Age
	Gender
Acuity/Priority	Elective/urgent/emergent
Comorbidities	Smoking
	Diabetes
	Morbid obesity
	Renal failure
	Hypertension
	Stroke
	COPD
	Peripheral vascular disease
	Cerebrovascular disease
Cardiac disease	Recent MI
	Type of angina
	Cardiogenic shock
	Preoperative arrhythmias
	Preop meds (diuretics, inotropes, antiarrhythmics, NTG)

       diabetes that render the patient more susceptible to the insults of cardiopulmonary bypass or complications from a low cardiac output state. Thus, accurate documentation of comorbidities is essential to any risk stratification model.

3. **Cardiac disease.** The nature and extent of cardiac disease and the urgency of surgery are important elements in determining surgical mortality risk, especially when the risk is high. Cardiac disease may also contribute to comorbidities, such as renal dysfunction, that may increase the length of stay and contribute to operative mortality. However, in patients at low to moderate cardiac risk, morbidity and mortality are predicted more commonly by comorbidities than by cardiac disease.

II.   Univariate Models

A. Univariate analysis is a rather simple model that assesses the association of an individual risk factor with a specific outcome, such as mortality. It uses chi-square and t tests to identify whether an association is present with high probability (P value < 0.05) or is due to random chance. An extensive univariate analysis for patients undergoing various types of open-heart surgery has been performed by the Society of Thoracic Surgeons (STS), which correlated pre-, intra-, and postoperative variables with surgical mortality (tables 4.2 through 4.4). Odds ratios are calculated that compare the outcome with and without the risk factor being present. For example, if the mortality is 2% for nondiabetics and 4% for diabetics, the odds ratio is 2.0 for diabetics.[1]

B. Calculation of operative risk is difficult using univariate data. Although each individual risk factor increases the risk of surgery, it is difficult to

Table 4.2 *Preoperative Factors and CABG Mortality in STS Database (1995–1996)*

Risk Variable	Risk Ratio[a]	Mortality (%)
Demographics		
Female	1.6	4.3
Age > 65	2.4	4.4
Comorbidities		
Renal failure (creat > 2.0)	3.4	9.6
Previous stroke	2.0	5.8
COPD	1.7	4.7
Diabetes	1.4	3.9
Cardiac-related		
Cardiogenic shock	7.6	21
Prior MI < 6 hours	5.1	11.9
On inotropic support	5.0	14.1
Prior MI 6–24 hours	4.0	9.2
Preoperative IABP	3.4	8.9
Emergency (nonsalvage)	2.8	6.2
Reoperative CABG	2.8	7.5
Congestive heart failure	2.8	7.0
PTCA within 6 h	2.6	7.7
Age > 65	2.4	4.2
Arrhythmias	2.2	5.8
EF < 50%	2.1	4.3
PCWP > 15	2.0	5.3
On IV NTG	1.7	4.5
Class IV	1.6	4.8
Left main	1.6	4.5
Urgent indication	1.5	3.3

[a]*Risk ratio = mortality rate with risk factor compared with mortality rate without risk factor being present. Overall CABG mortality among 230,730 operated upon in 1995–1996 was 3.1%.*

Table 4.3 *Intraoperative Factors and CABG Mortality in STS Database (1995–1996)*

Risk Variable	Risk Ratio	Mortality (%)
Intraoperative IABP	9.8	25.2
Antiarrhythmics leaving OR	3.1	8.4
Inotropic support leaving OR	3.1	5.2
Use of ventricular pacing	2.4	6.1
Use of atrial pacing	1.7	4.7
Blood Product Utilization		
Cryoprecipitate	5.3	15.1
Platelets	4.1	9.9
Fresh frozen plasma	4.1	9.7
Red blood cells	3.7	5.9

Table 4.4 *Postoperative Complications and CABG Mortality in the STS Database (1995–1996)*

Risk Variable	Incidence for 1st Operations (%)	Risk Ratio	Mortality (%)
Multisystem failure	0.6	29	74
Cardiac arrest	1.3	30	64
Renal failure (dialysis)	0.8	18	48
Septicemia	0.9	14	39
Renal failure (no dialysis: creat >2.0)	2.8	14	31
Ventilated >5 days	5.5	11	21
Permanent stroke	1.5	10	28
Tamponade	0.3	8	25
Anticoagulation-related	0.4	8	25
Perioperative MI	1.2	7	19
GI complication	2.0	6	17
Reexploration for bleeding	2.1	5	13
Deep sternal infection	0.6	4	11

assess the overall risk when multiple factors are present. The inherent shortcomings of univariate models mandate the use of multivariate analysis to evaluate further the independent association with morbidity or mortality of factors found to be significant by univariate analysis.

1. Risk factors are often interdependent, so the impact of similar risk factors in any model must be manipulated in some fashion to prevent overestimation of risk. For example, in the STS database, numerous variables are consistent with LV dysfunction. How should one calculate risk in the patient with cardiogenic shock within 21 days of an infarction when the patient has an elevated LVEDP and pulmonary capillary wedge pressure (PCWP) and requires preoperative inotropes and an intraaortic balloon pump (IABP)?

2. Certain risk factors identified in univariate models are reflective of other more independent variables that directly affect operative risk. For example, Table 4.3 shows that the use of any blood product significantly raised the risk of mortality by 3.7–5.3-fold. Although blood products can have adverse effects on pulmonary function and right ventricular performance, the mortality noted in patients receiving blood products is more commonly attributable to their use during complex procedures in elderly patients with preoperative anemia, extensive cardiac disease, and comorbidities.

C. Although some factors are discrete or dichotomous, such as gender or reoperation, others are continuous, such as patient age or ventricular function. Further subdividing continuous variables into multiple categories makes risk assessment very complex when numerous risk factors are being considered.

D. When dealing with continuous variables, it is important to define where the significant break in mortality occurs to obtain a more accurate assessment of risk. In the STS database, the odds ratio increased for an ejection fraction less than 50% and age older than 65 years. However, most studies suggest that the risk is not increased until the EF is less than 30% or age is greater than 75 years. This problem is evident no matter which type of analysis is performed.

III. Multivariate Regression Models

A. Multivariate regression models are designed to assess the independent association of variables with a specific outcome. In these models, only those variables found to be significant in univariate analysis are entered. Factors are added to or subtracted from the analysis until their relative weight or odds ratio can be determined. Logistic (or nonlinear) regression is used for dichotomous outcomes, such as death, whereas linear regression analysis is used for continuous outcomes, such as length of stay or hospital costs. One of the criticisms of these models is that data entry for an individual patient must be discarded if complete information is not provided.

B. Numerous risk factors for mortality have been identified in several major studies during the past 9 years.[2-9] Several factors represent routinely available information and represent the core variables from which operative mortality can be predicted with excellent accuracy.[8,9] They include, in decreasing order of significance:

   1. Urgency of surgery (emergent or urgent)
   2. Reoperation
   3. Older age
   4. Poor ventricular function
   5. Female gender
   6. Left main disease

C. Other less common but powerful risk factors must also be considered when predicting operative mortality. Inclusion of these factors is essential for an accurate assessment, especially when the risk is very high. Catastrophic conditions—such as cardiogenic shock, ventricular septal rupture, or ongoing CPR, as well as major comorbidities, such as dialysis-dependent renal failure and end-stage COPD—have significant impact on operative mortality and carry the highest odds ratios. Table 4.5 shows a comparison of risk factors identified in several major studies in order of significance. These include other so-called "level 1 variables," such as diabetes, cerebrovascular disease, and peripheral vascular disease, that are likely to be associated with increased mortality, but, just as importantly, have a significant impact on postoperative morbidity.

D. Multivariate models can be used in a variety of ways. Some allow for simple calculation of a risk based on multiplication of odds ratios, whereas others assign weights or points to each factor based on their odds ratio, which should reflect the relative contribution of each factor to mortality. The score derived from the weight of various factors can then be clinically correlated with ranges of mortality (0% to 5%, 5% to 8%, etc.). The most sophisticated models with extensive data entry require a computerized calculation to estimate the operative mortality.

   1. A simple multivariate model using odds ratios has been reported by the Department of Veteran Affairs.[6] A logit equation incorpo-

Table 4.5 Predictors of Operative Mortality in Major Studies (Multivariate analyses)[2-7]

Parsonnet[2]	Higgins[3] (Cleveland Clinic)	STS 1994[4]	NNE[5]	VA System[6]	NY State[7]
Catastrophic states (VSD)	Emergency	Emergency (salvage)	Age > 75	Reoperation	Disasters (VSD, cardiogenic shock)
Age > 80	Creat > 1.9	Reoperation	Emergency	Preoperative IABP	2nd reoperation
Dialysis-dependent renal failure	Severe LV dysfunction	Dialysis-dependent renal failure	Reoperation	IV NTG use	EF < 20%
Emergency	Reoperation	Cardiogenic shock	Age > 65	Cardiomegaly	Dialysis-dependent renal failure
Reoperation	Mitral regurgitation	Emergency (nonsalvage)	BSA < 1.6	Resting ST depression	1st reoperation
Age > 70	Age > 75	Creat > 1.5	Comorbidity score > 1	Peripheral vascular disease	CHF
EF < 30%	Prior vascular surgery	H/o stroke	Urgent operation	ASA classification	Diabetes
Diabetes	COPD	Female	LVEDP > 22	Cerebrovascular disease	Unstable angina
Morbid obesity	Anemia	Preop IABP	Age 60–64	Current diuretic	Valve operation
Hypertension	Diabetes	Peripheral vascular disease		Elevated creatinine	Left main

rating all variables with a P value $< .05$ in the multivariate logistic regression analysis was created to calculate the expected mortality. Mortality can be estimated simply by multiplying the odds ratios for each variable and then multiplying by the baseline mortality rate (table 4.6).

2. Two multivariate risk assessment models (Parsonnet[2] and Higgins[3]) have used scoring systems that allow for the bedside calculation of operative risk. Each factor found to be significant by multivariate analysis was assigned a relative weight based on its odds ratio, and the total score was correlated with ranges of mortality. Both models include pertinent demographic, cardiac, and noncardiac factors and have been validated clinically, although they tend to be somewhat inaccurate in estimating the mortality in very high-risk patients. The Cleveland Clinic model has also been used to determine morbidity and ICU length of stay after surgery (table 4.7 and figure 4.1).[13]

3. The Northern New England Model[5] included only seven clinical variables (age, gender, BSA, reoperation, ejection fraction, LVEDP, and surgical priority) and used the Charlson comorbidity index.[15] This index is based on assessment of 1-year, rather than 1-month, mortality data. Although nearly all comorbidity for cardiac surgical patients is accommodated by three factors (peripheral vascular disease, COPD, and diabetes, which had odds ratios of 2.9, 1.5, and 1.5, respectively), this index is overweighted with risk factors rarely seen in cardiac surgical patients (ulcer disease, leukemia, advanced liver disease, metastatic cancer, etc). Thus, if a patient had two of these factors, it would potentially increase surgical risk out of proportion to relevant comorbidities. Despite this criticism, excellent validation has been noted between the computer-generated estimate and the observed mortality.

Table 4.6 *Prediction of Operative Mortality in the Veterans Affairs Database[6]*

Risk Factor	Odds Ratio
Reoperation	2.2
Preoperative IABP	2.0
IV nitroglycerin	1.7
Cardiomegaly	1.5
Resting ST depression	1.4
Peripheral vascular disease	1.4
ASA classification	1.4
Current use of diuretics	1.3
Cerebrovascular disease	1.3
Congestive heart failure	1.2
Creatinine	1.2

The risk factors are identified and their odds ratios are multiplied by the baseline operative risk at a given institution to calculate an operative risk.

Table 4.7 *Cleveland Clinic Clinical Severity Scoring System[3]*

Preoperative Factor	Score
Emergency case	6
Creatinine >1.6–1.8	1
Creatinine ≥1.9	4
Severe LV dysfunction	3
Reoperation	3
Mitral regurgitation	3
Age 65–74	1
Age >75	2
Prior vascular surgery	2
COPD	2
Hematocrit <34%	2
Aortic stenosis	1
Weight ≤65 kg	1
Diabetes	1
Cerebrovascular disease	1

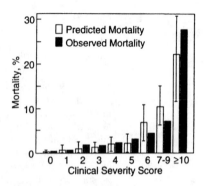

Figure 4.1 *The correlation of the clinical severity scoring system with mortality at the Cleveland Clinic. (Source: Higgins TL, Estafanous FG, Loop FD, et al. Stratification of morbidity and mortality outcome by preoperative risk factors coronary artery bypass patients. JAMA 1992;2657:234–8.)*

IV. Bayesian Analysis and Neural Networks (Artificial Intelligence)

A. Bayes' theorem basically states that one can predict the probability of an event based on the presence of a given factor, whether past, present, or potential. Based on an assessment of multiple factors, a conditional probability matrix is created. A predictive equation is then used to calculate the operative mortality based on the variables entered into the matrix. Because this calculation is rather complex, a computer-based iterative technique has been used that will determine operative outcome if the appropriate information is provided. The advantage of this model is that the results are not skewed by missing values.

B. This system was originally chosen by the Society of Thoracic Surgeons for analysis of predicted operative mortality rates. Significant variables (see table 4.1) are entered into the computer model which then calculates a patient's expected operative mortality based on national results. Currently, because data entry is more complete, the STS is using logistic regression analysis for its database.

C. Neural networks (artificial intelligence) are sophisticated models that have been evaluated as means of improving the accuracy of predicting mortality.[16] They mitigate some of the weaknesses of multivariate models which may not include uncommon variables that can have significant impact on outcome or may have missing data that can alter results. Generally, these models have not shown any greater predictive accuracy than the standard models previously mentioned. In higher risk patients, multivariate and Bayesian analyses tend to overestimate risk while neural networks underestimate risk.[17]

V.   Morbidity Analysis

A. Morbidity is noted in approximately 25–40% of patients after surgery. Awareness of potential risk factors and measures taken to optimize organ system function are critical to reducing the risk or severity of a particular complication. The more common complications, such as atrial fibrillation, are fairly benign but can have significant impact on hospital costs because of the number of patients who develop such problems. Less common complications may be associated with significant mortality and can be extremely costly (see table 4.4).

B. Prediction of increased LOS from preoperative variables is helpful in identifying patients with potentially increased hospital costs. Although increased LOS is more frequently associated with adverse events, a more prolonged recovery may simply be attributable to the insult of cardiopulmonary bypass and a complex surgical procedure in a very ill, often elderly, debilitated patient with multiple comorbidities.

C. Numerous publications have examined predictors of operative morbidity. Some provide a combined risk assessment for mortality and morbidity,[10,11,18] while others evaluate risk factors for postoperative morbidity with or without an evaluation of length of stay.[12,14,19,20] As with mortality studies, odds ratios can be calculated and then manipulated in such a way as to predict the overall probability of an adverse event. The risk factors identified in most but not all studies are similar to those associated with operative mortality. Commonly identified factors found to increase postoperative morbidity in six studies published through 1997 include, in relative order of significance (table 4.8):

1. Reoperations

2. Emergent procedure

3. Preoperative usage of an IABP

4. Congestive heart failure

5. CABG-valve surgery

6. Older age

7. Comorbidities in order of significance:

   a. Renal dysfunction

   b. Chronic obstructive pulmonary disease

   c. Diabetes

   d. Cerebrovascular disease

D. The significance of preexisting comorbidities or risk factors for postoperative morbidity is evident when the mortality associated with the development of complications is analyzed. Although increased morbidity may be inevitable in some patients, such as an elderly patient undergoing emergency surgery or a reoperation, the surgical outcome might be improved if additional perioperative measures are undertaken when risk factors are identified. Notable in the STS database (see table 4.4) are the following:

1. Renal failure that requires dialysis carries a mortality of nearly 50%. Optimizing renal function before, during, and after surgery is

Table 4.8 *Preoperative Predictors of Postoperative Morbidity or Increased Length of Stay in Major Studies*

Boston Univ[18]	Veterans Affairs[6]	Helsinki[19]	Pres-St. Luke's[12]	Albany[14]	Ontario[11]	Boston Univ[20]
Morbidity & Mortality	*Morbidity*	*Morbidity*	*Morbidity*	*Length of Stay*	*Length of Stay*	*Length of Stay*
Reoperation	Reoperation	Emergency	Emergency	Renal dysfunction	Emergency	Reoperation
Emergency	Preop IABP	Diabetes	Age ≥75	Previous stroke	Age ≥75	Valve-CABG
COPD	PVD	ST changes or nonsinus rhythm	MI within 3 mo	Peripheral vascular disease	Complex operation	Congestive heart failure
Pneumonia	Urgency	Low EF	CABG-valve	CHF	EF <20%	Insulin-dependent diabetes mellitus
ST >110	Diabetes	Age >70	Renal dysfunction	Age/RBC vol	Age 65–74	Creatinine ≥1.5
Age > 65	COPD	Creatinine >1.2	Cerebrovascular disease	Hypertension	EF 20–34%	Transfer to OR from CCU
BUN > 30	NYHA class	Diabetes	Reoperation	COPD	Reoperation	
Acute MI	CHF	COPD	Female		Urgent surgery	
Remote MI	Creatinine level	Cerebrovascular disease	Pulmonary hypertension			

Table 4.9   Model to Predict Combined Mortality and Morbidity[10]

Variable	Clinical Risk Score	Odds Ratio
Cardiogenic shock	7	29.9
Emergency	5	7.1
Urgent	4	3.5
Catheter-induced coronary closure	4	3.7
EF <30%	4	2.9
Age >75	3	2.9
Cardiomegaly	2	3.3
Peripheral vascular disease	2	1.7
Creatinine >1.9	2	2.6
Age 70–74	2	1.5
IDDM	2	2.5
NonIDDM	1	1.5
Low body mass index	1	1.4
Female	1	1.5
Reoperation	1	1.4
Age 65–69	1	1.4
Anemia	1	1.8
Cerebrovascular disease	1	1.6
COPD	1	1.4
Albumin <4 mg/dL	1	1.2
Creatinine 1.5–1.9	1	1.8
BUN >29 mg/dL	1	1.7
Congestive heart failure	1	2.3
Atrial arrhythmias	1	1.4

	Points	% Predicted
Mortality		
Low	0–4	0.2
Average	5–8	2
Moderate	9–11	6
High	12–18	30
Extremely high	19+	95
Morbidity		
Low	0–2	20
Moderate	3–5	50
High	6–8	74
Extremely high	9+	93

critical in patients with preexisting renal dysfunction. In fact, the odds ratio for mortality with a preoperative creatinine $>2\,mg/dL$ was 3.4.

2. Patients requiring mechanical ventilation for over 5 days have an operative mortality of over 20%. Preoperative treatment (use of antibiotics for pulmonary infiltrates or bronchitis, bronchodilators) and aggressive postoperative management (intraoperative fluid restriction and use of diuretics, use of bronchodilators and steroids, early mobilization and chest PT) may minimize the duration of mechanical ventilation.

3. Older age is associated with many costly or morbid complications, including atrial arrhythmias, mediastinal bleeding, renal dysfunction, and stroke. A permanent perioperative stroke carries a 28% mortality. Addressing carotid disease preoperatively, using epiaortic imaging in the operating room to identify ascending aortic or arch atherosclerosis, and maintaining a higher blood pressure on pump are a few examples of measures that should be considered in elderly patients to improve surgical results. Meticulous attention to hemostasis in elderly patients with fragile tissues can reduce the risk of bleeding, transfusions, tamponade, low cardiac output states, and subsequent respiratory and renal failure.

4. Reoperation for bleeding and the occurrence of tamponade carry significant mortality rates (13% and 25%, respectively). Reoperations, urgent surgery, older age, and renal dysfunction predispose to bleeding and require extra vigilance in the operating room. As noted above, the univariate analysis of the STS database showed that the use of intraoperative blood product transfusions significantly raised operative mortality. Presumably this is because of the clinical conditions that necessitated their use.

5. The mortality rate associated with all types of anticoagulation-related complications was approximately 25% in the STS database. Heparin may be used for atrial fibrillation, following embolic strokes, or for valve prostheses. Tamponade, gastrointestinal or retroperitoneal bleeding, or intracranial hemorrhage into infarcted areas may ensue. Strict criteria for usage of heparin, careful regulation of PTT and INRs, and vigilance for the insidious onset of tamponade are critical in any patient receiving anticoagulation after surgery.

E. A very simple and useful additive model was reported by the group at Allegheny General Hospital to predict both morbidity and mortality.[10] Stepwise logistic regression was used to assign weights to 24 variables, using morbidity and mortality as one dependent variable. The risk prediction model was validated with a high correlation coefficient (table 4.9).

References

1. The Society of Thoracic Surgeons. Data analyses of the Society of Thoracic Surgeons National Cardiac Surgery Database. Summit Medical, January, 1996.
2. Parsonnet V, Dean D, Bernstein AD. A method of uniform stratification of risk for evaluating the results of surgery in acquired adult heart disease. Circulation 1989;79(suppl 1):3–12.
3. Higgins TL, Estafanous FG, Loop FD, Beck GJ, Blum JM, Paranandi L. Stratification of morbidity and mortality outcome by preoperative risk factors in coronary artery bypass patients. A clinical severity score. JAMA 1992;267:234–8.
4. Edwards FH, Grover FL, Shroyer ALW, Schwartz M, Bero J. The Society of Thoracic Surgeons national cardiac surgery database: current risk assessment. Ann Thorac Surg 1997;63:903–8.
5. O'Connor GT, Plume SK, Olmstead EM, et al. Multivariate prediction of in-hospital mortality associated with coronary artery bypass graft surgery. Circulation 1992;85:2110–8.
6. Grover FL, Shroyer LW, Hammermeister KE. Calculating risk and outcome: the Veterans affairs database. Ann Thorac Surg 1996;62:S6–11.
7. Hannan EL, Kilburn H Jr, O'Donnell JF, Lukacik G, Shields EP. Adult open heart surgery in New York State. An analysis of risk factors and hospital mortality rates. JAMA 1990;264:2768–74.
8. Tu JV, Sykora K, Naylor CD, for the Steering committee of the cardiac care network of Ontario. Assessing the outcomes of coronary artery bypass graft surgery: how many risk factors is enough? J Am Coll Cardiol 1997;30:1317–23.
9. Jones RH, Hannan EL, Hammermeister KE, et al. Identification of preoperative variables needed for risk adjustment of short-term mortality after coronary artery bypass graft surgery. J Am Coll Cardiol 1996;28:1478–87.
10. Magovern JA, Sakert T, Magovern GJ Jr, et al. A model that predicts morbidity and mortality after coronary artery bypass grafting. J Am Coll Cardiol 1996;28:1147–53.
11. Tu JV, Jaglal SB, Naylor CD, and the Steering committee of the provincial adult cardiac care network of Ontario. Multicenter validation of a risk index for mortality, intensive care unit stay, and overall hospital length of stay after cardiac surgery. Circulation 1995;91:677–84.
12. Tuman KJ, McCarthy RJ, March RJ, Najafi H, Ivankovich AD. Morbidity and duration of ICU stay after cardiac surgery. A model for preoperative risk assessment. Chest 1992;102:36–44.
13. Higgins GL, Estafanous FG, Starr NJ, et al. Operative factors affecting morbidity and mortality risk following coronary bypass grafting. Anesth Analg 1995;80:S184.
14. Ferraris VA, Ferraris SP. Risk factors for postoperative morbidity. J Thorac Cardiovasc Surg 1996;111:731–41.
15. Charlson ME, Pompei P, Ales KI, Mackenzie CR. A new method of classifying prognostic comorbidity in longitudinal studies: development and validation. J Chron Dis 1987;40:373–83.
16. Lippman RP, Shahian DM. Coronary artery bypass risk prediction using neural networks. Ann Thorac Surg 1997;63:1635–43.
17. Grover FL. Cardiothoracic databases: where are we headed? Ann Thorac Surg 1997;63:1531–2.
18. Geraci JM, Rosen AK, Ash AS, McNiff KJ, Moskowitz MA. Predicting the occurrence of adverse events after coronary artery bypass surgery. Ann Intern Med 1993;118:18–24.

19. Kurki TSO, Kataja M. Preoperative prediction of postoperative morbidity in coronary artery bypass grafting. Ann Thorac Surg 1996;61:1740–5.
20. Lazar HL, Fitzgerald C, Gross S, Heeren T, Aldea GS, Shemin RJ. Determinants of length of stay after coronary artery bypass graft surgery. Circulation 1995;92(suppl 2):20–4.

5 Intraoperative Considerations in Cardiac Surgery

Anesthesia for Cardiac Surgery

Cardiopulmonary Bypass

Myocardial Protection

5   Intraoperative Considerations in Cardiac Surgery

Although excellence in pre- and postoperative care can often make the difference between an uneventful and a complicated recovery, the conduct of the intraoperative phase usually has the most significant impact on patient outcome. Performing a technically proficient, complete, and expeditious operation is only one component of this phase. Refinements in anesthetic technique and monitoring, cardiopulmonary bypass, and myocardial protection have enabled surgeons to operate successfully on extremely ill patients with far advanced cardiac disease. These patients, many of whom were previously considered inoperable, will now survive the operative period to provide a challenge to postoperative care. This chapter will describe briefly nonsurgical aspects of intraoperative care which significantly influence organ pathophysiology and the results of surgery. It should be kept in mind that the abnormal physiology of extracorporeal circulation can inflict new and sometimes poorly understood insults on nearly every organ system, which can be especially troublesome in patients with preexisting comorbidities.

I.   Anesthesia for Cardiac Surgery

The early postoperative course is determined not just by the technical quality of the surgical procedure, but to a large degree by the quality of care delivered by the anesthesiologist during the operative procedure. Newer and better anesthetic drugs, the use of antifibrinolytic drugs to minimize bleeding, transesophageal echocardiography, and more sophisticated understanding of inotropes have contributed a great deal to improved operative outcomes.

A. **Preoperative medications** should be administered 30 to 60 minutes before the patient is brought to the operating room. They are given to reduce the patient's anxiety and produce amnesia to allow for the safe insertion of monitoring lines without producing hemodynamic stress. Commonly used medications include morphine 0.1 mg/kg IM and scopolamine 0.3–0.4 mg/kg IM.

B. **Intraoperative monitoring**

1. Patients undergoing cardiac surgical procedures are extensively monitored. Hemodynamic alterations and myocardial ischemia occurring during the induction of anesthesia, the prebypass period, during cardiopulmonary bypass, and following resumption of cardiac activity can have significant adverse effects on myocardial function and recovery. It should be noted that even though both hypertension and tachycardia can increase myocardial oxygen demand, an increase in heart rate results in more myocardial ischemia at an equivalent increase in oxygen demand.[1]

2. Standard monitoring in the operating room consists of a five-lead ECG system, noninvasive blood pressure cuff, a radial (and occasionally femoral) arterial line, pulse oximetry, end-tidal CO_2, a Swan-Ganz pulmonary artery catheter to monitor filling pressures and cardiac outputs and assess for ischemia,[2,3] and a urinary Foley catheter to measure urine output and core body temperature. At

the conclusion of the operation, a left atrial line may be inserted if indicated, pacing wires are placed, and mediastinal and pleural chest tubes are connected to a thoracic drainage unit. Additional comments on the use of and complications associated with these monitoring lines are presented in Chapter 6.

3. Intraoperative transesophageal echocardiography (TEE) has become routine in many centers.[4-7] The probe is placed after the patient is anesthetized and usually before heparinization. TEE provides an analysis of regional and global right and left ventricular function and is very sensitive in detecting the presence of ischemia. It also evaluates valvular disease and images the aorta for atheromatous disease. Epiaortic imaging provides better visualization of the ascending aorta and arch when there are significant concerns about atheromatous disease. After bypass, TEE can be used to assess ventricular function, the presence of intracardiac air, and the efficacy of valvular repairs (see tables 2.3 and 2.4).

C. **Induction of anesthesia**

1. The selection of anesthetic agents is determined by the patient's cardiac disease, age, and comorbidities. Depending on the patient's coronary anatomy, ventricular function, and valvular pathology, anesthetic management should take into consideration the avoidance of myocardial depression, vasodilatation, tachycardia or bradycardia, fluid overload, and/or hypovolemia. Specific anesthetic concerns for various disease processes are presented in Chapter 1.

2. Cardiac anesthesia is provided by a combination of medications including induction agents, anxiolytics, amnestics, analgesics, muscle relaxants, and inhalational anesthetics (table 5.1). Induction agents include thiopental, propofol, etomidate, and the benzodiazepines. These are administered along with narcotics and neuromuscular blockers to produce muscle relaxation to facilitate intubation.

D. **Maintenance of anesthesia** is provided by the combination of low-dose narcotics, anxiolytics (midazolam or propofol), inhalational agents, and muscle relaxants (table 5.2). Bispectral EEG monitoring can be used to titrate and minimize the amount of medication required to maintain adequate anesthesia.

1. Traditional regimens that included high-dose fentanyl have been supplanted by protocols using low-dose fentanyl, sufentanil, or alfentanil.[8-10] The least expensive regimen combines low-dose fentanyl with an inhalational agent to facilitate early extubation. Sufentanil and alfentanil have half-lives of about 20–40 minutes and allow patients to awaken within hours of completion of the operation. Remifentanil is a very short-acting narcotic with a context-sensitive half-life of 3–5 minutes that may be beneficial in shorter operations and in elderly patients.

2. Midazolam has been shown to have an elimination half-life of over 10 hours in patients undergoing cardiac surgery.[11] Although some groups have achieved early extubation in patients receiving

Table 5.1 *Hemodynamic Effects of Commonly Used Anesthetic Agents*

	Heart Rate	Contractility	Systemic Vascular Resistance	Net Effect on Blood Pressure
Induction Agents				
Thiopental	↑	↓	↓	↓
Propofol	↓	↓	↓↓	↓↓
Etomidate	↔	↔	↔	↔
Anxiolytics				
Midazolam	↑	↔	↓	↓
Propofol	↓	↓	↓↓	↓↓
Lorazepam	↔	↔	↓	↓
Narcotics				
Fentanyl	↓	↔	↓	↓
Sufentanil	↓↓	↔	↓	↓
Alfentanil	↓	↔	↓	↓
Remifentanil	↓	↔	↓	↓
Muscle Relaxants				
Pancuronium	↑	↔	↔	↑
Vecuronium	↔	↔	↔	↔
Doxacurium	↔	↔	↔	↔
Atracurium	↔	↔	↓	↓
Pipecuronium	↔	↔	↔	↔
Succinylcholine	↑↓	↓	↔	↑↓

    midazolam throughout surgery, most groups limit its use to the pre-bypass period and then initiate a propofol infusion at the termination of bypass and continue it in the intensive care unit. When the patient is stable, the propofol is turned off and the patient is allowed to awaken.

3. Inhalational agents provide muscle relaxation and unconsciousness, but also depress the myocardium. They are generally used during cardiopulmonary bypass so that lower doses of intravenous medications can be given. Their vasodilator properties can be used to reduce blood pressure during bypass.

4. Muscle relaxants are given throughout the operation to offset the rigidity caused by narcotics and to suppress shivering during hypothermia. Adequate muscle relaxation might reduce some of the paraspinal muscle soreness often noted after surgery due to sternal retraction. Pancuronium is commonly used because it increases both heart rate and blood pressure and mitigates narcotic-induced bradycardia and hypotension. These hemodynamic changes are not noted with vecuronium and doxacurium.[12] Although some centers reverse muscle relaxants at the end of the operation, this can be detrimental if the patient becomes agitated and develops hemodynamic alterations. A conservative approach is to observe the patient in the ICU for several hours during which

Table 5.2 *Dosages and Metabolism of Commonly Used Anesthetic Agents*

	Usual Dosage	Duration of Action
Induction Agents		
Thiopental	3–5 mg/kg	5–10 min
Propofol	1–3 mg/kg → 10–100 µg/kg/min	2–8 min[a]
Etomidate	0.2–0.4 mg/kg → 5–10 µg/kg/min	3–8 min
Anxiolytics		
Propofol	25–75 µg/kg/min	Up to 20 min
Midazolam	2.5–5 mg IV q2h or 1–4 mg/h	Up to 10 h
Lorazepam	1–4 mg q4h or 0.02–0.05 mg/kg	4–6 h
Narcotics		
Fentanyl	5–25 µg/kg → 1–5 µg/kg	1–4 h
Sufentanil	1 µg/kg → 0.25–0.5 µg/kg/h	1–4 h
Alfentanil	50–75 µg/kg → 0.5–3.0 µg/kg/min	1.0–1.6 h
Remifentanil	1 µg/kg → 0.05–2 µg/kg/min	10 min
Muscle Relaxants		
Pancuronium	0.1 mg/kg → 0.01 mg/kg q1h	180–240 min[a]/0–60 min[b]
Vecuronium	0.1 mg/kg → 0.01 mg/kg q30–45 min	45–90 min[a]/25–40 min[b]
Doxacurium	0.06 mg/kg → 0.005 mg/kg q30 min	180–240 min[a]/45–60 min[b]
Atracurium	0.3–0.5 mg/kg → 0.2–0.4 mg/kg/h	30–45 min[a]/15–30 min[b]
Pipecuronium	0.08–1.0 mg/kg → 0.01 mg/kg/h	60–120 min[a]/40–60 min[b]
Succinylcholine	1 mg/kg	5–10 min

[a] After initial intubating dose.
[b] After repeat dose.

time most of the neuromuscular blockade dissipates and extubation can then be achieved.

E. **Prebypass considerations**

1. Antifibrinolytic drugs have been demonstrated unequivocally to reduce perioperative blood loss in cardiac operations and should be used for all cardiac surgical procedures.[13,14] Most protocols include giving the first dose at the time of skin incision or before heparinization, giving a dose in the pump prime, and administering a constant infusion during the operation. Epsilon-aminocaproic acid is inexpensive and effective when used for most cardiac procedures. Aprotinin is expensive and should be reserved for patients at high risk for bleeding (reoperations, hepatic dysfunction, known coagulopathy). The relative merits and various dosing regimens for these medications are discussed on pages 152–155.

2. A baseline activated clotting time (ACT) should be drawn after the operation has commenced and before systemic heparinization. Administration of 3–4 mg/kg of heparin is given by the anesthesiologist prior to cannulation for cardiopulmonary bypass. The ACT should be maintained over 480 seconds to minimize activation of the coagulation system and the formation of fibrin monomers in the extracorporeal circuit during bypass. Lower ACTs may be

acceptable with the use of heparin-coated circuits, although this remains controversial.[15–17] With the use of aprotinin, which itself raises the ACT level, kaolin ACTs maintained >480 seconds are acceptable, whereas celite ACTs must exceed 750 seconds to avoid underheparinization.[18] It should be noted that patients receiving preoperative heparin tend to be heparin-resistant in the operating room due to antithrombin III deficiency.[19] If additional heparin does not elevate the ACT, antithrombin III must be given, either in fresh frozen plasma or in a commercially available pooled product (Thrombate III™).

3. Avoidance of ischemia prior to initiating bypass remains critical. Identification of ischemic ECG changes, elevation in filling pressures, or regional wall motion abnormalities on transesophageal echocardiography require prompt attention.[2,3] Manual cardiac manipulation or blood loss during redo dissections, ongoing blood loss from leg incisions, and atrial fibrillation during atrial cannulation are a few of the potential insults that must be addressed in addition to the effects of the anesthetic agents selected. Judicious use of fluids and α-agents to counteract vasodilation, β-blockers or additional anesthetic agents for hypertension or tachycardia, and nitroglycerin for ischemia must be selected appropriately to maintain stable hemodynamics.

F. **Considerations during cardiopulmonary bypass**

1. The lungs are not ventilated during bypass.

2. A mean blood pressure of 55–65 mm Hg should be maintained using vasodilators (narcotics or inhalational anesthetics) or vasopressors (phenylephrine). If adequate flow is provided during bypass, organ system perfusion should be adequate. Cerebral blood flow is always of utmost concern and is determined primarily by arterial blood pressure, not by pump flow rate.[20] Nonetheless, cerebral blood flow is usually maintained by autoregulation until the pressure falls below 40 mm Hg. This response is, however, often inadequate in diabetic and hypertensive patients. Administration of cardioplegia is commonly associated with a transient profound decrease in systemic vascular resistance.

3. Measures to optimize renal function should be considered in patients with preoperative renal dysfunction (creatinine >1.5 mg/dL), especially in diabetic, hypertensive patients. These include use of mannitol (25 grams), dopamine (3 μg/kg/min),[21] furosemide, and perhaps diltiazem (3 μg/kg/min[22]) during bypass. Maintaining a higher mean perfusion pressure (around 80 mm Hg) during bypass and keeping the pump run as short as possible may also be beneficial. However, the major cause of postoperative renal dysfunction is a low output state, so maintenance of satisfactory hemodynamics at the termination of cardiopulmonary bypass is essential.

G. **Termination of bypass**

1. The lungs are ventilated, pacing is initiated if necessary, and bypass is weaned as described below.

2. Despite excellent myocardial protection, many patients with poor ventricular function, ongoing ischemia, or recent infarction require inotropic medications for several hours to support myocardial function. The anesthesiologist must work in concert with the surgeon in assessing myocardial function and the need for inotropes. Visual inspection of the heart, assessment of cardiac outputs and filling pressures with a Swan-Ganz catheter, and TEE imaging can be used to assess ventricular function. For example, evidence of new regional wall motion abnormalities may suggest technical problems with graft flow that can be remedied. The appropriate selection of inotropic agents is discussed in detail in Chapter 10.[23–25]

3. Protamine is administered to counteract the effects of heparin in a 1:1 ratio. Given in appropriate amounts, this should return the ACT to baseline. However, patients with significant thrombocytopenia or coagulopathies may still have an elevated ACT despite lack of heparin effect. This problem can be sorted out using the Medtronic Hepcon system, which measures heparin levels in the bloodstream. If bleeding persists and does not appear to be of a surgical nature, treatment must often be based on suspicion of the hematologic abnormality, unless the laboratory can rapidly provide the results of a PT, PTT, and platelet count. Generally, aprotinin,[26] clotting factors, including fresh frozen plasma, cryoprecipitate, and/or platelets are given. Obtaining a thromboelastogram or Sonoclot signature can be of value in ascertaining the hemostatic defect, although most patients usually receive "shotgun" therapy when bleeding is persistent. A further discussion of issues related to postoperative bleeding is presented in Chapter 8.

II.   Cardiopulmonary Bypass

A. Cardiopulmonary bypass (CPB) involves an extracorporeal circuit that provides systemic blood flow to the body while the heart and lungs are not functioning. Although not essential when surgery is performed on the surface of the heart, such as limited coronary bypass surgery, CPB is required when manipulation of the heart significantly compromises systemic blood pressure and when intracardiac surgery is performed.[27,28]

B. **The cardiopulmonary bypass circuit**

1. Venous blood drains by gravity from the right atrium or vena cavae into a reservoir, passes through an oxygenator/heat exchanger attached to a heating/cooling machine, and is returned to the arterial system through a filter using either a roller or centrifugal pump (figure 5.1).

   a. The arterial cannula is usually placed in the ascending aorta, but occasionally must be placed in a peripheral artery (usually the femoral and rarely the axillary artery) when cannulation of a calcified or atherosclerotic aorta is impossible or considered to substantially raise the risk of stroke from embolic debris.

   b. Active pump-assisted venous drainage using a centrifugal pump is being used more commonly during minimally

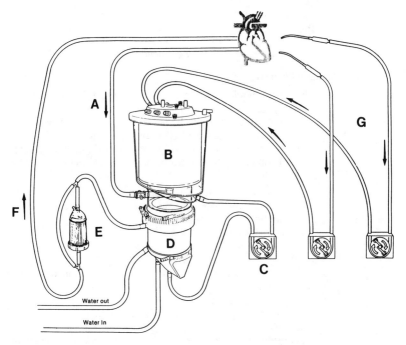

Figure 5.1 *The extracorporeal circuit. Blood drains by gravity through the (A) venous lines into a (B) cardiotomy reservoir, is (C) pumped through the (D) oxygenator/heat exchanger and (E) arterial line filter back into the (F) arterial circuit. Additional suction lines (G) can be used for intracardiac venting and scavenging of blood from the operative field.*

       invasive procedures. It augments venous drainage when small venous catheters are used.

2. Suction lines also return blood to the cardiotomy reservoir, into which the perfusionist can add medications. A blender regulates oxygen and carbon dioxide flow into the oxygenator. An additional cannula can be attached to an intracardiac vent, draining blood into the reservoir either by gravity or active suctioning by a roller pump head.

C. **Initiating bypass**

1. Systemic administration of 3–4 mg/kg of heparin with monitoring of heparin effect by an activated clotting time (ACT) is essential to minimize clotting within the extracorporeal circuit.

2. As the pump is turned on, nonpulsatile flow will be initiated with normovolemic hemodilution (the hematocrit will decrease 30% to 50% depending on the blood volume).[29] Back-draining of the prime from the pump before initiating bypass may minimize hemodilution and maintain a higher hematocrit.[30] Blood pressure should usually be maintained between 55–65 mmHg using

vasodilators (narcotics, inhalational agents, or propofol) or vaso-pressors (phenylephrine, norepinephrine) as noted above. The patient may be warmed or cooled, depending on the surgeon's preference and the operative procedure.[31]

D. **Terminating bypass**

1. The patient should be warmed to normothermia. The lungs are ventilated, pacing is initiated if necessary, and the heart is filled by restricting venous return as bypass flow is reduced and turned off. Low systemic resistance is common and α-agents and calcium chloride are useful to improve systemic blood pressure. Inotropic support should be considered for poor cardiac performance (see Chapter 10).

2. When the patient is stable, protamine is administered to reverse heparin effect (see page 162 for a discussion of protamine reactions), and the heart is decannulated. Hemostasis is achieved and the chest is closed.

E. **Adverse effects of CPB**

1. CPB activates numerous cascades, including the kallikrein, coagulation, and complement systems. One of the primary concerns is that of a systemic inflammatory response caused by release of proinflammatory cytokines. These contribute to neutrophil-endothelial adhesion which has been implicated in myocardial reperfusion damage, lung injury, and a generalized capillary leak.[32–35] Among other concerns resulting from CPB are a coagulopathy (dilution of clotting factors and platelets, platelet dysfunction), and renal and splanchnic hypoperfusion (causing renal dysfunction and GI complications).

2. Use of membrane oxygenators, heparin-coated circuits, centrifugal pumps, intraoperative steroids, leukocyte filters, or mannitol may reduce the extent of these derangements.[36] Aprotinin is a serine protease inhibitor that, when given in high doses, may ameliorate the consequences of the inflammatory cascade in addition to reducing blood loss.[36–38]

F. **Hypothermic circulatory arrest** is used in situations when the aorta cannot be clamped to perform an anastomosis to the aorta. The patient is cooled systemically to 18°–20°C at which the EEG is flat. The head is packed in ice and medications are often given (steroids, barbiturates) to potentially minimize cerebral injury. The arterial line is clamped and blood is drained from the circulation, taking care not to allow air entry in the lines. The "safe" upper limit for circulatory arrest at this temperature is 45–60 minutes. Administering blood from the pump retrograde into the brain through a cannula in the superior vena cava may extend this safe upper limit by providing some oxygen and nutrition to the brain. However, the primary benefit of retrograde perfusion is maintenance of cerebral hypothermia and flushing of air and debris out of the cerebral vessels.[39]

III. Myocardial Protection

A. An optimal surgical result depends on protecting the heart from damage that might ensue during a corrective operation. Some operations can be performed on a beating heart without the use of cardiopulmonary bypass, such as "minimally invasive" bypass surgery through a sternotomy or thoracotomy incision. Others can be performed on cardiopulmonary bypass with an empty beating heart (left ventricular aneurysm resection, closure of an atrial septal defect). However, nearly all intracardiac procedures and most coronary bypass operations require a quiet, bloodless field that allows for precise surgical techniques and prevents air embolism. This necessitates use of some form of "myocardial protection."

1. **Cardioplegia** is used by most surgeons to arrest the heart. Crossclamping of the aorta without the use of cardioplegia results in anaerobic metabolism and depletion of myocardial energy stores. Thus, without a reduction in myocardial metabolism, either by hypothermia or chemical cardiac arrest, crossclamping for more than 15–20 minutes would result in severe myocardial dysfunction.

2. There are two alternative techniques that are still used routinely by a few surgeons with satisfactory results, and have applications in special situations. **Intermittent ischemic arrest** involves clamping the aorta intermittently for short periods of time to perform the distal anastomoses. With the technique of **hypothermic fibrillatory arrest,** the aorta remains unclamped and distal anastomoses are performed with the heart cold and fibrillating at high perfusion pressures. This technique is useful when safe clamping of the aorta is not feasible because of extensive calcification or atherosclerosis.

B. **Principles of cardioplegia**[40–43]

1. Prompt **diastolic arrest** of the heart is achieved using potassium chloride (potassium channel openers are being investigated as alternative agents). The medium may be crystalloid, but is most commonly blood from the pump, which can provide oxygen and natural buffering agents. Supplemental additives include other buffers, agents to maintain slight hyperosmolarity, and those to maintain a low level of calcium. The oxygen demand of the heart is reduced nearly 90% by simply arresting the heart.

2. Traditionally, **hypothermia** was used alone and then in addition to cardioplegia to further reduce myocardial metabolism. However, the reduction in myocardial metabolism attributable to hypothermia is insignificant compared with that achieved by diastolic arrest (figure 5.2). Since enzyme and cellular reparative processes function better at normothermia, many surgeons use "warm cardioplegia" for myocardial protection. However, because of the tendency for the heart to resume electrical activity at normothermia, this must be given continuously or with only short periods of interruption to protect the heart. When given continuously, it can obscure the operative field. Terminal warm blood cardioplegia (so-called "hot shot") is commonly given just before removal of the aortic crossclamp because it has been shown to improve myocardial metabolism.

3. Cardioplegia may be administered antegrade into the aortic root or retrograde into the coronary sinus. The efficacy of the former is

ml/100 g/min

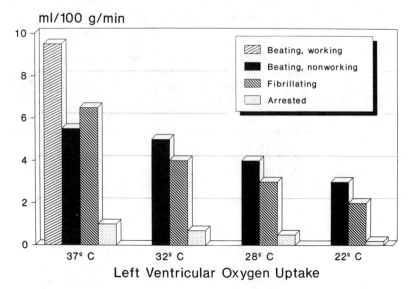

Figure 5.2 *Myocardial oxygen demand (mvO$_2$). Notice that the most significant decrease in mvO$_2$ occurs with the induction of the arrested state and secondarily by the production of hypothermia. (Modified with permission from Buckberg GD, Brazier JR, Nelson RL, Goldstein SM, McConnell DH, Cooper N. Studies of the effects of hypothermia on regional myocardial blood flow and metabolism during cardiopulmonary bypass. I. The adequately perfused beating, fibrillating, and arrested heart. J Thorac Cardiovasc Surg 1977;73:87–94.)*

somewhat compromised by severe coronary artery stenoses, it cannot be administered in patients with aortic insufficiency (except directly into the coronary ostia), and it can be cumbersome to readminister during aortic and mitral valve operations. However, retrograde cardioplegia is easy to administer, either intermittently or continuously, and does not interrupt the flow of the operation. It provides excellent myocardial protection, although concerns remain about protection of the right ventricle with this approach.

4. Various additives, including glutamate, aspartate, oxygen free-radical scavengers, adenosine, and other substrates have been added to cardioplegia solutions to improve myocardial protection, all with varying merit. Different mixtures of blood with cardioplegia (ranging from 2:1 to 8:1 to minimize hemodilution) have also been used. The variety of cardioplegia solutions is such that there are virtually as many different solutions used as there are surgical groups performing open-heart surgery.

References

1. Loeb HS, Saudye A, Croke RP, et al. Effects of pharmacologically-induced hypertension on myocardial ischemia and coronary hemodynamics in patients with fixed coronary obstruction. Circulation 1978;57:41–6.
2. Sanchez R, Wee M. Perioperative myocardial ischemia: early diagnosis using the pulmonary artery catheter. J Cardiothorac Vasc Anesthesia 1991;5:604–7.
3. Koide Y, Keehn L, Nomura T, Long T, Oka Y. Relationship of regional wall motion abnormalities detected by biplane transesophageal echocardiography and electrocardiographic changes in patients undergoing coronary artery bypass graft surgery. J Cardiothorac Vasc Anesthesia 1996;10:719–27.
4. Daniel WG, Mugge A. Transesophageal echocardiography. N Engl J Med 1995;332:1268–79.
5. Lazar HL, Plehn J. Intraoperative echocardiography. Ann Thorac Surg 1990;50:1010–8.
6. Murphy PM. Pro: intraoperative transesophageal echocardiography is a cost-effective strategy for cardiac surgical procedures. J Cardiothorac Vasc Anesthesia 1997; 11:246–9.
7. Kato M, Nakashima Y, Levine J, Goldinger PL, Oka Y. Does transesophageal echocardiography improve postoperative outcome in patients undergoing coronary artery bypass surgery? J Cardiothorac Vasc Anesthesia 1993;7:285–9.
8. Engelman RM, Rousou JA, Flack JE III, et al. Fast-track recovery of the coronary bypass patient. Ann Thorac Surg 1994;58:1742–6.
9. Collard E, Delire V, Mayne A, et al. Propofol-alfentanil versus fentanyl-midazolam in coronary artery surgery. J Cardiothorac Vasc Anesthesia 1996;10:869–76.
10. Engoren MC, Kraras C, Garcia G. Propofol-based versus fentanyl-isoflurane based anesthesia for cardiac surgery. J Cardiothorac Vasc Anesthesia 1998;12:177–81.
11. Maitre PO, Funk B, Crevoisier C, Ha HR. Pharmacokinetics of midazolam in patients recovering from cardiac surgery. Eur J Clin Pharmacol 1989;37:161–6.
12. Searle NR, Sahab P, Blain R, et al. Hemodynamic and pharmacodynamic comparison of doxacurium and high-dose vecuronium during coronary artery bypass surgery: a cost-benefit study. J Cardiothorac Vasc Anesthesia 1994;8:490–4.
13. Fremes SE, Wong BI, Lee E, et al. Metaanalysis of prophylactic drug treatment in the prevention of postoperative bleeding. Ann Thorac Surg 1994;58:1580–8.
14. Chen RH, Frazier OH, Cooley DA. Antifibrinolytic therapy in cardiac surgery. Texas Heart Inst J 1995;22:211–5.
15. von Segesser LK, Weiss BM, Garcia E, von Felten A, Turina MI. Reduction and elimination of systemic heparinization during cardiopulmonary bypass. J Thorac Cardiovasc Surg 1992;103:790–9.
16. Aldea GS, Doursounian M, O'Gara P, et al. Heparin-bonded circuits with a reduced anticoagulation protocol in primary CABG: a prospective, randomized study. Ann Thorac Surg 1996;62:410–8.
17. Kuitunen AH, Heikkila LJ, Selmenpera MT. Cardiopulmonary bypass with heparin-coated circuits and reduced systemic anticoagulation. Ann Thorac Surg 1997;63:438–44.
18. Dietrich W, Jochum M. Effect of celite and kaolin on activated clotting time in the presence of aprotinin: activated clotting time is reduced by binding of aprotinin to kaolin (letter). J Thorac Cardiovasc Surg 1995;1090:177–8.
19. Dietrich W, Spannagl M, Schramm W, Vogt W, Barankay A, Richter JA. The influence of preoperative anticoagulation on heparin response during cardiopulmonary bypass. J Thorac Cardiovasc Surg 1991;102:505–14.
20. Schwartz AE. Regulation of cerebral blood flow during hypothermic cardiopulmonary bypass. Review of experimental results and recommendations for clinical practice. CVE 1997;2:133–7.

21. Hines R. Pro: dopamine and renal preservation. J Cardiothorac Vasc Anesthesia 1995;9:333–4.
22. Zanardo G, Michielon P, Rosi P, et al. Effects of a continuous diltiazem infusion on renal function during cardiac surgery. J Cardiothorac Vasc Anesthesia 1993;7:711–6.
23. DiSesa VJ. Pharmacologic support for postoperative low cardiac output. Semin Thorac Cardiovasc Surg 1991;3:13–23.
24. Royster RL. Intraoperative administration of inotropes in cardiac surgery patients. J Cardiothorac Anesthesia 1990;4(suppl 5):17–28.
25. Butterworth J. Selecting an inotrope for the cardiac surgery patient. J Cardiothorac Vasc Anesthesia 1993;7(suppl 2):26–32.
26. Cicek S, Demirkilic U, Kuralay E, Ozal E, Tatar H. Postoperative aprotinin: effect on blood loss and transfusion requirements in cardiac operations. Ann Thorac Surg 1996;61:1372–6.
27. Deiss JM, Bojar RM. Cardiopulmonary bypass. In: Bojar RM. Adult cardiac surgery. Boston: Blackwell Scientific, 1992:1–36.
28. Utley JR. Cardiopulmonary bypass. CVE 1996;1:7–26.
29. Hall TS. The pathophysiology of cardiopulmonary bypass. The risks and benefits of hemodilution. Chest 1995;107:1125–33.
30. Rosengart TK, DeBois W, O'Hara M, et al. Retrograde autologous priming for cardiopulmonary bypass: a safe and effective means of decreasing hemodilution and transfusion requirements. J Thorac Cardiovasc Surg 1998;115:426–39.
31. Bert AA, Stearns GT, Feng W, Singh AK. Normothermic cardiopulmonary bypass. J Cardiothorac Vasc Anesthesia 1997;11:91–9.
32. Miller BE, Levy JH. The inflammatory response to cardiopulmonary bypass. J Cardiothorac Vasc Anesthesia 1997;11:355–66.
33. Downing SW, Edmunds LH Jr. Release of vasoactive substances during cardiopulmonary bypass. Ann Thorac Surg 1992;54:1236–43.
34. Boyle EM Jr, Pohlman TH, Johnson MC, Verrier ED. Endothelial cell injury in cardiovascular surgery: the systemic inflammatory response. Ann Thorac Surg 1997;63:277–84.
35. Hill GE. Cardiopulmonary bypass-induced inflammation: is it important? J Cardiothorac Vasc Anesthesia 1998;12(suppl 1):21–5.
36. Wan S, LeClerc JL, Vincent JL. Inflammatory response to cardiopulmonary bypass. Mechanisms involved and possible therapeutic strategies. Chest 1997;12:676–92.
37. Murkin JM. Cardiopulmonary bypass and the inflammatory response: a role for serine protease inhibitors? J Cardiothorac Vasc Anesthesia 1997;11:19–23.
38. Hill GE, Alonso AM, Spurzem JR, Stammers AH, Robbins RA. Aprotinin and methylprednisolone equally blunt cardiopulmonary bypass-induced inflammation in humans. J Thorac Cardiovasc Surg 1995;110:1658–62.
39. Coselli JF. Retrograde cerebral perfusion is an effective means of neural support during deep hypothermic circulatory arrest. Ann Thorac Surg 1997;64:908–12.
40. Buckberg GD, Beyersdorf F, Allen BS, Robertson JM. Integrated myocardial management: background and initial application. J Cardiac Surg 1995;10:68–89.
41. Hoffenberg EF, Ghomeshi HR, Deslauriers R, Salerno TA. Perspectives on myocardial protection. CVE 1997;2:3–10.
42. Buckberg GD. Update on current techniques of myocardial protection. Ann Thorac Surg 1995;60:805–14.
43. Beyersdorf F, Buckberg GD. Myocardial protection with blood cardioplegia during valve operations. J Heart Valve Dis 1994;3:388–403.

6 Admission to the ICU and Monitoring Techniques

Admission to the ICU

Monitoring in the ICU: Techniques and Problems

Summary of Guidelines for Removal of Lines and Tubes in the ICU

6   Admission to the ICU and Monitoring Techniques

I.   Admission to the ICU

A. The first critical phase of postoperative care starts at the completion of the surgical procedure. During transfer from the operating room table to an ICU bed, from one monitoring system to another, and from the operating room to the intensive care unit, the potential exists for airway and ventilation problems, sudden hypotension or hypertension, dysrhythmias, inadvertent medication changes, and unidentified problems with invasive catheters, monitoring, and bleeding. The electrocardiogram (ECG) and pressure tracings (arterial, pulmonary artery, and/or left atrial) are transferred one at a time from the operating room monitor to the transport module to ensure that the patient is monitored at all times. Ventilation is provided with a hand bag connected to a portable oxygen tank. Drug infusions should be placed on battery-powered infusion pumps to ensure accurate infusion rates. A selection of medications should always be available in the event of an emergency during transport.

B. On arrival in the ICU, the endotracheal tube is connected to a mechanical ventilator, and the ECG and pressure lines are transduced on the bedside monitor. The use of cartridges or modules that can be transferred directly from the operating room monitor to the transport module and then plugged directly into the ICU monitor can expedite access to hemodynamic information. Medication drip rates are readjusted on controlled infusion pumps, preferably using the same pumps that were used in the operating room to avoid temporary disconnection from the patient. The thoracic drainage system is connected to suction.

C. During this transition phase, attention is so often diverted away from the patient and toward connecting the tubes and lines to the ventilator and monitors that the patient's current status is frequently ignored. Therefore, it is critical that the accompanying anesthesia and/or surgical personnel assume responsibility for the patient's welfare by making sure that:

1. The patient is being well-ventilated by observing chest movement and auscultating bilateral breath sounds.

2. The ECG tracing demonstrates satisfactory rate and rhythm on the transport and then the bedside monitor.

3. The blood pressure is adequate on the portable monitor and remains so after the arterial line is transduced and calibrated on the bedside monitor.

D. Immediate assessment and response to abnormalities, whether real or spurious, is imperative. The two most common problems are a low blood pressure and an indecipherable ECG.

E. **Low blood pressure** is caused most commonly by hypovolemia or sudden termination of a drug infusion. It may also result from inadequate zeroing of the transducer, or kinking or transient occlusion of the line, producing a dampened tracing. If the transduced blood pressure is low, do the following:

1. Resume manual ventilation and listen for bilateral breath sounds.

2. Palpate the brachial or femoral arteries to confirm a pulse and a satisfactory blood pressure. Attach the blood pressure cuff above the radial arterial line site and take an auscultatory or occlusion blood pressure. This is done by inflating the cuff until the arterial tracing is obliterated; when the pressure tracing reappears, the systolic pressure can be read from the sphygmomanometer. **Never assume that a low blood pressure recording is caused by dampening of the arterial line unless a higher pressure can be confirmed by another method.** Insertion of an additional arterial monitoring line (usually in the femoral artery) may be indicated.

3. Make sure that all medication bottles are appropriately labeled and are connected to the patient and infusing at the designated rate through patent intravenous lines. **Note:** If hypotension is present, quickly ascertain whether the patient is receiving nitroprusside (in the silver wrapper), because this can precipitously and unexpectedly lower blood pressure.

4. Quickly examine the chest tubes for massive mediastinal bleeding.

5. Initial **treatment** of hypotension should include volume infusion, and, if there is no immediate response, administration of calcium chloride 300–500 mg IV. Vasoactive medications may be started or the rate of medications already being used can be adjusted. **If there is no response to these measures, and the ECG is abnormal, assume the worst and treat the patient as a cardiac arrest until the problem is sorted out.**

F. **An abnormal ECG** is usually caused by artifact with jostling or detachment of the ECG leads. If the arterial waveform is normal or the pulse oximeter (if attached) sounds normal, this is usually the case. However, if the arterial pressure is low or not transduced, the pulse is irregular or slow, or the monitor is difficult to interpret, palpate for a pulse and take the steps mentioned above. **If the blood pressure is undetectable and ECG reading is not available, assume the worst and treat the patient as a cardiac arrest.** Readjust the ECG leads on the patient and monitor. If interpretation remains difficult, attach a standard ECG machine to limb leads to ascertain the rhythm.

1. If ventricular fibrillation or tachycardia is present, immediate defibrillation and a cardiac arrest protocol are indicated.

2. If a pacemaker is being used, examine the connections and settings and confirm capture on an ECG.

3. Attach a pacemaker and initiate pacing if bradycardia or heart block is present.

4. Look for the undetected development of atrial fibrillation that can develop during atrioventricular pacing. This may account for a fall in cardiac output and blood pressure despite an adequate ventricular pacing rate.

5. Look for evidence of ischemia or other arrhythmias that may require treatment.

Table 6.1   *Initial Evaluation of the Patient in the Intensive Care Unit*

1. The patient should be examined thoroughly (heart, lungs, peripheral perfusion).
2. Hemodynamic measurements (central venous pressure [CVP], pulmonary artery diastolic [PAD], pulmonary capillary wedge [PCW] and left atrial [LA] pressures) should be obtained, cardiac output measured, and the systemic vascular resistance (SVR) calculated (see table 10.1).
3. A portable supine chest x-ray should be obtained. Specific attention should be paid to the position of the endotracheal tube and Swan-Ganz catheter, the width of the mediastinum, and the presence of a pneumothorax, fluid overload, atelectasis, or pleural effusion.
4. A 12-lead ECG should be reviewed for ischemic changes or arrhythmias.
5. Laboratory tests should be drawn (see table 6.2 for sample admission order sheet).

G. Once the patient's heart rate, rhythm, and blood pressure are found to be satisfactory and adequate ventilation from the ventilator is confirmed, a full report should be given to the ICU staff by the accompanying anesthesiologist and/or surgical house staff. This should include the patient's cardiac disease, comorbidities, operative procedure, intraoperative course, and special instructions for postoperative care. Further assessment as delineated in table 6.1 can then be carried out to address the subtleties of patient care.

II.   Monitoring in the ICU: Techniques and Problems

Careful monitoring is required in the early postoperative period to optimize patient management and outcome.[1,2] A continuous display of the ECG is provided and pressures derived from invasive catheters, including arterial, Swan-Ganz, and LA lines placed in the operating room, are transduced on bedside monitors. The endotracheal tube is securely connected to the mechanical ventilator and appropriate ventilator settings are selected. A continuous readout of the arterial oxygen saturation (SaO_2) determined by pulse oximetry should be displayed.[3] The drainage outputs of chest tubes and the Foley catheter are measured and recorded. Each invasive technique is used to provide an essential function or obtain special information about the patient's postoperative course, but each has potential complications. Each should be used only as long as necessary to maximize benefit while minimizing morbidity.

A. **Electrocardiographic display** on a bedside monitor is critical to allow for rapid interpretation of rhythm changes. The use of cartridge modules allows for the simultaneous display and recording of standard limb lead and atrial electrograms for the analysis of complex rhythms (see Chapter 10). A printout display monitor that has a short memory and is activated by abnormal rhythms is helpful in detecting the mechanism of arrhythmia development (such as an R-on-T phenomenon leading to ventricular tachycardia or fibrillation). ST segment analysis is provided by several monitoring systems, but abnormalities can be more thoroughly analyzed from a 12-lead ECG.

B. An endotracheal tube is used for mechanical ventilation during the early postoperative period. Confirmation of bilateral breath sounds and chest movement, rechecking of ventilator settings, and assessment of the adequacy of gas exchange are essential.

Table 6.2 *Typical Orders for Admission to the ICU*

1. Admit to SICU
2. Operation _____
3. Condition _____
4. Vital signs q15 minutes until stable, then q30 minutes
5. ECG, arterial and PA tracings on bedside monitor
6. Pulse oximetry on bedside monitor
7. Chest tubes to chest drainage system with 20 cm H_2O suction; record hourly
8. Urinary catheter to gravity drainage and record hourly
9. Elevate head of bed to 30°
10. Hourly I & O; daily weights
11. Cardiac output on arrival, q2h × 12 h, then prn
12. Ventilator settings
    FIO_2 _____ in SIMV mode
    IMV rate _____ breaths/min
    Tidal volume _____ mL
    PEEP _____ cm H_2O
13. Endotracheal suction q4h, then prn
14. NPO
15. NG tube to low suction
16. Cleanse incisions and apply dressings qd and as needed
17. Laboratory tests
    STAT ABGs, CBC, electrolytes, glucose
    STAT PT, PTT, platelet count if chest tube output >100/h
    STAT chest x-ray
    STAT ECG
    Every 4–6 hours and prn: Hct, K+
    ABGs 15 minutes and 4 hours after arrival, prior to weaning and prior to
        extubation

Medications
18. Allergies _____
19. D5/0.2% normal saline at 40 mL/h
20. Arterial line and distal Swan-Ganz port: heparin 250 U/250 mL NS at 3 mL/h
21. KCL 80 mEq/250 mL D5W via central line at _____ mEq/h to maintain K+
    4–4.5 mEq/L
22. Morphine sulfate 0.01–0.02 mg/kg continuous IV infusion; supplement with
    2–5 mg IV q1–2 h or prn for breakthrough pain
23. Ketorolac 15–30 mg IV q6h for breakthrough pain; D/C after 72 hours
24. Meperidine 25–50 mg IV prn, shivering
25. Propofol 25 μg/kg/min until stable, then wean over 30 minutes
26. Midazolam 2 mg IV q2h prn, agitation
27. Acetaminophen 650 mg PO/PR q3h, prn temp >38.5°C
28. Antibiotics:
    [   ] Cefazolin 1 g IV q8h × 6 doses
    [   ] Vancomycin 1 g IV q12h × 4 doses
29. Aspirin 75 mg per NG tube 7 hours after arrival in ICU; then enteric-coated
    aspirin 325 mg PO qd; hold if chest tube drainage over 100 mL/h
30. Antiarrhythmics:
31. Vasoactive medications:
32. Pacing:
33. Additional medications: (steroids, ulcer prophylaxis, neurologic medications, etc.)

1. **Pulse oximetry** is routinely used to assess on-line the status of peripheral perfusion and arterial oxygen saturation. It can draw attention to major problems with oxygenation and ventilation during the period of intubation and following extubation. Use of pulse oximetry obviates the need to draw arterial blood gases more than a few times during the period of intubation.

2. Suctioning should be performed gently every few hours or as necessary to maintain a tube free of secretions but not so frequently as to induce endobronchial trauma or bronchospasm. The endotracheal tube bypasses the protective mechanism of the upper airway and predisposes the patient to pulmonary infection. It should be removed as soon as the patient is maintaining satisfactory ventilation and oxygenation and is able to protect his or her airway. This is generally accomplished within 12 hours of surgery.

C. **Arterial lines** are generally placed in either the radial or femoral artery and are transduced on the bedside monitor. Accurate pressure recording depends on proper calibration and elimination of air from the transducer. Radial arterial pressure measurements may not reflect the central aortic pressure immediately after bypass, but this problem usually abates by the time the patient reaches the intensive care unit. In these situations, brachial or femoral arterial catheters provide a more accurate measurement.[4,5]

1. There is often a discrepancy noted between the auscultatory or occlusion blood pressure and that recorded digitally on the bedside monitor. This may be ascribed to the dynamic response characteristics of catheter-transducer systems.[6] The overdampening of signals usually results from gas bubbles within the fluid-filled system. Underdampening of signals is related to excessive compliance, length, or diameter of the tubing connecting the arterial line to the transducer. Most monitors are equipped with filters or resonance eliminators to reduce overshoot. If the intraarterial pressure appears to be dampened or exhibits overshoot, the analog display of the mean pressure is most reliable. The occlusion pressure is probably the most accurate measurement of the systolic pressure.

2. Arterial lines should be connected to continuous heparin flushes to improve patency rates and minimize thrombus formation. Nonetheless, maintaining a radial arterial line for more than 3 days is associated with an increased risk of vessel thrombosis and line sepsis.[7] Arterial lines are invaluable for sampling arterial blood gas specimens and obtaining blood for other laboratory tests, but they are often retained when invasive pressure monitoring is no longer essential but intravenous access for blood sampling is limited. Arterial lines should generally be removed when there is no longer a requirement for pharmacologic support and when satisfactory postextubation arterial blood gases have been achieved. A room air blood gas before removal may give a baseline assessment of the patient's oxygenation. If the patient requires continuous arterial pressure monitoring in the ICU, the line should be changed every 4 days.

      3. Attention must always be directed to perfusion of the hand when a radial arterial line is present. Removal is indicated urgently if hand ischemia develops. Fortunately, the incidence of serious complications associated with radial artery catheterization is extremely low.[8]

D. **Swan-Ganz pulmonary artery catheters** are usually placed before the induction of anesthesia, especially if left ventricular (LV) dysfunction is present. These catheters are useful for measuring left-sided filling pressures (PCWP), obtaining mixed venous oxygen saturations (SvO_2), and determining thermodilution cardiac outputs. Despite the nearly universal use of these catheters, studies have not conclusively demonstrated that they influence the outcome of cardiac surgery.[9,10]

      1. The catheter is usually inserted through an 8.5 F introducer placed into the internal jugular vein. It can also be placed through the external jugular or subclavian vein. Catheter placement from the arm or groin should be avoided in patients undergoing cardiac surgery.

      2. The catheter is passed into the right atrium and the balloon at the catheter tip is inflated. The catheter is advanced through the right ventricle and pulmonary artery (PA) into the pulmonary capillary wedge (PCW) position as confirmed by pressure tracings (figure 6.1). The pulmonary artery tracing should reappear when the balloon is deflated.

      3. The introducer sheath contains a side port that provides central venous access for the infusion of vasoactive medications and potassium.

      4. The proximal port of the Swan-Ganz catheter (30 cm from the tip) is used for central venous pressure (CVP) measurements from the right atrium and for fluid injections to determine the cardiac output. Care must be exercised when injecting sterile fluid for cardiac outputs to prevent bolusing of vasoactive medications that might be running through the CVP port. **Note:** One must **never** infuse anything through this port if the catheter has been pulled back so that the tip lies in the right atrium!

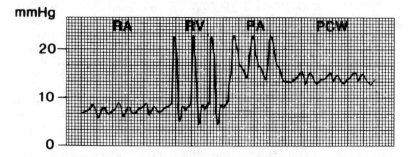

Figure 6.1 *Swan-Ganz catheter pressures. Intracardiac pressures are recorded from the distal (PA) port as the catheter is passed through the right atrium (RA), right ventricle (RV), and pulmonary artery (PA), into the pulmonary capillary wedge (PCW) position.*

5. The distal port should always be transduced and displayed on the bedside monitor to allow detection of catheter advancement into the permanent wedge position, which could result in pulmonary artery injury. Balloon inflation ("wedging" of the catheter) need not be performed more than once every few hours and the balloon should not be inflated for more than two respiratory cycles to prevent PA injury. Balloon inflation should be performed cautiously with minimal inflation volume or should be avoided entirely in patients with pulmonary hypertension. Medications should never be given through the distal PA port.

6. A variety of Swan-Ganz catheters are available that provide additional functions.

    a. Some catheters contain additional ports for volume infusion or placement of right atrial and ventricular pacing wires.[11] The latter is helpful during minimally invasive surgery when access to the heart is limited.

    b. Other catheters have been modified for assessment of continuous cardiac outputs[12] and online measurement of mixed venous O_2 saturations by fiberoptic oximetry.[13,14] The latter is valuable in patients with tricuspid regurgitation in whom thermodilution technology tends to underestimate the cardiac output.[15]

    c. Volumetric Swan-Ganz catheters use thermodilution to determine the right ventricular end-diastolic and end-systolic volumes, allowing for calculation of a right ventricular ejection fraction.[16] This is particularly valuable in patients with pulmonary hypertension and compromised right ventricular function.

7. Although there is a significant incidence of minor complications associated with the insertion and use of the Swan-Ganz catheter, serious life-threatening complications occur in less than 5% of patients.[17,18]

    a. Complications associated with insertion include:
        • Arrhythmias and heart block (especially in patients with bifascicular block)
        • Arterial puncture
        • Pneumothorax
        • Air embolism
        • Catheter knotting

    b. Complications of indwelling PA catheters include:
        • Arrhythmias and heart block
        • Heparin-induced thrombocytopenia (from heparin-coated catheters)
        • Infection
        • Pulmonary artery rupture and hemorrhage
        • Endocardial and valvular damage
        • Pulmonary infarction
        • Pulmonary infiltrates
        • Venous thrombosis

8. **Pulmonary artery perforation** is a very serious complication. It may occur during insertion of the catheter or during the surgical procedure when the catheter becomes rigid with hypothermia and advances into the lung when the heart is manipulated or the catheter is readvanced. It may also be noted in the ICU if the balloon is inflated in small pulmonary artery branches. Therefore, the position of the catheter should always be inspected on chest x-ray as soon as the patient arrives in the ICU or immediately after its insertion in the ICU. The catheter should be pulled back if it is located in the distal PA branches. Wedging is then reattempted.

   a. Perforation may lead to hemoptysis, bleeding into the endotracheal tube, or intrapleural hemorrhage. The chest x-ray may demonstrate a hematoma surrounding the tip of the catheter.

   b. If perforation is suspected, the catheter should be withdrawn and positive end-expiratory pressure (PEEP) added to the ventilator circuit. If bleeding persists, bronchoscopy can be performed with placement of a bronchial blocker to isolate the lung. Use of a double-lumen endotracheal tube or even a thoracotomy with pulmonary resection may be indicated for ongoing pulmonary hemorrhage.[19,20] Rarely, a false aneurysm of the pulmonary artery branches may develop. This has been treated by transcatheter embolization.[21]

9. The PA catheter should be removed when the patient no longer requires vasoactive drug support. If additional monitoring is required, a common practice is to electively replace the catheter every 4–5 days to prevent infection. There is, however, little evidence that this reduces the risk of bacteremia more than subsequent replacement for a clinical indication. Exchange over a guidewire should be avoided if the catheter is removed because of bacteremia. Otherwise, use of a guidewire reduces the risk of mechanical complications associated with insertion at a new site, and is associated with minimal or only a slightly increased risk of bacteremia.[22,23] If the catheter is removed but the introducer sheath is left in place for fluid or medication administration, the port must be covered with a small adhesive drape to minimize the risk of infection. A one-way valve present on most introducer sheaths eliminates the possibility of air embolism.

E. **Left atrial (LA) lines** are placed through the right superior pulmonary vein and passed into the left atrium during surgery.

   1. LA lines provide an accurate assessment of left-sided filling pressures, but are usually used only for patients with severe LV dysfunction or pulmonary hypertension. In the latter circumstance, they give a more accurate assessment of left ventricular filling when a high transpulmonary gradient is present. They also allow for pulmonary vasodilators to be infused into the central venous circulation while peripheral vasoconstrictors are infused directly into a left atrial line to maintain systemic resistance.[24] LA lines are helpful

during use of biventricular assist devices to assess the degree of left atrial filling.

2. An LA line should always be considered dangerous because of the risk of air embolism.[25] It must always be aspirated before being flushed to make sure there is no air or thrombus present within the system. It is then connected to a constant infusion flush line that includes an air filter to reduce the risk of systemic air embolism. The line should be removed when the chest tubes are still in place in the event that bleeding from the insertion site should occur.

F. **Chest tubes** are placed in the mediastinum and into the pleural spaces if they are entered during surgery. Drainage should be recorded hourly or more frequently if there is evidence of significant bleeding.

1. The chest tubes are connected to a drainage system to which 20 cm of H_2O suction is applied. The tubes should be gently milked or stripped to prevent blood from clotting within them. Aggressive stripping creates a negative pressure of up to -300 cm H_2O in the mediastinum. This may actually increase bleeding and is quite painful to the patient who has regained consciousness and is not heavily sedated. Suctioning of clotted chest tubes with endotracheal suction catheters should be discouraged because it may introduce infection.

2. Bloody drainage through chest tubes can be best observed if the tubes are not completely covered with tape. Plastic connectors must be tightly and securely attached to both the chest tubes and the drainage tubing to maintain sterility and prevent air leaks within the system.

3. A variety of collection systems are available for autotransfusion of shed mediastinal blood. The most cost-effective system allows for continuous autotransfusion from the collection chamber via an infusion pump and a 20-micron filter at a rate that approximates the previous hour's drainage. Autotransfusion should be considered primarily a volume infusion and a means of red cell salvage. It does not correct anemia because the hematocrit of the returned blood is less than 30% and it contains few clotting factors.[26]

G. The **urinary Foley catheter** is attached to gravity drainage and the urine output is recorded hourly. Urine output is an excellent measure of myocardial function, although it is subject to many variables.

1. Foley catheters incorporating temperature probes are frequently placed during surgery and can be used in the ICU to record the patient's core temperature.

2. The Foley catheter is usually removed on the first or second postoperative morning. It may be left in place if the patient is undergoing a significant diuresis or has a history of prostatic hypertrophy or urinary retention and has not been mobilized. The risk of urinary infection increases as the duration of indwelling catheter time lengthens, and prompt withdrawal should be considered in patients with prosthetic valves and grafts.

3. Suprapubic tubes should be left in place and clamped after several days to see if the patient can void per urethra.

H. **Nasogastric tubes** may be inserted in the operating room or after the patient's arrival in the ICU to aid with gastric decompression. Insertion may cause acute hypertension, bradycardia, tachycardia, or arrhythmias when the patient is not well sedated. Additional sedation may be required if insertion is difficult. Insertion may also cause nasopharyngeal bleeding if the patient is still heparinized (during surgery) or has a coagulopathy. Instillation of antacids to increase gastric pH is frequently used to reduce stress ulceration. However, sucralfate is preferable in patients requiring prolonged ventilation because antacids and H_2 blockers predispose to pneumonia by increasing the gastric pH.[27]

I. **Pacing wires.** Most surgeons place two atrial and two ventricular temporary epicardial pacing wire electrodes at the conclusion of open-heart surgery. If the pacing wires are being used, they must be securely attached to the patient and to the cable connector, and the cable must be securely attached to the pacing box. The pacemaker box itself should be easily accessible. **Everyone caring for the patient should understand how the particular pacemaker generator works.** Pacing wires that are not being used should be placed in insulating needle caps to isolate them from stray electrical currents that could potentially trigger arrhythmias.

III. Summary of Guidelines for Removal of Lines and Tubes in the ICU

A. The Swan-Ganz catheter should be removed when inotropic support and vasodilators are no longer necessary.

B. The arterial line should be removed after a stable postextubation blood gas has been obtained. An additional ABG obtained on room air is frequently worthwhile because it provides a relative indication of the patient's baseline postoperative oxygenation. The arterial line should not be left in place for blood sampling.

C. LA lines must be removed in the ICU while the chest tubes remain in place in the event that intrapericardial bleeding should occur.

D. The urinary catheter can be left in place if the patient is undergoing a vigorous diuresis or has an increased risk of urinary retention. It should otherwise be removed once the patient is mobilized out of bed, usually on the first or second postoperative day.

E. Chest tubes should be removed when the total drainage is less than 100 mL for 8 hours. Prolonging the duration of drainage after this criterion is met may increase total chest tube output without any effect on the incidence of postoperative effusions.[28] Mediastinal tubes should always be removed off suction, because graft avulsion might theoretically occur if suction is maintained. A chest x-ray is not essential after mediastinal tube removal, but should be performed after removal of pleural chest tubes to rule out a pneumothorax.

References

1. Wiedemann HP, Matthay MA, Matthay RA. Cardiovascular-pulmonary monitoring in the intensive care unit (Part 1). Chest 1984;85:537–49.

2. Wiedemann HP, Matthay MA, Matthay RA. Cardiovascular-pulmonary monitoring in the intensive care unit (Part 2). Chest 1984;85:656–68.

3. Bierman MI, Stein KL, Snyder JV. Pulse oximetry in the postoperative care of cardiac surgical patients. A randomized controlled trial. Chest 1992;102:1367–70.

4. Bazaral MG, Welch M, Golding LAR, Badhwar K. Comparison of brachial and radial arterial pressure monitoring in patients undergoing coronary artery bypass surgery. Anesthesiology 1990;73:38–45.

5. Mohr R, Lavee J, Goor DA. Inaccuracy of radial artery pressure measurement after cardiac operations. J Thorac Cardiovasc Surg 1987;94:286–90.

6. Gibbs NC, Gardner RM. Dynamics of invasive pressure monitoring systems: clinical and laboratory evaluation. Heart Lung 1988;17:43–51.

7. Bedford RF. Long-term radial artery cannulation: effects on subsequent vessel function. Crit Care Med 1978;6:64–7.

8. Slogoff S, Keats AS, Arlund C. On the safety of radial artery cannulation. Anesthesiology 1983;59:42–7.

9. Tuman KJ, McCarthy RJ, Spiess BD, et al. Effect of pulmonary artery catheterization on outcome in patients undergoing coronary artery surgery. Anesthesiology 1989;70:199–206.

10. Spackman TN. A theoretical evaluation of cost-effectiveness of pulmonary artery catheters in patients undergoing coronary artery surgery. J Cardiothorac Vasc Anesthesia 1994;8:570–6.

11. Risk SC, Brandon D, D'Ambra MN, et al. Indications for the use of pacing pulmonary artery catheters in cardiac surgery. J Cardiothorac Vasc Anesthesia 1992;6:275–9.

12. Segal J, Gaudiani V, Nishimura T. Continuous determination of cardiac output using a flow-directed Doppler pulmonary artery catheter. J Cardiothorac Anesthesia 1991;5:309–15.

13. Sommers MS, Stevenson JS, Hamlin RL, et al. Mixed venous oxygen saturation and oxygen partial pressure as predictors of cardiac index after coronary artery bypass grafting. Heart Lung 1993;22:112–20.

14. Scuderi PE, Bowton DL, Meredith JW, et al. A comparison of three pulmonary artery oximetry catheters in intensive care unit patients. Chest 1992;102:896–905.

15. Boerboom LE, Kinney TE, Olinger GN, Hoffmann RG. Validity of cardiac output measurement by the thermodilution method in the presence of acute tricuspid regurgitation. J Thorac Cardiovasc Surg 1993;106:636–42.

16. Hines R, Rafferty T. Right ventricular ejection fraction catheter: toy or tool? Pro: a useful monitor. J Cardiothorac Vasc Anesthesia 1993;7:236–40.

17. Boyd KD, Thomas SJ, Gold J, Boyd AD. A prospective study of complications of pulmonary artery catheterizations in 500 consecutive patients. Chest 1983;84:245–9.

18. Shah KB, Rao TLK, Laughlin S, El-Etr AA. A review of pulmonary artery catheterization in 6,245 patients. Anesthesiology 1984;61:271–5.

19. Urschel JD, Myerowitz PD. Catheter-induced pulmonary artery rupture in the setting of cardiopulmonary bypass. Ann Thorac Surg 1993;56:585–9.

20. Barash PG, Nardi D, Hammond G, et al. Catheter-induced pulmonary artery perforation. Mechanisms, management, and modifications. J Thorac Cardiovasc Surg 1981;82:5–12.

21. Karak P, Dimick R, Hamrick KM, Schwartzberg M, Saddenkni S. Immediate transcatheter embolization of Swan-Ganz catheter-induced pulmonary artery pseudoaneurysm. Chest 1997;111:1450–2.

22. Cobb DK, High KP, Sawyer RG, et al. A controlled trial of scheduled replacement of central venous and pulmonary-artery catheters. N Engl J Med 1992;327:1062–8.

23. Hagley MT, Martin B, Gast P, Traeger SM. Infectious and mechanical complications of central venous catheters placed by percutaneous venipuncture and over guidewires. Crit Care Med 1992;20:1426–30.

24. McEnany MT, Morgan RJ, Mundth ED, Austen WG. Circumvention of detrimental pulmonary vasoactivity of exogenous catecholamines in cardiac resuscitation. Surg Forum 1975;26:98–101.

25. Feerick AE, Church JA, Zwischenberger J, et al. Systemic gaseous microembolism during left atrial catheterization: a common occurrence? J Cardiothorac Vasc Anesthesia 1995;9:395–8.

26. Hartz RS, Smith JA, Green D. Autotransfusion after cardiac operation. Assessment of hemostatic factors. J Thorac Cardiovasc Surg 1988;96:178–82.

27. Apte NM, Karnad DR, Medhekar TP, Tilve GH, Morye S, Bhave GG. Gastric colonization and pneumonia in intubated critically ill patients receiving stress ulcer prophylaxis: a randomized, controlled trial. Crit Care Med 1992;20:590–3.

28. Smulders YM, Wiepking ME, Moulijn AC, et al. How soon should drainage tubes be removed after cardiac operations? Ann Thorac Surg 1989;48:540–3.

7 Early Postoperative Care: Basic Pathophysiology, Fast-Track Protocols, and Common Scenarios

7 Early Postoperative Care: Basic Pathophysiology, Fast-Track Protocols, and Common Scenarios

The early postoperative course for most patients undergoing cardiac surgery is characterized by a typical pattern of pathophysiologic derangements that benefits from standardized management.[1] The use of critical pathways provides guidelines for postoperative care and has been shown to expedite recovery by optimizing the delivery of care (see figure 12.1). Over the past few years, numerous changes have occurred in intraoperative and early postoperative management that have influenced how rapidly patients can recover from open-heart surgery. As discussed in Chapter 5, better intraoperative myocardial protection, improvements in cardiopulmonary bypass (CPB) technology, the advent of minimally invasive procedures, the availability of shorter-acting narcotics and amnestic agents, and the use of antifibrinolytic therapy have allowed for "fast-track recovery" of most patients following surgery.

This chapter will briefly summarize some of the practice changes that have impacted the early phase of postoperative recovery. It will then discuss aspects of postoperative care unique to various types of cardiac surgical procedures. The subsequent chapters will describe in greater detail the assessment and management of the major concerns of the postoperative period: mediastinal bleeding, respiratory, cardiovascular, renal, and metabolic problems.

I. Basic Pathophysiology During the First 24 Hours

A. Overview

1. Patients are commonly mildly hypothermic and fully anesthetized upon arrival in the ICU, requiring full mechanical ventilation for several hours.

2. Inotropic support may be required to terminate cardiopulmonary bypass and is usually maintained for at least 6 to 8 hours to optimize cardiac output as the heart recovers from the insult imposed by ischemia and reperfusion associated with cardioplegic arrest.

3. Urine output is usually copious because of hemodilution during surgery. Renal function is a good marker of hemodynamic function, although it is subject to numerous variables.

4. Patients may have mediastinal bleeding as a result of technical problems or a coagulopathy from a long bypass run.

5. Postoperative care requires an integration of a myriad of hemodynamic measurements and other laboratory tests to ensure a swift and uneventful recovery from surgery.

B. Warming from hypothermia to 37°C

1. Cardiopulmonary bypass is usually accompanied by systemic hypothermia to 25° to 32°C and is terminated after the patient has rewarmed to a core body temperature of at least 36°C. Nonetheless, progressive hypothermia may ensue from poor peripheral

perfusion, intraoperative heat loss from exposure to cool ambient temperatures in the operating room (especially during cases not requiring CPB), and anesthetic-induced inhibition of normal thermoregulatory control. Even patients maintained at systemic normothermia during surgery have a tendency to cool down several degrees before the conclusion of the operation. Patients usually arrive in the ICU at core temperatures of 34° to 35°C.

2. Although mild hypothermia may resolve with adequate tissue perfusion, more substantial hypothermia requires aggressive management because of potential adverse effects. Hypothermia may:

   a. Predispose to ventricular arrhythmias and lower the ventricular fibrillation threshold.

   b. Increase systemic vascular resistance (SVR) and cause hypertension. This may contribute to increased mediastinal bleeding; it raises afterload and myocardial oxygen demand, potentially depressing contractility and cardiac output; it may also elevate filling pressures and mask hypovolemia by producing peripheral vasoconstriction.

   c. Precipitate shivering which increases peripheral O_2 consumption and CO_2 production.[2]

   d. Produce a generalized impairment of the coagulation cascade.

3. Although peripheral vasoconstriction is a compensatory mechanism to provide core warming, it contributes to slow warming of peripheral tissues, especially when the cardiac output is marginal. Sodium nitroprusside is helpful in preventing the progressive hypothermia that is frequently noted after bypass by producing vasodilatation and improving peripheral perfusion.[3] However, it must be used cautiously in that progressive dilatation that accompanies both warming and improvement in cardiac output can produce profound hypotension if the patient becomes hypovolemic. It should be noted that central warming may be delayed in patients receiving pharmacologic vasodilators, such as propofol or nitroprusside. Core hypothermia may persist because peripheral vasodilatation augments heat loss.

4. Warming can be hastened by the use of warming blankets, radiant heating hoods, or heated humidifiers in the ventilator circuit. One study showed that forced-air warming systems (such as the "Bair Hugger" system) or a conductive electric overblanket were more effective than "space blankets" in limiting the duration of postoperative hypothermia, thus reducing shivering and oxygen consumption and expediting early extubation.[4-6] Another study comparing the "Warm Touch" forced air system (Mallinckrodt Medical, Inc.) with warm blankets and overhead heat lamps did not demonstrate any difference in rewarming efficacy.[7] Most of these methods minimize peripheral heat loss but do not directly promote core warming.

5. Patients may rapidly rewarm to 37°C and may occasionally "overwarm" to higher temperatures due to resetting of the central ther-

moregulating system. Narcotics, but not propofol, tend to increase the core temperature required for sweating and may contribute to this problem.[8,9] As noted above, warming may lead to profound peripheral vasodilatation and often hypotension in the presence of hypovolemia. Gradual vasodilatation with nitroprusside and concomitant volume infusion can minimize this problem (see postoperative scenarios III.A and III.B).

C. Control of mediastinal bleeding (see Chapter 8)

1. Numerous factors may predispose to mediastinal bleeding following cardiopulmonary bypass.[10,11] Most prominent are residual heparin effect, platelet dysfunction, clotting factor depletion, fibrinolysis, poor surgical technique, hypothermia, and postoperative hypertension.

2. Nearly all cardiac surgical units use one of the antifibrinolytic medications (aprotinin, epsilon-aminocaproic acid, tranexamic acid) to reduce intraoperative bleeding.[12] These medications not only inhibit fibrinolysis, but, to varying degrees, also preserve platelet function. Thus, intra- and postoperative bleeding have become relatively uncommon problems. Nonetheless, use of these medications is not a substitute for careful hemostasis in the operating room.

3. Careful monitoring of the extent of postoperative bleeding dictates the aggressiveness with which bleeding should be treated. Many patients with "nonsurgical" causes will drain about 100 mL/hour for several hours before bleeding eventually tapers. A faster rate of bleeding without evidence of diminution requires systematic evaluation and treatment (often prompting reexploration) as described in Chapter 8.

4. Recognition of the early signs of cardiac tamponade and the importance of prompt mediastinal exploration for severe bleeding or tamponade is critical to improving patient outcome.

D. Ventilatory support, emergence from anesthesia, weaning and extubation (see Chapter 9)

1. Most centers use narcotic-based anesthesia for cardiac surgery. This leaves the patient sedated upon arrival in the ICU, requiring mechanical ventilation for a short period of time. The initial inspired oxygen tension of 1.0 is gradually weaned to below 0.5 as long as the PaO_2 remains above 80 torr or the arterial oxygen saturation (SaO_2) exceeds 95%. Oxygenation is influenced by hemodynamic performance and fluid shifts into the lung interstitium during and soon after CPB. This is the result of a "capillary leak" that is produced by the various vasoactive substances released during extracorporeal circulation. The respiratory rate or tidal volume of the mechanical ventilator is adjusted to accommodate the increased CO_2 production that occurs with warming, awakening, and shivering.

2. Early extubation (within 8–12 hours) is feasible in most patients, but depends on the anesthetic agents used during surgery, med-

ications given in the ICU, the patient's age and comorbidities, the extent of the operative procedure, and the patient's hemodynamic performance.[13,14] High-dose fentanyl protocols have been supplanted by low-dose fentanyl regimens or shorter-acting narcotics (sufentanil, alfentanil, remifentanil).[15] Amnestic agents with long half-lives, such as midazolam, are given only in the prebypass period, and short-acting drugs, such as propofol, are commonly given after bypass and continued into the early postoperative period.[16,17] Although patients can be extubated fairly promptly by pharmacologic reversal of neuromuscular blockade, most centers prefer to observe patients for a few hours in the ICU and then consider weaning once the patient is stable.

3. As long as certain criteria are met (see page 189), there is no reason to exclude elderly patients or even those with impaired ventricular function or comorbidities from a protocol of early extubation. Even if it takes a few hours longer to extubate these patients than younger healthier ones, the benefits of an early extubation protocol usually translate into a quicker recovery from surgery.

E. **Analgesia and sedation**

1. An essential element of postoperative care is the provision of adequate analgesia and sedation.[18] Upon arrival in the unit, the patient remains anesthetized from the residual effects of the anesthetic agents used. However, with the trend toward earlier extubation, short-acting medications are essential to provide relief from pain and anxiety (especially about the endotracheal tube) while minimizing respiratory depression. For the patient in whom delayed extubation is anticipated—for example, when significant inotropic support or an intraaortic balloon pump (IABP) is required—a longer-acting sedative, such as midazolam, is acceptable.

2. Some centers that extubate patients fairly early after surgery give small doses of additional narcotics in the ICU, usually in combination with low-dose propofol. Just before the propofol is weaned off, a dose of indomethacin, 50 mg rectally, is given.

3. At our hospital, we prefer to administer morphine along with propofol to patients in the early postoperative period for relief of pain and anxiety. Rather than administering boluses of narcotics, a continuous infusion of morphine (0.02 mg/kg/hour for patients under age 65 and 0.01 mg/kg/hour for patients over age 65) is used. This usually produces minimal respiratory depression and can be continued after extubation. If the patient remains overly sedated, the infusion rate can be decreased. The hypertension that occasionally occurs after the propofol is stopped is treated with an antihypertensive agent, such as sodium nitroprusside.

4. Breakthrough pain in intubated patients may be treated with small additional doses of IV morphine or IV ketorolac (15–30 mg). Following extubation, the IV MS infusion can be continued until the patient is transferred out of the ICU. Many patients benefit from morphine delivered by a patient-controlled analgesia (PCA) pump

on the first postoperative day, although use of IV ketorolac (15–30 mg) may be sufficient.[19]

F. Hemodynamic support during a period of transient myocardial depression (see Chapter 10)

   1. Myocardial function is temporarily depressed as the heart recovers from the period of ischemia and reperfusion. Hypothermia and elevated levels of catecholamines lead to an increase in SVR and systemic hypertension, which increase afterload and depress myocardial performance.

   2. Serial assessments of filling pressures, cardiac output, and SVR allow for the appropriate selection of fluids, inotropes, and/or vasodilators to optimize preload, afterload, and contractility to provide hemodynamic support during this period of temporary myocardial depression. The objective is to maintain a cardiac index above $2.2\,L/min/m^2$ with a stable blood pressure (systolic 100 to 130 mm Hg or a mean pressure of 80 to 90 mm Hg). Adequacy of tissue oxygenation is the primary goal of hemodynamic management and can be assessed by measuring the mixed venous O_2 saturation (SvO_2) from the pulmonary artery port of the Swan-Ganz catheter (normal >65%).

   3. Atrial or atrioventricular pacing at a rate of 90 to 100 per minute is commonly required at the conclusion of surgery to achieve optimal hemodynamics. This is especially true in patients taking β-adrenergic blockers before surgery.

G. Fluid resuscitation to maintain filling pressures in the presence of a capillary leak and vasodilatation (see Chapter 11)

   1. Following cardiopulmonary bypass, the patient will be total body salt and water overloaded and should theoretically be aggressively diuresed. However, the use of cardiopulmonary bypass results in a "systemic inflammatory response" which produces a capillary leak. Furthermore, peripheral vasoconstriction masks intravascular hypovolemia despite adequate left-heart filling pressures.

   2. Fluid resuscitation is therefore necessary to offset the capillary leak and the vasodilatation that occurs from various medications and warming to normothermia. Crystalloid and colloid infusions are used to maintain intravascular volume, although this usually occurs at the expense of expansion of the interstitial space. After the capillary leak has ceased and hemodynamics have stabilized, the patient may be aggressively diuresed to eliminate the excessive salt and water administered during surgery and the early postoperative period.

   3. Various measures can be used in the operating room to minimize pulmonary compromise from fluid administration. Reducing the positive fluid balance during surgery is a major factor that improves the likelihood of successful early extubation and fosters a faster recovery from surgery. There is suggestive evidence that use of a membrane oxygenator, centrifugal pump, aprotinin,

steroids, and leukocyte filters during CPB may reduce the systemic inflammatory response and contribute to a faster recovery from surgery.[20–25]

II.   Fast-Track Protocols

A. Traditional postoperative management involved keeping the patient sedated overnight with plans for extubation in the early morning. However, numerous changes in intraoperative and postoperative management have changed this concept and made it possible for the majority of patients to be extubated within 12 hours (table 7.1). Early extubation is accomplished in patients who are more alert at an earlier stage of recovery, capable of being mobilized by the first postoperative day, and discharged routinely by the fourth day after uneventful and sometimes complex surgery.[13,14,25]

B. Preoperative considerations

1. Patient teaching using a simplified critical pathway

2. Careful evaluation of preoperative comorbidities

C. Intraoperative protocols

1. Alteration in anesthetic protocols: using short-acting anesthetic agents in the operating room (inhalational anesthetics, short-acting narcotics and anxiolytics).

2. Performing an expeditious and complete surgical procedure to minimize the duration of cardiopulmonary bypass and completely correct the underlying cardiac pathology. Performing "off pump" procedures when feasible.

3. Reducing intraoperative bleeding using antifibrinolytic drugs and precise surgical technique to avoid use of blood products.

4. Using the appropriate form of myocardial protection to optimize myocardial function.

5. Minimizing fluid administration in the operating room and using hemofiltration during bypass in patients with preexisting fluid overload.

6. Warming the patient to normothermia before concluding bypass.

7. Using measures to reduce the "systemic inflammatory response": membrane oxygenators, centrifugal pumps, aprotinin, steroids, leukocyte filters.

D. Postoperative care

1. Using shorter-acting sedatives and analgesics to minimize respiratory depression, permit early extubation, and expedite return of mental function and strength.

2. Selecting antihypertensive medications, rather than sedatives, to control hypertension.

3. Using meperidine rather than neuromuscular blockers for shivering.

4. Establishing a higher threshold for blood transfusions (hematocrit in the low 20s).

Table 7.1 *Options for a Fast-Track Protocol*

OPERATING ROOM

Anesthetic Agents	Fentanyl 5–10 µg/kg for induction, then 3–5 µg/kg/h
	Sufentanil 1 µg/kg for induction, then 0.25–0.5 µg/kg/h
	Alfentanil 50–75 µg/kg for induction, then 0.5–3.0 µg/kg/min
	Remifentanil 1 µg/kg for induction, then 0.05–2.0 µg/kg/min
Sedatives	Midazolam 2.5–5.0 mg before bypass
	Propofol 50–75 µg/kg/min (2–10 mg/kg/h) after bypass
Cardiopulmonary bypass	Withdrawal of autologous blood before starting bypass
	Warm to 37°C before terminating bypass
	Hemofiltration if fluid overloaded
	Echo imaging for aortic atherosclerosis
Myocardial protection	Antegrade/retrograde blood cardioplegia with terminal "hot shot"
Antifibrinolytic agents	Epsilon-aminocaproic acid 5 g at skin incision and in pump prime, and 1 g/h infusion
	Aprotinin 140 mg at skin incision and in pump prime, and 35 mg/h (high-risk cases)
Other medications	Methylprednisolone 1 g before bypass, then dexamethasone 4 mg IV q6h × 4
	Ranitidine 150 mg bid
	Triiodothyronine 0.8 µg/kg, then 0.113 µg/kg/h × 6 h (AF prophylaxis), or 10 µg × 2 in operating room, then T4 200 µg IV qd × 2 days

INTENSIVE CARE UNIT

Analgesia	Morphine infusion 0.01–0.02 mg/kg/h depending on age
	Ketorolac 15–30 mg IV after extubation
	PCA pump with morphine on POD #1
Anxiolysis	Propofol 25 µg/kg/min
Shivering	Meperidine 25–50 mg IV
Hypertension	Sodium nitroprusside/esmolol (avoid sedatives)
Anemia	Tolerate hematocrit of 22% if stable
Medications	Metoclopramide 10 mg tid
	Ranitidine 150 mg bid
	Magnesium sulfate 2 g on POD #1 (AF prophylaxis)
	Digoxin/metoprolol by POD #1 (AF prophylaxis)

5. Using metoclopramide to improve gastrointestinal motility and dietary intake.

6. Administering medications early to prevent atrial fibrillation (digoxin with β-blockers, magnesium sulfate, thyroid hormone).

7. Following a critical care pathway that defines daily expectations and events.

8. Mobilizing patients early and aggressively.

9. Initiating aggressive diuresis.

E. A full discussion of the merits and techniques for accomplishing early extubation are discussed in Chapter 9.

III.   Management of Common Postoperative Scenarios

There are several hemodynamic scenarios that are typically noted during the early phase of recovery from open-heart surgery. An understanding of these patterns allows therapeutic maneuvers to be undertaken in anticipation of hemodynamic changes, rather than as reactions to problems once they have occurred. Scenarios common to most patients undergoing cardiac surgical procedures using cardiopulmonary bypass will be presented first. Aspects of care unique to different types of adult cardiac surgical procedures will be discussed subsequently.

A. **Vasoconstriction from hypothermia with hypertension and borderline cardiac output**

1. The hypothermic patient will vasoconstrict in an attempt to increase core body temperature. The elevation in SVR may produce hypertension at a time when cardiac function is still somewhat depressed from surgery and requires inotropic support. These patients should be managed by a combination of fluid replacement to reach an LA or pulmonary capillary wedge pressure (PCWP) of 15 mm Hg, vasodilatation with sodium nitroprusside (SNP) to maintain a systolic pressure of 100 to 130 mm Hg (mean pressure 80 to 90 mm Hg), and inotropic support if the cardiac index remains less than $2.0 L/min/m^2$. Warming methods noted above should also be employed.

2. The use of SNP is beneficial in the vasoconstricted patient for several reasons:

   a. It lowers afterload, improving myocardial metabolism and LV function.

   b. It improves peripheral tissue perfusion. This minimizes the fall in core temperature after bypass.

   c. It facilitates gentle and adequate fluid administration.

3. Nitroprusside is administered starting at a dose of 0.1 μg/kg/min (often less) and titrating to a maximum of 8 μg/kg/min. As the SVR and blood pressure decrease, left-sided filling pressures will also fall, requiring the simultaneous infusion of fluids to maintain cardiac output. The optimal left-sided filling pressures depend on the state of myocardial contractility and compliance. Preload should generally not be raised above 18 to 20 mm Hg because of the deleterious effects of elevated wall tension on myocardial metabolism and function. However, if preload is allowed to fall too low during SNP infusion, the patient may become markedly hypovolemic and hypotensive when normothermia is achieved. The general principle is to "optimize preload → reduce afterload → optimize preload."

4. If the patient is vasoconstricted and the cardiac output is very marginal (e.g., CI $<2.0 L/min/m^2$), it is advisable to start an inotrope in addition to SNP. **Stopping an inotropic medication in a hypertensive patient without first ensuring that a satisfactory cardiac output is present can be very dangerous.** Some patients with very marginal cardiac function maintain a satisfactory blood pressure by intense vasoconstriction from enhanced sympathetic tone. Loss of

this compensatory mechanism may result in rapid deterioration from loss of perfusion pressure.

B. **Vasodilatation and hypotension during the rewarming phase**

1. Vasodilatation reduces filling pressures and, in the hypovolemic patient, may produce hypotension, even though the cardiac output may remain satisfactory. There are several reasons for a patient to vasodilate during the early postoperative period.

   a. Medications used for analgesia and anxiolysis are vasodilators (narcotics, propofol).

   b. Resolution of hypothermia leads to peripheral vasodilatation, which is accentuated in patients who warm to higher than 37°C.

   c. Improvement in cardiac output often leads to relaxation of peripheral vasoconstriction.

2. To avoid hypotension, fluid administration should be administered to maintain filling pressures. The quandary is whether crystalloid or colloid should be selected and how much should be given. If the basic reason for hypovolemia is a capillary leak syndrome, the use of colloid could be detrimental, because its oncotic elements may pass into the interstitial tissues and exacerbate tissue edema and compromise organ function. However, if vasodilatation of the peripheral and splanchnic beds is the major problem, then colloids should be preferable, because they will augment the intravascular volume to a greater extent than crystalloids (see figure 11.1). Generally, if the PCWP is not elevated, the amount of extravascular lung water will not be influenced significantly by whether colloid or crystalloid is infused.[26]

3. It is generally best to start with 500–1000 mL boluses of Ringer's lactate. If there is minimal increase in filling pressures, a colloid such as hetastarch may be chosen. It increases the intravascular volume more effectively than crystalloid and also longer than 5% albumin. The total infusion volume should be limited to 1500–1750 mL (20 mL/kg) per 24 hours to minimize adverse effects on the coagulation mechanism. Hetastarch should be avoided in the patient with significant mediastinal bleeding because it may increase bleeding.

4. There is often a tendency to administer a tremendous amount of fluid during the period of vasodilatation in order to maintain filling pressures and systemic blood pressure. Furthermore, most patients with satisfactory cardiac function are simultaneously producing a copious amount of urine. One should resist the temptation to "flood" the patient with fluid. Excessive fluid administration (>2 liters within 6 hours) may exacerbate interstitial edema and will delay extubation.[27] It also produces significant hemodilution, often necessitating blood transfusions for anemia, and reduces the levels of clotting factors, possibly increasing mediastinal bleeding and necessitating plasma or platelet administration.

5. **Preload should be increased only as necessary to maintain satisfactory cardiac output and tissue perfusion.** The response to fluid

administration is not always predictable and depends on the compliance of the left atrium and ventricle, the degree of "capillary leak," and the intensity of peripheral vasoconstriction.

    a. A minimal rise in filling pressures with repeated fluid challenges may reflect the beneficial relaxation of intense peripheral vasoconstriction that accompanies warming or an improvement in cardiac output. Once a satisfactory cardiac output has been achieved, an α-agent (phenylephrine or norepinephrine) can be used to maintain systemic blood pressure.

    b. A minimal rise in filling pressures may also indicate that fluid is leaking into the interstitial space rather than being retained in the intravascular space. This is especially prominent in sicker patients who have had a long duration of bypass and have a severe capillary leak syndrome. In these patients, it sometimes seems virtually impossible to maintain filling pressures despite the ongoing administration of large volumes of fluid. The use of inotropic agents to augment cardiac output or an α-agent to support SVR when the cardiac output is satisfactory may reduce the amount of fluid that needs to be administered.

    c. If filling pressures rise with fluid administration, but blood pressure and cardiac output remain marginal, left ventricular (LV) distention will increase stroke work and oxygen demand while decreasing coronary blood flow. At this point, additional inotropic support is usually necessary.

6. The following is a general guideline to hemodynamic management during the rewarming phase.

    a. If blood pressure is marginal, push the PCWP to 15 to 18 mmHg using crystalloid and then colloid. Once this level is reached, or if urine volume begins to match the infused volume, or if more than 2000mL of fluid has been administered and filling pressures are not rising, consider the following:

        i. If CI >2.5 L/min/m^2, use phenylephrine (pure α)

        ii. If CI is 2–2.5 L/min/m^2, use norepinephrine (α and β)

        iii. If CI <2 L/min/m^2, use an inotrope, then norepinephrine as needed

    b. Note: Use of an α-agent may not be able to minimize a capillary leak, but it does counteract vasodilatation. This may decrease the volume requirement and improve SVR and blood pressure with little effect on myocardial function.

C. **Copious urine output and falling PCWP.** Some patients will make inordinate amounts of urine, resulting in a reduction in filling pressures, blood pressure, and cardiac output. Several factors should be considered when determining why this might be occurring.

1. Is the patient on "renal dose" dopamine demonstrating renal vasodilatation and improved renal blood flow out of proportion to its hemodynamic effects? If so, and the patient requires inotropic support, consider changing to another drug, such as dobutamine or epinephrine.

2. Did the patient receive mannitol or furosemide in the operating room because of low urine output or hyperkalemia? Urine output is no longer a direct reflection of myocardial function when a diuretic has been administered. Excessive urine output often necessitates a significant amount of fluid administration to maintain filling pressures and confounds the selection of the appropriate fluid to administer (crystalloid vs. colloid).

3. Is the patient hyperglycemic and developing an osmotic diuresis? If so, check the blood glucose level, give an intravenous insulin bolus (5 units IV for each 50 mg/dL over 250 mg/dL), or use an insulin drip if significant hyperglycemia persists.

4. Does the patient have normal LV function and the kidneys are simply mobilizing excessive interstitial fluid from hemodilution on pump? This beneficial effect is often seen in healthy patients with a short CPB run, and reflects excellent cardiac output and renal function that should lead to a rapid postoperative recovery. However, copious urine output can be problematic when it lowers filling pressures, blood pressure, and cardiac output.

   a. The patient is putting out "crystalloid" in the urine and should have it replaced primarily with crystalloid (Ringer's lactate).

   b. The temptation should be resisted to administer too much colloid. It can produce significant hemodilution and may cause the hematocrit to fall despite the negative fluid balance achieved by the excellent urine output. Excessive colloid administration can also dilute levels of clotting factors and increase mediastinal bleeding. Furthermore, the provision of oncotic elements may contribute to a relative volume deficit in the interstitial and intracellular spaces.

   c. Volume should be administered to keep the fluid balance modestly negative during a phase of spontaneous diuresis. Use of an α-agent may maintain filling pressures and decrease the volume requirement in some of these patients.

D. **Normal left ventricular function, but low cardiac output**

1. A disturbing postoperative scenario is that of a low cardiac output syndrome associated with normal or elevated left-heart filling pressures but preserved ventricular function. This scenario is noted most commonly in small women with systemic hypertension who have small, hypertrophied LV cavities. It is more common in patients who have undergone mitral or aortic valve surgery.

2. The cause of this problem is not clear. It appears to represent an extreme form of diastolic dysfunction with reduced ventricular

compliance produced by myocardial edema from ischemic/reperfusion injury. Potential contributing factors include lack of AV synchrony with impaired ventricular filling, impaired right ventricular (RV) function, and perhaps excessive use of inotropic agents.

3. Based on hemodynamic data obtained from a Swan-Ganz catheter, it would appear that the low cardiac output is caused by impaired contractility. Therefore, it is usually managed by volume transfusions to elevate the PCWP and augment ventricular filling, inotropic support to improve stroke volume, atrial or AV pacing to improve ventricular filling, and afterload reduction. Although most of these measures are beneficial, they often lead to pulmonary congestion, little improvement in cardiac output, a reduction in renal blood flow, and progressive oliguria. The use of inotropes may also produce a significant sinus tachycardia that is detrimental to myocardial metabolism and recovery.

4. The use of transesophageal echocardiography (TEE) to assess myocardial function has been invaluable in the management of this problem. TEE will usually confirm a small LV chamber with excellent function. Fluid should be administered to raise the PCWP to about 20 to 25 mm Hg. This will increase the LV end-diastolic volume which tends to be smaller than would be suggested by pressure measurements because of poor LV compliance. Inotropic agents can usually be weaned, often without a change in stroke volume but with a decrease in heart rate, although they may be necessary to support RV function. Use of calcium-channel or β-blockers to improve diastolic relaxation is frequently beneficial. Aggressive diuresis to reduce interstitial edema while providing colloid (salt-poor albumin) to maintain intravascular volume may also improve diastolic relaxation. If the patient can survive the first few days of low output syndrome without end-organ dysfunction, a gradual improvement in cardiac output generally results.

5. Occasionally, a patient with markedly impaired RV function will present with marginal cardiac outputs and blood pressure despite preserved LV function. This may result from RV infarction or poor intraoperative protection of a hypertrophied right ventricle in patients with pulmonary hypertension. This is not uncommon in cardiac transplant recipients with preexisting pulmonary hypertension. The use of blood products also increases pulmonary vascular resistance and can exacerbate RV dysfunction. Fluid administration, inotropic support with medications such as amrinone or milrinone, and use of nitric oxide (a pure pulmonary vasodilator) may be beneficial (see page 228). If not, a circulatory assist device might be necessary.

IV.   Postoperative Considerations Following Specific Procedures

A.   Coronary artery bypass grafting (CABG)

1. The patient with excellent ventricular function usually requires a vasodilator (nitroprusside or nitroglycerin) to control hypertension more often than an inotrope. With the use of propofol, hyperten-

sion tends to be less common. Tachycardia is frequently present, especially in young anxious patients, and can be managed by β-blockers (esmolol) if cardiac output is satisfactory. Patients with a **hyperdynamic left ventricle** may develop progressive tachycardia when vasodilators are used to control hypertension. This should be managed by allowing the blood pressure to drift up to 140 systolic (mean 100 to 110) and then using β-blockers to control both the tachycardia and the hypertension.

2. **Inotropic support** is usually initiated at the termination of bypass and may be required for several hours in the ICU. The initial first-line drug may be dopamine, dobutamine, or epinephrine. The latter is least expensive and usually produces less tachycardia than the other drugs. If there is little response to one of these cate-cholamines, amrinone or milrinone is of great benefit in improving cardiac output. These medications are positive inotropes that produce systemic vasodilation which frequently requires the addition of norepinephrine to support systemic resistance. When hemodynamic performance remains very marginal, placement of an intraaortic balloon should be considered. In contrast to the cate-cholamines, the intraaortic balloon pump (IABP) can reduce myocardial oxygen demand and improve coronary perfusion. Support beyond 6 to 12 hours may be necessary if the patient has sustained a perioperative infarction or has a severely "stunned" myocardium that exhibits a prolonged period of dysfunction in the absence of infarction.

3. Intravenous lidocaine is often started in the operating room at the conclusion of CPB and continued on a prophylactic basis until the following morning. This may decrease the incidence of ventricular ectopy that may be associated with hypothermia, hemodynamic instability, or the presence of the endotracheal tube or Swan-Ganz catheter. Subsequent use of antiarrhythmic therapy should be based on the presence and severity of any arrhythmias as well as the patient's ejection fraction. Holter monitoring and/or electrophysiologic studies may be necessary to determine whether continued antiarrhythmic therapy is warranted for ventricular arrhythmias.

4. **Atrial fibrillation (AF)** is noted in about 30% of patients following CABG. It may be related to poor atrial preservation during surgery or to withdrawal of β-blockers. Most centers initiate β-blockers by the first postoperative morning (usually metoprolol 25–50 mg bid) because of the overwhelming evidence that β-blockers reduce the incidence of AF.[28] The concomitant administration of digoxin may lower the incidence of AF even further.[29] Magnesium sulfate has been shown to reduce the incidence of AF as well as aid in conversion to sinus rhythm. We routinely administer 2 grams at the termination of CPB and on POD #1.[30]

5. Close attention must be paid to the postoperative ECG. Evidence of ischemia may represent coronary spasm, incomplete revascularization, anastomotic stenosis, poor myocardial protection, or acute graft occlusion. Regardless of the etiology, intravenous nitroglycerin is usually indicated. Calcium-channel blockers (nifedipine 30 mg SL or diltiazem 0.25 mg/kg IV over 2 minutes, then 5–

15 mg/hour IV) are useful if coronary spasm is suspected. These medications may resolve ischemic changes or minimize infarct size if necrosis is already underway. Placement of an IABP should also be considered. If severe ischemia is felt to be caused by a problem with a bypass graft, emergency angiography or reexploration may be indicated.

6. For patients receiving radial artery grafts; diltiazem is given IV for 24 h and then PO for 6 months to prevent graft spasm.

7. The diagnosis of a perioperative **myocardial infarction** (MI) can be difficult to make, but is usually confirmed by persistent ECG changes and new regional wall motion abnormalities on echocardiography (see page 256). Elevation of cardiac enzymes (CK-MB, troponin T or I) may be noted, but they are commonly oversensitive markers of myocardial damage. Management consists of hemodynamic support and other standard measures. A common finding in the patient sustaining a small perioperative MI is a low SVR that requires a vasopressor for several days to support blood pressure. A more extensive infarction may require pharmacologic support or an IABP for longer periods of time and is associated with increased operative mortality and a decrease in long-term survival.

8. **Antiplatelet therapy** has been shown to inhibit platelet deposition on vein grafts and may delay or attenuate the development of fibrointimal hyperplasia and atherosclerosis. Starting enteric-coated aspirin 81–325 mg within 6–24 h of surgery and continuing for 1 year is recommended to improve graft patency.[31] It should be continued indefinitely because of its beneficial effects in patients with native coronary disease.

9. Patients undergoing **minimally invasive coronary surgery** (MIDCABs) are frequently extubated in the operating room or soon after arrival in the ICU. Attention should be directed toward the following:

   a. Respiratory status: most MIDCABs are performed through limited anterior thoracotomy incisions with one-lung anesthesia. The use of epidural analgesia (Duramorph) and intercostal bupivacaine (Marcaine) is helpful in reducing splinting and improving respiratory efforts in patients who might otherwise have significant chest wall pain from rib retraction, resection, or fracture.

   b. ECG: no pacing wires are placed after MIDCAB. A heart rate in the 60 to 70 range is usually acceptable. Atrial and ventricular pacing wires placed through the Swan-Ganz catheter can be used for bradycardia. The ECG should be carefully monitored for ischemia because anastomotic problems are more common when an anastomosis is performed on a beating, rather than an arrested heart. Ventricular pacing wires alone are usually placed after minimally invasive coronary operations using the Heartport system.

   c. Bleeding: Intrapericardial or intrapleural bleeding may originate from the chest wall, the anastomotic site, or side branches of the internal mammary artery (IMA). Blood will more readily accumulate in the pleural space during spontaneous ventilation. The possibility of bleeding should be monitored by observing chest tube drainage and a postoperative chest x-ray.

d. Anemia is unusual because there is no hemodilution attributable to CPB. However, a substantial amount of blood can be lost during construction of the anastomosis. Fluid retention is minimal and the copious urine output normally seen after CPB will not be noted. Diuretics are required less often than fluid administration to maintain urine output.

e. The incidence of atrial fibrillation does appear to be less than with a standard CABG, but still occurs fairly frequently.

B. Aortic valve surgery

1. Aortic stenosis (AS)

a. Aortic stenosis produces a hypertrophied, noncompliant left ventricle that depends on synchronous atrial and ventricular contractions for nearly 30% of its stroke volume. Postoperatively, it is imperative that sinus rhythm be present or that atrial or AV pacing be used. There should be a low threshold for cardioversion of atrial fibrillation because profound hemodynamic deterioration may occur, especially during the first 24 hours after surgery.

b. Adequate **preload** must be maintained (LA > 15 mm Hg) to ensure adequate LV filling. Filling pressures may rise rapidly with minimal volume infusion in patients with AS because of the noncompliant hypertrophied ventricle.

c. Although LV pressures often exceed 200 mm Hg in patients with AS, significant **systolic hypertension** is usually not seen at the conclusion of bypass despite the elimination of the transvalvular gradient and satisfactory myocardial protection. However, hypertension tends to develop after several hours in the ICU and must be controlled to reduce myocardial oxygen demand and protect the aortic suture line. Use of vasodilators for a hyperdynamic heart may reduce diastolic perfusion pressure and produce a tachycardia. Selective use of a β-blocker, such as esmolol, is very beneficial in this situation.

2. Aortic regurgitation (AR)

a. Aortic regurgitation produces both volume and pressure overload of the left ventricle, resulting in a dilated and frequently hypertrophied chamber. Maintenance of a supraventricular rhythm is important. Filling pressures often rise minimally despite large fluid challenges because of the enlarged, compliant left ventricle.

b. Despite the placement of a competent aortic valvular prosthesis, most patients with AR remain vasodilated after surgery and require the use of an α-agent, such as phenylephrine or norepinephrine, to maintain a satisfactory blood pressure. Systolic hypertension is better controlled with β-blockers than with vasodilators.

3. **Heart block** may complicate an aortic valve replacement (AVR) because of edema, hemorrhage, suturing, or débridement near the conduction system, which lies adjacent to the base of the right coronary cusp. Epicardial AV pacing may be necessary for several days. The presence of a bundle branch block following AVR is of adverse prognostic significance.[32] If complete heart block persists for more than 4 to 5 days, during which time edema or hemorrhage should subside, placement of a permanent DDD pacemaker should be considered.

4. **Anticoagulation**[33]

   a. Tissue valves: There is some evidence that short-term anticoagulation with warfarin may reduce the incidence of thromboembolism on aortic tissue valves, although other studies suggest that aspirin is just as effective as warfarin when used from the outset.[34–36] Warfarin is generally recommended for 3 months in younger patients or those with no contraindication to anticoagulation, and is then converted to aspirin. If warfarin is not used, aspirin 325 mg every day is prescribed.

   b. Mechanical valves: all patients should receive warfarin indefinitely to achieve an INR of 2.5–3.5 for tilting and bileaflet valves. Heparin may be started in the hospital, starting on POD #2–4 until the INR reaches the therapeutic range. More details on anticoagulation are discussed on pages 393–394.

C. **Mitral valve surgery**

1. **Mitral stenosis (MS).** Most patients with MS have a small LV cavity with preserved function. They are prone to a low cardiac output syndrome following surgery because of small LV end-diastolic and end-systolic volumes. Maintenance of adequate filling pressures is essential to ensure a satisfactory stroke volume. The "ideal" filling pressure varies for each patient, depending on the level of preexisting pulmonary hypertension and the degree of its reversibility. Hemodynamic support is more often required for RV rather than LV dysfunction.

   a. Postoperative ventilatory failure is not uncommon in patients with chronic MS as a result of pulmonary hypertension, fluid overload, and chronic cachexia with poor ventilatory reserve. Aggressive diuresis, nutritional support, and a plan for ventilatory support and weaning are essential.

   b. Most patients with MS are diuretic-dependent. Despite correction of their valvular abnormality, they usually require diuretics during the hospital stay to achieve their preoperative weight. They should be maintained on diuretics for several months after discharge.

2. **Mitral regurgitation (MR)** reduces LV wall stress by systolic unloading through the regurgitant valve. When mitral valve competence has been restored, there may be unmasking of LV dysfunction because of the greater systolic wall stress required to

achieve forward ejection. This may be attenuated to some degree by a reduction in volume overload. This so-called "afterload mismatch" may result in LV failure and require inotropic support and systemic unloading with vasodilators.[37] The problem is less significant after mitral valve repair or when MVR is performed with preservation of the chordae tendineae. Both right and LV dysfunction are frequently encountered after surgery for MR.

3. Hemodynamic management after mitral valve surgery is frequently directed toward reduction of pulmonary hypertension and improvement of RV function. Following surgery, RV failure may be precipitated by poor intraoperative myocardial protection and by factors that increase RV afterload, such as positive-pressure ventilation, increased extravascular lung water, blood product transfusions, blood gas and acid-base abnormalities, residual pulmonary vascular disease, and reversible pulmonary vascular spasm secondary to perfusion-related phenomena.

   a. Isolated RV dysfunction is manifest by a high central venous pressure, variable pulmonary artery (PA) pressures, a hypovolemic left ventricle, and a low cardiac output. Use of "volumetric" Swan-Ganz catheters can better define the degree of RV dysfunction by calculating an RV ejection fraction based on estimates of RV end-diastolic and end-systolic volumes.[38]

   b. LV filling pressures must be maintained at high levels (often well above 20 mm Hg) to ensure an adequate systemic cardiac output. Although there is some decrease in PA pressure after surgery, the degree and rapidity of reversibility of pulmonary hypertension are unpredictable. Optimal volume status can frequently be determined by observing myocardial function at various filling pressures at the conclusion of CPB. Various pharmacologic measures may be necessary to improve cardiac output once "adequate" filling pressures have been achieved.

      i. Pulmonary artery diastolic (PAD) pressures may give an inaccurate assessment of left heart filling because a significant transpulmonary gradient (PA mean pressure minus PCWP) is commonly present in patients with mitral and pulmonary vascular disease. PCW pressures give a more accurate assessment of left heart filling, although balloon inflation is best avoided in the presence of pulmonary hypertension because it carries an increased risk of pulmonary artery rupture. It can be attempted by inflating the balloon with the least volume of air necessary to achieve a wedge tracing.

      ii. Left atrial lines provide a more accurate pressure measurement and also permit the selective infusion of α-agents to counteract the systemic vasodilatation produced by various pulmonary vasodilators (see below).

      iii. A large quantity of fluid is frequently required to increase filling pressures because of increased left atrial and/or ventricular compliance. However, in the presence of severe RV dysfunction, attempts to achieve adequate left-sided filling may be futile and may lead to progressive RV dilatation and failure. Careful monitoring of the CVP and RV end-diastolic volumes may indicate when fluid challenges are detrimental rather than beneficial. Generally, if additional volume causes the CVP to rise above 15 without any improvement in cardiac output, further volume infusion should not be given. Inotropic support should be initiated or increased.

c. Inotropic drugs that reduce pulmonary vascular resistance (PVR) should be selected to support RV or LV function. Amrinone is effective in lowering the PVR and improving contractility while producing a modest tachycardia. Isoproterenol improves contractility and lowers the PVR, but its use is usually limited by a tachycardia.[39] Low-dose epinephrine or dobutamine may produce pulmonary vasodilatation, but the response is variable.

d. Direct pulmonary vasodilatation is best accomplished using nitric oxide, a selective pulmonary vasodilator. It is administered at 20–40 ppm through the ventilator.[40] Prostaglandin E_1 infused into the central circulation in doses <0.1 μg/kg/min is effective in reducing PA pres-sures without producing systemic hypotension.[39,41] Higher doses usually require infusion of a vasopressor, such as norepinephrine, directly into a left atrial line, to counteract systemic vasodilatation and maintain blood pressure. Nitroglycerin or nitroprusside are pulmonary vasodilators, but they usually reduce the systemic perfusion pressure as well.

4. Maintenance of **sinus rhythm** is beneficial to optimize cardiac output. Despite long-standing atrial fibrillation, it is frequently possible to AV pace the heart for several days after surgery. Maintenance of sinus rhythm beyond the early postoperative period is highly unlikely, however, when AF has been present for more than 1 year or the LA dimension exceeds 50 mm. Digoxin may be used for rate control, but type IA antiarrhythmics to maintain sinus rhythm are not indicated in the patient with chronic atrial fibrillation.

5. **Anticoagulation**

a. Tissue valves and mitral rings: warfarin should be given for 3 months to achieve an INR of 2.0–3.0 and should then be converted to aspirin 325 mg every day if the patient is in sinus rhythm. Warfarin should be continued indefinitely in patients with atrial fibrillation, an enlarged left atrium (>50 mm in diameter), or a history of thromboembolism. Use of heparin in the hospital is optional, but is advisable in the latter three circumstances.

b. Mechanical valves: warfarin to achieve an INR of 2.5–3.5 should be given indefinitely. The addition of aspirin 81–100 mg is safe and may further reduce the thromboembolic risk.[42] Heparin should be started on POD #2–4 if the INR has not reached the therapeutic range.

6. A dreaded complication of MVR is **left ventricular rupture,** presenting as cardiac tamponade or exsanguinating hemorrhage through the chest tubes. It usually occurs at the conclusion of surgery or soon after arrival in the ICU. LV rupture is usually the result of a technical mishap, but it can be precipitated by LV distention and excessive afterload. Repair usually requires CPB and carries a significant mortality rate.[43]

D. **Aortic dissections**

1. Most patients with dissections that involve the ascending aorta (type A dissections) undergo surgical repair. The reestablishment of vascular continuity involves suturing of a Dacron graft to very fragile tissues and can produce extensive bleeding from suture lines. In addition, surgical repair is predicated on stabilization of the entry site of the dissection but does not completely eliminate the distal false channel. Thus, surgery is palliative and leaves the patient predisposed to aneurysm formation within the false channel. Continued antihypertensive treatment is critical to improving long-term survival.

2. The antihypertensive regimen used in the early postoperative period must reduce systolic blood pressure and the force of cardiac contraction (dp/dt). The most common regimens are esmolol alone or esmolol combined with nitroprusside. The patient is then converted to oral medications, such as the β-blockers, calcium-channel blockers, or the angiotensin-converting enzyme (ACE) inhibitors.

3. Most repairs of type A dissections involve a period of deep hypothermic circulatory arrest. This may be complicated by intraoperative bleeding, which may be minimized by the use of aprotinin.[44] However, the latter has been associated with neurologic problems and renal dysfunction after circulatory arrest.[45] A careful preoperative neurologic evaluation is essential for comparison with potential postoperative deficits.

4. Patients undergoing surgery for repair of type B dissections may develop paraplegia and/or renal failure. A careful neurologic examination and measures to support renal function in the perioperative period are important.

E. **Thoracic aneurysms**

1. Thoracic aneurysms tend to develop in elderly patients with hypertension, chronic lung disease, and diffuse atherosclerosis, including cerebrovascular, coronary, and renovascular disease. Prevention or recognition of problems involving these organ systems is essential to achieving an uneventful recovery.

2. Repair of ascending aortic and arch aneurysms may involve use of deep hypothermic circulatory arrest, which is associated with a coagulopathy and potential neurologic insult.[44,46] Aggressive management of mediastinal bleeding and a careful neurologic evaluation before and after surgery are important.

3. Repair of descending thoracic and thoracoabdominal aneurysms involves a thoracotomy incision that can compromise ventilatory function. Use of an epidural catheter or PCA (patient-controlled analgesia) pump can ameliorate some of the associated pain without producing respiratory depression.

4. Crossclamping of the descending aorta can result in paraplegia or renal failure. Particular attention to pre- and postoperative neurologic evaluation and optimizing perioperative renal function is important. Delayed onset of paraplegia is uncommon, but has been described. It is often reversible with elevation of the blood pressure, cerebrospinal fluid drainage, and use of high-dose steroids.

F. **Left ventricular aneurysm resections and endocardial resections**

1. Patients undergoing resection of a LV aneurysm usually have markedly depressed LV function. Although ventricular size and geometry are better preserved using the endoaneurysmorrhaphy or endoventricular circular patch plasty techniques than with a linear closure, the stroke volume of the left ventricle after LVA repair is usually smaller after surgery. Achieving adequate filling pressures (usually a PCWP around 20–25 mmHg) is essential to optimize stroke volume. Filling pressures may rise precipitously with minimal volume infusion because of the small noncompliant LV chamber. Many patients generate a satisfactory cardiac output by virtue of a faster heart rate; this should not be reduced pharmacologically unless the stroke volume is satisfactory.

2. Hemodynamic support and the IABP are frequently necessary to allow weaning from bypass. Patients undergoing endocardial resections for ventricular tachycardia nearly always have LV aneurysms and similarly may require additional support.

3. The success rate of map-guided endocardial resection and cryoablation for ablating ventricular arrhythmias exceeds 80%, but persistent or recurrent arrhythmias will be noted in a few patients. They may be triggered by the use of inotropes that are arrhythmogenic. Lidocaine may be used prophylactically for 24 hours, but further antiarrhythmic therapy is not indicated unless ectopy persists. Postoperative electrophysiologic testing and Holter monitoring are performed to determine if the operation has been successful. If not, retesting is performed on antiarrhythmic drugs once therapeutic drug levels have been achieved.

4. Now that the equipment for map-guided resections is no longer manufactured, surgical treatment for ventricular arrhythmias involves blind endocardial resections and cryosurgery. Because this is less efficacious than map-guided resections, an ICD device is usually implanted before the patient is discharged home.

5. Anticoagulation with warfarin is generally used for 3 months following LVA resection.

G. **Implantable cardioverter defibrillator (ICD)**

1. ICDs are usually placed in the electrophysiology lab in patients with sustained ventricular tachycardia or other suspected life-

threatening arrhythmias. Patients are usually maintained on their antiarrhythmic drug regimen, since nearly 50% will require medication to control their arrhythmias.[47]

2. When the ICD device is placed in the operating room at the time of surgery, it is usually left in the inactive mode during the early postoperative period. Various abnormalities—including blood gas, acid-base, and fluid and electrolyte abnormalities, as well as a variety of medications—may increase the tendency to develop arrhythmias that could trigger the device and waste battery power. External defibrillator devices must be immediately available and should be used preferentially in the hospital setting. The patient is taken to the electrophysiology lab before hospital discharge to have the unit retested and activated. A card should be posted above the head of the patient's bed indicating the status of the ICD so that anyone who responds to an emergency knows whether the device is activated or not.

References

1. Higgins TL, Yared JP, Ryan T. Immediate postoperative care of cardiac surgical patients. J Cardiothorac Vasc Anesthesia 1996;10:643–58.
2. Frank SM, Fleisher LA, Olson KF, et al. Multivariate determinants of early postoperative oxygen consumption in elderly patients. Anesthesiology 1995;83:241–9.
3. Norback CR, Tinker JH. Hypothermia after cardiopulmonary bypass in man: amelioration by nitroprusside-induced vasodilatation during rewarming. Anesthesiology 1980;53:277–80.
4. Giesbrecht GG, Ducharme MB, McGuire JP. Comparison of forced-air patient warming systems for perioperative use. Anesthesiology 1994;80:671–9.
5. Cross MH, Davies JC, Shah MV. Post-operative warming in the cardiac patient: evaluation of the Bair Hugger convective warming system. J Cardiothorac Vasc Anesthesia 1994;8(suppl 3):80.
6. Pathi V, Berg GA, Morrison J, Cramp G, McLaren D, Faichney A. The benefits of active rewarming after cardiac operations: a randomized prospective trial. J Thorac Cardiovasc Surg 1996;111:637–41.
7. Villamaria FJ, Baisden CE, Hillis A, Rajad H, Rinaldi PA. Forced-air warming is no more effective than conventional methods for raising postoperative core temperature after cardiac surgery. J Cardiothorac Vasc Anesthesia 1997;11:708–11.
8. Kurz A, Go JC, Sessler DI, Kaer K, Larson MD, Bjorksten AR. Alfentanil slightly increases the sweating threshold and markedly reduces the vasoconstriction and shivering thresholds. Anesthesiology 1995;83:293–9.
9. Leslie K, Sessler DI, Bjorksten AR, et al. Propofol causes a dose-dependent decrease in the thermoregulatory threshold for vasoconstriction but has little effect on sweating. Anesthesiology 1994;81:353–60.
10. Woodman RC, Harker LA. Bleeding complications associated with cardiopulmonary bypass. Blood 1990;76:1680–97.
11. Czer LSC. Mediastinal bleeding after cardiac surgery: etiologies, diagnostic considerations, and blood conservation methods. J Cardiothorac Anesthesia 1989;3:760–75.
12. Fremes SE, Wong BI, Lee E, et al. Metaanalysis of prophylactic drug treatment in the prevention of postoperative bleeding. Ann Thorac Surg 1994;58:1580–8.
13. Higgins TL. Pro: early extubation is preferable to late extubation in patients following coronary artery surgery. J Cardiothorac Vasc Anesthesia 1992;6:488–93.
14. Verrier ED, Wright IH, Cochran RP, Spiess BD. Changes in cardiovascular surgical approaches to achieve early extubation. J Cardiothorac Vasc Anesthesia 1995;9(suppl 1):10–5.
15. Egan TD, Minto CF, Hermann DJ, Barr J, Muir KT, Shafer SL. Remifentanil versus alfentanil. Comparative pharmacokinetics and pharmacodynamics in healthy adult male volunteers. Anesthesiology 1996;84:821–33.
16. Mirenda J, Broyles G. Propofol as used for sedation in the ICU. Chest 1995; 108:539–48.
17. Roekaerts PMHJ, Huygen FJPM, de Lange S. Infusion of propofol versus midazolam for sedation in the intensive care unit following coronary artery surgery. J Cardiothorac Vasc Anesthesia 1993;7:142–7.
18. Wheeler AP. Sedation, analgesia, and paralysis in the intensive care unit. Chest 1993;104:566–77.
19. Ready LB, Brown CR, Stahlgren LH, et al. Evaluation of intravenous ketorolac administered by bolus or infusion for treatment of postoperative pain. A double-blind, placebo-controlled, multicenter study. Anesthesiology 1994;80:1277–86.
20. Gu YJ, Wang YS, Chiang BY, et al. Membrane oxygenator prevents lung reperfusion injury in canine cardiopulmonary bypass. Ann Thorac Surg 1991;51:573–8.

21. Hill GE, Alonso A, Spurzem JR, Stammers RH, Robbins RA. Aprotinin and methyl-prednisolone equally blunt cardiopulmonary bypass-induced inflammation in humans. J Thorac Cardiovasc Surg 1995;110:1658–62.

22. Jansen PGM, te Velthuis H, Huybregts RAJM, et al. Reduced complement activation and improved postoperative performance after cardiopulmonary bypass with heparin-coated circuits. J Thorac Cardiovasc Surg 1995;110:829–34.

23. Gu YJ, de Vries AJ, Boonstra PW, van Oeveren W. Leukocyte depletion results in improved lung function and reduced inflammatory response after cardiac surgery. J Thorac Cardiovasc Surg 1996;112:494–500.

24. Engelman RM, Rousou JA, Flack JE III, Deaton DW, Kalfin R, Das DK. Influence of steroids on complement and cytokine generation after cardiopulmonary bypass. Ann Thorac Surg 1995;60:801–4.

25. Engelman RM. Mechanisms to reduce hospital stays. Ann Thorac Surg 1996;61:S26–S29.

26. Gallagher JD, Moore RA, Kerns D, et al. Effects of colloid or crystalloid administration on pulmonary extravascular water in the postoperative period after coronary artery bypass grafting. Anesth Analg 1985;64:753–8.

27. Habbib R, Zacharias A, Engoren M. Determinants of prolonged mechanical ventilation after coronary artery bypass grafting. Ann Thorac Surg 1996;62:1164–71.

28. Kowey PR, Taylor JE, Rials SJ, Marinchak RA. Meta-analysis of the effectiveness of pro-phylactic drug therapy in preventing supraventricular arrhythmia early after coronary artery bypass grafting. Am J Cardiol 1992;69:963–5.

29. Roffman JA, Fieldman A. Digoxin and propranolol in the prophylaxis of supraventric-ular tachydysrhythmias after coronary artery bypass surgery. Ann Thorac Surg 1981;31:496–501.

30. Fanning WJ, Thomas CS Jr, Roach A, Tomichek R, Alford WC, Stoney WS Jr. Prophy-laxis of atrial fibrillation with magnesium sulfate after coronary artery bypass grafting. Ann Thorac Surg 1991;52:529–33.

31. Goldman S, Copeland J, Moritz T, et al. Saphenous vein graft patency 1 year after coro-nary artery bypass surgery and effects of antiplatelet therapy. Results of a Veterans Administration Cooperative Study. Circulation 1989;80:1190–7.

32. Thomas JL, Dickstein RA, Parker FB, et al. Prognostic significance of the development of left bundle conduction defects following aortic valve replacement. J Thorac Cardiovasc Surg 1982;84:382–6.

33. Stein PD, Alpert JS, Copeland J, Dalen JE, Goldman S, Turpie AGG. Antithrombotic therapy in patients with mechanical and biological prosthetic heart valves. Chest 1995;108(suppl):371S–379S.

34. Heras M, Chesebro JH, Fuster V, et al. High risk of early thromboemboli after bio-prosthetic cardiac valve replacement. J Am Coll Cardiol 1995;25:1111–9.

35. Blair KL, Hatton AC, White WD, et al. Comparison of anticoagulation regimens after Carpentier-Edwards aortic or mitral valve replacement. Circulation 1994;90(part 2):214–9.

36. Orszulak TA, Schaff HV, Mullany CJ, et al. Risk of thromboembolism with the aortic Carpentier-Edwards bioprosthesis. Ann Thorac Surg 1995;59:462–8.

37. Ross J Jr. Afterload mismatch in aortic and mitral valve disease: implications for surgi-cal therapy. J Am Coll Cardiol 1985;5:811–26.

38. Spinale FG, Smith AC, Carabello BA, Crawford FA. Right ventricular function com-puted by thermodilution and ventriculography. A comparison of methods. J Thorac Car-diovasc Surg 1990;99:141–52.

39. Camara ML, Aris A, Alvarez J, Padro JM, Caralps JM. Hemodynamic effects of prostaglandin E1 and isoproterenol early after cardiac operations for mitral stenosis. J Thorac Cardiovasc Surg 1992;103:1177–85.

40. Fullerton DA, McIntyre RC Jr. Inhaled nitric oxide: therapeutic applications in cardiothoracic surgery. Ann Thorac Surg 1996;61:1856–64.
41. D'Ambra MN, LaRaia PJ, Philbin DM, Watkins WD, Hilgenberg AD, Buckley MJ. Prostaglandin E_1: a new therapy for refractory right heart failure and pulmonary hypertension after mitral valve replacement. J Thorac Cardiovasc Surg 1985;89:567–72.
42. Meschengieser SS, Fondevila CG, Frontoth J, Santarelli MT, Lazzari MA. Low-intensity oral anticoagulation plus low-dose aspirin versus high-intensity oral anticoagulation alone: a randomized trial in patients with mechanical heart valves. J Thorac Cardiovasc Surg 1997;113:910–6.
43. Karlson KH, Ashraf MM, Berger RL. Rupture of the left ventricle following mitral valve replacement. Ann Thorac Surg 1988;46:590–7.
44. Royston D. A case for aprotinin in patients having deep hypothermic circulatory arrest. J Cardiac Surg 1997;12(suppl):215–21.
45. Sundt TM III, Kouchoukos NT, Saffitz JE, Murphy SF, Wareing TH, Stahl DJ. Renal dysfunction and intravascular coagulation with aprotinin and hypothermic circulatory arrest. Ann Thorac Surg 1993;55:1418–24.
46. de Figueiredo LFP, Coselli JS. Individual strategies of hemostasis for thoracic aortic surgery. J Cardiac Surg 1997;12(suppl):222–8.
47. Deutsch N, Hantler CB, Kirsh M. Perioperative management of the patient undergoing automatic internal cardioverter-defibrillator implantation. J Cardiothorac Anesthesia 1990;4:236–44.

8 Mediastinal Bleeding

8 Mediastinal Bleeding

I. Introduction

A. The use of cardiopulmonary bypass (CPB) during cardiac surgical procedures causes a significant disruption of the coagulation system.[1,2] Hemodilution from a crystalloid prime, systemic heparinization, and platelet activation in the extracorporeal circuit are a few of the important factors that influence perioperative hemostasis. In fact, heparinization, independent of the use of CPB, has been shown to cause platelet dysfunction and induce fibrinolysis.[3] Significant postoperative hypertension and hypothermia may also be contributory.[4]

B. Although postoperative bleeding gradually tapers in the majority of patients, persistent mediastinal bleeding may occur on occasion. Bleeding may produce hypovolemia or hemodynamic compromise from cardiac tamponade. In addition, it may require the use of various blood products to replace the shed blood or correct a coagulopathy. This may potentially contribute to respiratory insufficiency, right ventricular failure, transfusion reactions, and transmission of viral disease. Early aggressive management can often correct "nonsurgical" causes of mediastinal bleeding, but surgical reexploration is required in about 1–2% of patients for persistent bleeding.

C. All patients who have a median sternotomy incision for cardiac surgery have mediastinal drainage tubes placed at the conclusion of the operation. Pleural tubes are also placed if the pleural spaces have been entered. Upon arrival in the surgical ICU, the chest tubes are connected to a thoracic drainage system and placed to 20 cm of H_2O suction. They are gently milked or stripped to maintain patency. Autotransfusion of shed blood should be considered to reduce the requirement for homologous transfusion, although it is not cost-effective when the amount of drainage is insignificant.[5]

D. Chest tubes or drains are also placed after minimally invasive procedures. Usually one pleural tube is placed after minimally invasive direct coronary artery bypass (MIDCAB) procedures performed through a left thoracotomy or mitral valve procedures performed through a small right thoracotomy incision. Drains are placed after minimally invasive valve operations performed through either upper or transverse sternotomies or parasternal incisions.

II. Etiology of Mediastinal Bleeding[6,7]

Most significant mediastinal bleeding is surgical in nature. However, a "nonsurgical" cause, such as a coagulopathy from prolonged use of extracorporeal circulation, will occasionally be the source of persistent bleeding. No matter what the cause, persistent bleeding tends to be self-perpetuating by virtue of progressive depletion of clotting factors and platelets.

A. Surgical bleeding

1. Anastomotic sites (suture lines)

    2. Side branches of arterial or venous conduits

    3. Substernal soft tissues, sternal suture sites, bone marrow, periosteum

    4. Raw surfaces caused by previous surgery, pericarditis, or radiation therapy

B. Anticoagulant effect

    1. Residual heparin effect

        a. Inadequate heparin neutralization by protamine

        b. Heparin rebound

    2. Quantitative platelet defects

        a. Preoperative thrombocytopenia from medications (heparin, quinidine, antibiotics) or hypersplenism

        b. Hemodilution on CPB and consumption in the extracorporeal circuit, which reduce the platelet count by about 30% to 50%. Thrombocytopenia worsens as the duration of CPB lengthens.

        c. Protamine administration (which transiently reduces platelet count by about 30%).

    3. Qualitative platelet defects

        a. Preoperative platelet dysfunction from antiplatelet medications (aspirin, ticlopidine, clopidogrel), glycoprotein (GP) IIb/IIIa inhibitors (abciximab, tirofiban, eptifibatide) or uremia.

        b. Exposure of platelets to the CPB circuit with alpha-granule release and alteration of platelet membrane receptors. The degree of platelet dysfunction correlates with the duration of CPB and the degree of hypothermia after bypass.

    4. Depletion of coagulation factors

        a. Preoperative hepatic dysfunction, residual warfarin effect, vitamin K–dependent clotting factor deficiencies, von Willebrand's disease, thrombolytic therapy (which reduces factors I, II, V, and VIII).

        b. Hemodilution on CPB (which reduces most factors by 50% and factor V by 80%). This is most pronounced in patients with a small blood volume.

        c. Loss of clotting factors by intraoperative cell-saving devices

    5. Fibrinolysis (causes clotting factor degradation and platelet dysfunction)

        a. Preoperative use of thrombolytic agents

        b. Plasminogen activation during bypass

III. Prevention of Perioperative Blood Loss[8,9]

A. Abnormalities causing prolongation of the prothrombin time (PT) or partial thromboplastin time (PTT) should be identified and corrected, if possible.

B. **Warfarin** should be stopped 4 days before surgery to allow for resynthesis of vitamin K–dependent clotting factors and normalization of the international normalized ratio (INR).[10] In patients with atrial fibrillation or mechanical valves, consideration can be given to using intravenous heparin when the INR falls below the therapeutic range, although the risk of embolism during a brief period of subtherapeutic anticoagulation is considered to be quite low.[11]

C. **Aspirin** should be stopped 5 to 7 days before surgery, if feasible. Its use has been associated with increased perioperative blood loss in several studies.[12]

   1. Although aspirin inhibits platelet function, a bleeding time (BT) is usually normal. Nonetheless, a few patients with the so-called "intermediate syndrome of platelet dysfunction" will have an elevated BT after taking aspirin. Patients undergoing elective surgery should be told to stop their aspirin before surgery, but this is usually not feasible in patients requiring urgent surgery. It is neither cost-effective nor essential to delay surgery since the treatment of excessive intraoperative bleeding, if it occurs, can be based on the suspicion of platelet dysfunction (i.e., use of aprotinin, desmopressin, and/or platelet transfusions).[13,14]

   2. An abnormal bleeding time is usually noted in patients with platelet dysfunction attributable to uremia or von Willebrand's disease, as well as those with significant abnormalities in the coagulation system or profound anemia. However, little correlation has been noted between an elevated bleeding time and the extent of intraoperative bleeding.[15]

D. Two other antiplatelet agents that are being used in patients receiving coronary stents and may see more use in patients with acute coronary syndromes are ticlopidine and clopidogrel.

   1. **Ticlopidine** interferes with platelet membrane function by inhibiting ADP-induced platelet-fibrinogen binding and subsequent platelet-platelet interaction. This effect persists for the life of the platelet. Therefore, it is recommended that ticlopidine be stopped 10–14 days before an elective surgical procedure, if possible. Ticlopidine is often used with aspirin since it potentiates the effects of aspirin on platelet aggregation. If urgent surgery is required, exogenous platelets may be necessary to achieve adequate hemostasis. An abnormal bleeding time caused by ticlopidine can be normalized within 2 hours with methylprednisolone 20 mg IV.

   2. **Clopidogrel** is an analogue of ticlopidine that irreversibly modifies the platelet ADP receptor and thus inhibits the ADP-mediated activation of the GP IIb/IIIa receptor. Thus, its effects also last for the life of the platelet. It is recommended that it be stopped at least 7 days prior to an elective operation. The advantages of this medication over ticlopidine are its once daily dosing and a very low incidence of neutropenia.

E. **Abciximab (ReoPro)** is the Fab fragment of a monoclonal antibody that binds to the IIb/IIIa receptor on the surface of platelets. It inhibits platelet aggregation by preventing the binding of fibrinogen and von Willebrand's factor to this receptor site on activated platelets. It is used in high-risk angioplasty and stent procedures to improve patency rates and is given concomitantly with heparin and aspirin. It is also of benefit to patients with unstable angina and may prove beneficial as an adjunct to fibrinolytic therapy in patients with acute myocardial infarction.

1. Abciximab is usually given as a bolus dose of 0.25 mg/kg followed by a continuous infusion of 10 µg/min for 12 hours. This achieves 80% saturation of the receptor sites which is considered essential to render a damaged blood vessel nonreactive to platelets.

2. After the infusion is stopped, low levels of blockade persist for up to 10 days, but platelet function usually recovers within 48 hours. Although abnormal bleeding times and platelet aggregation tests are still abnormal in up to 25% of patients after 48 hours, there is little hemostatic compromise at receptor blockade levels less than 50%.[16]

3. Careful thought should be given to when emergency surgery might be considered if an artery were to occlude despite use of this medication.[17] Since most of the abciximab is bound to platelets immediately upon administration, it should not affect exogenously administered platelets. In the EPILOG and EPISTENT trials, use of abciximab before emergency surgery was not associated with increased bleeding, but platelet usage was usually required to achieve hemostasis. Nonetheless, it is theoretically more desirable to defer surgery at least 48 hours, if possible, to reduce the potential for significant perioperative hemorrhage.

4. Other GP IIb/IIIa inhibitors released during 1998 include **tirofiban** (Aggrastat®) and **eptifibatide** (Integrilin®). In contrast to abciximab, both of these medications are reversible antagonists of fibrinogen binding to the GP IIb/IIIa receptor. Thus, the time course of platelet inhibition parallels their plasma level. It is estimated that platelet aggregation is 90% of normal within 4–8 hours after stopping tirofiban and 50–80% of normal 4 hours after stopping eptifibatide.

F. Surgery should be delayed at least 24 hours, if possible, in patients receiving **thrombolytic therapy** for an acute evolving infarction. Increased perioperative bleeding may result from the persistent systemic hemostatic defects of thrombolytic agents that outlive their short half-lives (rt-PA = 5–8 min; urokinase = 15 min; streptokinase = 23 min). These effects include depletion of fibrinogen, reduction in factors II, V, and VIII levels, impairment of platelet aggregation, and the appearance of fibrin split products. When surgery must be performed on an emergency basis, the antifibrinolytic agents listed below should be used to minimize intraoperative hemorrhage. Cryoprecipitate is also helpful to replenish fibrinogen.

G. **Aprotinin** is a serine protease inhibitor that preserves adhesive platelet receptors (GPIb) during the early period of CPB and exhibits antifibrinolytic properties by inhibiting plasmin. In addition, when given in high doses, it inhibits kallikrein, blocking the contact phase of coagulation and inhibiting the intrinsic coagulation cascade. It has been unequivocally demonstrated to reduce blood loss, especially in reoperative procedures.[18–23] Many of the concerns about an increased risk of graft thrombosis and renal dysfunction have dissipated with attention to proper dosing and heparinization during surgery.[23–26]

1. Aprotinin is generally not cost-effective in primary operations, although it may reduce transfusion requirements. It should be used only for reoperations and other situations where the bleeding risk is increased (hepatic dysfunction, thrombocytopenia, uremia, very complex prolonged operations).[27]

2. Various dosing regimens have been described:

    a. High-dose aprotinin: 2 million kallikrein inactivator units (KIU) (280 mg) after the induction of anesthesia over 30 minutes, 2 million KIU (280 mg) in the pump prime, and a maintenance infusion of 0.5 million KIU/hour (70 mg/hour) until the completion of the operation. Aprotinin reduces the inflammatory response to cardiopulmonary bypass in a dose-dependent fashion, an effect probably only seen with this regimen.[28]

    b. Half-dose: 1 million KIU (140 mg) after induction, 1 million KIU (140 mg) in the pump prime, and a continuous infusion of 250,000 KIU/hour (35 mg/hour). **This dose is most commonly used** because of its efficacy and reduced cost compared with the high-dose protocol.

    c. "Minimal dose" and "ultra-low-dose" protocols have been proposed to reduce the cost of aprotinin use. Adding 1–2 million KIU to the pump prime is effective in reducing bleeding, but not in reducing the inflammatory response to bypass.[27,29–32] At this dose, aprotinin preserves platelet adhesive function and to a lesser degree inhibits fibrinolysis.[33] However, this dose is too low to inhibit kallikrein, and has been reported to produce a prothrombotic state and graft thrombosis.[9,27,30] Use of lower doses in the pump prime (250,000 KIU before bypass and in the pump prime) have not been shown to be effective in primary operations.[34]

    d. Rescue dose: administration of 2 million KIU as a rescue dose after bypass when significant nonsurgical bleeding is encountered has been effective in "stemming the tide" of blood loss, although there are concerns about its administration during a prothrombotic state, rather than when the patient is heparinized.[35] Use of lower doses (20,000 KIU) in the ICU for persistent bleeding has not been shown to be more effective than standard treatment.[36]

    e. Because aprotinin is excreted by the kidneys, lower doses should be used in patients with end-stage renal disease. Guidelines for dosing in patients with moderate renal dysfunction are not available, and it is not known whether aprotinin might be more likely to cause renal dysfunction in patients with preexisting kidney disease, in whom it might be beneficial because of uremic platelet dysfunction.

f. Aprotinin is removed by intraoperative hemofiltration; this must be taken into consideration when hemofiltration is used during surgery to remove fluid.

g. Aprotinin raises the activated clotting time (ACT) and can lead to underheparinization. Aprotinin is absorbed by kaolin, so a kaolin ACT greater than 480 seconds is adequate. It is not absorbed by celite, so a celite ACT must exceed 750 seconds.[37]

h. There has been a reported association of neurologic deficits and renal dysfunction in patients undergoing circulatory arrest with use of aprotinin.[38] These can be avoided by administering additional heparin before the period of circulatory arrest to achieve a higher ACT (some have recommended an ACT > 1000 seconds) and avoiding infusion of aprotinin during the arrest period. Alternatively, the aprotinin infusion can be initiated during the rewarming phase.[39]

i. Despite its antigenic properties, allergic reactions upon reexposure to aprotinin are relatively uncommon (about 3%).[40] Nonetheless, reexposure is best avoided within 6 months. A test dose of 10,000 KIU should be given to all reexposures, along with H_1 and H_2 blockers.

H. **Epsilon-aminocaproic acid** (EACA or Amicar) is an antifibrinolytic agent that, by virtue of inhibiting the conversion of plasminogen to plasmin, may also be beneficial in preserving platelet function. Several studies have shown its efficacy in reducing operative blood loss when used prophylactically.[41–43] It is generally the drug of choice for all first-time operations and anticipated uncomplicated reoperations.

1. One common regimen is to give 5 g after the induction of anesthesia, 5 g on pump, and 1 g/h during the procedure. Twice this dose is commonly used in patients weighing over 100 kg. Giving a 5–10 g dose only at the time of heparinization for bypass also reduces blood loss.[19,44]

2. Few adverse clinical effects have been noted with the use of EACA. However, studies have shown that a 10 g bolus or infusion is associated with renal tubular dysfunction, as monitored by urine β_2-microglobulin levels. This deserves further evaluation and is of concern in patients predisposed to postoperative renal dysfunction.[45]

3. EACA may prove beneficial when given as a rescue dose for significant bleeding, especially if fibrinolysis is present. However, more commonly, aprotinin is used in this situation. The combination of EACA and aprotinin must be considered cautiously because of the unknown interaction of these two medications in promoting a prothrombotic state (graft thrombosis, renal dysfunction, stroke, etc.).

4. There is no effect of EACA on the ACT.

5. EACA is very inexpensive (less than $2 for three vials in 1998).

I. **Tranexamic acid** (Cyklokapron) has similar properties to EACA. It has also been shown to reduce perioperative blood loss significantly.[43,46–48]

    1. Two commonly recommended regimens (10 g infusion over 2 hours starting at the time of anesthetic induction or a 2 g bolus and 8 g infusion during bypass) have been effective in reducing blood loss. However, a dose-response study showed that a 10 mg/kg loading dose followed by a 1 mg/kg/h infusion for 12 hours was just as effective as doses 4 times higher.[48]

    2. This medication is substantially more expensive than EACA with fairly equivalent efficacy. It is the third choice of the antifibrinolytic drugs.

J. **Autologous blood withdrawal** before instituting bypass protects platelets from the damaging effects of CPB. It has been demonstrated to preserve red cell mass and reduce transfusion requirements. However, its efficacy in reducing perioperative bleeding is controversial.[49]

K. The withdrawal of platelet-rich plasma (**platelet-rich plasmapheresis**) using a plasma separator at the beginning of the operation with its re-administration after protamine infusion improves hemostasis and reduces blood loss. Although this might be beneficial in reoperations, it is expensive, time-consuming, and of little benefit when prophylactic medications are used.[50–52]

L. **Heparin-induced thrombocytopenia (HIT)** may develop in patients receiving intravenous heparin for several days before surgery. Thus, it is very important to recheck the platelet count on a daily basis in these patients.

    1. HIT results from the development of a heparin-dependent IgG antibody that binds the heparin platelet factor 4 (PF4) complex on the surface of platelets, resulting in platelet activation and aggregation. Binding of PF4 to endothelial cells provides a target for antibody binding, resulting in endothelial damage, thrombosis, and disseminated intravascular coagulation. Use of heparin during CPB can produce disastrous consequences in patients with HIT, including uncontrollable hemorrhage from platelet depletion and arterial or venous thrombosis from platelet deposition.[53]

    2. Although surgery should ideally be delayed for several weeks until the platelet antibody has cleared and aggregation testing is negative, alternatives must be sought in the patient requiring an urgent surgical procedure.[54] These include:

        a. Five days of preoperative plasmapheresis followed by IgG 35 g IV.

        b. Aspirin and dipyridamole for pretreatment.

        c. Prostacyclin or iloprost instead of heparinization to prevent platelet aggregation.

        d. Ancrod to deplete fibrinogen allows for safe bypass without heparinization. This must be given over 12 to 24 hours (1.6 U/kg) to deplete fibrinogen levels to a level of 0.4–0.8 g/L.

    3. HIT is also associated with the use of low-molecular-weight heparins. Because of a high degree of in vitro cross-reactivity, these

compounds should not be given to patients with HIT.[55] Danaparoid sodium has little cross-reactivity and can be used in this situation, although there is a report of severe coagulation during CPB with its use.[56,57] Other medications, such as argatroban—a direct, selective, thrombin inhibitor—are being evaluated.[54]

M. **Meticulous surgical technique** is the mainstay of hemostasis. Warming the patient to normothermia before terminating bypass improves the function of the coagulation system.

IV.   Assessment of Bleeding in the ICU

Assessment of bleeding requires documentation of the amount of bloody drainage through the chest tubes, identification of potential causative factors, assessment of hemodynamic parameters, suspicion of possible undrained blood in the mediastinal and pleural spaces, and an ongoing awareness of the potential for cardiac tamponade. Tube patency, the pattern of drainage (sudden dump when turned vs. continuous drainage), and its color (arterial vs. venous) should be taken into consideration.

A. Quantitate the amount of chest tube drainage. Make sure that the chest tubes are patent; the extent of ongoing hemorrhage may be masked when the tubes have clotted or blood has drained into an open pleural space. **Note:** When patients are turned or moved, they will occasionally drain a significant volume of blood that has been accumulating in the chest for several hours. This may suggest the acute onset of bleeding and the need for surgical exploration. The presence of dark blood and minimal additional drainage are clues that this does not represent active bleeding. Serial chest x-rays may be helpful.

B. Assess hemodynamics with the Swan-Ganz catheter. Rising filling pressures and decreasing cardiac outputs may suggest the development of cardiac tamponade. Equilibration of intracardiac pressures may be noted with postoperative tamponade, but, more commonly, clot adjacent to the right or left atrium will produce intracardiac pressures that are also consistent with right or left ventricular failure, respectively. If hemodynamic measurements suggest borderline cardiac function and tamponade cannot be ruled out, whether the patient is bleeding or has stopped bleeding, transesophageal echocardiography is invaluable in making the correct diagnosis.[58]

C. Obtain a chest x-ray

1. Note the overall width of the mediastinum. A widened mediastinum may suggest undrained clotted blood accumulating within the pericardial cavity which could cause cardiac tamponade. Comparison of pre- and postoperative films can be misleading because of differences in technique. A repeat postoperative chest x-ray may be valuable, especially if bleeding tapers rapidly.

2. Note the distance between the edge of the Swan-Ganz catheter in the right atrium or the location of the right atrial pacing wires (if placed on the right atrial free wall) and the edge of the mediastinal silhouette. If this distance widens, suspect clot accumulation adjacent to the right atrium.

3. Note any accumulation of blood within the pleural space that has not drained through the pleural chest tubes.

D. Obtain coagulation studies upon arrival in the ICU. This is not necessary for patients with minimal mediastinal bleeding. However, if hemostasis was difficult to achieve in the operating room or hemorrhage persists, lab tests may be helpful in assessing whether a coagulopathy is contributing to mediastinal bleeding. Tests for some of the more common nonsurgical causes of bleeding (residual heparin effect, thrombocytopenia, and clotting factor deficiency) are readily available, but documentation of platelet dysfunction or fibrinolysis is more difficult. Although no individual test correlates that well with the amount of bleeding, together they can often direct interventions in a somewhat scientific manner.[59,60]

1. Prothrombin time (PT) assesses the extrinsic coagulation cascade. The PT may be slightly prolonged after a standard pump run, but clotting factor levels exceeding 30% of normal should allow for satisfactory hemostasis.

2. Partial thromboplastin time (PTT) assesses the intrinsic coagulation cascade and can also detect residual heparin effect.

3. Platelet count. Although platelet number is generally reduced by about 30–50% during bypass and most of the remaining platelets are dysfunctional, they usually suffice to produce hemostasis. Assessment of platelet function is costly (platelet aggregation studies) or ineffective (bleeding time, see below) after surgery and is rarely performed.

E. If a patient still has significant bleeding after standard corrective measures (protamine, fresh frozen plasma (FFP), cryoprecipitate, platelets, as indicated), surgical bleeding is usually present and requires reexploration. Infrequently, additional tests may be performed that can help identify specific correctable coagulation abnormalities.

1. Assessment of residual heparin effect with the ACT or heparin-protamine titration test. "Heparin rebound" may occur when heparin reappears in the bloodstream after protamine neutralization. This is more common in patients who have received large doses of heparin during bypass.[61] An elevated ACT or PTT in the ICU commonly reflects this phenomenon and can be reversed with additional doses of protamine.

a. The activated clotting time (ACT) qualitatively assesses the anticoagulant effect of heparin, but does not measure plasma heparin levels. Dose-response curves relating the heparin dose to its effect on the ACT can be used to ensure adequate anticoagulation during surgery (ACT > 480 seconds) and determine a neutralizing dose of protamine to return the ACT to baseline. However, the ACT is influenced by many factors besides heparin, including hypothermia, hemodilution, and depletion of coagulation factors (especially factor I). Although moderate thrombocytopenia has not been shown to increase the ACT in patients with normally functioning platelets, it does seem to increase it when associated with platelet dysfunction after bypass.[62] Thus, although additional protamine can be administered for a slightly elevated ACT, it will not necessarily return the ACT to its baseline value.

b. The heparin-protamine titration test (HPT), performed with the Medtronic Hepcon system, directly quantitates the amount of circulating heparin in the bloodstream. This allows for calculation of the appropriate dose of protamine to neutralize the remaining heparin.

2. Assessment for fibrinolysis (D-dimers). Achievement of an ACT greater than 480 seconds minimizes activation of the coagulation system and the development of secondary fibrinolysis during bypass. However, the efficacy of the antifibrinolytic drugs in minimizing bleeding has refocused attention on the possible contribution of fibrinolysis to postoperative hemorrhage. Fibrinolysis is associated with an elevated PT and PTT; decreased levels of factors I (fibrinogen < 150mg/dL), V, and VIII; and rapid euglobulin clot lysis. The presence of D-dimers indicates the presence of fibrin monomers and confirms the diagnosis of fibrinolysis. Test results can be confounded by the autotransfusion of shed blood, which contains large amounts of fibrin monomers,[63] and by blood products already given. The thromboelastogram has a distinct contour with fibrinolysis and may be helpful. "Rescue" aprotinin, and perhaps EACA, should be considered when fibrinolysis is suspected or documented.

3. Assessment of platelet function (bleeding time). In addition to a reduction in platelet number, platelet dysfunction is usually present after CPB. An abnormal bleeding time (>10 minutes) indicates abnormal platelet aggregation and adhesiveness. Postoperatively, the bleeding time is disproportionately prolonged when the platelet count is less than 100,000, and it is elevated more when the patient is hypothermic.[4] Unfortunately, bleeding times are notoriously inaccurate and nonreproducible in the postoperative patient. The bleeding time may also be influenced by a low hematocrit because platelet function may be impaired when the hematocrit is less than 30%.[64] Red cells increase platelet-to-platelet interaction and facilitate the interaction of platelets with the subendothelium.[8]

4. A **thromboelastogram** (figure 8.1) may occasionally be of value. It is a readily available test that gives a qualitative measurement of clot strength. It evaluates the interaction of platelets with the coagulation cascade from the onset of clot formation through clot lysis. Although an abnormal thromboelastogram pattern is not always a sensitive predictor of postbypass bleeding, it is more accurate than routine coagulation studies in identifying the exact hemostatic abnormality present during persistent bleeding and can direct the appropriate therapy.[65,66] Unfortunately, this test is time-consuming and patients have usually already received "shotgun" therapy that could correct any of the abnormalities detected by the thromboelastogram.

5. **Sonoclot analysis** (figure 8.2) is another viscoelastic method of evaluating clot formation and retraction that allows for assessment

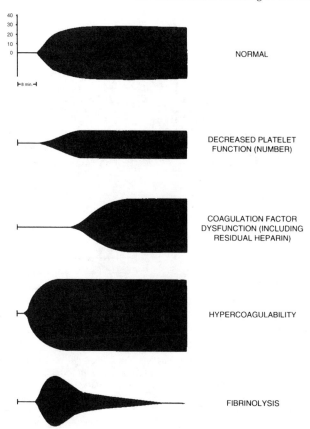

Figure 8.1 *Representative thromboelastogram tracings. (Reproduced by permission from Tuman KJ, McCarthy RJ, Ivankovich AD. The thromboelastograph: is it the solution to coagulation problems? Cardiothoracic and vascular anesthesia update. 1991;2;chapter 8:1–13.)*

of coagulation factor, fibrinogen, and platelet activity. The device measures the changing impedance to movement imposed by the developing clot on a small probe that vibrates at an ultrasonic frequency within a blood sample. Studies have suggested that both a thromboelastogram and Sonoclot are more predictive of bleeding than routine coagulation studies. This device has seen limited use, but can direct appropriate therapy in patients with persistent bleeding.[66,67]

6. Assessment of levels of individual clotting factors can be performed, but is rarely indicated, since all of the clotting factors are replaced by FFP or cryoprecipitate (especially fibrinogen).

F. An **echocardiogram** is invaluable in differentiating poor myocardial function from cardiac tamponade when there is evidence of hemodynamic

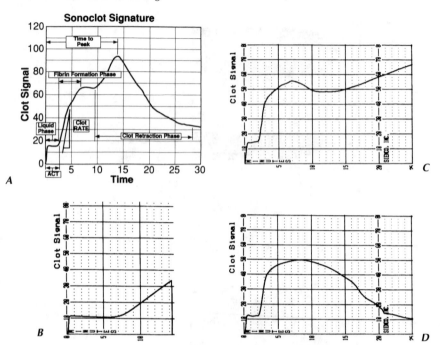

Figure 8.2   *Representative Sonoclot tracings. (A) The Sonoclot signature assesses the liquid phase of initial clot formation, the rate of fibrin and clot formation, further fibrinogenesis and platelet-fibrin interaction, a peak impedance after completion of fibrin formation, and a downward slope as platelets induce contraction of the completed clot. (B) Heparinization. (C) Poor platelet function (slow clot retraction). (D) Hyperfibrinolysis (no tightening associated with clot retraction). (Courtesy of Sienco, Inc.)*

compromise. Tamponade should be suspected when there is excessive bleeding, bleeding that has abruptly stopped, or minimal chest tube drainage caused by clotted tubes or drainage into the pleural space. A transesophageal echocardiogram is more accurate than a transthoracic study in detecting clot behind the heart.

V.   Treatment of Mediastinal Bleeding (table 8.1)

Although there is no role for prophylactic blood product transfusions in the prevention of bleeding following open-heart surgery, persistent bleeding must be treated immediately and aggressively based on the suspected etiology of hemorrhage. The longer a patient bleeds, the worse the coagulopathy becomes. In general, the most benign and least invasive treatments should be considered first. If a patient was "dry" at the time of closure and suddenly starts bleeding, the source is usually surgical in nature and requires reexploration. In contrast, the patient with persistent bleeding may have a surgical or medical cause for the bleeding.[68]

A.   Ensure chest tube patency. Ongoing bleeding without drainage leads to tamponade.

Table 8.1   *Management of Postoperative Mediastinal Bleeding*

1. Explore early for significant ongoing bleeding or tamponade
2. Ensure that chest tubes are patent
3. Warm patient to normothermia
4. Control hypertension and shivering
5. Check results of coagulation studies (PT, PTT, platelet count)
6. Protamine 25 mg IV for two doses
7. Aprotinin 1–2 million KIU IV over 10 minutes
8. Packed cells if hematocrit <26%
9. Platelets, 1 U/10 kg
10. Fresh frozen plasma, 2–4 units (5–10 mL/kg)
11. Cryoprecipitate, 1 U/10 kg
12. Desmopressin (DDAVP) 0.3 µg/kg IV over 20 minutes (if suspect platelet dysfunction from uremia or aspirin)

B. Warm the patient to 37°C. Hypothermia produces a generalized suppression of the coagulation mechanism and also impairs platelet function.[4] The use of a heated humidifier in the ventilator circuit, a warming blanket, or a radiant heat shield is beneficial and will reduce the tendency toward shivering.

C. Control hypertension with vasodilators (nitroprusside) or β-blockers (esmolol for the hyperdynamic heart) (see Chapter 10).

D. Control agitation if the patient is awake with short-acting sedatives:

   1. Propofol 25 µg/kg/min
   2. Midazolam 2.5–5.0 mg IV q1–2h
   3. Morphine 2.5–5 mg IV q1–2h

E. Control shivering with:

   1. Meperidine 25–50 mg IV
   2. Pancuronium 0.1 mg/kg IV over 5 to 10 minutes, then 0.01 mg/kg q1h or a continuous infusion of 2–4 mg/h (always with sedation)

F. Correct abnormalities in the coagulation studies sent on admission to the ICU (PT, PTT, platelet count). If bleeding persists after corrective measures have been taken, these tests should be repeated to reassess the status of the coagulation system. Further testing is rarely indicated, as discussed above.
   Note: Aggressive treatment with blood components may be indicated in the patient with marked mediastinal hemorrhage within the first few hours of arrival in the ICU. The results of coagulation tests are frequently not available at this time. Their use can be justified because depletion of clotting factors and platelets will be progressive during persistent bleeding. Furthermore, platelet transfusions are helpful because platelet dysfunction is usually present.

   1. Elevated PT implies the need for clotting factors provided by FFP and/or cryoprecipitate.

2. Elevated PTT suggests a problem with the intrinsic coagulation cascade or persistent heparin effect. Administration of protamine, FFP, and/or cryoprecipitate may be indicated.

   Note: These blood samples are usually obtained from lines with heparin flushes. If the studies are markedly abnormal or inconsistent with the amount of bleeding (e.g., elevated PT or PTT but minimal hemorrhage), they should be repeated and drawn through nonheparinized lines.

3. A platelet count below 100,000/μL suggests the need for platelet transfusions. Platelets should not be transfused when bleeding is insignificant unless the count falls below 30,000, at which point spontaneous bleeding may occur. Because platelets are also dysfunctional after bypass, suspicion of a qualitative defect in the actively bleeding patient may be treated with platelets, even if the platelet count exceeds 100,000.

   Note: Blood transfusions are often neglected in the bleeding patient when plasma and platelet transfusions are administered. A borderline hematocrit in the bleeding patient requires concomitant blood transfusion to maintain a hematocrit at a reasonable level (>26% to 28%) and to optimize platelet function.

G. Administer **protamine** in 25 mg increments for two doses if the PTT is elevated.

1. Heparin is usually reversed with protamine in a 1:1 ratio (mg per mg) at the conclusion of CPB. Residual heparin effect may be detected by an abnormal heparin-protamine test or an elevated ACT, although the latter is subject to many other variables. An elevated PTT will also be present. In general, the longer the duration of CPB, the greater the amount of protamine necessary to neutralize heparin effect. Furthermore, the greater the dose of heparin given, the greater the amount of postoperative bleeding.[61] A hypocoagulable state ("heparin rebound") has occasionally been noted several hours after successful neutralization, either from protamine metabolism or from release of heparin from tissue stores.

2. Protamine itself is an anticoagulant. Although a dose exceeding that of heparin by 3:1 is usually necessary to produce this effect, studies have demonstrated that an elevated PT from protamine itself may occur when the ratio exceeds 1.5:1.[69]

3. If protamine was well tolerated in the operating room, an adverse reaction will be distinctly unusual in the ICU, especially because small doses are given at slow rates (5 mg/min). However, most protamine reactions are unrelated to the dose or rate of administration.

4. Protamine reactions have been divided into three categories:[70,71]

   a. **Type I.** Systemic hypotension from rapid administration (entire neutralizing dose after CPB given within 3 minutes). This is probably caused by a histamine-related reduction in systemic and pulmonary vascular resistance. It can be avoided by infusing the protamine over a 10–15 minute period.

b. **Type II.** Anaphylactic or anaphylactoid reaction resulting in hypotension, bronchospasm, flushing, and edema.

  i. IIA. Idiosyncratic IgE- or IgG-mediated anaphylactic reaction. Release of histamine and leukotrienes produces a systemic capillary leak causing hypotension and edema. This tends to occur within the first 10 minutes of administration.

  ii. IIB. Immediate nonimmunologic anaphylactoid reaction.

  iii. IIC. Delayed reactions, usually occurring 20 minutes or more after the protamine infusion has been started, probably related to complement activation and leukotriene release, producing wheezing, hypovolemia, and noncardiogenic pulmonary edema from a pulmonary capillary leak.

c. **Type III.** Catastrophic pulmonary vasoconstriction manifested by elevated PA pressures, systemic hypotension from peripheral vasodilatation, decreased LA pressures, right ventricular dilatation, and myocardial depression. This reaction tends to occur about 10 to 20 minutes after the protamine infusion has started. One proposed mechanism involves activation of complement by the heparin-protamine complex that triggers leukocyte aggregation and release of liposomal enzymes that damage pulmonary tissue leading to pulmonary edema. Activation of the arachidonic acid pathway produces thromboxane which constricts the pulmonary vessels. Pulmonary vasoconstriction usually abates after about 10 minutes.

d. Prevention of protamine reactions is usually not possible.[72] Skin testing has not proved of any value. In patients considered at high risk—such as those with fish allergies, a vasectomy, or taking NPH insulin—type II reactions might be attenuated by the prophylactic use of histamine blockers (cimetidine 300 mg IV, diphenhydramine 50 mg IV) and steroids (hydrocortisone 100 mg IV). This common practice has not been shown clinically to be of much benefit.

e. Treatment of protamine reactions involves correction of hemodynamic abnormalities that are identified. In the operating room, reinstitution of cardiopulmonary bypass is often necessary. After the chest has been closed, measures must be taken to support systemic blood pressure while reversing pulmonary vasoconstriction if it is also present. The following plan may be effective:

  i. Calcium chloride 500 mg IV to support systemic resistance and provide some inotropic support

  ii. α-agents (phenylephrine, norepinephrine) to support systemic resistance

  iii. β-agents for inotropic support that can also reduce pulmonary resistance (low-dose epinephrine, dobutamine, amrinone)

       iv. Drugs to reduce preload and pulmonary pressures (nitroglycerin, prostaglandin E_1)[73]

       v. Aminophylline for wheezing

      vi. Readministration of heparin has been used to reverse the protamine reaction.[74]

H. **Aprotinin** 140–280 mg given as a rescue dose over 15 minutes. This inhibits fibrinolysis and has other poorly understood benefits in promoting clotting. It theoretically should be reserved for patients with normal clotting studies in whom fibrinolysis is confirmed by the presence of D-dimers (for fear of precipitating intravascular clotting), but it seems to be effective when used empirically.[35]

I. **Desmopressin** (DDAVP) 0.3–0.4 µg/kg IV over 20 minutes. A slow infusion may attenuate the peripheral vasodilatation and hypotension that often follows DDAVP infusion.[75] Peak effects are seen in 30–60 minutes.

    1. Bleeding following cardiac surgery is often secondary to an acquired defect in the formation of the platelet plug caused by a deficiency in von Willebrand's factor. DDAVP increases the level of procoagulant activity (VIII:c) and raises the level of von Willebrand's factor (VIII:vWF) by approximately 50% by releasing it from tissue stores. These factors are responsible for promoting platelet adhesion to the subendothelium.

    2. In clinical studies of patients undergoing uncomplicated coronary bypass surgery, prophylactic use of DDAVP has not been shown to significantly alter platelet aggregation, bleeding time, or postoperative blood loss.[76–78]

    3. DDAVP shortens the bleeding time in patients with uremia, liver disease, and aspirin ingestion. A randomized study has demonstrated reduced blood loss with DDAVP in patients taking aspirin before surgery.[14] In addition, DDAVP has been shown to reduce the bleeding time and improve hemostasis in patients with significant intraoperative bleeding in whom there is evidence of severe platelet dysfunction.[79,80] Thus it can be recommended as an adjunct to blood component therapy in this situation (usually in uremic patients or those on aspirin), although it is difficult to prove whether it is of much benefit.

J. **Red cell transfusions**

    1. The safe lower limit for the hematocrit in the stable patient following open-heart surgery is probably around 22–24%.[81–83] However, such a degree of anemia may be dangerous during a period of significant bleeding because it may contribute to ischemia or hemodynamic compromise. It is therefore safest in the bleeding patient to administer blood when the hematocrit is less than 26%. This can maintain a margin of safety, especially when there is ongoing blood loss and the administration of blood components will produce significant hemodilution.

    2. Blood filters of 170 micron pore size must be used for all blood transfusions. Filters of 20–40 micron pore size are more effective

in removing microaggregates of fibrin, platelet debris, and leukocytes that accumulate in stored blood. These filters have been shown to decrease the incidence of nonhemolytic febrile transfusion reactions. They may also reduce the incidence of pulmonary complications and attenuate the increase in pulmonary vascular resistance often seen after multiple blood product transfusions which can compromise right ventricular function. Although they have been recommended for the third and every subsequent unit of blood, their use for all transfusions may be justified. Micropore filters should always be used with autotransfused blood.

3. Blood lines should be primed with isotonic solutions (preferably normal saline). Ringer's lactate should not be used because it contains calcium and can theoretically precipitate clotting in intravenous tubing. D5W is hypotonic and will produce significant red cell hemolysis.

   Note: Care should be taken to avoid transfusing cold blood products. Blood warmers should generally be used if the patient receives rapid transfusions. If one unit is to be transfused, it should be allowed to sit at ambient room temperature or under a heating hood for several minutes to warm.

4. **Packed red blood cells** have an average hematocrit of 70% and one unit will raise the hematocrit of a 70 kg man by 3%. At least 70% of transfused cells survive 24 hours, and these cells have a normal life span. Because packed cells contain no clotting factors, administration of fresh frozen plasma should be considered to replace clotting factors if a large number of units (generally more than 5) is given over a short period of time. Each unit of packed cells has about a 0.03% risk of transmitting hepatitis C (which accounts for more than 95% of cases of hepatitis)[84] and a 0.004% risk of transmitting the HIV virus.[85]

5. **Fresh whole blood** (less than 6 hours old) has a hematocrit of about 35% and contains clotting factors and platelets. One unit has been shown to provide equivalent, if not superior, hemostasis to the effect of 10 units of platelets.[86] It is probably the best replacement product, but, unfortunately, most blood banks fractionate blood into components and fresh whole blood is usually not available for use.

6. **Cell saver blood** (shed and washed in the operating room) is rinsed with heparinized saline and is devoid of clotting factors and platelets. Up to 12% of the heparin may be retained after centrifugation. If returned to the patient in large quantities, administration of additional protamine may be necessary. The survival of washed red blood cells is equivalent to that of nonprocessed blood.[87]

7. **Hemofiltration blood** is obtained by placing a hemofilter in the extracorporeal circuit. This provides concentrated red cells and also preserves platelets and clotting factors. Studies have shown superior blood salvage and hemostasis with use of the hemofilter when compared with cell-saving devices.[88]

8. **Autotransfusion** of shed mediastinal blood can be used as a means of blood salvage. It is not associated with the risk of febrile, allergic, or transfusion reactions. Blood may be reinfused from soft plastic collection bags or directly from the plastic shell via a pump and a 20–40 micron filter. This is cost-effective in reducing homologous blood transfusions when more than 250 mL is transfused (usually during the first 4 hours after surgery).[5,89,90] Shed blood usually does not clot because it has undergone fibrinolysis (unless the hemorrhage is extremely rapid).

a. This blood has a fairly low hematocrit, very low levels of factors VIII and fibrinogen, about 60,000 platelets/μL, most of which are dysfunctional, and significant levels of fibrin split products (FSPs).[91] Reinfusion of moderate volumes does not alter coagulation parameters significantly or increase postoperative bleeding, and has been shown to reduce homologous transfusion requirements. It should be considered a source of "volume" rather than a red cell transfusion to treat anemia, and should be supplemented with FFP, cryoprecipitate, platelets, and PRBCs as indicated.

b. In contrast, autotransfusion of more than 1500 mL should be avoided because it reinfuses fibrin monomers and reduces levels of other clotting factors, producing a coagulopathy and potentially increasing bleeding.[63,89,90] It is associated with elevation in the PT and PTT, reduction in fibrinogen levels, and increased levels of D-dimers, spuriously suggesting the presence of fibrinolysis. Washing with the cell-saver device can eliminate the high titers of fibrin split products present in shed mediastinal blood.[63] Generally, if a patient bleeds more than 1000 mL within 6 hours of surgery, reexploration is indicated.

c. An autotransfusion system should not be used if Avitene (microfibrillar collagen hemostat) was used during surgery to achieve hemostasis in the mediastinum.[92] This topical hemostat passes through most filters and can embolize, resulting in organ damage if administered intravenously.

K. **Platelets** should be given to the bleeding patient if the platelet count is less than 100,000/μL. Furthermore, because platelets are dysfunctional in patients receiving antiplatelet medications or GP IIb/IIIa inhibitors and following a long duration of CPB, one should not hesitate to administer platelets for ongoing bleeding even if the platelet count is greater than 100,000. Platelets are not indicated if the patient is not bleeding unless the count is perilously low (<20–30,000/μL).
Note: Platelet function is also impaired when the hematocrit is less than 30%. Thus, raising the hematocrit toward 30% should be considered to improve platelet function.[8,64]

1. One unit of platelets contains 70% of the platelets in a unit of fresh blood. Standard transfusions should be 1 unit/10 kg (i.e., 7 units to a 70 kg patient) and each unit transfused should increase the platelet count by 7–10,000/μL. Platelets stored at room tempera-

ture can be used for up to 5 days and have a life span of 8 days. Those stored at 40°C are useful for only 24 hours (only 50% to 70% of total platelet activity is present at 6 hours) and have a life span of only 2 to 3 days.

2. ABO compatibility should be observed for platelets, but is not essential. Because each unit is derived from one donor, one unit of platelets has a similar risk of transmitting hepatitis and HIV as one unit of blood.

3. Platelets should be administered through a 170 micron filter. Depth filters of smaller micron size should not be used because they will remove platelets. However, the 40 micron Pall SQ40S transfusion filter has been shown to allow passage of over 90% of platelets while trapping leukocytes.[93] The Pall LRF10 filter is specifically designed to remove leukocytes from platelet transfusions. The use of these filters may be beneficial in reducing the risk of allergic reactions caused by red and white cells present in platelet packs. Pretreatment with diphenhydramine (50 mg IV), cimetidine (300 mg IV) (H_1 and H_2 blockers), and steroids (hydrocortisone 100 mg IV) might also attenuate these reactions, but is usually not necessary.

L. **Fresh frozen plasma** (FFP) contains all clotting factors except platelets and should be considered the colloid of choice when significant mediastinal bleeding is present as long as the hematocrit remains satisfactory. In situations where the PT is normal but there is ongoing bleeding, one should not hesitate to administer FFP because only 30% of the normal levels of various clotting factors need to be present to have a normal PT. Additional loss of clotting factors during ongoing bleeding will impair subsequent hemostasis.

1. One unit of FFP contains about 250 mL. The amount usually given is 5–10 mL/kg (approximately 2–4 units for the average adult).

2. FFP should be ABO compatible, transfused within 2 hours of thawing, and given through a 170 micron filter. Because each unit is derived from one donor, FFP has a similar risk of transmitting hepatitis or HIV as one unit of blood.

3. FFP should be given to patients with antithrombin III (AT-III) deficiency in whom severe heparin resistance is noted in the operating room. To minimize volume infusions, a concentrated source of AT-III is available (Thrombate III).
   Note: The administration of plasma and platelets not only provides clotting factors, but also raises filling pressures. These blood products will therefore lower the hematocrit and can precipitate fluid overload. If the hematocrit is less than 26% or not yet available and the patient is bleeding, anticipate the need for blood if other volume is being administered. Remember that the hematocrit does not change with acute blood loss until replacement fluids are administered.

M. **Cryoprecipitate**

1. One bag of cryoprecipitate contains about 20–25 mL and is derived from one donor. It provides approximately 40–50% of the original plasma content of factor VIII and von Willebrand's factor and is

also a source of factors I (fibrinogen) and XIII. It is usually pooled from several donors into a larger bag of 10 units (200–250 mL). The amount that is routinely given is 0.1 unit/kg (e.g., 7 units to a 70 kg patient).

2. Cryoprecipitate is especially beneficial for patients with von Willebrand's disease or documented hypofibrinogenemia. It may also be of benefit to patients requiring surgery soon after thrombolytic therapy, which reduces the levels of fibrinogen significantly.

3. Cryoprecipitate should be given rapidly through a 170 micron filter within 6 hours of thawing. ABO compatibility should be observed, but is not essential.

N. **Calcium chloride** 1 g IV (10 mL of 10% solution) over 15 minutes may be administered if the patient has received multiple transfusions during a short period of time (e.g., more than 10 units within 1–2 hours). The citrate used as a preservative in CPD blood binds calcium, but hypocalcemia is unusual because of the rapid metabolism of citrate by the liver. If hypocalcemia is present, as it often is following CPB, calcium chloride is preferable to calcium gluconate because it provides 3 times more ionized calcium.

O. Hetastarch 6% in saline (Hespan) and 5% albumin are colloid solutions that are used as volume expanders.[94] They should generally be avoided in the bleeding patient unless blood components are not available and the patient is hypovolemic. Their dilutional effect on clotting factors can be minimized by limiting infusion volume to 1500 mL per day (about 20–25 mL/kg). Higher doses of hetastarch can produce a coagulopathy by reducing levels of factor VIII moieties, impairing fibrin clot formation, and enhancing fibrinolysis.

VI.   Guidelines for Mediastinal Reexploration

A. The presence of untapering mediastinal bleeding or suspected cardiac tamponade is an indication for urgent mediastinal reexploration. Emergency reexploration in the intensive care unit is indicated for exsanguinating hemorrhage or tamponade with incipient cardiac arrest. The acute onset of rapid bleeding suggests a surgical etiology as does persistent bleeding in the absence of a specific hemostatic defect. General guidelines for reexploration include a bleeding rate of:

1. 500 mL/h for 1 hour
2. 400 mL/h for 2 hours
3. 300 mL/h for 3 hours

B. Reexploration for bleeding is associated with increased operative mortality and morbidity, often because of a delay in returning the patient to the operating room and the necessity for open-chest resuscitation in the intensive care unit.[95–100] Early reexploration for persistent hemorrhage may reduce the requirement for homologous transfusions, the risk of respiratory insufficiency, and may also lower the wound infection rate associated with an undrained mediastinal hematoma.[101] Emergency exploration in the ICU for tamponade or bleeding is associated with a high survival rate, in contrast to emergency thoracotomy for malignant arrhythmias or a myocardial infarction.[99]

C. The diagnosis of cardiac tamponade is suggested by hemodynamic compromise with elevated filling pressures, usually in a patient with significant mediastinal bleeding or significant bleeding that has stopped. Therefore, the following might be identified:

1. Sudden cessation of significant mediastinal bleeding

2. Low cardiac output and hypotension with respiratory variation and narrowing of the pulse pressure
Note: Positive-pressure ventilation reverses and accentuates the blood pressure response to respiration. During early inspiration, compression of pulmonary capacitance vessels augments left heart filling and blood pressure; however, in late inspiration, decreased left heart filling and blood pressure occur. This is in contradistinction to the fall in blood pressure noted with spontaneous inspiration. Thus, classic pulsus paradoxus is not an applicable sign of tamponade in the ventilated patient.

3. Equilibration of intracardiac pressures with RA = PCW = LA pressure resulting from increased intrapericardial pressure. **Note:** It is not unusual for clot to accumulate next to the right or left atrium and cause unequal elevations of RA and LA pressures.[102,103]

4. Widening of the mediastinum on chest x-ray

5. Compensatory tachycardia

6. Dysrhythmias

7. Decreased ECG voltage

8. Electromechanical dissociation

D. The diagnosis of tamponade can occasionally be very difficult to make. The scenario of hypotension, tachycardia, and elevated filling pressures with moderate mediastinal bleeding is not an uncommon scenario in a patient with marginal myocardial function. If hemodynamics do not improve after volume infusion and inotropic support, tamponade may be present. If time allows, an **echocardiogram** should be performed to differentiate ventricular failure from tamponade. Transthoracic echocardiography may not be able to identify the presence of posterior clot compressing the left heart chambers, but a transesophageal study should make the diagnosis. The presence of left ventricular diastolic collapse is a reliable sign of tamponade.[104] When echocardiography is not available or the patient has very tenuous hemodynamics, emergency mediastinal exploration may be necessary to make the appropriate diagnosis.

E. Emergency reexploration is indicated for exsanguinating hemorrhage or tamponade with incipient cardiac arrest. Every member of the house staff must be thoroughly familiar with the location and use of emergency thoracotomy equipment as he or she may be the only individual available to perform an emergency sternotomy and save a patient's life.

VII.   Technique of Emergency Resternotomy

A. Remove dressing.

B. Pour antiseptic on skin.

C. Place four towels around the sternotomy incision.

D. Open the wound down to the sternum with a knife. If skin staples are present, make the incision lateral to the staples.

E. If sternal wires were used, cut with a wire cutter; if a wire cutter is not available, untwist the wires with a heavy needle holder until they fatigue and break.

F. Place the sternal retractor to expose the heart (a one-piece retractor is essential).

G. Place a finger over the bleeding site and suction the remainder of the chest.

H. Resuscitate with volume through central or peripheral lines.

I. Internal massage may be necessary if the chest is opened for cardiac arrest or marginal blood pressure. An experienced individual can achieve satisfactory compression using one-hand massage, placing the fingers behind the heart and compressing against the thenar eminence. However, in inexperienced hands, perforation of the heart may occur. Therefore, it is generally recommended that two hands be used, compressing the heart between the left hand, placed behind and around the left ventricular apex, and the palm and flattened fingers of the right hand anteriorly. Attention to the location of bypass grafts is critical (especially the internal mammary artery graft).

J. Control major and then minor bleeding sites. Manual control of a bleeding site should be obtained as the chest is suctioned and the patient receives volume resuscitation. Only then should specific attention be made to placing sutures or ties to control bleeding. Manual control can usually minimize bleeding and "buys time" until a more experienced person arrives or the operating room can be made available.
Note: If the patient remains hemodynamically unstable, it is preferable to resuscitate the patient in the ICU rather than rush the patient to the operating room. Invariably the bleeding site can be controlled and the patient stabilized.

K. Irrigate the mediastinum extensively with warm saline or antibiotic solution and consider leaving drainage catheters for postoperative antibiotic irrigation.

References

1. Czer LSC. Mediastinal bleeding after cardiac surgery: etiologies, diagnostic considerations, and blood conservation methods. J Cardiothorac Anesthesia 1989;3:760–75.
2. Woodman RC, Harker LA. Bleeding complications associated with cardiopulmonary bypass. Blood 1990;76:1680–97.
3. Khuri SF, Valeri CR, Loscalzo J, et al. Heparin causes platelet dysfunction and induces fibrinolysis before cardiopulmonary bypass. Ann Thorac Surg 1995;60:1008–14.
4. Valeri CR, Khabbaz K, Khuri SF, et al. Effect of skin temperature on platelet function in patients undergoing extracorporeal bypass. J Thorac Cardiovasc Surg 1992; 104:108–16.
5. Dietrich W. Pro: shed mediastinal blood retransfusion should be used routinely in cardiac surgery. J Cardiothorac Vasc Anesthesia 1995;9:95–9.
6. Mammen EF, Koets MH, Washington BC, et al. Hemostasis changes during cardiopulmonary bypass surgery. Semin Thromb Hemost 1985;11:281–92.
7. Kalter RD, Saul CM, Wetstein L, Soriano C, Reiss RF. Cardiopulmonary bypass. Associated hemostatic abnormalities. J Thorac Cardiovasc Surg 1979;77:427–35.
8. Hardy JF, Bélisle S, Janvier G, Samama M. Reduction in requirements for allogeneic blood products: nonpharmacologic means. Ann Thorac Surg 1996;62:1935–43.
9. Janssens M, Hartstein G, David JL. Reduction in requirements for allogeneic blood products: pharmacologic means. Ann Thorac Surg 1996;62:1944–50.
10. White RH, McKittrick T, Hutchinson R, Twitchell J. Temporary discontinuation of warfarin therapy: changes in the international normalized ratio. Ann Int Med 1995;122:40–2.
11. Kearon C, Hirsh J. Management of anticoagulation before and after elective surgery. N Engl J Med 1997;336:1506–11.
12. Sethi GK, Copeland JG, Goldman S, et al. Implications of preoperative administration of aspirin in patients undergoing coronary artery bypass grafting. J Am Coll Cardiol 1990;15:15–20.
13. Murkin JM, Lux J, Shannon NA, et al. Aprotinin significantly decreases bleeding and transfusion requirements in patients receiving aspirin and undergoing cardiac operations. J Thorac Cardiovasc Surg 1994;107:554–61.
14. Gratz I, Koehler J, Olsen D, et al. The effect of desmopressin acetate on postoperative hemorrhage in patients receiving aspirin therapy before coronary artery bypass operations. J Thorac Cardiovasc Surg 1992;104:1417–22.
15. Lind SE. The bleeding time does not predict surgical bleeding. Blood 1991;77:2547–52.
16. Coller BS. Monitoring platelet GP IIa/IIIb antagonist therapy. Circulation 1997;96:3828–32.
17. Alvarez JM. Emergency coronary bypass grafting for failed percutaneous coronary artery stenting: increased costs and platelet transfusion requirements after the use of abciximab. J Thorac Cardiovasc Surg 1998;115:472–3.
18. Fremes SE, Wong BI, Lee E, et al. Metaanalysis of prophylactic drug treatment in the prevention of postoperative bleeding. Ann Thorac Surg 1994;58:1580–8.
19. Chen RH, Frazier OH, Cooley DA. Antifibrinolytic therapy in cardiac surgery. Tex Heart Inst J 1995;22:211–5.
20. Bidstrup BP, Royston D, Sapsford RN, Taylor KM. Reduction in blood loss and blood use after cardiopulmonary bypass with high dose aprotinin (Trasylol). J Thorac Cardiovasc Surg 1989;97:364–72.
21. van Oeveren W, Harder MP, Roozendaal KJ, Eijsman L, Wildevuur CRH. Aprotinin protects platelets against the initial effect of cardiopulmonary bypass. J Thorac Cardiovasc Surg 1990;99:788–97.

22. Westaby S. Aprotinin in perspective. Ann Thorac Surg 1993;55:1033–41.

23. Blauhut B, Gross C, Necek S, Doran JE, Spath P, Lundsgaard-Hansen P. Effects of high-dose aprotinin on blood loss, platelet function, fibrinolysis, complement, and renal function after cardiopulmonary bypass. J Thorac Cardiovasc Surg 1991;101:958–67.

24. Lemmer JH Jr, Stanford W, Bonney SL, et al. Aprotinin for coronary artery bypass grafting: effect on postoperative renal function. Ann Thorac Surg 1995;59:132–6.

25. Cosgrove DM III, Heric B, Lytle BW, et al. Aprotinin therapy for reoperative myocardial revascularization: a placebo-controlled study. Ann Thorac Surg 1992;54:1031–8.

26. Lemmer JH Jr, Stanford W, Bonney SL, et al. Aprotinin for coronary bypass operations: efficacy, safety, and influence on early saphenous vein graft patency. A multicenter, randomized, double-blind, placebo-controlled study. J Thorac Cardiovasc Surg 1994;107:543–53.

27. Lemmer JH Jr, Dilling EW, Morton JR, et al. Aprotinin for primary coronary artery bypass grafting: a multicenter trial of three dose regimens. Ann Thorac Surg 1996;62:1659–68.

28. Diego RP, Mihalakakos PJ, Hexum TD, Hill GE. Methylprednisolone and full-dose aprotinin reduce reperfusion injury after cardiopulmonary bypass. J Cardiothorac Vasc Anesthesia 1997;11:29–31.

29. Liu B, Tengborn L, Larson G, et al. Half-dose aprotinin preserves hemostatic function in patients undergoing bypass operations. Ann Thorac Surg 1995;59:1534–40.

30. Hayashida N, Isomura T, Sato T, Maruyama H, Kosuga K, Aoyagi S. Effects of minimal-dose aprotinin on coronary artery bypass grafting. J Thorac Cardiovasc Surg 1997;114:261–9.

31. Hardy JF, Bélisle S, Couturier A, Robitaille D. Randomized, placebo-controlled, double-blind study of an ultra-low-dose aprotinin regimen in reoperative and/or complex cardiac operations. J Cardiac Surg 1997;12:15–22.

32. Ashraf S, Tian Y, Cowan D, et al. "Low-dose" aprotinin modifies hemostasis but not proinflammatory cytokine release. Ann Thorac Surg 1997;63:68–73.

33. Speekenbrink RGH, Wildebuur CRH, Sturk A, Eijsman L. Low-dose and high-dose aprotinin improve hemostasis in coronary operations. J Thorac Cardiovasc Surg 1996;112:523–30.

34. Alvarez JM, Quiney NF, McMillan D, et al. The use of ultra-low-dose aprotinin to reduce blood loss in cardiac surgery. J Cardiothorac Vasc Anesthesia 1995;9:29–33.

35. Cicek S, Demirkilic U, Kuralay E, Ozal E, Tatar H. Postoperative aprotinin: effect on blood loss and transfusion requirements in cardiac operations. Ann Thorac Surg 1996;61:1372–6.

36. Hardy JF, Roy M, Perrault J, et al. Low-dose aprotinin to control bleeding after cardiopulmonary bypass. Presented at the American Society of Anesthesiologists 1997 Annual meeting. San Diego, CA, October 1997.

37. Dietrich W, Jochum M. Effect of celite and kaolin on activated clotting time in the presence of aprotinin: activated clotting time is reduced by binding of aprotinin to kaolin (letter). J Thorac Cardiovasc Surg 1995;109:177–8.

38. Sundt TM III, Kouchoukos NT, Saffitz JE, Murphy SF, Wareing TH, Stahl DJ. Renal dysfunction and intravascular coagulation with aprotinin and hypothermic circulatory arrest. Ann Thorac Surg 1993;55:1418–24.

39. Royston D. A case for aprotinin in patients having deep hypothermic circulatory arrest. J Cardiac Surg 1997;12(suppl):215–21.

40. Dietrich W, Spath P, Ebell A, Richter JA. Prevalence of anaphylactic reactions to aprotinin: analysis of two hundred forty-eight reexposures to aprotinin in heart operations. J Thorac Cardiovasc Surg 1997;113:194–201.

41. Daily PO, Lamphere JA, Dembitsky WP, Adamson RM, Dans NF. Effect of prophylactic epsilon-aminocaproic acid on blood loss and transfusion requirements in

patients undergoing first-time coronary artery bypass grafting. A randomized, prospective, double-blind study. J Thorac Cardiovasc Surg 1994;108:99–108.

42. Vander Salm, Kaur S, Lancey RA, et al. Reduction of bleeding after heart operations through the prophylactic use of epsilon-aminocaproic acid. J Thorac Cardiovasc Surg 1996;112:1098–107.

43. Karski JM, Teasdale SJ, Norman PH, Carroll JA, Weisel RD, Glynn MFX. Prevention of postbypass bleeding with tranexamic acid and ε-aminocaproic acid. J Cardiothorac Vasc Anesthesia 1993;7:431–5.

44. Arom KV, Emery RW. Decreased postoperative drainage with addition of ε-aminocaproic acid before cardiopulmonary bypass. Ann Thorac Surg 1994; 57:1108–13.

45. Garwood S, Mathew J, Barash PG, Hines R. Reduced blood loss at the expense of renal function: is epsilon-aminocaproic acid a blow to the kidney? Presented at the American Society of Anesthesiologists 1997 Annual meeting, San Diego, CA, October 1997.

46. Karski JM, Teasdale SJ, Norman P, et al. Prevention of bleeding after cardiopulmonary bypass with high-dose tranexamic acid. Double-blind, randomized clinical trial. J Thorac Cardiovasc Surg 1995;110:835–42.

47. Rousou JA, Engelman RM, Flack JE III, Deaton DW, Owen SG. Tranexamic acid significantly reduces blood loss associated with coronary revascularization. Ann Thorac Surg 1995;59:671–5.

48. Horrow JA, Van Riper DR, Strong MD, Grunewald KE, Parmet JL. The dose-response relationship of tranexamic acid. Anesthesiology 1995;82:383–92.

49. Helm RE, Klemperer JD, Rosengart TK, et al. Intraoperative autologous blood donation preserves red cell mass but does not decrease postoperative bleeding. Ann Thorac Surg 1996;62:1431–41.

50. Jones JW, McCoy TA, Rawitscher RE, Lindsley DA. Effects of intraoperative plasmapheresis on blood loss in cardiac surgery. Ann Thorac Surg 1990;49:585–90.

51. Shore-Lesserson L, Reich DL, DePerio M, Silvay G. Autologous platelet-rich plasmapheresis: risk versus benefit in repeat cardiac operations. Anesth Analg 1995; 81:229–35.

52. Christenson JT, Reuse J, Badel P, Simonet F, Schmuziger M. Plateletpheresis before redo CABG diminishes excessive blood transfusion. Ann Thorac Surg 1996; 62:1373–9.

53. Walls JT, Curtis JJ, Silver D, Boley TM, Schmaltz TA, Naarawong W. Heparin-induced thrombocytopenia in open heart surgical patients: sequelae of late recognition. Ann Thorac Surg 1992;53:787–91.

54. Shorten GD, Comunale ME. Heparin-induced thrombocytopenia. J Cardiothorac Vasc Anesthesia 1996;10:521–30.

55. Warkentin TE, Levine MN, Hirsh J, et al. Heparin-induced thrombocytopenia in patients treated with low-molecular-weight heparin or unfractionated heparin. N Engl J Med 1995;332:1330–5.

56. Chong BH, Ismail F, Cade J, et al. Heparin-induced thrombocytopenia; studies with a new molecular weight heparinoid Org 10172. Blood 1989;73:1592–6.

57. Grocott HP, Root J, Berkowitz SD, de Bruijn N, Landolfo K. Coagulation complicating cardiopulmonary bypass in a patient with heparin-induced thrombocytopenia receiving the heparinoid, Danaparoid sodium. J Cardiothorac Vasc Anesthesia 1997;11:875–7.

58. Russo AM, O'Connor WH, Waxman HL. Atypical presentations and echocardiographic findings in patients with cardiac tamponade occurring early and later after cardiac surgery. Chest 1993;104:71–8.

59. Nuttall GA, Oliver WC, Ereth MH, Santrach PJ. Coagulation tests predict bleeding after cardiopulmonary bypass. J Cardiothorac Vasc Anesthesia 1997;11:815–23.

60. Gelb AB, Roth RI, Levin J, et al. Changes in blood coagulation during and following cardiopulmonary bypass. Lack of correlation with clinical bleeding. Am J Clin Pathol 1996;106:87–99.

61. Gravlee GP, Rogers AT, Dudas LM, et al. Heparin management protocol for cardiopulmonary bypass influences postoperative heparin rebound but not bleeding. Anesthesiology 1992;76:393–401.

62. Ammar T, Fisher CF, Sarier K, Coller BS. The effects of thrombocytopenia on the activated coagulation time. Anesth Analg 1996;83:1185–8.

63. Griffith LD, Billman GF, Daily PO, Lane TA. Apparent coagulopathy caused by infusion of shed mediastinal blood and its prevention by washing of the infusate. Ann Thorac Surg 1989;47:400–6.

64. Fernandez F, Goudable C, Sie P, et al. Low haematocrit and prolonged bleeding time in uremic patients: effect of red cell transfusions. Br J Haematol 1985;59:139–48.

65. Wang JS, Lin CY, Hung WT, et al. Thromboelastogram fails to predict postoperative hemorrhage in cardiac patients. Ann Thorac Surg 1992;53:435–9.

66. Tuman KJ, Spiess BD, McCarthy RJ, Ivankovich AD. Comparison of viscoelastic measures of coagulation after cardiopulmonary bypass. Anesth Analg 1989;69:69–75.

67. Hett DA, Walker D, Pilkington SN, Smith DC. Sonoclot analysis. Brit J Anaesthesia 1995;75:771–6.

68. Hartstein G, Janssens M. Treatment of excessive mediastinal bleeding after cardiopulmonary bypass. Ann Thorac Surg 1996;62:1951–4.

69. Vertrees RA, Engelman RM, Breyer RH, Johnson J III, Auvil J, Rousou JA. Protamine-induced anticoagulation following coronary bypass. Proc Am Acad Cardiovasc Perfusion 1986;7:94–7.

70. Horrow JC. Protamine allergy. J Cardiothorac Anesthesia 1988;2:225–42.

71. Horrow JC. Heparin reversal of protamine toxicity: have we come full circle? J Cardiothorac Anesthesia 1990;4:539–42.

72. Weiler JM, Gellhaus MA, Carter JG, et al. A prospective study of the risk of an immediate adverse reaction to protamine sulfate during cardiopulmonary bypass surgery. J Allergy Clin Immunol 1990;85:713–9.

73. Whitman GJR, Martel D, Weiss M, et al. Reversal of protamine-induced catastrophic pulmonary vasoconstriction by prostaglandin E_1. Ann Thorac Surg 1990;50:303–5.

74. Lock R, Hessell EA II. Probable reversal of protamine reactions by heparin administration. J Cardiothorac Anesthesia 1990;4:604–8.

75. Frankville DD, Harper GB, Lake CL, Johns RA. Hemodynamic consequences of desmopressin administration after cardiopulmonary bypass. Anesthesiology 1991;74:988–96.

76. Horrow JC, Van Riper DF, Strong MD, Brodsky I, Parmet JL. Hemostatic effects of tranexamic acid and desmopressin during cardiac surgery. Circulation 1991;84:2063–70.

77. Lazenby WD, Russo I, Zadeh BJ, et al. Treatment with desmopressin acetate in routine coronary artery bypass surgery to improve postoperative hemostasis. Circulation 1990;82(suppl 4):413–9.

78. Andersson TLG, Solem JO, Tengborn L, Vinge E. Effects of desmopressin acetate on platelet aggregation, von Willebrand factor, and blood loss after cardiac surgery with extracorporeal circulation. Circulation 1990;81:872–8.

79. Czer LSC, Bateman TM, Gray RJ, et al. Treatment of severe platelet dysfunction and hemorrhage after cardiopulmonary bypass: reduction in blood product usage with desmopressin. J Am Coll Cardiol 1987;9:1139–47.

80. Ansell J, Klassen V, Lew R, et al. Does desmopressin acetate prophylaxis reduce

blood loss after valvular heart operations? A randomized, double-blind study. J Thorac Cardiovasc Surg 1992;104:117–23.

81. Johnson RG, Thurer RL, Kruskal MS, et al. Comparison of two transfusion strategies after elective operations for myocardial revascularization. J Thorac Cardiovasc Surg 1992;104:307–14.

82. Doak GJ, Hall RI. Does hemoglobin concentration affect perioperative myocardial lactate flux in patients undergoing coronary artery bypass surgery? Anesth Analg 1995;80:910–6.

83. Baron JG. Which lower value of haematocrit or haemoglobin concentration should guide the transfusion of red blood cell concentrates during and after extracorporeal circulation? Ann Fr Anesth Réanim 1995;14(suppl):21–7.

84. Donahue JG, Munoz A, Ness PM, et al. The declining risk of post-transfusion hepatitis C virus infection. N Engl J Med 1992;327:369–73.

85. Nelson KE, Donahue JG, Munoz A, et al. Transmission of retroviruses from seronegative donors by transfusion during cardiac surgery. A multicenter study of HIV-1 and HTLV-I/II infections. Ann Intern Med 1992;117:554–9.

86. Mohr R, Martinowitz U, Lavee J, Amroch D, Ramot B, Goor DA. The hemostatic effects of transfusing fresh whole blood versus platelet concentrates after cardiac operations. J Thorac Cardiovasc Surg 1988;96:530–4.

87. Ansell J, Parilla N, King M, et al. Survival of autotransfused red blood cells recovered from the surgical field during cardiovascular operations. J Thorac Cardiovasc Surg 1982;84:387–91.

88. Boldt J, Zickmann B, Fedderson B, Herold C, Dapper F, Hempelman G. Six different hemofiltration devices for blood conservation in cardiac surgery. Ann Thorac Surg 1991;51:747–53.

89. Axford TC, Dearani JA, Ragno G, et al. Safety and therapeutic effectiveness of reinfused shed blood after open heart surgery. Ann Thorac Surg 1994;57:615–22.

90. Vertrees RA, Conti VR, Lick SD, Zwischenberger JB, McDaniel LB, Schulman G. Adverse effects of postoperative infusion of shed mediastinal blood. Ann Thorac Surg 1996;62:717–23.

91. Hartz R, Smith JA, Green D. Autotransfusion after cardiac operation. Assessment of hemostatic factors. J Thorac Cardiovasc Surg 1988;96:178–82.

92. Robiscek F, Duncan GD, Born GVR, Wilkinson HA, Masters TN, McClure M. Inherent dangers of simultaneous application of microfibrillar collagen hemostat and blood-saving devices. J Thorac Cardiovasc Surg 1986;92:766–70.

93. Snyder EL, Hezzey A, Cooper-Smith M, James R. Effect of microaggregate blood filtration on platelet concentrates in vitro. Transfusion 1981;21:427–34.

94. Kirklin JK, Lell WA, Kouchoukos NT. Hydroxyethylstarch versus albumin for colloid infusion following cardiopulmonary bypass in patients undergoing myocardial revascularization. Ann Thorac Surg 1984;37:40–6.

95. The Society of Thoracic Surgeons. Data analyses of The Society of Thoracic Surgeons National Cardiac Surgery Database, January 1996. Summit Medical Systems, 1996.

96. Unsworth-White MJ, Herriot A, Valencia O, et al. Resternotomy for bleeding after cardiac operation: a marker for increased morbidity and mortality. Ann Thorac Surg 1995;59:664–7.

97. Moulton MJ, Creswell LL, Mackey ME, Cox JL, Rosenbloom M. Reexploration for bleeding is a risk factor for adverse outcomes after cardiac operations. J Thorac Cardiovasc Surg 1996;111:1037–46.

98. Kaiser GC, Naunheim KS, Fiore AC, et al. Reoperation in the intensive care unit. Ann Thorac Surg 1990;49:903–8.

99. Anthi A, Tzelepis GE, Alivizatos P, Michalis A, Palatianos GM, Geroulanos S. Unex-

pected cardiac arrest after cardiac surgery. Incidence, predisposing causes, and outcome of open chest cardiopulmonary resuscitation. Chest 1997;113:15–9.

100. McKowen RL, Magovern GJ, Liebler GA, Park SB, Burkholder JA, Maher TD. Infectious complications and cost-effectiveness of open resuscitation in the surgical intensive care unit after cardiac surgery. Ann Thorac Surg 1985;40:388–92.

101. Talamonti MS, LoCicero J III, Hoyne WP, Sanders JH, Michaelis LL. Early reexploration for excessive postoperative bleeding lowers wound complication rates in open heart surgery. Am Surgeon 1987;53:102–4.

102. Bateman T, Gray R, Chaux A, et al. Right atrial tamponade complicating cardiac operation. Clinical, hemodynamic, and scintigraphic correlates. J Thorac Cardiovasc Surg 1982;84:413–9.

103. Torelli J, Marwick TH, Salcedo EE. Left atrial tamponade: diagnosis by transesophageal echocardiography. J Am Soc Echocardiogr 1991;4:413–4.

104. Schwartz SL, Pandian NG, Cao QL, Hsu TL, Aronovitz M, Diehl JT. Left ventricular diastolic collapse in regional left heart tamponade. An experimental echocardiographic and hemodynamic study. J Am Coll Cardiol 1993;22:907–13.

9 Respiratory Management

9   Respiratory Management

I.   General Comments

A.   The majority of cardiac surgical procedures are performed through a median sternotomy incision with the use of cardiopulmonary bypass. These two factors can produce changes in pulmonary function and chest wall mechanics that can adversely affect the efficiency of oxygenation and ventilation.[1,2] Nonetheless, with the use of narcotic-based anesthesia, most patients can be successfully weaned from the ventilator in a short period of time without significant pulmonary sequelae. Protocols to accomplish "early extubation" within 6 to 12 hours of surgery have proven beneficial in reducing pulmonary complications, encouraging earlier mobilization, and reducing length of stay in the hospital.[3,4]

B.   The degree of respiratory impairment differs, to varying degrees, in patients undergoing minimally invasive operations.

1.   Minimally invasive coronary surgery usually involves a left anterior thoracotomy incision for performance of a left internal mammary artery to left anterior descending artery (LAD) anastomosis without the use of cardiopulmonary bypass. These patients are frequently extubated in the operating room or soon after arrival in the ICU. Aside from some chest wall discomfort, they generally have few pulmonary complications.

2.   Minimally invasive valve procedures are performed through mini-sternotomy or small chest incisions but require the use of CPB. With the Heartport system, mitral valve operations and coronary artery bypass grafting (CABGs) can be performed through small right and left thoracotomy incisions, respectively, with use of CPB. Although the adverse effects of CPB on lung function should be relatively comparable to those of a sternotomy incision, there is less effect on chest wall mechanics and patients seem to recover faster when smaller incisions are made. Patients are frequently extubated in the operating room or soon thereafter.

C.   An understanding of the postoperative changes in pulmonary function, routine pulmonary management, and contributing factors to respiratory dysfunction allows for the early identification and treatment of problems, thus optimizing the recovery of pulmonary function. The majority of comments in this chapter pertain to patients who have undergone procedures using CPB.

II.   Postoperative Changes in Pulmonary Function

A.   During the early postoperative period, the principal mechanisms underlying borderline oxygenation are ventilation/perfusion ($\dot{V}/\dot{Q}$) mismatch and intrapulmonary shunting.[5] Contributing factors include:

1.   Atelectasis from the effects of general anesthesia and extracorporeal circulation (inadequate surfactant production from pulmonary hypoperfusion, small airway closure from release of various vasoactive mediators).

2. Cardiogenic pulmonary edema from hemodilution, reduction in oncotic pressure, or ventricular dysfunction with elevated pulmonary artery pressures.

3. Noncardiogenic interstitial pulmonary edema from the endothelial dysfunction that accompanies the "systemic inflammatory response"; contributory factors include:

   a. Complement activation

   b. Release of vasoactive substances and proinflammatory cytokines which promote neutrophil-endothelial cell interaction and expression of adhesion molecules

   c. Pulmonary sequestration of activated neutrophils with release of proteolytic enzymes and oxygen-free radicals that may damage tissue

   d. Blood product transfusions

4. Pleural effusions or atelectasis associated with harvesting of the internal mammary artery (IMA).

5. Diaphragmatic dysfunction from phrenic nerve injury. This may result from the use of iced saline slush in the pericardial well or from direct injury or devascularization from harvesting of the IMA.

B. These changes are noted to varying degrees in nearly all patients, but usually have minimal impact on the ability to wean and extubate most patients within the first 6 to 12 hours after surgery. In approximately 5% of patients, further mechanical ventilatory support is necessary, either because of marked hemodynamic compromise, poor oxygenation, or inadequate ventilation.

III.   Routine Ventilator, Sedation, and Analgesia Management

A. Patients are placed on a volume-cycled respirator in the synchronized intermittent mandatory ventilation (SIMV) mode upon arrival in the ICU. They remain anesthetized from the residual effects of narcotics, anxiolytic medications (midazolam or propofol), and muscle relaxants given during surgery. Before the patient breathes spontaneously, controlled ventilation improves the efficiency of gas exchange and decreases oxygen consumption by reducing the work of breathing. This is very important during the first few postoperative hours when hypothermia, acid-base and electrolyte disturbances, and hemodynamic instability are most pronounced.

B. Initial ventilator settings are as follows:

   Tidal volume: 10–12 mL/kg
   IMV rate: 8–10 breaths/min
   Fraction of inspired oxygen (FIO_2): 1.0
   Positive end-expiratory pressure (PEEP): 5 cm H_2O

C. Tidal volume and respiratory rate are selected to achieve a minute ventilation of approximately 100 to 120 mL/kg/min. Patients with chronic obstructive pulmonary disease (COPD) often benefit from lower respiratory rates and higher tidal volumes with increased flow rates. This allows satisfactory time for the expiratory phase and can reduce the potential for the development of high levels of "auto-PEEP" that can develop in patients with obstructive lung disease and produce adverse hemodynamic effects.[6] Lower tidal volumes with higher respiratory rates are often beneficial for patients with restrictive lung disease.

D. A low level (5 cm H_2O) of PEEP is routinely added to the respiratory circuit to prevent atelectasis. This level should not have any impact on cardiac function.[7] However, higher levels must be used judiciously because of adverse effects on venous return and right and left ventricular function.[8,9] Caution is required especially when the patient is hypovolemic from peripheral vasodilatation or when impaired right ventricular function is already present.[9]

E. **Continuous pulse oximetry** is used during mechanical ventilation with display of the arterial oxygen saturation (SaO_2) on the bedside monitor. This can bring attention to abrupt changes in oxygenation and obviates the need to obtain arterial blood gases (ABGs) on a frequent basis in the stable patient. Concern should be raised when the SaO_2 is less than 95%. **Capnography** (end-tidal CO_2) can also be used as a relative assessment of the level of $PaCO_2$ but is inaccurate when $\dot{V}/\dot{Q}$ mismatch is present. For example, the end-tidal CO_2 will be much lower than the $PaCO_2$ when there is an increase in physiologic dead space (increased $\dot{V}/\dot{Q}$). It is also affected by the degree of CO_2 production, the minute ventilation, and the cardiac output. An abrupt change in the contour of the capnogram signifies an acute problem with the patient's ventilatory status, hemodynamics, or metabolic state.

F. A chest x-ray should be checked after the patient's arrival in the ICU. The position of the endotracheal tube, Swan-Ganz catheter, and intraaortic balloon should be identified. The lung fields should be evaluated for lung expansion/atelectasis, pneumothorax, undrained pleural effusion, pulmonary edema, or infiltrates. Attention should be paid to the width of the mediastinum, primarily for later comparison in the event of postoperative hemorrhage. Some have argued that the routine chest x-ray has little yield in the absence of a specific clinical indication, but experience with this controversial approach is limited.[10,11]

G. The initial arterial blood gas should be checked about 15 to 20 minutes after arrival in the ICU. The FIO_2 is reduced to 0.40 and the tidal volume and respiratory rate are adjusted to maintain the ABGs within a normal range. The extent of hypothermia should be taken into consideration when making these adjustments, anticipating that the PCO_2 will rise as the patient warms. The metabolic demand and CO_2 production are decreased 10% for every degree less than 37°C. Acceptable ABGs include:

PaO_2 > 80 torr (SaO_2 > 95%)
$PaCO_2$ = 32 to 48 torr
pH = 7.32 to 7.48

H. Adequate sedation and analgesia are provided in the early postoperative period by the residual effects of narcotics and anxiolytics used during surgery. Inhibition of the stress response and minimization of pain and anxiety are important at this time to minimize myocardial ischemia and hypertension.

1. In centers that extubate patients within a few hours of arrival in the ICU, no additional sedatives may be given since mild sedation is present from the residual effects of intraoperative medications. Midazolam should not be given after bypass because it has a half-life of over 10 hours after surgery.[12,13] Therefore, propofol 25 µg/kg/min is commonly used until the patient satisfies criteria for ventilatory weaning (see page 190).[13–15] Patients normally awaken within 20 minutes of termination of a propofol infusion, although it may take several more hours before they can be extubated.

2. Optimal pain management consists of a continuous infusion of a low-dose narcotic such as morphine sulfate (MS) (0.01–0.02 mg/kg/hour) to blunt the sympathetic response and alleviate pain. This may be given intravenously or via an epidural catheter.[16] Such a protocol avoids the respiratory depression and pain associated with the peaks and valleys of bolus doses of medication. Thus, it may be given safely after the patient is extubated. Ketorolac (Toradol) 30 mg IV can be used for breakthrough pain during the IV MS infusion or later to decrease oral narcotic requirements.[17] Its use should be limited to 72 hours, and it should be avoided in patients with renal dysfunction.

3. Some groups administer indomethacin 50 mg rectally just before terminating the propofol infusion and find that few patients require additional narcotics.[18]

I. Arterial blood gases should be checked if there is a significant change in the patient's clinical picture or if noninvasive monitoring (pulse oximetry or end-tidal CO_2) suggest a problem. A cautious approach is to check the ABGs after 4–6 hours, before initiating weaning, and just before extubation.

J. Once criteria for weaning have been met, the IMV rate is gradually decreased, and if satisfactory mechanics and ABGs are present, the patient is extubated.

K. A discussion of weaning and extubation criteria and the merits of early versus late extubation are presented on pages 187–193.

IV. Basic Concepts of Oxygenation

A. One of the primary goals of mechanical ventilation is the achievement of satisfactory arterial oxygenation. Although this is usually assessed by the arterial PaO_2, it should be remembered that the PaO_2 is an indirect measurement of the oxygen saturation of hemoglobin (Hb) in the blood.

B. Blood oxygen content is determined primarily by the amount of oxygen bound to Hb (the arterial oxygen saturation or SaO_2) and to a minimal extent by the oxygen dissolved in solution (the PaO_2). Each gram of Hb can transport 1.39 mL of oxygen/100 mL of blood (vol%), whereas each 100 torr of PaO_2 transports 0.031 vol%. Thus, correction of anemia does significantly more to improve blood oxygen content than does raising the level of dissolved oxygen (PaO_2) by increasing the FIO_2.

1. The oxygen-Hb dissociation curve demonstrates the relationship between PaO_2 and O_2 saturation (figure 9.1). The amount of

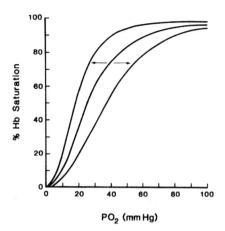

Figure 9.1 *Oxygen–hemoglobin dissociation curve. The sigmoid curve delineates the saturation of hemoglobin at increasing levels of PO_2. Note that a PO_2 of 65 torr corresponds to a saturation of 90%. Higher levels of PO_2 produce only small increments in blood oxygen content, but a PO_2 below this level results in a precipitous fall in O_2 saturation. A shift of the curve to the left, as is noted with alkalosis and hypothermia, increases the affinity of hemoglobin for oxygen and decreases tissue oxygen delivery. A shift to the right occurs with acidosis and improves tissue oxygen delivery.*

oxygen delivered to tissues depends on a number of factors that can affect this relationship. A shift to the left, as noted with hypothermia and alkalosis, indicates more avid binding of oxygen and less release to the tissues, whereas a shift to the right, noted with acidosis, improves tissue oxygen delivery.

2. Note that a PaO_2 of 65 torr corresponds to an O_2 saturation of 90%, but this lies at the shoulder of the sigmoid curve. Below this level, a small decrease in PaO_2 causes a precipitous fall in O_2 saturation. Therefore, although a PaO_2 of 60 to 70 torr is certainly acceptable, there is little margin of safety in the event of a sudden change in hematocrit, cardiac output, or ventilator function.

3. The relationship between PaO_2 and oxygen saturation also dissociates when methemoglobinemia (metHb) is present. This occurs when more than 1% of available Hb is in an oxidized form and unable to bind oxygen. It has been noted in patients receiving high-dose IV nitroglycerin (over $10\,\mu g/kg/min$ for several days), especially when hepatic or renal dysfunction is present.[19] When metHb is present, the PaO_2 may be very high but the true O_2 saturation measured directly by oximetry is very low. Thus, ischemia may be exacerbated by undetected hypoxemia. It should be remembered that the O_2 saturation reported back from the blood gas laboratory is calculated from a nomogram based on the PaO_2, pH, and temperature—it is not measured directly.

4. Pulse oximetry is beneficial in measuring O_2 saturations continuously when the PO_2 is low, but it will overestimate the O_2 saturation when methemoglobinemia is present.

5. The amount of oxygen available to tissues depends not just on the SaO_2, pH, and the blood Hb content, but also on the cardiac output. An attempt to improve oxygen saturation at the expense of a decrease in cardiac output is counterproductive. This may be noted when levels of PEEP are increased in the hypovolemic patient.

C. The PaO_2 is generally used to assess the adequacy of oxygenation. Some centers use the alveolar-arterial oxygen difference ($D(A-a)O_2$) to ascertain the efficiency of gas exchange in the lungs because it is a very sensitive index of pulmonary dysfunction. This is calculated according to the following equation:

$$D(A-a)O_2 = (FIO_2)(713) - PaO_2 - PaCO_2/0.8$$

In general, a PaO_2 less than 300 torr or a $D(A-a)O_2$ greater than 350 on 100% oxygen indicates suboptimal oxygenation that should be investigated. "Respiratory insufficiency" in the ventilated patient is defined by a PaO_2 less than 60 torr with an FIO_2 of 0.5 or greater. Diagnosis and management of this problem are discussed in Section IX of this chapter.

D. In patients with normal pulmonary function, the PaO_2 may be well over 500 torr on 100% oxygen immediately after surgery. The FIO_2 should be gradually decreased to 0.40 as tolerated to prevent adsorption atelectasis and oxygen toxicity. It should not be lowered any farther, even if the PaO_2 seems high, in order to maintain a safety margin for oxygenation in the event that hypotension, dysrhythmias, bleeding, or a pneumothorax should suddenly develop.

E. Some patients with chronic pulmonary disease have a relatively "fixed shunt" with a PaO_2 of 60 to 70 torr despite a high FIO_2 and moderate levels of PEEP. If possible, it is best to avoid an FIO_2 greater than 0.5 for more than a few days to avoid complications associated with oxygen toxicity. Keep in mind that a PaO_2 of 65 torr corresponds to an O_2 saturation of 90% and is acceptable in these patients.

V.   Basic Concepts of Alveolar Ventilation

A. The second goal of mechanical ventilation is that of alveolar ventilation, which regulates the level of PCO_2. This is controlled by setting the tidal volume and the respiratory rate on the ventilator and should provide a minute ventilation of approximately 8 to 12 L/min. The level of PCO_2 is determined most reliably by the arterial blood gases. Noninvasive monitoring with end-tidal CO_2 gives a reasonably accurate assessment of $PaCO_2$, although the correlation depends on the amount of physiologic dead space.

B. **Hypocarbia**

1. Mild hypocarbia (PCO_2 of 30 to 35 torr) is quite acceptable in the immediate postoperative period, especially when the patient is hypothermic. It produces a mild respiratory alkalosis that:

   a. Decreases the patient's respiratory drive.

   b. Allows for increased CO_2 production to occur from the increased metabolic rate associated with warming and shivering without producing respiratory acidosis. Remember that the metabolic rate is decreased 10% for every degree below 37°C and most patients return to the ICU from the operating room with a core temperature between 33° and 35°C.

        c. Compensates for the mild metabolic acidosis that frequently develops from hypoperfusion and peripheral vasoconstriction when the patient is still hypothermic.

  2. A more profound respiratory alkalosis has potential detrimental effects and must be avoided.

        a. It leads to hypokalemia and may predispose to ventricular arrhythmias.

        b. It shifts the oxygen–hemoglobin dissociation curve to the left, decreasing oxygen release to the tissues.

        c. **Note:** Hypocarbia with a normal pH is masking a metabolic acidosis. With improved tissue perfusion, acids are more readily cleared and excreted and the metabolic acidosis usually improves. However, when the metabolic rate increases with warming and CO_2 production increases, a combined respiratory and metabolic acidosis can occur and may prove deleterious to myocardial function. Prompt treatment of a significant metabolic component with sodium bicarbonate may minimize adverse effects resulting from the combined acidosis.

  3. **Treatment** of hypocarbia is best accomplished by lowering the IMV rate. The amount of dead space in the tubing can also be increased. Adding 10% of the tidal volume in mL/kg to the tubing will raise the PCO_2 approximately 5 torr.

        a. Although the addition of PEEP to the ventilator circuit usually prevents alveolar collapse by maintaining volume in the lungs above the critical closing volume, it is best not to decrease the tidal volume below 8 to 10 mL/kg to avoid alveolar hypoventilation and atelectasis. The tidal volume should be decreased only if peak inspiratory pressures are excessively high (over 40 cm H_2O).

        b. If hypocarbia is noted in a patient who is "breathing over" the ventilator, options include, depending on the clinical scenario:

            i. Converting the patient from the SIMV to the control mode ventilation (CMV) or pressure support ventilation (PSV) mode

           ii. Giving additional sedation to minimize respiratory drive

         iii. Weaning the patient by reducing the respiratory rate

C. **Hypercarbia**

  1. Hypercarbia indicates that the minute ventilation provided by the ventilator is inadequate to meet ventilatory demands. Adjustment of ventilator settings must accommodate the progressive increase in PCO_2 that occurs during the early postoperative period as the metabolic rate increases from warming and postanesthetic shivering. As the patient is being weaned, a PCO_2 in the range of 48 to 50 torr is usually acceptable, as the patient is still somewhat

sedated. Higher levels of PCO_2 usually mean that the patient is not awake enough to maintain adequate ventilation.

2. A lower tidal volume may be requested by the surgeon to minimize tension on a short IMA pedicle. In these patients, it is preferable to increase the IMV rate rather than the tidal volume to compensate for an elevated PCO_2.

3. During weaning from mechanical ventilation, hypercarbia may represent compensatory hypoventilation in response to a metabolic alkalosis. This frequently results from aggressive diuresis in the early postoperative period. Use of acetazolamide (Diamox) 250–500 mg IV q6h in conjunction with other diuretics is beneficial in correcting a primary metabolic alkalosis. However, the metabolic component should not be corrected in patients with chronic CO_2 retention.

4. **Manifestations** of significant hypercarbia and respiratory acidosis include:

    a. Tachycardia

    b. Hypertension

    c. Arrhythmias

    d. Pulmonary hypertension

5. **Treatment**

    a. Moderate hypercarbia is corrected in the fully ventilated patient by increasing either the tidal volume or the respiratory rate.

    b. Significant hypercarbia usually indicates a mechanical problem such as ventilator malfunction, endotracheal tube malposition, or a pneumothorax. The latter may still be present even when bilateral breath sounds seem to be heard above all the other extraneous noises of the ICU setting. Temporary hand bag ventilation, alteration of ventilator settings, repositioning of the endotracheal tube, or insertion of a chest tube will usually resolve the problem.

    c. Sedation can be obtained with short-acting narcotics or other sedatives. These include:

        i. Propofol 25 µg/kg/min

        ii. Morphine sulfate 2.5–5 mg IV q1–2 h

        iii. Midazolam 2.5–5.0 mg IV q1h or 2 mg/h as a continuous infusion. This can reduce the total narcotic requirement but will delay extubation.

        iv. Fentanyl drip can be used when a more prolonged period of sedation is indicated. The usual dose is a 50–100 µg IV bolus over 5 minutes followed by a drip of 50–200 µg/h of a 2.5 mg/250 mL mix.

    d. Shivering is best controlled using meperidine 25–50 mg IV. However, persistent shivering that is deleterious to hemodynamics may be controlled with pharmacologic paralysis.[20] **It is important never to paralyze an awake patient without also administering sedation.**

  i. Pancuronium 0.1 mg/kg IV over 5 to 10 minutes, then 0.01 mg/kg q1h or a 2–4 mg/h continuous infusion

  ii. Vecuronium 0.1 mg/kg IV, then 0.01 mg/kg q30–45 min or a 2–6 mg/h continuous infusion

  iii. Atracurium 0.3–0.5 mg/kg IV, then a 0.4–0.6 mg/kg/h (about 6–10 µg/kg/min) continuous infusion

e. Some patients appear to "fight the ventilator" and seem unable to breathe in synchrony with delivered breaths. Although this problem is less common with the IMV mode, it may be noted in patients with hypoxia, mental confusion or delirium, inadequate sedation, or diaphragmatic dysfunction from phrenic nerve paresis. Some patients become very agitated when spontaneous breaths are initiated against high levels of PEEP.

  i. It is important to assess the adequacy of ventilation and oxygenation first.

  ii. If these are satisfactory, additional sedation and/or paralysis should be used and full ventilation resumed in the CMV mode. PEEP levels should be decreased to 5 cm H_2O or less if PaO_2 permits.

  iii. Pressure support ventilation (see page 204) increases the comfort of the spontaneously breathing patient and improves synchronization with IMV ventilation.

6. The persistence of hypercarbia despite standard therapeutic measures usually indicates significant ventilatory failure. This will be discussed later in this chapter.

VI. The Concept of Early Extubation

A. The traditional method of ventilatory support involved keeping the patient sedated overnight with plans for weaning in the morning.

1. Advantages of this approach were that it:

a. Allowed time for hemodynamic recovery, cessation of mediastinal bleeding, warming to normothermia, and dissipation of the anesthetic agents.

b. Allowed for use of additional sedative medications that blunted the sympathetic response and reduced metabolic demand and the work of breathing. Some studies have suggested that there is a significant incidence of postoperative myocardial ischemia that can be ameliorated by adequate intensive analgesia.[21]

c. Permitted a prolonged period of positive pressure ventilation and PEEP that improved arterial oxygenation.

2. Disadvantages of this approach included:

   a. Impaired right ventricular function caused by positive-pressure ventilation
   b. Increased volume requirements
   c. Additional sedation required to tolerate the endotracheal tube
   d. Ventilator-associated morbidity
   e. Use of bolus doses of narcotics, which required higher doses and provided less effective analgesia and more prolonged respiratory depression
   f. Increased costs

B. Early extubation protocols were initially conceived for financial reasons, primarily to move patients out of the ICU faster, expedite hospital discharge, and reduce costs. Subsequent studies have shown, however, that early extubation is beneficial for nearly all patients in expediting recovery and has become the standard of care.[3,4,18,22–32]

   1. The concerns and potential disadvantages of this approach include:

      a. Increased sympathetic tone leading to tachycardia and hypertension: peak incidence of ischemia occurs at 2 hours with peak depression in ventricular function at 4–6 hours
      b. Increased risk of bleeding if patient is hypertensive
      c. More pain if less analgesia is given
      d. Pain and splinting may cause atelectasis from hypoventilation; possibly higher risk of reintubation
      e. Higher metabolic demand may impair recovery
      f. Newer drugs are more expensive

   2. However, most of these concerns have not borne out, and advantages of early extubation have been shown to be:

      a. Avoidance of the prolonged use of positive-pressure ventilation improves hemodynamic performance. There is improved venous return, reduction in right ventricular afterload, and augmented left ventricular filling, which produce a higher cardiac output.
      b. Faster awakening with use of shorter-acting narcotics and anxiolytic agents, such as sufentanil and propofol. Propofol infusions can be continued for as long as necessary if other issues—such as bleeding, hypothermia, or impaired cardiac function—are present and can allow the patient to awaken within minutes of its cessation.
      c. Attenuation of the sympathetic response has been achieved by continuous low-dose narcotic infusions. Thoracic epidural analgesia decreases the postoperative hormonal stress response and improves cardiac and respiratory function.[16]
      d. Improved ciliary function and mucous transport, reducing the risk of pneumonia.

      e. No increase in respiratory morbidity, myocardial ischemia or hypertension, with earlier patient mobilization and discharge from the hospital.

C. **Selection of patients for early extubation**

1. The selection of patients for early extubation should not be restrictive. Factors to be taken into consideration include the patient's age, preexisting lung disease, status of left ventricular function, extent of the operative procedure, the duration of cardiopulmonary bypass, and the type of anesthetic agents used.

2. Numerous factors have been identified as predictors of delayed extubation. It is noteworthy that demographic factors and comorbidities, rather than preoperative spirometry, are the major determinants of delayed extubation. These factors include:[29–31]

    a. Older age

    b. Females and lower body surface area

    c. NYHA class IV/CHF requiring use of diuretics

    d. Reoperations

    e. Urgent/emergent cases

    f. Intraoperative fluid retention

    g. Bleeding and need for a blood transfusion

    h. Postoperative low output states, need for an intraaortic balloon pump (IABP)

    i. Postoperative stroke

3. Although many patients with these risk factors may be less likely to satisfy weaning and extubation criteria early in the postoperative course, there should be no reason to exclude them preoperatively from anesthetic and pharmacologic management protocols in the ICU that would otherwise favor early extubation.[32] If intraoperative or postoperative events dictate that prolonged intubation is necessary, shorter-acting medications can be continued or changed. Extubation should be performed when clinically indicated and should not be dictated by a rigid time schedule.

4. However, there are some patients who can be identified before surgery who will most likely require more prolonged ventilatory support after surgery (table 9.1). It is more cost-effective to use standard medications (fentanyl/midazolam/morphine) to keep these patients comfortably intubated and supported for longer periods of time and wean them at a more optimal time.

5. Intraoperative exclusionary criteria for early extubation tend to be relative. For example, a patient with marginal myocardial function in the operating room, a long pump run, or a coagulopathy may dramatically improve within hours of arrival in the ICU and can be successfully weaned and extubated nearly "on schedule." The presence of postoperative exclusionary criteria can either delay extubation for several hours or days, in which case consideration should be given to alternative pharmacologic management.

Table 9.1 *Exclusionary Criteria for Early Extubation*

Preoperative Criteria	Intraoperative Criteria	Postoperative Criteria
Pulmonary edema	Deep hypothermic circulatory arrest	Mediastinal bleeding
Intubated	Coagulopathy	Hemodynamic instability/need for an IABP
Cardiogenic shock	Severe myocardial dysfunction	Respiratory failure/hypoxic
Sepsis	Long pump run >4–6 hours	Stroke

D. The essential elements of a fast-track recovery program were presented in table 7.1 and are repeated in table 9.2. In addition to the intraoperative considerations discussed on page 128, postoperative considerations in the ICU include:

1. Provision of analgesia in doses to minimize pain and respiratory depression; residual narcotic effect from the operating room may suffice, but a continuous low-dose narcotic infusion is usually helpful.

2. Use of short-acting anxiolytics that allow a patient to awaken within minutes of its discontinuation (propofol).

3. Use of antihypertensive medications, rather than sedatives, to control hypertension.

4. Higher threshold for blood transfusions (hematocrit in the low 20s).

5. Aggressive diuresis once hemodynamics have stabilized.

6. Metoclopramide to improve gastrointestinal motility and improve dietary intake.[26,27]

7. Following a critical care pathway (see table 12.1).

8. Early mobilization.

VII.   Ventilatory Weaning and Extubation

A. **Criteria for weaning.** Weaning depends on the willingness of the nursing and medical staff to wean and extubate patients when each patient is ready, not when it is convenient for the staff or after a certain time interval has passed.

1. Awake with stimulation

2. Chest tube drainage <50 mL/h

3. Hemodynamic stability

   a. Cardiac index >2.2 L/min/m^2 on minimal pressor support

   b. Blood pressure <140 mm Hg on/off medications

   c. No arrhythmias

4. Core temperature >35.5°C

5. Evidence of reversal of neuromuscular blockade

6. Satisfactory oxygenation (PaO$_2$ > 70 torr on 50% FIO$_2$ and 5 cm of PEEP) and ventilation

Table 9.2 *Options for a Fast-Track Protocol*

OPERATING ROOM

Anesthetic agents	Fentanyl 5–10 µg/kg for induction, then 3–5 µg/kg/h
	Sufentanil 1 µg/kg for induction, then 0.25–0.5 µg/kg/h
	Alfentanil 50–75 µg/kg for induction, then 0.5–3 µg/kg/min
	Remifentanil 1 µg/kg for induction, then 0.05–2 µg/kg/min
Sedatives	Midazolam 2.5–5 mg before bypass
	Propofol 50–75 µg/kg/min (2–10 mg/kg/h) after bypass
Cardiopulmonary bypass	Withdrawal of autologous blood before starting bypass
	Warm to 37°C before terminating bypass
	Hemofiltration if fluid overloaded
	Echo imaging for aortic atherosclerosis
Myocardial protection	Antegrade/retrograde blood cardioplegia with terminal "hot shot"
Antifibrinolytic agents	Epsilon-aminocaproic acid, 5 g at skin incision and on pump, 1g/h infusion
	Aprotinin 140 mg at skin incision and on pump and 35 mg/h (high-risk cases)
Other medications	Methylprednisolone 1 g before bypass, then dexamethasone 4 mg IV every 6 hours × 4
	Triiodothyronine 0.8 µg/kg, then 0.113 µg/kg/h × 6 hours (AF prophylaxis), or 10 µg × 2 in operating room then T4 200 µg IV qd × 2 days[32]

INTENSIVE CARE UNIT

Analgesia	Morphine infusion, 0.01–0.02 mg/kg/h depending on age Ketorolac 15–30 mg IV after extubation
	PCA pump with morphine on POD #1
Anxiolysis	Propofol 25 µg/kg/min
Shivering	Meperidine 25–50 mg IV
Hypertension	Sodium nitroprusside/esmolol (avoid sedatives)
Anemia	Tolerate hematocrit of 22% if stable
Other medications	Metoclopramide 10 mg tid
	Ranitidine 150 mg bid
	Magnesium sulfate 2 g on POD #1 (AF prophylaxis)
	Digoxin/metoprolol by POD #1 (AF prophylaxis)

B. **Method of weaning**[33]

   1. Minimize sedation.

   2. Maintain the FIO_2 at 0.5 or below with a PEEP of no more than 5 to 8 cm H_2O. If the patient still requires a higher level of PEEP, weaning is usually not indicated. If oxygenation is satisfactory, lower the PEEP in 3–5 cm H_2O intervals to 5 cm and initiate weaning.

   3. Weaning is usually accomplished using an SIMV wean. The IMV rate is reduced by two breaths every 30 minutes with observation of SaO_2. An ABG is then checked on continuous positive airway

pressure (CPAP) of 5 cm H_2O. If the ABGs and respiratory mechanics are acceptable (see extubation criteria below), the endotracheal tube is removed. Alternatively, a T-piece wean (spontaneous respiration without CPAP) can be performed. The patient is placed on a T-piece for 30 minutes and if the criteria are met, the patient is extubated.[34]

4. Weaning should be stopped and ventilation resumed at a higher rate if:

a. Systolic blood pressure increases >20 mm Hg

b. Heart rate increases >20 beats/min or to over 110

c. Respiratory rate increases >10 breaths/min or to over 30

d. Arrhythmias develop or become more frequent

e. SaO_2 falls below 90% or PaO_2 falls to less than 60 torr

f. End-tidal CO_2 changes more than 10 points from baseline or PCO_2 rises above 50 torr

g. pH falls below 7.30

5. **Note:** A rise in PA pressure is often the first hemodynamic abnormality noted in the patient who is not tolerating weaning very well. Tachypnea is the first clinical sign of ineffective weaning.

C. **Extubation criteria** include the weaning criteria listed above, as well as:

1. Awake without stimulation

2. Acceptable respiratory mechanics

a. Vital capacity >10 to 15 mL/kg

b. Negative inspiratory force >25 cm H_2O

c. Spontaneous respiratory rate <24/minute

d. Rapid shallow breathing index (respiratory rate/tidal volume in liters) <100

3. Acceptable arterial blood gases on 5 cm or less of CPAP

a. PaO_2 > 70 torr on an FIO_2 less than 0.5

b. PCO_2 < 48 torr

c. pH 7.32–7.45

Extubation may be accomplished from CPAP or from T-piece. Although oxygenation may be slightly better during a CPAP than a T-piece trial, post-extubation oxygenation is frequently better in patients weaned with T-piece because the PaO_2 declines less than in patients who were extubated from CPAP.[35,36]

D. **Note**

1. If the patient was very difficult to intubate in the operating room, make absolutely certain that the ABGs and respiratory mechanics are satisfactory before extubation. Early extubation in the middle of the night should be performed cautiously in these patients. An individual experienced in difficult intubations should be present. A flexible laryngoscope or bronchoscope should also be available.

2. Elderly patients and those with more advanced cardiac disease or hepatic dysfunction often take longer to awaken from anesthesia even if sedatives are not administered. It is important to resist the temptation to reverse the narcotic effect with naloxone. This medication can precipitate severe pain, anxiety, hypertension, dysrhythmias, and bleeding, and may result in recurrent respiratory depression when its effects have worn off. Similarly, flumazenil to reverse benzodiazepines should be avoided early in the postoperative period. If a patient fails to awaken after 24 hours, one might consider use of these agents. **Naloxone** (Narcan) is given in 0.1–0.2 mg IV increments every 3 minutes. **Flumazenil** is given in a dose of 0.2 mg IV over 30 seconds, followed by doses of 0.3 mg, then 0.5 mg every 30 seconds, if necessary, to a maximum of 3 mg in one hour.

3. Many patients, especially those who have received supplemental narcotics, will demonstrate excellent respiratory mechanics when stimulated, but then drift off to sleep and become apneic. Constricted pupils may be noted in patients with persistent narcotic effect.

4. Do not confuse comfortable breathing with persistent narcotic or sedative effect.

VIII. Postextubation Respiratory Care

A. After extubation, the patient's breathing pattern and hemodynamics are observed. Occasionally, especially in patients who were difficult to intubate, laryngeal stridor may be prominent and may require steroids (dexamethasone 4 mg IV) or even reintubation.

B. Because the median sternotomy incision is associated with moderate discomfort and decreased chest wall compliance, patients tend to splint, take shallow breaths, and cough poorly. Oxygenation may be compromised by fluid overload and atelectasis from poor inspiratory effort. It is advisable to supply 40–70% humidified oxygen by face mask for a few days. Diuretics can be given until the patient has reached his or her preoperative weight. The patient should be mobilized and encouraged to cough and take deep breaths.[37] An incentive spirometer is very beneficial in maintaining the functional residual capacity (FRC) and preventing atelectasis. Chest physical therapy may be necessary for patients with underlying lung disease, borderline pulmonary function, or copious secretions. Albuterol administered via nebulizer is frequently beneficial.

C. Satisfactory narcotic analgesia is very helpful in improving the patient's respiratory effort. Use of ketorolac after extubation reduces the narcotic requirement in patients with moderate to severe pain.[17] A patient-controlled analgesia (PCA) pump allows patients to titrate their analgesia to a desired level of pain relief.[38] Narcotics, such as morphine or fentanyl, can be given at frequent intervals (every 5–10 minutes) producing a relatively constant plasma drug concentration. Improved comfort is generally achieved with this method compared with use of larger drug boluses given at less frequent intervals that produce fluctuating drug concentrations. Morphine administered via a thoracic epidural catheter has been found to decrease the postoperative hormonal stress response and improve cardiac and respiratory function.[16]

D. Patients who have undergone CABG with use of the IMA may require more attention to postoperative respiratory care. When the IMA is harvested, the pleural space is usually entered and the blood supply to the intercostal muscles may be reduced. Use of the IMA is associated with:

1. A higher incidence of pleural effusions, lower lobe atelectasis, and pulmonary edema when the pleural space has been entered.[39]

2. Significant reduction in peak expiratory flow rates (FEV$_1$, FVC), FRC, and expiratory reserve volume, that may be exacerbated by the presence of pleural chest tubes.[2,40–42]

3. Potential phrenic nerve injury or devascularization contributing to diaphragmatic dysfunction.[43] This is more frequent in diabetic patients.[44]

IX. Acute Respiratory Insufficiency

A. Respiratory insufficiency generally results from a severe pre- or intraoperative cardiopulmonary insult, often superimposed on preexisting lung disease. Patients predisposed to pulmonary complications include those with COPD, advanced age, depressed left ventricular function and congestive heart failure (CHF), obesity, diabetes, and a current smoking history.[45,46] Preoperative treatment of bronchitis and bronchospasm, aggressive diuresis in patients with CHF, and improvement in nutritional status can optimize a patient's baseline pulmonary function in attempts to minimize postoperative morbidity. Although prolonged ventilatory support is indicated in only about 5% of patients, the associated mortality exceeds 20% and most commonly results from infection and multisystem organ failure.[47–49]

B. Respiratory insufficiency is present when there is evidence of inadequate oxygenation (PO$_2$ < 60 torr on 0.5 FIO$_2$) or ventilation (PCO$_2$ > 50 torr) during mechanical ventilatory support. It may become manifest during attempts at weaning or during spontaneous respiration following extubation. The end result of oxygenation failure is tissue hypoxia and end-organ failure.

C. **Etiology.** During the first 48 hours, oxygenation problems predominate and can produce tissue hypoxia. Inadequate ventilation (hypercapnia) is usually the result of a mechanical problem.

1. Inadequate O$_2$ delivery and ventilation (mechanical problems)

   a. Ventilator malfunction

   b. Improper ventilator settings: low FIO$_2$, tidal volume, or respiratory rate

   c. Endotracheal tube problems: cuff leak, incorrect endotracheal tube placement (larynx, mainstem bronchus, esophagus), kinking or occlusion of the tube

2. Low cardiac output states leading to mixed venous desaturation, venous admixture, and hypoxemia

3. Pulmonary problems

    a. Atelectasis or lobar collapse

    b. Pulmonary edema

        i. Cardiogenic from fluid overload and/or left ventricular dysfunction

        ii. Noncardiogenic from pulmonary endothelial injury with increased microvascular permeability. This may be related to complement activation leukocyte activation, or release of other inflammatory mediators associated with extracorporeal circulation. This problem is more prominent as the duration of bypass lengthens and is more common in patients receiving multiple blood transfusions.[50,51]

        iii. Reduced colloid oncotic pressure from hemodilution on bypass.[52]

    c. Pneumonia

    d. Intrinsic pulmonary disease (COPD)

    e. Severe bronchospasm or air trapping

    f. Microembolization from blood transfusions

4. Intrapleural problems

    a. Pneumothorax

    b. Hemothorax or pleural effusion

5. Metabolic problems: shivering leading to increased peripheral oxygen extraction.

6. Pharmacologic causes: drugs that inhibit hypoxic pulmonary vasoconstriction (nitroglycerin, nitroprusside, calcium-channel blockers, ACE inhibitors).[53]

D. The acute development of shortness of breath or an abrupt change in ABGs after an uneventful early postoperative course should raise suspicion of the following problems:

1. Pneumothorax

2. Atelectasis or lobar collapse from poor inspiratory effort

3. Aspiration pneumonia

4. Acute pulmonary edema (from ischemia, LV dysfunction, or undetected renal insufficiency)

5. Pulmonary embolism

E. **Manifestations**

1. Tachypnea (rate >30 breaths/min) with shallow breaths

2. Paradoxical inward movement of the abdomen during inspiration ("abdominal paradox")

3. Agitation, diaphoresis, obtundation, or mental status changes

4. Tachycardia or bradycardia

    5. Arrhythmias

    6. Hypertension or hypotension

F. **Assessment and management** of acute respiratory insufficiency during mechanical ventilation (table 9.3)

1. **Examine the patient:** auscultate for bilateral breath sounds and listen over the stomach to make sure the tube has not slipped into the larynx or been placed in the esophagus.

2. **Increase the FIO$_2$ to 100%** until the causative factors have been identified. **Manually ventilate** with a resuscitation bag (Ambu) if ventilator malfunction is suspected. This not only provides ventilation but also permits an assessment of pulmonary compliance. **Note:** Make sure the gas line on the bag is attached to the oxygen (green) and not the room air (yellow) connector and the gas has been turned on.

3. **Ensure adequate alveolar ventilation**

    a. **Check ventilator function** and settings and optimize the following:

        i. Tidal volume

        ii. Ventilator trigger sensitivity

        iii. Inspiratory flow rate (increase peak flow rate for patients with COPD, especially if bronchospasm is present)

    b. **Obtain a chest x-ray** looking for any of the potential etiologic factors listed above; specifically note any mechanical problems that can be corrected by simple repositioning of the endotracheal tube or chest tube insertion.

    c. **Repeat the ABGs.**

Note: An acute increase in peak inspiratory pressure may signify the development of a pneumothorax, although it can also result from severe bronchospasm, flash pulmonary edema, mainstem intubation, or an obstructed airway (copious secretions, the patient biting the endotracheal tube).

4. **Assess and optimize hemodynamic status.** A Swan-Ganz catheter should be inserted to assess the patient's fluid status and cardiac output. A low cardiac output not only reduces oxygen delivery, but also lowers the mixed venous oxygen saturation, increasing venous admixture and further decreasing the PaO$_2$. Inotropic support or diuresis may be indicated. An echocardiogram may be helpful in identifying a contributory problem (LV dysfunction, tamponade, mitral regurgitation, recurrent ventricular septal defect).

5. Add **PEEP** to the respiratory circuit to improve oxygenation and wean the FIO$_2$ to less than 0.5. An FIO$_2$ of greater than 0.5 improves PaO$_2$ to a very minimal extent if the intrapulmonary shunt exceeds 20%. This is true because it is not possible to oxygenate perfused but nonventilated alveoli to eliminate venous admixture. Furthermore, maintenance of an FIO$_2$ exceeding 0.5 for several days can

Table 9.3   *Management of Acute Respiratory Insufficiency*

1. Examine patient, ventilator settings and function, arterial blood gases (ABGs), and chest x-ray
2. Hand ventilate with 100% oxygen; increase FIO_2 on ventilator until problem is sorted out
3. Ensure alveolar ventilation by correcting mechanical problems (adjust ventilator, reposition endotracheal tube, insert chest tube)
4. Assess and optimize hemodynamics
5. Add PEEP in 2.5–5 cm H_2O increments while decreasing FIO_2 to 0.5 or less; serially evaluate cardiac output at higher levels of PEEP to ensure optimal systemic oxygen delivery
6. Consider sedation or paralysis if patient–ventilator dyssynchrony
7. Treat identifiable problems:
   a. Diuretics for pulmonary edema
   b. Antibiotics for pneumonia
   c. Bronchodilators for bronchospasm
   d. Transfuse for low hematocrit (<26%)
8. Perform chest physiotherapy
9. Begin nutritional supplementation

produce alveolar-capillary damage, alveolar collapse, and stiff, noncompliant lungs (so-called "oxygen toxicity").

   a. PEEP recruits previously closed alveoli to increase the surface area for oxygen exchange, thus increasing the FRC and preventing early airway closure. PEEP thus improves oxygenation and allows for a lowering of the FIO_2. PEEP decreases intrapulmonary shunting by causing a redistribution of lung water from the alveoli to the perivascular interstitial space. PEEP does not decrease extravascular lung water content.

   b. A baseline level of 5 cm of PEEP is added for all patients admitted to the ICU. This substitutes for the loss of the "physiologic PEEP" of normal breathing resulting from the presence of the endotracheal tube. If oxygenation remains poor, PEEP is added in increments of 2.5–5.0 cm H_2O until oxygenation has improved. Caution must be exercised because PEEP creates positive airway and intrathoracic pressures. This may produce adverse hemodynamic consequences and impair oxygen transport and tissue oxygenation. The optimal level of PEEP can be determined by observation of the arterial waveform and serial reassessments of cardiac function. Improving oxygenation with PEEP while depressing the cardiac output is counterproductive, because a low cardiac output not only reduces oxygen delivery, but also lowers the mixed venous oxygen saturation, increasing venous admixture and further decreasing the PaO_2.

      i. PEEP decreases venous return and increases pulmonary vascular resistance (PVR) and right ventricular (RV) afterload, resulting in depressed RV output in the presence of hypovolemia. The decrease in right-sided filling reduces left ventricular end-diastolic volume and cardiac output. Volume infusion is necessary to counteract this effect before increasing the level of PEEP.

ii. In patients with intrinsic pulmonary disease and especially adult respiratory distress syndrome (ARDS), the PVR may be elevated. Increasing levels of PEEP may produce RV failure and dilatation, shifting the interventricular septum and compromising filling and compliance of the left ventricle. In these patients, volume infusion must be given cautiously.

iii. Adding high levels of PEEP to patients with severe COPD may overdistend alveoli that are highly compliant and poorly perfused, resulting in increased $\dot{V}/\dot{Q}$ shunting and progressive hypoxia.

c. High levels of PEEP can result in "barotrauma" (pneumothorax, pneumomediastinum), which can compromise ventilation and produce acute hemodynamic embarrassment. Barotrauma is caused by alveolar overdistention, and is attributable more directly to the severity of the underlying lung disease than to the peak airway pressure.[54]

d. **Note:** Care must be exercised when suctioning a patient on high levels of PEEP. Oxygenation can become very marginal when PEEP has been temporarily discontinued.[55] A PEEP valve should be used during manual ventilation if the patient's oxygenation is dependent on PEEP.

e. The interpretation of pressure tracings from a pulmonary artery catheter is influenced by PEEP. The measured CVP, PA, and LA pressures are elevated, but transmural filling pressures, which determine the gradient for venous return, are decreased because pressure is transmitted through the lungs to the pleural space. A general rule is that the true wedge pressure is equal to the measured pressure minus half of the PEEP level at end-expiration. In situations in which the alveolar pressure exceeds that in the pulmonary vessels (e.g., during hypovolemia), the PCWP will reflect the intraalveolar pressure and not the left atrial pressure. If ventilation is discontinued to obtain PA pressure measurements in the hypovolemic patient, hypoxemia may develop and persist for up to 1 hour.[56]

6. **Sedation** with/without paralysis often improves gas exchange by improving the efficiency of ventilation. It can relax the diaphragm and chest wall and reduce the energy expenditure or "oxygen cost" of breathing.

7. Additional supportive measures

a. **Diuresis** (usually with IV furosemide) often improves oxygenation in the early postoperative period when pulmonary interstitial edema may impair gas exchange.

b. Obtain sputum cultures and add **antibiotics** to treat pneumonia.

c. **Bronchodilators** for bronchospasm to reduce airway resistance (see page 207). Steroids may be useful for the patient with severe COPD.

d. **Blood transfusions** to treat anemia and improve tissue oxygenation. Remember that the primary concern in patients with arterial hypoxemia is tissue hypoxia.

e. **Bronchoscopy** may be beneficial when postural drainage and suctioning are unable to resolve atelectasis because of the presence of tenacious secretions.

8. Methods of mechanical ventilation for patients requiring more than one week of ventilatory support are discussed below.

X. Chronic Respiratory Failure

A. **Etiology.** Inability to wean the patient from the ventilator within 48–72 hours after surgery may be caused by problems that primarily impair oxygenation and/or produce primary ventilatory insufficiency. Although many patients can be weaned after a few days of additional ventilatory support once contributory factors have been treated, a few will progress to a phase of chronic respiratory insufficiency with ventilator dependence.[57]

1. The extreme form of respiratory insufficiency is the development of the adult respiratory distress syndrome (ARDS). This represents a nonspecific diffuse pulmonary injury with noncardiogenic pulmonary edema. It is characterized by stiff, noncompliant lungs with severe impairment to gas exchange from alveolar-capillary damage, interstitial edema, and atelectasis. ARDS can produce both oxygenation and ventilatory failure. ARDS usually results from an acute insult, such as pneumonia, interstitial pulmonary edema, or cardiogenic or septic shock, superimposed on preexisting lung disease. Occasionally, no specific precipitating factors other than the use of cardiopulmonary bypass or blood products can be implicated.[58,59]

2. **Hypoxia.** The persistence of oxygenation problems beyond 48–72 hours usually indicates severe cardiac failure or an acute parenchymal lung problem. These are frequently superimposed on preexisting problems, such as preoperative acute pulmonary edema, pulmonary hypertension, or COPD. The primary causes are:

a. Hemodynamic instability, especially a low cardiac output state that requires multiple pressors. This increases the oxygen cost of breathing and can produce both hypoxemia and hypercarbia.

b. Parenchymal problems

i. Interstitial pulmonary edema, either noncardiogenic (capillary leak or sepsis) or cardiogenic (CHF)

ii. ARDS

iii. Pneumonia

iv. Lower airway obstruction (bronchitis, secretions, bronchospasm) often associated with COPD

3. **Hypercarbia.** Primary ventilatory failure is caused by an imbalance between ventilatory capacity and demand and is the most common reason for failure to wean a patient from the ventilator. The patient is incapable of generating the respiratory effort necessary to sustain the "work of breathing," a term that refers to the work necessary to overcome the impedance to ventilation produced by the disease process and the resistance of the ventilator circuitry. Contributory factors include:

   a. Increased CO_2 production and ventilatory demand

      i. Sepsis, fever, chills

      ii. Pain, anxiety

      iii. Hypothyroidism

      iv. Catabolic states

      v. Carbohydrate overfeeding

   b. Decreased respiratory drive

      i. Altered mental status (medications) or encephalopathy

      ii. Stroke

      iii. Sleep deprivation

   c. Decreased respiratory muscle function

      i. Significant obesity

      ii. Protein malnutrition with muscle weakness

      iii. Critical illness polyneuropathy (see page 404)[60]

      iv. Metabolic abnormalities (hypophosphatemia, hyper- or hypomagnesemia, hypokalemia, hypocalcemia)

      v. Diaphragmatic paralysis from phrenic nerve injury. This may be caused by the use of iced slush within the pericardial well during cardioplegic arrest. Unilateral paralysis usually does not cause ventilatory insufficiency unless there is severe underlying lung disease. Bilateral paralysis may require prolonged ventilatory support, although recovery can usually be anticipated within a year.[61,62]

B. **Manifestations** are similar to those noted above for acute respiratory insufficiency. The most prominent clinical signs of inability to wean are:

   1. Tachypnea (rate >30 breaths/min) with shallow breaths

   2. Paradoxical inward movement of the abdomen during inspiration ("abdominal paradox")

C. **Management** involves measures to optimize cardiac performance, improve intrinsic pulmonary function, reduce the ventilatory demand, and strengthen the respiratory muscles.

   1. Improve hemodynamic status with inotropic support. Pulmonary vasodilators, such as nitroprusside and nitroglycerin, should generally be avoided because they can increase intrapulmonary shunting by preventing hypoxic vasoconstriction.

   2. Treat hypoxemia and reduce the impedance to ventilation

  a. Ventilatory support preferably with pressure support ventilation and PEEP (see next section)

  b. Suctioning, chest PT, positioning

  c. Diuretics for fluid overload

  d. Antibiotics for pneumonia

  e. Bronchodilators for bronchospasm (see last section of this chapter)

  f. Transfusions for significant anemia (hematocrit $< 26\%$)

3. **Tracheostomy.** A common practice is to delay tracheostomy for 2–3 weeks in the belief that it predisposes the patient to a mediastinal wound infection. However, if the need for continued support is recognized after 10 days, it is practical and safe to perform a tracheostomy at that time. Persistent laryngotracheal intubation leads to laryngeal damage and swallowing dysfunction. Tracheostomy reduces airway resistance and glottic trauma, improves suctioning, lowers the risk of sinusitis, often allows the patient to eat, and generally makes the patient look and feel better. Tracheostomy can be performed percutaneously (see Appendix 9) or via a standard surgical approach. The former is associated with less tracheal stenosis at follow-up. Alternatively, a cricothyroidotomy can be performed.[63–68]

4. Reduce the minute ventilation requirement

  a. Analgesia for pain and sedatives for anxiety. Excessive sedation must be avoided because it inhibits the central respiratory drive.

  b. Treat infections (sepsis, pneumonia) with antibiotics and reduce fever with acetaminophen. There is evidence that prophylactic antibiotics administered intravenously and into the oropharynx and stomach (selective decontamination of the gut) during periods of prolonged ventilatory support can reduce the incidence of lower respiratory tract infection.[69] However, this is a costly measure that has not been shown to reduce overall mortality. Most centers prefer to use antibiotics only when infection is present to prevent the development of antibiotic-resistant pneumonia. Use of sucralfate as stress ulcer prophylaxis should be considered rather than histamine blockers, which raise the gastric pH and can increase the incidence of pneumonia.[70]

5. Improve respiratory drive and neuromuscular weakness

  a. Provide adequate nutrition to achieve positive nitrogen balance and improve respiratory muscle strength and immune competence. Overfeeding with carbohydrates or fats can increase CO_2 production which adds to the ventilatory burden. A tube feeding such as Pulmocare should be considered.

  b. Select the appropriate mode of ventilatory support to reduce the work of breathing and train the respiratory muscles to support spontaneous ventilation.

    c. Physical therapy.

    d. Optimize acid-base, electrolyte, and endocrine (thyroid) status. Metabolic alkalosis and hypothyroidism inhibit the central respiratory drive.

    e. Evaluate diaphragmatic motion during fluoroscopy ("sniff test"). Diaphragmatic plication may improve respiratory function in patients with ventilator dependence caused by unilateral diaphragmatic dysfunction.[71]

D. Methods of ventilatory support and weaning[72–74]

1. **Full ventilatory support** is usually indicated for several days to rest the respiratory muscles while the underlying disease processes are treated and nutrition is optimized. Support may be provided using volume-preset modes (controlled ventilation) or pressure-controlled ventilation (see below). Providing full support can reduce the work of breathing and improve the efficiency of gas exchange in the patient who is sedated and/or paralyzed.

2. **Partial ventilatory support** can be provided by a variety of ventilator modes.

    a. **Volume-preset modes.** Most patients are placed on "volume ventilators" that deliver a set tidal volume. A limit is set on the peak pressure to avoid barotrauma. Patients with non-compliant, stiff lungs or bronchospastic airways can be difficult to ventilate in this mode because some of the preset tidal volume may not be delivered once the peak pressure limit is reached. This system is best for patients with normal or increased compliance (emphysema).

        i. **Assist-control ventilation (A/C ventilation).** The ventilator delivers a breath when triggered by the patient's inspiratory effort or at preset intervals if no breath is taken.

        ii. **Intermittent mandatory ventilation (IMV).** The patient may breath spontaneously but also receives positive-pressure breaths at a preset volume and rate. Spontaneous breaths require opening of a demand valve that can increase the work of breathing, a problem which can be overcome by the use of a continuous-flow or flow-by system.

        iii. **Synchronized intermittent mandatory ventilation (SIMV).** The patient breathes spontaneously, but at preset intervals the next spontaneous breath is augmented by a full tidal volume from the ventilator. This mode uses a demand-flow system to provide the gas for spontaneous inspiration.

    b. **Pressure-preset or volume-variable modes.** "Pressure ventilators" deliver gas flow up to a set pressure limit. The amount of gas flow delivered (the tidal volume) depends on the compliance of the lungs and airway resistance. This system ensures delivery of a more consistent tidal volume to patients with increased airway resistance (bronchospasm, restrictive lung disease). It is best avoided in patients with emphysema, in whom overinflation of the lungs can occur at low pressures.

    i. **Pressure-controlled ventilation (PCV)** allows the clinician to preset the peak airway pressure and the inspiratory time. A breath is then delivered at predetermined intervals. PCV is primarily a form of full ventilatory support. It can be used to provide inverse ratio ventilation.

    ii. **Pressure support ventilation (PSV)** differs from other ventilator modes in that the patient's inspiratory effort is augmented by a selected level of inspiratory pressure. The patient sets the respiratory rate, flow rate, and inspiratory time. The tidal volume is determined by the level of pressure support, the patient's inspiratory effort, lung compliance, and resistance of the circuitry and the patient's airway. This mode is flow-cycled, not time-cycled.

  c. After a period of full support, a method of weaning should be selected. When the patient begins spontaneous respirations, controlled ventilation will suppress the patient's respiratory drive and lead to respiratory muscle atrophy. Frequent triggering of the ventilator in the assist mode may result in alveolar hyperventilation. Furthermore, the patient's efforts may persist despite the machine's superimposed breath, leading to increased respiratory muscle fatigue. Therefore, the IMV and PSV modes are preferable for weaning.

3. The "rapid shallow breathing index," the ratio of the respiratory rate/tidal volume in liters during spontaneous ventilation for one minute, is considered to be a sensitive indicator of the ability to wean. In one study, values less than 100 breaths/min/L were highly predictive of successful weaning.[75] Another study, however, found little difference in the ability to extubate when the index was greater or less than 105.[76]

4. **T-piece weaning**

  a. Periods of full support (rest) or partial weaning are alternated with periods of independent spontaneous ventilation (stress). A gradual increase in the duration of independent breathing can increase the strength and endurance of the respiratory muscles. However, the sudden transition to a complete workload is usually not well tolerated during the early phase of recovery from severe ventilatory failure and may result in profound respiratory muscle fatigue.

  b. A study comparing PSV, IMV, and daily and twice daily T-piece weaning found that either form of T-piece weaning permitted earlier extubation.[77]

5. **Intermittent mandatory ventilation (IMV)**

  a. The patient's spontaneous breaths are interspersed with a full tidal volume delivered by the ventilator at a designated rate.

During the weaning process, the IMV rate is gradually decreased and the patient assumes a greater proportion of the minute ventilation. Because the energy expenditure of the respiratory muscles increases as the IMV rate is lowered, lowering of the IMV rate during the day can be coupled with complete rest at night to avoid muscle fatigue. When the patient can maintain spontaneous ventilation for a prolonged period of time, extubation can be accomplished.

b. The work of breathing with an IMV system (as well as with CPAP) is reduced using a continuous flow or flow-by system, rather than a demand-flow system. With the latter, a decrease in the airway system pressure ("pressure sensitivity") caused by the patient's spontaneous inspiration opens a demand valve to receive fresh gas. In contrast, with the flow-by system, the system delivers a predetermined gas flow to the circuit prior to inspiration and is measured at the exhalation port every 20 msec. When the patient's inspiratory flow reaches a preset threshold limit ("flow sensitivity"), the ventilator adds gas to maintain positive airway pressure and provide the inspired gas.[78] Thus, fresh gas is available to the patient as soon as an inspiratory effort is initiated and the delay between the inspiratory effort and the supply of gas to the patient is minimized.

c. The use of pressure support concomitantly with IMV can also reduce the work of breathing during the patient's spontaneous respirations. Weaning can be accomplished by initially reducing the IMV rate and subsequently reducing the level of pressure support. The duration of spontaneous ventilation on low levels of pressure support or CPAP is then extended and the patient is extubated.

6. **Pressure support ventilation (PSV)**[79-82]

a. The patient's spontaneous inspiration triggers the ventilator to deliver gas flow to the circuit until a selected amount of inspiratory pressure is achieved. Airway pressure remains constant by automatic adjustment of the flow rate as long as the patient maintains an inspiratory effort. Gas flow stops when the flow rate demand decreases below 25% of the initial peak inspiratory flow rate, and exhalation is then allowed to occur passively.

b. The patient's effort controls the inspiratory time and flow rate (tidal volume/inspiratory time), the expiratory time, the respiratory rate, and the tidal volume. The eventual amount of inspired tidal volume depends on the level of PSV, the patient's respiratory effort, and the resistance of the airway, which may be increased by small endotracheal tubes, secretions, bronchospasm, and decreased lung compliance.

c. The advantage of PSV is that it reduces the work of breathing by overcoming the impedance of the ventilatory circuitry and supplying some of the pressure work required to initiate ventilation. Because the patient controls most of the parameters during the respiratory cycle, PSV results in more comfortable breathing for the patient. Lower peak airway pressures, slower respiratory rates, and higher tidal volumes can be achieved with PSV than with other modes of ventilation. It is beneficial for the patient who is out of synchrony with the ventilator (i.e., "fighting the ventilator").

d. High levels of pressure support (>20 cm H_2O) can provide full ventilation with a tidal volume of 10–12 mL/kg. This represents total unloading of the ventilatory muscles in a manner comparable to CMV. Its use should be restricted to brief periods of time (less than 72–96 hours) to prevent atrophy of the respiratory muscles.

e. Lower levels of PSV produce partial unloading of the ventilator muscles and prevent respiratory (diaphragmatic) muscle fatigue. By reducing the work of ventilation, PSV can recondition the respiratory muscles to assume more spontaneous ventilation without producing excessive energy expenditure. It thus may expedite the weaning process. The actual level of support depends on the level of PSV and system impedances.

f. PSV is initially set at a pressure around 15–20 cm H_2O. It is then reduced gradually and the patient is observed carefully for fatigue. The shallow breathing index is a valuable means of assessing the efficacy of a PSV wean. Significant unloading is considered to be present when the patient's respiratory rate is less than 20/min and should correspond to a tidal volume of 10–12 mL/kg. Weaning options include:

    i. Increasing the duration of spontaneous ventilation with PSV during the daytime ("sprinting") with full support at night. If the patient tolerates PSV for 12 hours, the level of PSV is gradually reduced by 2 cm H_2O intervals daily or every other day, and the tidal volume and respiratory rate are assessed. Extubation is accomplished when the patient is able to breathe comfortably for 24 hours at low levels of PSV (around 6–8 cm H_2O support).

    ii. PSV with IMV. A level of partial PSV support is selected and the IMV rate is gradually decreased. When the IMV rate has been reduced to less than 4 breaths, the PSV level is weaned as discussed above.

g. Potential disadvantages of PSV

    i. PSV requires an intact respiratory drive to trigger the ventilator. Inadequate ventilation will result if the patient is apneic or has an unstable neurologic status, respiratory drive, or mechanics.

    ii. Cardiac output may be compromised because airway pressure is always positive. With IMV weaning, there is a phase of negative intrathoracic pressure that can augment venous return.

       iii. Shallow tidal volumes from poor inspiratory effort may lead to atelectasis.

       iv. A gas leak in the system may prevent PSV from being terminated, producing persistently high airway pressures and hemodynamic compromise.

       v. In-line nebulizers (for bronchodilators) are in the inspiratory limb and may make it difficult for the patient to initiate a breath to trigger PSV.

7. There are several other forms of positive pressure ventilation that have been investigated for use in patients with chronic respiratory failure. These include inverse ratio ventilation, airway pressure release ventilation, and proportional assist ventilation. These techniques may improve oxygenation in patients with severe hypoxemia.[82]

XI. Other Acute Respiratory Complications

A. Respiratory complications may occur during the period of mechanical ventilation, soon after extubation, or later during convalescence on the postoperative floor. The management of these complications must be individualized, taking the patient's overall medical condition, the extent and nature of the surgical procedure, the precipitating factors, and the phase of recovery into consideration. The complications that are noted frequently in the ICU setting are discussed here. Others that are seen more commonly on the postoperative floor are discussed in Chapter 12.

B. **Pneumothorax.** Although a chest tube is placed into an opened pleural space at the conclusion of surgery, a small opening into the pleural space may occasionally be missed (usually caused by passage of a sternal wire through the pleura). An immediate postoperative chest x-ray will usually demonstrate a pneumothorax. A chest tube should be placed at this time, regardless of the size of the pneumothorax, because the patient will be on positive pressure ventilation. Less commonly, a pneumothorax will be absent on the initial x-ray but evident on subsequent films.

1. Always consider the possibility of a pneumothorax (possibly tension) when deteriorating ABGs or hemodynamic instability develop for no obvious reason after several hours of stability. The first sign is often a sudden increase in the peak inspiratory pressure, indicated by repeated alarming of the ventilator.

2. Evidence of an air leak in the chest drainage system frequently indicates loose connections, rather than a leak from the lung. However, chest tubes should never be removed until it is confirmed that an air leak is not the result of an intrapleural or parenchymal problem.

3. Progressive subcutaneous emphysema may develop in a variety of circumstances. If the chest tubes have been removed, it usually results from an air leak exiting chest tube holes in the pleura and entering the subcutaneous space. In patients with severe emphysema or bronchospastic airways, it may result from alveolar rupture. A pneumothorax may or may not be present. Nonetheless, management usually requires placement of unilateral or bilateral chest tubes, and, if the emphysema is severe, performing decompressing skin incisions in the upper chest or neck.

4. A chest x-ray should always be performed after the removal of pleural chest tubes. A small pneumothorax (<20%) can be observed with serial films. However, aspiration of the pleural space or placement of a new chest tube is indicated if the pneumothorax exceeds 20%.

C. **Bronchospasm** can occur at the termination of surgery and can produce difficulty with sternal closure. Severe bronchospasm and air trapping developing in the ICU can produce difficulties with mechanical ventilation as well as hemodynamic problems that can mimic cardiac tamponade. Bronchospasm can be precipitated by fluid overload, drug reactions, blood product transfusions, or the use of β-blockers, and it can occur in patients without known COPD or bronchospastic airways. Treatment involves the following:

1. **Inhalational bronchodilators** delivered by nebulizer or metered dose inhaler (MDI) are helpful during mechanical ventilation as well as after extubation (table 9.4). The combination of albuterol and ipratropium (Combivent) provides the best bronchodilatation.[83,84]

   a. Albuterol (Ventolin, Proventil) 0.5 mL of 0.5% solution (2.5 mg) in 2.5 mL normal saline q4–6h

   b. Ipratropium (Atrovent), 2.5 mL of 0.02% in 2.5 mL normal saline q6–8h or 2 puffs q6–8h

   c. Metaproterenol (Alupent, Metaprel) 0.2–0.3 mL of 5% solution in 2.5 mL normal saline q4–6h

   d. Isoetharine (Brethaire, Bronkosol) 0.5 mL of 1% solution in 2.5 mL normal saline q4–6h

   e. Racemic epinephrine 0.5 mL of 0.25% solution in 3.5 mL normal saline q4h

2. **IV aminophylline** has several beneficial effects. It is a bronchodilator, a mild diuretic, increases the respiratory drive, improves respiratory muscle function, and it may decrease the pulmonary artery pressure and improve right ventricular function. However, it is arrhythmogenic and chronotropic and must be used cautiously in patients with tenuous hemodynamics. Nonetheless, the tachycardia that may be present frequently improves when bronchospasm resolves.

   a. IV aminophylline is given as a 5–8 mg/kg load over 30 minutes followed by a continuous infusion. The maintenance dosage in mg/kg ideal body weight/h should be 0.6 for nonsmokers, 0.9 for smokers, and 0.3 for patients with cardiac decompensation or liver disease.

Table 9.4 *Comparison of Adrenergic Bronchodilators*

	β_1	β_2	Potency	Onset (min)	Duration (hours)
Albuterol	+	++++	++++	5	4–6
Metaproterenol	+	+++	+++	1–5	4
Isoetharine	++	+++	++	1–6	2–3

   b. When PO theophylline is substituted for IV aminophylline, the appropriate dose can be calculated from either of the following two formulas:

   total daily dose = (mg/h IV aminophylline) (24 h) (0.8)

   or

   10 × (mg/h IV aminophylline) = dose of theophylline bid

   The IV infusion is stopped immediately after the first oral dose.

   c. The dose of sustained-release theophylline (Theodur) is 200–300 mg q8–12h.

   d. Therapeutic levels are 10–20 μg/mL.

3. Epinephrine can be selected as an inotrope if cardiac output is marginal because it is an excellent bronchodilator. Since it is also a strong positive chronotrope, it must be used cautiously when sinus tachycardia is present.

4. **Corticosteroids** are frequently beneficial when bronchospasm is refractory to the above measures. They may increase airway responsiveness to other β-agonists.

   a. Methylprednisolone (Solumedrol) 0.5–1 mg/kg IV q6h × 2–7 days

   b. Convert to prednisone 1 mg/kg/day and wean over a 1–2 week period.

5. **Note:** β-blockers are generally contraindicated during episodes of bronchospasm. However, patients with a history of bronchospastic airways can frequently tolerate the selective β-blockers, such as esmolol, metoprolol, and atenolol.[85]

References

1. Matthay MA, Wiener-Kronish JP. Respiratory management after cardiac surgery. Chest 1989;95:424–34.
2. Shapira N, Zabatino SM, Ahmed S, Murphy DMF, Sullivan D, Lemole GM. Determinants of pulmonary function in patients undergoing coronary bypass operations. Ann Thorac Surg 1990;50:268–73.
3. Cheng DCH, Karski J, Peniston C, et al. Early tracheal extubation after coronary artery bypass graft surgery reduces costs and improves resource use. A prospective, randomized, controlled trial. Anesthesiology 1996;85:1300–10.
4. Cheng DCH, Karski J, Peniston C, et al. Morbidity outcome in early versus conventional tracheal extubation after coronary artery bypass grafting: a prospective randomized controlled trial. J Thorac Cardiovasc Surg 1996;112:755–64.
5. Hachenberg T, Tenling A, Nystrom SO, Tyden H, Hedenstierna G. Ventilation-perfusion inequality in patients undergoing cardiac surgery. Anesthesiology 1994;80:509–19.
6. Pepe PE, Marini JJ. Occult positive end-expiratory pressure in mechanically ventilated patients with airflow obstruction. The Auto-PEEP effect. Am Rev Respir Dis 1982;126:166–70.
7. Valta P, Takala J, Elissa NT, Milic-Emili J. Effects of PEEP on respiratory mechanics after open heart surgery. Chest 1992;102:227–33.
8. Van Trigt P, Spray TL, Pasque MK, et al. The effect of PEEP on left ventricular diastolic dimensions and systolic performance following myocardial revascularization. Ann Thorac Surg 1982;33:585–92.
9. Boldt J, King D, v Bormann B, Scheld H, Hempelmann G. Influence of PEEP ventilation immediately after cardiopulmonary bypass on right ventricular function. Chest 1988;94:566–71.
10. Hornick PI, Harris P, Cousins C, Taylor KM, Keogh BE. Assessment of the value of the immediate postoperative chest radiograph after cardiac operation. Ann Thorac Surg 1995;59:1150–4.
11. O'Brien W, Karski JM, Cheng D, Carroll-Munro J, Peniston C, Sandler A. Routine chest roentgenography on admission to intensive care unit after heart operations: is it of any value? J Thorac Cardiovasc Surg 1997;113:130–3.
12. Maitre PO, Funk B, Crevoisier C, Ha HR. Pharmacokinetics of midazolam in patients recovering from cardiac surgery. Eur J Clin Pharmacol 1989;37:161–6.
13. Higgins TL, Yared JP, Estafanous FG, Coyle JP, Ko HK, Goodale DB. Propofol versus midazolam for intensive care unit sedation after coronary artery bypass grafting. Crit Care Med 1994;22:1415–23.
14. Mirenda J, Broyles G. Propofol as used for sedation in the ICU. Chest 1995;108:539–48.
15. Myles PS, Buckland MR, Weeks AM, et al. Hemodynamic effects, myocardial ischemia, and timing of tracheal extubation with propofol-based anesthesia for cardiac surgery. Anesth Analg 1997;84:12–9.
16. El-Baz N, Goldin M. Continuous epidural infusion of morphine for pain relief after cardiac operations. J Thorac Cardiovasc Surg 1987;93:878–83.
17. Ready LB, Brown CR, Stahlgren LH, et al. Evaluation of intravenous ketorolac administered by bolus or infusion for treatment of postoperative pain. A double-blind, placebo-controlled, multicenter study. Anesthesiology 1994;80:1277–86.
18. Karski JM. Practical aspects of early extubation in cardiac surgery. J Cardiothorac Vasc Anesthesia 1995;9(suppl 1):30–3.
19. Bojar RM, Rastegar H, Payne DD, et al. Methemoglobinemia from intravenous nitroglycerin: a word of caution. Ann Thorac Surg 1987;43:332–4.

20. Isenstein DA, Venner DS, Duggan J. Neuromuscular blockade in the intensive care unit. Chest 1992;102:1258–66.

21. Mangano DT, Siciliano D, Hollenberg M, et al. Postoperative myocardial ischemia. Therapeutic trials using intensive analgesia following surgery. Anesthesiology 1992; 76:342–53.

22. Gall SA Jr, Olsen CO, Reves JG, et al. Beneficial effects of endotracheal extubation on ventricular performance. Implications for early extubation after cardiac operations. J Thorac Cardiovasc Surg 1988;95:819–27.

23. Hickey RF, Cason BA. Timing of tracheal extubation in adult cardiac surgery patients. J Cardiac Surg 1995;10:340–8.

24. Higgins TL. Pro: early endotracheal extubation is preferable to late extubation in patients following coronary artery surgery. J Cardiothorac Anesthesia 1992;6:488–93.

25. Higgins TL. Safety issues regarding early extubation after coronary artery bypass surgery. J Cardiothorac Vasc Anesthesia 1995;9(suppl 1):24–9.

26. Engelman RM, Rousou JA, Flack JE III, et al. Fast-track recovery of the coronary bypass patient. Ann Thorac Surg 1994;58:1742–6.

27. Engelman RM. Mechanisms to reduce hospital stays. Ann Thorac Surg 1996;61:S26–9.

28. Gordon GR, England MR, Panza WS, et al. Early recovery from CABG surgery: practice changes and their effect on ICU utilization, costs, and pulmonary complications. Anesth Analg 1996;82:SCA45.

29. Arom KV, Emery RW, Petersen RJ, Schwartz M. Cost-effectiveness and predictors of early extubation. Ann Thorac Surg 1995;60:127–32.

30. Habib RH, Zacharias A, Engoren M. Determinants of prolonged mechanical ventilation after coronary artery bypass grafting. Ann Thorac Surg 1996;62:1164–71.

31. Bando K, Sun K, Binford RS, Sharp TG. Determinants of longer duration of endotracheal intubation after adult cardiac operations. Ann Thorac Surg 1997;63: 1026–33.

32. Ott RA, Gutfinger DE, Miller MP, Alimadadian H, Tanner TM. Rapid recovery after coronary artery bypass grafting: is the elderly patient eligible? Ann Thorac Surg 1997;63:634–9.

33. Tobin MJ, Yang K. Weaning from mechanical ventilation. Crit Care Clin 1990; 6:725–47.

34. Tomlinson JR, Miller KS, Lorch DG, Smith L, Reines HD, Sahn SA. A prospective comparison of IMV and T-piece weaning from mechanical ventilation. Chest 1989;96: 348–52.

35. Jones DP, Byrne P, Morgan C. Positive end-expiratory pressure vs T-piece. Extubation after mechanical ventilation. Chest 1991;100:1655–9.

36. Annest SJ, Gottlieb M, Paloski WH, et al. Detrimental effects of removing end-expiratory pressure prior to endotracheal extubation. Ann Surg 1980;191:539–45.

37. Stiller K, Montarello J, Wallace M, et al. Efficacy of breathing and coughing exercises in the prevention of pulmonary complications after coronary artery surgery. Chest 1994;105:741–7.

38. Glass PSA, Estok P, Ginsberg B, Goldberg JS, Sladen RN. Use of patient-controlled analgesia to compare the efficacy of epidural to intravenous fentanyl administration. Anesth Analg 1992;74:345–51.

39. Gilbert TB, Barnas GM, Sequeira AJ. Impact of pleurotomy, continuous positive airway pressure, and fluid balance during cardiopulmonary bypass on lung mechanics and oxygenation. J Cardiothorac Vasc Anesthesia 1996;10:844–9.

40. Berrizbeitia LD, Tessler S, Jacobowitz IJ, Kaplan P, Budzilowicz L, Cunningham JN. Effect of sternotomy and coronary bypass surgery on postoperative mechanics. Comparison of internal mammary and saphenous vein bypass grafts. Chest 1989; 96:873–6.

41. Hurlbut D, Myers ML, Lefcoe M, Goldbach M. Pleuropulmonary morbidity: internal thoracic artery versus saphenous vein graft. Ann Thorac Surg 1990;50:959–64.
42. Higgins TL, Barrett C, Riden DJ, Roberts MM, Coyle JP. Influence of pleural and mediastinal chest tubes on respiration following coronary artery bypass grafting (CABG). Chest 1989;96(suppl):237S.
43. O'Brien JW, Johnson SH, VanSteyn SJ, et al. Effects of internal mammary artery dissection on phrenic nerve perfusion and function. Ann Thorac Surg 1991;52:182–8.
44. Yamazaki K, Kato H, Tsujimoto S, Kitamura R. Diabetes mellitus, internal thoracic artery grafting, and the risk of an elevated hemidiaphragm after coronary artery bypass surgery. J Cardiothorac Vasc Anesthesia 1994;8:437–40.
45. Cohen A, Katz M, Katz R, Hauptman E, Schachner A. Chronic obstructive pulmonary disease in patients undergoing coronary artery bypass grafting. J Thorac Cardiovasc Surg 1995;109:574–81.
46. Spivack SD, Shinozaki T, Albertini JJ, Deane R. Preoperative prediction of postoperative respiratory outcome. Coronary artery bypass grafting. Chest 1996;109:1222–30.
47. Kollef MH, Wragge T, Pasque C. Determinants of mortality and multiorgan dysfunction in cardiac surgery patients requiring prolonged mechanical ventilation. Chest 1995;107:1395–401.
48. The Society of Thoracic Surgeons. Data analyses of The Society of Thoracic Surgeons National Cardiac Surgery Database, January 1996. Summit Medical Systems, 1996.
49. Bevelaqua F, Garritan S, Haas F, Salazar-Schicchi J, Axen K, Reggiani JL. Complications after cardiac operations in patients with severe pulmonary impairment. Ann Thorac Surg 1990;50:602–6.
50. Maggart M, Stewart S. The mechanisms and management of noncardiogenic pulmonary edema following cardiopulmonary bypass. Ann Thorac Surg 1987;43:231–6.
51. Louagie Y, Gonzalez E, Jamart J, Bulliard G, Schoevaerdts. Postcardiopulmonary bypass lung edema. A preventable complication? Chest 1993;103:86–95.
52. Klancke KA, Assey ME, Kratz JM, Crawford FA. Postoperative pulmonary edema in postcoronary artery bypass graft patients. Relationship of total serum protein and colloid oncotic pressures. Chest 1983;84:529–34.
53. Cutaia M, Rounds S. Hypoxic pulmonary vasoconstriction. Physiologic significance, mechanism, and clinical relevance. Chest 1990;97:706–15.
54. Marcy TW. Barotrauma: detection, recognition and management. Chest 1993;104: 578–84.
55. Bodai BI, Blaisdell FW. Discontinuance of positive end-expiratory pressure during suctioning: effect on oxygenation in patients with adult respiratory distress syndrome. Surg Forum 1981;31:311–2.
56. Schwartz SZ, Shoemaker WC, Nolan-Avila LS. Effects of blood volume and discontinuance of ventilation on pulmonary vascular pressures and blood gases in patients with low levels of positive end-expiratory pressure. Crit Care Med 1987;15:671–5.
57. Marini JJ. The physiologic determinants of ventilator dependence. Resp Care 1986;31: 271–82.
58. Kollef MH, Schuster DP. The acute respiratory distress syndrome. N Engl J Med 1995;332:27–37.
59. Peruzzi WT, Franklin ML, Shapiro BA. New concepts and therapies of adult respiratory distress syndrome. J Cardiothorac Vasc Anesthesia 1997;11:771–86.
60. Hund EF, Fogel W, Krieger D, DeGeorgia M, Hacke W. Critical illness polyneuropathy: clinical findings and outcomes of a frequent cause of neuromuscular weaning failure. Crit Care Med 1996;24:1328–33.
61. Chandler KW, Rozas CJ, Kory RC, Goldman AL. Bilateral diaphragmatic paralysis complicates local cardiac hypothermia during open heart operation. Am J Med 1984;77: 243–9.

62. Wilcox PG, Paré PD, Pardy RL. Recovery after unilateral phrenic injury associated with coronary artery revascularization. Chest 1990;98:661–6.
63. Locicero J III, McCann B, Massad M, Joob AW. Prolonged ventilatory support after open-heart surgery. Crit Care Med 1992;20:990–2.
64. Tolep K, Getch CL, Criner GJ. Swallowing dysfunction in patients receiving prolonged mechanical ventilation. Chest 1996;109:167–72.
65. Stone DJ, Bogdonoff DL. Airway considerations in the management of patients requiring long-term endotracheal intubation. Anesth Analg 1992;74:276–87.
66. Friedman Y, Fildes J, Mizock B, et al. Comparison of percutaneous and surgical tracheostomies. Chest 1996;110:480–5.
67. van Heurn LWE, Goei R, de Pleog I, Ramsey G, Brink PRG. Late complications of percutaneous dilatational tracheotomy. Chest 1996;110:1572–6.
68. O'Connor JV, Reddy K, Ergin MA, Griepp RB. Cricothyroidotomy for prolonged ventilatory support after cardiac operations. Ann Thorac Surg 1985;39:353–4.
69. Heyland DK, Cook DJ, Jaeschke R, Griffith L, Lee HN, Guyatt GH. Selective decontamination of the digestive tract. An overview. Chest 1994;105:1221–9.
70. Apte NM, Karnad DR, Medhekar TP, Tilve G, Morye S, Bhave GG. Gastric colonization and pneumonia in intubated critically ill patients receiving stress ulcer prophylaxis: a randomized, controlled trial. Crit Care Med 1992;20:590–3.
71. Graham DR, Kaplan D, Evans CC, Hind CRK, Donnelly RJ. Diaphragmatic plication for unilateral diaphragmatic paralysis: a 10-year experience. Ann Thorac Surg 1990;49:248–52.
72. Tobin TJ. Mechanical ventilation. N Engl J Med 1994;330:1056–61.
73. Shapiro BA, Vender JS, Peruzzi WT. Airway pressure therapy for cardiac surgical patients: state of the art and clinical controversies. J Cardiothorac Vasc Anesthesia 1992;6:735–48.
74. Slutsky AS. Mechanical ventilation. Chest 1993;104:1833–59.
75. Yang KL, Tobin MJ. A prospective study of indexes predicting the outcome of trials of weaning from mechanical ventilation. N Engl J Med 1991;324:1445–50.
76. Lee KH, Hui KP, Chan TB, Tan WC, Lim TK. Rapid shallow breathing (frequency-tidal volume ratio) did not predict extubation outcome. Chest 1994;105:540–3.
77. Esteban A, Frutos F, Tobin MJ, et al. A comparison of four methods of weaning patients from mechanical ventilation. N Engl J Med 1995;332:345–50.
78. Sassoon CSH, Giron AE, Ely EA, Light RW. Inspiratory work of breathing in flow-by and demand-flow continuous positive airway pressure. Crit Care Med 1989;17:1108–14.
79. Hurst JM, Branson RD, Davis K Jr, Barrette RR. Cardiopulmonary effects of pressure support ventilation. Arch Surg 1989;124:1067–70.
80. Banner MJ, Kirby RR, MacIntyre NR. Patient and ventilator work of breathing and ventilatory muscle loads at different levels of pressure support ventilation. Chest 1991;100:531–3.
81. Brochard L, Harf A, Lorino H, Lemaire F. Inspiratory pressure support prevents diaphragmatic fatigue during weaning from mechanical ventilation. Am Rev Resp Dis 1989;139:513–21.
82. Sassoon CSH. Positive pressure ventilation. Alternate modes. Chest 1991;100:1421–9.
83. Nelson HS. β-adrenergic bronchodilators. N Engl J Med 1995;333:499–506.
84. The COMBIVENT Inhalation Solution Study Group. Routine nebulized ipratropium and albuterol together are better than either alone in COPD. Chest 1997;112:1514–21.
85. Gold MR, Dec GW, Cocca-Spofford D, Thompson BT. Esmolol and ventilatory function in cardiac patients with COPD. Chest 1991;100:1215–8.

10 Cardiovascular Management

10   Cardiovascular Management

The achievement of satisfactory hemodynamic performance is the primary objective of postoperative cardiac surgical management. Optimal cardiac function ensures adequate perfusion and oxygenation of other organ systems and improves the chances for an uneventful recovery from surgery. Even brief periods of cardiac dysfunction can lead to organ system ischemia and a variety of potentially life-threatening complications. This chapter presents a few basic concepts in cardiovascular management and then reviews the evaluation and management of the low cardiac output syndrome, hypertension, and rhythm disturbances that can contribute to compromised cardiovascular function.

I.   Basic Principles

The important concepts of postoperative cardiac care are those of cardiac output, tissue oxygenation, and the ratio of myocardial oxygen supply and demand. Ideally, one should strive to obtain a cardiac index greater than $2.2 \, L/min/m^2$ with a normal mixed venous oxygen saturation while optimizing the oxygen supply:demand ratio.

   A.   **Cardiac output** is determined by the stroke volume and heart rate ($CO = SV \times HR$). The stroke volume represents the left ventricular end-diastolic volume (LVEDV) minus the left ventricular end-systolic volume (LVESV) and is calculated by dividing the cardiac output by the heart rate. The three major determinants of stroke volume are preload, afterload, and contractility.[1]

   1.   **Preload** refers to the left ventricular end-diastolic fiber length or end-diastolic volume. Postoperatively, the status of left ventricular filling can only be assessed accurately by echocardiography. However, it is routinely assessed indirectly by measuring left heart filling pressures, which include the pulmonary artery diastolic (PAD), pulmonary capillary wedge (PCW), and left atrial (LA) pressures. The relationship between filling pressures and volumes is determined by ventricular compliance.

   a.   Generally, the closer the site of assessment to the left ventricle, the closer the correlation to the LVEDP. Thus, the correlation is best for LA > PCW > PAD. The PAD pressure generally correlates with the PCWP, but is frequently higher than the PCWP in patients with preexisting pulmonary hypertension or intrinsic pulmonary disease who may have an increased transpulmonary gradient (equal to the PA mean pressure minus the PCWP). Thus, in these situations, the PAD may significantly overestimate left ventricular volume.

   b.   Filling pressures must be interpreted cautiously in the early postoperative period.[2–4] There is often a poor correlation of PAD and PCW pressures with the LVEDV early after surgery because of a change in ventricular compliance caused by myocardial edema from cardiopulmonary bypass and the use of cardioplegia solutions. Furthermore, the release of various inflammatory substances during bypass and the use of blood products may increase pulmonary vascular resistance (PVR). The patient with a stiff ventricular chamber (hypertension, S/P aortic valve replacement for aortic steno-sis) may require high filling pressures to achieve adequate ventricular filling.

c. For patients with relatively normal ventricular function, many centers do not use Swan-Ganz catheters, relying on central venous pressure (CVP) measurements to assess preload. Although this is an inaccurate means of assessing preload in the diseased heart, it gives a fairly good approx-imation of left heart filling in the normal heart. Generally, if the CVP exceeds 15–18 mm Hg, inotropic support is indi-cated. If the patient has other signs of low cardiac output (poor oxygenation, tapering urine output, acidosis), insertion of a Swan-Ganz catheter will allow for a more objective evaluation of the problem.

2. **Afterload** refers to the left ventricular wall tension during systole. It is determined by both the preload (Laplace's law relating radius to wall tension) and the systemic vascular resistance (SVR) against which the heart must eject after the period of isovolumic contrac-tion. The SVR can be calculated from measurements obtained from the Swan-Ganz catheter (table 10.1). It should be kept in mind that

Table 10.1   *Hemodynamic Formulas*

Formula	Normal Values
Cardiac output (CO) and index (CI)	
$CO = SV \times HR$	4–8 L/min
$CI = CO/BSA$	2.5–4.0 L/min/m^2
Stroke volume (SV)	
$SV = \dfrac{CO(L/min) \times 1000\,(mL/L)}{HR}$	60–100 mL/beat (1 mL/kg/beat)
Stroke volume index (SVI)	
$SVI = SV/BSA$	33–47 mL/beat/m^2
Mean arterial pressure (MAP)	
$MAP = DP + \dfrac{SP - DP}{3}$	70–100 mm Hg
Systemic vascular resistance (SVR)	
$SVR = \dfrac{MAP - CVP}{CO} \times 80$	800–1200 dyne-sec/cm^5
Pulmonary vascular resistance (PVR)	
$PVR = \dfrac{PAP - PCWP}{CO} \times 80$	50–250 dyne-sec/cm^5
Left ventricular stroke work index (LVSWI)	
$LVSWI = SVI \times (MAP - PCW) \times 0.0136$	45–75 mg-M/beat/m^2

BSA = body surface area; CVP = central venous pressure; DP = diastolic pressure; HR = heart rate; PAP = mean pulmonary artery pressure; PCWP = pulmonary capillary wedge pressure; SP = systolic pressure.

the equation to calculate SVR is based on the cardiac output, not the cardiac index (thus, the SVR index is more precise). Therefore, it will be higher in the smaller patient at a comparable cardiac index. An elevated SVR can be selectively lowered with vasodilators to improve stroke volume, often in combination with volume infusions and inotropic agents.

3. **Contractility** is the intrinsic strength of myocardial contraction at constant preload and afterload. However, it can be improved by increasing preload or heart rate, decreasing the afterload, or using inotropic medications.[5] Although contractility (i.e., the ejection fraction) is best assessed by echocardiography, it is usually inferred from an analysis of the cardiac output and filling pressures.

4. The assessment of cardiac output after surgery is obtained by thermodilution technology using a Swan-Ganz catheter and bedside computer. A measured aliquot of volume is infused into the CVP port of the catheter and the thermistor near the tip measures the pattern of temperature change, from which the computer calculates the cardiac output. A continuous cardiac output catheter system is available and beneficial for online assessment and pharmacologic manipulation when hemodynamics are tenuous.[6]

5. The presence of a low cardiac output does not imply that ventricular function is impaired. It is also noted with slow heart rates, hypovolemia, and with a small, stiff ventricular chamber. In contrast, a satisfactory cardiac index may accompany significant ventricular dysfunction when the left ventricle is dilated, especially if a severe tachycardia is present. Thus, the treatment of a low cardiac output state must take into account all of the factors mentioned above to determine the appropriate treatment.

B. **Tissue oxygenation**

1. Oxygen transport to tissues is the basic principle upon which hemodynamic support should be based. It is determined by the cardiac output (CO), the hemoglobin (Hb) level, and the arterial oxygen saturation (SaO_2). This is represented by the equation:

$$O_2 \text{ delivery} = CO(Hb \times \%sat)(1.39) + (PaO_2)(0.0031)$$

where 1.39 is the milliliters of oxygen transported per gram of hemoglobin and 0.0031 is the solubility coefficient of oxygen dissolved in solution (mL/torr of PaO_2).

2. It should be noted in the above equation that the majority of oxygen transported to the tissues is in the form of oxygen bound to hemoglobin, not dissolved in solution. Thus, one of the major factors lowering O_2 delivery in the postoperative period is a low hematocrit. Increasing the hemoglobin level by 1 g/dL can increase blood oxygen content by 1.39 vol%, whereas an increase in PaO_2 of 100 torr will only transport an additional 0.3 vol% of oxygen.

3. Studies have suggested that the safe lower limit for hematocrit in the early postoperative period to maintain adequate tissue oxygenation is probably around 22–24%.[7,8] Because this may reduce

tissue oxygen delivery to less than 60% of normal, it is imperative that arterial oxygen saturation be close to 100% and cardiac output be optimized to achieve adequate O_2 delivery. Once an arterial saturation of 95–100% has been achieved, there is little additional benefit of maintaining a high FIO_2 and PaO_2.

4. The threshold for administering blood transfusions has increased in recent years, with more than 50% of patients receiving no blood products after surgery. However, blood transfusions should be considered in patients who might benefit from additional oxygen delivery (elderly patients, poor ventricular function, ischemic ECG changes, hypotension, or tachycardia).

5. **Mixed venous oxygen saturation** (SvO_2) can be used to assess the adequacy of tissue perfusion and oxygenation. PA catheters using reflective fiberoptic oximetry are available to monitor the SvO_2 in the pulmonary artery on a continuous basis. Intermittent SvO_2 measurements can be measured from blood samples obtained from the distal PA port of the Swan-Ganz catheter. A change of 10% in the SvO_2 can occur before any change is noted in hemodynamic parameters. Despite its theoretical benefit, numerous studies have shown SvO_2 measurements to be unreliable and insensitive in predicting the cardiac output.[9]

    a. In the postoperative cardiac surgical patient, a fall in SvO_2 generally reflects decreased oxygen delivery or increased oxygen extraction by tissues and is suggestive of a reduction in cardiac output. However, other constantly changing factors that affect oxygen supply and demand may also influence SvO_2 and must be taken into consideration. These include shivering, temperature, anemia, alteration in FIO_2, and the efficiency of alveolar gas exchange. The Fick equation, which uses the arteriovenous oxygen content difference to determine cardiac output, can be rearranged as follows:

    $$SvO_2 = SaO_2 - \frac{\dot{V}O_2}{Hb \times 1.39 \times CO} \times 10$$

    where:
    SvO_2 = mixed venous oxygen saturation
    SaO_2 = arterial O_2 saturation
    $\dot{V}O_2$ = oxygen consumption
    normal PvO_2 = 40 torr and SvO_2 = 75%
    normal PaO_2 = 100 torr and SaO_2 = 99%

    b. This equation indicates that a decrease in SvO_2 may result from a decrease in SaO_2, cardiac output, or hemoglobin level, or an increase in oxygen consumption.

    c. When the arterial O_2 saturation is normal ($SaO_2 > 95\%$), a $PvO_2 < 30$ torr or an $SvO_2 < 60$–65% suggests the presence of a decreased cardiac output and the need for further assessment and therapeutic intervention. Conversely, a rise in SvO_2 reflects less oxygen extraction as seen during hypothermia, sepsis, or intracardiac or significant peripheral arteriovenous shunting. In several of these situations, oxygen delivery or utilization may be impaired and an otherwise "normal" cardiac output is insufficient to provide adequate tissue oxygenation.

6. When the cardiac index exceeds $2.2\,L/min/m^2$ and the arterial oxygen saturation is adequate (>95%), it may be inferred that oxygen delivery to the tissues is satisfactory. Thus, SvO_2 measurements to assess oxygen delivery are not necessary. However, there are a few situations when calculation of tissue oxygenation may be valuable in assessing cardiac function:

   a. The thermodilution cardiac output is unreliable (tricuspid regurgitation, improperly positioned Swan-Ganz catheter) or not available (Swan-Ganz catheter has not been placed or cannot be placed, such as the patient with a mechanical tricuspid valve or central venous thrombosis).

   b. The thermodilution cardiac output may seem spuriously low and inconsistent with the clinical scenario (malfunctioning Swan-Ganz catheter or incorrect calibration of computer). A normal SvO_2 indicates that the cardiac output is sufficient to meet tissue metabolic demands.

   c. The patient has a marginal cardiac output, and on-line assessment of mixed venous oxygen saturation can provide up-to-date information as to the status of cardiac function.

C. **Myocardial oxygen supply and demand**

   1. **Myocardial O_2 demand** (mvO_2) is influenced by factors similar to those that determine cardiac output (afterload, preload, heart rate, and contractility). Reducing afterload will reduce mvO_2 and improve cardiac output, whereas an increase in any of the other three factors will improve cardiac output at the expense of an increase in mvO_2. Preoperative management of the patient with ischemic heart disease is directed toward minimizing O_2 demand.[10]

   2. **Myocardial O_2 supply** is determined by coronary blood flow (affected by native or graft stenosis or spasm), the duration of diastole, coronary perfusion pressure, the hemoglobin level, and the arterial oxygen saturation. When complete revascularization has been achieved, postoperative management is directed toward optimizing factors that improve O_2 supply.

      a. A heart rate of 80 to 90/min should be achieved and excessive tachycardia and arrhythmias must be avoided.

      b. An adequate perfusion pressure (mean pressure 80–90 mm Hg) should be maintained, taking care to avoid both hypotension and hypertension from elevated SVR.

      c. Ventricular distention must be minimized by avoiding excessive preload, reducing the SVR, and improving cardiac function with inotropic drugs.

       d. Although increasing the hematocrit would ideally optimize oxygen delivery further, myocardial ischemia should not occur in the well-protected, revascularized heart unless the hematocrit drops into the low 20s.[7,8]

II. Low Cardiac Output Syndrome

A. General comments

1. The achievement of a satisfactory cardiac output is the primary objective of postoperative cardiovascular management. Hemodynamic norms for the patient recovering uneventfully from cardiac surgery are a cardiac index (CI) greater than $2.5\,L/min/m^2$, an LA or PCW pressure below 20 mm Hg, and a heart rate below 100/min. The patient should have warm, well-perfused extremities with an excellent urine output.

2. Myocardial function generally declines for about 6–8 hours following surgery—presumably from ischemic/reperfusion injury—before returning to baseline within 24 hours.[11] It is during this period that temporary inotropic support is often required to optimize hemodynamic performance. Drugs that were used to terminate cardiopulmonary bypass should generally be continued for this brief period of time and can be weaned once an improvement in cardiac output is noted.

3. When marginal ventricular function is present, compensatory mechanisms develop from sympathetic autonomic stimulation and endogenous catecholamine production. These increase heart rate, contractility, and arterial and venous tone, elevating both preload and afterload. All of these factors may improve cardiac output or systemic blood pressure, but may also increase myocardial oxygen demand. Consequently, they may be detrimental to the ischemic or depressed myocardium. In fact, studies have documented a significant incidence of asymptomatic ischemia following coronary bypass surgery.[12,13] Subtle findings, such as a progressive tachycardia or cool extremities, should alert the astute clinician to the need for early intervention. It cannot be overemphasized that observing trends in hemodynamic parameters, rather than absolute numbers, is important when evaluating a patient's progress or deterioration.

4. When compensatory mechanisms are exhausted, the advanced clinical manifestations of the low cardiac output syndrome will be noted. These include:

       a. Poor peripheral perfusion with pale, cool extremities and diaphoresis

       b. Pulmonary congestion and poor oxygenation

       c. Impaired renal perfusion and oliguria

       d. Metabolic acidosis

5. The use of sophisticated invasive monitoring to continuously evaluate a patient's hemodynamic status allows for appropriate therapeutic interventions to be undertaken before these advanced clinical signs become apparent. Intervention is indicated for a low

Table 10.2 *Management of Hemodynamic Problems*

BP	PCWP	CO	SVR	Plan
↓	↓	↓	↓	Volume
N	↑	N	↑	Diuretic or venodilator
↓	↑	↓	↑	Inotrope
↑	↑	↓	↑	Vasodilator
↑↓	↑	↓	↑	Inotrope/vasodilator/IABP
↓	N	N	↓	α-agent

↑ = increased; ↓ = decreased; N = normal; ↑↓ = variable.

cardiac output state, defined as a cardiac index below 2.0 L/min/m², usually associated with left-sided filling pressures exceeding 20 mm Hg and an SVR exceeding 1500 dyne-sec/cm⁵.

6. A general scheme for the management of postoperative hemodynamic problems is presented in table 10.2.

B. **Etiology.** A low cardiac output state may result from abnormal preload, contractility, heart rate, or afterload.

   1. Decreased left ventricular preload

      a. Hypovolemia (bleeding, vasodilatation from warming, vasodilators, narcotics, or sedatives)

      b. Cardiac tamponade

      c. Positive pressure ventilation and PEEP

      d. Right ventricular dysfunction (RV infarction, pulmonary hypertension)

      e. Tension pneumothorax

   2. Decreased contractility

      a. Low ejection fraction

      b. Myocardial "stunning," ischemia or infarction

         i. Poor intraoperative myocardial protection

         ii. Incomplete myocardial revascularization

         iii. Anastomotic stenosis

         iv. Coronary artery spasm

      c. Hypoxia, hypercarbia, acidosis

   3. Tachy- and bradyarrhythmias

      a. Tachycardia with reduced cardiac filling time

      b. Bradycardia

      c. Atrial arrhythmias with loss of atrial contraction

      d. Ventricular arrhythmias

   4. Increased afterload

      a. Vasoconstriction

      b. Fluid overload

5. Diastolic dysfunction (a common finding after cardioplegic arrest)[14]

6. Syndromes associated with cardiovascular instability and hypotension

   a. Sepsis (hypotension from a reduction in SVR; hyperdynamic early and myocardial depression at a later stage)

   b. Anaphylactic reactions (blood products, drugs)

   c. Adrenal insufficiency (primary or in the patient on preoperative steroids)

   d. Protamine reaction

C. **Assessment** (concerns noted in parentheses)

   1. Bedside physical examination (breath sounds, murmurs, extremities)

   2. Obtain hemodynamic measurements: assess filling pressures and determine cardiac output with a Swan-Ganz catheter; calculate SVR; measure SvO_2.

   3. Analysis of arterial blood gases (hypoxia, hypercarbia, acidosis/alkalosis), hematocrit (anemia), and serum potassium (hypo- or hyperkalemia)

   4. Electrocardiogram (ischemia, arrhythmias)

   5. Chest x-ray (pneumothorax, endotracheal tube position)

   6. Urinary output (oliguria)

   7. Chest tube drainage (mediastinal bleeding)

   8. Echocardiography is very helpful when the nature of the problem is difficult to determine. Along with hemodynamic measurements, it can help define whether a low cardiac output state is related to left ventricular systolic or diastolic dysfunction, right ventricular systolic dysfunction, or cardiac tamponade. **Transesophageal echocardiography** provides better and more complete information than a transthoracic study and can be readily performed in the intubated patient. It should always be considered when the clinical picture is consistent with tamponade but a transthoracic study is inconclusive.[15]

D. **Treatment** (table 10.3)[16]

   1. Ensure satisfactory **oxygenation** and **ventilation** (see Chapter 9).

   2. Treat **ischemia** or **coronary spasm** if suspected to be present. Myocardial ischemia often responds to intravenous nitroglycerin but may require further investigation if it persists. Coronary spasm (see page 255) can be difficult to diagnose but usually responds to a calcium-channel blocker, such as sublingual nifedipine or intravenous diltiazem.

   3. Optimize **preload** by raising filling pressures with volume infusion to an LA or PCW pressure of about 18–20 mm Hg. This may be all that is necessary to achieve a satisfactory cardiac output. Volume infusion is preferable to atrial pacing for improving cardiac output

Table 10.3 *Management of Low Cardiac Output Syndrome*

1. Look for noncardiac correctable causes (respiratory, acid-base, electrolytes)
2. Treat ischemia or coronary spasm
3. Optimize preload (PCW or LA pressure of 15–18 mm Hg)
4. Optimize heart rate at 90–100 beats/min with pacing
5. Control arrhythmias
6. Assess cardiac output and start inotrope if cardiac index is $<2.0 L/min/m^2$
   - Dopamine (if low SVR) or dobutamine (if high SVR)
   - Epinephrine unless arrhythmias or tachycardia
   - Amrinone
   - Insert IABP
7. Calculate SVR and start vasodilator if SVR is >1500
   - Nitroprusside if high filling pressures, SVR, and blood pressure
   - Nitroglycerin if high filling pressures or evidence of coronary ischemia or spasm
8. If SVR is low:
   - Use norepinephrine if marginal cardiac output
   - Use phenylephrine if satisfactory cardiac output
9. Give blood transfusion if hematocrit $<26\%$

because it produces less metabolic demand on the recovering myocardium.[17]

a. The ideal PCW or LA pressure can often be determined from the preoperative catheterization data or pressures noted at the conclusion of CPB in the operating room. For patients with preserved LV function, an LA pressure around 15 mm Hg is ideal. For patients with poor LV function, a stiff hypertrophied ventricle with diastolic dysfunction, a small LV chamber (mitral stenosis or after LVA resection), or preexisting pulmonary hypertension from mitral valve disease, the LA pressure must often be in the low 20s.

b. The response to volume infusion may be variable. Failure of filling pressures to rise with volume may result from the capillary leak that is present during the early postoperative period. It may also result from vasodilatation associated with rewarming or the use of medications with vasodilator properties, such as propofol or narcotics. However, it may also reflect the beneficial attenuation of peripheral vasoconstriction that is attributable to an improvement in cardiac output caused by the volume infusion. As the SVR and afterload gradually decrease, the cardiac output may improve further without an increase in preload.

c. A rise in filling pressures without improvement in cardiac output may adversely affect myocardial performance as well as the function of other organ systems. At this point, inotropic support may be necessary. Thus, careful observation of the response to volume infusion is imperative.

    i. Excessive preload increases left ventricular wall tension and may exacerbate ischemia by increasing myocardial oxygen demand and decreasing the transmyocardial gradient (aortic diastolic minus LV diastolic pressure) for coronary blood flow. It may also impair myocardial contractility.

    ii. Excessive preload may lead to interstitial edema of the lungs, resulting in increased extravascular lung water, ventilation/perfusion abnormalities, and hypoxemia.

    iii. Excessive preload in the patient with right ventricular dysfunction may impair myocardial blood flow to the RV resulting in progressive ischemia. A distended RV may contribute to left ventricular dysfunction because of overdistention and septal shift that impairs left ventricular distensibility.

    iv. The presence of right or biventricular dysfunction may produce systemic venous hypertension which may reduce perfusion pressure to other organ systems. This may affect the kidneys (causing oliguria), the gastrointestinal tract (splanchnic congestion, jaundice, ileus), or the brain (contributing to altered mental status).

4. The **heart rate and rhythm** should be stabilized. All attempts should be made to achieve atrioventricular synchrony with a heart rate of 90 to 100/min. This may require atrial (AOO or AAI) or atrioventricular (DDD or DVI) pacing. These modalities take advantage of the 20–30% improvement in cardiac output provided by atrial contraction that will not be achieved with ventricular pacing alone. This is especially important in the hypertrophied ventricle. Antiarrhythmic drugs should be used as necessary to control ventricular ectopy or slow the response to atrial fibrillation.

5. **Improve contractility** with inotropic agents (see page 229).

6. **Reduce afterload** with vasodilators if the cardiac output is marginal while carefully monitoring systemic blood pressure to avoid hypotension (see page 264). Vasodilators must be used cautiously when the cardiac index is very poor, because an elevated SVR from intense vasoconstriction is often a compensatory mechanism in low cardiac output states to maintain central perfusion. If the calculated SVR exceeds 1500, vasodilators may be indicated either alone or in combination with inotropic medications.

    a. The use of inotropic agents in the early postoperative period may seem paradoxical in that augmented cardiac output is being achieved at the expense of an increase in oxygen demand (e.g., increased heart rate and contractility). However, the *major* determinant of oxygen demand is the pressure work that the left ventricle must perform. This is reflected by the afterload, which is determined by preload and SVR. Inotropic drugs that are used to increase contractility do not necessarily increase oxygen demand in the failing heart because they reduce preload, afterload, and frequently the heart rate as a result of improved cardiac function.

b. **Note:** The presence of a satisfactory or elevated blood pressure (BP) is not necessarily a sign of good cardiac performance. Blood pressure is related directly to the cardiac output and the systemic vascular resistance (BP = CO × SVR). In the early postoperative period, myocardial function may be marginal despite normal or elevated blood pressure because of an elevated SVR resulting from augmented sympathetic tone and peripheral vasoconstriction. Vasodilators can be used to reduce afterload in the presence of elevated filling pressures, thus reducing myocardial ischemia and improving myocardial function. However, **withdrawal of inotropic support in the hypertensive patient should be considered only after a satisfactory cardiac output has been documented**. Otherwise, acute deterioration may ensue.

c. **Note:** One should not be deceived into concluding that myocardial function is satisfactory when the cardiac output is "adequate" but is being maintained by fast heart rates at low stroke volumes.

   i. Tachycardia is often an ominous sign of acute myocardial ischemia or infarction, and it may render the borderline heart ischemic.[12,13] The stroke volume index (SVI) is an excellent method of assessing myocardial function. Unless the patient is hypovolemic, a low SVI (less than 30 mL/beat/m^2) indicates poor myocardial function for which inotropic support is usually indicated. Although β-blockers would theoretically be beneficial to control tachycardia in the injured or ischemic heart, they are poorly tolerated in the presence of LV dysfunction and must be avoided.

   ii. Sinus tachycardia may represent a beneficial compensatory mechanism for a small stroke volume in patients with a small left ventricular chamber (S/P LVA resection, S/P MVR for mitral stenosis) or merely when the patient is hypovolemic. In this situation, attempts to slow the heart rate pharmacologically may compromise the cardiac output significantly.

   iii. Similarly, tachycardia is common in patients with marked left ventricular hypertrophy and diastolic dysfunction. In these patients, the cardiac output may be marginal despite preserved ventricular function because of a small noncompliant LV chamber. β-blockers or calcium-channel blockers can be used to slow the heart rate after adequate volume replacement has been achieved, but must be used with extreme caution.

   iv. Tachycardia accompanying a large stroke volume is often seen in young patients with preserved ventricular function or in hypertrophied hearts after aortic valve replacement. It can be treated safely with a β-blocker, such as esmolol.

7. **Maintain blood pressure**

   a. If the patient has a satisfactory cardiac output but low systemic resistance and a low blood pressure, moderate volume infusion may improve the blood pressure. This scenario is common in sedated patients receiving medications that have potent vasodilator properties. Maintenance of peripheral vascular tone with low-dose norepinephrine or phenylephrine is preferable to "flooding" the patient with volume, which is often futile and potentially deleterious. Norepinephrine is preferred when the cardiac output is marginal because it has β-agonist properties, whereas phenylephrine is a pure α-agonist. Some patients respond better to norepinephrine than phenylephrine, and others just the reverse.

   b. If both the blood pressure and cardiac output remain marginal despite all of the above therapeutic measures, including multiple inotropes, norepinephrine can be used to augment central perfusion pressure. Although it may have adverse effects on organ system perfusion, especially the kidney, maintenance of coronary perfusion pressure is beneficial to myocardial metabolism. However, if the cardiac output remains low despite augmentation of perfusion pressure (mean pressure 80 to 90 mm Hg), physiologic support with an **intraaortic balloon** should be considered strongly.

   c. When refractory vasodilatory hypotension accompanies a satisfactory cardiac output after CPB, it may represent a condition of autonomic failure. In one study, levels of vasopressin were found to be low in most normotensive patients after bypass but were inappropriately low for patients with vasodilatory hypotension. Furthermore, the ability to vasoconstrict to maintain blood pressure may be impaired in patients taking ACE inhibitors (which block the renin-angiotensin system) or amiodarone (which blocks sympathetic stimulation by α and β blockade). **Arginine vasopressin** (AVP) acts on vasomotor V1 and renal V2 receptors and, given in a dose of 0.1–0.4 units/min, can restore blood pressure in these patients. It can often be given in low doses because patients with vasodilatory shock tend to be hypersensitive to its effects. It also improves renal perfusion in that it constricts the efferent rather than the afferent arterioles, in contradistinction to the effects of α-agents on renal perfusion.[18,19,19a]

8. Correct **anemia** with blood transfusions. The hematocrit is usually maintained above 24% in the postoperative period, but transfusions should be considered for hemodynamic instability or evidence of myocardial ischemia.

9. If the patient cannot be weaned from bypass or has hemodynamic evidence of severe ventricular dysfunction despite maximal medical therapy and the intraaortic balloon pump (IABP), use of **a**

circulatory assist device should be considered. This is discussed on page 247.

E. **Right ventricular failure and pulmonary hypertension**

1. A low cardiac output state may be the result of right ventricular (RV) failure, producing inadequate filling of the left heart. Patients may be predisposed to RV dysfunction because of preexisting conditions, such as:

    a. Right coronary artery disease

    b. Right ventricular infarction

    c. Pulmonary hypertension associated with mitral/aortic disease or in patients undergoing heart transplantation, especially with an undersized donor heart and a prolonged ischemic time.

2. However, RV systolic dysfunction may also occur in patients with no known preexisting RV problems. It may be attributable to:

    a. Poor myocardial protection/cooling

    b. Prolonged ischemic times/myocardial stunning

    c. Coronary embolism of air, thrombi, or particulate matter

    d. Systemic hypotension, which contributes to RV ischemia, especially if PA and RV pressures are elevated

    e. Acute pulmonary hypertension from:
        - Vasoactive substances associated with blood product transfusions and cardiopulmonary bypass
        - LV dysfunction
        - Protamine reaction
        - Hypoxia and acidosis

    f. RV pressure overload: intrinsic pulmonary disease, adult respiratory distress syndrome (ARDS), pulmonary embolism

3. RV dysfunction may be identified by a high RA/PCW pressure ratio, although this is usually unreliable when LV dysfunction is also present. RV ejection fraction thermodilution catheters and echocardiography are very helpful in assessing the status of RV function.[20]

4. RV dysfunction may contribute to progressive LV dysfunction. When the RV dilates, it shifts the interventricular septum leftward, impairing LV distensibility. Progressive LV dysfunction may reduce systemic perfusion pressure, causing RV ischemia, and may elevate pulmonary artery pressures and RV afterload.[16]

5. The goals of treatment are to optimize RV preload, maintain systemic perfusion pressure, improve RV contractility, and reduce RV afterload by reducing pulmonary vascular resistance.

    a. RV preload must be raised cautiously to avoid the adverse effects of RV dilatation on RV myocardial blood flow and LV function. Generally, the RA pressure should be increased to 15 to 18 mm Hg. If no improvement in cardiac output ensues when the RA pressure is further increased by 3 mm Hg, additional volume infusions should be avoided.

b. Atrioventricular conduction is essential.

c. Correction of hypothermia and hypoxemia, and hyperventilation to eliminate respiratory acidosis will decrease pulmonary vascular resistance (acidosis rather than hypercarbia is most deleterious).

d. Medications that can provide a positive inotropic effect while reducing the pulmonary artery pressure are usually selected.

  i. The phosphodiesterase inhibitors, amrinone and milrinone, are very beneficial in achieving these goals, although they are usually associated with systemic hypotension as well.

  ii. Isoproterenol, while effective in accomplishing these goals, usually causes a significant tachycardia and is rarely used today.

e. Pulmonary vasodilators can also be of great benefit.

  i. **Prostaglandin E₁** is a potent pulmonary vasodilator that may also produce systemic hypotension.[21,22] When given in doses $<0.1\,\mu g/kg/min$, hypotension can be avoided. Use of higher doses may necessitate an infusion of norepinephrine to counteract the decrease in systemic vascular resistance. To minimize adverse effects on the pulmonary vasculature, this should be given directly into a left atrial line.

  ii. Inhaled **nitric oxide** (NO), also known as endothelium-derived relaxing factor, is a selective pulmonary vasodilator with minimal effect on systemic vascular resistance. Thus, it is capable of decreasing RV afterload and augmenting RV performance while maintaining systemic perfusion pressure to minimize ischemia. The usual dose is 20–40 ppm administered into the ventilatory circuit. The circuit must be designed to optimally mix O_2 and NO to generate a low level of NO_2, which is toxic to lung tissue. Measurements of the concentration of NO in the inhaled limb and NO_2 in the exhalation limb of the ventilatory circuit by chemiluminescence are essential during delivery. Ideally, a scavenger system should be attached to the exhaust port of the ventilator.[23]

    • NO should be weaned slowly to prevent a rebound increase in pulmonary vascular resistance. A general guideline is to decrease the dose no more than 20% every 30 minutes. Inhalation can be stopped once 6 ppm is reached.
    • One study has demonstrated that NO is more effective in patients undergoing coronary surgery than valve surgery, perhaps because the pulmonary bed is less reactive in valve patients.[24]
    • NO does not increase intrapulmonary shunting. It may reverse the hypoxic vasoconstriction that

is frequently noted with other pulmonary vasodilators (such as nitroprusside).

- When pulmonary hypertension is refractory to nitric oxide, the addition of dipyridamole 0.2 mg/kg IV may reduce RV afterload.[25] Dipyridamole blocks the hydrolysis of cyclic GMP in vascular smooth muscle and may also attenuate rebound pulmonary hypertension noted after NO withdrawal.

- NO in the bloodstream is rapidly metabolized to methemoglobin (metHb) and levels should be monitored; methemoglobinemia is rarely noted in adults, but can be a significant problem in young children.

   iii. Adenosine administered at a rate of 500 µg/kg/min produces significant selective pulmonary vasodilatation with subsequent increase in cardiac output.[26]

F. **Diastolic dysfunction** can be caused by impaired systolic relaxation or decreased diastolic compliance, often with an inappropriate tachycardia.[27] These problems may result from a prolonged episode of ischemia with subsequent reperfusion injury and are most prominent in the small, hypertrophied, hyperdynamic heart. The end result is a low cardiac output syndrome with a small left ventricular chamber at end-diastole yet high left-sided filling pressures. This problem can be difficult to manage and often results in end-organ dysfunction, such as renal failure, which progresses until the diastolic dysfunction improves. Although inotropic drugs are frequently given, they are of little benefit. In contrast, ACE inhibitors may improve diastolic compliance; lusitropic drugs, such as the calcium-channel blockers, may improve impaired systolic relaxation; and bradycardic drugs, such as β-blockers or calcium-channel blockers, can be used for an inappropriate tachycardia. Aggressive diuresis may also be beneficial in reducing myocardial edema that might contribute to reduced compliance.

III. Inotropic and Vasoactive Drugs

A. General comments

1. A variety of vasoactive medications are available to provide hemodynamic support for the patient with marginal myocardial function. The selection of a particular drug depends on an understanding of its mechanism of action and limitations to its use. The majority of vasoactive medications are catecholamines, the effects of which depend on their interaction with α- and β-adrenergic receptors. They elevate levels of intracellular cyclic AMP (cAMP) by β-adrenergic stimulation of adenylate cyclase.[16,28-30] In contrast, the phosphodiesterase inhibitors (amrinone, milrinone) elevate cAMP levels by inhibiting cAMP degradation. Elevation of cAMP augments calcium influx into myocardial cells and increases contractility.

   - α_1 and α_2 stimulation result in increased systemic and pulmonary vascular resistance. Cardiac α_1 receptors increase contractility and decrease the heart rate.

Table 10.4 *Hemodynamic Effects of Vasoactive Medications*

Medication	SVR	HR	PCW	CI	MAP	MVO₂
Dopamine	↓↑	↑↑	↑	↑	↓↑	↑
Dobutamine	↓	↑↑	↓	↑	↓↔↑	↑↔
Epinephrine	↓↑	↑↑	↓↑	↑	↑	↑
Amrinone/milrinone	↓↓	↑	↓	↑	↓↑	↓
Isoproterenol	↓↓	↑↑↑	↓	↑	↓↑	↑
Calcium chloride	↑↑	↔	↑	↑	↑↑	↑
Norepinephrine	↑↑↑	↑	↑↑	↑	↑↑↑	↑
Phenylephrine	↑↑	↔	↑	↔	↑↑	↔↑

↑ = increased; ↓ = decreased; ↔ = no change; ↓↑ = variable effect.
Note:
1. The effect may vary with dosage level (particularly dopamine and epinephrine), in which case the effect seen at low dose is indicated by the first arrow.
2. The relative effect is indicated by the number of arrows.
3. For some medications, an improvement in MAP may occur from the positive inotropic effect despite a reduction in SVR.
4. The effects of amrinone and calcium are not mediated by α- and β-receptors.

- β₁ stimulation results in increased contractility (inotropy), heart rate (chronotropy), and conduction (dromotropy).
- β₂ stimulation results in peripheral vasodilatation and bronchodilatation.

2. The net effects of medications that share α and β properties usually depend on the dosage level and are summarized in table 10.4. Concomitant use of several medications with selective effects may minimize the side effects of higher doses of individual medications. For example:

- Low-dose dopamine can be used to improve renal perfusion while another inotrope is used to improve myocardial performance.
- Inotropes with vasoconstrictive (α) properties can be combined with vasodilators to reduce SVR.
- Catecholamines can be combined with the phosphodiesterase inhibitors (amrinone or milrinone) to provide additive inotropic effects while achieving pulmonary and systemic vasodilatation.
- α-agents can be infused directly into the left atrium to improve SVR while a pulmonary vasodilator is infused into the right heart.

3. All vasoactive medications should be administered via controlled infusion pumps and through a central line to ensure intravenous access and prevent infiltration into peripheral tissues. The standard mixes and dosage ranges are listed in table 10.5.

4. The benefits of most vasoactive medications are noted when adequate blood levels are achieved in the systemic circulation. However, higher levels can be reached by drug infusion into the left atrium rather than the central venous circulation, which results

Table 10.5 *Mixes and Dosage Ranges for Vasoactive Medications*

Medication	Mix	Dosage Range
Dopamine	400 mg/250 mL	2–20 µg/kg/min
Dobutamine	500 mg/250 mL	2–20 µg/kg/min
Epinephrine	1 mg/250 mL	1–4 µg/min
Amrinone	200 mg/200 mL	0.75 mg/kg bolus, then 10–15 µg/kg/min
Milrinone	20 mg/200 mL	50 µg/kg bolus, then 0.375–0.75 µg/kg/min
Isoproterenol	1 mg/250 mL	0.5–10 µg/min
Norepinephrine	4 mg/250 mL	2–100 µg/min
Phenylephrine	40 mg/250 mL	10–500 µg/min

Note: *X mg placed in 250 mL gives an infusion rate of X µg (mg divided by 1000) in 15 drops of solution. For example, a 200 mg/250 mL mix gives a drip of 200 µg in 15 drops. 60 microdrops = 1 mL. 15 drops/min = 15 mL/hour.*
Note: *The final volume of the mix reflects the total volume; thus for amrinone, 50 mL of amrinone is added to 150 mL to achieve a total volume of 200 mL. For all of the other medications, the drug volume is very small.*

in partial removal or inactivation of these drugs by the lungs. Furthermore, infusion of medications such as norepinephrine or epinephrine through a left atrial line will minimize elevation of the pulmonary vascular resistance, which may contribute to RV dysfunction.[31,32]

B. **Epinephrine**

1. **Hemodynamic effects**

    a. Epinephrine is a potent β_1 inotropic agent that increases cardiac output by an increase in heart rate and contractility. At doses less than 2 µg/min, it has a β_2 effect that produces mild peripheral vasodilatation, but the blood pressure is usually maintained or elevated by the increase in cardiac output. At doses greater than 2 µg/min, α effects will increase SVR and raise the blood pressure significantly, with possible adverse effects on myocardial oxygen metabolism and function. Even at low doses, epinephrine often produces a metabolic acidosis.

    b. Epinephrine has strong β_2 properties that produce bronchodilatation.

    c. Its usefulness is often limited by the development of arrhythmias or tachycardia. One comparative study did show, however, that epinephrine at a dose of 2 µg/min caused less tachycardia than dobutamine given at a dose of 5 µg/kg/min.[33]

    d. Epinephrine delivered through a left atrial line produces a higher cardiac index with lower pulmonary pressures and pulmonary vascular resistance than when delivered through a central venous line. This may be beneficial in the patient with RV dysfunction in whom an increase in RV afterload would not be well tolerated.[31] In this situation, however, amrinone (see below) would be the preferred drug.

2. **Indications**

    a. Borderline cardiac output in the absence of tachycardia or ventricular ectopy. It can be used as a first-line drug at low doses because of its efficacy and low cost. Many centers use it as a second-line drug after dopamine or dobutamine.

    b. When the heart requires pacing for a slow heart rate. Epinephrine is frequently beneficial in improving the atrium's responsiveness to pacing at the conclusion of bypass.

    c. Bronchospasm when an inotrope is also required.

    d. Anaphylaxis (protamine reaction)

    e. Resuscitation from cardiac arrest

3. **Dosage**: starting dose is 1 µg/min (about 0.015 µg/kg/min) with a mix of 1 mg/250 mL. Dosage can be increased to 4 µg/min. Higher doses are rarely indicated in patients following cardiac surgery.

C. **Dopamine**

1. **Hemodynamic effects** depend on the dosage administered.

    a. At doses of 2–3 µg/kg/min, dopamine has a selective "dopaminergic" effect that dilates the renal arteries, producing an increase in renal blood flow and urine output. A mild β_2 effect decreases peripheral resistance and may reduce blood pressure. Even at this low dosage level, a profound tachycardia may be noted despite lack of any inotropic effect.

    b. At doses of 3–8 µg/kg/min, dopamine has a strong β_1 inotropic effect that improves contractility, and, to a variable degree, increases heart rate and the potential for arrhythmogenesis. The dopaminergic effects are still present.

    c. At doses greater than 8 µg/kg/min, there are increasing inotropic effects, but also predominant α effects that occur directly and by endogenous release of norepinephrine. These effects raise the SVR, systemic blood pressure, and filling pressures, and may adversely affect myocardial oxygen consumption and ventricular function. Concomitant use of a vasodilator, such as nitroprusside, to counteract these α effects allows for the best augmentation of cardiac output.

    d. Dopamine may increase AV conduction in atrial fibrillation/flutter.[34]

2. **Indications**

    a. Usually a first-line drug for a low cardiac output state, especially when the SVR is low and the blood pressure is marginal. Its use may be limited by the development of a profound tachycardia, even at very low doses, and occasionally by excessive urine output. In these situations, another inotrope should be selected.

    b. Beneficial to improve renal perfusion and urine output in patients with or without preexisting renal dysfunction.

This benefit may be observed during surgery as well as postoperatively.

3. **Starting dose** is 2 μg/kg/min with a mix of 400 mg/250 mL. Dosage can be increased to 20 μg/kg/min.

D. Dobutamine

1. **Hemodynamic effects**

   a. Dobutamine is a positive inotropic agent with a strong β_1 effect that increases contractility and heart rate and a mild β_2 effect that reduces SVR. There is minimal α_1 activity on the heart and peripheral vasculature. The effect on heart rate is variable and a profound tachycardia may limit its use. Blood pressure may fall slightly because of the vasodilating effect, but is generally maintained by the augmented inotropic state.

   b. Dobutamine has been compared with dopamine in several studies. Although both drugs increase myocardial oxygen demand to a comparable degree, only dobutamine is able to match this increase with augmented myocardial blood flow.[35] Furthermore, in contrast to dopamine, dobutamine reduces left ventricular wall stress by lowering preload and afterload. These changes improve myocardial oxygen balance and can further improve myocardial function.[36] This is particularly evident in volume overloaded hearts (valve replacement for mitral or aortic regurgitation).[37]

2. **Indications**

   a. Most useful when the cardiac output is marginal and there is a mild elevation in SVR. Its use is usually restricted by development of a tachycardia.

   b. Useful if dopamine produces a profound tachycardia or excessive urine output.

   c. Has a synergistic effect in improving cardiac output when used with a phosphodiesterase inhibitor (amrinone/milrinone).

3. **Starting dose** is 2 μg/kg/min using a mix of 500 mg/250 mL. Dosage can be increased to 20 μg/kg/min.

E. Amrinone (Inocor) and milrinone (Primacor)

1. **Hemodynamic effects**

   a. These are phosphodiesterase-III inhibitors that can be classified as "inodilators."[38] They improve cardiac output by reducing systemic and pulmonary vascular resistance and by a moderate positive inotropic effect. There is usually a modest increase in heart rate, a lowering of filling pressures (and thus a decrease in myocardial oxygen demand), and a moderate reduction in systemic blood pressure. Although the unloading effect produced by the decrease in SVR may contribute a great deal to their efficacy, an α-agent (phenylephrine or norepinephrine) is frequently required to maintain systemic blood pressure.

b. Because they have a different mechanism of action, synergistic effects on ventricular performance are noted when they are used with one of the catecholamines, such as dobutamine or epinephrine.[39–41]

c. When compared with dobutamine, amrinone has been shown to be associated with less increase in heart rate and fewer atrial and ventricular arrhythmias. Although a comparable increase in cardiac output can be achieved, amrinone may be associated with less increase in myocardial oxygen demand and a lower incidence of perioperative infarction.[41] Furthermore, amrinone, but not dobutamine, may reduce coronary vascular resistance, contributing to an improvement in the myocardial oxygen supply:demand ratio.[42]

2. **Indications**

a. Poor cardiac output without initial response to catecholamines or when their use is limited by tachycardia.

b. Right ventricular dysfunction associated with an elevation in PVR (pulmonary hypertension in mitral valve or cardiac transplant patients). These drugs increase RV contractility and lower PVR.

3. **Advantages and disadvantages**

a. These medications have long elimination half-lives (3.6 hours for amrinone and 2.3 hours for milrinone), which is even longer in patients with low cardiac output states. Thus, an intraoperative bolus can be used to terminate bypass and provide a few hours of additional inotropic support without the need for a continuous infusion. This should be considered due to the expense of these medications.

b. Because the hemodynamic effects persist for several hours after the drug infusion is discontinued (in contrast to the short duration of action of the catecholamines), the patient must be observed carefully for deteriorating myocardial function for several hours as the medication's effects wear off.

c. Amrinone has been associated with the development of thrombocytopenia. Therefore, platelet counts must be monitored on a daily basis. In contrast, thrombocytopenia is very rare with milrinone, which is often used for weeks at a time in patients awaiting transplantation.[43]

d. Milrinone (and presumably amrinone) causes vasodilatation of arterial conduits. Thus, it may prove beneficial in the patient with suspected coronary spasm who requires inotropic support.[44]

4. **Starting doses**

a. Amrinone: 0.75 mg/kg bolus over 10 minutes followed by a continuous infusion of 10–15 µg/kg/min with a mix of 200 mg/200 mL of normal saline. When given during surgery, a 1.5 mg/kg bolus is usually required to achieve a satisfactory plasma concentration.[45]

b. Milrinone: 50 μg/kg IV bolus over 10 minutes, followed by a continuous infusion of 0.375–0.75 μg/kg/min of a 20 mg/200 mL solution.[46,47]

F. **Isoproterenol**

1. **Hemodynamic effects**

   a. Isoproterenol has strong β_1 effects that increase cardiac output by a moderate increase in contractility and a marked increase in heart rate. Although its β_2 effect lowers SVR to a slight degree, the increased myocardial O_2 demand caused by the tachycardia limits its utility in coronary bypass patients. Isoproterenol may produce ischemia out of proportion to its chronotropic effects, and it also predisposes to ventricular arrhythmias.

   b. Isoproterenol's β_2 effect lowers pulmonary vascular resistance and reduces right heart afterload.

   c. There is a strong β_2 bronchodilatation effect.

2. **Indications**

   a. Right ventricular dysfunction associated with an elevation in PVR. Isoproterenol is both an inotrope and a pulmonary vasodilator. Like amrinone, it is particularly helpful following mitral valve surgery in patients with preexisting pulmonary hypertension.[22] It is also of value in reducing PVR, increasing heart rate, and causing ventricular relaxation following heart transplantation. Because it causes such a profound tachycardia, it has generally been supplanted by amrinone/milrinone.

   b. Bronchospasm when an inotrope is required.

   c. Bradycardia in the absence of functioning pacemaker wires. It is commonly used after heart transplantation to maintain a heart rate of 100 to 110/min.

3. **Starting dose** is 0.5 μg/min with a mix of 1 mg/250 mL. It can be increased to about 10 μg/min.

G. **Norepinephrine**

1. **Hemodynamic effects**

   a. Norepinephrine is a powerful catecholamine with both α- and β-adrenergic properties. Its predominant α effect raises SVR and blood pressure, while the β_1 effect increases contractility. The heart rate usually increases from the β effects.

   b. By increasing afterload and contractility, it usually increases myocardial oxygen demand and may prove detrimental to the ischemic or marginal myocardium. It also reduces organ system perfusion, increasing the risk of renal or visceral ischemia.

2. **Indications**

    a. Low blood pressure caused by a low SVR. This is often noted when the patient warms and vasodilates. Use of a pure α-agent is feasible if the cardiac index exceeds 2.5 L/min/m², but norepinephrine can provide some inotropic support if the cardiac index is borderline. If the cardiac index is below 2.0 L/min/m², another inotrope should probably be used in addition to or in place of norepinephrine.

    b. Norepinephrine is frequently effective in raising the blood pressure when little effect has been obtained from phenylephrine (and vice versa).

    c. It has been used as an inotrope to improve cardiac output in conjunction with a vasodilator, such as phentolamine or sodium nitroprusside, which counteracts its α effects, but this combination is used infrequently.[48]

3. **Starting dose** is 2 µg/min with a mix of 4 mg/250 mL. The dose may be increased as necessary to achieve a satisfactory blood pressure.

H. **Phenylephrine**

1. **Hemodynamic effects**

    a. Phenylephrine is a pure α-agent that increases SVR and may cause a reflex decrease in heart rate. Myocardial function may be compromised if an excessive increase in afterload is produced by phenylephrine; however, it is frequently improved by an elevation in coronary perfusion pressure that resolves myocardial ischemia.

    b. Phenylephrine has no direct cardiac effects.

2. **Indications**

    a. Hypotension from low SVR with a satisfactory cardiac output. This scenario is commonly noted at the termination of bypass and is the primary indication for its use. Comparable hemodynamics may also be noted in the ICU as the patient warms and vasodilates. The patient should be given volume infusions initially, but can then be supported with phenylephrine to maintain a systemic blood pressure around 100–110 mm Hg. Significantly higher pressures should be avoided to minimize the adverse effects of an elevated SVR on myocardial function.

    b. Phenylephrine can be used preoperatively to treat ischemia by maintaining perfusion pressure while nitroglycerin is used to reduce preload.

3. **Advantages and disadvantages**

    a. Patients often become refractory to the effects of phenylephrine after several hours of use, necessitating a change to norepinephrine. Conversely, some patients respond very poorly to norepinephrine and have an immediate blood pressure response to low-dose phenylephrine.

      b. By providing no cardiac support other than an increase in central perfusion pressures, phenylephrine has limited indications.

4. **Starting dose** is 10 μg/min with a mix of 40 mg/250 mL. The dosage can be increased as necessary (up to 500 μg/min) to maintain a satisfactory blood pressure.

I. **Calcium chloride**

1. **Hemodynamic effects.** Calcium chloride provides ionized calcium, which produces a strong but transient inotropic effect if hypocalcemia is present and a more sustained increase in SVR, even if normocalcemia is present.[49] There is little effect on heart rate. Calcium's inotropic effect is independent of any effect on cAMP. Calcium salts may attenuate the cardiotonic effects of catecholamines, such as dobutamine or epinephrine, but there is little effect on the efficacy of amrinone.[50]

2. **Indications**

      a. Frequently used at the termination of CPB to augment systemic blood pressure by either its positive inotropic or vasoconstrictive effect.

      b. To support myocardial function or blood pressure on an emergency basis until further assessment and intervention can be undertaken. *Note:* Calcium is not recommended for routine use during a cardiac arrest.

      c. Hyperkalemia (K^+ > 6.0 mEq/L)

3. **Usual dose** is 0.5–1 g slow IV bolus.

J. **Triiodothyronine (T_3)**

1. **Hemodynamic effects**

      a. T_3 has been shown to increase cardiac output and lower systemic vascular resistance in patients with depressed ventricular function.[51,52] Its positive inotropic effect results from increased aerobic metabolism and synthesis of high-energy phosphates. It causes a dose-dependent increase in myocyte contractile performance that is independent of and additive to β-adrenergic stimulation.[53]

      b. Randomized studies have not demonstrated a decrease in inotropic requirement or an improvement in overall outcome with use of T_3 upon weaning from bypass.[54] However, significant improvement in hemodynamics has been demonstrated in patients with impaired ventricular function.[55]

      c. There is some evidence that T_3 may reduce the incidence of postoperative atrial fibrillation through an unknown mechanism.[56]

2. **Indications.** The current role for T_3 appears to be as salvage when bypass cannot be terminated with maximal inotropic support and the IABP. Further evidence of its efficacy in reducing the incidence of atrial fibrillation might justify the cost of its routine use.

3. **Dosage** in various studies ranges from 0.05–0.8 µg/kg IV. We have commonly used a 20 µg IV bolus for inotropic support, although several recent studies have used a dose of 0.8 µg/kg in the operating room, followed by an infusion of 0.12 µg/kg/h for 6 hours.[52,54–56]

K. **Other modalities to treat low cardiac output**

1. **Glucose-insulin-potassium (GIK).** GIK has been demonstrated to have an inotropic effect on the failing myocardium after cardioplegic arrest. It provides metabolic support to the myocardium by increasing anaerobic glycolysis, lowering free fatty acid levels, preserving intracellular glycogen stores, and stabilizing membrane function. The mixture contains 50% glucose, 80 units/L of regular insulin, and 100 mEq/L of potassium infused at a rate of 1 mL/kg/h.[57,58]

2. **Enoximone** is a phosphodiesterase inhibitor with hemodynamic effects similar to those of amrinone. It decreases systemic, pulmonary, and coronary resistance, and has a positive inotropic effect with minimal alteration in heart rate.[59] Its vasodilating properties may be less than those of amrinone, but it still usually requires a vasoconstrictor to offset the vasodilatory effects of the bolus injection. It also has a synergistic effect when given with a catecholamine. It is not associated with the development of thrombocytopenia. It is given as a 0.5–1.0 mg/kg bolus at the termination of bypass.

L. **Selection of vasoactive medications**

1. The selection of a vasoactive medication should be based on several factors:

   a. An adequate understanding of the underlying cardiac pathophysiology derived from hemodynamic measurements and often echocardiography.

   b. Knowledge of the α, β, or nonadrenergic hemodynamic effects of these medications and their anticipated influence on preload, afterload, heart rate, and contractility.

2. Vasoactive medications are usually started in the operating room and maintained for about 6–12 hours while the heart recovers from the period of ischemia/reperfusion. The doses are adjusted as the patient's hemodynamic parameters improve. Occasionally, when the heart demonstrates persistent "stunning" or has sustained an intraoperative infarction, pharmacologic support and/or an IABP may be necessary for several days.

3. When the cardiac index is satisfactory ($>2.2 L/min/m^2$) but the blood pressure is low, an α-agent should be selected. Phenylephrine is commonly used in the operating room, but norepinephrine is probably a better drug to use in that it provides some β effects that are beneficial during the early phase of myocardial recovery. Systolic blood pressure need only be maintained around 100 mm Hg (mean pressure >80 mm Hg) to minimize the increase in afterload.

4. When the cardiac index remains marginal ($<$2.0–2.2 L/min/m^2) after optimizing volume status, heart rate and rhythm, an inotropic agent should be selected. The first-line drugs are usually dopamine, dobutamine, or epinephrine. The major limitation to their use is the development of tachycardia, which tends to be less prominent with use of low-dose epinephrine.[33] At inotropic levels, dopamine and epinephrine tend to raise SVR, whereas dobutamine lowers SVR. If a satisfactory cardiac output has been achieved and the blood pressure is elevated, addition of a vasodilator is beneficial. If the blood pressure is low, an α-agent can be added.

5. If the cardiac output remains marginal despite moderate doses of drugs (dopamine 10 μg/kg/min, dobutamine 10 μg/kg/min, epinephrine 3–4 μg/min), a second drug should be selected. If dopamine or dobutamine was used initially, epinephrine is usually chosen unless a tachycardia is present. If epinephrine was used initially, dobutamine or amrinone is added. Amrinone usually causes a significant increase in cardiac output, but frequently requires use of norepinephrine to maintain SVR. The β effect of norepinephrine may further improve contractility, but it can increase the heart rate. The α effect may reduce organ system perfusion (especially renal blood flow) and it may compromise flow in arterial conduits (such as the IMA or radial artery).[60] If the cardiac index remains marginal despite the use of two medications, an intraaortic balloon should be inserted.

6. If the patient cannot be weaned from bypass or has hemodynamic evidence of cardiogenic shock (PCWP $>$ 20 mm Hg, CI $<$ 2.0 L/min/m^2) despite medications and the IABP, a circulatory assist device should be considered.

M. Vasoactive medications provide specific hemodynamic benefits, but their use may be limited by the development of adverse effects. Nearly all of the catecholamines will increase myocardial oxygen demand by increasing heart rate and contractility. Other side effects that may necessitate changing to or addition of another medication include:

1. Arrhythmogenesis and tachycardia (epinephrine, isoproterenol, dobutamine, dopamine)

2. Vasoconstriction and poor renal, splanchnic, and peripheral perfusion (norepinephrine, phenylephrine)

3. Vasodilatation that requires α-agents to support systemic blood pressure with potential adverse effects on renal perfusion (amrinone)

4. Excessive urine output (dopamine)

5. Thrombocytopenia (amrinone)

6. Cyanide and thiocyanate toxicity (nitroprusside)

7. Methemoglobinemia (nitroglycerin)

N. **Weaning of vasoactive medications**

1. α-agents should generally be weaned first. Their use should ideally be restricted to increasing the SVR to support blood pressure when

the cardiac output is satisfactory. However, there are circumstances when α-agents are required to maintain cerebral and coronary perfusion in the face of a poor cardiac output. In these desperate life-saving situations, the resultant intense peripheral vasoconstriction can compromise organ system and peripheral perfusion, causing renal, mesenteric, and peripheral ischemia, acidosis, and frequently death.

   a. In the routine patient, SVR and blood pressure increase when the anesthetic and sedative medications wear off, the patient awakens and develops increased intrinsic sympathetic tone, and when myocardial function improves. At this point the α-agents can be stopped.

   b. When amrinone or the IABP is used to support myocardial function, an α-agent is frequently required to counteract the excellent unloading and decrease in SVR that is achieved. It may not be possible to wean the α-agent before the amrinone or IABP is weaned, because the patient may become hypotensive despite an excellent cardiac output. It is usually necessary to wean the α-agent in conjunction with the weaning of the other modalities.

   c. An occasional patient who has sustained a small perioperative infarction will have an excellent cardiac output but a low SVR. This requires temporary α support until the blood pressure improves spontaneously.

2. The stronger positive inotropes with the most potential detrimental effects on myocardial metabolism should be weaned next. Those that possess α properties should be decreased to doses at which these effects do not occur.

   a. Epinephrine should be weaned first. The dosage should preferably be kept at 2 μg/min or less to avoid any α effects. Another drug should be selected if epinephrine causes tachycardia or arrhythmias.

   b. Dobutamine (which lacks any α effects) and dopamine should then be weaned, starting with the drug given at the higher dosage. Dopamine should be decreased to doses less than 8–10 μg/kg/min, at which point its α effects should dissipate but the β effects will be maintained. If tachycardia or an excessive urine output is present, another drug should be selected.

   c. Amrinone has few deleterious effects on myocardial function, although the concomitant use of an α-agent to support SVR might compromise renal perfusion. Because of its long half-life, amrinone should be weaned hours before the withdrawal of other major support modalities (IABP). It can usually be weaned from the maintenance dose of 10–15 μg/kg/min by halving the dose and then stopping it a few hours later. The cardiac output must be monitored to observe for potential deterioration in myocardial function that may occur several hours after the infusion has been stopped. Not infrequently, the patient may require the reinstitution of inotropic support at that point. Early weaning of amrinone (or conversion to milrinone) should also be considered when the patient develops progressive thrombocytopenia. It is not always clear whether this is caused by amrinone or other coexisting problems, such as heparin-induced thrombocytopenia or IABP-induced platelet destruction.

d. IABP removal may be performed once the patient is on low doses of inotropic support, such as epinephrine at 1 µg/min or dobutamine or dopamine at 5 µg/kg/min.

e. The use of vasoactive medications in patients on circulatory assist devices depends on the extent of support provided and the function of the unsupported ventricle. In patients receiving univentricular support, inotropic medications may be necessary to improve function of the unassisted ventricle. Patients with biventricular support are usually given only α-agents to support systemic resistance. If the device is being used for temporary support, rather than as a bridge to transplantation, inotropes may be given to assess ventricular function and reserve as flows are transiently reduced. If ventricular function is recovering, a drug such as milrinone may be given to allow for successful removal of the device.

O. Vasodilators are commonly used during the early phase of postoperative recovery to reduce blood pressure when the patient is hypothermic, vasoconstricted, and hypertensive. They are weaned off as the patient vasodilates to maintain a systolic blood pressure of 100–120 mm Hg. Vasodilators may also be used alone or in conjunction with inotropic medications to improve myocardial function by lowering SVR. In this situation, they are weaned concomitantly with the inotropes, depending on the cardiac output and the blood pressure.

1. Continued use of antihypertensive medications is usually required in patients with a preexisting history of hypertension. The potent intravenous vasodilators used in the ICU should then be converted to oral medications. The appropriate selection of medication depends on the status of myocardial and renal function. The more commonly used medications include β-blockers, calcium-channel blockers, venodilators (nitrates), and the angiotensin-converting enzyme (ACE) inhibitors. The latter should be considered in patients with poor ventricular function (ejection fraction <35%) because of their beneficial effects on myocardial performance and survival.

2. Oral medications can be given down the nasogastric tube. If the patient cannot take oral drugs or has an ileus, medications such as topical nitroglycerin, intravenous nicardipine or diltiazem, or sublingual nifedipine can be used. These do not require continuous on-line arterial monitoring.

IV. Intraaortic Balloon Counterpulsation

Intraaortic balloon counterpulsation is a technique that provides hemodynamic support and/or control of ischemia both before and after surgery.[61] In contrast to most inotropic agents, the intraaortic balloon pump (IABP) provides physiologic assistance to the failing heart by decreasing myocardial oxygen demand and improving coronary perfusion. Although it is an invasive technique with several potential complications, it has proven invaluable in improving the results of surgery in high-risk patients and allowing for the survival of many patients with postcardiotomy ventricular dysfunction. The survival rate of patients requiring postoperative IABP support approximates 60% to 70%.[62]

A. **Indications**

1. Perioperative ischemia

2. Unloading for cardiogenic shock or mechanical complications of myocardial infarction (acute mitral regurgitation, ventricular septal rupture)

3. Postoperative low cardiac output syndrome unresponsive to moderate doses of inotropic agents

4. Acute deterioration of myocardial function to provide temporary support or a bridge to transplantation

B. **Contraindications**

1. Aortic insufficiency

2. Aortic dissection

3. Severe aortic and peripheral vascular atherosclerosis (balloon can be inserted via the ascending aorta)

C. **Principles**

1. It reduces the impedance to LV ejection ("unloads the heart") by rapid deflation just before ventricular systole.

2. It increases diastolic coronary perfusion pressure by rapid inflation just after aortic valve closure.

3. This sequence reduces the time-tension index (systolic wall tension) and increases the diastolic pressure-time index, favorably altering the myocardial oxygen supply : demand ratio.

D. **Insertion techniques**

1. Percutaneous insertion is performed by the Seldinger technique, placing the balloon through a sheath and over a guidewire. The sheath can be left in place or removed from the artery (especially if the femoral artery is small). Some systems are "sheathless" to minimize occlusion of the femoral vessels, but can lead to shearing of the balloon in patients with significant aortoiliac atherosclerosis. The balloon is situated just distal to the left subclavian artery (figure 10.1). Percutaneous insertion is associated with a significant risk of limb ischemia in patients with known peripheral vascular disease.[63]

2. Surgical insertion can be accomplished by exposing the femoral artery and placing the balloon through a sidearm graft or directly into the vessel through an arteriotomy or a percutaneous sheath. Transthoracic balloon placement via the ascending aorta may be necessary if severe aortoiliac disease is present.

DIASTOLE   SYSTOLE

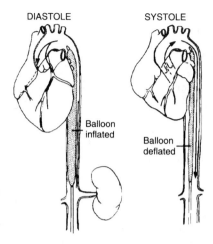

Balloon
inflated

Balloon
deflated

Figure 10.1 *The intraaortic balloon is
positioned just distal to the left subclavian
artery. Balloon inflation occurs in early
diastole and improves coronary perfusion
pressure. Deflation occurs just before
systole to reduce the impedance to left
ventricular ejection. (Reproduced with
permission from Maccioli GA, Lucas WJ,
Norfleet EA. The intra-aortic balloon
pump: a review. J Cardiothorac Anesthesia
1988;2:365–73.)*

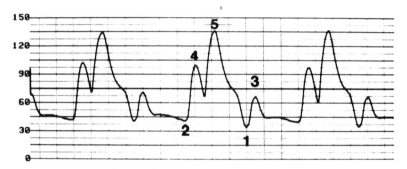

Figure 10.2 *Intraaortic balloon tracing at 1:2 inflation ratio. Note that the balloon
aortic end-diastolic pressure (1) is lower than the patient's aortic end-diastolic pressure
(2), and the balloon-assisted peak systolic pressure (3) is lower than the systolic pressure
that is generated without a preceding assisted beat (4). These changes reflect a decreased
impedance to ejection during systole. Coronary perfusion pressure is increased by
diastolic augmentation achieved by balloon inflation (5).*

    E. **IABP timing** is performed from the ECG or the arterial waveform.

        1. ECG: input to the balloon console is provided from skin leads or
the bedside monitor. Inflation is set for the peak of the T wave
at the end of systole with deflation set just before or on the R wave.
The use of bipolar pacing eliminates the interpretation of pacing
spikes as QRS complexes by the console.

        2. Arterial waveform: inflation should occur at the dicrotic notch with
deflation just before the onset of the aortic upstroke. This method
is especially useful in the operating room where electrocautery
may interfere with the ECG signal.

        3. A typical arterial waveform during a 1:2 ratio of IABP inflation is
demonstrated in figure 10.2. This shows the systolic unloading

(decrease in the balloon-assisted systolic and diastolic pressures) and the diastolic augmentation that are achieved with the IABP.

F. **IABP problems and complications**

1. **Inability to balloon.** Once the balloon is situated properly and has unwrapped, satisfactory ballooning should be achieved by proper timing of inflation and deflation. However, unsatisfactory ballooning can occur in the following situations.

    a. Unipolar atrial pacing. This produces a large atrial pacing spike that can be interpreted by the console as a QRS complex leading to inappropriate inflation. Use of bipolar pacing eliminates this problem. Most monitoring equipment suppresses pacing signals.

    b. Rapid rates. Some balloon consoles are unable to inflate and deflate fast enough to accommodate heart rates over 150 (usually when there is a rapid ventricular response to atrial fibrillation). Augmentation can be performed at a 1:2 ratio.

    c. Arrhythmias. Atrial and ventricular ectopy can disrupt normal inflation and deflation patterns and must be treated.

    d. Volume loss from the balloon detected by the console monitor alarms. This indicates a leak in the system, either at the connectors or from the balloon itself. Volume loss may also indicate that the balloon has not unwrapped properly, preventing proper inflation.

    e. Balloon rupture. When blood appears in the balloon tubing, the balloon has perforated. Escape of gas (usually helium) from the balloon into the bloodstream can occur. The balloon must be removed immediately. Difficulty with removal (balloon entrapment) may be encountered if thrombus forms within the balloon. Most consoles have alarms that will call attention to this problem and will prevent the device from inflating.

2. **Vascular complications**

    a. Catastrophic complications such as aortic dissection or rupture of the iliac artery or aorta are fortunately very uncommon. Paraplegia can result from development of a periadventitial aortic hematoma or embolization of atherosclerotic debris.

    b. Embolization to visceral vessels, especially the renal arteries, can occur in the presence of significant aortic atherosclerosis. Renal ischemia may occur if the balloon is situated too low and inflates below the level of the diaphragm. This apparently does not affect mesenteric flow.[64,65] Restriction of flow in an internal mammary artery may occur if the balloon has been passed too proximally and wedges into the subclavian artery.[66]

    c. Distal ischemia is the most common complication of indwelling balloons, occurring in about 5–10% of patients.

It is seen more commonly when the balloon has been placed percutaneously. The balloon and sheath occupy a substantial proportion of the cross-sectional area of the femoral artery and can compromise distal perfusion. This is especially true in women with small femoral arteries and patients with iliofemoral occlusive disease. Thrombosis near the insertion site or distal thromboembolism can occur. Use of intravenous heparin (maintaining a PTT of 1.5–2 times control) is advisable to minimize ischemic and thromboembolic problems if the balloon remains in place for more than a few days after surgery.

d. The presence of distal pulses or Doppler signals must be assessed in all patients with an IABP. Although distal perfusion may improve if ischemia is caused temporarily by peripheral vasoconstriction from hypothermia, a low cardiac output state, or use of vasopressors, persistent ischemia jeopardizes the viability of the distal leg. Options at this time include:

   i. Removing the sheath from the femoral artery if the balloon has been placed percutaneously.

   ii. Removing the balloon if the patient appears to be hemodynamically stable; femoral exploration is indicated if adequate distal perfusion cannot be obtained.

   iii. Removing the balloon and placing it in the contralateral femoral artery if the patient is IABP-dependent. Using a balloon with a smaller caliber sheath (9.5F) may be helpful.

   iv. Performing a femoro-femoral bypass if the contralateral pulse is satisfactory.

   v. Considering placement of a transthoracic balloon.

e. Long-term follow-up of patients treated with the IABP has shown that nearly 20% will develop evidence of progressive lower limb ischemia. This is more common in patients who have smoked cigarettes, had developed acute ischemia during IABP usage, or had the IABP inserted during a period of cardiogenic shock.[67]

3. **Thrombocytopenia**. The mechanical action of persistent inflation and deflation activates and destroys circulating platelets. It is not always clear whether progressive thrombocytopenia is caused by the IABP or medications that the patient may be receiving, such as heparin or amrinone. Platelet counts must be checked at least on a daily basis.

G. Weaning of the IABP

1. IABP support can be withdrawn when the cardiac output is satisfactory on minimal inotropic support (usually less than 5 μg/kg/min of either dopamine or dobutamine or 1 μg/min of epinephrine). However, earlier removal may be indicated if complications develop, such as leg ischemia, balloon malfunction, thrombocytopenia, or infection.

2. Weaning is initiated by decreasing the inflation ratio from 1:1 to 1:2 for about 4–6 hours, and then to 1:3 or 1:4 (depending on which console device is used) for a few more hours.

3. Removal can be achieved if hemodynamics remain stable when the inflation ratio is reduced. Serial measurements of filling pressures and cardiac outputs should be evaluated. Remember that the IABP produces efficient unloading, and the blood pressure usually is lower on the bedside monitor during balloon assistance than with an unassisted beat (actually the diastolic pressure is higher, but the true systolic pressure is lower). Thus, visual improvement in blood pressure with weaning of the IABP is not, by itself, a sensitive measure of the patient's progress.

H. IABP removal techniques

1. Balloons inserted by the percutaneous technique can usually be removed percutaneously. This is performed by compressing the groin distal to the insertion site as the balloon is removed, allowing blood to flush out the skin wound for several heart beats, and then compressing just proximal to the skin hole where the arterial puncture site is located (figure 10.3).[68] Pressure must be maintained for at least 45 minutes to ensure satisfactory thrombus formation at the puncture site.

2. **Note:** Coagulation parameters must be corrected before percutaneous removal or the patient may require groin exploration for persistent hemorrhage or a false aneurysm.

3. Surgical removal should be considered in patients with small or diseased vessels and in those with very weak pulses or Doppler

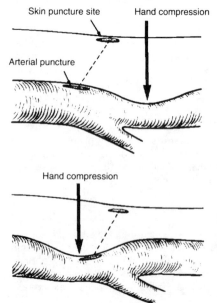

Skin puncture site   Hand compression

Arterial puncture

Hand compression

Figure 10.3 *Technique of percutaneous balloon removal. Initial compression is held below the level of the arterial puncture site to allow for flushing of blood. However, subsequent pressure should be maintained over the arterial puncture site to prevent bleeding. Note that the hole in the artery lies more cephalad than the hole in the skin. (Modified from Rodigas PC, Finnegan JO. Technique for removal of percutaneously placed intraaortic balloons. Ann Thorac Surg 1992;40:80–1.)*

signals with the balloon in place.[69] These are patients in whom a thrombectomy and embolectomy may be anticipated. If the IABP has been in place for more than 5 days, percutaneous removal can be performed, but there is a greater chance that surgical repair of the femoral artery may be required.

V.   Circulatory Assist Devices

A. If a patient cannot be weaned from cardiopulmonary bypass despite maximal pharmacologic support and use of the IABP, consideration should be given to placement of a circulatory assist device.[70,71] These devices provide flow to support the systemic or pulmonary circulation while awaiting recovery of myocardial function. Short-term devices (nonimplantable) should be considered when recovery of function is anticipated. However, when chances for recovery are remote—often due to extensive perioperative infarction or biventricular failure—circulatory assist with long-term (implantable) devices should be considered only if the patient is considered a suitable candidate for transplantation.[72] Use of pulsatile pumps can usually improve multiorgan system function and improve the clinical status of potential transplant recipients.[73]

B. **Left ventricular assist devices (LVADs)**

1. LVADs provide systemic perfusion while decompressing the left ventricle, permitting it to undergo metabolic and functional recovery. LV wall stress is reduced by about 80% with a 40% decrease in myocardial oxygen demand. LVAD flow is dependent on adequate intravascular volume and right ventricular function.

2. **Indications**. See table 10.6.

Table 10.6   *Indications for Circulatory Assist Devices*

1. Complete and adequate cardiac surgical procedure

2. Correction of all metabolic problems (ABGs, acid-base, electrolytes)

3. Inability to wean from bypass despite maximal pharmacologic therapy and use of the IABP

4. Cardiac index $<1.8–2\,L/min/m^2$

LVAD	RVAD	BiVAD
Systolic BP $<90\,mmHg$	RA pressure $>20\,mmHg$	RA pressure $>20–25\,mmHg$
LA pressure $>20\,mmHg$	LA pressure $<15\,mmHg$	LA pressure $>20\,mmHg$
SVR >2100 dynes-sec/cm^5	No TR	No TR
Urine output $<20\,mL/h$		Inability to maintain LVAD flow $>2.0\,L/min/m^2$ with RA pressure $>20\,mmHg$

LVAD = left ventricular assist device; RVAD = right ventricular assist device; BiVAD = biventricular assist device.

3. **Technique.** Depending on the device used, drainage is provided from the left atrium or left ventricle with return of blood to the aorta (figure 10.4). A left atrial catheter may be inserted for accurate monitoring of filling pressures.

4. **Management** during LVAD support

   a. LVAD flow is initiated to achieve a systemic flow of 2.2 L/min/m² with an LA pressure of 10–15 mm Hg. Inability to achieve satisfactory flow indicates either hypovolemia, improper position of the drainage catheter, or RV failure. Adequacy of tissue perfusion can be assessed by mixed venous oxygen saturations.

   b. Inotropic support should generally be stopped to decrease myocardial oxygen demand, but it may be required to support moderate RV dysfunction. α-agents may be necessary to support systemic resistance, aiming to maintain a mean arterial pressure >75 mm Hg.

   c. Heparinization to achieve an ACT of 175–200 seconds is recommended for most assist devices (except the HeartMate) once perioperative bleeding has ceased. An initial infusion of 500 units/h of heparin usually suffices, although most patients become heparin resistant. If pump flow is transiently

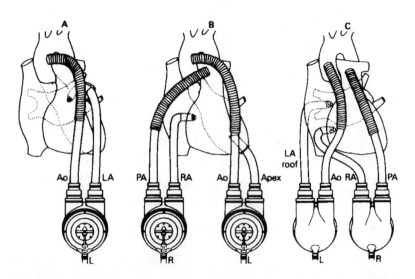

Figure 10.4 *Cannulation techniques for ventricular assist devices. (A) LVAD with left atrial and aortic cannulation. (B) BiVAD setup. The RVAD consists of right atrial and pulmonary artery cannulation. The LVAD cannulation sites are the left ventricular apex and the aorta. (C) BiVAD setup with LVAD drainage from the roof of the left atrium. The Thoratec device is demonstrated in this diagram, but the cannulation sites are similar for nearly all assist devices. (Reprinted with permission of the New England Journal of Medicine, from Farrar DJ, Hill JD, Gray LA Jr, et al. Heterotopic prosthetic ventricles as a bridge to cardiac transplantation. A multicenter study in 29 patients. N Engl J Med 1988;318:333–40.)*

decreased to less than 1.5 L/min, additional heparinization is recommended to achieve an ACT of 200–250 seconds.

d. After at least 48 hours of support, left ventricular function is assessed by transesophageal echocardiography (TEE) during partial support. If there is recovery of function, flow may be weaned to a minimal flow rate of 2 L/min (to reduce the risk of thromboembolism) with careful observation of hemodynamic parameters (cardiac output, filling pressures, systemic pressure). Low-dose inotropic support can be initiated during the weaning process. Soon thereafter, the patient can be brought to the operating room and the heart observed for a short period of time at low flow. If the heart can sustain adequate hemodynamics and appears by echocardiography to have recovered adequate function, the device is removed. If an IABP was used (in patients with nonpulsatile devices), it can generally be removed the day following LVAD removal.

5. **Overall results.** Weaning has been accomplished in about 50% of patients receiving LVAD assist with 25–30% of patients surviving to be discharged from the hospital. Improved survival is noted in patients with preserved RV function, no evidence of a perioperative MI, and recovery of LV function within 48–72 hours. In patients receiving the HeartMate device, almost 70% of patients have survived to be successfully transplanted.

C. **Right ventricular assist devices (RVADs)**

1. RVADs provide support of the pulmonary circulation while decompressing the right ventricle allowing it to recover function. RV failure may result from RV infarction, worsening of preexisting RV dysfunction caused by pulmonary hypertension, or poor intraoperative protection. One of the main contributing factors to RV dysfunction is elevation in pulmonary vascular resistance, which can often be attributed to the activation of cytokine pathways from blood products. Achieving satisfactory systemic flow depends on adequate LV function.[74]

2. **Indications**. See table 10.6.

3. **Technique.** Drainage is provided from the right atrium with return of desaturated blood to the pulmonary artery (see figure 10.4).

4. **Management** during RVAD support

a. RVAD flow is initiated to achieve a flow rate of 2.2 L/min/m^2, increasing the LA pressure to 15 mm Hg while maintaining an RA pressure of 5–10 mm Hg. Inability to achieve satisfactory flow rates may indicate hypovolemia or improper position of the drainage catheter. If the intravascular volume is adequate, systemic hypotension may be the result of impaired LV function that may require inotropic, IABP, or LVAD support. It may also result from systemic vasodilatation that requires use of an α-agent. TEE is helpful in evaluating the status of LV function.

     b. The requirement for heparinization is similar to that for LVADs.

     c. Assessment of myocardial recovery by TEE and weaning of the device are similar to LVADs. Thermodilution cardiac outputs can be used to determine right ventricular recovery when the flow rate is transiently reduced to low levels of support.

  5. **Overall results.** Patients receiving RVADs have a poor prognosis. Weaning has been accomplished in about 35% of patients with 25% of patients surviving to be discharged from the hospital.

D. Biventricular assist devices (BiVADs)

  1. Biventricular failure is noted in about 10–15% of patients who require assist devices after bypass. BiVADs provide support of both the pulmonary and systemic circulations and can function during periods of ventricular fibrillation. Although the need for assistance may not be evident from the outset, left ventricular decompression often unmasks dysfunction of the right ventricle by increasing septal shift and RV stroke work.[75] Other factors contributing to RV dysfunction include an increase in PVR from blood transfusions, LV dysfunction, or vasopressors, and RV ischemia from systemic hypotension.

     a. Hemodynamic risk factors for RV failure after LVAD placement are not well defined. One study did not find any correlation between pulmonary hypertension, RA pressure, RV ejection fraction, cardiac index or the need for an RVAD.[76] Another reported that an RA pressure greater than 20 mm Hg and a transpulmonary gradient greater than 16 mm before LVAD implantation and a decrease in mean PA pressure of less than 10 mm Hg after LVAD placement were predictors of RV dysfunction after LVAD implantation.[77]

     b. Nitric oxide is very beneficial in reducing RV afterload after LVAD implantation and can often obviate the need to place an RV assist device.[78]

  2. **Indications.** See table 10.6.

  3. **Technique.** BiVAD support incorporates the techniques noted above for LVAD and RVAD connections (see figure 10.4).

  4. **Management** during BiVAD support

     a. Sequential manipulations of RVAD and LVAD flow are used to achieve a systemic flow rate of 2.2 L/min/m². The RVAD flow is increased to raise the LA pressure to 15 to 20 mm Hg, and then the LVAD flow is increased to reduce the LA pressure to 5 to 10 mm Hg. Inability to achieve satisfactory flow rates usually indicates hypovolemia or catheter malposition. Left- and right-sided flow rates may differ because of varying contributions of the native ventricles to pulmonary or systemic flow.

     b. Heparin requirements are similar to those noted above.

c. Assessment of recovery and weaning are similar to the methods described for RVAD and LVAD devices.

5. **Overall results**. Weaning has been accomplished in about 35% of patients, with only 20% of patients surviving to be discharged from the hospital. These poor results reflect the adverse impact of biventricular failure on survival.

E. **Devices available to provide ventricular assist**

1. **Nonpulsatile pumps**

a. Nonpulsatile centrifugal pumps (Bio-Medicus, Sarns Delphin) are the most readily available and easy-to-use systems for uni- or biventricular support. They can only be used for short-term support (about 7–10 days) because hemolysis and end-organ damage may develop with longer-term use.

b. The Hemopump is a nonpulsatile rotary pump that uses axial flow technology to withdraw blood from the left ventricle and pump it into the aorta. This device is inserted through the femoral artery and situated across the aortic valve into the left ventricle. It has been shown to improve blood supply to ischemic zones and produce diastolic and systolic unloading.

2. **Pulsatile pumps**

a. The Abiomed BVS 5000 system is a pulsatile pneumatic device that is located at the patient's bedside (figures 10.5 and 10.6). It can provide uni- or biventricular support. It is indicated primarily for temporary support, and its use should generally be restricted to about 2 weeks. It functions in series with the heart, with ejection occurring once the bladder has reached a designated volume. It requires anticoagulation with an ACT of 150–200 seconds. One of its drawbacks is the formation of fibrinous clot in the outflow chamber that may give rise to thromboembolism.

b. The Thoratec VAD is a pulsatile pneumatic paracorporeal device that lies on the abdominal wall. The patient is tethered only by the pneumatic drive line. Two separate units are required for biventricular support. This device can provide long-term temporary support and can be used as a bridge to transplantation. It also requires full anticoagulation.

c. The ThermoCardiosystems HeartMate 1000 VAD is an implantable, pulsatile, pneumatic device that can provide only left ventricular assist (figure 10.7). Blood drains from the LV apex through a valve into the device which then ejects when the chamber is filled or at a fixed rate.

i. This device has a unique textured surface that decreases the risk of thromboembolism and does not require heparinization until the flow rate is reduced below 2 L/min. Most patients can be managed with aspirin alone.

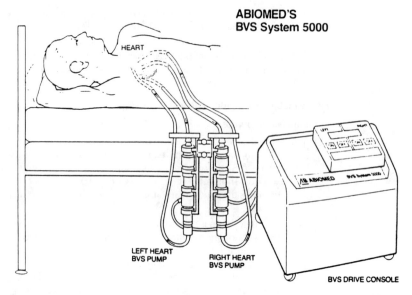

Figure 10.5   *The Abiomed BVS 5000 System. The devices are located at the patient's bedside and are connected to the drive console for pneumatic activation. (Courtesy of Abiomed, Inc.)*

    ii. This device is used nearly exclusively as a bridge to transplantation. Its low complication rate and efficacy in providing pulsatile flow allow for correction of pre-existing organ system dysfunction prior to transplantation. Nearly 70% of patients receiving the device are successfully transplanted.

    iii. A vented electric system has been undergoing investigative trials since 1991 and should be commercially available in mid-1998. This system allows the patient to ambulate with a battery pack instead of being tethered to a pneumatic drive line.

    iv. If a patient receiving a HeartMate requires RVAD support, the Abiomed system is usually selected.

  d.   The Novacor LVAS is an implantable, pulsatile, electrical device that can provide only left ventricular assist. It functions like the HeartMate system and also has a relatively low incidence of thromboembolism but does require anticoagulation. This device is used nearly exclusively as a bridge to transplantation.

F.   **Complications**. Continuing improvements in biocompatibility have reduced the incidence of thromboembolism and blood element damage associated with the long-term use of the pneumatic and electrically-driven circulatory assist devices. However, common complications include the following:

ABIOMED BVS 5000 BLOOD PUMP

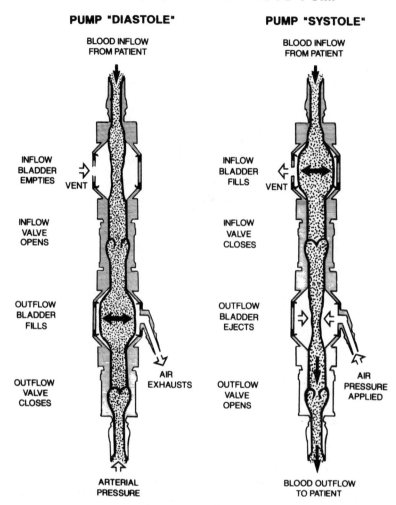

Figure 10.6 *The Abiomed BVS 5000 System. A cross-sectional view of the heart pumps during systole and diastole. (Courtesy of Abiomed, Inc.)*

1. Mediastinal bleeding. Use of aprotinin at the time of device implantation has been successful in reducing transfusion requirements. Nonetheless, because of the large dead space around the catheters in the mediastinum, many patients require reexploration for evacuation of mediastinal clot that can cause tamponade (manifest by inadequate drainage into the device). Contributing factors are the requirement for anticoagulation for most devices and the occurrence of fibrinolysis and platelet activation due to the extracorporeal circuit.[79]

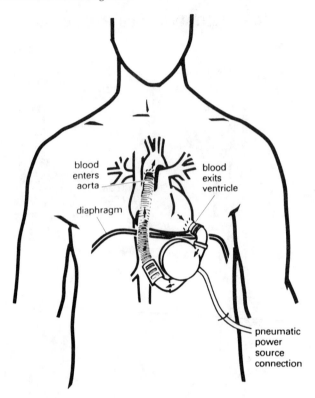

blood enters aorta

blood exits ventricle

diaphragm

pneumatic power source connection

Figure 10.7   *The HeartMate 1000 LVAD system. The device rests in a preperitoneal pocket in the left upper quadrant. Blood enters the device through an apical cannulation site and is pumped through a graft sewn to the ascending aorta. Porcine valves are incorporated into inflow and outflow grafts. (Courtesy of ThermoCardiosystems, Inc.)*

2. Mediastinitis and sepsis. The risk of infection with most devices ranges between 25–45%. Commonly the patient is debilitated, malnourished, and poorly mobilized and has numerous intravascular and other invasive catheters that can become colonized. Infection also predisposes to thromboembolism. The infection risk is reduced if the cannulas are brought out through separate stab wounds and the sternum can be closed primarily. The risk is lowest with the implantable devices. The presence of infection, unless it involves the blood contacting surfaces, has not been shown to impair survival or the results of transplantation for patients receiving the HeartMate device.

3. Thromboembolism resulting in stroke has been noted in about 10% of patients, although the incidence is only about 3% in patients with the HeartMate device, even in the absence of anticoagulation. Clot formation within other devices occurs despite careful attention to anticoagulation.

4. Malignant ventricular arrhythmias may develop as a result of myocardial ischemia, infarction, or the use of catecholamines. They may also originate from an arrhythmogenic focus in a dilated myopathic ventricle. BiVADs function during VF, as can LVADs as long as the PVR is not high. Fibrillation may foster thrombus formation in the ventricles and should be treated aggressively.

5. Renal failure is less common with pulsatile devices and is usually caused by prolonged episodes of hypotension or low cardiac output prior to insertion of the devices.

6. Respiratory failure is usually attributable to a prolonged duration of cardiopulmonary bypass, sepsis, use of multiple blood products, and perhaps a long period of nonpulsatile flow with certain devices.

7. Vasodilatory shock due to inappropriately low levels of vasopressin is not uncommon in patients requiring placement of LVADs. In fact, vasopressin hypersensitivity may be noted. Use of arginine vasopressin 0.1 U/min effectively increases mean arterial pressure in these patients.[19]

VI. Special Concerns

A. **Coronary vasospasm** has become increasingly recognized as a cause of postoperative morbidity and mortality following coronary artery bypass grafting (CABG). It can affect normal coronary arteries, bypassed vessels, saphenous vein grafts, or arterial grafts (IMA, radial or gastroepiploic artery).[80]

1. **Etiology** is speculative; it is possibly related to calcium infusions, hypothermia, increased α-adrenergic tone, release of platelet thromboxane A_2, or rebound from withdrawal of calcium-channel blockers used preoperatively. It is more commonly noted in young women with small coronary arteries.

2. **Diagnosis** of spasm can be extremely difficult to make. It is generally manifested by:
   a. ST elevation in multiple leads
   b. Hemodynamic collapse (low cardiac output, hypotension)
   c. Ventricular arrhythmias
   d. Heart block

3. The differential diagnosis of the scenario of cardiovascular instability, arrhythmias, and ECG changes must include other potential problems, such as preexisting myocardial dysfunction or ventricular arrhythmias, myocardial ischemia or infarction, reperfusion injury, or graft stenosis or occlusion subsequent to an operation. Coronary angiography may be necessary to make the appropriate diagnosis if there is no response to therapy. Angiography will usually demonstrate sluggish flow through grafts, diffuse spasm, and poor flow into distal native vessels. Resolution of spasm with intracoronary nitroglycerin or verapamil confirms the diagnosis. Differentiation from technical problems at the anastomosis can be difficult due to poor flow. If there is little response to pharmacologic manipulation, reexploration may be indicated.

4. **Treatment**

    a. Optimize oxygenation and correct acidosis

    b. Optimize preload, afterload, heart rate, and contractility. If an inotrope is indicated, amrinone or milrinone are the best choices in that they are potent vasodilators of the internal mammary artery and perhaps of native vessels as well.[44]

    c. Select a calcium-channel blocker:

        i. Nifedipine 10 mg SL, then 30 mg per NG every 6 hours

        ii. IV diltiazem drip: 0.25 mg/kg IV bolus over 2 minutes, followed by a repeat bolus of 0.35 mg/kg 15 minutes later. A continuous infusion is then given at a rate of 5–15 mg/h using a 250 mg/250 mL mix.

        iii. IV verapamil drip: 0.1 mg/kg bolus, followed by a 2–5 µg/kg/min infusion of a 120 mg/250 mL mix.

    d. IV nitroglycerin starting at 0.5 µg/kg/min and raise as tolerated (this may improve ischemia, but usually does not resolve vasospasm).

    e. When taking orally: Isordil 20 mg SL q4h, nifedipine 30 mg PO q6h, or diltiazem 30 mg PO q8h.

B. **Perioperative myocardial infarction** occurs in less than 5% of patients undergoing cardiac surgery. Depending on its extent, it may be of little consequence to the patient or it may result in a low output state or malignant arrhythmias. Generally, a hemodynamically significant infarction results in increased perioperative mortality and reduced long-term survival.[81,82]

1. **Predisposing factors**

    a. Left main or diffuse three-vessel disease

    b. Unstable angina (especially following a failed angioplasty)

    c. Poor LV function (LVEDP >15 mm Hg, low ejection fraction)

    d. Left ventricular hypertrophy

    e. Coronary endarterectomy

    f. Long aortic crossclamp period

2. **Mechanisms**

    a. Undetected preoperative myocardial necrosis. Studies have shown that an elevated level of troponin T, indicative of myocardial cell damage that is not detectable by other means, is common in unstable patients.[83]

    b. Prolonged ischemia during anesthetic induction or before the establishment of coronary reperfusion. This is usually caused by tachycardia, hypertension/hypotension, or ventricular distention, but may occasionally result from acute thrombosis of a critically narrowed artery or stenotic vein graft at reoperation.

    c. Inadequate myocardial protection

    d. Reperfusion injury following cardioplegic arrest

    e. Incomplete revascularization

    f. Anastomotic stenosis

    g. Graft thrombosis

    h. Embolization of debris down coronary arteries (usually in patent but atherosclerotic vein grafts during reoperations)

    i. Ventricular distention

    j. Intracoronary air embolism

3. **Diagnosis.** The diagnosis of a perioperative MI is usually entertained by the combination of new ECG changes (new Q waves or ST changes) with evidence of new regional or global wall motion abnormalities by echocardiography or radionuclide ventriculography. However, several factors must be considered before concluding that myocardial necrosis has occurred.

    a. Severe postcardiotomy ventricular dysfunction may suggest the development of an MI, but often represents a prolonged period of reversible myocardial depression ("stunning") that can recover after several days of pharmacologic or mechanical support. However, the persistence of new regional wall motion abnormalities on serial evaluations is more consistent with the occurrence of a perioperative MI.

    b. New Q waves on the ECG are noted in about 5% of patients after surgery. Up to 20% of new Q waves are considered to be false positives, representing areas of altered depolarization or unmasking of old infarcts. The presence of ST segment depression, deep T wave inversions, ventricular tachyarrhythmias, or a new bundle branch block that persist for over 48 hours suggests some degree of myocardial injury.

    c. Creatine kinase (CK) levels over 1000 IU/L with a CK-MB fraction over 80–100 IU/mL are usually associated with perioperative infarctions, but are too sensitive to be of predictive value. CK-MB levels can be elevated by atriotomy or ventriculotomy incisions, myocardial trauma, reperfusion ventricular fibrillation, reperfusion of severely ischemic zones, and by autotransfusion of shed mediastinal blood.[84] There is usually little correlation between the CK-MB level and the size of an infarction. Thus, by itself, the CK-MB is an unreliable determinant of perioperative infarction.

    d. Troponin I and T (TnI and TnT) are very sensitive and specific biochemical markers of myocardial cell injury.[85] Levels rise within hours of myocardial damage, peak on days 2–5 (in contrast to the rapid fall in CK levels) and remain elevated for 7 days. Since they can detect a minor amount of myocardial damage, they may be useful in assessing the adequacy of myocardial protection, but may be too sensitive to be of clinical significance. It has been proposed that a TnI concentration $<15\mu g/L$ within 24–48 hours after surgery indicates absence of a perioperative MI.[86] Although both TnI and TnT can be used as markers, TnT is also elevated in patients with chronic renal insufficiency. It should be noted that there is some increase in TnT levels after defibrillation of VF, but minimal increase after cardioversion for atrial fibrillation.[87]

e. Technetium (Tc)-99 SPECT scanning is very sensitive in detecting small areas of infarction. However, such subtle findings are of little relevance in that patients without adverse hemodynamic consequences from a perioperative MI have a favorable prognosis.[88]

4. **Presentation and treatment**

a. **Intraoperative ischemia.** Identification of regional wall motion abnormalities by transesophageal echocardiography is the most sensitive means of assessing intraoperative myocardial ischemia. These changes precede evidence of ischemia noted with Swan-Ganz monitoring (elevation of PA pressures) or the ECG (ST segment elevation). Aggressive treatment to reduce myocardial oxygen demand and maintain perfusion pressure is essential to lower the risk of perioperative MI.

b. **Postcardiotomy low cardiac output syndrome with/ without ECG evidence of ischemia.** The occurrence of severe postcardiotomy ventricular dysfunction, whether caused by ischemia, "stunning," or an infarction, requires careful evaluation and treatment.

   i. If myocardial dysfunction or ischemia is noted in the operating room, the adequacy of the operative procedure should be reevaluated. Supplemental grafts or graft revision may be necessary. IABP or circulatory assist devices may be indicated.

   ii. The incidence of asymptomatic postoperative ischemia has been reported to be as high as 50% in one study and should draw attention to means to optimize postoperative cardiac function while minimizing the increase in oxygen demand.[12]

   iii. If ECG changes are detected upon arrival in the ICU, intravenous nitroglycerin or calcium-channel blockers (if spasm is suspected) should be used. Placement of an IABP, and possible graft revision with or without coronary angiography, should be considered to prevent an infarct or minimize infarct size.

   iv. Treatment of a hemodynamically significant MI involves supportive care until arrhythmias and hemodynamic instability resolve. Cardiac output should be optimized by judicious manipulation of preload, contractility, afterload, and heart rate. Excessive volume infusions and tachycardia produced by inotropic agents may increase myocardial oxygen demand and worsen an ischemic insult. Use of amrinone/milrinone and/or reduction of afterload with vasodilators or the IABP will minimize oxygen consumption. It is difficult to treat the sinus tachycardia that is frequently present in low cardiac output states because it usually represents a compensatory mechanism to maintain cardiac output. Sinus tachycardia is frequently a sign of an "injured heart" and can perpetuate myocardial ischemia and damage.

c. **Good cardiac output but low SVR**. The patient sustaining a small perioperative infarction may have a normal cardiac output accompanied by systemic hypotension. This syndrome usually requires use of an α-agent for several days to maintain an adequate systemic blood pressure until SVR returns to normal.

d. **Persistent ventricular ectopy** should be treated with lidocaine and standard oral antiarrhythmic medications. Holter monitoring should be used subsequently to evaluate the severity of the arrhythmias. Therapy should be continued only for symptomatic life-threatening arrhythmias because of the unclear benefit of long-term antiarrhythmic therapy. Electrophysiologic testing should be employed to evaluate the necessity for and the response to therapy.

e. Some patients will have an infarction diagnosed by electrocardiographic, enzymatic, or functional criteria but will demonstrate no clinical or hemodynamic sequelae. These patients do not require any special treatment.

5. **Prognosis**

a. An uncomplicated infarction does not influence operative mortality or long-term survival. Despite a return to baseline ventricular function, however, the heart may fail to demonstrate functional improvement during exercise.[89]

b. In contrast, a hemodynamically significant MI (i.e., one presenting as a low cardiac output syndrome or malignant arrhythmias) does increase operative mortality and decrease long-term survival.

c. The prognosis following a perioperative infarction is determined primarily by the adequacy of revascularization and the residual ejection fraction. One study reported that the prognosis for patients sustaining an MI with an ejection fraction greater than 40% and with complete revascularization was comparable to patients not developing a perioperative infarction.[90]

C. **Cardiac arrest** is a dreaded complication of any cardiac operation. Despite a well-preserved myocardium and judicious pharmacologic support, cardiac arrest can occur unexpectedly during transport from the operating room, in the ICU, or later during convalescence on the floor. It must be managed immediately to prevent severe neurologic sequelae from compromising the results of a successful cardiopulmonary resuscitation (CPR).[91,92]

1. **Etiology and assessment.** Evaluation to determine the possible cause of a cardiac arrest should be undertaken as the resuscitation is under way. Considerations include some problems that are easily remediable and others that can be difficult to correct.

a. Listen to the chest, check the ventilator function, arterial blood gases (ABGs), acid-base and electrolyte status. If patient is not intubated, secure an airway, administer oxygen, and then intubate.

   - Severe ventilatory or oxygenation disturbance (hypoxia, hypercarbia from pneumothorax, endotracheal tube displacement)
   - Severe acid-base and electrolyte disturbances (acidosis, hypo- or hyperkalemia)

b. Check the chest tube drainage and review the chest x-ray.

   - Acute impairment of venous return (tension pneumothorax, cardiac tamponade—occasionally with sudden cessation of massive bleeding)
   - Acute hypovolemia (massive mediastinal bleeding)

c. Assess whether inotropes, vasopressors, and vasodilators are being administered at the correct rate.

   - Inadvertent cessation of inotropic support
   - Profound vasodilatation from bolusing of nitroprusside

d. Examine the cardiac monitor and ECG.

   - Third-degree heart block (may occur spontaneously or if AV pacing fails in a patient with complete heart block)
   - Acute ischemia (graft thrombosis, anastomotic problem, coronary spasm)
   - Ventricular tachyarrhythmias (ventricular tachycardia or fibrillation)

2. **Management of cardiac arrest in the ICU**

a. Hand ventilate with 100% oxygen at a rate of 15–20/min; listen for bilateral breath sounds. Intubate after establishing an adequate airway and initiating ventilation.

b. Assess current rhythm from monitor:

   i. **Ventricular tachycardia or fibrillation (VT/VF)** necessitates immediate defibrillation with 200 joules; if unsuccessful, increase to 300 and then 360 joules.

   ii. **Asystole:** turn on the atrial and/or ventricular pacing wires.

c. Initiate external cardiac massage at a rate of 100/min if unable to defibrillate or establish pacing within 30 seconds. Efficient massage can provide about 25% of the normal cardiac output. Massage can result in disruption of the sternal closure, injury to bypass grafts, or damage to the ventricular myocardium from prosthetic valves. This potential damage can be minimized if compressions are delayed for a **very short period of time** to prepare and use the defibrillator or attach the pacing wires to a pacemaker.

d. **Ventricular fibrillation and pulseless ventricular tachycardia**

   - **Defibrillation** is essential for VF or pulseless VT and should be repeated with increasing energy levels (200, 300, 360 J).

- **Epinephrine** 1 mg IV (10 mL of 1:10,000 solution) should be given if VT/VF persists or recurs after three attempts at defibrillation. It may be repeated every 3–5 minutes.
- Antiarrhythmic drugs may improve the success of defibrillation and should be used for persistent/recurrent VT/VF or malignant ventricular ectopy. Defibrillation should be repeated after each dose of medication.
- Use **lidocaine** first as a 1.0–1.5 mg/kg bolus followed by 0.5–0.75 mg/kg boluses every 5 minutes to a total dose of 3 mg/kg; then start a continuous drip of 2–4 mg/min.
- **Bretylium** should be used for VF or VT refractory to lidocaine; an initial bolus of 5 mg/kg may be followed by one of 10 mg/kg every 5 minutes to a total dose of 30 mg/kg; then start a drip of 2 mg/min.
- **Magnesium sulfate** 1–2 g in 50 mL of D5W IV may be helpful for refractory VF or torsades de pointes.
- **Procainamide** should be used for refractory VF. Give 30 mg/min IV until the arrhythmia is suppressed, hypotension occurs, the QRS complex widens to 50% of its original width, or a total dose of 17 mg/kg is given; then start an infusion of 1–4 mg/min.
- **Amiodarone** may be considered when the patient is refractory to all other measures. It is given as 150 mg IV over 15 min followed by an infusion of 1 mg/min for 6 hours, then 0.5 mg/min for 18 hours with conversion to oral dosing if necessary.

e. **Asystole** that is unresponsive to epicardial pacing
  - Attempt **transcutaneous pacing.**
  - **Epinephrine** bolus 1 mg IV (10 mL of a 1:10,000 solution) every 3–5 minutes; an infusion of 2–10 μg/min can be used for bradycardia.
  - **Atropine** 1 mg IV with repeat doses of 0.5–1.0 mg every 3–5 minutes to a total dose of 0.04 mg/kg.

f. **Bradycardia** that is unresponsive to epicardial pacing
  - **Atropine** 1 mg IV with repeat doses of 0.5–1.0 mg every 3–5 minutes to a total dose of 0.04 mg/kg.
  - Attempt **transcutaneous pacing.**
  - **Dopamine** 5–20 mg/kg/min (200 μg/250 mL mix).
  - **Epinephrine** 2–10 μg/min (1 mg/250 mL mix).
  - **Isoproterenol** infusion 2–10 μg/min (2 μg = 30 drops/min of a 1 mg/250 mL mix).

g. **Pulseless electrical activity** refers to a variety of rhythms that are associated with no detectable blood pressure (including electromechanical dissociation, or EMD). It is therefore important to palpate for a pulse and not be deceived by pacing spikes or the patient's QRS complex on the monitor which may represent isolated electrical activity without any effective myocardial contraction. **Epinephrine** 0.5–1.0 mL of a 1:10,000 solution should be given. Common contributing factors and their treatment include:

- Hypovolemia: volume infusions
- Hypoxia: hand ventilation with 100% oxygen
- Cardiac tamponade: pericardiocentesis, subxiphoid exploration, or emergency reopening of sternotomy incision
- Tension pneumothorax: needle decompression
- Massive pulmonary embolism: consider thrombolytics or surgery
- Massive acute myocardial infarction
- Severe acidosis: sodium bicarbonate
- Hyperkalemia: calcium chloride, glucose/insulin/bicarbonate drip
- Drug overdose (digoxin, β-blockers, calcium-channel blockers): lavage, activated charcoal

h. **Persistent hypotension**. Reestablishment of satisfactory myocardial blood flow is the most important element in a successful resuscitation. Because coronary perfusion occurs during compression "diastole" (i.e., when the aortic pressure exceeds the right atrial pressure), elevation of SVR and coronary perfusion pressure is critical. This is best achieved with medications that have predominantly α properties.

- **Epinephrine** is a mixed α- and β-agonist with predominant α properties at the dosage recommended.
- Norepinephrine, methoxamine, and phenylephrine have been equally effective in resuscitation from VF because of their predominant α activity. None of them is currently recommended during CPR.

  i. If the patient cannot be resuscitated within 5 to 10 minutes of the time of cardiac arrest, open chest massage should be strongly considered (see page 169). Internal cardiac massage is nearly twice as effective as closed chest compressions in increasing forward blood flow.

i. **Sodium bicarbonate** should not be given routinely for the attended arrest during which excellent ventilation and cardiac compressions are achieved. Administration of NaHCO$_3$ can depress cerebral and myocardial function, reduce SVR, exacerbate central venous acidosis, inactivate catecholamines administered simultaneously, and impair oxygen release to tissues. Its use should be guided by the results of ABGs drawn every 10 minutes during the arrest. It is given in doses of 1 mEq/kg, with half this dose readministered 10 minutes later if ABGs are not available.

j. **Calcium chloride** 2 mL of a 10% solution (about 2–4 mg/kg) can be given for hypocalcemia, hyperkalemia, or persistent calcium-channel blockade. Calcium may otherwise contribute to intracellular damage during periods of ischemia, and thus is not routinely recommended during a cardiac arrest.

3. **Management on the postoperative floor**. If the patient is no longer intubated, basic life support should be initiated.

  a. Secure an airway and initiate ventilation (15 to 20/min).

  b. Start external cardiac compressions (100/min).

  c. Defibrillate for VT/VF.

  d. Establish intravenous access for medications.

  e. **Note**: Lidocaine and epinephrine are very effective when given down an endotracheal tube if intravenous access is not yet available. Two to 2.5 times the usual intravenous dose should be diluted in 10 mL of normal saline.[93]

  f. Advanced life support as delineated above should then be employed.

VII. Systemic Hypertension

A. General comments

1. Systemic hypertension is a frequent occurrence after open-heart surgery. It commonly results from enhanced sympathetic nervous system activity caused by elevated levels of norepinephrine, renin-angiotensin, and vasopressin associated with the use of extracorporeal circulation. Hypertension is noted more commonly in patients with preserved ventricular function, preoperative hypertension, and preoperative use of β-blockers, and in those undergoing surgery for aortic valve disease.[94–96]

2. Hypertension may result from either elevated systemic vascular resistance or hyperdynamic myocardial performance, or both. Therefore, it is imperative that cardiac hemodynamics be assessed before therapeutic interventions are initiated. **One should never assume that hypertension is the result of hyperdynamic cardiac performance.** Withdrawal of inotropic support when hypertension is present may lead to rapid deterioration if the cardiac output is marginal and the SVR is markedly elevated.

3. Systemic hypertension that requires treatment in the postoperative cardiac patient can be defined arbitrarily as a systolic blood pressure >140 mm Hg or a mean arterial pressure >110 mm Hg. Aggressive treatment is warranted to minimize the potential adverse effects of hypertension. It increases afterload and can precipitate myocardial ischemia, dysrhythmias, or myocardial failure. It also contributes to mediastinal bleeding, potential suture line disruption, aortic dissection, and stroke.

B. Etiology

1. The hormonal milieu of cardiopulmonary bypass (elevated norepinephrine, renin-angiotensin, vasopressin)

2. Vasoconstriction from hypothermia, vasopressors, or a low cardiac output state

3. Fever, anxiety, pain, consciousness

4. Abnormal arterial blood gases (hypoxia, hypercarbia, acidosis)

5. Pharyngeal manipulation (readjusting an endotracheal tube, placing a nasogastric tube or echo probe)

6. Hyperdynamic LV syndrome

   a. S/p aortic valve replacement

   b. S/p coronary bypass grafting with normal LV function

7. Altered baroreceptor function: following combined CABG-carotid endarterectomy

8. Severe acute hypoglycemia

C. **Assessment**

1. Careful patient examination

2. Assessment of cardiac hemodynamics

3. Arterial blood gases, serum potassium, hematocrit, chest x-ray, and ECG

D. **Treatment.** Systolic pressure should be maintained between 110 and 130 mm Hg (mean arterial pressure around 90 mm Hg). The objective is to reduce SVR sufficiently enough to reduce myocardial oxygen demand without compromising coronary perfusion pressure. A secondary benefit is frequently an improvement in myocardial function. Ideally, an antihypertensive agent should prevent myocardial ischemia without any adverse effects on heart rate, AV conduction, or myocardial contractility.

1. Ensure satisfactory oxygenation and ventilation.

2. Use vasodilator medications if the cardiac output is satisfactory.

3. Provide inotropic support along with vasodilators if the cardiac output is marginal (CI < 2.0–2.2 L/min/m^2)

4. Sedate with propofol 25 µg/kg/min (2–6 mg/kg/hour), midazolam 2.5–5 mg IV, or morphine 2.5–5 mg IV. With the trend toward earlier extubation, sedation should be minimized unless hypertension is labile and difficult to control with antihypertensive medications. However, in the fully ventilated patient in whom delayed extubation is anticipated, sedation is an appropriate first step in the control of hypertension.

5. Control shivering with meperidine 25–50 mg IV or pharmacologic paralysis (**always** with sedation).

VIII.   Vasodilators and Antihypertensive Medications

A variety of medications can be used to control systemic hypertension (table 10.7). Their hemodynamic effects depend on the status of intravascular volume and myocardial function, and the site at which they exert their antihypertensive action. Vasodilators may reduce blood pressure by increasing venous capacitance or reducing arterial resistance. Other antihypertensive medications reduce blood pressure by inhibiting central adrenergic discharge or exerting a negative inotropic effect, a property also shared by several of the vasodilators. Thus, a careful cardiac assessment is required to ensure that the appropriate medication is selected.[94-96]

A. **Sodium nitroprusside (SNP)**

1. **Hemodynamic effects**

   a. SNP primarily relaxes arterial smooth muscle and reduces systemic and pulmonary vascular resistance. It also reduces

Table 10.7 *Mixes and Dosage Ranges for IV Antihypertensive Medications*

Medication	Mix	Dosage Range
Nitroprusside	50 mg/250 mL	0.1–10 µg/kg/min
Nitroglycerin	50 mg/250 mL	0.1–10 µg/kg/min
Calcium-channel blockers		
Nicardipine	50 mg/250 mL	2.5 mg over 5 min; repeat ×4 at 10 min intervals, then 2–4 mg/h
Diltiazem	250 mg/250 mL	0.25 mg/kg over 2 min, then 0.35 mg/kg over 2 min, then 5–15 mg/h
Verapamil	120 mg/250 mL	0.1 mg/kg bolus over 2 min, then 2–5 µg/kg/min
β-blockers		
Esmolol	2.5 g/250 mL	0.25–0.5 mg/kg bolus over 1 min then 50–200 µg/kg/min
Labetalol	200 mg/200 mL	1–4 mg/min
Prostaglandin E$_1$	5 mg/250 mL	0.03–0.2 µg/kg/min

preload by producing venous dilatation. These effects lower systemic blood pressure and reduce elevated filling pressures, resulting in an improvement in left ventricular function. Maintenance or improvement in cardiac output usually requires a volume infusion to restore filling pressures to an optimal level. The theory is "optimize preload → reduce afterload → restore preload." The development of a reflex tachycardia during SNP infusion usually reflects hypovolemia, and it may increase myocardial oxygen demand.

   b. SNP should be avoided in the ischemic heart. It dilates resistance vessels in the coronary circulation and can produce a coronary steal syndrome by shunting blood away from ischemic zones. In addition, if filling pressures do not decrease when systemic perfusion pressure falls, the diastolic transmyocardial gradient for coronary blood flow will be reduced, potentially producing myocardial ischemia.[97]

   c. SNP is a **very dangerous drug** which always requires close monitoring with an indwelling arterial cannula. It has a very rapid onset of action (within seconds) and can lower blood pressure precipitously. Fortunately, its effects dissipate within 1–2 minutes.

 2. **Indications**

   a. To control hypertension caused by an increase in SVR. SNP is the best antihypertensive drug to use if cardiac function is marginal, filling pressures are elevated, and SVR is high.

   b. To improve myocardial function when the SVR is elevated, whether systemic hypertension is present or not. The best results are often obtained with concomitant inotropic support.

   c. To reduce pulmonary artery pressures in the patient with pulmonary hypertension to improve RV function. This benefit is usually offset by simultaneous systemic vasodilatation.

3. The usual starting dose is 0.1 µg/kg/min with a mix of 50 mg/250 mL. The bottle must be wrapped in aluminum foil to prevent metabolic breakdown from light. The dose is gradually increased to a maximum of 10 µg/kg/min.

4. **Adverse effects**

   a. Potentiation of myocardial ischemia from a reduction in diastolic perfusion pressure, shunting of blood from ischemic zones, or reflex tachycardia.

   b. Reflex increase in contractility and *dp/dt* that must be treated with β-blockers in a patient with an aortic dissection.

   c. Inhibition of hypoxic vasoconstriction, which produces ventilation-perfusion mismatch and hypoxia.

   d. Tachyphylaxis to its vasodilating effects

   e. **Cyanide toxicity**. Nitroprusside is metabolized to cyanide, which is then converted to thiocyanate in the liver. Cyanide toxicity, manifested by metabolic acidosis and an elevated mixed venous PO_2, may occur when large doses (>8 µg/kg/min) are given for several days (cumulative dose >1 mg/kg over 12–24 hours) or if hepatic dysfunction is present. Moderate cyanide toxicity is treated by converting the cyanide to thiocyanate for its excretion by the kidneys.

      i. Sodium bicarbonate for metabolic acidosis in doses of 1 mEq/kg.

     ii. Sodium thiosulfate, 150 mg/kg IV (approximately 12.5 g in a 50 mL D5W solution given over 10 minutes)

   f. **Thiocyanate toxicity** (level >5 mg/dL) may develop from chronic use of SNP, especially when there is impaired renal excretion of this metabolite. It is manifested by dyspnea, vomiting, and mental status changes with dizziness, headache, and loss of consciousness. **Treatment** of both severe cyanide and thiocyanate toxicity involves use of nitrite preparations to induce methemoglobin formation. Methemoglobin combines with cyanide to form cyan-methemoglobin, which is nontoxic.

      i. Amyl nitrite inhalation of 1 ampule over 15 seconds

     ii Sodium nitrite 5 mg/kg IV slow push. This is usually given at a rate of 2.5 mL/min of a 3% solution to a total of 10–15 mL. One-half of this dose can be used subsequently if toxicity recurs.

    iii. Sodium thiosulfate in the dose noted above can then be administered to convert the cyanide that is gradually dissociated from cyanmethemoglobin into thiocyanate for excretion.

B. **Nitroglycerin (NTG)**

   1. **Hemodynamic effects**

      a. NTG is primarily a venodilator that lowers blood pressure by reducing preload, filling pressures, stroke volume, and cardiac output. If filling pressures are satisfactory, NTG will maintain aortic diastolic perfusion pressure, although at high doses, some arterial vasodilatation does occur. In the presence of hypovolemia or a marginal cardiac output, NTG should be avoided, because it will lower cardiac output further and produce a reflex tachycardia.

      b. NTG dilates coronary conductance vessels and improves blood flow to ischemic zones.[97]

   2. **Indications**

      a. **Hypertension** in association with myocardial ischemia or high filling pressures

      b. ECG changes of **myocardial ischemia**

      c. **Coronary spasm** (beneficial when given intracoronary, but not as useful as calcium-channel blockers when given intravenously)

      d. **Pulmonary hypertension** after mitral valve replacement to reduce right ventricular afterload and improve RV function

      e. **Preoperative ischemia**. NTG is useful before revascularization to reduce preload while phenylephrine is used to maintain coronary perfusion pressure.

   3. Starting dose is 0.1 µg/kg/min with a mix of 50 mg/250 mL. The dose can be titrated up to 10 µg/kg/min. It must be administered through non–polyvinyl chloride (PVC) tubing because PVC tubing absorbs up to 80% of the NTG.

   4. **Adverse effects**. Nitroglycerin is metabolized by the liver to nitrites, which oxidize hemoglobin to methemoglobin (metHb). Methemoglobinemia and impaired oxygen transport can occur if the patient receives excessive doses of intravenous NTG (over 10 µg/kg/min for several days) or has renal or hepatic dysfunction. The diagnosis is suggested by the presence of chocolate-brown blood and an elevated PaO_2, yet a low oxygen saturation measured by oximetry. It can be confirmed by an elevated metHb level (>1% of total hemoglobin). Symptoms (cyanosis, progressive weakness, and acidosis) are usually not noted until the metHb level exceeds 15–20%. The treatment is IV methylene blue 1 mg/kg of a 1% solution.[98]

C. **β-blockers**

   1. **Hemodynamic effects**

      a. In contrast to the vasodilating drugs, β-blockers reduce blood pressure primarily by their negative inotropic and chronotropic effects. They reduce contractility, lowering the stroke volume and cardiac output, and also slow the heart rate by depressing the SA node. Their antihypertensive activity may also be attributable to a decrease in central sympathetic outflow and suppression of renin activity.

   b. β-blockers slow AV conduction and can precipitate heart block. Pacemaker backup should be available when intravenous β-blockers are given. This electrophysiologic effect is beneficial in reducing the ventricular rate response to atrial tachyarrhythmias.

2. **Indication.** Control of postoperative systolic hypertension associated with a satisfactory cardiac output. β-blockers are especially beneficial in the hyperdynamic, tachycardic heart that is often noted in patients with normal preoperative LV function and/or LV hypertrophy. **Note:** Intravenous β-blockers should be avoided in hypertensive patients with compromised cardiac output.

3. **Esmolol** is a cardioselective, ultrafast, short-acting β-blocker with an onset of action of 2 minutes, reaching a steady state level in 5 minutes, and with reversal of effect in 10–20 minutes.[99] Because of its very short duration of action, esmolol is the β-blocker of choice in the ICU for transient hypertension control in the hemodynamically unstable patient.

   a. Esmolol must be used with extreme caution when the cardiac output is marginal. Frequently, blood pressure and cardiac output are maintained by fast heart rates at low stroke volumes. Use of esmolol in this circumstance will often reduce blood pressure and cardiac output by a negative inotropic effect with little reduction in heart rate. Even in patients with an excellent cardiac output, the reduction in blood pressure is generally more prominent than the decrease in heart rate.

   b. Esmolol can be used safely in the patient with a history of bronchospasm because of its cardioselectivity.

   c. The recommended initial dose is a 0.25–0.5 mg/kg load over 1 minute, followed by 50 µg/kg/min over 4 minutes. Because patients tend to be very sensitive to esmolol in the immediate postoperative period, a smaller test dose should be considered to determine its effect on heart rate and blood pressure. If an adequate antihypertensive effect is not achieved, a repeat loading dose is given, then a maintenance infusion of 100 µg/kg/min is given over 4 minutes. Two more reloading doses can be given with additional 50 µg/kg/min increases in the maintenance infusion rate. Little additional effect is gained at a dose over 200 µg/kg/min.

   d. The mix for continuous infusion is 2.5 g/250 mL.

4. **Labetalol** has both α- and β-blocking properties as well as a direct vasodilatory effect. The ratio of β:α effects is 3:1 for the oral form and 7:1 for the intravenous form. In the postoperative cardiac surgical patient, the primary mechanisms by which intravenous labetalol reduces blood pressure are its negative inotropic and chronotropic effects. The α-blocking effect prevents reflex vasoconstriction.[100]

      a. The onset of action for intravenous labetalol is rapid with a maximum blood pressure response at 5 minutes for bolus injection and 10–15 minutes for a continuous infusion. Because the approximate duration of action is 6 hours, labetalol is useful when a longer-acting antihypertensive drug is desired.

      b. Labetalol is given as a 0.25 mg/kg bolus over 2 minutes with subsequent doses of 0.5 mg/kg every 15 minutes until effect is achieved (to a total dose of 300 mg).

      c. Alternatively, a continuous intravenous infusion can be given at a rate of 1–4 mg/min, mixing 40 mL of the 5 mg/mL solution in 160 mL (200 mg/200 mL).

  5. **Metoprolol** is a cardioselective β-blocker that can be used for control of hypertension after surgery. However, the primary indications for its intravenous use are control of ischemia and slowing of the ventricular response to atrial fibrillation. It is given in 5 mg increments every 5 minutes for up to 3 doses until effect is achieved. The onset of action is 2–3 minutes, with a peak effect in 20 minutes and a duration of action of up to 5 hours for a 5 mg dose. Oral metoprolol is commonly used in doses of 25–100 mg bid for control of postoperative systolic hypertension.

  6. **Propranolol** is a noncardioselective β-blocker administered intravenously in 0.5 mg increments up to 0.1 mg/kg. The onset of action is 2–5 minutes with a peak effect in 10–15 minutes; the effect may last several hours. Like metoprolol, it is rarely used in intravenous form for control of hypertension, especially because of its long duration of action (compared with esmolol) and its negative inotropic effects.

D. Calcium-channel blockers

  1. **Hemodynamic effects**

      a. The calcium-channel blockers are very effective for control of hypertension after surgery, primarily by relaxing vascular smooth muscle and producing peripheral vasodilatation. A variety of medications are available that have differing effects on cardiovascular hemodynamics and electrophysiology (table 10.8).[100–106]

      b. Other beneficial effects may include coronary vasodilatation, negative inotropy, a reduction in SA nodal automaticity (slowing the sinus mechanism), and slowing of AV nodal conduction (decreasing the ventricular rate response to atrial tachyarrhythmias).

  2. **Indications**

      a. Hypertension with satisfactory cardiac output; beneficial if there is evidence of myocardial ischemia. Nicardipine can be used if there is evidence of compromised ventricular function, but diltiazem and verapamil should be avoided because of their negative inotropic properties.

      b. Coronary spasm (diltiazem, nifedipine, verapamil).

Table 10.8 *Effects of Calcium-Channel Blockers*

	Nicardipine	Diltiazem	Verapamil	Nifedipine	Isradipine
Inotropy	0	↓	↓↓	0	0
Heart rate	0↑	↓	↓	↑	0↑
AV conduction	0	↓↓	↓↓	0	0
Systemic resistance	↓↓	↓↓	↓↓	↓↓	↓↓
Coronary vascular resistance	↓↓	↓↓	↓↓	↓↓	↓↓

↑ = *increased;* ↓ = *decreased;* 0 = *no effect.*

    c. Slowing the ventricular response to atrial fibrillation/flutter (diltiazem, verapamil).

    d. Oral agents are used for the treatment of systemic hypertension and ischemic heart disease.

3. Nicardipine

    a. Nicardipine reduces blood pressure by a reduction in SVR. It lacks a negative inotropic effect, produces a minimal increase in heart rate, and has no effect on AV conduction. It has been shown to be very effective and safe in controlling postoperative hypertension and may provide more stable blood pressure control than SNP.[101–103]

    b. Advantages over sodium nitroprusside

        i. Nicardipine improves cardiac output with less reduction in filling pressures than SNP (which also causes venodilatation), thus necessitating less volume infusion.

        ii. It avoids the reflex tachycardia and coronary steal that could lead to myocardial ischemia.

        iii. It is a potent coronary vasodilator that may improve the distribution of blood flow to ischemic zones.

    c. Disadvantages

        i. Despite a rapid onset of action (1–2 minutes), nicardipine has a longer duration of action than SNP, with an elimination half-life of 40 minutes. Nonetheless, it can be titrated for optimal control of hypertension.

        ii. It does increase ventilation/perfusion mismatch and can produce hypoxemia.[103]

    d. The dose is 2.5 mg over 5 minutes, repeated every 10 minutes to a total dose of 12.5 mg. An infusion of 2–4 mg/h is then begun, using a 50 mg/250 mL mix.

4. Diltiazem

    a. Diltiazem reduces systemic blood pressure by lowering SVR. However, it depresses systolic function by a negative inotropic effect and should be avoided if cardiac output is marginal. Furthermore, because it slows the heart rate, it will reduce cardiac output. Nonetheless, the slowing of a tachy-cardia in a patient with a satisfactory cardiac output may be beneficial in improving myocardial oxygen metabolism.[104]

b. **Indications**

    i. Slowing ventricular response to atrial fibrillation. Diltiazem slows AV conduction and can produce heart block; therefore, pacemaker backup must be available when it is administered intravenously.

    ii. Prevention of arterial graft spasm (specifically, the radial artery)

    iii. Treatment of coronary artery spasm (diltiazem is a potent coronary vasodilator)

    iv. Systemic hypertension (especially when associated with spasm or atrial fibrillation)

c. IV dosage is a 0.25 mg/kg bolus over 2 minutes, which may be followed by a repeat bolus of 0.35 mg/kg 15 minutes later. A continuous infusion is then given at a rate of 5–15 mg/h with a 250 mg/250 mL mix.

5. **Verapamil**

a. Verapamil reduces systemic blood pressure by lowering SVR, but it also has moderate negative inotropic, chronotropic, and dromotropic effects that depress contractility, slow the heart rate, and depress AV conduction. In the early postoperative period, indications for its use are similar to those of diltiazem.

b. IV dosage is a 0.1 mg/kg IV bolus, followed by a 2–5 µg/kg/min continuous infusion of a 120 mg/250 mL mix.

6. **Other calcium-channel blockers**

a. **Nifedipine** is a potent arterial vasodilator that lowers blood pressure by reducing SVR. This is frequently accompanied by a baroreceptor-mediated reflex tachycardia and a slight reflex increase in cardiac inotropy and AV conduction. Nifedipine is beneficial to treat coronary spasm because it is a potent coronary vasodilator. It also reduces PVR and pulmonary artery pressures. Although there are reports of its use in intravenous form for control of postoperative hypertension, it is primarily given SL or orally in a dose of 10–30 mg q4h.[104,105]

b. **Isradipine** has effects similar to those of nicardipine. It reduces blood pressure and improves cardiac output by a reduction in SVR, with minimal effect on filling pressures and no negative inotropic effects. Some studies report a moderate reflex tachycardia, while others note no change in heart rate. There is no effect on AV conduction. Isradipine also improves coronary flow by reducing coronary vascular resistance, but it has little effect on the pulmonary circulation. Intravenous use is investigational and it is more commonly used as an oral antihypertensive agent.[106]

    c. **Amlodipine** similarly reduces SVR and blood pressure and may improve cardiac output due to a decrease in afterload. It has no negative inotropic effects and no effect on the SA node or AV nodal conduction. It produces a gradual decrease in blood pressure that persists for 24 hours after an oral dose. Thus, it is indicated for long-term control of hypertension in the stable patient. It is given in doses of 2.5–10 mg qd.

E. **Enalaprilat** is an intravenous angiotensin-converting enzyme (ACE) inhibitor. It inhibits activation of the renin-angiotensin system and also blunts the increase in other vasoactive substances that normally rise with cardiopulmonary bypass (catecholamines, endothelin, and atrial natriuretic peptide).

    1. Enalaprilat reduces blood pressure by producing balanced arterial and venous vasodilatation without a reflex increase in heart rate. It thus reduces preload and afterload and reduces myocardial oxygen demand. It also does not produce hypoxic vasoconstriction, having no effect on gas exchange and oxygen delivery.

    2. The recommended dose is 0.625–1.25 mg IV given over 15 minutes q6h. However, studies in the literature have used either bolus doses of 0.06 mg/kg (approximately a 4 mg bolus) or continuous infusions of 1 mg/h with doubling of the dose every 30 minutes until effect (to a total dose of 10 mg).[107,108]

    3. Initial clinical response after a bolus dose is noted in 15 minutes with peak effect in 4 hours. This drug can be considered in the hemodynamically stable patient with hypertension and depressed ventricular function who is unable to tolerate oral medications. It can subsequently be converted to the oral form of enalapril, giving 5 mg qd (half this dose if creatinine clearance is <30 mL/min).

F. **Hydralazine**

    1. Hydralazine is a direct arteriolar vasodilator that decreases SVR and systemic blood pressure. The reduction in afterload may improve myocardial function, but is usually accompanied by a compensatory tachycardia.

    2. **Indication:** Frequently used as a substitute for potent intravenous antihypertensive medications if the patient is hemodynamically stable but remains hypertensive several days after surgery. It is beneficial when the patient cannot take or absorb oral medications or if toxicity from or resistance to other intravenous antihypertensive medications develops.

    3. The usual dose is 20–40 mg IM q4h or 5 mg IV q15min until effect. The onset of action after intravenous injection is about 5–10 minutes with a peak effect at 20 minutes and a duration of action of 3–4 hours. Thus, it is difficult to titrate and should not be used if the patient is hemodynamically unstable. However, a continuous infusion of 1.5 µg/kg/min has been used in postoperative cardiac patients with excellent reduction in afterload.[109]

G. **Fenoldopam mesylate**

1. Fenoldopam is a rapid-acting vasodilator that became available in late 1997. It activates D1-like dopamine receptors, resulting in peripheral arterial, coronary, mesenteric, and renal vasodilatation. This is accompanied by a reflex tachycardia. It dilates both renal afferent and efferent arterioles, resulting in an increase in renal blood flow. It also produces hypokalemia, either through a direct drug effect or enhanced K^+-Na^+ exchange.

2. **Indications:** severe hypertension when rapid and reversible effect is necessary. There have been only a few reports of its use in cardiac surgical patients as of late 1998.[187]

3. It is given as a continuous infusion starting at 0.05 to 1 µg/kg/min using a 10 mg/250 mL mix. The dose may be increased in 0.05–0.1 µg/kg/min increments every 15 minutes until effect is achieved (to a maximum infusion rate of 0.3 µg/kg/min). An infusion of 0.03 µg/kg/min may improve renal perfusion without producing any hemodynamic effects.[188]

H. **Prostaglandin E₁ (PGE₁)**

1. PGE₁ is a very potent direct systemic and pulmonary vasodilator. Its sole use in adults is for refractory right heart failure resulting from pulmonary hypertension. This is noted most commonly in patients following mitral valve surgery or cardiac transplantation.

2. It must be infused into the right-sided circulation (central line or CVP port of the Swan-Ganz catheter) to minimize systemic hypotension. If necessary, a vasopressor, such as norepinephrine, may be infused simultaneously into a left atrial line to minimize this effect.

3. The starting dose is 0.03 µg/kg/min and may be increased to 0.2 µg/kg/min. Systemic vasodilatation requiring vasopressor support is usually noted at doses exceeding 0.1 µg/kg/min.[22]

I. **Selection of the appropriate antihypertensive medication**

1. When filling pressures are high and the cardiac output is marginal, an arterial vasodilator, such as **nitroprusside,** should be selected. It will reduce preload and afterload by producing arterial (and some venous) dilatation, and will often improve cardiac output. Consideration should be given to using inotropic agents and vasodilators together to optimally augment cardiac function. **Nicardipine** reduces SVR without any negative inotropic or chronotropic effects and can be used effectively in this situation. Its longer duration of action may prove detrimental if used during a period of hemodynamic instability.

2. When filling pressures are high and the cardiac output is satisfactory, a venodilator, such as **nitroglycerin,** may be beneficial. This will reduce venous return, filling pressures, stroke volume, cardiac output, and blood pressure. However, nitroglycerin is best avoided when hypovolemia or a marginal cardiac output is present.

3. When the heart is hyperdynamic with adequate filling pressures, a high cardiac output, and frequently tachycardia, medications with

negative inotropic and chronotropic properties such as **esmolol** or the calcium-channel blockers (**diltiazem, verapamil**), should be selected. These medications are beneficial in improving myocardial oxygen metabolism, especially when there is evidence of ischemia.

4. Once the patient is able to tolerate oral medications, other medications can be used to control hypertension or reduce afterload to improve myocardial performance. Long-acting preparations are more convenient and should be instituted once the patient is stable. These include:

   a. ACE inhibitors for patients with impaired ventricular function (use cautiously in the presence of renal dysfunction) (see Appendix 2).

   b. Calcium-channel blockers

   c. β-blockers can also be used for control of systolic hypertension and are frequently beneficial in reducing the incidence of postoperative atrial arrhythmias as well. **Carvedilol** is an α- and β-blocker that is beneficial in patients with impaired ventricular function.

IX.   Pacing Wires and Pacemakers

Two temporary right atrial and two right ventricular epicardial pacing wire electrodes are usually placed at the conclusion of all open-heart procedures. These pacing wires have both diagnostic and therapeutic utility.[110]

A. **Diagnostic.** Atrial pacing wires can be used to record atrial activity in both unipolar and bipolar modes. With suitably equipped monitors, these recordings can be obtained simultaneously with standard limb leads to distinguish among atrial and junctional arrhythmias and differentiate them from more life-threatening ventricular arrhythmias. Simultaneous ECG and atrial electrogram (AEG) tracings for each of the most commonly encountered postoperative arrhythmias are provided in the next section. The technique for obtaining atrial wire tracings is either of the following:

1. A multichannel recorder can be used to print simultaneous monitor ECG and atrial electrograms. Most current monitoring systems have cartridges with three leads for recording the AEG: two of them represent the arm leads and are connected with alligator clips to the atrial pacing wires; the third represents a left leg lead and is attached to an electrode pad over the patient's flank. When the monitor channel for the AEG is set on lead I, a bipolar AEG is obtained (figure 10.8). This shows a large atrial complex and a very small or undetectable ventricular complex. When the AEG monitor channel is set on leads II or III, a unipolar atrial electrogram is obtained. This demonstrates a large atrial and slightly smaller ventricular complex.

2. When a standard ECG machine is used, the two arm leads are connected to the atrial wires with alligator clips, and the leg leads are attached to the right and left legs. A bipolar atrial electrogram will be recorded on lead I and a unipolar atrial electrogram on lead II or III. Alternatively, the atrial wires can be connected to the V leads.

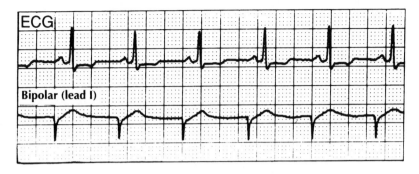

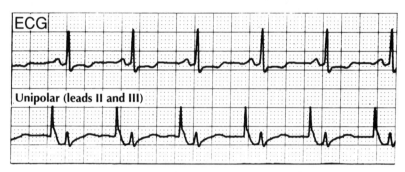

Figure 10.8 *Sinus rhythm in simultaneous monitor leads and AEGs. In the upper tracing, note that the bipolar AEG (lead I) produces predominantly an atrial complex with essentially no visible ventricular complex. In contrast, the unipolar tracing (leads II and III) on the bottom shows both a large atrial wave and a smaller ventricular complex.*

Bipolar electrograms give a better assessment of atrial activity than do unipolar electrograms and can distinguish between sinus tachycardia and atrial arrhythmias. However, because the AEG and standard ECG tracings are not obtained simultaneously, a unipolar tracing is required to differentiate sinus from junctional tachycardia because it can demonstrate the relationship between the larger atrial and smaller ventricular complexes.

B. **Therapeutic**

1. Optimal hemodynamics are achieved at a heart rate of 90 beats/min in the immediate postoperative period. Use of pacing wires to increase the heart rate is preferable to the use of positive chronotropic agents that have other effects on myocardial function. Atrial or AV pacing will nearly always demonstrate superior hemodynamics to ventricular pacing. Because AV delay is often prolonged after bypass, shortening it artificially using AV pacing can improve hemodynamics, especially in patients with impaired ventricular function.[111]

2. Reentrant rhythms can be terminated by rapid pacing. Rapid atrial pacing can terminate type I atrial flutter (flutter rate less than 350)

and other paroxysmal supraventricular tachycardias. Rapid ventricular pacing can terminate ventricular tachycardia.

C. **Pacing nomenclature**

1. The sophistication and reprogrammability of permanent pacemaker systems led to the establishment of a joint nomenclature by the North American Society of Pacing & Electrophysiology (NASPE) and the British Pacing & Electrophysiology Group (BPEG). This nomenclature, referred to as the NBG code, classifies pacemakers by their exact mode of function (see table 10.9).

2. Use of the first three letters is helpful in understanding the temporary pacemaker systems that are used after cardiac surgical procedures (see table 10.10). The most common modes are AOO (atrial pacing), VVI (ventricular demand pacing), DVI (AV sequential pacing), and, with the newer external units, DDD (AV sequential demand pacing).

D. **Atrial pacing**

1. Atrial bipolar pacing is achieved by connecting both atrial electrodes to the pacemaker. This produces a smaller pacing stimulus artifact on a monitor than unipolar pacing and can often be difficult to detect even in multiple leads (figure 10.9). It does, however, prevent intraaortic balloon consoles from misinterpreting large pacing spikes as QRS complexes.

2. Atrial pacing can also be achieved using transesophageal electrodes or a pacing catheter placed through Paceport Swan-Ganz catheters. These are particularly beneficial during minimally invasive surgery.[112]

3. Pacing is usually accomplished in the AOO mode. The usual settings are a pulse amplitude of 10 to 20mA in the asynchronous mode (insensitive to the ECG signal), set at a rate faster than the intrinsic heart rate. With the Medtronic Model 5346 DDD external pacemaker, AAI demand pacing may be accomplished if atrial sensing is satisfactory.

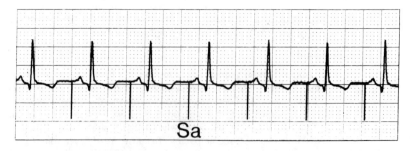

Figure 10.9 *Atrial pacing at a rate of 95 beats/min. The atrial pacing stimulus artifact (Sa) is well seen in this tracing, but is frequently difficult to identify on the monitor. The height of the atrial pacing spike may be increased on the monitor for better visualization, or it may be decreased to prevent problems with ECG interpretation or intraaortic balloon tracking.*

Table 10.9 NBG Pacemaker Identification Codes

				Code Positions	
I	II	III	IV	V	
Chamber Paced	Chamber Sensed	Response to Sensing	Programmable Functions	Antitachyarrhythmia Functions	
V-ventricle	V-ventricle	T-triggers pacing	P-programmable rate and/or output	P-antitachyarrhythmia	
A-atrium	A-atrium	I-inhibits pacing	M-multiprogrammable	S-shock	
D-double	D-double	D-triggers and inhibits pacing	C-communicating functions (telemetry)	D-dual (pacer & shock)	
0-none	0-none	0-none	R-rate modulation	0-none	
S-single chamber	S-single chamber		0-none		

Table 10.10 *Temporary Pacing Modes Used after Heart Surgery*

Code Positions			Description
I	II	III	
A	O	O	Asynchronous atrial pacing
A	A	I	Atrial demand pacing
V	O	O	Asynchronous ventricular pacing (do not use)
V	V	I	Ventricular demand pacing
D	O	O	Asynchronous AV pacing (do not use)
D	V	I	AV sequential pacing (ventricular demand)
D	D	D	AV pacing (both chambers sense)

A = atrium; V = ventricle; D = both chambers; O = does not apply.

4. **Indications.** Atrial pacing requires the ability to capture the atrium as well as normal conduction though the AV node. It is ineffective during atrial fibrillation/flutter.

   a. Sinus bradycardia

   b. Suppression of premature ventricular complexes: set at a rate slightly faster than the sinus mechanism

   c. Suppression of premature atrial complexes

   d. Slow junctional rhythm

   e. Overdriving supraventricular tachycardias (atrial flutter, paroxysmal atrial or AV junctional reentrant tachycardia). Rapid atrial pacing can interrupt a reentrant circuit and convert it to sinus rhythm or a nonsustained rhythm, such as atrial fibrillation, which may terminate spontaneously.

E. **Technique of overdrive pacing**

1. Overdrive pacing is accomplished using a pacemaker that can produce rates as high as 800 beats/min (figures 10.10 and 10.11). When attaching pacemaker wires to the generator, **be absolutely certain** that the atrial wires, not the ventricular wires, are being attached. In addition, pacing initially 10–15 beats/min above the ventricular rate will confirm that the ventricle is not being paced, which has been noted to happen when atrial pacing wires are placed close to the ventricle.

2. The patient must be attached to an ECG monitor during rapid atrial pacing. Bipolar pacing should be used to minimize distortion of the atrial complex. Pacing spikes are often best identified by evaluation of lead II.

3. Turn the pacer to full mA (20) and to a rate about 10 beats faster than the tachycardia or flutter rate. When the atrium has been captured, increase the rate slowly until the morphology of the flutter waves changes (atrial complexes become positive). This is usually about 20–30% above the atrial flutter rate. Pacing for up to one minute may be required.

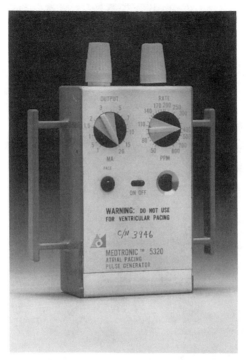

Figure 10.10 *Rapid atrial pacer. This pacer can produce rates as high as 800 beats/min and is used to terminate supraventricular reentrant rhythms, especially atrial flutter.*

4. The pacer should be turned off abruptly. Sinus rhythm, a pause followed by sinus rhythm, atrial fibrillation, or recurrent flutter may be noted (figure 10.12). If severe bradycardia develops, the pacemaker may be turned on at a rate around 60 until the sinus mechanism recovers.

F. **Atrioventricular pacing**

1. AV pacing is achieved by connecting both atrial wires to the atrial inlets and both ventricular wires to the ventricular inlets of an AV pacer (figures 10.11 and 10.13). If two ventricular wires are not available or functioning, an atrial or skin lead can be used as a ground (the positive electrode) for ventricular pacing.

2. The old standard AV sequential demand pacemaker (figure 10.13) can provide AOO, VVI, DVI, and DOO pacing. The atrial and ventricular outputs are both set at 10–20 mA with a PR interval of 150 ms. The demand mode is usually recommended because it prevents competitive ventricular rhythms that might occur in the asynchronous mode. However, "cross-talk" between the atrial pacing and ventricular sensing mechanisms can inhibit the ventricular response in the demand mode and necessitate use of the asyn-

Figure 10.11 *Medtronic Model 5346 DDD temporary pulse generator. This sophisticated programmable pacemaker can provide a variety of pacing modes, including those available on the model 5330 (figure. 10.13) as well as the DDD mode. This model has rapid atrial pacing capabilities and an emergency button that activates VVI pacing.*

chronous mode. Cardiac output can often be improved by increasing or decreasing the PR interval to alter ventricular filling time. The ECG will demonstrate both pacing spikes, although the atrial spike is often difficult to detect (figure 10.14).

3. The newer external temporary pacemakers can provide a wide variety of pacing modes (see figure 10.11). In addition to the standard modes already noted, they can provide DDD pacing and rapid atrial burst pacing. DDD pacing has several advantages, including the ability to sense a fast atrial rate and produce a synchronized ventricular contraction, as well as a reduced risk of triggering atrial, junctional, and pacemaker-induced arrhythmias.

   a. Careful monitoring is necessary in the event that the pacemaker tracks the atrial signal in atrial fibrillation/flutter, resulting in a very fast ventricular response. However, setting an appropriate upper rate limit on these pacemakers usually prevents this complication.

   b. Occasionally, a pacemaker-mediated tachycardia can develop from repetitive retrograde conduction from premature

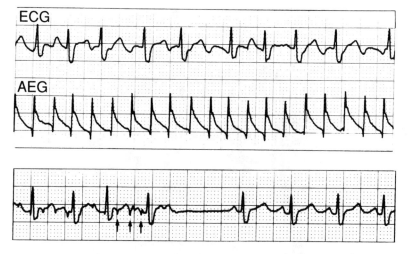

Figure 10.12   *Rapid atrial bipolar pacing of atrial flutter in sequential ECG tracings. The upper tracing confirms the rhythm as type I atrial flutter (rate of 300 beats/min) with variable AV block. In the lower tracing, rapid atrial pacing at a slightly faster rate entrains the atrium; the pacer is turned off and sinus rhythm resumes after a brief pause. The arrows indicate the atrial pacing stimulus artifact.*

ventricular complexes that produces atrial deflections that are sensed and tracked.

4. **Indications**

   a. Complete heart block

   b. Second-degree heart block to achieve 1:1 conduction

   c. First-degree heart block if 1:1 conduction cannot be achieved at a faster rate because of a long PR interval.

   d. DDD or VDD pacing for fast atrial rates with second- or third-degree heart block. In this situation, the ventricle will be stimulated after the pacemaker senses the atrial activity, establishing a fixed PR interval.

5. Additional comments

   a. Sequential AV pacing is ineffective during atrial fibrillation/flutter.

   b. AV pacing is always preferable to ventricular pacing because of the atrial contribution to ventricular filling. This is especially important in noncompliant ventricles in which atrial contraction contributes up to 20–30% of the cardiac output.

   c. If sudden hemodynamic deterioration occurs during AV pacing, consider the possibility that atrial fibrillation has occurred with loss of atrial contraction. If AV conduction is slow, the ECG will demonstrate two pacing spikes with a QRS complex suggesting AV sequential pacing, although only ventricular pacing is present.

Figure 10.13 *AV sequential demand pacer (model 5330). The PR interval is usually set at 150 ms, with a stimulus strength of 10 to 20 mA. The threshold should be measured by decreasing the mA until there is failure to capture. Pacing can be accomplished in either the asynchronous (DOO) or demand (DVI) mode.*

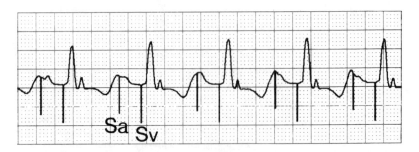

Figure 10.14 *Atrioventricular (AV) pacing at a rate of 100 beats/min with a PR interval of about 160 ms. The P wave is often very poorly seen between the pacing stimulus artifacts (atrial = Sa, ventricular = Sv).*

G. **Ventricular pacing**

1. Ventricular pacing is achieved by connecting the two ventricular wires to the pulse generator for bipolar pacing or connecting one ventricular wire to the negative pole and an indifferent electrode (skin wire) to the positive pole for unipolar pacing.

2. The pacemaker is used in the VVI mode. The ventricular output is set at 10–20 mA in the synchronous (demand) mode. Otherwise it may discharge on the T wave and trigger ventricular fibrillation. The rate selected depends on whether the pacemaker is being used for bradycardia backup, pacing at a therapeutic rate, or overdrive pacing (figure 10.15).

3. **Indications**
   a. A slow ventricular response to atrial fibrillation or flutter
   b. Failure of atrial pacing to maintain heart rate
   c. Ventricular tachycardia (overdrive pacing)

4. If a patient is dependent on AV or ventricular pacing, the pacing threshold must be tested. Gradually lower the mA until there is no capture. If the mA necessary to generate electrical activity is rising or exceeds 10 mA, consideration should be given to placement of a transvenous pacing system (temporary or permanent).

5. If the pacemaker is in the demand mode, testing the sensing threshold is worthwhile. Turn the rate to 50 (or less than the sinus or ventricular rate) and gradually increase the sensitivity until the "pacing" light, rather than the "sensing" light flashes. This gives an indication of the size of the R wave that is required for sensing. If the pacemaker requires a large R wave, it may start inappropriate pacing, instead of sensing, when smaller R waves are encountered.

H. **Potential problems with epicardial pacing wire electrodes**

1. **Failure to function** may result from:
   a. Faulty connections of the connecting cord to the pacing wires or the pulse generator
   b. Faulty pulse generator function (low battery)

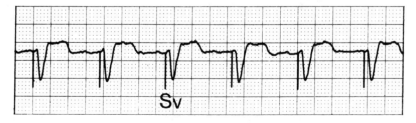

Figure 10.15 *Ventricular pacing at a rate of 80 beats/min, demonstrating the wide ventricular complex. Because the patient's own mechanism is slower, the pacemaker produces all of the ventricular complexes. Sv = ventricular pacing stimulus artifact.*

      c. Undetected development of atrial fibrillation causing failure of atrial capture

      d. Electrodes located in areas of poor electrical contact and high threshold

      e. Undetected detachment of the wire electrode from the atrial or ventricular epicardium

2. **Options** to restore pacemaker function include:

      a. Checking all connections; changing the connecting cord

      b. Increasing the output of the pulse generator to maximum current (20 mA)

      c. Using a different wire electrode as the negative (conducting) electrode

      d. Unipolarizing the pacemaker by attaching the positive lead to a surface ECG electrode or skin pacing wire

      e. Converting to ventricular pacing if the atrial stimulus fails to produce capture

      f. Using a chronotrope, such as epinephrine or isoproterenol, to increase the intrinsic rate and possibly increase atrial sensitivity to the pacing stimulus

      g. Placing a transvenous pacing wire if the patient has heart block or severe bradycardia and is pacer-dependent

3. **Change in threshold.** The pacing threshold rises from the time of implantation because of edema, inflammation, or the formation of scar tissue near the electrodes. If an advanced degree of heart block persists for over 1 week, consideration should be given to the placement of a permanent transvenous pacemaker system.

4. **Oversensing problems.** If the atrial activity of atrial fibrillation/flutter is sensed during DDD pacing, a very fast ventricular response will be noted. The upper rate limit should be programmed to prevent this. If this is not possible, the pacemaker should be converted to the VVI mode. Oversensing of T waves may lead to inhibition of VVI pacing.

5. **Competition with the patient's own rhythm.** When atrial or ventricular ectopy occurs during asynchronous pacing, the pacemaker may be set at a rate similar to the patient's intrinsic mechanism. Turning off the pacemaker will eliminate the problem.

6. **Inadvertent triggering of ventricular tachycardia or fibrillation.** Use of ventricular pacing in the asynchronous mode can potentially trigger ventricular ectopy by competing with the patient's own mechanism. Ventricular pacing must always be accomplished in the demand mode (DVI, VVI, DDD). Pacing wires that are not being used should be electrically isolated to prevent stray AC or DC current near the wires from triggering VF. Wires should be placed in needle caps and left in accessible locations.

7. **Mediastinal bleeding** can occur if rigid pacing wires are placed close to bypass grafts, shearing them by intermittent contact during

ventricular contractions. Similar damage can also occur during pacing wire removal. Bleeding from atrial or ventricular surfaces can occur if the wires are sewn too securely to the heart and excessive traction is applied for their removal. The patient should be observed carefully for signs of tamponade for several hours after removal of epicardial wires.

8. **Inability to remove the wire electrodes from the heart.** The wire can be caught beneath a tight suture on the heart, or more likely, under a sternal wire or subcutaneous suture. Constant gentle traction, allowing the heart to "beat the wire loose" should be applied. A lateral chest x-ray may reveal where the wires are entrapped. If the wires cannot be removed, they should be pulled out as far as possible, cut off at the skin level, and allowed to retract. Infection can occur in pacing wire tracts, but it is unusual.

I. **Other temporary pacing modes**

1. Newer defibrillator/monitors have the capability of providing transcutaneous pacing. This is most useful in emergency situations when epicardial pacing wires fail to function. Sedation may be required for patients who cannot tolerate the external pacing stimulus. This should not be relied upon for more than a few hours because ventricular capture frequently deteriorates over time.

2. Placement of a 4–5F temporary transvenous ventricular pacing wire is indicated if the patient is pacemaker-dependent and the threshold of the epicardial wires is high or the wires fail to function. These wires are usually placed through an introducer in the internal jugular or subclavian vein. Several brands have balloon tips that assist in floating the pacing wire into the apex of the right ventricle, although fluoroscopy may occasionally be required.

3. Some Swan-Ganz catheters have extra channels that open into the right atrium and ventricle (Paceport catheters) through which pacing catheters can be placed. This is convenient during and following minimally invasive cardiac operations. It is also helpful in emergency situations, since central venous access has already been achieved. These pacing probes should not be relied upon for chronic pacing in the pacemaker-dependent patient.

4. Transesophageal atrial pacing is valuable during minimally invasive procedures and can be used in the intensive care unit on a temporary basis.[112]

X. Cardiac Arrhythmias

The development of cardiac arrhythmias following open-heart surgery is fairly common. Supraventricular arrhythmias, especially atrial fibrillation, are noted in about 30% of patients. Ventricular ectopy is noted less commonly and usually reflects some degree of myocardial injury. Whereas atrial fibrillation is usually benign, ventricular arrhythmias may warrant further evaluation and treatment because of their potentially life-threatening nature.

The mechanisms underlying the development of most arrhythmias are those of altered automaticity (impulse formation) and conductivity (impulse conduction).

Table 10.11   *Treatment of Common Arrhythmias*

Arrhythmia	Treatment
1. Sinus bradycardia	Pacing: atrial or AV > ventricular
	Atropine
	Chronotropic medication
2. Third-degree heart block	Pacing: AV > ventricular
	Isoproterenol
3. Sinus tachycardia	Treat cause
	β-blocker
4. Premature atrial complexes (PACs)	No treatment
	Atrial pacing
	Digoxin
	Quinidine/procainamide
	β-blocker
	Verapamil
	Magnesium sulfate
5. Atrial fibrillation	Cardioversion if hemodynamically compromised
	Rate control: diltiazem/verapamil
	β-blocker
	digoxin
	Convert: procainamide/quinidine
	propafenone/ibutilide/amiodarone
	electrical cardioversion
	V-pace if slow response
6. Atrial flutter	Cardioversion if compromised
	Rapid atrial pacing
	See atrial fibrillation
7. Slow junctional rhythm	Pacing (atrial > AV > ventricular)
	Chronotropic medication
8. Other supraventricular tachycardias (PAT or AVNRT)	Atrial overdrive pacing
	Cardioversion
	Adenosine
	Verapamil/diltiazem
	β-blocker
	Digoxin
9. Nonparoxysmal AV junctional tachycardia	On digoxin: stop digoxin
	potassium
	phenytoin
	Not on digoxin: digoxin
10. Premature ventricular complexes (PVCs)	Treat hypokalemia
	Atrial overdrive pacing
	Lidocaine
	Procainamide
11. Ventricular tachycardia/ fibrillation	Defibrillation
	Lidocaine
	Bretylium
	Procainamide
	Amiodarone

An understanding of these mechanisms and the electrophysiologic effects of the antiarrhythmic drugs has provided a rational basis for their use (see page 314).[113] The treatment of arrhythmias commonly noted after open-heart surgery is summarized in table 10.11.[114]

A. **Etiology**. Although the factors that contribute to the development of various cardiac arrhythmias may differ, there are several common causes that should be considered.

    1. Cardiac problems

        a. Underlying heart disease

        b. Preexisting arrhythmias

        c. Myocardial ischemia or infarction

        d. Poor intraoperative myocardial protection

        e. Pericardial inflammation

    2. Respiratory problems

        a. Endotracheal tube irritation or misplacement

        b. Hypoxia, hypercarbia, acidosis

        c. Pneumothorax

    3. Electrolyte imbalance (hypo- or hyperkalemia, hypomagnesemia)

    4. Intracardiac monitoring lines (PA catheter)

    5. Surgical trauma (atriotomy, ventriculotomy, dissection near the conduction system)

    6. Drugs (digoxin, vasoactive medications)

    7. Hypothermia

    8. Fever, anxiety, pain

    9. Gastric dilatation

B. **Assessment**

    1. Check the arterial blood gases, ventilator function, position of the endotracheal tube, and chest x-ray for mechanical problems.

    2. Check serum electrolytes (especially potassium).

    3. Review a 12-lead ECG for ischemia and a more detailed examination of the arrhythmia. If the diagnosis is not clearcut, obtain an atrial electrogram (AEG). This is frequently beneficial in differentiating among some of the more common arrhythmias by providing an amplified tracing of atrial activity.

C. **Sinus bradycardia**

    1. Sinus bradycardia is present when the sinus rate is less than 60 beats/min. It is frequently caused by persistent β-blockade and the use of narcotics, and may result in atrial, junctional, or ventricular escape rhythms.

    2. Because sinus bradycardia reduces cardiac output, the heart rate should be maintained around 90 beats/min following the termination of CPB to optimize hemodynamics. An increase in heart rate can improve myocardial contractility and cardiac output.

3. **Diagnosis**. See figure 10.16.

4. **Treatment**

   a. Atrial pacing should be used to take advantage of the 20–30% increase in stroke volume that results from the contribution of atrial filling. This is particularly important in the early postoperative period when reperfusion and myocardial edema impair ventricular compliance and cause diastolic dysfunction. Atrial contraction is especially important in patients with LV hypertrophy (aortic valve disease, systemic hypertension).

   b. AV pacing should be used if abnormal AV conduction is present (second- or third-degree AV block).

   c. If pacing wires were not placed at the conclusion of surgery or if they fail to function, atropine, 0.01 mg/kg IV (usually 0.5–1 mg IV), or one of the catecholamines can be used to stimulate the sinus mechanism. Either epinephrine 1–2 µg/min or isoproterenol 0.3–4 µg/min (starting at 5 microdrops/min of a 1 mg/250 mL mix) is often useful. However, these medications (as well as dopamine and dobutamine) not only increase the heart rate, but have other hemodynamic effects as well.

   d. Ventricular pacing can be used if the atrium fails to capture or there is little response to pharmacologic management. It will nearly always produce less effective hemodynamics than a supraventricular mechanism. If the ventricular pacing wires fail to function, the other pacing modes listed on page 285 can be considered.

   e. Patients with known sick sinus or tachy-brady syndrome often have problems with slow heart rates postoperatively and may require placement of a permanent pacemaker.

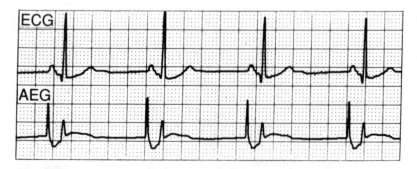

Figure 10.16 *Sinus bradycardia at a rate of 54 beats/min recorded simultaneously in lead I and a unipolar AEG. The AEG demonstrates the larger atrial complex, a PR interval of 0.18 ms, and the smaller ventricular complex.*

f. Following heart transplantation, recovery of sinus and AV node function may take up to 4 weeks, and pacemaker implantation can be deferred as long as the sensitivity of the epicardial wires remains satisfactory. Aminophylline is often beneficial in stimulating the sinus mechanism in transplant patients with sinus node dysfunction.[115]

D. **Conduction abnormalities and heart block**

1. Transient disturbances of AV conduction are noted in about 25% of patients following coronary bypass surgery. They are more frequent when cold cardioplegic arrest is used for myocardial protection, especially when calcium-channel blockers are used as additives.

   a. Conduction abnormalities are more common in patients with compromised LV function, hypertension, severe coronary disease (especially right-sided), long aortic crossclamp periods, and extremely low myocardial temperatures. These findings suggest that ischemic or cold injury to the conduction system may be responsible for these problems. Although most will resolve within 24–48 hours, the persistence of a new left bundle branch block (LBBB) suggests the possible occurrence of a perioperative infarction.[116–118]

   b. Conduction abnormalities occurring after aortic valve replacement (AVR) may be caused by hemorrhage, edema, suturing, or débridement near the conduction system. Although persistent conduction abnormalities do not appear to influence the long-term prognosis after CABG, LBBB is an ominous prognostic sign after AVR.[119]

   c. Exposure of the mitral valve by the biatrial transseptal approach involves division of the sinus node artery and anterior internodal pathways. Although some studies have not documented a higher incidence of postoperative rhythm disturbances, others have shown a high incidence of ectopic atrial rhythms, junctional rhythms, and varying degrees of heart block. Nearly 20% of patients may require a permanent pacer for bradycardia or complete heart block when this approach is used.[120,121]

2. **Diagnosis.** See figures 10.17 through 10.21.

3. **Treatment**

   a. Temporary atrial and ventricular pacing wires are invaluable in the management of heart block in the immediate postoperative period.

   b. **First-degree AV block** usually does not require treatment (see figure 10.17). If the PR interval is markedly prolonged, attempts to achieve faster atrial pacing will not achieve 1:1 conduction because the AV node will remain refractory when the next impulse arrives. This will produce functional second-degree heart block. AV pacing in the DDD or DVI

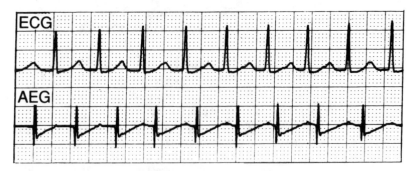

Figure 10.17 *First-degree AV block recorded simultaneously in lead II and a bipolar AEG. The PR interval is approximately 0.26 ms.*

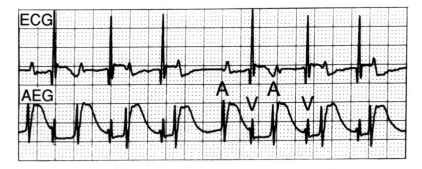

Figure 10.18 *Mobitz type I (Wenckebach) second-degree block. The unipolar AEG demonstrates a constant atrial rate of 120 with progressive lengthening of the A-V (PR) intervals until the ventricular complex is dropped. In the AEG, the atrial activity is represented by the larger of the two complexes (A = atrial complex, V = ventricular complex).*

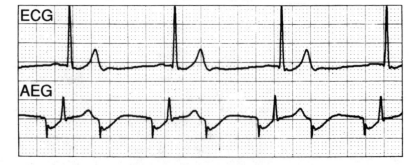

Figure 10.19 *Mobitz type II second-degree block. Atrial activity is present at a rate of 100 beats/min with 2:1 block, producing a ventricular rate of 50 beats/min.*

mode can be used in this situation. As previously noted, shortening a prolonged AV interval can significantly improve hemodynamics, especially in patients with impaired LV function.[111]

c. **Second-degree AV block**

   i. Mobitz type I (Wenckebach) is characterized by progressive PR interval prolongation culminating in a nonconducted P wave (see figure 10.18). This usually does not require treatment unless the ventricular rate is slow. In this situation, it can be treated by AV pacing (DVI) at a slightly faster rate, or, if the atrial rate is too fast to overdrive, by DDD pacing.

   ii. Mobitz type II is characterized by intermittent nonconducted P waves without progressive PR elongation (see figure 10.19). If the ventricular rate is too slow, AV pacing in the DVI or DDD mode should be used.

d. **Complete heart block** requires AV pacing in the DVI mode if there is atrial inactivity or a slow atrial rate. The DVI mode may increase the risk of developing atrial fibrillation if frequent PACs are present. The DDD mode is used if there is a moderately fast atrial rate. Ventricular pacing should be used if atrial fibrillation/flutter is present (see figure 10.20). Pacing is usually not necessary when there is AV dissociation with an adequate junctional or idioventricular rate. However, it can be accomplished with DDD pacing if the atrial rate is not too fast (see figure 10.21).

e. If heart block persists, the patient's medications should be reviewed. β-blockers and calcium-channel blockers should be used very cautiously, if at all. If digoxin has been used, a drug level should be checked. If complete heart block persists for more than 1 week after bypass or valve surgery, a permanent pacemaker system should be placed.

f. About 40% of patients in whom permanent pacemakers are placed are not dependent on their system at follow-up. The most significant predictor of pacemaker dependency is its insertion for complete heart block.[122]

g. Depression of AV nodal function following cardiac transplantation may take up to 4 weeks to resolve. Epicardial pacing wires or aminophylline may be used to defer pacemaker implantation.

E. **Sinus tachycardia**

1. Sinus tachycardia is present when the sinus rate exceeds 100 beats/min. It generally occurs at rates less than 130. A faster and regular ventricular rate suggests the presence of paroxysmal supraventricular (atrial or junctional) tachycardia or atrial flutter with 2:1 block.

2. Fast heart rates are detrimental to myocardial metabolism. They can exacerbate myocardial ischemia by increasing oxygen demand

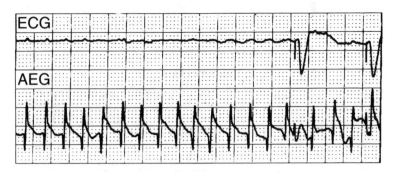

Figure 10.20 *Complete AV block. The AEG demonstrates type I atrial flutter, but the monitor ECG shows no ventricular complex until ventricular pacing is initiated.*

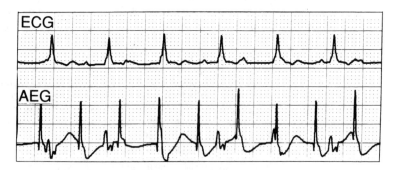

Figure 10.21 *Complete AV block with AV dissociation. The unipolar AEG demonstrates an atrial rate of 140 (large spikes) with no clearcut relationship to the QRS complex, which represents a junctional mechanism at a rate of 100 beats/min.*

and decreasing the time for diastolic coronary perfusion. They also reduce the time for ventricular filling and can reduce stroke volume, especially in patients with LVH and diastolic dysfunction.

3. **Etiology**

   a. Benign hyperdynamic reflex response related to sympathetic overactivity:
      - Pain, anxiety, fever
      - Low stroke volumes (hypovolemia, small LV chamber, severe LV hypertrophy)
      - Adrenergic rebound (patient on β-blockers preoperatively)
      - Drugs (catecholamines, pancuronium)
      - Gastric dilatation
      - Anemia
      - Hypermetabolic states (sepsis)

   b. Compensatory response to myocardial injury or impaired cardiorespiratory status:

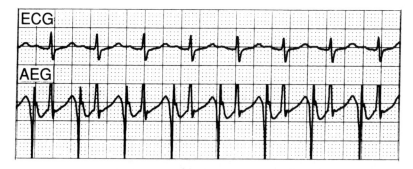

Figure 10.22 *Sinus tachycardia at a rate of 130 beats/min on simultaneous recordings of monitor lead II and a unipolar AEG. Note the larger atrial and smaller ventricular complex in the unipolar AEG tracing, which demonstrates the 1:1 AV conduction.*

- Abnormal arterial blood gases
- Myocardial ischemia or infarction
- Cardiac tamponade
- Tension pneumothorax

4. **Diagnosis.** See figure 10.22.

5. **Treatment**

a. Correction of the underlying cause

b. Sedation and analgesia

c. β-blockers can be used if the heart is hyperdynamic with an excellent cardiac output. They must be used cautiously, however, when cardiac function is marginal. Tachycardia is a compensatory mechanism to maintain cardiac output when the stroke volume is low, so attempts to slow the heart rate may prove detrimental. Even when the cardiac output is satisfactory, β-blockers often lower the blood pressure significantly more than they reduce the heart rate.

    i. Esmolol 0.25–0.5 mg/kg IV over 1 minute, followed by a continuous infusion of 50–200 μg/kg/min. A trial bolus of 0.125–0.25 mg/kg is frequently beneficial in determining whether the patient can tolerate esmolol.

    ii. Metoprolol in 5 mg IV increments

    iii. Propranolol in 0.5 mg IV increments
    Note: β-blockers should be used cautiously in the absence of functional pacing wires. They generally should not be given at the same time as intravenous calcium-channel blockers.

d. Calcium-channel blockers have mild negative chronotropic effects on the SA node, but they do not play a major role in the treatment of sinus tachycardia.

e. Selective bradycardic agents such as zatebradine are drugs that act specifically at the SA node but have no effect on contractility, ventricular relaxation, or coronary blood flow. They have seen little clinical use to date, but have been shown experimentally to enhance the inotropic effects of catecholamines by virtue of a reduction in heart rate that increases subendocardial flow per beat, leading to an improvement in regional contractile function.[123,124] These medications should be avoided when the tachycardia is compensatory to maintain cardiac output.

F. **Premature atrial complexes (PACs)**

1. PACs are premature beats arising in the atrium that generally have a different configuration than the normal P wave and produce a PR interval that exceeds 120 ms. Although benign, they often herald the development of atrial fibrillation or flutter, which may not be well tolerated in the early postoperative period. This conversion can be very difficult to prevent.

2. Magnesium sulfate may be beneficial in reducing the incidence of PACs in the immediate postoperative period. The dose is 2 g in 100 mL solution.

3. **Diagnosis.** See figure 10.23.

4. **Treatment**

    a. PACs generally do not need to be treated. Several of the antiarrhythmic medications that are used to slow the ventricular response to atrial fibrillation may actually increase the risk of developing atrial fibrillation if PACs are present.

    b. Atrial pacing at a faster rate may suppress PACs, but it may also trigger atrial arrhythmias and induce atrial fibrillation. If PACs occur during atrial pacing, suspect competition with the patient's own rhythm.

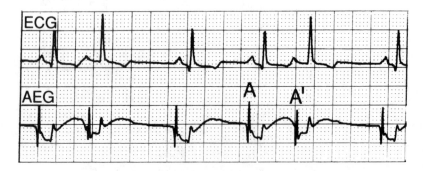

Figure 10.23 *Premature atrial complexes (PACs) in monitor lead II and a unipolar AEG. Note the slightly different morphology of the normal (A) and premature (A') atrial complexes and the slightly shorter PR interval following the PACs that indicates a focus different from the sinus node. The PR interval exceeds 120 ms, thus differentiating these beats from premature junctional complexes.*

    c.   Digoxin 0.25 mg IV q6h × 4 doses, then 0.25 mg PO qd. Digoxin is useful in decreasing the frequency of PACs and slows conduction through the AV node if AF does develop. However, by increasing conduction velocity in the atrium, digoxin can theoretically increase the risk of developing atrial fibrillation if PACs are present.

    d.   Quinidine or procainamide after full digitalization. These type IA antiarrhythmic medications slow conduction through the atrium and may decrease the incidence of PACs. However, they can accelerate AV conduction if atrial flutter develops. At the conclusion of surgery, intravenous procainamide may be selected as an antiarrhythmic because of its beneficial effects in treating both atrial and ventricular ectopy. The doses of these medications are noted in the next section.

    e.   β-blockers and verapamil are occasionally successful in decreasing the incidence of PACs and will slow AV conduction if atrial fibrillation develops subsequently.

G. Atrial fibrillation or flutter

1. Atrial fibrillation (atrial rate >380) and flutter (atrial rate generally <380) are the most common arrhythmias noted after open-heart surgery. Despite various prophylactic measures to decrease their incidence, they still occur in about 25–30% of patients. The underlying mechanism is probably increased dispersion of repolarization, but predisposing factors have not been well identified. The incidence is greater in older patients, those with a history of atrial arrhythmias, lung disease (especially when requiring prolonged postoperative ventilation), right coronary artery stenosis, valve disease, and patients not receiving β-blockers after surgery.[125–129]

2. The potential adverse effects of these rhythms are a compromise in cardiac hemodynamics and systemic thromboembolism from left atrial thrombus.[130] Because of the resources required to treat atrial fibrillation once it occurs, it has a substantial impact on hospital costs.[129,131]

3. These arrhythmias occur most commonly on the second and third postoperative day. By that time, myocardial function has recovered to baseline and few adverse hemodynamic effects are noted. However, when atrial tachyarrhythmias occur during the first 24 hours or when the patient is hemodynamically unstable, a rapid ventricular response can precipitate ischemia and lower cardiac output by eliminating the atrial contribution to ventricular filling. This can be troublesome in patients with marginal myocardial function or noncompliant ventricles that derive 30% of their stroke volume from atrial contraction.

4. After the initial 24 hours, atrial fibrillation is frequently an incidental finding on the ECG monitor. Symptoms such as palpitations, nausea, fatigue, or lightheadedness may be noted, especially in patients with LV hypertrophy or poor ventricular function.

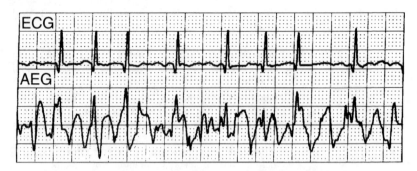

Figure 10.24 *Atrial fibrillation with a ventricular response of 130 beats/min. The AEG demonstrates the chaotic atrial activity that is characteristic of atrial fibrillation.*

5. **Etiology**
   a. Poor atrial preservation during aortic crossclamping
   b. Adrenergic rebound in patients taking β-blockers preoperatively
   c. Enhanced sympathetic activity (elevated norepinephrine levels)[132]
   d. Surgical trauma or pericardial inflammation
   e. Atrial distention
   f. Metabolic derangements (hypoxia, hypokalemia, hypomagnesemia)

6. **Diagnosis.** See figures 10.24 and 10.25.

7. **Prevention**
   a. Initiation of low-dose β-blockers starting within 12–24 hours of surgery is effective in lowering the incidence of these arrhythmias. Metoprolol 25–50 mg bid, propranolol 10 mg qid, or atenolol 25 mg qd, are used most commonly.[133,134] The addition of digoxin to one of the β-blockers may increase efficacy, although digoxin alone is not effective.[135]
   b. Magnesium sulfate (2 g in 100 mL) is effective in decreasing the number of episodes of postoperative atrial fibrillation.[136,137]
   c. Intraoperative use of triiodothyronine 0.8 μg/kg (about 50–80 μg) at the time of removal of the crossclamp and a 6 hour infusion of 0.113 μg/kg/h (8–11 μg/h) has been shown to halve the rate of atrial fibrillation.[56]
   d. Sotalol is a β-blocker with class III antiarrhythmic properties that, at a dose of 40 mg q6–8h, is more effective than both metoprolol and propranolol in preventing supraventricular tachyarrhythmias.[138,139] However, because of the risk of side effects (hypotension, bradycardia, QT prolongation, and torsades de pointes), it has not seen much use to date.

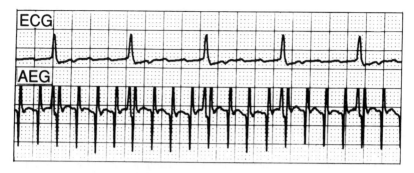

Figure 10.25 *Atrial flutter with 4:1 AV block. The unipolar AEG demonstrates an atrial rate of about 300 with a ventricular response of about 75 beats/min.*

e. Amiodarone is effective in reducing the incidence of atrial fibrillation if adequate tissue levels are achieved. One study showed that amiodarone, given for 600 mg qd × 7 days preoperatively, then 200 mg qd until discharge, halved the rate of atrial fibrillation and slowed the ventricular response to AF. At this dosage level, very few side effects were noted.[140]

f. Dual site atrial pacing may be effective in reducing the incidence of atrial fibrillation. It is theorized that intraatrial conduction delays may contribute to atrial fibrillation. Dual site pacing alters the atrial activation sequence and may achieve electrical resynchronization and more uniform electrical activation of the atria. So far, it has been found to be effective in reducing the incidence of atrial fibrillation only in patients receiving β-blockers.[141]

g. The efficacy of numerous other medications in preventing atrial fibrillation has been studied. These include digoxin alone, procainamide, verapamil, and diltiazem. Although some reports have been favorable, the general consensus is that these drugs are not efficacious and/or are not well tolerated.[142-145]

8. **Treatment** for the unstable patient initially involves cardioversion; for the stable patient, the plan involves rate control, anticoagulation if atrial fibrillation persists, and attempts to achieve conversion to sinus rhythm (table 10.12).[146-148]

a. **Cardioversion** with 50–100 J should always be considered first if there is evidence of significant hemodynamic compromise. This is more common in the early postoperative period when myocardial function is moderately depressed. **Note:** There is an increased risk of precipitating malignant ventricular arrhythmias if cardioversion is attempted when the digoxin level is significantly elevated, especially if hypokalemia or hypercalcemia is also present. Lidocaine or phenytoin should be available.

Table 10.12   *Management Protocols for Atrial Fibrillation/Flutter*

1. Prophylaxis
   a. Magnesium sulfate 2 g IV after CPB and on first postoperative morning
   b. Metoprolol 25–50 mg PO (per NG tube) starting 8 hours after surgery
   c. Digoxin 0.25 mg IV q6h starting 8 hours after surgery
   d. Alternatives (based on current literature)
      • Dual site atrial pacing
      • Sotalol 40 mg q6–8h
      • Amiodarone 600 mg qd × 7 preoperatively, then 200 mg qd
      • Triiodothyronine 0.8 μg/kg at the time of removal of the crossclamp and a 6-hour infusion of 0.113 μg/kg/hour

2. Treatment
   a. Cardioversion with 50–100 J if unstable
   b. Rapid atrial pace if atrial flutter
   c. Increase prophylactic β-blocker dose if hemodynamically stable
   d. Rate control:
      • IV diltiazem 0.25 mg/kg IV over 2 minutes; followed 15 minutes later by 0.35 mg/kg over 2 minutes; followed by a continuous infusion of 10–15 mg/h, if necessary
      • Other options: verapamil, β-blockers, magnesium sulfate
   e. Conversion to sinus rhythm and anticoagulation
      • Magnesium sulfate 2 g IV
      • Option #1: heparin/warfarin after 24 hours of atrial fibrillation and discharge home in atrial fibrillation
      • Option #2: Procan SR 500 mg q6h or quinidine gluconate 324 mg tid sulfate until conversion occurs; heparinization necessary after 24 hours
      • Option #3: procainamide 10 mg/kg IV over 30 minutes followed by attempt at cardioversion (within 24 hours of onset of atrial fibrillation); TEE essential if cardioversion attempted after 24–36 hours without anticoagulation
        If unsuccessful: heparinize and give warfarin; discharge home in atrial fibrillation
        If successful: continue oral procainamide for 4 weeks; if cardioversion is performed after 36–48 hours, consider 3–4 weeks of warfarin
      • Option #4: use of type IC and III antiarrhythmic medications
        Propafenone 1 mg/kg IV over 2 minutes, followed 10 minutes later by another 1 mg/kg dose
        Ibutilide 1 mg infusion over 10 minutes (0.01 mg/kg if <60 kg) with a second infusion 10 minutes later
        Amiodarone 150 mg over 30 minutes followed by an infusion of 1 mg/min × 6 h, then 1 g/day, if necessary
        Sotalol 80 mg q4h × 4 doses

b. **Rapid atrial pacing** should be attempted to convert atrial flutter (see figure 10.12 and page 278 for technique of rapid atrial pacing). It is usually successful in converting only type I flutter (atrial rate less than 350). A variety of type IA, IC, and III antiarrhythmics (procainamide, propafenone, and ibutilide) increase the efficacy of rapid atrial pacing by prolonging the atrial flutter cycle length. The type IA drugs do not alter or may increase the duration of the excitable gap in the reentrant circuit, whereas the type III agents shorten the excitable gap. Although the latter may limit the ability of pacing to capture tissue in the reentrant circuit, equivalent efficacy has been noted.[149,150]

c. **Rate control** can be achieved most readily with one of the rapid-acting intravenous medications and more chronically by use of digoxin. Once the rate has been controlled, the IV medications can be converted to PO.

   i. **Diltiazem** is given in a dose of 0.25 mg/kg IV over 2 minutes, followed 15 minutes later by 0.35 mg/kg over 2 minutes, followed by a continuous infusion of 10–15 mg/h, if necessary.[151] Heart rate response is noted in about 3 minutes with a peak effect within 7 minutes. The reduction in heart rate lasts 1–3 hours after a bolus dose. The median duration of action is 7 hours after a 24 hour continuous infusion. Diltiazem is more effective in slowing the ventricular response to atrial fibrillation than flutter.

   - Hypotension is the most common side effect but is seen less frequently than with verapamil. Because diltiazem has a mild negative inotropic effect, it must be used cautiously in patients with compromised ventricular function.

   - Diltiazem is extremely effective in slowing the ventricular response, but converts only about 20% of patients to sinus rhythm.

   - **Note:** Extreme caution must be used when administering any IV calcium-channel blocker concomitantly with an IV β-blocker because of the risk of inducing complete AV block. Availability of functional pacing wires is essential.

   ii. **Verapamil** can be used as an alternative to diltiazem because of its lower cost, although it is associated with more hypotension and has a shorter duration of action.

   - The dose is 2.5–5.0 mg IV q15min until the heart rate slows. It may be given intermittently or as a continuous drip of 2–5 µg/kg/min. The onset of action is only 1–3 minutes, but the duration of action is relatively short, with a half-life of only 15 minutes.

   - Verapamil is a negative inotrope and a vasodilator. Hypotension is not uncommon when doses greater than 2.5 mg are given. This can usually be reversed with fluid administration, or, if necessary, with calcium chloride.

- As with diltiazem, control of the ventricular response is the major therapeutic effect. Reversion to sinus rhythm is noted in only 10% of cases.[152,153]

iii. **Magnesium sulfate** is not quite as effective as the calcium-channel blockers in reducing the ventricular response, but it is much more effective in converting patients to sinus rhythm (60% within 4 hours with a dose of 2 g).[153]

iv. **Esmolol** is another alternative to achieve rapid rate control. However, because of its hypotensive effect, it usually requires arterial line monitoring, whereas IV bolus doses of calcium-channel blockers are usually safer and do not require aggressive monitoring. One advantage of esmolol is that it achieves conversion to sinus rhythm in about 50% of patients.[152]

- The dose is 0.125–0.5 mg/kg IV over 1 minute, followed by an infusion of 50–200 μg/kg/min.
- Intravenous esmolol has an onset of action of 2 minutes with reversal of effect in 10–20 minutes. Its short duration of action makes it safer than the longer-acting β-blockers if adverse effects develop, such as bronchospasm, conduction disturbances, LV dysfunction, or excessive bradycardia. Because of its negative inotropic effects, esmolol must be used cautiously in patients with borderline ventricular function.

v. **Propranolol** or **metoprolol** are inexpensive medications that are very effective in achieving rate control and conversion to sinus rhythm. They have negative inotropic effects that are fairly comparable to the calcium-channel blockers. It is unfortunate that these medications have gone out of vogue because they generally are very safe and extremely effective.

- Propranolol is given in 0.5 mg IV increments q30min PRN up to 0.1 mg/kg. The onset of action is 2–5 minutes with peak effect in 30 minutes and a variable duration of action.
- Metoprolol is given in 5 mg IV increments q5min up to a total dose of 15 mg. The onset of action is 2–3 minutes with a peak effect noted at 20 minutes. The duration of action is approximately 5 hours.

vi. Concomitant with the selection of one of the preceding medications, **digoxin** should be started because of its efficacy in chronically slowing the ventricular response. If it was given along with β-blockers for prophylactic therapy, drug levels should be optimized to achieve the best response. It is the safest drug to use in the patient with significant ventricular dysfunction.

- The initial dose is 0.5 mg IV, followed by 0.25 mg IV q4–6h × 3 doses (up to a total dose of 1.25 mg within 24 hours—less in elderly patients), and then 0.125–0.25 mg qd.
- The onset of action of IV digoxin is about 30 minutes with a peak effect in 2–3 hours.
- The ventricular response to atrial fibrillation tends to be resistant to digoxin in the early postoperative period because its vagotonic effect on the AV node is offset by the increased sympathetic tone that contributes to the rapid ventricular response at this time.[154] Therefore, it is usually of little value in the acute postoperative setting and nearly always requires the addition of either calcium-channel blockers or β-blockers for rate control. Furthermore, higher doses are required to directly depress the AV node in the early postoperative period, at which time there is a narrow therapeutic range between efficacy and toxicity.
- Digoxin is ineffective in converting atrial fibrillation back to sinus rhythm, and it is also ineffective in preventing paroxysmal atrial fibrillation.[155] In fact, digoxin may render the atrium more susceptible to the development of atrial fibrillation because it increases atrial excitability and conduction velocity, reduces the atrial refractory period, and increases the number of fibrillatory wavelets. Thus, paroxysmal atrial fibrillation may actually be more frequent, of longer duration, and faster.
- Because digoxin may increase the fibrillation rate, it may convert atrial flutter to fibrillation. If the latter occurs, the ventricular response may be easier to control.
- The serum potassium level should be over 4.0 mEq/L when digoxin is given because hypokalemia may precipitate digoxin-toxic rhythms.
- Digoxin levels should always be drawn at least 6 hours after the last oral dose or 4 hours after the last IV dose to reflect serum steady-state levels accurately.
- Additional comments on digoxin toxicity are found on page 321.

d. **Anticoagulation.** Heparinization should be considered for patients with recurrent or persistent atrial fibrillation to minimize the risk of stroke from embolization of left atrial thrombus. In one study, it was noted that 14% of patients developed thrombus and 39% had spontaneous echo contrast in the left atrium within 3 days of the development of atrial fibrillation.[156] Generally, heparin should be started within 24–36 hours of the development of atrial fibrillation to minimize the risk of thrombus formation.

    i. Cardioversion can usually be performed safely within 24–36 hours without anticoagulation. If anticoagulation is not given for more than 36 hours, atrial thrombus should be excluded by TEE.[157] However, even in this situation, thromboembolism can occur after cardioversion, either because TEE is not sensitive enough to detect all thrombi or because subsequent de novo thrombus forms due to mechanical atrial inactivity that may persist after electrical cardioversion.[158] Therefore, in the patient undergoing successful cardioversion beyond 36–48 hours, anticoagulation should be given for 3–4 weeks unless there are contraindications to its use. It is usually not necessary if cardioversion is performed earlier.

    ii. If a patient cannot be converted, warfarin should be given for 3 weeks before an elective cardioversion is attempted. If successful, warfarin is continued for an additional 4 weeks because of persistent mechanical atrial dysfunction.[148,159]

e. **Conversion to sinus rhythm.** The use of type IA medications to convert patients to sinus rhythm is successful about 60% of the time, but often is ineffective, time-consuming, frustrating, and costly. Options include the following:

    i. Magnesium sulfate (2 g IV over 15 minutes) is a benign and relatively effective means of converting patients back to sinus rhythm, with a conversion rate of 60% within 4 hours in one study.[153]

    ii. A brief course of IV procainamide (10 mg/kg over 20–60 minutes, followed by a 2 mg/min infusion), followed within 12 hours by an attempt at electrical cardioversion. This may avoid the need to heparinize the patient if performed within 36 hours of the onset of atrial fibrillation. If successful, the procainamide is continued for 4 weeks. If unsuccessful, it is stopped and the patient is anticoagulated and rate-controlled. As noted above, if a patient has not been anticoagulated, it is reasonably safe to perform electrical cardioversion if atrial thrombus is excluded by a careful transesophageal echocardiogram, but anticoagulation should be considered following a successful cardioversion.[157]

    iii. A course of oral procainamide or quinidine will be successful in about 60% of patients. However, gastrointestinal side effects and QT prolongation are major concerns with these medications. Because they have a vagolytic effect that can accelerate AV conduction in atrial fibrillation/flutter, they should be given only after the ventricular rate has been controlled.

- **Procainamide** is usually given IV or PO. Advantages over quinidine are that its gastrointestinal side effects are usually anorexia and nausea, but uncommonly diarrhea; it does not influence digoxin levels; and it has less of a proarrhythmic effect than quinidine. The usual dose is:

  Intravenous: 10 mg/kg load (100 mg q5min), then a 2–4 mg/min infusion

  Oral: Procan-SR 500–1000 mg q6h, or Procanbid 500–1000 mg bid.

  If converting IV to PO, stop the IV infusion when the PO dose is given.

- **Quinidine** is usually administered orally, because it may cause hypotension when given IV and is poorly absorbed when given IM. Therefore, it is usually not given if the patient is still NPO. The usual dose is:

  Quinidine sulfate 200 mg PO q2h × 4 doses or 300 mg PO q3h × 3 doses, then quinidine gluconate 324–486 mg PO q8h.

  Its disadvantages are that it:

  - Causes diarrhea in a significant percentage of patients.
  - Raises digoxin levels by nearly 50% and may produce digoxin toxicity if levels are not monitored carefully. Digoxin levels should generally be halved when quinidine is used.
  - It may produce thrombocytopenia and can cause a drug fever.
  - It is more proarrhythmic than procainamide, and can produce ventricular arrhythmias (such as torsades de pointes) even at therapeutic levels.

iv. The type IC and III antiarrhythmics have been successful in converting a significant number of patients with recent-onset atrial fibrillation back to sinus rhythm. However, very few studies have evaluated patients developing atrial fibrillation after cardiac surgical procedures. Chronic use of these medications should only be considered for symptomatic, refractory atrial fibrillation because of their proarrhythmic effects.

- **Propafenone** 1 mg/kg IV over 2 minutes, followed 10 minutes later by another 1 mg/kg dose, converts about 67% of patients with atrial fibrillation and 30% of patients with atrial flutter of short duration to sinus rhythm. It is effective in slowing the ventricular response if conversion does not occur. The conversion rate occurs more slowly with one oral dose of 600 mg, but is comparable at 8 hours.[160]
- **Ibutilide** 1 mg infusion over 10 minutes (0.01 mg/kg if <60 kg) with a second infusion 10

minutes later, if necessary. This converts about 30–50% of patients with atrial fibrillation and 50–70% with atrial flutter. Mean time to conversion is about 30 minutes. Because of the proarrhythmic risk, the infusion should be stopped as soon as the arrhythmia has terminated, ventricular tachycardia occurs, or there is marked prolongation of the QT interval.[161] Ibutilide is particularly useful in patients with poor ventricular function or chronic lung disease.

- **Amiodarone** can be given intravenously to slow the ventricular response or convert patients with refractory atrial fibrillation to sinus rhythm. It is used more commonly for long-term maintenance of sinus rhythm after electrical cardioversion, especially in patients with depressed LV function. It is given in a dose of 150 mg over 1 h, then 1 mg/min for 6h. Conversion has been noted in about 65% of patients with atrial fibrillation, but takes longer (4–6 hours) than propafenone. Amiodarone should be considered for the patient with renal dysfunction, in whom it is best to avoid procainamide.[162]

- **Sotalol** 80 mg q4h × 4 doses is effective in converting about 50% of patients to sinus rhythm. As noted above, its β-blocking properties are frequently not tolerated and nearly half the patients cannot tolerate this dosing because of bradycardia or hypotension.[163]

v. Carotid sinus massage is often recommended as a diagnostic modality to differentiate among various arrhythmias by slowing the ventricular response to atrial tachyarrhythmias. However, it must be used with caution in patients with coronary artery disease, not only because it may precipitate asystole, but because it may produce an embolic stroke in patients with coexistent carotid artery disease.

H. **Other supraventricular tachycardias (SVTs)**

1. This designation refers to a tachycardia of sudden onset that arises either in the atrium (paroxysmal atrial tachycardia or PAT) or in the AV nodal region (AV nodal reentrant tachycardia or AVNRT). These rhythms usually occur at a rate of 150–250 and are uncommon after cardiac surgery. PAT with AV block may be associated with ischemic heart disease and commonly results from digoxin toxicity. As with any arrhythmia causing a rapid ventricular response, immediate treatment is indicated because of potential adverse effects on myocardial metabolism and function.

2. **Diagnosis**. Differentiation among sinus tachycardia, PAT, AVNRT, and atrial flutter with 2:1 block may require examination of an atrial electrogram. See figure 10.26.

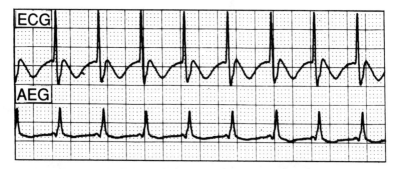

Figure 10.26 *AV junctional tachycardia at a rate of about 140 beats/min recorded in simultaneous monitor and bipolar AEG tracings. Note the nearly simultaneous occurrence of retrograde atrial activation in the AEG and the antegrade ventricular activation in the monitor lead.*

3. **Treatment**

   a. Rapid atrial overdrive pacing may capture the atrium and cause reversion to sinus rhythm.

   b. Cardioversion should be considered if there is evidence of hemodynamic compromise.

   c. Vagal stimulation will often break a reentrant rhythm involving the AV node. Carotid sinus massage must be used cautiously as noted above.

   d. Adenosine produces transient high-grade AV block and is successful in terminating SVT caused by AVNRT.[164] The dose is 6 mg by rapid IV injection via a central line followed by a saline flush. A repeat dose of 12 mg may be given 2 minutes later. The half-life of adenosine is only 10 seconds.

   e. Calcium-channel blockers are effective in converting AVNRT to sinus rhythm in about 90% of patients.

      i. Diltiazem 0.25 mg/kg IV over 2 minutes, followed 15 minutes later by 0.35 mg/kg, if necessary.[165]

      ii. Verapamil 2.5–10 mg IV over 5–10 minutes

   f. Additional measures that can be used for AVNRT if the above fail include:

      i. Digoxin 0.5 mg IV in a patient not previously on digoxin

      ii. Propranolol 1 mg IV q5 min to total dose of 0.2 mg/kg

      iii. Edrophonium 5 mg slow IV push followed by a 10 mg dose

   g. PAT with block is usually associated with digoxin toxicity and treatment should be provided accordingly:

      i. Digoxin should be withheld and a digoxin level obtained

      ii. Administration of potassium chloride

       iii. Digibind (digoxin immune Fab [ovine]) starting at a dose of 400 mg (10 vials) over 30 minutes if severe digoxin toxicity

       iv. Phenytoin (Dilantin) 250 mg IV over 5 minutes

I. **AV junctional rhythm and nonparoxysmal AV junctional tachycardia**

1. An AV junctional rhythm occurs when junctional tissue has a faster intrinsic rate than the sinus node. When it occurs at a rate less than 60 beats/min, it is termed a junctional escape rhythm.

2. Nonparoxysmal AV junctional tachycardia occurs at a rate of 70–130 beats/min. In the postoperative patient, this rhythm may reflect digitalis toxicity, pericarditis, or an inferior infarction. Its presence may be suggested by a regularized ventricular rate with underlying atrial fibrillation and can be confirmed with an atrial electrogram.

3. As with any nonatrial rhythm, cardiac output is diminished by lack of synchronous atrial and ventricular contractions.

4. **Diagnosis**. See figures 10.26 and 10.27. The focus may be localized by the relationship of the P wave to the QRS on a surface ECG (short PR interval if high nodal, invisible P wave if mid-nodal, and P wave following the QRS if low nodal). The P-QRS relationship is more evident on an atrial electrogram.

5. **Treatment**

   a. Slow junctional rhythm

      i. Atrial pacing if AV conduction is normal.

      ii. AV pacing if AV conduction is depressed.

      iii. Use of a vasoactive drug with chronotropic β_1 action to stimulate the sinus mechanism. Any drug the patient is receiving that might slow the sinus mechanism should be stopped.

   b. Nonparoxysmal junctional tachycardia

      i. If the patient is receiving digoxin, it should be stopped. Severe digoxin toxicity may be treated with Digibind.

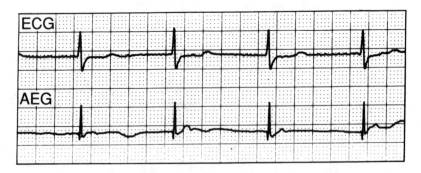

Figure 10.27 *Slow junctional rhythm at a rate of 54 beats/min. Note the simultaneous occurrence of atrial and ventricular activation.*

Use of potassium, lidocaine, phenytoin, or propranolol may be helpful.

ii. Overdrive pacing at a faster rate may establish AV synchrony.

iii. If the patient is not on digoxin, it should be started. If the rhythm is not well tolerated, use of a β-blocker or calcium-channel blocker can be considered to slow the junctional focus with use of atrial or AV pacing to establish AV synchrony.

J. **Premature ventricular complexes (PVCs)**

1. Ventricular ectopy is fairly common in survivors of myocardial infarction and is often generated from ectopic foci adjacent to scar tissue. Thus, if present before surgery, it commonly persists afterward, although ischemia-induced ectopy may be improved.

2. PVCs are fairly uncommon after complete revascularization with good myocardial protection. When they develop de novo, they may reflect transient perioperative phenomena, such augmented sympathetic tone or increased levels of catecholamines (endogenous or exogenous), irritation from a Swan-Ganz catheter or endotracheal tube, an abnormal acid-base status, or hypoxemia (see Section X.A). Thus, most PVCs are self-limited, benign, and not predictive of more serious, life-threatening arrhythmias, such as ventricular tachycardia or fibrillation.

3. However, PVCs developing de novo may also reflect poor intraoperative protection, myocardial ischemia or infarction—and may, in fact, herald these malignant arrhythmias. Therefore, some surgical groups believe that even occasional PVCs should never be ignored in the early postoperative period. During the first 24 hours after surgery, when a multitude of cardiac and noncardiac precipitating factors may be present, evaluating and treating any ventricular ectopy has potential benefits and little risk. Continued short-term antiarrhythmic therapy (for 12–36 hours) is warranted for patients with depressed LV function (ejection fraction <40%) and complex ventricular ectopy. It is usually not necessary for patients with normal ventricular function.[166,167]

4. **Diagnosis**. See figure 10.28.

5. **Treatment**

    a. Correct the serum potassium with an intravenous KCl infusion at a rate up to 10–20 mEq/h through a central line. Some patients require potassium levels between 4.5–5.0 mEq/L to eliminate ventricular ectopy.

    b. Atrial pace at a rate exceeding the current sinus rate ("overdrive pacing") unless tachycardia is present.

    c. Administer lidocaine 1 mg/kg with 1–2 repeat doses of 0.5 mg/kg 10 minutes apart. A continuous infusion of 1–2 mg/min of a 1 g/250 mL mix should be started. Do not exceed 4 mg/min to avoid seizure activity. Consider the patient's size and hepatic function when calculating a maximum dose (usually 3 mg/kg).

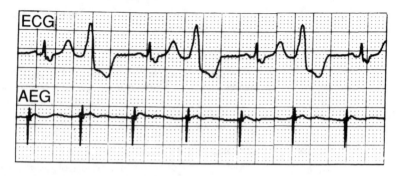

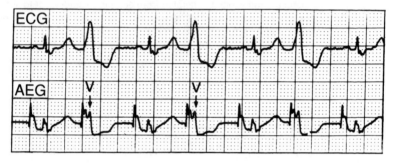

Figure 10.28 *Premature ventricular complexes (ventricular bigeminy) recorded simultaneously from monitor lead II and bipolar (upper) and unipolar (upper) AEGs. Note the wide complex of unifocal morphology representing the PVC on the ECG. The bipolar AEG shows that the interval between atrial complexes is maintained despite the PVCs. The unipolar tracing shows that the PVC directly follows the sinus beat but leaves the ventricle refractory to the following beat, producing a full compensatory pause. V = premature ventricular complex.*

        d.   Magnesium sulfate (2 g in 100 mL) administered at the termination of bypass has been shown to reduce the incidence of ventricular ectopy.[168]

K. **Ventricular tachycardia (VT) and ventricular fibrillation (VF)**

   1. **Etiology**

        a.   Ventricular tachyarrhythmias result from disorders of impulse formation or propagation. When they occur preoperatively on the basis of ischemia, resolution may be anticipated with complete revascularization of the ischemic zones. However, reperfusion of ischemic zones can also trigger de novo arrhythmias. If the patient has a history of VT, usually as a consequence of a previous myocardial infarction, it will not be improved and may be exacerbated by revascularization.

        b.   Malignant ventricular arrhythmias arising de novo after surgery warrant further evaluation by electrophysiologic testing.[169–172]

    i. Monomorphic VT is usually noted in patients with a previous myocardial infarction and depressed LV function, often with formation of an LV aneurysm. The border zone between scar and viable tissue provides the electrophysiologic substrate for a reentry mechanism which passes through myocyte bands surviving within the infarct. Reperfusion of these zones may provoke new onset monomorphic VT after surgery.

    ii. Polymorphic VT is usually caused by increased dispersion of repolarization in areas of reperfused ischemia or infarction. Triggered activity in the form of delayed afterdepolarizations and occasionally enhanced automaticity are the electrophysiologic mechanisms behind the formation of these arrhythmias. Their occurrence may be facilitated by perioperative phenomena such as hemodynamic instability, use of catecholamines or intrinsic sympathetic activity, withdrawal of β-blockers, and other metabolic problems. Similarly, ventricular fibrillation may be triggered by an acute ischemic insult.

  c. If the patient has a VVI or DDD pacemaker, the use of electrocautery during surgery can inactivate the sensing circuit, converting it to the VOO mode. This may result in bizarre-appearing arrhythmias and may trigger ventricular fibrillation. These pacemakers must be evaluated upon arrival in the ICU and reprogrammed if necessary.[173]

2. **Diagnosis.** See figures 10.29 and 10.30.

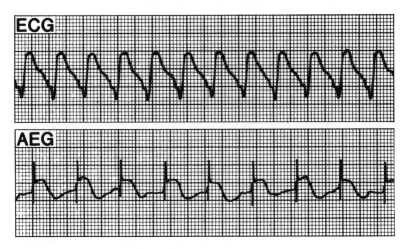

Figure 10.29   *Ventricular tachycardia recorded simultaneously in lead II and a bipolar AEG. There is dissociation between the sinus tachycardia at a rate of 115 beats/min noted in the AEG and the wide complex ventricular tachycardia occurring at a rate of 160 beats/min noted in the monitor lead.*

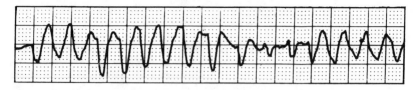

Figure 10.30 *Ventricular fibrillation on monitor lead.*

3. **Evaluation**

   a.   Although the prognosis of ventricular arrhythmias is favorable for patients with preserved LV function, it is less favorable when ventricular function is impaired.[174] Therefore, any patient with sustained VT following surgery should be evaluated by electrophysiologic testing. Therapy will vary depending on the status of LV function, the inducibility of VT, and whether the VT is monomorphic or polymorphic.

   b.   Since polymorphic VT is usually associated with myocardial infarction or ischemia, it should prompt further evaluation for ongoing ischemia. This may involve coronary arteriography to identify potential graft occlusion or an anastomotic stenosis, which may be a correctable problem.

4. **Treatment**

   a.   The incidence and severity of early postoperative arrhythmias is lessened by the administration of magnesium sulfate.[168]

   b.   The protocol for management of cardiac arrest should be instituted when **pulseless VT or VF** occur (see pages 260–262). These rhythms must be recognized immediately and treated with electrical defibrillation (starting at 200 Joules and increasing to 360 J) while initiating antiarrhythmic therapy.

   i.   If a patient develops refractory VT or VF unresponsive to repeated defibrillation attempts and multiple antiarrhythmic medications, **open thoracotomy** should be performed without hesitation, although it is only occasionally of benefit.

   ii.   **Note:** If defibrillation equipment is available, it is often preferable to hold off on external cardiac massage for the very brief period of time necessary to prepare equipment and perform defibrillation. External cardiac massage can disrupt the sternal closure, damage fresh grafts, or produce injury to cardiac structures from rigid prosthetic valves.

   iii. Antiarrhythmic medications should be started to prevent the recurrence of life-threatening arrhythmias. Electrophysiologic testing may be indicated to assess for inducibility of VT and for the efficacy of the antiarrhythmic medications. Placement of an implantable cardioverter-defibrillator (ICD) should be considered for these patients.

   c. Sustained VT (lasting over 30 seconds) may occur without hemodynamic compromise.

       i. Lidocaine should be given first in the doses noted on page 307.

      ii. Ventricular overdrive pacing can terminate the reentry circuit.

    iii. Cardioversion is indicated for persistent VT or hemodynamic compromise.

    iv. Bretylium 5 mg/kg, then a 2 mg/min infusion.

     v. Procainamide 30 mg/min up to 15 mg/kg, then a 2–4 mg/min infusion

    vi. Amiodarone 150 mg over 15–30 minutes, then 1 mg/min for 6–12 hours, then 0.5 mg/min

   d. Monomorphic VT is inducible in 80% of patients with spontaneous VT and is usually associated with a remote infarct and an arrhythmogenic substrate causing a reentry mechanism. This usually requires antiarrhythmic therapy (usually amiodarone), possible ablation, and/or placement of an ICD.

   e. Polymorphic VT is usually associated with ischemia or reperfusion arrhythmias and is often transient. Therapy must be individualized.[175]

   f. **Note:** Drug treatment for ventricular (as well as atrial) arrhythmias must be selected cautiously. Because of their mechanism of action, many of the antiarrhythmic drugs have proarrhythmic effects that could offset any benefit being derived from control of the primary arrhythmia.[176,177]

5. **Torsades de pointes** is a form of polymorphic VT that is associated with QT prolongation.[178] It usually occurs as a complication of type IA and III antiarrhythmic agents, especially during hypokalemia. Among the medications that can contribute to torsades are metoclopramide and high-dose haloperidol (>35 mg/day) used for agitation in the ICU.[179] The mechanism involves early afterdepolarizations (EADs) and triggered activity.

   a. Typical ECG changes involve labile QT intervals, prominent U waves, and a "pause-dependent" onset of the arrhythmia (figure 10.31).

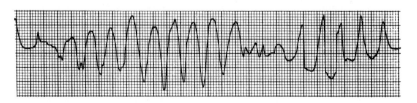

Figure 10.31 *Torsades de pointes on monitor lead. Note how the QRS complex appears to "twist" around the isoelectric baseline. Torsades is usually initiated by a premature ventricular complex discharging at the end of a T wave, usually associated with a long QT interval.*

    b.   Treatment entails:

        i. Cardioversion immediately for hemodynamic compromise or prolonged episodes (usually VF is suspected)

        ii. Correct hypokalemia (shortens the QT interval)

        iii. Ventricular pacing at 90–100 beats/min or isoproterenol 1–4 µg/min (shortens the action potential to prevent EADs and triggered activity)

        iv. Magnesium sulfate 1–2 g and β-blockers (eliminate triggered activity to prevent recurrence but do not shorten the QT interval)

XI.   Antiarrhythmic Medications

A variety of medications are available for the control of supraventricular and ventricular arrhythmias (table 10.13). A basic understanding of their mechanism of action is critical to the intelligent selection of these drugs for the treatment of various arrhythmias.[113,114,177,180–183]

A. **Electrophysiologic classification of antiarrhythmic medications**

Class I	**Sodium-channel blockers**	
	Class IA	Quinidine
		Procainamide
		Disopyramide
	Class IB	Lidocaine
		Mexiletine
		Phenytoin
	Class IC	Propafenone
Class II	**β-adrenergic blockers**	
Class III	**Potassium-channel blockers**	
	Amiodarone	
	Bretylium	
	Ibutilide	
	Sotalol	
Class IV	**Calcium-channel blockers**	

B. Table 10.14 shows the effects of the various classes of antiarrhythmic drugs on automaticity, conduction velocity, and the effective refractory period (ERP). The appropriate class of antiarrhythmic drug that can be selected for the management of the common arrhythmias is as follows:

    1. Alterations in automaticity

        a. Sinus tachycardia (sinus node): classes II, IV

        b. Ventricular ectopy (Purkinje and ventricular fibers): classes IA, IB, IC, II, III

        c. Digoxin-toxic ectopy (delayed afterdepolarizations): classes IB, IC, II, IV

Table 10.13 *Doses and Therapeutic Levels of Common Antiarrhythmic Drugs*

Drug	Intravenous	Oral	Therapeutic Levels
Amiodarone	150 mg over 15–30 min, then 1 mg/min × 6 h, then 1 g/day	600–1600 mg PO qd load for 10–14 days, then 200–600 mg qd	1–2.5 μg/mL
Bretylium	Load: 5–10 mg/kg Drip: 2–4 mg/min (1 g/250 mL)	—	0.04–0.9 μg/mL
Digoxin	0.25 mg IV q6h × 4 → 0.25 mg qd	0.25 mg q6h for 4 doses, then 0.25 mg qd	0.5–1.5 ng/mL
Disopyramide	—	100–200 mg q6h	2–5 μg/mL
Lidocaine	Load: 1 mg/kg → 0.5 mg/kg 1–2 times 10 min apart Drip: 2–4 mg/min (1 g/250 mL)	—	1–5 μg/mL
Procainamide	Load: 100 mg q5 min up to 1000 mg (10 mg/kg) Drip: 1–4 mg/min (1 g/250 mL)	Procan SR 0.5–1 g q6h Procanbid 1–2.5 g q12h	4–10 μg/mL (Procan) 2–8 μg/mL (NAPA)
Quinidine	—	200 mg q3h for 4 doses or 300 mg q3h for 3 doses, then sulfate 200 mg q6h or gluconate 324–486 mg q8h	3–5 μg/mL

   2. Alterations in conduction velocity and ERP

      a. Conversion of atrial fibrillation (atrium): classes IA, IC, III

      b. To slow the response to atrial fibrillation (AV node); conversion of AVNRT: classes IC, II, IV, digoxin

      c. Ventricular tachycardia (interrupt reentrant circuits in His-Purkinje fibers or ventricle): classes IA, IB, IC, III.

C. **Note:** The clinical indications listed below for each of the antiarrhythmic medications are those for which there is documented efficacy. FDA approval has not necessarily been provided for each of these indications.

D. **Quinidine**

   1. Clinical indications

      • Conversion or prevention of paroxysmal atrial fibrillation/ flutter

Table 10.14   *Electrophysiologic Properties of Antiarrhythmic Drugs*

Property		Class IA	Class IB	Class IC	Class II	Class III	Class IV
Automaticity							
SA node		—	—	—	↓	—	↓
Vent ectopic foci (Purkinje)		↓	↓	↓	↓	—	—
Delayed afterdepolarizations*		—	↓	↓	↓	—	↓
Conduction							
Atria	CV	↓	—	↓	—	—	—
	ERP	↑	—	↑	—	—	—
AV node	CV	—	—	↓	↓	—	↓
	ERP	—	—	↑	↑	—	↑
His-Purkinje	CV	↓	↓	↓	—	—	—
	ERP	↓	↑	↑	↑	—	—
Ventricle	CV	↓	↓	↓	—	—	—
	ERP	↑	↓	↑	—	↑	—

CV = conduction velocity; ERP = effective refractory period
* Mechanism of digoxin-induced ventricular ectopy

- • Suppression of premature supraventricular and ventricular complexes and sustained ventricular tachyarrhythmias
- • Wolff-Parkinson-White (WPW) syndrome (slows conduction over accessory pathways)

2. Dose: quinidine sulfate 300 mg q3h PO × 3 doses, then 200–300 mg q6h or quinidine gluconate 324–486 mg q8h; give with antacid (ALTernaGEL) to minimize gastrointestinal side effects

3. Metabolism: hepatic

4. Therapeutic level: 3–5 µg/mL

5. Hemodynamic effects: negative inotropy and decreased SVR from rapid IV injection

6. Special electrophysiologic concerns

   a. Slowing of the atrial rate in atrial flutter and vagolytic effects on AV conduction may increase the ventricular response to atrial fibrillation/flutter. Digoxin should be used first to prevent accelerated AV conduction.

   b. Evidence of toxicity: prolongation of QT interval (>500 ms); slowing of SA or AV nodal conduction; torsades de pointes

   c. Use of quinidine in patients with postoperative atrial fibrillation (after conversion or with failure to convert) must be weighed against its potential risks, such as its proarrhythmic effects.[184]

   d. Quinidine generally doubles the digoxin level; it decreases the renal excretion of digoxin and displaces digoxin from peripheral binding sites. Thus the digoxin dose should be reduced by 50%.

7. Noncardiac side effects: gastrointestinal upset and diarrhea (less with gluconate than sulfate), cinchonism, drug fever, thrombocytopenia, hemolytic anemia, hepatitis

E. **Procainamide**

1. Clinical indications

   - Conversion or prevention of paroxysmal atrial fibrillation
   - Suppression of premature supraventricular and ventricular complexes and sustained ventricular tachyarrhythmias
   - WPW syndrome (slows conduction over accessory pathways)

2. Dose

   a. IV: 100 mg q5min up to 1000 mg (never more than 50 mg/min), then a 2–4 mg/min drip (1 g/250 mL mix)

   b. PO: 500–1000 mg load, then 375 mg q3h of procainamide HCL; sustained release preparations are more commonly used (Procan-SR 500–1000 mg q6h or Procanbid 1–2.5 g q12h = 50 mg/kg/day)

   c. Conversion of IV to PO: Give one-quarter of the total daily IV dose as Procan SR q6h or one-half as Procanbid; stop the IV infusion immediately after the first oral dose.

3. Metabolism: hepatic to active metabolite N-acetylprocainamide (NAPA) and then excreted by the kidneys

4. Therapeutic level: 4–10 μg/mL of procainamide and 2–8 μg/mL of NAPA

5. Hemodynamic effects: decreases SVR, negative inotrope in high doses

6. Special electrophysiologic concerns

   a. Slowing of the atrial rate in atrial flutter and vagolytic effects on AV conduction (less so than quinidine) may increase the ventricular response to atrial fibrillation/flutter. Prior use of digoxin to prevent accelerated AV conduction must be accomplished first.

   b. Evidence of toxicity

      i. QT prolongation and polymorphic VT

      ii. Myocardial depression

      iii. NAPA has different electrophysiologic properties than procainamide. It may accumulate in patients with heart and renal failure. It has a longer half-life than procainamide (7 hours vs. 4 hours) and can lead to cardiac toxicity, including early afterdepolarizations, triggered activity, and ventricular arrhythmias, including torsades de pointes.

7. Noncardiac side effects: gastrointestinal (nausea, anorexia), central nervous system (insomnia, psychosis, depression), rash, drug fever, agranulocytosis, lupus-like syndrome with long-term use

F. **Disopyramide (Norpace)**

1. Clinical indications
   - Suppression of ventricular and supraventricular arrhythmias
   - Termination and prevention of recurrence of AVNRT
   - Conversion or prevention of atrial fibrillation
   - WPW syndrome (slows conduction over accessory pathways)
2. Dose: 100–200 mg PO q6h
3. Metabolism: 65% renal, 35% hepatic
4. Hemodynamic effects: strong negative inotrope
5. Therapeutic level: 2–5 µg/mL
6. Special electrophysiologic concerns
   a. Slowing of the atrial rate in atrial flutter and vagolytic effects on AV conduction require prior use of digoxin to prevent accelerated AV conduction.
   b. May cause torsades de pointes or other ventricular tachyarrhythmias associated with QT prolongation.
7. Noncardiac side effects: anticholinergic (urinary retention, constipation, blurred vision), nausea, dizziness, insomnia

G. **Lidocaine**

1. Clinical indications: premature ventricular complexes and ventricular tachyarrhythmias
2. Dose
   a. 1 mg/kg IV followed by a continuous infusion of 2–4 mg/min (1 g/250 mL mix); a dose of 0.5 mg/kg may be given 20 minutes later to achieve a stable plasma concentration.
   b. A rebolus of 0.5 mg/kg should be given to increase plasma levels if the infusion rate is increased.
3. Metabolism: hepatic; half-life is 15 minutes after one dose and 2 hours with constant infusion (often longer with hepatic impairment)
4. Therapeutic level: 1–5 µg/mL
5. Hemodynamic effects: none in the absence of severe LV dysfunction
6. Noncardiac side effects: CNS (dizziness, delirium, tremors, seizures), GI (nausea)

H. **Mexiletine**

1. Clinical indication: symptomatic ventricular tachyarrhythmias
2. Dose: 200–300 mg PO q8h
3. Metabolism: hepatic
4. Therapeutic levels: 1–2 µg/mL
5. Hemodynamic effects: none
6. Noncardiac side effects are noted in 40% of patients: CNS (tremor, dysarthria, paresthesias, confusion, drowsiness, diplopia), GI upset

I. **Phenytoin**

1. Clinical indication: digoxin-toxic ventricular ectopy

2. Dose

    a. IV: 100 mg q5min up to 1 g, then 100 mg q6–8h

    b. PO: 300 mg q2h for 3 doses, then 100 mg q8h starting 24 hours later

    Note: a therapeutic level may take 6–12 days to achieve without a load.

3. Metabolism: hepatic

4. Therapeutic levels: 10–20 μg/mL

5. Hemodynamic effect: rapid intravenous infusion may lead to hypotension and cardiac arrest.

6. Noncardiac side effects: CNS (nystagmus, dizziness, vertigo, drowsiness), GI (nausea, anorexia, epigastric discomfort)

7. Special concerns

    a. Phenytoin has a pH of 13 and will crystallize if mixed with an acidic solution.

    b. Serum level is increased by warfarin and decreased by phenobarbital.

J. **Propafenone**

1. Clinical indications
    - Life-threatening ventricular tachyarrhythmias
    - Conversion of atrial fibrillation
    - Conversion of AVNRT

2. Dose

    a. PO: 150–300 mg q8h

    b. IV: 1 mg/kg IV over 2 minutes, followed 10 minutes later by another 1 mg/kg dose (used for conversion of atrial fibrillation)

3. Metabolism: hepatic

4. Therapeutic level: 0.2–3.0 μg/mL

5. Hemodynamic effects: negative inotrope in patients with compromised ventricular function

6. Special electrophysiologic concerns

    a. Proarrhythmic effects are noted in 5% of patients.

    b. Has some β-blocker activity and can produce AV block and sinus node depression.

    c. It doubles the digoxin level.

7. Noncardiac side effects are noted in 15% of patients: CNS (dizziness, diplopia), GI upset.

K. **β-adrenergic blockers**

1. Clinical indications
   - Prevention of atrial arrhythmias after cardiac surgery
   - Rapid ventricular response to atrial fibrillation/flutter
   - Sinus tachycardia
   - Ventricular arrhythmias associated with digoxin toxicity, myocardial ischemia, or QT prolongation
   - AVNRT and reciprocating tachycardias in WPW syndrome

2. Doses
   a. Propranolol
      i. IV: 0.5 mg q5min up to 0.2 mg/kg
      ii. PO: 10–80 mg q6h
   b. Metoprolol (relative potency is 2.5:1 for IV:PO)
      i. IV: 5 mg q5min for 3 doses
      ii. PO: 25–50 mg q12h
   c. Esmolol: 500 μg/kg load IV, then 50–200 μg/kg/min drip

3. Metabolism: hepatic (propranolol, metoprolol, timolol), renal (atenolol), blood (esmolol)

4. Therapeutic level (propranolol): 1.0–2.5 μg/mL

5. Hemodynamic and electrophysiologic effects: negative inotropes; can produce hypotension, bradycardia, and heart block

6. Noncardiac side effects: bronchospasm (less with the cardioselective β-blockers atenolol and metoprolol), diarrhea, impotence, depression, intermittent claudication

L. **Amiodarone**[185]

1. Clinical indications
   - Recurrent ventricular tachyarrhythmias
   - Prevention/treatment of postoperative atrial fibrillation
   - Recurrent paroxysmal atrial fibrillation/flutter or AVNRT, with or without WPW syndrome

2. Dose
   a. PO: 600–1600 mg orally qd, load for 10–14 days, then 200–600 mg qd
   b. IV: 150 mg over 30–60 min (over 15 min for intractable VF), then 1 mg/min × 6 h, then 1 g/day

3. Metabolism: hepatic (half-life of 50 days)

4. Therapeutic level: 1.0–2.5 μg/mL

5. Hemodynamic effects: β-blocker; coronary and peripheral vasodilator (α-adrenergic effect)

6. Special electrophysiologic concerns
   a. May produce bradycardia and heart block
   b. Prolongs the QT interval but rarely causes ventricular arrhythmias

      c. Proarrhythmic effects (primarily bradycardias) are noted in about 30% of patients.

      d. Reduces clearance (and therefore increases serum levels) of drugs metabolized by the liver. These include **digoxin,** quinidine, procainamide, and **warfarin.** Doses of these medications should be reduced by about one-half.

7. Noncardiac side effects are noted in more than 50% of patients, especially during chronic therapy. These include pulmonary toxicity, hepatic dysfunction, corneal microdeposits (in nearly all patients), photosensitivity, GI upset, CNS (tremor, ataxia, paresthesias), neuropathy.

M. **Bretylium**

1. Clinical indication: refractory ventricular tachycardia or fibrillation in the ICU setting

2. Dose: 5–10 mg/kg IV bolus, followed by a continuous infusion of 2–4 mg/min (1 g/250 mL mix)

3. Metabolism: renal

4. Therapeutic level: 0.04–0.9 µg/mL

5. Hemodynamic effects: initially hypertension and tachycardia with increased cardiac output from norepinephrine release; then hypotension from decreased SVR

6. Noncardiac side effects: GI (nausea and vomiting)

N. **Ibutilide**

1. Clinical indication: conversion of recent-onset atrial fibrillation and flutter

2. Dose: 1 mg IV over 10 minutes × 2 (0.01 mg/kg if less than 60 kg)

3. Metabolism: hepatic

4. Therapeutic level: unknown

5. Hemodynamic effects: no significant hemodynamic effects

6. Special electrophysiologic concerns

      a. Dose-related prolongation of the QT interval (avoid if the QT interval exceeds 440 ms). QT prolongation may contribute to torsades de pointes, but sustained polymorphic VT may occur even in the absence of a prolonged QT interval.

      b. Monomorphic or polymorphic VT (sustained or nonsustained) is noted in about 10% of patients; careful monitoring in the ICU is essential for 4 hours after an administered dose (half-life is 6 hours) or until the QT interval has returned to baseline.

7. Noncardiac side effects: headache, nausea

O. **Sotalol**

1. Clinical indications

     • Prevention and conversion of atrial arrhythmias after cardiac surgery

- Suppression of premature ventricular complexes and ventricular tachyarrhythmias
- Conversion of AVNRT

2. Dose: 80–160 mg PO bid

3. Metabolism: excreted unchanged in the urine

4. Hemodynamic effects: causes a decrease in heart rate with some negative inotropic effect

5. Special electrophysiologic effects

   a. Exhibits β-blocking and class III effects

   b. Produces torsades de pointes or proarrhythmic effects in about 4% of patients. Torsades is dose-related and predictable from the QT interval.

6. Side effects: fatigue, dyspnea, dizziness, heart failure, nausea, and vomiting

P. **Calcium-channel blockers** (verapamil and diltiazem)

1. Clinical indications
   - Rapid ventricular response to atrial fibrillation/flutter
   - AVNRT and reciprocating tachycardias of WPW syndrome (**not** atrial fibrillation in WPW syndrome)
   - Ischemic ventricular ectopy

2. Doses

   a. Diltiazem

      i. IV: 0.25 mg/kg IV bolus over 2 minutes, with a repeat bolus of 0.35 mg/kg 15 minutes later; then a continuous infusion of 10–15 mg/h (250 mg/250 mL mix).

      ii. PO: 30–90 mg q8h

   b. Verapamil

      i. IV: 2.5–10 mg bolus over 1 minute with repeat dose in 30 minutes; then a continuous infusion of 2–5 µg/kg/min (120 mg/250 mL mix)

      ii. PO: 80–160 mg q8h

3. Metabolism: hepatic

4. Therapeutic level: 0.1–0.15 µg/mL (verapamil)

5. Hemodynamic effects: mild negative inotropes, hypotension from decreased SVR

6. Special electrophysiologic effects

   a. Can precipitate asystole, bradycardia, or heart block when used concomitantly with intravenous β-blockers

   b. Verapamil reduces clearance of digoxin and increases the digoxin level by about 35%.

   c. Noncardiac side effects: GI (constipation, nausea), headache, dizziness, elevation in liver function tests

Q. **Adenosine**[164]

1. Clinical indication: paroxysmal supraventricular tachycardias with AV nodal reentry (AVNRT)

2. Dose: 6 mg rapid IV injection followed by a saline flush; a second dose of 12 mg may be given 2 minutes later if necessary.

3. Metabolism: rapidly degraded in blood, with a half-life of less than 10 seconds

4. Electrophysiologic effects: produces transient high-grade AV block that can be used to unmask atrial activity to differentiate the causes of narrow and wide complex tachycardias. It may also produce asystole.

5. Side effects: flushing, dyspnea, or chest pressure of very brief duration

R. **Digoxin**

1. Clinical indications
   - Rapid ventricular response to atrial fibrillation/flutter
   - Recurrent PSVT

2. Dose
   a. IV: 0.5 mg, then 0.25 mg q4–6h to total dose of 1.0–1.25 mg, then 0.125–0.25 mg qd
   b. PO: 0.5 mg, then 0.25 mg q4–6h to total dose of 1.25 mg, then 0.25 mg qd
      i. Maintenance dose depends on serum level and therapeutic effect.
      ii. Dose is 0.125 mg qod for patients in renal failure.
      iii. IV dose is two-thirds of the PO dose.

3. Metabolism: renal

4. Therapeutic level: 1–2 ng/mL (drawn not less than 6 hours after an oral dose or 4 hours after an IV dose)
   a. Serum levels are increased by medications that reduce its clearance or volume of distribution—thus digoxin dosing should be reduced accordingly.
   b. Levels are increased by quinidine (by 100%), verapamil (by 35%), amiodarone (by 70% to 100%).

5. Hemodynamic effects: slight inotropic effect, peripheral vasodilatation

6. Special electrophysiologic concerns: see comments below on digoxin toxicity.

7. Noncardiac side effects: GI (anorexia, nausea, vomiting), CNS (headache, fatigue, confusion, seizures), visual symptoms

S. **Comments on digoxin toxicity**

1. Digoxin remains one of the most commonly prescribed medications following cardiac surgery.[186] It is used primarily to slow the ventricular response to atrial fibrillation/flutter by virtue of its vagotonic effect (at low dose) and a direct effect (high dose) on the AV node. It is less effective than other medications in slowing the ventricular response to atrial fibrillation in the early postoperative period at which time the window between therapeutic and toxic levels is rather narrow. Patients may be predisposed to

digoxin toxicity in the early postoperative period for a number of reasons.

   a. Increased sensitivity to digoxin may be related to augmented sympathetic tone, myocardial ischemia, electrolyte imbalance (hyper- or hypokalemia, hypercalcemia, hypomagnesemia), acid-base imbalance, or use of vasoactive or antiarrhythmic drugs (quinidine or verapamil).

   b. Large doses are frequently given to achieve effect because arrhythmias tend to be less responsive to digoxin in the immediate postoperative period when the vagotonic effect is offset by increased sympathetic tone. This often raises the serum level above the therapeutic range. Digoxin is usually loaded intravenously, with patients receiving up to 1.25 mg within a 24-hour period to achieve a therapeutic effect. Maintenance doses are usually given IV in the ICU, but should be two-thirds of the usual PO dose. Giving maintenance doses of 0.25 mg IV frequently raises serum digoxin levels to toxic levels.

   c. The volume of distribution is less in many elderly patients with decreased lean body mass.

   d. The high urinary output noted in the immediate postbypass period produces a profound potassium diuresis that lowers serum potassium levels. Hypokalemia predisposes to digoxin toxicity.

   e. Hypomagnesemia is very common in the immediate postoperative period and also predisposes the patient to digoxin toxicity.

   f. Renal excretion may be impaired in patients with chronic renal insufficiency. Elderly patients have reduced glomerular filtration rates and excrete digoxin less efficiently.

2. Digoxin toxicity should be considered in any patient receiving digoxin who develops a change in rhythm. These changes include, in decreasing order of frequency:

   a. Premature ventricular complexes (multiform and bigeminy)

   b. Nonparoxysmal AV junctional tachycardia

   c. AV block: first-degree or Wenckebach second-degree block

   d. Paroxysmal atrial tachycardia with 2:1 block

   e. Ventricular tachycardia (especially bidirectional VT at a rate of 140 to 180 beats/min)

   f. Sinus bradycardia or SA block

3. Digoxin toxicity in a patient with atrial fibrillation is usually manifested by:

   a. Slow ventricular response (<50/min)

   b. AV dissociation with AV junctional escape or accelerated junctional rhythm. Thus, the development of a regular rhythm may represent digoxin toxicity, not a return to sinus rhythm.

4. Treatment

  a. Bradyarrhythmias are treated by atrial, AV, or ventricular pacing, depending on the underlying atrial rhythm and the status of AV conduction. Atropine can be used, but isoproterenol should be avoided because it may induce malignant ventricular arrhythmias.

  b. Tachyarrhythmias

    i. Potassium chloride, except in the presence of high-grade AV block, because hyperkalemia can potentiate the depressant effect of digoxin on AV conduction

    ii. Lidocaine at usual doses

    iii. Phenytoin (Dilantin), 100 mg IV every 5 minutes to a maximum of 1 g, then 100–200 mg PO q8h

  c. Digibind (digoxin immune Fab [Ovine]) 400 mg (10 vials) IV, which may repeated in several hours, can be used for life-threatening digoxin toxicity.

5. Special concerns

  a. Correct assessment of serum digoxin levels requires measurement of steady-state levels. Therefore, digoxin levels should be drawn at least 6 hours after an oral dose and at least 4 hours after an IV dose. Levels drawn during the period of drug loading are of little value.

  b. Digoxin toxicity decreases the threshold for postcardioversion malignant arrhythmias. This may be exacerbated when hypokalemia or hypercalcemia is present. Use of lidocaine, phenytoin, or lower energy levels should be considered.

  c. Dialysis is ineffective in removing digoxin. Its half-life is 36–48 hours.

References

1. Thys DM, Kaplan JA. Cardiovascular physiology: an overview. J Cardiothorac Anesthesia 1989;3:2–9.
2. Douglas PS, Edmunds LH, Sutton MSJ, Geer R, Harken AH, Reichek N. Unreliability of hemodynamic indexes of left ventricular size during cardiac surgery. Ann Thorac Surg 1987;44:31–4.
3. Mammana RB, Hiro S, Levitsky S, Thomas PA, Plachetka J. Inaccuracy of pulmonary capillary wedge pressure when compared to left atrial pressure in the early postsurgical period. J Thorac Cardiovasc Surg 1982;84:420–5.
4. Hansen RM, Viquerat CE, Matthay MA, et al. Poor correlation between pulmonary arterial wedge pressure and left ventricular end-diastolic volume after coronary artery bypass surgery. Anesthesiology 1986;64:764–70.
5. Eichhorn EJ, Diehl JT, Konstam MA, Payne DD, Salem DN, Cleveland RJ. Left ventricular inotropic effect of atrial pacing after coronary artery bypass grafting. Am J Cardiol 1989;63:687–92.
6. Yelderman ML, Ramsay MA, Quinn MD, Paulsen AW, McKown RC, Gilman PH. Continuous thermodilution cardiac output measurement in intensive care unit patients. J Cardiothorac Vasc Anesthesia 1992;6:270–4.
7. Johnson RG, Thurer RL, Kruskall MS, et al. Comparison of two transfusion strategies after elective operations for myocardial revascularization. J Thorac Cardiovasc Surg 1992;104:307–14.
8. Doak GJ, Hall RI. Does hemoglobin concentration affect perioperative myocardial lactate flux in patients undergoing coronary artery bypass surgery? Anesth Analg 1995;80:910–6.
9. Sommers MS, Stevenson JS, Hamlin RL, Ivey TD, Russell AC. Mixed venous oxygen saturation and oxygen partial pressure as predictors of cardiac index after coronary artery bypass grafting. Heart Lung 1993;22:112–20.
10. Ardehali A, Ports TA. Myocardial oxygen supply and demand. Chest 1990;98:699–705.
11. Breisblatt WM, Stein KL, Wolfe CJ, et al. Acute myocardial dysfunction and recovery: a common occurrence after coronary bypass surgery. J Am Coll Cardiol 1990;15:1261–9.
12. Smith RC, Leung JM, Mangano DT. Postoperative myocardial ischemia in patients undergoing coronary artery bypass surgery. Anesthesiology 1991;74:464–73.
13. Jain U. Myocardial ischemia after cardiopulmonary bypass. J Cardiac Surg 1995;10:520–6.
14. Casthely PA, Shah C, Mekhjian H, et al. Left ventricular diastolic function after coronary artery bypass grafting: a correlative study with three different myocardial protection techniques. J Thorac Cardiovasc Sug 1997;114:254–60.
15. Reichert CLA, Visser CA, Koolen JJ, et al. Transesophageal echocardiography in hypotensive patients after cardiac operations. Comparison with hemodynamic parameters. J Thorac Cardiovasc Surg 1992;104:321–6.
16. Doyle AR, Dhir AK, Moors AH, Latimer RD. Treatment of perioperative low cardiac output syndrome. Ann Thorac Surg 1995;59:S3–11.
17. Weisel RD, Burns RJ, Baird RJ, et al. A comparison of volume loading and atrial pacing following aortocoronary bypass. Ann Thorac Surg 1983;36:332–44.
18. Argenziano M, Choudhri AF, Moazami M, et al. Vasodilatory hypotension after cardiopulmonary bypass: risk factors and potential mechanisms. Circulation 1997;96(suppl 1):I-680.

19. Argenziano M, Choudhri AF, Oz MC, Rose EA, Smith CR, Landry DW. A prospective randomized trial of arginine vasopressin in the treatment of vasodilatory shock after left ventricular assist device placement. Circulation 1997;96(suppl II):II-286–90.

19a. Mets B, Michler RE, Delphin ED, Oz MC, Landry DW. Refractory vasodilation after cardiopulmonary bypass for heart transplantation in recipients on combined amiodarone and angiotensin-converting enzyme inhibitor therapy: a role for vasopressin administration. J Cardiothorac Vasc Anesthesia 1998;12:326–9.

20. Davila-Roman VG, Waggoner AD, Hopkins WE, Barzilai B. Right ventricular dysfunction in low output syndrome after cardiac operations: assessment by transesophageal echocardiography. Ann Thorac Surg 1995;60:1081–6.

21. D'Ambra MN, LaRaia PJ, Philbin DM, Watkins WD, Hilgenberg AD, Buckley MJ. Prostaglandin E_1. A new therapy for refractory right heart failure and pulmonary hypertension after mitral valve replacement. J Thorac Cardiovasc Surg 1985; 89:567–72.

22. Camara ML, Aris A, Alvarez J, Padro JM, Caralps JM. Hemodynamic effects of prostaglandin E_1 and isoproterenol early after cardiac operations for mitral stenosis. J Thorac Cardiovasc Surg 1992;103:1177–85.

23. Fullerton DA, McIntyre RC Jr. Inhaled nitric oxide: therapeutic applications in cardiothoracic surgery. Ann Thorac Surg 1996;61:1856–64.

24. Fullerton DA, Jaggers J, Wollmering MM, Piedalue F, Grover FL, McIntyre RC Jr. Variable response to inhaled nitric oxide after cardiac surgery. Ann Thorac Surg 1997;63:1251–6.

25. Fullerton DA, Jaggers J, Piedalue F, Grover FL, McIntyre RC Jr. Effective control of refractory pulmonary hypertension after cardiac operations. J Thorac Cardiovasc Surg 1997;113:363–70.

26. Fullerton DA, Jones SD, Grover FL, McIntyre RC Jr. Adenosine effectively controls pulmonary hypertension after cardiac operations. Ann Thorac Surg 1996; 61:1118–24.

27. Brutsaert DL, Sys SU, Gillebert TC. Diastolic dysfunction in post-cardiac surgical management. J Cardiothorac Vasc Anesthesia 1993;7(suppl 1):18–20.

28. DiSesa VJ. Pharmacologic support for postoperative low cardiac output. Sem Thorac Cardiovasc Surg 1991;3:13–23.

29. Royster RL. Intraoperative administration of inotropes in cardiac surgery patients. J Cardiothorac Anesthesia 1990;4(suppl 5):17–28.

30. Levy JH. Support of the perioperative failing heart with preexisting ventricular dysfunction: currently available options. J Cardiothorac Vasc Anesthesia 1993;7(suppl 2):46–51.

31. Aral A, Oguz M, Ozberrak H, et al. Hemodynamic advantages of left atrial epinephrine administration in open heart surgery. Ann Thorac Surg 1997;64:1046–9.

32. Hochberg MS, Gielchinsky I, Parsonnet V, Hussain SM, Fisch D. Pulmonary inactivation of vasopressors following cardiac operations. Ann Thorac Surg 1986; 41:200–3.

33. Butterworth JF IV, Prielipp RC, Royster RL, et al. Dobutamine increases heart rate more than epinephrine in patients recovering from aortocoronary bypass surgery. J Cardiothorac Vasc Anesthesia 1992;6:535–41.

34. Gelfman DM, Ornato JP, Gonzalez ER. Dopamine-induced increase in atrioventricular conduction in atrial fibrillation-flutter. Clin Cardiol 1987;10:671–3.

35. Fowler MB, Alderman EL, Oesterle SN, et al. Dobutamine and dopamine after cardiac surgery: greater augmentation of myocardial blood flow with dobutamine. Circulation 1984;70(suppl I):I-103–11.

36. Van Trigt P, Spray TL, Pasque MK, Peyton RB, Pellom GL, Wechsler AS. The comparative effects of dopamine and dobutamine on ventricular mechanics after coro-

nary artery bypass grafting: a pressure-dimension analysis. Circulation 1984;70(suppl I):I-112–7.

37. DiSesa VJ, Brown E, Mudge GH Jr, Collins JJ Jr, Cohn LH. Hemodynamic comparison of dopamine and dobutamine in the postoperative volume-loaded, pressure-loaded, and normal ventricle. J Thorac Cardiovasc Surg 1982;83:256–63.

38. Butterworth JF IV. Use of amrinone in cardiac surgery patients. J Cardiothorac Vasc Anesthesia 1993;7:1–7.

39. Royster RL, Butterworth JF IV, Prielipp RC, Robertie PG, Kon ND. A randomized, blinded trial of amrinone, epinephrine, and amrinone/epinephrine after cardiopulmonary bypass (CPB). Anesthesiology 1991;75:A148.

40. Olsen KH, Kluger J, Fieldman A. Combination high dose amrinone and dopamine in the management of moribund cardiogenic shock after open heart surgery. Chest 1988;94:503–6.

41. Dupuis JY, Bondy R, Cattran C, Nathan HJ, Wynands JE. Amrinone and dobutamine as primary treatment of low cardiac output syndrome following coronary artery surgery: a comparison of their effects on hemodynamics and outcome. J Cardiothorac Vasc Anesthesia 1992;6:542–53.

42. Ko W, Zelano JA, Fahey AL, et al. The effects of amrinone versus dobutamine on myocardial mechanics after hypothermic global ischemia. J Thorac Cardiovasc Surg 1993;105:1015–24.

43. Kikura M, Lee MK, Safon RA, Bailey JM, Levy JH. The effects of milrinone on platelets in patients undergoing cardiac surgery. Anesth Analg 1995;81:44–8.

44. Liu JJ, Doolan LA, Xie B, Chen JR, Buxton BF. Direct vasodilator effect of milrinone, an inotropic drug, on arterial coronary bypass grafts. J Thorac Cardiovasc Surg 1997;113:108–13.

45. Bailey JM, Levy JH, Rogers HG, Szlam G, Hug CC Jr. Pharmacokinetics of amrinone during cardiac surgery. Anesthesiology 1991;75:961–8.

46. Bailey JM, Levy JH, Kikura M, Szlam G, Hug CC Jr. Pharmacokinetics of intravenous milrinone in patients undergoing cardiac surgery. Anesthesiology 1994;81:616–22.

47. Butterworth JF IV, Hines RL, Royster RL, James RL. A pharmacokinetic and pharmacodynamic evaluation of milrinone in adults undergoing cardiac surgery. Anesth Analg 1995;81:783–92.

48. Kirsh MM, Bove E, Detmer M, Hill A, Knight P. The use of levarterenol and phentolamine in patients with low cardiac output following open-heart surgery. Ann Thorac Surg 1980;29:26–31.

49. Drop LJ, Scheidegger D. Plasma ionized concentration: important determinant of the hemodynamic response to calcium infusion. J Thorac Cardiovasc Surg 1980;79:425–31.

50. Butterworth JF, Zaloga GP, Prielipp RD, Tucker WY Jr, Royster RL. Calcium inhibits the cardiac stimulating properties of dobutamine but not of amrinone. Chest 1992;101:174–80.

51. Novitzky D, Cooper DKC, Barton CI, et al. Triiodothyronine as an inotropic agent after open heart surgery. J Thorac Cardiovasc Surg 1989;98:972–8.

52. Klemperer JD, Klein I, Gomez M, et al. Thyroid hormone treatment after coronary-artery bypass surgery. N Engl J Med 1995;333:1522–7.

53. Walker JD, Crawford FA Jr, Mukherjee R, Zile MR, Spinale FG. Direct effects of acute administration of 3,5,3' triiodo-L-thyronine on myocyte function. Ann Thorac Surg 1994;58:851–6.

54. Bennett-Guerrero E, Jimenez JL, White WD, D'Amico EB, Baldwin BI, Schwinn DA. Cardiovascular effects of intravenous triiodothyronine in patients undergoing coronary artery bypass graft surgery. A randomized, double-blind, placebo-controlled trial. JAMA 1996;275:687–92.

55. Mullis-Jansson S, Corwin SJ, Delphin E, Jackson DT, Williams MR. A double blind placebo controlled study of the effect of triiodothyronine upon cardiac performance and outcome following coronary artery bypass surgery. Circulation 1996;94(suppl I): I-171.

56. Klemperer JD, Klein IL, Ojamaa K, et al. Triiodothyronine therapy lowers the incidence of atrial fibrillation after cardiac operations. Ann Thorac Surg 1996;61: 1323–9.

57. Coleman GM, Gradinac S, Taegtmeyer H, Sweeney M, Frazier OH. Efficacy of metabolic support with glucose-insulin-potassium for left ventricular pump failure after aortocoronary bypass surgery. Circulation 1989;80(suppl I):I-91–6.

58. Lazar HL, Philippides G, Fitzgerald C, Lancaster D, Shemin RJ, Apstein C. Glucose-insulin-potassium enhance recovery after urgent coronary artery bypass grafting. J Thorac Cardiovasc Surg 1997;113:354–62.

59. Boldt J, Kling D, Zickmann B, Dapper F, Hempelmann G. Efficacy of the phosphodiesterase inhibitor enoximone in complicated cardiac surgery. Chest 1990;98: 53–8.

60. Dzimiri N, Chester AH, Allen SP, Duran C, Yacoub MH. Vascular reactivity of arterial coronary artery bypass grafts—implications for their performance. Clin Cardiol 1996;19:165–71.

61. Maccioli GA, Lucas WJ, Norfleet EA. The intra-aortic balloon pump: a review. J Cardiothorac Anesthesia 1988;2:365–73.

62. Torchiana DF, Hirsch G, Buckley MJ, et al. Intraaortic balloon pumping for cardiac support: trends in practice and outcome, 1968 to 1995. J Thorac Cardiovasc Surg 1997;113:758–69.

63. Kvilekval KHV, Mason RA, Newton GB, Anagnostopoulos CE, Vlay SC, Giron F. Complications of percutaneous intra-aortic balloon pump use in patients with peripheral vascular disease. Arch Surg 1991;126:621–3.

64. Shimamoto H, Kawazoe K, Kito H, Fujita T, Shimamoto Y. Does juxtamesenteric placement of intra-aortic balloon interrupt superior mesenteric flow? Clin Cardiol 1992;15:285–90.

65. Swartz MT, Sakamoto T, Arai H, et al. Effects of intraaortic balloon position on renal artery blood flow. Ann Thorac Surg 1992;53:604–10.

66. Rodigas PC, Bridges KG. Occlusion of left internal mammary artery with intra-aortic balloon: clinical implications. J Thorac Cardiovasc Surg 1986;91:142–3.

67. Funk M, Ford CF, Foell DR, et al. Frequency of long-term lower limb ischemia associated with intraaortic balloon pump use. Am J Cardiol 1992;70:1195–9.

68. Rodigas PC, Finnegan JO. Technique for removal of percutaneously placed intraaortic balloons. Ann Thorac Surg 1985;40:80–1.

69. Rohrer MJ, Sullivan CA, McLaughlin DJ, Cutler BS. A prospective randomized study comparing surgical and percutaneous removal of intraaortic balloon pump. J Thorac Cardiovasc Surg 1992;103:569–72.

70. Pennington DG, ed. Mechanical circulatory support. Semin Thorac Cardiovasc Surg 1994;6:129–94.

71. Argenziano M, Oz MC, Rose EA. The continuing evolution of mechanical ventricular assistance. Curr Prob Surg 1997;34:318–86.

72. Oz MC, Rose EA, Levin HR. Selection criteria for placement of left ventricular assist devices. Am Heart J 1995;129:173–7.

73. Burnett CM, Duncan JM, Frazier OH, Sweeney MS, Vega JD, Radovancenic B. Improved multiorgan function after prolonged univentricular support. Ann Thorac Surg 1993;55:65–71.

74. Chen JM, Levin HR, Rose EA, et al. Experience with right ventricular assist devices for perioperative right-sided circulatory failure. Ann Thorac Surg 1996;61:305–10.

75. Park CH, Nishimura K, Kitano M, Matsuda K, Okamoto Y, Ban T. Analysis of right ventricular function during bypass of the left side of the heart by afterload alterations in both normal and failing hearts. J Thorac Cardiovasc Surg 1996; 111:1092–102.

76. Fukamachi K, McCarthy PM, Smedira NG, Vargo RL, Starling RC, Young JB. Risk factors for perioperative RV failure after implantable LVAD insertion. Circulation 1997;96(suppl I):I-299.

77. Nakatani S, Thomas JD, Savage RM, Vargo RL, Smedira NG, McCarthy PM. Prediction of right ventricular dysfunction after left ventricular assist device implantation. Circulation 1996;94(suppl II):II-216–21.

78. Wagner F, Dandel M, Günther G, et al. Nitric oxide inhalation in the treatment of right ventricular dysfunction following left ventricular assist device implantation. Circulation 1997;96(suppl 2):II-291–6.

79. Spanier T, Oz M, Levin H, et al. Activation of coagulation and fibrinolytic pathways in patients with left ventricular assist devices. J Thorac Cardiovasc Surg 1996;112: 1090–7.

80. Lemmer JH Jr, Kirsh MM. Coronary artery spasm following coronary artery surgery. Ann Thorac Surg 1988;46:108–15.

81. Jain U. Myocardial infarction during coronary artery bypass surgery. J Cardiothorac Vasc Anesthesia 1992;6:612–23.

82. Tuman KJ. Perioperative myocardial infarction. Semin Thorac Cardiovasc Surg 1991;3:47–52.

83. Machler H, Metzler H, Sabin K, et al. Preoperative myocardial cell damage in patients with unstable angina undergoing coronary artery bypass graft surgery. Anesthesiology 1994;81:1324–31.

84. Schmidt H, Mortensen PE, Folsgaard SL, Jensen EA. Cardiac enzymes and autotransfusion of shed mediastinal blood after myocardial revascularization. Ann Thorac Surg 1997;63:1288–92.

85. Birdi I, Angelini GD, Bryan AJ. Biochemical markers of myocardial injury during cardiac operations. Ann Thorac Surg 1997;63:879–84.

86. Alyanakian MA, Dehoux M, Chatel D, et al. Cardiac troponin I in diagnosis of perioperative myocardial infarction after cardiac surgery. J Cardiothorac Vasc Anesthesia 1998;12:288–94.

87. Runsiö M, Kallner A, Kallner G, Rosenqvist M, Bergfeldt L. Myocardial injury after electrical therapy for cardiac arrhythmias assessed by troponin-T release. Am J Cardiol 1997;79:1241–5.

88. Burns RJ, Gladstone PJ, Tremblay PC, et al. Myocardial infarction determined by technetium-99m pyrophosphate single-photon tomography complicating elective coronary artery bypass grafting for angina pectoris. Am J Cardiol 1989;63:1429–34.

89. Robert AJ, Spies SM, Lichtenthal PR, et al. Changes in left ventricular performance related to perioperative myocardial infarction in coronary artery bypass surgery. Ann Thorac Surg 1983;35:516–24.

90. Force T, Hibberd P, Weeks G, et al. Perioperative myocardial infarction after coronary artery bypass surgery. Clinical significance and approach to risk stratification. Circulation 1990;82:903–12.

91. Emergency Cardiac Care Committee and Subcommittees, American Heart Association. Guidelines for cardiopulmonary resuscitation and emergency cardiac care. III. Adult advanced cardiac life support. JAMA 1992;268:2199–241.

92. Cummins RO, ed. Textbook of advanced cardiac life support. American Heart Association, 1994.

93. Prengel AW, Lindner KH, Hahnel J, Ahnefeld FW. Endotracheal and endobronchial

lidocaine administration: effects on plasma lidocaine concentration and blood gases. Crit Care Med 1991;19:911–5.

94. Gray RJ. Postcardiac surgical hypertension. J Cardiothorac Anesthesia 1988;2: 678–82.

95. van Zwieten PA, van Wezel HB. Antihypertensive drug treatment in the perioperative period. J Cardiothorac Vasc Anesthesia 1993;7:213–26.

96. Kaplan JA, Guffin AV. Perioperative management of hypertension and tachycardia. J Cardiothorac Anesthesia 1990;4:7–12.

97. Fremes SE, Weisel RD, Mickle DAG, et al. A comparison of nitroglycerin and nitroprusside: I. Treatment of postoperative hypertension. Ann Thorac Surg 1985;39: 53–60.

98. Bojar RM, Rastegar H, Payne DD, et al. Methemoglobinemia from intravenous nitroglycerin: a word of caution. Ann Thorac Surg 1987;43:332–4.

99. Kataria B, Dubois M, Lea D, et al. Evaluation of intravenous esmolol for treatment of postoperative hypertension. J Cardiothorac Anesthesia 1990;4:13–6.

100. Sladen RN, Klamerus KJ, Swafford MWG, et al. Labetalol for the control of elevated blood pressure following coronary artery bypass grafting. J Cardiothorac Anesthesia 1990;4:210–21.

101. David D, Dubois C, Loria Y. Comparison of nicardipine and sodium nitroprusside in the treatment of paroxysmal hypertension following aortocoronary bypass surgery. J Cardiothorac Vasc Anesthesia 1991;5:357–61.

102. IV Nicardipine Study Group. Efficacy and safety of intravenous nicardipine in the control of postoperative hypertension. Chest 1991;99:393–8.

103. Vincent JL, Berlot G, Preiser JC, Engelman E, Dereume JP, Khan RJ. Intravenous nicardipine in the treatment of postoperative arterial hypertension. J Cardiothorac Vasc Anesthesia 1997;11:160–4.

104. Mullen JC, Miller DR, Weisel RD, et al. Postoperative hypertension: a comparison of diltiazem, nifedipine, and nitroprusside. J Thorac Cardiovasc Surg 1988;96: 122–32.

105. Nathan HJ, Laganière S, Dubé L, et al. Intravenous nifedipine to treat hypertension after coronary artery revascularization surgery. A comparison with sodium nitroprusside. Anesth Analg 1992;74:809–17.

106. Leslie J, Brister N, Levy JH, et al. Treatment of postoperative hypertension after coronary artery bypass surgery. Double-blind comparison of intravenous isradipine and sodium nitroprusside. Circulation 1994;90(part II):II-256–61.

107. Boldt J, Schindler E, Wollbruck M, Gorlach G, Hempelmann G. Cardiorespiratory response of intravenous angiotensin-converting enzyme inhibitor enalaprilat in hypertensive cardiac surgery patients. J Cardiothorac Vasc Anesthesia 1995;9: 44–9.

108. Tohmo H, Karanko M, Klossner J, et al. Enalaprilat decreases plasma endothelin and atrial natriuretic peptide levels and preload in patients with left ventricular dysfunction after cardiac surgery. J Cardiothorac Vasc Anesthesia 1997;11:585–90.

109. Swartz MT, Kaiser GC, Willman VL, Codd JE, Tyras DH, Barner HB. Continuous hydralazine infusion for afterload reduction. Ann Thorac Surg 1981;32:188–92.

110. Waldo AL, MacLean WAH. Diagnosis and treatment of cardiac arrhythmias following open heart surgery. Emphasis on the use of atrial and ventricular epicardial wire electrodes. Mount Kisco, New York: Futura Publishing, 1983.

111. Broka SM, Ducart AR, Collard EL, et al. Hemodynamic benefit of optimizing atrioventricular delay after cardiopulmonary bypass. J Cardiothorac Vasc Anesthesia 1997;11:723–8.

112. Atlee JL III, Pattison CZ, Mathews EL, Hedman AG. Transesophageal atrial pacing for intraoperative sinus bradycardia or AV junctional rhythm: feasibility as prophy-

laxis in 200 anesthetized adults and hemodynamic effects of treatment. J Cardiothorac Vasc Anesthesia 1993;7:436–41.

113. Weng JT, Smith DE, Moulder PV. Antiarrhythmic drugs: electrophysiological basis of their clinical usage. Ann Thorac Surg 1986;41:106–12.

114. Feeley TW. Management of postoperative arrhythmias. J Cardiothorac Vasc Anesthesia 1997;11(suppl 1):10–5.

115. Bertolet BD, Eagle DA, Conti JB, Mills RM, Belardinelli L. Bradycardia after heart transplantation: reversal with theophylline. J Am Coll Cardiol 1996;28:396–9.

116. Hippelainen M, Mustonen P, Manninen H, Rehnberg S. Predictors of conduction disturbances after coronary bypass grafting. Ann Thorac Surg 1994;57:1284–8.

117. Caspi J, Amar R, Elami A, Safadi T, Ammar R, Merin G. Frequency and significance of complete atrioventricular block after coronary artery bypass grafting. Am J Cardiol 1989;63:526–9.

118. Baerman JM, Kirsh MM, de Buitleir M, et al. Natural history and determinants of conduction defects following coronary artery bypass surgery. Ann Thorac Surg 1987;44:150–3.

119. Thomas JL, Dickstein RA, Parker FB, et al. Prognostic significance of the development of left bundle conduction defects following aortic valve replacement. J Thorac Cardiovasc Surg 1982;84:382–6.

120. Gaudino M, Alessandrini F, Glieca F, et al. Conventional left atrial versus superior septal approach for mitral valve replacement. Ann Thorac Surg 1997;63:1123–7.

121. Utley JR, Leyland SA, Nguyenduy T. Comparison of outcomes with three atrial incisions for mitral valve operations. Right lateral, superior septal, and transseptal. J Thorac Cardiovasc Surg 1995;109:582–7.

122. Glikson M, Dearani JA, Hyberger LK, Schaff HV, Hammill SC, Hayes DL. Indications, effectiveness, and long-term dependency in permanent pacing after cardiac surgery. Am J Cardiol 1997;80:1309–13.

123. Wynsen JC, O'Brien PD, Warltier DC. Zatebradine, a specific bradycardic agent, enhances the positive inotropic actions of dobutamine in ischemic myocardium. J Am Coll Cardiol 1994;23:233–41.

124. Breall JA, Watanabe J, Grossman W. Effect of zatebradine on contractility, relaxation, and coronary blood flow. J Am Coll Cardiol 1993;21:461–7.

125. Ommen SR, Odell JA, Stanton MS. Atrial arrhythmias after cardiothoracic surgery. N Engl J Med 1997;336:1429–34.

126. Hashimoto K, Ilstrup DM, Schaff HV. Influence of clinical and hemodynamic variables on risk of supraventricular tachycardia after coronary artery bypass. J Thorac Cardiovasc Surg 1991;101:56–65.

127. Mendes LA, Connelly GP, McKenney PA, et al. Right coronary artery stenosis: an independent predictor of atrial fibrillation after coronary artery bypass surgery. J Am Coll Cardiol 1995;25:198–202.

128. Leitch JW, Thomson D, Baird DK, Harris PJ. The importance of age as a predictor of atrial fibrillation and flutter after coronary artery bypass grafting. J Thorac Cardiovasc Surg 1990;100:338–42.

129. Aranki SF, Shaw DP, Adams DH, et al. Predictors of atrial fibrillation after coronary artery surgery. Current trends and impact on hospital resources. Circulation 1996;94:390–7.

130. Creswell LL, Schuessler RB, Rosenbloom M, Cox JL. Hazards of postoperative atrial arrhythmias. Ann Thorac Surg 1993;56:539–49.

131. Mathew JP, Parks R, Savino JS, et al. Atrial fibrillation following coronary artery bypass surgery. Predictors, outcomes, and resource utilization. JAMA 1996;276:300–6.

132. Kalman JM, Munawar M, Howes LG, et al. Atrial fibrillation after coronary artery bypass grafting is associated with sympathetic activation. Ann Thorac Surg 1995;60:1709–15.
133. Andrews TC, Reimold SC, Berlin JA, Antman EM. Prevention of supraventricular arrhythmias after coronary artery bypass surgery. A meta-analysis of randomized controlled trials. Circulation 1991;84(suppl 3):III-236–44.
134. Kowey PR, Taylor JE, Rials SJ, Marinchak RA. Meta-analysis of the effectiveness of prophylactic drug therapy in preventing supraventricular arrhythmia early after coronary artery bypass grafting. Am J Cardiol 1992;69:963–5.
135. Roffman JA, Fieldman A. Digoxin and propranolol in the prophylaxis of supraventricular tachydysrhythmias after coronary artery bypass surgery. Ann Thorac Surg 1981;31:496–500.
136. Fanning WJ, Thomas CS Jr, Roach A, Tomichek R, Alford WC, Stoney WS Jr. Prophylaxis of atrial fibrillation with magnesium sulfate after coronary artery bypass grafting. Ann Thorac Surg 1991;52:529–33.
137. Nurözler F, Tokgözoglu L, Pasaoglu I, Boke E, Ersoy U, Bozer AY. Atrial fibrillation after coronary bypass surgery: predictors and the role of $MgSO_4$ replacement. J Cardiac Surg 1996;11:421–7.
138. Suttorp MJ, Kingma JH, Gin RMTJ, et al. Efficacy and safety of low- and high-dose sotalol versus propranolol in the prevention of supraventricular tachyarrhythmias early after coronary artery bypass operations. J Thorac Cardiovasc Surg 1990;100:921–6.
139. Abdulrahman O, Dale HT, Theman TE, Krall J, Hallenar M. Low dose sotalol compared with metoprolol in the prevention of supraventricular arrhythmias (SVA) after cardiac surgery. Circulation 1997;96(suppl I):I-26.
140. Daoud EG, Strickberger SA, Man KC, et al. Preoperative amiodarone as prophylaxis against atrial fibrillation after heart surgery. N Engl J Med 1997;337:1785–91.
141. Mittleman RS, Hill MRS, Mehra R, et al. Evaluation of the effectiveness of right atrial and biatrial pacing for the prevention of atrial fibrillation (AF) after coronary artery bypass surgery (CABG). Circulation 1996;94(suppl I):I-68.
142. Laub GW, Janeira L, Muralidharan S, et al. Prophylactic procainamide for prevention of atrial fibrillation after coronary artery bypass grafting; a prospective, double-blind, randomized, placebo-controlled pilot study. Crit Care Med 1993;21:1474–8.
143. Hannes W, Fasol R, Zajonc H, et al. Diltiazem provides anti-ischemic and anti-arrhythmic protection in patients undergoing coronary bypass grafting. Eur J Cardiothorac Surg 1993;7:239–45.
144. Seitelberger R, Hannes W, Gleichauf M, Keilich M, Christoph M, Fasol R. Effects of diltiazem on perioperative ischemia, arrhythmias, and myocardial function in patients undergoing elective coronary bypass grafting. J Thorac Cardiovasc Surg 1994;107:811–21.
145. Davison R, Hartz R, Kaplan K, Parker M, Feiereisel P, Michaelis L. Prophylaxis of supraventricular tachyarrhythmia after coronary bypass surgery with oral verapamil: a randomized, double-blind trial. Ann Thorac Surg 1995;39:336–9.
146. Anderson JL. Acute treatment of atrial fibrillation and flutter. Am J Cardiol 1996;78:17–21.
147. Olchansky B. Management of atrial fibrillation after coronary artery bypass graft. Am J Cardiol 1996;78(suppl 8A):27–34.
148. Prystowksky EN, Benson DW Jr, Fuster V, et al. Management of patients with atrial fibrillation. A statement for healthcare professionals from the subcommittee on electrocardiography and electrophysiology, American Heart Association. Circulation 1996;93:1262–77.
149. Stambler BS, Wood MA, Ellenbogen KA. Comparative efficacy of intravenous ibu-

tilide versus procainamide for enhancing termination of atrial flutter by atrial over-drive pacing. Am J Cardiol 1996;77:960–6.

150. D'Este D, Bertaglia E, Mantovan R, Zanocco Z, Franceschi M, Pascotto P. Efficacy of intravenous propafenone in termination of atrial flutter by overdrive trans-esophageal pacing previously ineffective. Am J Cardiol 1997;79:500–2.

151. Ellenbogen KA, Dias VC, Cardello FP, et al. Safety and efficacy of intravenous dilti-azem in atrial fibrillation or atrial flutter. Am J Cardiol 1995;75:45–9.

152. Platia EV, Michelson EL, Porterfield JK, Das G. Esmolol versus verapamil in the acute treatment of atrial fibrillation or atrial flutter. Am J Cardiol 1989;63:925–9.

153. Gullestad L, Birkeland K, Molstad P, Hoyer MM, Vanberg P, Kjekshus J. The effect of magnesium versus verapamil on supraventricular arrhythmias. Clin Cardiol 1993;16:429–34.

154. Falk RH, Leavitt JI. Digoxin for atrial fibrillation: a drug whose time has gone? Ann Intern Med 1991;114:573–5.

155. Falk RH, Knowlton AA, Bernard SA, Gotlief NE, Battinelli NJ. Digoxin for convert-ing recent-onset atrial fibrillation to sinus rhythm. A randomized, double-blinded trial. Ann Int Med 1987;106:503–6.

156. Stoddard MF, Dawkins PR, Prince CR, Ammash NM. Left atrial appendage thrombus is not uncommon in patients with acute atrial fibrillation and a recent embolic event: a transesophageal echocardiographic study. J Am Coll Cardiol 1995;25:452–9.

157. Manning WJ, Silverman DI, Keighley CS, Oettgen P, Douglas PS. Transesophageal echocardiographically facilitated early cardioversion from atrial fibrillation using short-term anticoagulation: final results of a prospective 4.5-year study. J Am Coll Cardiol 1995;25:1354–61.

158. Black IW, Fatkin D, Sagar KB, et al. Exclusion of atrial thrombus by transesophageal echocardiography does not preclude embolism after cardioversion of atrial fibrilla-tion. A multicenter study. Circulation 1994;89:2509–13.

159. Harjai KJ, Mobarek SK, Cheirif J, Boulos LM, Murgo JP, Abi-Samra F. Clinical vari-ables affecting recovery of left atrial mechanical function after cardioversion from atrial fibrillation. J Am Coll Cardiol 1997;30:481–6.

160. Boriani G, Capucci A, Lenzi T, Sanguinetti M, Bagnani B. Propafenone for conver-sion of recent-onset atrial fibrillation. A controlled comparison between oral loading dose and intravenous administration. Chest 1995;108:355–8.

161. Ellenbogan KA, Clemo HF, Stambler BS, Wood MA, Vander Lugt JT. Efficacy of ibu-tilide for termination of atrial fibrillation and flutter. Am J Cardiol 1996;78(suppl 8A):42–5.

162. Larbuisson R, Venneman I, Stiels B. The efficacy and safety of intravenous propafenone versus intravenous amiodarone in the conversion of atrial fibrillation or flutter after cardiac surgery. J Cardiothorac Vasc Anesthesia 1996;10:229–34.

163. Halinen MO, Huttunen M, Paakkinen S, Tarssanen L. Comparison of sotalol with digoxin-quinidine for conversion of acute atrial fibrillation to sinus rhythm (the sotalol-digoxin-quinidine trial). Am J Cardiol 1995;76:495–8.

164. Wilbur SL, Marchlinski FE. Adenosine as an antiarrhythmic agent. Am J Cardiol 1997;79(12A):30–7.

165. Dougherty AH, Jackman WM, Naccarelli GV, Friday KJ, Dias VC, for the IV Dilti-azem Study group. Acute conversion of paroxysmal supraventricular tachycardia with intravenous diltiazem. Am J Cardiol 1992;70:587–92.

166. Discher TJ, Kumar P. Pro: antiarrhythmic drugs should be used to suppress ventric-ular ectopy in the perioperative period. J Cardiothorac Vasc Anesthesia 1994;8:699–700.

167. Miller SM, Mayer RC. Con: antiarrhythmic drugs should not be used to suppress

ventricular ectopy in the perioperative period. J Cardiothorac Vasc Anesthesia 1994;8:701–3.

168. England MR, Gordon G, Salem M, Chernow B. Magnesium administration and dysrhythmias after cardiac surgery. JAMA 1992;268:2395–402.

169. Topol EJ, Lerman BB, Baughman KL, Platia EV, Griffith LSC. De novo refractory ventricular tachyarrhythmias after coronary revascularization. Am J Cardiol 1986;57: 57–9.

170. Kron IL, DiMarco JP, Harman PK, et al. Unanticipated postoperative ventricular tachyarrhythmias. Ann Thorac Surg 1984;38:317–22.

171. Azar RR, Berns E, Seecharran B, Veronneau J, Lippman N, Kluger J. De novo monomorphic and polymorphic ventricular tachycardia following coronary artery bypass grafting. Am J Cardiol 1997;80:76–8.

172. Saxon LA, Wiener I, Natterson PD, Laks H, Drinkwater D, Stevenson WG. Monomorphic versus polymorphic ventricular tachycardia after coronary artery bypass grafting. Am J Cardiol 1995;75:403–5.

173. Lamas GA, Antman EM, Gold JP, Braunwald NS, Collins JJ. Pacemaker backup-mode reversion and injury during cardiac surgery. Ann Thorac Surg 1986;41:155–7.

174. Rubin DA, Nieminski KE, Monteferrante JC, et al. Ventricular arrhythmias after coronary artery bypass graft surgery: incidence, risk factors, and long-term prognosis. J Am Coll Cardiol 1985;6:307–10.

175. Dhein S, Muller A, Gerwin R, Klaus W. Comparative study on the proarrhythmic effects of some antiarrhythmic agents. Circulation 1993;87:617–30.

176. Prystowski EN. Proarrhythmia during drug treatment of supraventricular tachycardia: paradoxical risk of sinus rhythm for sudden death. Am J Cardiol 1996;78(suppl 8A):35–41.

177. Landers MD, Reiter MJ. General principles of antiarrhythmic therapy for ventricular tachyarrhythmias. Am J Cardiol 1997;80(suppl 8A):31G–44G.

178. Roden DM. A practical approach to torsades de pointes. Clin Cardiol 1997;20: 285–90.

179. Sharma ND, Rosman HS, Padhi ID, Tisdale JE. Torsades de pointes associated with intravenous haloperidol in critically ill patients. Am J Cardiol 1998;81:238–40.

180. Podrid PJ. Antiarrhythmic drug therapy (Part 1). Benefits and hazards. Chest 1985;88:452–60.

181. Podrid PJ. Antiarrhythmic drug therapy (Part 2). Benefits and hazards. Chest 1985;88:618–24.

182. Zipes DP. Management of cardiac arrhythmias: pharmacological, electrical, and surgical techniques. In: Braunwald E, ed. Heart disease. A textbook of cardiovascular medicine. 5th ed. Philadelphia: WB Saunders, 1997:593–639.

183. Zipes DP. Specific arrhythmias: diagnosis and treatment. In: Braunwald E, ed. Heart disease. A textbook of cardiovascular medicine. 5th ed. Philadelphia: WB Saunders, 1997:640–704.

184. Grace AA, Camm AJ. Quinidine. N Engl J Med 1998;338:35–45.

185. Kowey PR, Marinchak RA, Rials SJ, Filart RA. Intravenous amiodarone. Am J Cardiol 1997;29:1190–8.

186. Bhatia SJS, Smith TW. Digitalis toxicity: mechanisms, diagnosis, and management. J Cardiac Surg 1987;2:453–65.

187. Hill AJ, Feneck RO, Walesby RK. A comparison of fenoldopam and nitroprusside in the control of hypertension following coronary artery surgery. J Cardiothorac Vasc Anesthesia 1993;7:279–84.

188. Garwood S, Hines R. Perioperative renal preservation: dopexamine and fenoldopam—new agents to augment renal performance. Sem Anesthesia, Periop Medicine, Pain 1998;17:308–18.

11 Fluid Management, Renal and Metabolic Problems

11 Fluid Management, Renal and Metabolic Problems

The use of extracorporeal circulation, anesthetic agents, and vasoactive drugs that provide hemodynamic support during open-heart surgery have significant effects on renal perfusion, vasomotor tone, and fluid redistribution. Being aware of the factors that influence renal function, taking measures to optimize renal perfusion, and paying attention to the early signs of renal dysfunction are essential to reduce the incidence of postoperative oliguria and renal insufficiency. These considerations can often make the difference between an uneventful recovery and a stormy postoperative course complicated by cardiac, respiratory, or renal failure.

There are several important concepts in fluid and electrolyte balance that must be understood to direct fluid management in the postoperative cardiac surgical patient. The influence of cardiopulmonary bypass on fluid shifts and other metabolic parameters must also be appreciated to optimize postoperative care.

I. Body Water Distribution

Approximately 60% of the body weight is water, with two-thirds of this residing in the intracellular space and one-third in the extracellular space. In the latter, two-thirds is in the interstitial space (the so-called "third space"), and one-third constitutes the intravascular volume.

A. Water moves freely among all three compartments and will shift so as to normalize serum osmolarity (which generally reflects the serum sodium concentration).

B. Sodium moves freely between the intravascular and interstitial spaces but does not move passively into cells. Therefore, if a patient receives a hypotonic sodium load (e.g., 0.45% saline) which would lower the serum osmolarity and sodium concentration, water will move from the extracellular space into the intracellular space to normalize these values. The presence of a low serum sodium concentration in the postoperative patient usually indicates total body water overload.

C. Protein remains within the intravascular space and is the primary determinant of plasma oncotic pressure. If colloid or protein is administered, plasma oncotic pressure will increase and fluid will be drawn into the intravascular space from the interstitial space. Conversely, if serum albumin is low, fluid will tend to shift into the interstitial space, contributing to tissue edema.

D. Starling's law governs the influence of hydrostatic and oncotic pressures on fluid shifts. For example, elevated hydrostatic pressure (e.g., increased pulmonary capillary wedge pressure, or PCWP) or lower intravascular colloid oncotic pressure (e.g., low serum albumin) will shift fluid into the lung interstitium. Conversely, raising the intravascular oncotic pressure with colloid (e.g., hetastarch, albumin) will tend to draw fluid from the lung interstitium back into the intravascular space.

E. Starling's law describes fluid shifts in the absence of abnormalities in membrane integrity. However, extracorporeal circulation is associated with the so-called "systemic inflammatory response," which results in increased membrane permeability and a transient capillary leak.[1] When this leak is present, fluid administration to maintain intravascular volume, whether crystalloid or colloid, will partially shift into the interstitial space. Although the most frequent manifestation of a capillary leak is increased extravascular lung water that impairs oxygenation, expansion of the interstitial space may also contribute to cerebral edema (mental obtundation), hepatic congestion (jaundice), splanchnic congestion (ileus), and impaired renal perfusion.

II.   Effects of Cardiopulmonary Bypass on Renal and Metabolic Parameters

The use of extracorporeal circulation during open-heart surgery is associated with significant pathophysiologic and endocrine abnormalities that influence fluid shifts, vasomotor tone, organ system perfusion, and carbohydrate and lipid metabolism.[2] Low-flow, hypothermic, nonpulsatile perfusion with hemodilution reduces renal blood flow (RBF), decreases the glomerular filtration rate (GFR) out of proportion to the decrease in RBF, and may produce some degree of tubular injury. Despite the complex effects of cardiopulmonary bypass (CPB) on renal function, postoperative renal dysfunction is relatively uncommon in the absence of preexisting renal disease, significant hypotension during bypass, or low cardiac output states following bypass.

A. **Humoral effects**

1. Increased release of renin and aldosterone results in sodium retention and potassium excretion.

2. Elevation in angiotensin II levels produces renal vasoconstriction.

3. An increase in vasopressin secretion produces an increase in systemic vascular resistance. The marked elevation of this hormone produces a paradoxical sodium and water diuresis by directly impairing tubular absorption.

4. Increased levels of atrial natriuretic factor (ANF) and urodilan (a natriuretic-vasorelaxant peptide) increase natriuresis and diuresis after bypass.[3] These effects may be reproduced by the exogenous administration of ANF (7.5 pmol/kg/min) after surgery.[4]

5. Marked elevation in epinephrine levels causes peripheral vasoconstriction and intraorgan redistribution of blood flow. Epinephrine also impairs insulin release, contributing to hyperglycemia.

6. Elevation in norepinephrine levels occurs early during CPB and contributes to postoperative hypertension.

7. Elevation of plasma-free cortisol after CPB contributes to sodium retention and enhanced potassium excretion.

8. Impaired insulin secretion and peripheral insulin resistance resulting from elevated epinephrine levels and hypothermia produce hyperglycemia.

B. **Hypothermia** decreases renal cortical blood flow by producing vasoconstriction. It also decreases GFR slightly, decreases renal tubular function, and reduces free water and osmolar clearance. These effects are offset to some degree by hemodilution during CPB. During the phase of rewarming, vasodilatation and hyperemia of tissue beds result in "third spacing" of fluid.

C. **Hemodilution** with a crystalloid prime reduces plasma oncotic pressure, promoting movement of fluid from the vascular space into the interstitial space. A reduction in viscosity increases outer renal cortical blood flow, leading to an increase in urine output, free water clearance, and sodium and potassium excretion.[5]

D. Other vasoactive substances released during CPB include complement, kallikrein, and bradykinin, which alter vascular tone and contribute to the generalized inflammatory response that increases capillary permeability.

E. **Medications.** Nitroglycerin, nitroprusside, calcium-channel blockers, inhalational anesthetics, narcotics, and anxiolytics (midazolam, propofol) can produce significant vasodilatation that increases fluid requirements.[6]

F. **Ischemic/reperfusion injury** associated with the use of cardioplegia for myocardial protection can produce myocardial edema, a reduction in diastolic compliance, and impairment of myocardial function. This may alter the relationship between the left-sided filling pressures and left ventricular end-diastolic volume (LVEDV).

III. Routine Fluid Management in the Early Postoperative Period

A. As a result of hemodilution on cardiopulmonary bypass, most patients are in a state of total body sodium and water overload at the conclusion of the operation, being about 5–10% above their preoperative weight. Cardiac filling pressures do not necessarily reflect this state because of the capillary leak that accompanies CPB and the progressive vasodilatation that occurs as the patient warms to normothermia. Therefore, fluid must invariably be administered to maintain intravascular volume and cardiac hemodynamics at the expense of expansion of the interstitial space. It should be noted that early extubation is helpful in reducing fluid requirements because it eliminates the adverse effects of positive pressure ventilation on venous return and ventricular function.

B. The requirement for fluid administration occurs at a time when the kidneys are often excreting large amounts of urine. If ventricular function is satisfactory, cardiac output is primarily preload-dependent, necessitating volume infusions to maintain hemodynamics and compensate for the excessive urine output. The selection of which type of fluid to administer to maintain filling pressures is controversial and can be confusing.

C. Clearly, any fluid infused during a period of altered capillary membrane integrity will expand the interstitial space, but fluids that can more effectively expand the intravascular space while minimizing expansion of the interstitial space should be preferable.[7,8] As shown in figure 11.1, blood and colloids are superior to hypotonic or even isotonic crystalloid solutions in expanding the intravascular volume. Thus, sodium-rich colloids (5% albumin in saline, 6% hetastarch in saline) are often selected. However, these solutions are costly and sometimes not available. If the patient is oxygenating well and maintaining an excellent urine output,

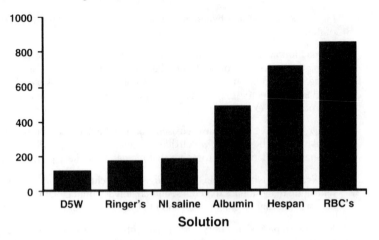

Figure 11.1 *Increase in intravascular volume noted after a 1.5 hour infusion of 1000 mL of various solutions to postoperative patients. Note that colloids produce a greater increase in volume than crystalloid solutions. Hespan = 6% hetastarch. Albumin = 5% albumin. Ringer's = lactated Ringer's solution. Nl saline = 0.9% saline.*

administering a moderate amount of crystalloid (1.0–1.5 liters of normal saline or Ringer's lactate) should suffice to raise filling pressures without significant adverse effects.[9]

D. It cannot be overemphasized that the purpose of postoperative fluid administration is to maintain **adequate** intravascular volume to ensure **satisfactory** cardiac output and tissue perfusion. Administration of excessive volume to maintain high filling pressures and the highest possible cardiac output can be detrimental to pulmonary function and will often delay extubation. In addition, expansion of the intravascular volume may decrease the hematocrit and the level of clotting factors, possibly necessitating homologous blood or plasma transfusions.

E. When cardiac function is satisfactory but there is an ongoing volume requirement to maintain filling pressures or blood pressure, often from a combination of the capillary leak, vasodilatation, or excellent urine output, "flooding" the patient with volume should be resisted. After 1.5–2.0 liters of fluid is given, an α-agent, such as phenylephrine or norepinephrine, should be considered to limit fluid administration. However, if both the cardiac output and urine output remain marginal after fluid administration, α-agents are best avoided and other measures noted below (low-dose dopamine and inotropic support) should be considered. Generally, diuretics are best avoided in the first 6 hours after surgery unless inexplicable oliguria, pulmonary edema, or borderline oxygenation is present.

F. When the patient has achieved a stable core temperature and the capillary leak has ceased, usually within the first 6–12 hours, filling pressures will stabilize or rise with little fluid administration. By this time, myocardial function has usually recovered, inotropic support can be withdrawn gradually, and the patient can be extubated. Diuresis should be initiated to excrete the excess salt and water administered during CPB and the early postoperative period. Patients who have undergone operations that require long periods of bypass or who have persistent low output syndromes may experience a longer period of "capillary leak" that requires further fluid administration to maintain filling pressures.

G. Diuresis can be augmented most efficiently by the use of loop diuretics. Most patients with preserved renal function respond to furosemide (Lasix) 10–20 mg IV. A gentle continuous diuresis may be obtained in patients with hemodynamic instability but significant fluid overload by using a bolus dose followed by a continuous infusion of 0.1–0.5 mg/kg/h (usually 10 mg/h) of furosemide.[10,11] This decreases total dosage requirements and usually improves the diuretic response, especially in patients who are diuretic "tolerant." Diuretics are continued in intravenous or oral form until the patient has achieved his or her preoperative weight. Commonly used oral diuretics include furosemide (which usually requires potassium replacement) and the potassium-sparing diuretics, such as triamterene or spironolactone combined with a thiazide (Dyazide and Aldactazide).

H. Guidelines for the hemodynamic and fluid management of typical postoperative scenarios are presented in Chapter 7.

IV. Prevention of Renal Dysfunction

A. Preoperative renal dysfunction is a major determinant of postoperative morbidity and mortality. The mortality rate for patients undergoing coronary artery bypass or valve surgery with a preoperative creatinine >1.5–2.0 mg/dL ranged from 9–15% in several recent studies.[12–15] Thus, the presence of renal insufficiency should lead to a search for potentially treatable causes that might lower the risk of progressive dysfunction postoperatively. Identifying and correcting these contributing factors before surgery and using prophylactic measures during and after surgery to optimize renal perfusion may ameliorate the complications associated with the development of renal failure.

B. **Risk factors** for the development of postoperative renal dysfunction[12–14]

1. Preoperative factors

   a. Preexisting renal dysfunction (creatinine >1.5 mg/dL)

   b. Older age

   c. Left ventricular dysfunction, especially when resulting in congestive heart failure

   d. Emergency operations

   e. The combination of hypertension, diabetes, and peripheral vascular disease

2. Intraoperative factors

   a. Concomitant CABG-valve operations

   b. Mitral valve operations

   c. Use of deep hypothermic circulatory arrest

   d. Long durations of bypass

Table 11.1 *Factors Contributing to Preoperative and Postoperative Renal Insufficiency*

Preoperative factors	Low cardiac output states/hypotension (cardiogenic shock from acute MI, mechanical complications of MI)
	Medications that interfere with renal autoregulation (ACE inhibitors, NSAIDs)
	Nephrotoxins (contrast-induced ATN, especially in diabetic vasculopaths), medications (metformin, aminoglycosides)
	Renal atheroembolism (catheterization, IABP)
	Interstitial nephritis (antibiotics, NSAIDs, furosemide, cimetidine)
	Glomerulonephritis (endocarditis)
Intraoperative factors	Cardiopulmonary bypass (nonpulsatile, low flow, low-pressure perfusion which reduces RBF and GFR)
	Low cardiac output syndrome/hypotension after CPB
	Hemolysis and hemoglobinuria from prolonged duration of CPB
Postoperative factors	Low cardiac output states (decreased contractility, hypovolemia, absent AV synchrony in hypertrophied hearts)
	Hypotension
	Intense vasoconstriction (low-flow states, α-agents)
	Atheroembolism (IABP)
	Sepsis
	Medications (cephalosporins, aminoglycosides, ACE inhibitors)

C. Elevation of the blood urea nitrogen (BUN) and creatinine are commonly used to diagnose the presence of renal insufficiency. A more precise assessment of the extent of renal dysfunction can be obtained from the creatinine clearance (C_{cr}), which approximates the GFR. In the steady state, this can be estimated from the serum creatinine with the following equation:

$$\frac{(140 - \text{age}) \times \text{weight in kg}}{72 \times Cr} \times 0.85 \text{ for females}$$

A more precise calculation requires collection of a 24-hour urine specimen:

$$C_{cr} = (U_{cr}/P_{cr}) \times (\text{volume}/1440 \text{ minutes})$$

where U_{cr} and P_{cr} are the urinary and plasma creatinine concentrations. The C_{cr} can be used to determine the appropriate doses of medications to prevent drug toxicity.

D. A number of etiologic mechanisms may contribute to preoperative acute renal insufficiency (table 11.1). They may be prerenal (reduced renal perfusion), renal (intrinsic renal insults), or postrenal (obstructive uropathy). When the kidneys have sustained an acute preoperative insult, they seem to be particularly sensitive to the nonpulsatile flow of cardiopulmonary bypass and to tenuous postcardiotomy hemodynamics. The BUN and creatinine should therefore be allowed to return to baseline before proceeding with surgery.

E. Patients with chronic renal failure (CRF) are more susceptible to fluid overload, hyponatremia, hyperkalemia, and metabolic acidosis in the perioperative period. Patients on chronic dialysis should be dialyzed within the 24 hours before and after surgery. Intraoperative hemodialysis should also be performed to reduce the positive fluid balance. With judicious management, patients with CRF undergoing elective surgery have a surgical risk fairly comparable to that of patients with normal renal function. However, the risk is significantly higher in patients with advanced cardiac symptoms or those undergoing urgent surgery.[16,17] The initial postoperative creatinine usually decreases from hemodilution and then rises back to its baseline value. Patients with CRF tolerate perioperative insults quite poorly, however, and a rise in BUN and creatinine is not uncommon when a low cardiac output syndrome is present.

F. **Preoperative measures**

1. Ensure adequate hydration (0.45% NS at 75 mL/h) before, during, and after contrast studies. Use of mannitol and/or furosemide may be helpful in augmenting urine output, but may actually increase the risk of developing acute renal dysfunction.

2. Repeat the serum creatinine 12–24 hours after contrast studies and defer surgery, if possible, until the creatinine has returned to baseline.

3. Identify and eliminate any medications with adverse effects on renal function, especially nonsteroidal antiinflammatory drugs (NSAIDs), ACE inhibitors, and metformin.

4. Optimize hemodynamic status with inotropes, vasodilators, and/or the intraaortic balloon. More often then not, emergency surgery is indicated in patients requiring such support. Aggressive intra- and postoperative renal management should be instituted to minimize the inevitable, but frequently transient, deterioration in renal function.

5. Correct other acid-base or metabolic abnormalities associated with renal insufficiency, such as hyponatremia, hyper- or hypokalemia, hypomagnesemia, hyperphosphatemia, metabolic acidosis (from CRF) or alkalosis (from diuretics).

G. **Intraoperative measures** to improve renal blood flow and prevent kidney damage should be considered in patients with an elevated BUN or creatinine or with known risk factors for the development of perioperative renal dysfunction.

1. Give mannitol (25 g), dopamine (3 μg/kg/min), and furosemide (20–100 mg) during bypass.

2. Maintain a higher mean perfusion pressure (around 80 mm Hg) during bypass.

3. Keep the pump run as short as possible. Extremely long pump runs may also produce hemoglobinuria.

4. Consider use of a calcium-channel blocker during surgery.

   a. **Diltiazem** reduces renal vascular resistance by dilating afferent arterioles, resulting in an increase in renal blood and GFR. It also causes a redistribution of intrarenal blood flow. Diltiazem increases sodium excretion and creatinine and free water clearance by an increase in GFR and a direct effect on tubular reabsorption. This offsets the reflex sympathetic activation of the renin-angiotensin-aldosterone system resulting from vasodilatation.

b.   Diltiazem may also minimize the increase in calcium influx into renal tubular cells that is noted during ischemia. This decreases levels of intracellular adenosine triphosphate (ATP) and may contribute to renal dysfunction after heart surgery.

c.   The use of diltiazem has been somewhat limited by concerns about its vasodilatory properties, because it is usually desirable to maintain a higher perfusion pressure during bypass in patients with renal dysfunction. In fact, one study showed that an intraoperative infusion of diltiazem (usually given as a 0.1 mg/kg bolus, followed by a continuous infusion of 2 µg/kg/min) contributed to the delayed onset of azotemia and renal dysfunction after surgery.[18–20]

5.   Consider use of fenoldopam 0.03 µg/kg/min (see page 273).

6.   Consider hemofiltration during the pump run if the patient was in heart failure before surgery or the urine output is marginal during the operation.

7.   Use aprotinin to minimize postbypass hemorrhage attributable to suspected uremic platelet dysfunction. Consideration may also be given to use of desmopressin, cryoprecipitate, or platelet transfusions to reduce bleeding.

V.   Postoperative Oliguria and Renal Insufficiency

A.   The use of hemodilution during CPB expands the extracellular volume and invariably produces an excellent urine output in the immediate postoperative period. Oliguria is considered to be present in the postoperative cardiac surgical patient when the urine output is **less than 0.5 mL/kg/h**. Although a low urine output may be associated with an excellent cardiac output, it is usually a manifestation of an acute renal insult during surgery or the early postoperative period, such as prolonged hypotension or a low cardiac output state.

1.   Some degree of postoperative renal dysfunction (probably best defined as an increase in serum creatinine to more than 50% of the preoperative level), affects about 7–10% of patients undergoing cardiac surgery. In patients with preexisting renal dysfunction or risk factors for its development, even an uneventful operation may be associated with a rise in creatinine despite the absence of oliguria (**nonoliguric renal failure**). This usually reflects less renal damage and is associated with a mortality rate of about 10%.[14] Most patients can be managed by judicious fluid administration and high-dose diuretics to optimize urine output while awaiting spontaneous recovery of renal function.

2.   **Oliguric renal failure** requiring postoperative dialysis is noted in about 2% of patients and is associated with a 50% mortality

rate.[12–15,21] This mortality rate has not changed over the past 10 to 15 years despite the early institution of various forms of dialysis and general improvements in postoperative care. This reflects the higher risk population undergoing surgery and the morbidity of conditions frequently associated with renal failure, such as low cardiac output states, respiratory failure, infection, and stroke. In one study, the occurrence of three of these factors before or during the first 48 hours after initiating hemodialysis was associated with a 90% mortality in contrast to only 15% when none were present.[21]

B. **Etiology of postoperative renal insufficiency** (see table 11.1)

   1. Despite the complex effects of low-flow, low-pressure, nonpulsatile perfusion with hemodilution and hypothermia on renal function, renal failure is most commonly the result of a **low cardiac output state.** A common contributing factor is intense peripheral vasoconstriction, often related to use of α-agents such as phenylephrine or norepinephrine. The primary impact of oliguria is noted during the first few 12–24 hours after surgery when fluid overload and hyperkalemia can lead to pulmonary and myocardial complications and impair recovery from surgery.

   2. The kidneys have a tremendous capacity to autoregulate and maintain RBF, GFR, filtration fraction, and tubular reabsorption in the face of reduced renal perfusion pressure. Intrinsic renal mechanisms that maintain autoregulation include a reduction in afferent arteriolar resistance and an increase in efferent arteriolar resistance. When a low cardiac output or hypotension persists or potent vasopressor medications are used, the filtration reserve is exhausted, resulting in intense renal vasoconstriction and a fall in GFR. The development of renal failure often represents a continuum in which these compensatory mechanisms for prerenal problems are exhausted and ischemic acute tubular necrosis (ATN) develops.[22]

   3. Thus, the management of both prerenal azotemia and ATN is fairly comparable. If prerenal insults can be corrected fairly readily, ATN should not develop. If the prerenal insults are prolonged, various degrees of ATN may occur. Prompt attention to the correction of potential causes along with judicious fluid administration, inotropic support, and high-dose diuretics may minimize the degree of decompensation and the severity of renal failure.

C. Three patterns of acute renal failure have been described following open-heart surgery (figure 11.2.)[23] In the first, termed **abbreviated acute renal failure (ARF)**, a transient intraoperative insult occurs that causes renal ischemia. The serum creatinine peaks on the fourth postoperative day and then returns to normal. In the second pattern, termed **overt ARF,** the acute insult is followed by a more prolonged period of cardiac dysfunction. The creatinine usually rises to a higher level and returns toward baseline gradually over the course of several weeks, once hemodynamics improve. The third pattern, **protracted ARF,** is characterized by an initial insult followed by a period of cardiac dysfunction that resolves. Just as the creatinine begins to fall, another insult occurs, often from sepsis or a hypotensive

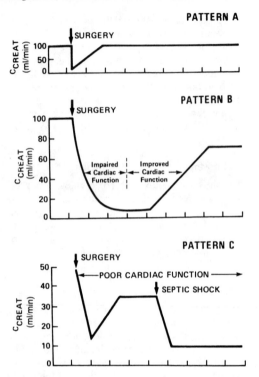

Figure 11.2 *Patterns of acute renal failure observed after open heart surgery.*
(A) Abbreviated ARF. (B) Overt ARF. (C) Protracted ARF. The reduction in creatinine
clearance (C_{creat}) noted here is paralleled by a rise in serum creatinine. (Reproduced with
permission of the Massachusetts Medical Society from Myers BD, Moran SM.
Hemodynamically mediated acute renal failure. N Engl J Med 1986;314:97–105.)

event (ventricular tachycardia, rapid atrial fibrillation, gastrointestinal
bleeding), that triggers a progressive, often irreversible rise in creatinine.
Oliguria accompanying the rise in creatinine may adversely affect pulmonary function and can be offset by the early use of a form of dialysis.

D. **Assessment** (table 11.2)[24]

    1. Assess cardiac hemodynamics (filling pressures, cardiac output).

    2. Assess for use of drugs with adverse effects on renal function.

    3. Obtain a serum BUN, creatinine, electrolytes, and osmolarity.
       Note: An elevation in creatinine with parallel rise in BUN is fre-
       quently noted with ATN. In contrast, a disproportionate rise in BUN
       with little rise in creatinine may reflect a prerenal process or
       increased protein intake, total parenteral nutrition, gastrointestinal
       bleeding, hypercatabolism, or steroid administration.

    4. Examine the urinary sediment. Epithelial or granular ("muddy
       brown") casts are indicative of ATN. In contrast, hyaline and fine
       granular casts are seen in prerenal failure.

Table 11.2 *Evaluation of the Etiology of Oliguria*

	Prerenal	Renal
BUN/Cr	>20:1	<10:1
U/P creatinine	>40	<20
U_{osm}	>500	<350
U/P osmolality	>1.5	<1.1
Urine specific gravity	>1.020	1.010
U_{Na} (mEq/L)	<20	>40
FE_{Na}	<1%	>2%
$U_{Na}/(U_{cr}/P_{cr})$*	<1	>1

* Renal failure index.

5. Measure the urine sodium (U_{Na}), creatinine (U_{Cr}), and osmolarity (U_{osm}). These measurements may be helpful in differentiating pre-renal from renal causes, but are rarely of value since most patients have already received high doses of diuretics, which may alter the interpretation of the results.

   a. The fractional excretion of sodium (FE_{Na}) is useful in differentiating prerenal and renal etiologies. This is calculated by the following formula:

   $$FE_{Na} = \frac{U_{Na} \times P_{creat}}{P_{Na} \times U_{creat}} \times 100$$

   where U and P are the urinary and plasma concentrations of sodium and creatinine, respectively.

   b. In the oliguric patient, an FE_{Na} above 1–2% is noted in patients who develop ATN, whereas an FE_{Na} <1% reflects retained tubular function with absorption of sodium and water, suggesting a prerenal problem. With an improvement in hemodynamics, a rise in FE_{Na} may be noted during re-covery of renal function due to sodium mobilization.[25] However, a low FE_{Na} with a low FE_{K+} may be noted in patients with ATN associated with contrast nephrotoxicity or hepatorenal syndrome.

6. Monitor other electrolytes, blood glucose, and acid-base balance frequently.

7. Obtain a renal ultrasound to rule out obstruction.

E. **Management of oliguria** (table 11.3)

   1. Ensure that the Foley catheter is within the bladder and is patent. Irrigate with saline if necessary or consider changing the catheter empirically.

   2. Optimize cardiac function before administering a diuretic. Al-though urine output is generally a reflection of the cardiac output, this is not necessarily the case. Oliguria may be present when the cardiac output is satisfactory and polyuria is occasionally noted when hemodynamics are marginal.

Table 11.3 *Management of Low Urine Output*

1. Ensure that Foley catheter is in the bladder and is patent
2. Optimize cardiac function
   - Treat hypovolemia
   - Control arrhythmias
   - Improve contractility
   - Reduce elevated afterload
3. Renal-dose dopamine 1–3 μg/kg/min
4. Diuretics
   - Increasing doses of furosemide (up to 500 mg IV) or a continuous infusion of 10–60 mg/h
   - Add chlorothiazide 500 mg IV
5. If above fail:
   - Limit fluid to insensible losses
   - Readjust drug doses
   - Avoid potassium supplements
   - Nutrition: Essential amino acid diet
     High nitrogen tube feeds if on dialysis (Nepro)
     TPN with 4.25% amino acid/35% dextrose
6. Consider early ultrafiltration or dialysis

   a. Optimize preload

   b. Optimize heart rate and treat arrhythmias

   c. Improve contractility with inotropes

   d. Reduce afterload with vasodilators and try to eliminate vasoconstrictive drugs; avoid ACE inhibitors.

      i. The reduction in systemic blood pressure should not be overly aggressive, because patients with preexisting hypertension and chronic renal insufficiency often require a higher blood pressure (130–150 mm Hg systolic) to maintain renal perfusion.

      ii. **Note:** The use of amrinone or milrinone to improve cardiac output is frequently accompanied by a reduction in SVR that requires norepinephrine to maintain systemic blood pressure. The renal vasoconstrictive effects of norepinephrine frequently reduce RBF despite the improvement in cardiac output. This adverse effect on RBF may be counteracted by the concomitant use of low-dose dopamine, although there may be no increase in GFR or urine output.[26,27]

   e. If cardiac output remains marginal despite the use of multiple inotropes, consider the placement of an intraaortic balloon pump (IABP). This may result in an abrupt and dramatic increase in urine output.

3. "Renal-dose" dopamine (2–3 μg/kg/min) increases RBF by direct renal vasodilatation, increases GFR, and directly inhibits tubular solute reabsorption, leading to increased sodium and water excretion.[28]

a. When the cardiac output is satisfactory, low-dose dopamine can be given to improve RBF. If the cardiac output is marginal, a higher dose of dopamine (5–10 µg/kg/min) may be used to provide a positive inotropic effect. More commonly, however, renal-dose dopamine should be used as an adjunct to another inotropic agent.

b. One study of critically ill patients demonstrated that renal-dose dopamine increased urine output without improving creatinine clearance, whereas dobutamine given at a dose of approximately 2.5 µg/kg/min improved creatinine clearance without increasing urine output.[29]

c. Once a patient has developed acute renal insufficiency, dopamine has not been shown in most studies to produce a statistically significant improvement in urine output.[30]

4. A diuretic should then be selected if oliguria persists. Diuretics probably have little direct effect on renal functional recovery and the natural history of ATN, but a diuretic can often convert oliguric to nonoliguric renal failure if it is administered early after the onset of renal failure,[31] thus minimizing the adverse impact of fluid retention on pulmonary function.

a. One of the loop diuretics is chosen first. They inhibit sodium reabsorption in the ascending limb of the loop of Henle and increase solute (sodium) presentation to the distal tubules. By inhibiting tubular water reabsorption, they increase solute and free water clearance and prevent tubular obstruction. They may also, to a lesser extent, increase RBF and GFR. These include the following:

   i. Furosemide may be given in incremental doses starting at 10 mg IV to improve urine output; once the patient has developed acute renal failure, the initial dose is usually 80 mg IV, with doubling of the dose up to 320 mg to a cumulative maximum of 1 g in 24 hours.

   ii. Ethacrynic acid 50–100 mg IV

   iii. Bumetanide 2–10 mg IV

   Note: High doses of these diuretics should be administered slowly (over 5 minutes) to minimize the risk of ototoxicity.

b. A gentle sustained diuresis can be obtained using a continuous intravenous furosemide drip starting at 10 mg/h and increasing to a maximum of 60 mg/h.[10,11] This is particularly beneficial in patients who are poorly responsive to bolus doses of furosemide.

c. Even if the urine output fails to improve with one diuretic, an excellent response may be achieved with another or by combining one of these loop diuretics with chlorothiazide 500 mg IV or metolazone (Zaroxolyn) 5–10 mg PO or per NG tube.[32]

d. The combination of dopamine and furosemide may be synergistic because the renal vasodilatation and improved RBF produced by dopamine improve the delivery of furosemide to the distal tubules and increase solute diuresis.[33]

   e. **Note:** The patient taking diuretics before surgery may demonstrate "diuretic tolerance." In this situation, a low urine output may be present despite an excellent cardiac output. There is usually a prompt response to loop diuretics in doses comparable to those taken preoperatively or, if necessary, given continuously. The addition of oral or intravenous thiazides may also be beneficial.[32]

   f. **Note:** Mannitol is an osmotic diuretic that is frequently used to maintain urine output during surgery. It improves tubular flow and reduces tubular cell swelling. Nonetheless, it is best avoided in the postoperative period because its oncotic effect mobilizes fluid into the intravascular space. This could theoretically lead to pulmonary edema if fluid overload is present and urine output does not improve.

5. Maintain an alkaline urine if there is evidence of hemoglobinuria.

F. **Management of established renal failure**

1. Optimize hemodynamics. Maintain a higher blood pressure (systolic of 130–150 mm Hg) in hypertensive patients.

2. Restrict fluids with mL/mL of fluid replacement (i.e., input = output) plus 500 mL D5/0.2% normal saline/day (about 200 mL/m^2/day). Daily weights are helpful in assessing changes in day-to-day fluid status, but must also take into consideration the influence of nutritional status on body mass.

3. Monitor electrolytes and blood glucose

   a. Avoid potassium supplements and medications that increase potassium levels (β-blockers). Correct hyperkalemia as described on pages 358–359.

   b. Hyponatremia should be treated with fluid restriction.

   c. Metabolic acidosis should be corrected if serum bicarbonate falls below 15 mEq/L.

   d. Correct hyperglycemia and abnormalities of calcium, phosphate, or magnesium metabolism.

4. Medications

   a. Give antacid medications (H$_2$ blockers, omeprazole) to reduce the risk of gastrointestinal bleeding.

   b. Eliminate drugs that impair renal function (aminoglycosides, NSAIDs, ACE-inhibitors)

   c. Adjust doses of medications that are excreted or metabolized by the kidneys (particularly digoxin, procainamide, and antibiotics) (see Appendixes 1 and 2).

5. Remove the Foley catheter and catheterize daily or as needed, depending on urine output. Culture the urine.

6. Nutrition

   a. If the patient is able to eat, an essential amino acid diet should be used. Protein should not be restricted if the patient is on peritoneal dialysis or hemodialysis, because these procedures are associated with significant nitrogen loss. Hemodialysis can result in the loss of 3–5 g/h of protein and peritoneal dialysis may remove 40–60 g/day of protein. Patients should receive approximately 1.5 g/kg/day of protein if they are on dialysis.

b. If the patient is unable to eat, a high nitrogen tube feeding, such as Nepro, can be used if the patient is on dialysis. For most patients with acute renal insufficiency, there is no need to alter the amount of protein and standard tube feedings can be used. In patients with chronic renal insufficiency that does not require dialysis, a low protein supplement, such as Suplena, can be used to provide 0.5–0.8 g/kg/day of protein (see Appendixes 3 and 4).

c. If the patient is unable to tolerate enteral feedings, total parenteral nutrition (TPN) using a 4.25% amino acid/35% dextrose solution that contains no potassium, magnesium, or phosphate is recommended.

7. Obtain studies that might delineate the cause of renal failure if there is no identifiable etiology. A renal ultrasound (for kidney size and obstruction) or renal scan (if a renal embolus is suspected) may be helpful.

8. Consider the prompt initiation of dialysis or ultrafiltration.

VI. Hemofiltration and Dialysis (table 11.4)[34,35]

A. General comments

1. Early initiation of one of the various forms of hemofiltration or dialysis may be beneficial following heart surgery when persistent oliguria or a progressive rise in serum creatinine occurs. Although the mortality rate of patients requiring dialysis after surgery is approximately 50%, it is hoped that the early initiation of hemofiltration to minimize the development of other complicating factors, such as respiratory failure and infection, will improve patient survival.

Table 11.4 *Techniques of Dialysis*

If the patient has:	HD	CVVH	CVVHD	CAVH	CAVHD	PD
Unstable hemodynamics	−	+++	+++	++	++	++
Contraindication to heparin	++	+	+	+	+	++
Vascular access problems	+++	+++	+++	−	−	++
Volume overload	++	+++	+++	+++	+++	+
Hyperkalemia	+++	++	+++	++	+++	+
Severe uremia	+++	+	++	+	++	+
Respiratory compromise	++	+++	+++	+++	+++	−

HD, hemodialysis; CVVH, continuous venovenous hemofiltration; CVVHD, continuous venovenous hemodialysis; CAVH, continuous arteriovenous hemofiltration; CAVHD, continuous arteriovenous hemodialysis; PD, peritoneal dialysis.
− = avoid, + = useful, ++ = better, +++ = even better.

2. General **indications** for dialysis or ultrafiltration are:
   a. Hypervolemia
   b. Hyperkalemia
   c. Progressive acidosis
   d. Progressive uremia (BUN over 80 mg/dL) or rise in serum creatinine of greater than 1.5 mg/dL per day
   e. Uremia associated with pericarditis, encephalopathy, seizures, or coagulopathy
3. The form of hemofiltration to be selected should depend on its indication, the hemodynamic stability of the patient, and the availability of vascular access. Newer technology that allows continuous hemofiltration using only venous access has abrogated concern in unstable patients or those with limited arterial access.

B. **Intermittent hemodialysis (HD)**
   1. **Principle.** Solute passes by diffusion down a concentration gradient from the blood, across a hollow-fiber semipermeable membrane, and into a dialysate bath. Some solute is also transported by convection resulting from a difference in hydrostatic pressure.
   2. **Indications.** Severe fluid overload, hyperkalemia, acid-base imbalances, or a hypercatabolic state in the hemodynamically stable patient. HD is the most rapid means of correcting these problems.
   3. **Access.** Standard intermittent HD is performed using a single 12F double-lumen catheter placed in the internal jugular or, if only a few dialysis treatments are anticipated, in the femoral vein. Insertion in the subclavian vein should be avoided because of the high incidence of venous thrombosis. To reduce the infection risk in patients requiring more extended periods of dialysis, a double-lumen PermCath can be placed into the internal jugular vein and brought through a subcutaneous tunnel. Subsequently, a fistula can be created for permanent dialysis.
   4. **Technique.** Intermittent HD is performed over a 3–4 hour period. The blood is pumped into the dialysis cartridge at a rate of 300–500 mL/min, while the dialysate solution is infused at a rate of 500 mL/min in a direction countercurrent to blood flow. The system is rinsed initially with 5000 units of heparin, but no additional heparinization is necessary.
   5. **Limitations**
      a. Circulatory instability from hypovolemia or blunted sympathetic reflexes commonly occurs during intermittent HD because a large volume of fluid is removed in a short period of time. Volume shifts that contribute to neuromuscular and hemodynamic problems can be attenuated by the use of higher sodium levels in the dialysate solution. Colloid or blood transfusions and hemodynamic support (usually with α-agents) are frequently necessary. Therefore, HD is best avoided in the hemodynamically unstable patient.
      b. Dialysis machines are complex, costly, and require special expertise. Although other forms of hemofiltration are effec-

tive in removing fluid, especially in the unstable patient, intermittent HD remains the most efficient means of removing solute and correcting severe acid-base abnormalities.

C. **Continuous venovenous hemofiltration (CVVH) or hemodialysis with filtration (CVVHD)**

   1. **Principle.** An occlusive pump is included in a circuit that actively withdraws blood from the venous system, pumps it through a diafilter, and returns it to the venous system. For CVVHD, dialysis fluid runs countercurrent to the direction of blood flow within the diafilter. Solute then passes by diffusion down a concentration gradient across a hemofilter into the dialysate solution.

   2. **Indications.** Management of fluid overload, especially in the hemodynamically unstable or hypotensive patient. Slow correction of electrolyte imbalance can be achieved with CVVH using a crystalloid solution of different composition as replacement fluid. Severe electrolyte imbalance or hypercatabolic states are better managed with CVVHD.

   3. **Access** is obtained using a 12F double-lumen catheter (12 gauge for each lumen) placed in the internal jugular or femoral vein.

   4. **Technique** (figure 11.3)

      a. A hemofilter (Renalflo HF700) is attached downstream to an occlusive pump and heparin is infused into the inflow portion of the circuit to maintain a dialyzer output (venous) PTT of 45–60 sec. The pump is usually set to deliver blood at a rate of 100 mL/min and the ultrafiltrate rate is usually set at 999 mL/h. The blood then passes through a bubble trap air detector and is returned to the patient.

      b. For CVVHD, dialysis fluid (Dianeal 1.5% with 4 mL of 23% NaCl per 2 L bag) is infused into the dialysis cartridge at a rate of 999 mL/h.

      c. Replacement fluid (usually solutions alternately containing calcium gluconate and $NaCO_3$) is infused into the inflow circuit or the venous chamber. The amount administered is dictated by the desired negative fluid balance per hour. Alternatively, the infusion of a sodium citrate solution prefilter with administration of calcium post-filter obviates the need for heparinization and $NaCO_3$ administration.

   5. **Limitations**

      a. Heparinization is required in the circuit to prevent clotting (unless sodium citrate is used as noted).

      b. The pump adds some complexity and cost to the system compared with arteriovenous hemofiltration.

      c. CVVH usually suffices to achieve satisfactory solute clearance, but CVVHD may be selected to achieve more thorough clearance.

   6. **Comments.** The availability of CVVH has simplified the management of fluid overload in the hemodynamically unstable patient.

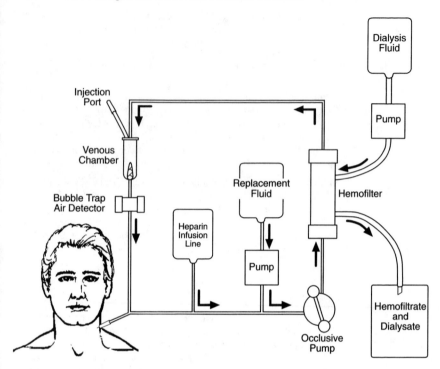

Figure 11.3 *Continuous venovenous hemofiltration (CVVH). An occlusive pump withdraws blood from the venous circuit, pumps it through a diafilter, and returns it to the venous system through a double-lumen catheter placed in the internal jugular vein. Dialysis is accomplished by infusing a dialysate solution into the diafilter in a direction countercurrent to blood flow.*

Arterial access is not required, and the system will function well in the hypotensive patient. CVVH has become the preferred technique for acute hemofiltration in the ICU setting, especially in the unstable patient.

D. **Continuous arteriovenous hemofiltration (CAVH) or hemodialysis with filtration (CAVHD)**

1. **Principle**

   a. The hydrostatic pressure provided by the blood pressure drives protein-free fluid across a membrane by convection. The rate of formation of the ultrafiltrate depends primarily on the transmembrane gradient (the difference in hydraulic pressure between the blood and ultrafiltrate compartments), the blood flow in the system, and the size of the membrane. The gradient can be increased by connecting the ultrafil-trate compartment to a suction device. Alteration in serum electrolyte composition depends on the volume of ultra-filtrate removed and the composition and amount of fluid replacement.

b. With CAVHD, the convection principle of CAVH is combined with the diffusion principle of hemodialysis with passage of solute down a concentration gradient across a hemofilter into a dialysate solution.

c. The use of a continuous technique avoids the hemodynamic instability noted with conventional HD, which removes large volumes of fluid in a short period of time.

2. **Indications**

    a. Fluid overload, especially in a hemodynamically unstable patient. CAVH may remove fluid at a faster rate than hemodialysis without producing hypotension. Moderate electrolyte imbalance can be corrected by replacing the ultrafiltrate with a crystalloid solution of different composition (for example, one that is potassium-free). This system is very helpful in patients requiring biventricular assist devices because the driving pressure can be provided by the pump.

    b. CAVHD is more effective for severe hyperkalemia or hypercatabolic states.

3. **Access.** 10F cannulas (Vascaths) are placed in the femoral artery and vein.

4. **Technique**

    a. The hemofilter is connected as shown in figure 11.4. The filter is flushed with 2 liters of normal saline containing 5000 units of heparin/liter, and 10 units/kg/h are continuously infused into the arterial line. Ultrafiltration can occur as long as the systolic pressure exceeds 60 mm Hg. Drainage can be increased by connecting the diafilter to suction and decreased by clamping down on the ultrafiltrate drainage tube or adjusting the relative heights of the filter and the collection bag. Approximately 300–1000 mL can be removed per hour. Reduction in serum solute and urea levels is accomplished by fluid replacement given at a rate slightly less than the previous hour's drainage (see CVVH replacement fluid above). This allows for a precise determination of the desired fluid balance which must be monitored on an hourly basis.

    b. For CAVHD, a dialysate solution is infused into the filter countercurrent to the direction of blood flow at rates of 999 mL/h. Total fluid clearance approximates 20–25 mL/min (1200–1500 mL/h).

5. **Limitations**

    a. CAVH is inadequate for severe electrolyte or acid-base imbalances or for solute removal in hypercatabolic states, but CAVHD can be used.

    b. Both techniques are ineffective in the hypotensive patient because arterial pressure dictates the rate of blood flow into the filter.

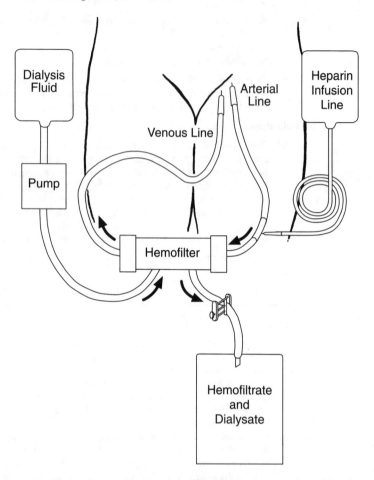

Figure 11.4 *Continuous arteriovenous hemofiltration (CAVH) is performed by placing a hemofilter between the arterial and venous lines. Heparinized saline is infused through a controlled infusion pump into the arterial line. The effluent flows into a collection bag. The rate of ultrafiltration may be decreased by clamping down on the effluent line. Continuous AV hemodiafiltration is performed by infusing a dialysate solution into the filter in a direction countercurrent to blood flow.*

    c. The rapid removal of fluid can result in hypovolemia and hemodynamic instability. This is counteracted by the administration of intravenous fluid at a rate slightly less than the rate of ultrafiltration. Alternatively, the rate of fluid withdrawal can be minimized to allow for a slow withdrawal of fluid without concern for solute clearance (so-called "slow continuous ultrafiltration" or SCUF).

    d. Arterial (as well as venous) access is required and can be problematic in the patient with peripheral vascular disease.

The risk of femoral artery thrombosis exceeds 5%. Bacterial colonization of the catheters can occur if they remain in place for an extended period of time.

   e. Heparinization is required to prevent clotting within the filter, which can occur during periods of low blood flow.

   f. With CAVHD, electrolyte imbalance (hyponatremia) and hyperglycemia may develop and require careful monitoring and appropriate modification of the dialysate solution.

   g. CAVHD is effective in removing solute by dialysis, but is a more complex setup than standard CAVH.

   h. Because of the drawbacks of the system (arterial access, heparinization, limited efficacy in hypotensive patients), CAVH has generally been replaced by CVVH.

E. **Peritoneal dialysis (PD)**

   1. **Principle.** Solute passes down an osmotic gradient by diffusion from the blood, across the rich capillary network of the peritoneal membrane, and into a dialysate solution that is infused into the abdominal cavity. The efficiency of ultrafiltration and solute removal depends primarily on the glucose composition of the dialysate solution, but also on the volume infused and the intraabdominal dwell time.

   2. **Indications.** Hypervolemia, hyperkalemia, or uremia in the hemodynamically unstable patient. PD is especially valuable in patients with vascular access problems or contraindications to heparinization.

   3. **Access.** An indwelling dialysis catheter (Tenckhoff catheter) with multiple sideholes is placed by surgical cutdown just below the umbilicus and positioned in the pelvis. The presence of intraabdominal adhesions may make insertion difficult and may impair drainage.

   4. **Technique.** Exchanges are performed using a dialysate solution with varying glucose concentrations (1.5%, 2.5%, or 4.25%) to remove more or less volume and solute. The infusion volume is limited to 2 liters to minimize intraabdominal distention. Using an automatic cycler, the solution is usually infused for 10 minutes, allowed to dwell for 45 minutes, and then drained for 20 minutes. A 1.5% dextrose solution will withdraw approximately 100 mL of volume with a 1-hour dwell, whereas the 4.25% solution will extract about 300–400 mL.

   5. **Limitations**

      a. PD is less effective than hemodialysis in removing urea (hypercatabolic states) and solute (hyperkalemia).

      b. Abdominal distention from a 2-liter infusion may produce respiratory compromise during the dwell period.

      c. Absorption of glucose from the dialysate can increase the respiratory quotient and worsen ventilatory failure.

      d. Peritonitis develops in about 5% of patients.

e. Significant protein loss may develop unless the patient receives adequate nutrition.

6. **Additional comments.** The main advantages of PD are that arterial access is not required and heparinization is avoided. However, with the availability of CVVH, PD is rarely used today. The production of abdominal distention and glucose absorption greatly impedes respiratory function in the postoperative patient. The only situation when PD is currently used is the patient on chronic PD prior to surgery with a well-functioning catheter.

VII. Hyperkalemia

A. **Etiology**

1. High-volume, high-potassium cardioplegia solutions used in the operating room. The potassium load is usually eliminated promptly by normally functioning kidneys, but hyperkalemia can be problematic in patients with intrinsic renal dysfunction or oliguria from other causes.

2. Low cardiac output states associated with oliguria. Potassium levels may rise with alarming and life-threatening rapidity.

3. Severe tissue ischemia, whether peripheral (from severe peripheral vascular disease or complication of an IABP) or intraabdominal (mesenteric ischemia). Hyperkalemia is often the first clue to the existence of these problems.

4. Acute and chronic renal insufficiency

   Note: Remember that hyperkalemia is exacerbated by acidosis, which often accompanies low output or ischemic syndromes. A 0.2-unit change in pH produces about a 1 mEq/L change in serum potassium concentration.

B. **Manifestations** are predominantly electrocardiographic. An asystolic arrest may occur when the potassium rises rapidly to a level exceeding 6.5 mEq/L. The ECG changes of hyperkalemia do not always develop in classic progressive fashion and are more related to the rate of rise of serum potassium than to the absolute level. These changes include:

1. Peaked T waves

2. ST depression

3. Smaller R waves

4. Prolonged PR interval

5. Loss of P waves

6. QRS widening, bradycardia, asystole, ventricular fibrillation

When the heart is being paced, hyperkalemia may result in failure to respond to the pacemaker stimulus.

C. **Treatment** entails shifting potassium into cells and increasing its excretion from the body.

1. Optimize cardiac function

2. If there is evidence of advanced cardiac toxicity ($K^+ > 6.0$ mEq/L), administer calcium gluconate 5–10 mL of a 10% solution (0.5–1 g) IV over 15 minutes.

3. Shift potassium into cells

    a. $NaHCO_3$ (1 amp = 50 mEq/L) to correct acidosis and raise the pH to 7.40–7.50. A mild respiratory alkalosis can also be produced by increasing the respiratory rate on the ventilator.

    b. Regular insulin 10 units/25 g of 50% dextrose IV

    c. Aerosolized β-agonists by nebulizer. They may improve potassium uptake into cells.

4. Enhance potassium excretion

    a. Furosemide 10–200 mg IV

    b. Kayexalate enema 50 g in water enema or 50 g PO with sorbitol

    c. Dialysis

D. **Note:** Make sure the patient is not receiving any exogenous potassium. Stop any medications that can increase the serum potassium level (e.g., β-blockers, potassium-sparing diuretics).

VIII. Hypokalemia

A. **Etiology**

1. Profound diuresis without adequate potassium replacement. Potassium excretion parallels the urine output after bypass, which tends to be copious because of hemodilution. The use of potent diuretics, especially during surgery, may produce a significant diuresis in the early postoperative period.

2. Insulin to treat hyperglycemia

3. Alkalosis (metabolic or respiratory)

4. Significant nasogastric tube drainage

B. **Manifestations.** Hypokalemia promotes atrial, junctional, or ventricular ectopy, and enhances digoxin-induced arrhythmias. The ECG may demonstrate flattened ST segments, decreased T wave amplitude, and the presence of U waves.

C. **Treatment.** Potassium replacement may resolve ectopic beats by several mechanisms that alter automaticity and conduction.

1. It is essential that renal function and urine output be evaluated before a KCl drip is started, because acute hyperkalemia can develop very rapidly when oliguria or renal dysfunction is present. A slower infusion rate is advisable in this situation, with frequent rechecking of the serum potassium level.

2. In the ICU setting, KCl is administered through a central line at a rate of 10–20 mEq/h (mix of 80 mEq/250 mL). The serum potassium rises approximately 0.1 mEq/L for each 2 mEq of KCl administered.

3. When a central line is not present, a concentrated potassium drip cannot be administered peripherally because it scleroses veins. The maximum concentration of KCl that can be administered peripherally is 60 mEq/L. Oral potassium (usually 10–20 mEq tablets) is somewhat unpalatable, but coated preparations are available.

IX. Hypocalcemia

A. Calcium plays a complex role in myocardial reperfusion damage and myocardial energetics. Ionized calcium (normal = 1.1–1.3 mmol/L) should be measured because total calcium levels, which are affected by protein binding, are usually reduced during surgery because of hemodilution, hypothermia, shifts in pH, and the use of citrated blood. Hypocalcemia is usually associated with prolongation of the QT interval on the ECG tracing.

B. **Treatment**

1. It is common practice to empirically administer a 500 mg bolus of calcium chloride at the termination of bypass to support SVR (if the ionized calcium is normal) and/or increase myocardial contractility (if the ionized calcium is low).[36–38]

2. It is questionable whether treatment of hypocalcemia identified in the ICU is of any value in improving cardiovascular function. In fact, calcium salts may attenuate the cardiotonic effects of catecholamines, such as dobutamine or epinephrine, although they have little effect on the efficacy of amrinone.[39] Nonetheless, if the ionized calcium level is measured and found to be less than 1 mmol/L, calcium gluconate (10 mL of 10% solution) may be given, although there is no clear benefit to doing so. Calcium chloride is best avoided for "asymptomatic hypocalcemia" to minimize any acute hemodynamic effects.

3. Calcium chloride (0.5–1.0 g IV) may be given in emergency situations to provide temporary circulatory support when a low cardiac output syndrome or acute hypotension develops suddenly. The transient improvement in hemodynamics allows time for analysis of causative factors and the institution of other pharmacologic support. $CaCl_2$ should not be given routinely during a cardiac arrest.

X. Hypomagnesemia

A. Magnesium plays a role in energy metabolism and cardiac impulse generation. Low levels have been associated with coronary spasm, prolonged ventilatory support, and a higher incidence of postoperative atrial and ventricular arrhythmias, especially digoxin-related arrhythmias.

B. Magnesium levels (normal = 1.5–2 mEq/L) are usually not measured during surgery, but they are reduced in more than 70% of patients studied.[40] This may be the result of diuretic usage or simple hemodilution.

C. Administration of magnesium sulfate (2 g in 100 mL solution) to raise the serum level to 2 mEq/L has been shown to reduce the incidence of postoperative atrial and ventricular dysrhythmias.[41,42] In addition, magnesium has been found to inhibit the vasoconstrictive response to epinephrine, but not its cardiotonic effects.[43] We routinely administer 2 g of $MgSO_4$ at the conclusion of bypass and on the first postoperative morning.

XI. Metabolic Acidosis

A. Etiology

1. Low cardiac output states with peripheral vasoconstriction or poor peripheral perfusion. This scenario is often noted in the immediate postoperative period when the patient not only has marginal myocardial function but is also hypothermic.

2. Intraabdominal catastrophes, such as mesenteric ischemia secondary to a low-flow state; the latter should always be suspected in the patient with unexplained persistent acidemia.

3. Sepsis

4. High doses of sodium nitroprusside

5. Renal failure

6. Diabetic ketoacidosis

B. Effects

1. Adverse effects from metabolic acidemia are usually not noted until the pH is less than 7.20.[44] A pure metabolic acidosis (low serum bicarbonate with acidemic pH) may be noted in the heavily sedated patient in whom there is no respiratory compensation. However, compensatory hyperventilation will usually occur during synchronized intermittent mandatory ventilation (SIMV) or spontaneous ventilation to decrease the PCO_2 and neutralize the pH to minimize these effects. Nonetheless, some of the deleterious effects of metabolic acidemia may be related to the metabolic products associated with the acidemia rather than the absolute level of pH, although they may be reversed by administration of sodium bicarbonate.

2. The presence of progressive or significant metabolic acidosis (as assessed by the serum bicarbonate level) may be an indication of a serious ongoing problem that must be corrected before adverse consequences occur. These include:

    a. Cardiovascular effects

    - Decreased contractility and cardiac output; reduction in hepatic and renal blood flow
    - Attenuation of the positive inotropic effects of catecholamines[45]
    - Venoconstriction and arteriolar dilatation, which increase filling pressures and decrease systemic pressures
    - Increased pulmonary vascular resistance (PVR)
    - Sensitization to reentrant arrhythmias and reduction in the threshold for ventricular fibrillation

    b. Respiratory effects

    - Dyspnea and tachypnea
    - Decreased respiratory muscle strength

    c. Metabolic changes
- Increased metabolic demands
- Hyperglycemia caused by tissue insulin resistance and inhibition of anaerobic glycolysis
- Decreased hepatic update and increased hepatic production of lactate
- Hyperkalemia
- Increased protein catabolism

    d. Cerebral function
- Inhibition of brain metabolism and cell volume regulation
- Obtundation and coma

3. **Lactic acidosis** reflects impaired tissue oxygenation and anaerobic metabolism resulting from circulatory failure. The acidosis is self-perpetuating in that excess lactate is being produced at a time when there is suppression of hepatic lactate utilization. Both the lactate ion and the acidemia individually contribute to potential cardiovascular dysfunction. Elevated lactate levels ($>2\,mEq/L$) should raise suspicion of a low cardiac output state or severe tissue ischemia.

C. **Treatment** should be directed toward reversal of the underlying cause. However, correction of a primary metabolic acidosis (not that which compensates for a primary respiratory alkalosis) should be considered when the serum bicarbonate is less than $15\,mEq/L$ (base deficit greater than 8 to $10\,mmol/L$). Treatment is especially important when the etiology of the acidosis is unclear or not imminently remediable. If there has been adequate respiratory compensation, this correction should take place slowly, allowing the patient's respiratory drive to decrease to reduce the risk of producing alkalemia.

1. **Sodium bicarbonate** is administered in a dose calculated from the following equation:

$$0.5 \times body\ weight\ in\ kg \times base\ deficit = mEq\ NaHCO_3$$

This should be administered over several hours in the patient with severe metabolic acidemia.

2. **Carbicarb** is an equimolar solution of sodium bicarbonate and sodium carbonate.[46] One of its advantages over standard $NaHCO_3$ is that is does not undergo significant breakdown into CO_2 and H_2O. The recommended dose is:

$$0.2 \times kg \times base\ deficit = mEq\ sodium$$

3. **Tromethamine** $0.3\,M$ (THAM or Tris buffer) can be used if the patient has developed hypernatremia from multiple doses of $NaHCO_3$. It also limits CO_2 generation.

$$kg \times base\ deficit = mL\ of\ 0.3\,M\ THAM$$

XII.   Metabolic Alkalosis

A. **Etiology**

1.   Excessive diuresis, especially from the loop diuretics

2.   Nasogastric drainage with inadequate electrolyte replacement by intravenous solutions

3.   Total parenteral nutrition with inappropriate solute composition

4.   Secondary as compensation for respiratory acidosis

B. **Adverse effects**[47]

1.   Lowers the serum potassium level, potentially leading to atrial and ventricular arrhythmias (especially digoxin-induced arrhythmias) and to neuromuscular weakness.

2.   Has an adverse effect on the cardiovascular response to catecholamines that is comparable to that of acidosis.[45]

3.   Shifts the oxygen-hemoglobin dissociation curve to the left, impairing oxygen delivery to the tissues (this effect is offset in chronic metabolic alkalosis by an increase in 2,3 DPG in red cells).

4.   Produces arteriolar constriction, which can compromise cerebral and coronary perfusion. Neurologic abnormalities including headache, seizures, tetany, and lethargy may occur, probably because of the associated hypocalcemia induced by alkalosis. These effects are usually seen with a pH > 7.60.

5.   Decreases the central respiratory drive, leading to hypoventilation, CO_2 retention, and potentially hypoxemia.

C. **Treatment**

1.   Metabolic alkalosis is sustained by hypovolemia ("contraction alkalosis"), hypokalemia, and hypochloremia. Thus, therapy should be directed toward correction of these factors.

2.   Potential contributors to alkalosis should be assessed.

    a.   Reduce doses of loop diuretics or thiazides. Use **acetazolamide** (Diamox) 250–500 mg IV in conjunction with a loop diuretic. This has a fairly weak diuretic effect when used alone. Use potassium-sparing diuretics (most are available only in oral form).

    b.   Loss of gastric acid through a nasogastric tube can be reduced using H_2-blockers or omeprazole.

    c.   Avoid lactate (lactated Ringer's solution) and acetate (common in parenteral nutrition solutions) that are metabolized to bicarbonate.

3.   The administration of chloride, usually as KCl or NaCl, is the primary treatment for metabolic alkalosis. The selection of the appropriate solute depends on the potassium concentration and the volume status. The rate of administration of intravenous KCl is usually limited to 20 Eq/h, but it can be slightly faster if the patient has significant hypokalemia and an ongoing profound diuresis.

4. **Hydrochloric acid** 0.1 N (100 mEq/L) may be administered through a central line at a rate of 10–20 mEq/h. It is rarely required in cardiac surgical patients. The total dose can be calculated based on a bicarbonate space of 50% body weight from either of the two following methods:

    a.   Chloride deficit:

$$mEq \ HCL = 0.5 \times kg \times (103 - measured \ chloride)$$

    b.   Base-excess method:

$$mEq \ HCL = \frac{0.5 \times kg \times base \ excess}{2}$$

If a profound alkalosis is present, these doses should be given over 12 hours with intermittent reevaluation.

XIII.   Hyperglycemia

A. **Etiology**

1. Impaired insulin production and peripheral insulin resistance during bypass resulting from elevated levels of the counterregulatory hormones, including cortisol, epinephrine, and growth hormone.

2. Total parenteral nutrition with inadequate insulin response.

3. Sepsis (often the first manifestation of an occult sternal wound infection or an intraabdominal process).

B. **Manifestations.** Hyperglycemia contributes to excessive urine output from an osmotic diuresis, impairs wound healing, increases the risk of infection, and may impair blood pressure regulation.[48,49]

C. **Treatment**

1. Blood glucose in diabetic patients should be monitored every 6 hours in the ICU. Because subcutaneous absorption is unreliable, insulin should be given intravenously. An intravenous bolus may be sufficient for moderate hyperglycemia (BS ≤ 300 mg/dL), giving 5 units of regular insulin IV for each 50 mg/dL over 200 mg/dL). However, an insulin bolus is rapidly cleared from the blood and may lower the potassium level without affecting the blood glucose. When the blood glucose exceeds 300 mg/dL, a continuous insulin infusion is preferable to maintain the blood glucose less than 200 mg/dL. The usual dose is 0.1 U/kg/h (about 5–10 U/h) using a 100 unit regular insulin/100 mL normal saline mix. Blood glucose levels should be repeated within a few hours to determine the patient's sensitivity to insulin.

2. Patients with type I diabetes mellitus should have their insulin doses gradually increased back to preoperative levels depending on blood glucose levels. It is preferable to use a lower dose of intermediate-acting insulin initially (usually one-half of the usual dose) and supplement it with regular insulin as necessary. The glucose level may be higher than suspected from the patient's oral intake because of

the residual elevation of counterregulatory hormones from the operation. Insulin doses may be increased when the patient becomes more active and has an improved caloric intake.

3. In type II diabetics, oral hypoglycemic medications should be restarted once the patient is taking a normal diet. Nonetheless, daily blood sugars should be obtained during the first postoperative week because many patients have a poor appetite and their blood sugar remains less than 200 mg/dL on no medications.

D. **Hyperosmolar, hyperglycemic, nonketotic coma** has been reported in type II diabetics following surgery. It commonly develops 4–7 days after surgery and is manifested by polyuria in association with a rising BUN or serum sodium. The resultant dehydration, often exacerbated by gastrointestinal bleeding or use of high-nitrogen, hyperosmolar tube feedings, results in the hyperosmolar state.[50] Gradual correction of hypovolemia, hyperglycemia, hypokalemia, and hypernatremia is indicated.

E. **Diabetic ketoacidosis** is rarely seen following cardiac surgery, but may be noted in type I diabetics. Standard management with saline infusions, an insulin drip, and correction of potassium and acid-base abnormalities should be followed.

XIV. Hypothyroidism

A. Hypothyroidism is difficult to treat preoperatively in the patient with ischemic heart disease because thyroid replacement can precipitate ischemic symptoms.

B. **Manifestations** include decreased myocardial contractility, bradycardia, high peripheral resistance, diastolic hypertension, and low cardiac output. Cardiac surgery is well tolerated in most patients with mild to moderate hypothyroidism.[51] Ventricular dysfunction is rarely noted upon weaning from bypass.

C. **Treatment**

1. Should postcardiotomy ventricular dysfunction occur, 0.05 mg of IV levothyroxine (T_4) or 0.05–2 µg/kg of triiodothyronine (T_3) can be given in conjunction with an inotrope such as amrinone that does not depend on β-receptors for its action.[52,53]

2. For the hypothyroid patient who has tolerated surgery uneventfully, treatment is initiated postoperatively with T_4 (Synthroid) 0.05 mg orally each day and subsequently increased depending on TSH and T_4 levels. If the patient is unable to take an oral dose, one-half of the oral dose can be given intravenously.

3. If the patient is severely hypothyroid, consultation with an endocrinologist is imperative. Doses of T_4 that have been recommended include an initial IV dose of 0.4 mg, followed by 3 days of 0.1–0.2 mg IV daily, and then a maintenance dose of 0.05 mg PO qd.

XV. Adrenal Insufficiency

A. Adrenal insufficiency is a rare complication of cardiac surgery that may result from adrenal hemorrhage associated with heparinization and stress in an elderly patient.[54,55]

B. **Manifestations** include flank pain, nonspecific gastrointestinal complaints (anorexia, nausea, vomiting, ileus, abdominal pain or distention), fever, and delirium. Late signs include hyperkalemia, hyponatremia, and hypotension with poor response to vasopressors. The clinical scenario can be confused with sepsis.

C. **Diagnosis** is confirmed by low serum cortisol levels and failure of cortisol levels to rise after a 25 unit ACTH challenge.

D. **Treatment** is with 100 mg of hydrocortisone IV q8h as well as administration of glucose and normal saline. If additional mineralocorticoid is needed, 0.05–0.2 mg of fludrocortisone can be given every day.

XVI. Pituitary Abnormalities

A. **Pituitary apoplexy**

1. **Etiology**

   a. Ischemia, edema, or hemorrhage of an undetected pituitary tumor.

   b. CPB with heparinization and low cerebral blood flow may be contributory.

2. **Presentation.** Compression of the optic chiasm and parasellar structures results in ophthalmoplegia, visual loss, and headache.[56]

3. **Treatment**

   a. Decrease intracerebral edema with hyperventilation, mannitol, and steroids (dexamethasone 10 mg q6h).

   b. Urgent hypophysectomy if no improvement.

B. **Diabetes insipidus.** This is a rare complication of cardiac surgery that may produce polyuria due to diminished production of ADH. Documentation of a urine osmolarity of 50–100 mOsm/L should raise suspicion of the diagnosis. Treatment involves use of arginine vasopressin, 5–10 units IM tid.

References

1. Boyle EM Jr, Pohlman TH, Johnson MC, Verrier ED. Endothelial cell injury in cardiovascular surgery: the systemic inflammatory response. Ann Thorac Surg 1997;63:277–84.

2. Swain JA. Endocrine responses to cardiopulmonary bypass. In: Utley JR, ed. Pathophysiology and techniques of cardiopulmonary bypass. Baltimore: Williams and Wilkins, 1982;I:24–33.

3. Sehested J, Wacker B, Forssmann WG, Schmitzer E. Natriuresis after cardiopulmonary bypass: relationship to urodilan, atrial natriuretic factor, antidiuretic hormone, and aldosterone. J Thorac Cardiovasc Surg 1997;114:666–71.

4. Bergman A, Odar-Cederlof I, Westman L, Ohqvist G. Effects of human atrial natriuretic peptide in patients after coronary artery bypass surgery. J Cardiothorac Vasc Anesthesia 1996;10:490–6.

5. Utley J. Renal function and fluid balance with cardiopulmonary bypass. In: Gravlee GP, Davis RF, Utley JR, eds. Cardiopulmonary bypass. Principles and practice. Baltimore: Williams & Wilkins, 1993:488–508.

6. Tuman KJ, Keane DM, Spiess BD, McCarthy RJ, Silins AI, Ivankovich AD. Effects of high-dose fentanyl on fluid and vasopressor requirements after cardiac surgery. J Cardiothorac Anesthesia 1988;2:419–29.

7. Lamke LO, Liljedahl SO. Plasma volume changes after infusion of various plasma expanders. Resuscitation 1976;5:93–102.

8. London MJ. Plasma volume expansion in cardiovascular surgery: practical realities, theoretical concerns. J Cardiothorac Anesthesia 1988;2:39–49.

9. Gallagher JD, Moore RA, Kerns D, et al. Effects of colloid or crystalloid administration on pulmonary extravascular water in the postoperative period after coronary artery bypass grafting. Anesth Analg 1985;64:753–8.

10. Martin SJ, Danziger LH. Continuous infusion of loop diuretics in the critically ill: a review of the literature. Crit Care Med 1994;22:1323–9.

11. Krasna MJ, Scott GE, Scholz PM, Spotnitz AJ, Mackenzie JW, Penn F. Postoperative enhancement of urinary output in patients with acute renal failure using continuous furosemide therapy. Chest 1986;89:294–5.

12. Andersson LG, Ekroth R, Bratteby LE, Hallhagen S, Wesslen O. Acute renal failure after coronary surgery—a study of incidence and risk factors in 2009 consecutive patients. Thorac Cardiovasc Surg 1993;41:237–41.

13. Corwin HL, Sprague SM, DeLaria GA, Norusis MJ. Acute renal failure associated with cardiac operations. A case-control study. J Thorac Cardiovasc Surg 1989;98:1107–12.

14. Zanardo G, Michielon P, Paccagnella A, et al. Acute renal failure in the patient undergoing cardiac operation. Prevalence, mortality rate, and main risk factors. J Thorac Cardiovasc Surg 1994;107:1489–95.

15. The Society of Thoracic Surgeons. Data analyses of The Society of Thoracic Surgeons National Cardiac Surgery Database, January 1996. Summit Medical Systems, 1996.

16. Deutsch E, Bernstein RC, Addonizio VP, Kussmaul WG III. Coronary artery bypass surgery in patients on chronic hemodialysis. A case-control study. Ann Intern Med 1989;110:369–72.

17. Ko W, Kreiger KH, Isom OW. Cardiopulmonary bypass procedures in dialysis patients. Ann Thorac Surg 1993;55:677–84.

18. Amano J, Suzuki A, Sunamori M, Tofukuji M. Effect of calcium antagonist diltiazem on renal function in open heart surgery. Chest 1995;107:1260–5.

19. Zanardo G, Michielon P, Rosi P, et al. Effects of a continuous diltiazem infusion on renal function during cardiac surgery. J Cardiothorac Vasc Anesthesia 1993;7:711–6.

20. Young EW, Diab, A, Kirsh MM. Intravenous diltiazem and acute renal failure after cardiac operations. Ann Thorac Surg 1998;65:1316–9.
21. Lange HW, Aeppli DM, Brown DC. Survival of patients with acute renal failure requiring dialysis after open heart surgery: early prognostic indicators. Am Heart J 1987;113:1138–43.
22. Badr KF, Ichikawa I. Prerenal failure: a deleterious shift from renal compensation to decompensation. N Engl J Med 1988;319:623–9.
23. Myers BD, Moran SM. Hemodynamically mediated acute renal failure. N Engl J Med 1986;314:97–105.
24. Klahr S, Miller SB. Acute oliguria. N Engl J Med 1998;338:671–5.
25. Hilberman M, Cerby GC, Spencer RJ, Stinson EB. Sequential pathophysiological changes characterizing the progression from renal dysfunction to acute renal failure following cardiac operation. J Thorac Cardiovasc Surg 1980;79:838–44.
26. Schaer GL, Fink MP, Parillo JE. Norepinephrine alone versus norepinephrine plus low-dose dopamine: enhanced renal blood flow with combination pressor therapy. Crit Care Med 1985;13:492–6.
27. Richer M, Robert S, Lebel M. Renal hemodynamics during norepinephrine and low-dose dopamine infusions in man. Crit Care Med 1996;24:1150–6.
28. Hilberman M, Maseda J, Stinson EB, et al. The diuretic properties of dopamine in patients after open-heart operation. Anesthesiology 1984;61:489–94.
29. Duke GJ, Briedis JH, Weaver RA. Renal support in critically ill patients: low-dose dopamine or low-dose dobutamine? Crit Care Med 1994;22:1919–25.
30. Denton MD, Chertow GM, Brady HR. "Renal-dose" dopamine for the treatment of acute renal failure: scientific rationale, experimental studies and clinical trials. Kidney Int 1996;50:4–14.
31. Majumdar S, Kjellstrand CM. Why do we use diuretics in acute renal failure? Semin Dial 1996;9:454–9.
32. Vanky F, Broquist M, Svedjeholm R. Addition of a thiazide: an effective remedy for furosemide resistance after cardiac operations. Ann Thorac Surg 1997;63:993–7.
33. Lindner A. Synergism of dopamine and furosemide in diuretic-resistant, oliguric acute renal failure. Nephron 1983;33:121–6.
34. Pastan S, Bailey J. Dialysis therapy. N Engl J Med 1998;338:1428–37.
35. Forni LG, Hilton PJ. Continuous hemofiltration in the treatment of acute renal failure. N Engl J Med 1997;336:1303–9.
36. DiNardo JA. Pro: calcium is routinely indicated during separation from cardiopulmonary bypass. J Cardiothorac Vasc Anesthesia 1997;11:905–7.
37. Prielipp R, Butterworth J. Con: calcium is not routinely indicated during separation from cardiopulmonary bypass. J Cardiothorac Vasc Anesthesia 1997;11:908–12.
38. Drop LJ, Scheidegger D. Plasma ionized calcium concentration. Important determinant of the hemodynamic response to calcium infusion. J Thorac Cardiovasc Surg 1980;79:425–31.
39. Butterworth JF, Zaloga GP, Prielipp RC, Tucker WY Jr, Royster RL. Calcium inhibits the cardiac stimulating properties of dobutamine but not of amrinone. Chest 1992;101:174–80.
40. Aglio LS, Stanford GG, Maddi R, Boyd JL III, Nussbaum S, Chernow B. Hypomagnesemia is common following cardiac surgery. J Cardiothorac Vasc Anesthesia 1991;5:201–8.
41. England MR, Gordon G, Salem M, Chernow B. Magnesium administration and dysrhythmias after cardiac surgery. A placebo-controlled, double-blind, randomized trial. JAMA 1992;268:2395–402.
42. Fanning WJ, Thomas CS Jr, Roach A, Tomichek R, Alford WC, Stoney WS Jr. Prophy-

laxis of atrial fibrillation with magnesium sulfate after coronary artery bypass grafting. Ann Thorac Surg 1991;52:529–33.

43. Prielipp RC, Zaloga GP, Butterworth JF IV, et al. Magnesium inhibits the hypertensive but not the cardiotonic actions of low-dose epinephrine. Anesthesiology 1991;74: 973–9.

44. Adrogué HJ, Madias NE. Management of life-threatening acid-base disorders. First of two parts. N Engl J Med 1998;338:26–34.

45. Kaplan JA, Guffin AV, Yin A. The effects of metabolic acidosis and alkalosis on the response to sympathomimetic drug in dogs. J Cardiothorac Anesthesia 1988;2:481–7.

46. Leung JM, Landow L, Franks M, et al. Safety and efficacy of intravenous Carbicarb® in patients undergoing surgery: comparison with sodium bicarbonate in the treatment of mild metabolic acidosis. Crit Care Med 1994;22:1540–9.

47. Adrogué HJ, Madias NE. Management of life-threatening acid-base disorders. Second of two parts. N Engl J Med 1998;338:107–11.

48. Hoogwerf BJ, Sheeler LR, Licata AA. Endocrine management of the open heart surgical patient. Sem Thorac Cardiovasc Surg 1991;3:75–80.

49. Zerr KJ, Furnary AP, Grunkemeier GL, Bookin S, Kanhere V, Starr A. Glucose control lowers the risk of wound infection in diabetics after open heart operations. Ann Thorac Surg 1997;63:356–61.

50. Seki S. Clinical features of hyperosmolar hyperglycemic nonketotic diabetic coma associated with cardiac operations. J Thorac Cardiovasc Surg 1986;91:867–73.

51. Drucker DJ, Burrow GNM. Cardiovascular surgery in the hypothyroid patient. Arch Int Med 1985;145:1585–7.

52. Whitten CW, Latson TW, Klein KS, Elmore J, Spencer R, Duggar P. Anesthetic management of a hypothyroid cardiac surgical patient. J Cardiothorac Vasc Anesthesia 1991;5:156–9.

53. Novitzky D, Cooper DKC, Barton CI, et al. Triiodothyronine as an inotropic agent after open heart surgery. J Thorac Cardiovasc Surg 1989;98:972–8.

54. Alford WC, Meador CK, Mihalevich J, et al. Acute adrenal insufficiency following cardiac surgical procedures. J Thorac Cardiovasc Surg 1979;78:489–93.

55. Sutherland FWH, Naik SK. Acute adrenal insufficiency after coronary artery bypass grafting. Ann Thorac Surg 1996;62:1516–7.

56. Cooper DM, Bazaral MG, Furlan AJ, et al. Pituitary apoplexy: a complication of cardiac surgery. Ann Thorac Surg 1986;41:547–50.

12 Post-ICU Care and Other Complications

12 Post-ICU Care and Other Complications

I. General Comments

A. Following a brief stay in the intensive care unit, most patients undergoing cardiac surgical procedures follow a routine pattern of recovery. The use of fast-track protocols and critical pathways ensures that the health care team and the patient have a clear understanding of what to expect at different junctures during recovery. Critical pathways are designed to standardize care and identify variances from the expected. However, they are not a substitute for careful patient examination which may identify problems that might otherwise be ignored by rigid adherence to protocols.

B. Most patients are transferred to an intermediate care unit or the postoperative cardiac surgical floor on the first postoperative day. Invasive monitoring is no longer used, although bedside telemetry should be considered for several days to identify arrhythmias. It should be remembered that patients are still in an early phase of recovery from surgery with many physiologic derangements still present. Restoring the patient to a normal physiologic state requires careful attention to the prevention, identification, and treatment of complications that may develop at any time during the hospital stay. A detailed daily examination of the patient must be performed with particular attention paid to each organ system. Orders must be thought out carefully and written on an individualized basis to ensure the best possible postoperative care.

C. Although postoperative complications are more common in elderly patients and those with comorbidities, they may still develop unpredictably in low-risk, healthy patients despite an uneventful surgical procedure and early postoperative course. Problems such as atrial arrhythmias are very common and quite benign, with little influence on the patient's hospital course or long-term prognosis. In contrast, less common complications, such as stroke, mediastinitis, tamponade, renal failure, or an acute abdomen, may be devastating, resulting in early death or prolonged hospitalization with multisystem organ failure (see table 4.4).[1]

II. Transfer from the ICU and Postoperative Routines

The patient undergoing a routine recovery from surgery is usually extubated within 12 hours and is off all inotropic support by the first postoperative morning. The following interventions are standardized and can be followed on a delayed basis for patients requiring a few additional days of care in the ICU. An example of the critical pathway for patients undergoing coronary artery bypass grafting (CABG) at New England Medical Center is noted in table 12.1. Typical orders for transfer to the postoperative floor are noted in table 12.2.

A. Postoperative night

1. Wean vasoactive medications

2. Wean from ventilator and extubate

Table 12.1 Critical Pathway for Coronary Artery Bypass Grafting

	Preop Day or Office Visit	Day of Surgery	POD #1	POD #2–3	POD #4–5
CARDIOVASCULAR	Bilateral BP Height & weight	Monitor & treat: bleeding shivering arrhythmias hemodynamics Meds (start 8 h postop): ASA Digoxin Metoprolol	VS q2h Telemetry D/C neck and arterial lines Meds: 2 g MgSO$_4$	VS q4–8h Telemetry	VS before D/C Remove pacing wires
RESPIRATORY	RA ABGs if COPD	Wean to extubate within 12–16 hours IS W/A q1h	40% face mask or nasal cannula IS W/A q1h Splinted cough	Nasal cannula at 2–4 L/min for O$_2$ sat < 95% IS W/A q1h Splinted cough	Room air
FLUIDS & ELECTROLYTES		I&O q1h Keep u/o > 1 mL/kg/h	Weight I&O q2h Furosemide IV	Weight I&O qshift Furosemide IV	Weight Furosemide IV/PO until at preop weight
WOUNDS & DRAINS	Hibiclens shower	OR dressing × 12 h Monitor/manage CT drainage	DSD with Betadine wipe to wounds & pacing wire sites D/C CT when total drainage <100 mL/last 8 h CT dressing intact × 48 h	DSD with Betadine wipe to wounds and pacing wire sites	Wounds open to air; DSD with Betadine wipe to pacing wire sites Remove staples early AM before D/C
PAIN CONTROL		Continuous IV MS	IV → PCA MS IV ketorolac	Oxycodone or Tylenol #3	Oxycodone or Tylenol #3

NUTRITION/GI	NPO after MN	NPO NGT to low suction	D/C NG tube Clear liquids	Advance to hi cal, hi protein, NAS diet ADA for diabetics Metamucil/Colace	Progress on diet
ACTIVITY	Ambulatory	OOB to chair × 1 after extubation	OOB to chair q8h	Ambulate × 3 in room with assist, then in hallway × 4	Ambulate × 6 in hallway; stair climb 12 stairs × 1
TESTS & LABS	CXR, ECG, PT, PTT, plts, CBC, LBC, LFTs, U/A	On arrival: CXR, ECG, CBC, K+ ABG, If bleeding: PT, PTT, plts Obtain K+ q4h × 3	CXR after CT removal LBC, CBC PT (on warfarin)	K+ if on furosemide PT (on warfarin) PTT (on heparin)	CXR, ECG, CBC, LBC day before discharge Echo for valve patients
ANTICOAGULATION	D/C warfarin 4 days before surgery	Start warfarin for valve patients	Warfarin (valve patients)	Start heparin POD #3 if subtherapeutic INR (mechanical valves)	Warfarin (valve patients)
DISCHARGE PLANNING	Home assessment	Reevaluate home situation		D/C planning status discussed by care team with discharge planners	
TEACHING	Videos, critical pathway, NPO, shower instructions, incentive spirometry				Patient and family attend discharge class or view discharge video Nutrition instructions Medication instructions

Table 12.2 *Transfer Orders from the ICU*

1. Transfer to: _____
2. Procedure: _____
3. Condition: _____
4. Vital signs q4h
5. Weigh daily
6. I&O qshift
7. Diet
   ❑ NPO
   ❑ Clear liquids/no added salt
   ❑ Full liquids/no added salt
   ❑ High protein, hi calorie/no added salt
   ❑ _____ mL fluid restriction
   ❑ _____ calorie ADA diet
8. Activity
   ❑ Bed rest
   ❑ OOB and ambulate with assistance
9. Foley to gravity drainage; D/C at _____ ; due to void in 8 h
10. Elastic anti-embolism stockings
11. Dry sterile dressing changes qd until POD #4
12. ECG telemetry
13. Temporary pacemaker settings:
14. Respiratory care
    ❑ Oxygen via nasal prongs at 6 L/min
    ❑ Incentive spirometer q1h when awake
15. Laboratory studies
    ❑ CBC, K^+, BUN, creatinine q3 days (depending on renal function or
      requirement for diuretics)
    ❑ Daily PT, PTT if on heparin/warfarin
    ❑ Daily platelet count if on heparin
    ❑ Chest x-ray, ECG, CBC, electrolytes, BUN, creatinine day prior to discharge

Medications
16. Allergies: _____
17. Antibiotics:
    ❑ Vancomycin 1 g IV q12h, D/C on ___/___/___
    ❑ Cefazolin 1 g IV q8h, D/C on ___/___/___
18. Pain medication
    ❑ Morphine sulfate via PCA pump or 10 mg IM q3h PRN severe pain
    ❑ Ketorolac 15–30 mg IV q6h PRN pain, D/C after 72 hours
    ❑ Acetaminophen with oxycodone (Percocet) 1 tab PO q4h PRN pain
    ❑ Acetaminophen with codeine (Tylenol #3) 1–2 tabs PO q4h PRN pain
19. Acetaminophen 650 mg PO q3h PRN temp > 38.5°C
20. Chloral hydrate 500 mg PO qhs prn sleep
21. Saline lock with 1 mL NS flush q8h and PRN
22. Albuterol 2.5 mg/5 mL NS via nebulizer q4h PRN
23. GI medications
    ❑ Milk of magnesia 30 mL po qhs PRN
    ❑ Metamucil 12 g in H_2O qd PRN constipation
    ❑ Docusate (Colace) 100 mg bid
    ❑ Dulcolax suppository PR qd PRN constipation

Table 12.2   *continued*

24. Anticoagulation:
    - ❑ Enteric-coated aspirin 325 mg PO qd (coronary bypass patients)
    - ❑ Heparin 25,000 U/500 mL D5W at _____U/h starting on _____,
    - ❑ Coumadin _____ mg PO qd starting on _____; daily dose check with HO
25. Cardiac medications:
    - ❑ Digoxin
    - ❑ β-blockers
    - ❑ Antihypertensives
    - ❑ Diltiazem 100 mg/100 mL NS @ _____ mg/h × 24 h, then 30 mg qID
      (radial artery grafts)
26. Other medications
    - ❑ Furosemide
    - ❑ Potassium chloride
    - ❑ Prochlorperazine 10 mg IM/IV q6h prn nausea
    - ❑ Preoperative medications (insulin, oral hypoglycemics, thyroid
      replacement, psychotropic medications, etc.)

    3. Remove nasogastric tube
    4. Remove Swan-Ganz and arterial lines
    5. Get patient out of bed (OOB) in a chair
    6. Start warfarin for valve patients

B. POD #1

    1. Remove chest tubes
    2. Transfer to floor; place on telemetry and pulse oximetry × 48 hours
    3. OOB and ambulate
    4. Advance diet
    5. Remove Foley catheter

C. POD #2–3

    1. Stop antibiotics (after 36–48 hours)
    2. Advance diet to achieve satisfactory nutrition
    3. Increase activity level
    4. Continue diuresis to preoperative weight
    5. Commence early planning for home services or rehabilitation

D. POD #3–4

    1. Consider heparin for patients receiving mechanical valves
    2. Obtain predischarge laboratory data (hematocrit, electrolytes,
       BUN, creatinine, chest x-ray, ECG)
    3. Remove pacing wires
    4. Perform discharge teaching

E.   POD #4–5

1.   Remove skin sutures or clips and place Steri-Strips; leave sutures if there is an anticipated problem with wound healing (steroids)

2.   Discharge home

III. Differential Diagnosis of Common Postoperative Symptoms

The development of chest pain, shortness of breath, fever, or just feeling "plain lousy" during the early convalescent period is not unusual. Although the cause of these signs and symptoms may be benign, they should not be taken lightly because they may indicate the presence of potentially serious problems that warrant investigation. Careful questioning and examination of the patient can prioritize diagnoses, direct the evaluation, and lead to prompt and appropriate treatment.

A.   **Chest pain**

1.   **Differential diagnosis.** The development of chest pain following cardiac surgery often raises the suspicion of myocardial ischemia, but the differential diagnosis must include several other potential causes. The greatest fear to a patient is that the recurrence of chest pain indicates a failed operation; the surgeon meanwhile may purposely try to provide alternative explanations. Diagnoses that should be considered include:

a.   Myocardial ischemia

b.   Musculoskeletal pain

c.   Sternal wound infection

d.   Pericarditis

e.   Pneumothorax

f.   Pneumonia

g.   Pulmonary embolism

h.   Esophagitis/ulcer/gastroesophageal reflux

2.   **Evaluation.** The chest x-ray and ECG often provide the appropriate diagnosis and may direct additional testing. Consultation with the cardiology service is essential in managing patients with a suspected cardiac origin to their chest pain. Stress testing or even coronary angiography may be warranted. Other diagnostic modalities include echocardiography, ventilation/perfusion ($\dot{V}/\dot{Q}$) scanning, and sternal wound aspiration.

B.   **Shortness of breath**

1.   **Differential diagnosis.** The most common benign factors that contribute to shortness of breath are anxiety and chest wall discomfort with splinting. However, significant shortness of breath, its acute onset, or deterioration in pulmonary status should heighten one's awareness of a significant problem. The problem may be of a primary pulmonary nature, but it may also be a consequence of cardiac or renal dysfunction. Diagnoses to be considered include:

a.   Pleuropulmonary problems

i.   Atelectasis and hypoxia from mucus plugging or poor inspiratory effort

        ii. Pneumothorax

       iii. Pneumonia (aspiration)

       iv. Bronchospasm

        v. An enlarging pleural effusion

       vi. Pulmonary embolism

   b. Cardiopulmonary problems—low cardiac output states or acute pulmonary edema caused by:

        i. Cardiac tamponade (low cardiac output state, metabolic acidosis, and compensatory tachypnea)

       ii. Acute myocardial ischemia (graft problem, uncorrected mitral regurgitation (MR) precipitated by ischemia or systemic hypertension)

       iii. Fluid overload (often secondary to renal dysfunction)

       iv. Diastolic dysfunction

        v. Recurrent VSD or MR

       vi. Atrial or ventricular tachyarrhythmias

   c. Compensatory response to metabolic acidosis (sepsis, low cardiac output state)

  2. **Evaluation.** Careful lung examination may reveal absent breath sounds or diffuse rales/rhonchi suggesting a parenchymal process or pulmonary edema. Clinical evidence of cardiac tamponade (muffled heart sounds, pulsus paradoxus) should be sought. An arterial blood gas (ABG), chest x-ray, and ECG should be obtained. An echocardiogram gives an assessment of ventricular function, valve dysfunction, or recurrent shunting, and may also identify a large pericardial effusion or tamponade. A $\dot{V}/\dot{Q}$ scan should be performed if a pulmonary embolism is suspected.

C. **Fever**

  1. **Differential diagnosis.** Fever is very common during the first 48 to 72 hours and is usually caused by atelectasis from splinting and poor respiratory effort. Thorough evaluation of recurrent fevers is warranted after the first 72 hours.[2] Potential causes of postoperative fever include:

   a. Atelectasis or pneumonia

   b. Leg wound infections

   c. Urinary tract infections

   d. Sternal wound infection

   e. Drug fever

   f. Sinusitis

   g. An intraabdominal process

   h. Catheter sepsis

   i. Endocarditis

   j. Decubitus ulcer

   k. Postpericardiotomy syndrome

   l. Deep venous thrombosis and pulmonary embolism

2. **Evaluation.** The lungs and chest and leg incisions should be examined carefully. A CBC with differential, chest x-ray, and appropriate cultures should be performed. If the WBC is normal, a drug fever may be present. Occult sternal infections may be investigated with a chest CT scan, but needle aspiration should be performed if suspicion is high.

3. **Treatment.** It is ideally best to defer antibiotic therapy until an organism has been identified. However, a broad-spectrum antibiotic may be initiated based on the presumed source and organisms involved. This is especially important in patients who have received prosthetic material (valves, grafts). A more narrow-spectrum antibiotic may be substituted subsequently. Occasionally a patient will have a fever and elevated WBC with no evident source, but will respond to a brief course of antibiotics. Further comments on nosocomial infections are found on page 395.

IV.   Respiratory Care and Complications

A. Respiratory function is still impaired when the patient is transferred to the postoperative floor. Common manifestations are shortness of breath or arterial desaturation detected by pulse oximetry. These usually result from residual fluid overload combined with a poor inspiratory effort and atelectasis from chest wall splinting. Other contributing factors—such as pneumonia, enlarging pleural effusions, or pneumothorax—can be identified by examination and chest x-rays. Standard orders should include:

1. Supplemental oxygen via nasal cannula at 2–6 L/min

2. Frequent use of incentive spirometry

3. Progressive mobilization

4. Provision of adequate, but not excessive analgesia. Patient-controlled analgesia (usually morphine) is particularly beneficial for 1–2 days following surgery, and may be supplemented with other pain medications, such as ketorolac (Toradol) 15–30 mg IV q6h for a few days. Most patients obtain adequate analgesia with oral medications 2–3 days after surgery and seem to do better with regular, rather than PRN, pain medications.

5. Chest physical therapy and bronchodilators administered via nebulizers can be used for copious secretions or bronchospasm, respectively.

B. Significant decompensation of respiratory function is uncommon in patients without preexisting lung disease or a history of heavy smoking. Potential pleuropulmonary contributory factors were noted above in Section IIIB. However, arterial desaturation may be a sign of cardiac disease (myocardial ischemia or mitral regurgitation), cardiac tamponade, or an early manifestation of renal dysfunction with progressive oliguria.

C. The management of respiratory insufficiency and bronchospasm was discussed in Chapter 9. Some of the less common complications, which include diaphragmatic dysfunction from phrenic nerve paresis, pulmonary embolism, and chylothorax, are discussed below.

D. **Diaphragm dysfunction from phrenic nerve injury**

1. **Etiology**

   a. Cold injury to the phrenic nerve along the pericardium from use of iced saline slush. Avoidance of iced slush has been shown to reduce the incidence of phrenic nerve paresis.[3,4]

   b. Direct surgical injury to the phrenic nerve in the upper mediastinum during proximal dissection of the internal mammary artery (IMA). This may also occur when making a V-incision in the pericardium to allow for better lie of the IMA pedicle.

   c. Phrenic nerve devascularization during IMA harvest. It has been proposed that dissection of the IMA may make the phrenic nerve more vulnerable to hypothermia, stretch, and ischemia.

   d. **Note:** diaphragmatic dysfunction is more common in diabetic patients, particularly if the IMA has been harvested.[5]

2. **Presentation**

   a. Most patients with unilateral phrenic nerve paresis have few respiratory symptoms and are extubated uneventfully. Difficulty weaning, shortness of breath, and the requirement for reintubation may be noted in patients with severe chronic obstructive pulmonary disease (COPD).[6] The diagnosis is usually made by noting elevation of a hemidiaphragm (usually the left) on a chest x-ray after the patient is extubated, although it may be obscured by lower lobe atelectasis or a pleural effusion.

   b. Bilateral phrenic nerve palsy usually produces tachypnea, paradoxical abdominal breathing, and CO_2 retention during attempts to wean from mechanical ventilation.

   c. **Note:** Consideration should always be given to the possibility of an elevated left hemidiaphragm when a left pleural effusion is present. The position of the gastric bubble should identify the position of the diaphragm. A decubitus film may identify the size of the effusion. The location of the diaphragm must be given careful thought before a thoracentesis or tube thoracostomy is performed.

3. **Evaluation**

   a. Chest x-ray will demonstrate an elevated hemidiaphragm during spontaneous ventilation. This will not be evident during mechanical ventilation.

   b. Diaphragmatic fluoroscopy ("sniff test") will demonstrate paradoxical upward motion of the diaphragm during spontaneous inspiration if unilateral paralysis is present.

   c. Phrenic nerve stimulation and measurement of transdiaphragmatic pressures can confirm the diagnosis of bilateral diaphragmatic dysfunction.

4. **Treatment** is supportive until phrenic nerve function recovers, which may take up to 2 years. Diaphragmatic plication can provide

significant symptomatic and objective improvement in patients with marked dyspnea from unilateral paralysis.[7] Ventilatory support is usually necessary for patients with bilateral involvement. Some patients can be managed at home with a cuirass respirator or a rocking bed.

E. **Pulmonary embolism** (PE) is extremely uncommon in patients undergoing open-heart surgery, with an incidence of about 0.5%. The risk is quite low because of the use of systemic heparinization and hemodilution during surgery and the presence of thrombocytopenia and platelet dysfunction in the early postoperative period.[8]

1. **Risk factors**

    a. Prolonged preoperative hospitalization or bed rest

    b. Recent groin catheterization

    c. Hyperlipidemia, which is associated with a hypercoagulable state and platelet activation.[9]

    d. Postoperative congestive heart failure, prolonged bed rest, or development of deep venous thrombosis (DVT). In patients developing DVT, the risk of PE is increased by a perioperative MI or atrial fibrillation.[10]

2. **Manifestations.** Pleuritic chest pain and shortness of breath are usually present. The acute onset of these symptoms distinguishes them from typical postoperative respiratory symptoms. The new onset of atrial fibrillation, sinus tachycardia, or fever of unknown origin may be clues to the diagnosis.

3. **Assessment.** ABGs, chest x-ray, and ECG should be obtained. Unfortunately, all of these tests are nonspecific and relatively insensitive. A $\dot{V}/\dot{Q}$ scan should be performed and must be carefully correlated with a chest x-ray to rule out false positive studies. A low PaO_2 may be difficult to interpret, but comparison with the last PaO_2 obtained in the ICU may be helpful. A positive venous noninvasive study of the lower extremities in association with respiratory symptoms and hypoxia is suggestive evidence of a pulmonary embolism. A pulmonary arteriogram should be considered to provide a definitive diagnosis if the $\dot{V}/\dot{Q}$ scan is indeterminate or there is a contraindication to anticoagulation.

4. **Treatment** entails bed rest and anticoagulation with IV heparin for 1 week, followed by warfarin for 6 months. An IVC filter is recommended for recurrent pulmonary embolism despite therapeutic anticoagulation or when anticoagulation is contraindicated. The mortality rate of postoperative pulmonary embolism is about 25% because of its high recurrence rate. Thus, a form of IVC interruption should be considered following a significant embolus, even if anticoagulation can be used safely.[10]

F. **Chylothorax** is a rare complication of intrapericardial cardiac surgery.[11] Injury to tributaries of the thoracic duct can occur during proximal mobilization of the IMA near the subclavian vessels or during surgery of the distal aortic arch. Chylothorax is more common after congenital heart operations requiring dissection near the jugular-subclavian confluence. It may also be caused by subclavian vein thrombosis or injury to collaterals from the right bronchomediastinal trunk as it crosses the midline.

1. **Manifestations.** An enlarging pleural effusion or tamponade (chylopericardium) will be noted if the chest tubes have been removed. If they remain in place, turbulent milky drainage will be present and exacerbated by dietary fat.

2. **Diagnosis.** Chyle is sterile, contains large quantities of lymphocytes, and is rich in triglycerides (>110 mg/dL is diagnostic). Staining with Sudan III can distinguish chyle from purulent fluid.

3. **Treatment.** Conservative management with chest tube drainage, elimination of fat from the diet, and medium-chain triglycerides will often be successful. If drainage persists for more than 1–2 weeks, further intervention is indicated. Instillation of doxycycline may be effective for moderate persistent drainage. Clipping of a leaking lymphatic tributary may be performed thoracoscopically or through a left thoracotomy. Rarely will direct ligation of the thoracic duct in the area of injury be indicated. Thoracic duct ligation low in the mediastinum through a right thoracotomy incision is an alternative approach for a persistent problem.

V.   Cardiac Care and Complications

The evaluation and management of complications most commonly noted in the intensive care unit are presented in Chapter 10. These included low cardiac output states, perioperative infarction, cardiac arrest, coronary spasm, hypertension, and arrhythmias. This section will discuss several cardiac problems commonly noted during subsequent convalescence.

A. **Atrial arrhythmias.** Approximately 25–30% of patients undergoing open-heart surgery will develop atrial arrhythmias, usually beginning on the second or third postoperative day. They are more common in elderly patients and those with a history of atrial arrhythmias before surgery.[12,13] A rapid ventricular response and loss of atrial contraction may precipitate ischemia or lower the cardiac output and blood pressure. Although the development of atrial fibrillation (AF) is frequently an incidental finding on the ECG monitor, symptoms such as palpitations, nausea, fatigue, or lightheadedness may be noted, especially in patients with left ventricular hypertrophy or poor ventricular function.

1. **Prophylaxis.** Only β-blockers have been consistently shown to be effective in reducing the incidence of postoperative AF, especially if they were taken before surgery.[14] We start metoprolol 25–50 mg bid on the first postoperative night or the following morning. There is some evidence that the combined use of digoxin and a β-blocker is the most effective regimen to prevent postoperative AF.[15] Magnesium sulfate is effective in AF prophylaxis and we routinely give 2 g after cardiopulmonary bypass (CPB) and on the first postoperative morning.[16]

2. **Rate-control vs. cardioversion.** Atrial fibrillation may predispose to the formation of thrombus in the left atrium and to embolic strokes. One study showed a fivefold increase in the incidence of postoperative neurologic events in patients developing AF, although

another did not demonstrate any increase in morbidity.[13,17] Thus, maintaining the patient in sinus rhythm is beneficial for both hemodynamic performance and reduction in thromboembolic risk. However, attempts to convert a patient to sinus rhythm can be time-consuming, expensive, and frustrating.

    a.   Rate control must be achieved first, usually with diltiazem added to the regimen of digoxin and metoprolol.[18]

    b.   Conversion may be attempted with a short course of a type IA drug such as procainamide, following which electrical cardioversion may be performed. The latter should be considered promptly if type IA agents are ineffective after 24–36 hours, thus shortening the patient's length of stay.

    c.   Heparinization should be considered for patients with recurrent or persistent AF to minimize the risk of stroke from embolization of left atrial thrombus, which may form within 3 days of the development of AF.[19] If a patient cannot be converted, warfarin should be given for 3 weeks before subsequent cardioversion is attempted. If successful, warfarin is continued for an additional 4 weeks because mechanical atrial dysfunction persists after electrical cardioversion.[20,21]

3.   The diagnosis, assessment, and treatment of supraventricular arrhythmias are discussed in detail on pages 295–304 and summarized in table 10.12.

B. **Ventricular arrhythmias** can develop at any time after surgery and are usually related to myocardial ischemia or injury (see pages 307–312). Although preexisting ischemic-related ventricular ectopy may be improved by surgery, there is usually little change in, and often worsening of, the preoperative pattern of ventricular ectopy, especially nonsustained ventricular tachycardia.[22]

1.   Some centers use prophylactic lidocaine for 12 hours after surgery. If ventricular ectopy persists, it is important to assess its significance because most antiarrhythmic drugs have proarrhythmic effects and are not benign. Holter monitoring should be performed off antiarrhythmic drugs to quantitate the amount and severity of the arrhythmia.

2.   In general, evidence of ventricular tachycardia requires electrophysiologic evaluation, drug therapy, and possible use of an implantable cardioverter-defibrillator (ICD). Symptomatic high-grade ventricular ectopy, especially if associated with poor ventricular function, usually requires treatment. Asymptomatic ectopy in a patient with preserved ventricular function usually does not require treatment.

C. **Complete (third-degree) heart block** is not infrequent following open-heart procedures performed using cardioplegic arrest, but it usually resolves within several hours. Epicardial pacing wires are used to provide AV pacing until normal conduction returns. In the event that the patient remains pacemaker-dependent, the pacing thresholds of the epicardial wires should be assessed daily. If the threshold is rising rapidly, a temporary pacing wire may be inserted, and placement of a permanent pacemaker system should be considered soon thereafter. Generally, a permanent pacemaker is placed if heart block persists for more than one week.

1. Heart block is most common after aortic valve surgery because of the proximity of the conduction system to the aortic annulus. It is occasionally noted after redo mitral valve surgery.

2. Transient heart block will frequently occur following CABG, but usually resolves within several hours. Complete heart block that persists beyond 6 hours may be caused by a perioperative MI.[23] Interestingly, studies have shown that AV block usually resolves within 2 months in patients in whom pacemakers were placed.[24]

3. Preexisting sick sinus syndrome (SSS) is often more evident after surgery and documentation of several second pauses off medications is an indication for a pacemaker.

D. **Hypertension.** Blood pressure tends to return to its preoperative level several days after surgery once myocardial function has returned to baseline and the patient has been mobilized. A decrease in systolic blood pressure from preoperative levels may be noted in patients experiencing a perioperative infarction. In contrast, patients with aortic stenosis may develop significant systolic hypertension following aortic valve replacement (AVR). Oral medications must be substituted for the potent intravenous drugs used in the ICU. If blood pressure was well controlled before surgery, the same medications should usually be restarted. Other considerations when selecting an antihypertensive medication include:

1. Poor ventricular function: use one of the ACE inhibitors. (See Appendix 2 on page 449.)

2. Sinus tachycardia with good left ventricular (LV) function, evidence of residual myocardial ischemia: use a β-blocker.

3. Coronary spasm or use of a radial artery graft: use a calcium-channel blocker (diltiazem, verapamil, nicardipine). These are excellent first-line medications to use in patients without significant ventricular dysfunction.

E. **Recurrent myocardial ischemia.** Recurrent ischemia following CABG is usually manifested by ischemic ECG changes or angina. It may lead to a low output state, congestive heart failure, myocardial infarction, ventricular arrhythmias, or sudden death.

1. **Contributing factors**

a. Acute graft thrombosis

b. Anastomotic narrowing

c. Unbypassed, diseased coronary arteries (incomplete revascularization)

d. Coronary spasm

e. Hypoperfusion syndromes (replacing a moderately diseased vein graft with a small IMA at reoperation).

2. **Evaluation**

    a. Empiric use of calcium-channel blockers may be of diagnostic and therapeutic value for suspected coronary spasm (see page 255).

    b. Urgent coronary arteriography should be considered when there are significant ECG changes. It may identify a technical problem with a graft or confirm the diagnosis of spasm.

    c. Stress imaging with dipyridamole-thallium/sestamibi can be performed to identify the presence of myocardial ischemia. This differentiates between ischemic and nonischemic causes of chest pain.

3. **Treatment**

    a. Intensification of a medical regimen with nitrates and β-blockers is frequently the most appropriate treatment course.

    b. If a technical problem with a graft is identified, the patient should be returned to the operating room for graft revision or additional grafting. Occasionally, an angioplasty can be performed. If spasm is identified, intracoronary nitroglycerin (NTG) or verapamil may be helpful. Not uncommonly, however, the coronary vessels supplying the ischemic zone are small and diffusely diseased, leaving small areas of the heart potentially ischemic. These vessels may not have been considered bypassable, or the graft flow was limited by small vessel size and runoff.

    c. The long-term results of coronary bypass surgery are influenced by the development of atherosclerotic disease in bypass conduits, unbypassed native arteries, or native arteries beyond the bypass sites. Factors that can improve these results include use of the IMA, abstinence from smoking, control of hypercholesterolemia, and use of aspirin for 1 year.[25] The late development of ischemia has also been attributed on rare occasion to a coronary steal syndrome, either from a coronary-subclavian steal or an IMA-pulmonary artery fistula.[26,27]

F. **Delayed tamponade.** Pericardial effusions are noted in nearly 50% of patients following surgery but usually resolve completely. A small percentage of patients will have effusions that gradually increase in size and produce a low cardiac output state and tamponade. This may be noted within the first week of surgery or weeks to months later. Suspicion of this problem must remain high because symptoms often develop insidiously and are frequently difficult to differentiate from those noted in patients recovering slowly from surgery.[28] **This is one of the most serious, yet most potentially correctable of all postoperative problems**.

1. **Etiology**

    a. Slow intrapericardial bleeding from heparin or warfarin (even when anticoagulation is well-regulated). This may originate from soft tissues or raw pericardium and infrequently from surgically identifiable sites.

b. Acute hemorrhage from graft injury caused by indwelling pacing wires or during their removal, or myocardial rupture from vent sites, infarction, or prosthetic valves.

c. Serous or serosanguineous effusions, occasionally from the postpericardiotomy syndrome, but frequently of unknown etiology.

d. Chylopericardium (extremely rare)

2. **Presentation.** A low output state may produce a low-grade fever, malaise, shortness of breath, anorexia, or nausea. These symptoms are frequently ascribed to medications or simply a slow recovery from surgery. Jugular venous distention, a pericardial rub, hypotension, and a pulsus paradoxus are often noted. Frequently, the first sign is a decrease in urine output with rise in BUN and creatinine, with the development of progressive renal dysfunction reflecting the low output state. Acute hemorrhage—usually after removal of pacing wires—will present as refractory hypotension and the clinical picture of acute cardiac tamponade.

3. **Evaluation.** A chest x-ray may reveal enlargement of the cardiac silhouette, but frequently is normal, depending on the site and rapidity of blood accumulation. Two-dimensional echocardiography can identify the pericardial effusion, confirm tamponade physiology, and also assess the status of ventricular function. Transesophageal echocardiography (TEE) is more sensitive than the transthoracic approach in detecting posterior fluid collections. If clinical suspicion remains high and the transthoracic image is suboptimal, a TEE should be strongly considered.

4. **Treatment**

a. Mediastinal exploration is indicated for active bleeding.

b. Pericardiocentesis is the least invasive means of draining a large effusion that has produced cardiac tamponade. This is usually performed in the cardiac catheterization laboratory under ECG or two-dimensional echocardiographic guidance.[29,30]

c. Subxiphoid exploration should be considered when the echocardiogram suggests that the fluid collection will not be approachable percutaneously (usually posterior collections) or is loculated. If this is insufficient, the entire sternal incision may need to be opened.

d. A pericardial "window" or limited pericardiectomy through a left thoracotomy approach should be considered for loculated posterior effusions or recurrent effusions several weeks after surgery.

e. Antiinflammatory medications or steroids can be used for large effusions attributable to postpericardiotomy syndrome that have not produced hemodynamic compromise.

G. **Postpericardiotomy syndrome** (PPS) has been reported in nearly 20% of patients following open-heart surgery and is considered to represent an autoimmune inflammatory response.[31,32] It may occur within the first week of surgery or several weeks to months later. PPS is more common in younger patients and those with a history of pericarditis or steroid usage. It must be aggressively treated because it may contribute to cardiac tamponade, early vein graft closure, or constrictive pericarditis.

1. **Presentation.** Fever, precordial chest pain, and a pericardial rub are the diagnostic criteria. Malaise, arthralgias, and pleural or pericardial effusions may also be present.

2. **Evaluation.** Lymphocytosis and an elevated erythrocyte sedimentation rate (ESR) are noted, but a fever work-up is negative. Pleural or pericardial effusions are usually demonstrable by chest x-ray and echocardiography.

3. **Treatment**

   a. Aspirin should be used as the initial treatment. If there is minimal symptomatic relief, a one-week course of nonsteroidal antiinflammatory agents (ibuprofen 400 mg qid or indomethacin 25 mg tid taken with meals or antacids) is 90% effective. Aspirin should be stopped if these medications are used to minimize gastric irritation. Prednisone can be used if symptoms persist.

   b. Pericardiocentesis may be necessary to drain a large symptomatic pericardial effusion.

   c. Pericardiectomy is recommended for recurrent large effusions.

H. **Constrictive pericarditis** is a late complication of cardiac surgery that is rare despite the development of dense adhesions that form within the mediastinum following surgery. It has been noted in patients with early postpericardiotomy syndrome, previous mediastinal radiation, and those with a significant postoperative hemopericardium.[28,33]

1. **Presentation.** The patient will note the insidious onset of dyspnea on exertion, chest pain, and fatigue. Peripheral edema and jugular venous distention are common, but pulsus paradoxus is infrequent.

2. **Evaluation**

   a. Chest x-ray is frequently normal in the absence of a pericardial effusion.

   b. Two-dimensional echocardiography will demonstrate pericardial thickening and occasionally a small pericardial effusion.

   c. CT scan identifies the thickness of the pericardium and the presence of pericardial fluid.

   d. Right heart catheterization provides the most definitive information. It will document the equilibration of diastolic pressures and demonstrate a diastolic dip-plateau pattern ("square-root" sign) in the right ventricular pressure tracing.

3. **Treatment.** Pericardiectomy is indicated for clinically significant constriction. It is usually best performed through a sternotomy incision, which allows for adequate decortication of the right atrium and ventricle and much of the left ventricle. It also allows for the

institution of cardiopulmonary bypass in the event of a difficult or bloody operation. Relief of epicardial constriction is difficult and may result in surgical damage to bypass grafts or significant bleeding. A "waffle" or "turtle shell" procedure is performed with crisscrossing incisions made in the epicardial scar to relieve the constriction.

I. **Chylopericardium** is rare following adult open-heart surgery, but it is encountered occasionally following congenital heart surgery. It results from operative injury to the thoracic duct or pericardial lymphatics or thrombosis at the subclavian-jugular confluence.[28]

   1. **Presentation.** Milky drainage from mediastinal chest tubes or signs and symptoms of cardiac tamponade may be present.

   2. **Diagnosis.** High levels of triglycerides and positive staining for fat with Sudan III will confirm the presence of chyle.

   3. **Treatment.** Drainage with a pericardial tube and dietary fat restriction with use of medium-chain triglycerides may suffice. If drainage persists, a pericardiectomy and/or thoracic duct ligation low in the mediastinum may be indicated.

VI. Renal, Metabolic, and Fluid Management and Complications

A. **Routine care**

   1. Most patients are still substantially above their preoperative weight when transferred to the postoperative floor. Comparison of the patient's preoperative weight with daily weights obtained postoperatively is a guide to the use of diuretics to excrete excess fluid. Achievement of dry body weight may require more aggressive diuresis if congestive heart failure was present before surgery. In the chronically ill patient, preoperative weight may be achieved despite fluid overload due to poor nutrition.

   2. Dietary restriction (sodium and water) need not be overly strict in most cases. With the availability of potent diuretics to achieve negative fluid balance and the common problem of a poor appetite after surgery, it is more important to provide palatable food without restriction to improve the patient's caloric intake.

   3. If a patient required diuretics before surgery (especially valve patients and those with poor myocardial function), it is advisable to continue them upon discharge from the hospital, even if preoperative weight has been attained.

B. **Transient renal failure** (see also Chapter 11). Patients with chronic renal insufficiency and those with stormy postoperative courses marked by a low cardiac output state may develop evidence of progressive renal dysfunction. Diuretics are useful in reducing the immediate postoperative fluid overload and preventing the development of oliguric renal failure. However, postoperative management can be very difficult on the postoperative floor when methods of monitoring intravascular volume are limited. Attempts must be made to maintain adequate intravascular volume to prevent prerenal azotemia without producing pulmonary edema. Simultaneously, diuretics are commonly given to create negative fluid balance while the BUN and creatinine are rising. Treatment is especially difficult when myocardial function is borderline.

1. A common scenario is gradual elevation in the BUN and creatinine with low serum sodium reflective of persistent total body water and salt overload. In most patients, the renal dysfunction is transient as long as cardiac output has returned to baseline. These patients are usually treated with diuretics, achieving a gradual diuresis with maintenance of intravascular volume.

2. If fluid retention persists and the BUN continues to rise, further evaluation and treatment are indicated. **Rising BUN and creatinine of unclear etiology, especially when associated with new onset oliguria, should always raise the suspicion of delayed tamponade**. An echocardiogram should be performed to assess myocardial function and rule out tamponade. The patient may require return to the ICU for intravenous inotropic support, dopamine, ultrafiltration, or dialysis.

C. **Hyperkalemia** usually occurs in association with renal dysfunction. Its manifestations and treatment are discussed on page 358. Particular attention should be directed to stopping any exogenous potassium intake and assessing renal function.

D. **Hyperglycemia** in diabetics is a common postoperative problem. The blood glucose level may be elevated due to residual elevation of the counterregulatory hormones (glucagon, cortisol) after surgery. There is some evidence that stringent control of blood sugar during the early postoperative period may reduce the incidence of wound infection.[34]

1. Insulin resistance is commonly noted during the early postoperative period. Patients with type I diabetes mellitus should have their insulin doses gradually increased back to preoperative levels depending on oral intake and blood glucose levels. It is preferable to use a lower dose of intermediate-acting insulin initially and supplement it with regular insulin as necessary.

2. Oral hypoglycemics can be restarted once the patient has an adequate oral intake, usually starting at half the usual dose. Nonetheless, daily blood sugars should be obtained during the first postoperative week because many patients have a poor appetite and their blood sugar remains less than 200 mg/dL on no medications.

E. Other electrolyte and endocrine complications are fairly unusual once the patient has been transferred to the postoperative floor. Chapter 11 discusses the evaluation and management of some of these problems.

VII. Hematologic Complications and Anticoagulation Regimens

A. **Anemia**

1. With the use of antifibrinolytic drugs during surgery (ε-aminocaproic acid and aprotinin) and other blood conservation

measures, more than 50% of patients undergoing bypass surgery do not require any blood transfusions. Nonetheless, hemodilution and blood loss during surgery result in a postoperative hematocrit of 25–30% in most patients. Hematocrits in the low to mid-20s are considered safe for most patients. However, transfusion should be considered for elderly patients, those who feel significantly weak and fatigued, and those with ECG changes, hypotension, or significant tachycardia.

2. Although the hematocrit may rise gradually with postoperative diuresis, it frequently will not increase because of the shortened red cell life span caused by extracorporeal circulation and the loss of 30% of transfused red cells within 24 hours of transfusion.

3. Any patient with a hematocrit below 30% should be placed on iron therapy (ferrous sulfate or gluconate 300 mg tid for 1 month) at the time of discharge. Exogenous iron may not be necessary, however, if the patient has received multiple transfusions because of the storage of iron from hemolyzed cells.[35]

4. Consideration may also be given to use of recombinant erythropoietin (Epogen) to stimulate red cell production (50–100 U/kg SC tiw).

B. **Thrombocytopenia** is caused by platelet destruction and hemodilution during extracorporeal circulation, but platelet counts gradually return to normal within several days. Impaired hemostasis noted in the early postoperative period is caused more commonly by platelet dysfunction produced during bypass. However, platelet dysfunction is less common with use of the antifibrinolytic drugs which achieve some of their effectiveness by reducing platelet activation on pump.

1. **Etiology**

   a. Platelet depletion or dilution during CPB

   b. Excessive bleeding without platelet replacement therapy

   c. Use of the intraaortic balloon

   d. Medications that may reduce the platelet count (heparin, amrinone, cimetidine)

2. **Treatment.** Platelet transfusions are indicated:

   a. When the platelet count is less than 20–30,000/μL

   b. For ongoing bleeding when the platelet count is less than 100,000/μL. Platelet administration may be considered when the platelet count is higher if platelet dysfunction is suspected.

   c. For a planned surgical procedure (such as a percutaneous intraaortic balloon pump removal) when the platelet count is <60,000/μL.

3. **Heparin-induced thrombotic thrombocytopenia** (HIT) is a very serious complication of heparin therapy with a high mortality rate. It is caused by the formation of IgG antibodies that bind to the heparin-platelet factor 4 (PF4) complex, producing platelet activation that releases more PF4. When heparin is depleted by this

process, PF4 then binds to heparin-like glycosaminoglycans on the surface of endothelial cells, providing a target for antibody binding. This results in endothelial damage, thrombosis, and disseminated intravascular coagulation. This syndrome is recognized clinically by arterial and/or venous thrombosis from platelet aggregation, often associated with bleeding from profound thrombocytopenia.[36–40]

    a. Once HIT is suspected, all heparin infusions, whether used for therapeutic purposes or line flushes, must be stopped immediately and alternative anticoagulation initiated if necessary. All heparin-coated intravascular catheters (including the Swan-Ganz catheter) should be removed.

    b. The diagnosis can be confirmed by in vitro platelet aggregation testing.

    c. Alternatives for the patient requiring cardiac surgery were presented on page 155. If the patient requires anticoagulation postoperatively, initiate therapy with warfarin; if urgent anticoagulation is indicated and the international normalized ratio (INR) is subtherapeutic, there are several alternatives

        i. Aspirin +/− dipyridamole

        ii. Low-molecular-weight dextran (Rheomacrodex), 20 mL/hour. Because of the small risk of an anaphylactic reaction, dextran 1 (Promit), 20 mL, should be given over 60 seconds, 1–2 minutes before starting the infusion. This may be best for patients at high risk of thromboembolism (mechanical mitral valve with atrial fibrillation, history of recurrent DVT).

        iii. **Note:** although low-molecular-weight heparins (LMWH) are less commonly associated with HIT, the possibility of cross-reactivity with the antibody that causes this problem is 80%; therefore, LMWHs should not be used in patients with documented HIT.[36,40]

        iv. Danaparoid sodium (ORG 10172 or Orgaran) can be used because cross-reactivity is only 10% (testing for cross-reactivity should still be performed).[38] One recommended regimen is 2500 units IV, followed by 400 U/h for 4 h, then 300 U/h for 4 h, then 150–200 U/h to maintain anti-Xa levels between 0.5–0.8 U/mL; alternatively, subsequent doses of 1250 U may be given q8–12h.[41]

    d. **Note:** Platelet counts must be monitored on a daily basis in any patient receiving heparin. A falling platelet count or heparin resistance may be an indication for in vitro aggregation testing to identify HIT.

  C. **Coronary bypass surgery.** Antiplatelet therapy is recommended for one year to increase saphenous vein graft patency. Aspirin 81 mg qd is given down the nasogastric tube starting 7 hours postoperatively and then taken orally in a dose of 325 mg qd.[25] Aspirin should be given indefinitely for all patients including those receiving only arterial conduits, because of its beneficial effect on the primary and secondary prevention of coronary events.[42] Warfarin should be considered to improve graft patency when an extensive coronary endarterectomy has been performed, although there is little evidence that this is actually beneficial. Aspirin should be given in low doses along with warfarin because of its antiplatelet effects.

D. **Prosthetic heart valves** (table 12.3). Heart valves are more susceptible to thromboembolic complications during the first 3 months after implantation during which time warfarin is generally recommended. It is then continued indefinitely for mechanical valves and converted to aspirin for tissue valves. Warfarin is continued indefinitely if atrial fibrillation is present. Intravenous heparin should start around POD #2–4 in patients considered at high risk for thromboembolism (older age, atrial fibrillation, large left atrium, history of thromboembolism). Its use must always be weighed against the potential risk of pericardial bleeding and tamponade.[43]

1. **Tissue valves**

   a. Aortic valves are ideally treated with 3 months of warfarin to achieve an INR of 2.0–3.0 and then changed to aspirin 325 mg qd. There is some evidence that short-term anticoagulation with warfarin may reduce the incidence of thromboembolism on aortic tissue valves.[44] However, other studies have demonstrated equivalent protection from thromboembolism using just aspirin.[45,46] Therefore, in patients in whom the risk of anticoagulation is increased, aspirin 325 mg should provide adequate protection.

   b. Patients receiving mitral valves or mitral rings should receive warfarin to achieve an INR of 2.0–3.0. Aspirin can then be

Table 12.3 *Recommended Anticoagulation Regimens for Prosthetic Heart Valves*

	Warfarin	Antiplatelet Drugs
AVR—mechanical	INR 2.0–3.0 indefinitely	Aspirin 81–100 mg qd or dipyridamole 100 mg qid
AVR—tissue	INR 2.0–3.0 for 3 months Elderly: none	Aspirin 325 mg qd after 3 months Aspirin 325 mg qd
MVR—mechanical	INR 2.5–3.5 indefinitely	Aspirin 81–100 mg qd or dipyridamole 100 mg qid
MVR—tissue or MV repair	INR 2.0–3.0 for 3 months; continue indefinitely if atrial fibrillation and consider if history of thromboembolism or left atrial size >50 mm	Aspirin 325 mg qd after 3 months
AVR-MVR— mechanical	INR 3.0–4.5 indefinitely	Aspirin 81–100 mg qd or dipyridamole 100 mg qid
AVR-MVR—tissue	INR 2.0–3.0 for 3 months	Aspirin 325 mg qd after 3 months
Atrial fibrillation with any of above	Continue warfarin indefinitely	

substituted after 3 months if sinus rhythm is present. In the high-risk patient, warfarin should be continued indefinitely. The addition of aspirin might be beneficial for these patients. Patients with pericardial ring annuloplasties should take aspirin alone.

2. **Mechanical valves**

   a. Warfarin is given to achieve an INR of 2.5–3.5 for current mechanical heart valve prostheses in any position. However, for patients receiving double valves or with older valves (Bjork-Shiley, Starr-Edwards), the target INR is 3.0–4.5.

   b. The thromboembolic risk can be lowered safely with the addition of either aspirin 81–100 mg or dipyridamole 100 mg qid.[43,47–49] These should be added if thromboembolism occurs despite adequate anticoagulation with warfarin alone.

   c. If bleeding develops despite well-regulated anticoagulation, the warfarin dose should be lowered to achieve an INR around 2.0–3.0 and both dipyridamole 100 mg qid and aspirin 660 mg/day should be added. If bleeding persists, reoperation should be considered to replace the mechanical valve with a tissue valve.

3. **Dosing and overanticoagulation.** The dosing of warfarin should be carefully individualized to avoid rapid overanticoagulation. An initial dose of 5 mg is given to most patients. However, 2.5 mg should be given to small elderly women, patients with hepatic dysfunction, chronic illness, and those receiving antibiotics. Potential dangers of overanticoagulation include cardiac tamponade from intrapericardial bleeding, and gastrointestinal, intracranial, or retroperitoneal hemorrhage.

   a. If the patient is bleeding with an elevated INR, fresh frozen plasma is indicated.

   b. If the patient has no evidence of bleeding, general recomendations for treatment of the overanticoagulated patient are:

      i. INR > 10, hold warfarin and give fresh frozen plasma

      ii. INR > 6, hold warfarin for 1–2 days and restart when INR is <4

      iii. INR 4–6, reduce the dose of warfarin for a few days

   c. Vitamin K can be used in patients who require urgent surgery; giving small doses of 1–3 mg SC or IV (over 30 minutes) for an INR of 6–10 should lower the INR to the therapeutic range within 24 hours.[50] However, in patients with mechanical valves who are overanticoagulated, vitamin K should be avoided because it may produce a hypercoagulable state and render subsequent anticoagulation very difficult. If the patient is bleeding, however, vitamin K can be considered (10 mg SC or IV). Heparin can be used once the bleeding has stopped if the INR is subtherapeutic. It can be continued until the patient becomes responsive to warfarin.

VIII.   Wound Care and Infectious Complications

A.   General comments

1.   Prophylactic antibiotics should be given for 36–48 hours starting just before surgery. First- or second-generation cephalosporins (cefazolin or cefamandole) are commonly used because of their effectiveness against gram-positive cocci. Vancomycin is substituted if there is a penicillin allergy. Even though vancomycin is probably the most effective antibiotic in preventing sternal wound infections, its use should be confined to patients receiving prosthetic material (valves, grafts) because of its added cost and the risk of promoting the growth of resistant organisms (i.e., vancomycin-resistant enterococci).[51,52]

2.   Antibiotics can be stopped if chest tubes, the endotracheal tube, Foley catheter, or even an intraaortic balloon remain in place. Prolonging antibiotic therapy for several days while an intraaortic balloon pump (IABP) is in place does not reduce the risk of infection.[53]

3.   Wounds should be cleansed and covered with a dressing every day for the first 3 postoperative days. Subsequent coverage is not necessary unless drainage is noted. All drainage should be cultured and sterile occlusive dressings applied.

B.   Nosocomial infections develop in 12–20% of patients undergoing cardiac surgery. They most commonly affect the surgical sites, respiratory and urinary tracts, and are associated with increased length of stay, multisystem organ failure, and increased mortality. Two studies have shown a four- to fivefold increase in operative mortality for patients developing nosocomial infections after cardiac surgery.[54,55]

1.   Risk factors for the development of a nosocomial infection include:

   a.   Older age

   b.   Female gender

   c.   Long, complex operations (valve + CABG)

   d.   Urgent operations

   e.   Prolonged duration of mechanical ventilation

   f.   Prolonged duration of urinary tract catheterization

   g.   Empiric use of postoperative antibiotics

   h.   Requirement for blood transfusions

2.   One study showed that use of chlorhexidine gluconate 0.12% oral rinse preoperatively and in the ICU reduced the incidence of nosocomial respiratory infections by 70% and also reduced mortality rate in cardiac surgical patients.[56]

C.   Sternal wound infections complicate about 2% of cardiac surgical procedures performed via a median sternotomy. *Staphylococcus aureus* and *S. epidermidis* are the most common pathogens encountered, despite the use of prophylactic antibiotics specifically directed at these organisms. Sternal infections are a major source of physical, emotional, and economic stress,

although advances in plastic surgical coverage techniques have improved results dramatically.[57-65]

1. **Risk factors**
    a. Diabetes mellitus
    b. Obesity
    c. Chronic obstructive pulmonary disease
    d. Prolonged ventilatory support
    e. Bilateral IMA usage, specifically in diabetics[60]
    f. Excessive mediastinal bleeding, reexploration for bleeding, or multiple transfusions
    g. Older age
    h. Impaired nutritional status (low serum albumin)
    i. Low cardiac output syndromes requiring inotropic support
    j. Reoperations
    k. Prolonged duration of CPB or surgical procedure

2. **Presentation** can be either overt or occult. Infections usually present about 10 days after the surgical procedure.[65]
    a. Minor/superficial: serous drainage, cellulitis, localized area of wound breakdown with purulent drainage
    b. Major/deep incisional (deep subcutaneous, osteomyelitis, mediastinitis): any of the above, but usually significant purulent drainage, often with an unstable sternum. Sternal instability may be noted when mediastinitis is present, but, in the absence of other clinical evidence, may represent a sterile dehiscence.
    c. Inexplicable chest wall pain or tenderness, fever, gram-positive bacteremia, or leukocytosis should raise suspicion of a major sternal wound infection. Sternal wound infections account for more than 50% of postoperative gram-positive bacteremias.[66] Occult infections are particularly common in diabetic patients who often mount a very poor inflammatory response and may present several weeks after surgery with extensive purulent mediastinitis but few systemic signs.
    d. A chronic draining sinus tract is a common delayed presentation of chronic osteomyelitis.

3. **Evaluation**
    a. Culture of purulent drainage may identify the organisms and direct the antibiotic therapy.
    b. Wound aspiration may diagnose an infection when purulent drainage is not present and the infection is occult.
    c. Chest CT scanning may be beneficial if the infection is indolent. Loss of the integrity of retrosternal soft tissue fat planes and loculated retrosternal abscesses are suggestive of deep-seated mediastinal infection. However, it can be very

difficult to distinguish infection from hematoma formation and fibrin tracts in the retrosternal space. CT scanning is generally neither sensitive nor specific enough to be of much help in the early postoperative setting.[67,68]

    d. Indium-111 leukocyte scanning may identify an early sternal infection.[68]

    e. Occasionally, the infection will have to "declare itself" by spontaneous drainage when other diagnostic techniques are inconclusive but the clinical suspicion remains high.

4. **Treatment**

    a. Minor infections usually respond to intravenous antibiotics, opening of the wound, and local wound care. Persistence of a sinus tract or multiple areas of recurrent breakdown suggest a deeper-seated infection, often involving the sternal sutures. This usually requires surgical exploration rather than dressing changes ad infinitum.

    b. Major infections require mediastinal exploration for débridement of infected tissues, removal of foreign bodies, drainage, and elimination of dead space. Antibiotic therapy is generally recommended for 6 weeks.

        i. The closed method entails placement of substernal drainage catheters for postoperative antibiotic irrigation (usually 0.5% povidone-iodine). This may be successful if performed within 3 weeks of surgery when mediastinal tissues are pliable enough to eliminate dead space.[64] However, rewiring of the débrided sternum may not provide a stable chest and may predispose the patient to chronic osteomyelitis.

        ii. The open method is used for severe mediastinitis, chronic osteomyelitis, recalcitrant infections, or extensive subcutaneous involvement that extends down to the sternum and contaminates the sternal wires. In this situation, full exploration is essential because the degree of bony involvement or mediastinitis may not be evident. Sternal débridement with placement of muscle flaps (pectoralis major or rectus abdominis) or omentum simultaneously or after several days of dressing changes to clean up the wound is very successful in treating these infections.[69–71] One disadvantage of leaving the wound open for dressing changes is the risk of right ventricular rupture, especially if sternal débridement has been inadequate.[72] It is important to augment the patient's nutritional status to ensure a satisfactory result from flap coverage.

D. **Leg wound infections** are an underappreciated source of postoperative morbidity. Infections and poor wound healing are noted in up to 10% of patients and may result from poor surgical technique with creation of flaps, failure to eliminate dead space, use of excessive suture material, or hematoma formation. They are more common in females and patients with severe peripheral vascular disease, diabetes, and obesity.[73]

1. **Presentation**

   a. Cellulitis

   b. Wound breakdown with purulent drainage

   c. Skin necrosis from thin flaps or a large subcutaneous hematoma; formation of eschar

2. **Prevention**

   a. Careful surgical technique: avoid tissue trauma, minimize flap formation, obtain meticulous hemostasis, avoid excessive suture material and tissue strangulation. Use of skip incisions or minimally invasive endoscopic techniques may be beneficial in reducing the incidence and severity of infection.

   b. Placement of suction drains to eliminate dead space underneath flaps.

3. **Treatment** requires antibiotics and débridement. If a large hematoma or necrotic skin edges are present, early return to the operating room should be considered to evacuate the hematoma and close the leg primarily. This may lessen morbidity and reduce the duration of hospitalization.[74]

E. Antibiotic prophylaxis for dental or surgical procedures is mandatory for all patients with prosthetic valves and grafts. The 1997 AHA recommendations for prevention of bacterial endocarditis are shown in table 12.4.[75,76]

IX.   Neurologic Complications

Neurologic complications are dreaded sequelae of cardiac surgical procedures. Focal neurologic events complicate approximately 2% of cardiac procedures requiring cardiopulmonary bypass, although this may increase as more patients with advanced age and diffuse vascular disease undergo cardiac surgery. Neurologic deficits resulting from intraoperative events are usually noted within the first 24–48 hours of surgery. However, a small proportion of deficits may develop later during the hospital stay, usually as a result of postoperative hemodynamic instability or atrial fibrillation. The etiology of neurologic deficits remains enigmatic in a small proportion of patients.

A. **Central nervous system deficits**

   1. **Risk factors** have been described in numerous publications[77–83] and have also been combined in one multicenter study to determine a preoperative stroke risk index.[84]

      a. Preoperative factors

         • Preexisting cerebrovascular disease (especially history of a stroke)

         • Increasing age (risk of up to 10% in patients older than age 75)

         • Presence of a carotid bruit

         • Diabetes mellitus

Table 12.4 *Antibiotic Prophylaxis to Prevent Endocarditis in Adult Patients*

Dental/oral/respiratory/esophageal procedures

Standard regimen	Amoxicillin 2.0 g PO 1 h before procedure
Unable to take PO medications	Ampicillin 2.0 g IV/IM within 30 min of starting procedure
Penicillin allergic	Clindamycin 600 mg, cephalexin 2 g, or clarithromycin 500 mg PO 1 h before procedure
Penicillin allergic and unable to take PO	Clindamycin 600 mg or cefazolin 1 g IV within 30 min of starting procedure

GI/GU procedures

High-risk	Ampicillin 2 g IM/IV plus gentamicin 1.5 mg/kg IV/IM within 30 min of starting procedure; then ampicillin 1 g IM/IV or amoxicillin 1 g PO 6 h later
High-risk, but ampicillin/amoxicillin allergic	Vancomycin 1 g IV over 1–2 h plus gentamicin 1.5 mg/kg IV within 30 min of starting procedure
Moderate-risk	Amoxicillin 2 g PO 1 h before procedure or ampicillin 2 g IM/IV within 30 min of starting procedure
Moderate-risk, but ampicillin/ amoxicillin allergic	Vancomycin 1 g IV over 1–2 h within 30 min of starting procedure

Source: Dajani AS, Taubert KA, Wilson W, et al. Prevention of bacterial endocarditis. Recommendations by the American Heart Association. JAMA 1997;277:1794–1908; Circulation 1997;96:358–66.
1. *High-risk: prosthetic heart valves (including homografts), history of endocarditis, prosthetic intravascular grafts*
2. *Moderate-risk: valvular heart disease, hypertrophic cardiomyopathy, mitral valve prolapse with valvar regurgitation and/or thickened leaflets*
3. *Not required: pacemakers, implantable defibrillators, transesophageal echocardiography[76]*

- Hypertension
- Peripheral vascular disease
- Poor LV function

    b. Intraoperative/postoperative findings/events

- Ascending aortic atherosclerosis and calcification[85]
- Left ventricular mural thrombus
- Opening of a cardiac chamber during surgery
- Long duration of CPB
- Normothermic bypass (controversial)[86]
- Perioperative hypotension or cardiac arrest
- Postoperative atrial fibrillation

  2. **Mechanisms**

    a. Particulate embolism is the most common cause of stroke. One study using transcranial Doppler ultrasonography documented a significant incidence of cerebral complications when more than 60 microemboli were detected during surgery.[87] Sources may be:

- Atherosclerotic aorta (during cannulation or clamping)
- Left atrial or left ventricular thrombus
- Air embolism
- Platelet-fibrin debris from carotid ulceration
- Solid or gaseous microembolism debris from the extra-corporeal circuit

b. Cerebral hypoperfusion may be the result of systemic hypotension or impaired regional cerebral blood flow. The latter may result from intra- or extracranial carotid disease. During cardiopulmonary bypass with nonpulsatile perfusion, cerebral autoregulation can maintain cerebral blood flow down to a mean pressure of about 40 mm Hg. However, the influence of hypothermia, blood gas regulation (alpha vs. pH stat), diabetes, and preexisting hypertension on the adequacy of cerebral flow is not well defined. Of particular concern is the potential for cerebral hypoperfusion during a postoperative hypotensive event. This may result in a watershed infarct, especially in patients with uncorrected carotid disease.

3. **Presentation** depends primarily on the site and extent of the cerebral insult. Common presentations include:

a. Transient ischemic attacks (TIAs) or reversible neurologic deficits (RNDs)

b. Focal deficits
- Hemiparesis or hemiplegia
- Aphasia, dysarthria, and hand incoordination
- Visual deficits (caused by retinal emboli, occipital lobe infarction, or anterior ischemic optic neuropathy)[88]

c. Severe confusion

d. Coma

4. **Prevention** of neurologic complications requires the identification and appropriate treatment of potential precipitating factors.

a. Preoperative evaluation for extracranial carotid disease should be considered in any patient with current or remote neurologic symptoms. Noninvasive studies followed by carotid arteriography, if indicated, may identify carotid disease that should be corrected before or at the same time as cardiac surgery.

b. **Symptomatic** carotid disease always warrants carotid endarterectomy (CE) either prior to or at the time of cardiac surgery. A combined CABG-CE should be performed in the patient with unstable angina or significant myocardium at risk if neurologic symptoms are present.[89–93]

c. **Asymptomatic** carotid disease is usually detected by the presence of a carotid bruit, which should be evaluated by noninvasive testing. The presence of a carotid bruit and documented severe carotid stenosis is associated with an increased risk of stroke.[94,95] Although still controversial, there is a trend toward performance of a combined CABG-CE in asymptomatic patients with high-grade unilateral disease because of excellent current results and overall reduced cost.[89–93] The risk of stroke in asymptomatic patients with bilateral disease is high during isolated CABG[95] and remains high with combined procedures.[91] This is particularly true in patients with unilateral occlusion.[78,89,91]

    d. Intraoperative transesophageal or epiaortic echocardiography can be used to identify aortic atherosclerosis that might alter cannulation and clamping techniques to prevent manipulation of a diseased ascending aorta.[96] Other measures that reduce the risk of embolic stroke are careful removal of left ventricular thrombus, meticulous valve débridement and irrigation, and complete removal of air from the left heart after intracardiac procedures. The latter can be very difficult during minimally invasive surgery. Use of a single aortic crossclamp technique to avoid application of a partial-exclusion clamp is also beneficial.[97] Use of the membrane oxygenator and an arterial filter may reduce microembolism from the bypass circuit.[98]

    e. Use of a higher mean arterial pressure during CPB may be beneficial to patients with hypertension or known intracranial vascular disease.

    f. Techniques that identify cerebral hypoperfusion or cerebral embolization during bypass include EEG monitoring, transcranial Doppler, and retinal fluorescein angiography with digital image analysis.[98,99] However, these are expensive, somewhat inconvenient, and have not achieved widespread usage.

5. **Evaluation** requires an assessment of the degree of functional impairment by careful neurologic examination, identification of the anatomic extent of cerebral infarction on CT scan with particular attention to evidence of hemorrhage, and evaluation for a possible source of the stroke that might require additional attention (echocardiogram, carotid noninvasive studies).

6. **Treatment**

    a. Heparin is generally recommended for embolic strokes once a CT scan has demonstrated no evidence of intracranial hemorrhage. However, the possibility of subsequent hemorrhage into an infarct zone should be weighed when deciding if heparinization is indicated. Heparin may be beneficial to improve cerebral microcirculatory flow or prevent propagation of intracardiac thrombus, but is of unclear benefit in preventing further aortic atheroembolism from dislodged plaque.

    b. Standard measures to reduce intracranial pressure may be indicated depending on the extent of cerebral infarction.

      c. A carotid endarterectomy may be considered for patients with severe carotid stenosis and postoperative transient neurologic deficits or small strokes.

      d. Early institution of physical therapy is important.

7. **Prognosis** is favorable for patients with small or temporary deficits. The mortality rate in the Society of Thoracic Surgeons (STS) database for patients suffering permanent strokes was 28%.[1] The outlook for comatose patients is extremely poor, with over 50% dying or remaining in a vegetative state.

B. **Encephalopathy and delirium** represent an acute change in a patient's mental status. They are fairly common after open-heart surgery, with an incidence of approximately 30%.[100] The mechanism of delirium is frequently not clear. It may be related to mild cerebral hypoperfusion associated with intracranial small vessel disease or may result from microemboli from the use of cardiopulmonary bypass. It is usually transient and has a fluctuating course, but it can be very disturbing to the patient and his or her family.

1. **Risk factors**

      a. Older age

      b. Recent alcoholism

      c. Preoperative organic brain disease (mild degrees of cognitive dysfunction or dementia)

      d. Severe cardiac disease

      e. Multiple associated medical illnesses

      f. Complex and prolonged surgical procedures on CPB

2. **Common causes**

      a. Medication toxicity (including benzodiazepines and analgesics)

      b. Metabolic disturbances

      c. Alcohol withdrawal

      d. Low cardiac output syndromes; this may include periods of marginal cerebral blood flow during bypass that are just above the threshold for cerebral infarction.

      e. Hypoxia

      f. Sepsis

      g. Recent/new stroke

3. **Manifestations**

      a. Disorientation and confusion

      b. Lethargy or agitation

      c. Paranoia and hallucinations

4. **Evaluation**

      a. Review of current medications and drug levels

      b. Identification of possible history of recent alcoholism or substance abuse

    c. Neurologic examination

    d. ABGs, electrolytes, BUN, creatinine, CBC, magnesium, calcium, cultures

5. **Management**

    a. Soft restraints, side rails

    b. Correct metabolic abnormalities

    c. Stop inappropriate medications

    d. Control agitation with haloperidol 2.5–5.0 mg PO/IM/IV q6h.[101] However, minimize sedating drugs, such as diphenhydramine or the benzodiazepines. The latter are very poorly tolerated in elderly patients, often exacerbating confusion and producing either agitation or stupor; benzodiazepines can be reversed using flumazenil 0.2 mg IV given over 30 seconds, followed by doses of 0.3 mg, then 0.5 mg every 30 seconds, if necessary, to a total dose of 3 mg over 1 hour.[102]

    e. Treat suspected alcohol withdrawal:

        i. Benzodiazepines—lorazepam, diazepam, or chlordiazepoxide (Librium)—with gradual wean

        ii. Thiamine 50–100 mg IM bid, folate 1 mg qd

    f. Psychotherapy: reassurance and support

C. **Seizures** may accompany cerebral insults from hypoxia, or air and particulate emboli. However, they can also result from medication overdoses (e.g., lidocaine). Contributing factors should be addressed and the patient evaluated by a neurologist. CT scan, EEG, or anticonvulsant therapy with phenytoin should be considered upon advice from the neurologist.

D. **Neuropsychologic or cognitive dysfunction** is extremely common after surgery, with an incidence ranging between 30 and 80% in various studies. It may be subtle, as measured by a sophisticated battery of neuropsychologic tests, and it may be transient or long-lasting. Older age, more severe cardiac disease, long duration of bypass, and perhaps low perfusion pressures during CPB correlate with the incidence of neuropsychologic dysfunction. The finding that hypothermic bypass, alpha stat pH management, membrane oxygenators, and arterial line filters are associated with a lower incidence of dysfunction suggests that microembolism plays a major role in its development.[103–105] One randomized trial demonstrated that neuropsychologic dysfunction was significantly more common in patients undergoing normothermic cardiopulmonary bypass.[106]

E. **Psychiatric problems** are fairly common in patients undergoing open heart surgery. Anxiety and depression occur frequently in patients with known psychiatric disorders, but are also noted in patients who have lost family members due to coronary disease. Exacerbation of preexisting disorders, such as affective (manic-depressive) and personality disorders is also not unusual. A psychiatrist with an interest in postoperative problems is invaluable in helping patients resolve distressing psychiatric symptoms and in providing advice on the appropriate use of psychotropic medications.[107]

F. **Critical illness polyneuropathy** is a syndrome of unknown etiology that complicates the course of sepsis and multisystem organ failure. It usually presents as failure to wean from the ventilator due to weakness of the diaphragm and chest wall muscles. Axonal degeneration is the underlying pathologic process and is manifested by proximal muscle atrophy and paresis, decreased deep tendon reflexes, and, in some cases, by laryngeal and pharyngeal weakness, producing swallowing difficulties. It may produce motor and sensory deficits and can be diagnosed by electromyography. The syndrome is self-limited and has no specific treatment other than supportive care (ventilatory support and physical therapy). It must be distinguished from other causes of postoperative muscle weakness, such as medications, nutritional deficiency, disuse atrophy, or other neuromuscular disorders.[108,109]

G. **Brachial plexus injuries**

1. **Etiology.** Stretch of the inferior cords of the brachial plexus by sternal retraction or elevation is probably the most common cause of this injury. The incidence may be minimized by caudad placement of the retractor and opening it only as much as necessary for adequate exposure. Injuries are significantly more common in patients in whom the IMA is harvested, suggesting that asymmetric sternal retraction may play a causal role.[110,111]

2. **Presentation.** Numbness, paresthesia, weakness, and occasionally sharp pains are noted in the ulnar nerve distribution. In more extreme forms, the median or radial nerve distribution may be involved. Radial nerve deficits are more likely to be caused by direct arm compression by retraction bars used for the IMA takedown.

3. **Evaluation.** If the deficit persists, EMG may be useful in assessing the extent of the deficit and the return of function, but it does not need to be performed routinely.

4. **Treatment.** Symptoms usually resolve over several months. Physical therapy is essential to maintain motor tone. Amitriptyline (Elavil) 10–25 mg q5h, and carbamazepine (Tegretol) 100 mg tid are often helpful for pain associated with nerve injury.

H. **Recurrent laryngeal nerve palsy** is a rare complication that has been described following coronary bypass surgery from injury during IMA mobilization. Laryngoscopic examination will confirm vocal cord paresis.[112]

I. **Phrenic nerve palsy** (see page 381)

J. **Pituitary apoplexy** (see page 366)

X. Gastrointestinal Complications

Gastrointestinal complications affect about 1–2% of patients undergoing open-heart surgery. Because they frequently occur in critically ill patients, they are associated with a significant mortality rate. The common pathophysiologic mechanism is a low cardiac output state, which produces sympathetic vasoconstriction and hypoperfusion of the splanchnic bed. This contributes to inadequate tissue perfusion, mucosal ischemia, and the so-called "acute GI focal necrosis syndrome." Changes that are seen may include stress ulceration, mucosal atrophy, bacterial overgrowth from stress ulcer prophylaxis, and loss of barrier function with increased permeability. These changes may potentially lead to bacterial translocation, sepsis, and multiorgan failure.[113] Use of preventive measures and prompt, aggressive surgical intervention are necessary to decrease the mortality associated with these complications.[114-119]

A. **Routine care and common complaints.** Most patients have a nasogastric tube inserted in the operating room before heparinization or after its reversal with protamine. This maintains gastric decompression during positive pressure ventilation, removes gastric contents to minimize the risk of aspiration, decreases gastric acidity, and allows for the administration of oral medications and antacids in the ICU. The tube is usually removed after extubation if bowel sounds are present. An oral diet is then advanced from clear liquids to a regular diet.

1. Anorexia, nausea, and a distaste for food are fairly common complaints after surgery and may be attributable to the side effects of medications (narcotics, type IA antiarrhythmics) and possibly to mineral deficiency (especially zinc).

a. Metoclopramide (Reglan) 10–20 mg IM qid may stimulate gastrointestinal motility and decrease the incidence of postoperative nausea and distention.

b. Cisapride (Propulsid) 10 mg PO qid accelerates gastric emptying and may be given to reduce symptoms of nocturnal heartburn due to gastroesophageal reflux.

c. H_2 blockers or omeprazole may also be of benefit.

2. Diarrhea may accompany the use of quinidine, but may also develop from *Clostridium difficile* colitis even when the duration of antibiotic therapy is short.

3. Constipation is a common problem after surgery. Preoperative enemas are usually not given, narcotics are used for analgesia, and elderly patients are often poorly mobilized for several days. Milk of magnesia, bulk laxatives (Metamucil) or stool softeners (Colace) may be helpful in older patients.

B. **Differential diagnosis of acute abdominal pain**

1. **Manifestations.** The presence of an acute intraabdominal process can be difficult to detect in critically ill patients in the ICU setting. It is frequently suspected by the presence of fever, an elevation in WBC count, marked tenderness to abdominal palpation, hemodynamic evidence of sepsis, or positive blood cultures. Arriving at the appropriate diagnosis can be even more challenging.

2. **Etiology**

a. Cholecystitis (acalculous or calculous)

b. Perforated viscus (gastric or duodenal ulceration, diverticulitis)

c. Pancreatitis

      d. Mesenteric ischemia or ischemic colitis

      e. *Clostridium difficile* colitis

      f. Severe paralytic ileus (occasionally idiopathic [Ogilvie's syndrome], but frequently associated with an acute inflammatory process or colitis)

      g. Small bowel or colonic obstruction

      h. Retroperitoneal bleeding

      i. Severe constipation

      j. Urinary tract infection

      k. Bladder distention

  3. **Risk factors**[114–119]

      a. Perioperative low cardiac output or hypotension, frequently requiring use of vasopressors or the intraaortic balloon pump (IABP)

      b. Long duration of cardiopulmonary bypass

      c. Older age

      d. Respiratory failure requiring prolonged ventilatory support

      e. Poor nutritional status in long-term patients

      f. Valve surgery

      g. Emergency surgery

  4. **Evaluation**

      a. A review of preexisting conditions

      b. Serial abdominal examinations

      c. Laboratory tests: KUB (for obstruction or ileus), semiupright chest x-ray (for free air under the diaphragm), liver function tests (LFTs), serum amylase and lipase, *C. difficile* titer if diarrhea is present.

      d. An upper abdominal ultrasound or HIDA scan should be performed if biliary tract obstruction is suspected.

      e. Abdominal CT scanning, peritoneal lavage, or laparoscopy may be helpful.

      f. A mesenteric arteriogram can be performed if mesenteric ischemia is suspected.

  5. **Treatment.** An exploratory laparotomy may be required to make the appropriate diagnosis. General surgery consultation should be obtained from the outset because early exploration may reduce the high mortality associated with the development of gastrointestinal complications. Although many patients with these complications are very ill and often septic, they are usually better able to tolerate exploration after cardiac surgery than they had been before.

C. **Paralytic ileus** occasionally persists for several days after surgery. It is frequently a benign, self-limited problem, but occasionally it may reflect sepsis or severe intraabdominal pathology.

1. **Contributing factors**
   a. Gastric distention (possibly related to vagal injury)
   b. Congestion of the hepatic or splanchnic bed (from poor venous drainage during surgery or systemic venous hypertension)
   c. Inflammatory processes (e.g., cholecystitis, pancreatitis)
   d. Retroperitoneal bleeding (from groin catheterization, but occasionally spontaneously in an anticoagulated patient)
   e. *Clostridium difficile* colitis
   f. Mesenteric ischemia
   g. Drugs (narcotics)

2. **Evaluation**
   a. Serial patient examinations for inflammatory signs, distention, return of bowel sounds
   b. Laboratory tests: KUB, CBC, amylase, liver function tests, *C. difficile* titers

3. **Management.** Keeping the patient NPO with nasogastric decompression will prevent gastric distention until peristaltic activity returns. A rectal tube may also be beneficial when colonic distention is marked. Therapy must also be directed at any identifiable precipitating process. Occasionally, Ogilvie's syndrome of colonic "pseudo-obstruction" will develop and necessitate colonoscopy or exploration if bowel rupture appears imminent. Total parenteral nutrition should be provided.

D. **Cholecystitis**

1. **Etiology.** Cholecystitis is noted more commonly in older patients and those with prolonged pump times, suggesting that hypoperfusion is a contributing factor. In addition, fasting, parenteral nutrition, and narcotics can decrease gallbladder contractility and produce biliary stasis. Acalculous rather than calculous cholecystitis is usually present.

2. **Evaluation**
   a. Serial abdominal examinations may draw attention to an inflammatory process in the right upper quadrant.
   b. Liver function tests (ALT, AST, bilirubin, alkaline phosphatase) may suggest extrahepatic biliary obstruction.
   c. Right upper quadrant (RUQ) ultrasound or HIDA scan can identify a dilated gallbladder and biliary obstruction.

3. **Treatment**
   a. Cholecystostomy is often recommended in critically ill patients, but it is not adequate treatment when gangrene is present.
   b. Cholecystectomy (open or laparoscopic) is the preferred procedure unless the patient is considered too ill to tolerate the procedure.

E. **Upper gastrointestinal (GI) bleeding**

1. **Etiology.** Upper GI bleeding usually results from stress ulceration and is more common in elderly patients and those with gastritis or preexisting ulcer disease. A thorough preoperative history and physical examination (stigmata of liver disease, stool guaiac) may identify patients at increased risk of developing postoperative GI bleeding. Postoperative risk factors that may increase gastric acidity, produce mucosal ischemia, reduce the mucosal defense mechanism, or precipitate bleeding include:[120,121]

    a. Respiratory failure

    b. Low cardiac output states producing splanchnic hypoperfusion

    c. Anticoagulation from medications (aspirin, heparin, or warfarin) or a coagulopathy (thrombocytopenia, elevated PT from hepatic dysfunction or poor nutrition)

2. **Prophylaxis.** Any patient with a history of ulcer disease or gastritis should receive medications in the ICU to prevent stress-related mucosal damage and potential GI bleeding. In addition, any patient on prolonged ventilatory support or with a coagulopathy should receive stress ulcer prophylaxis. Numerous medications have been shown to provide comparable prophylaxis against stress ulceration:

    a. Sucralfate 1 g q6h can be given orally or down a nasogastric tube. It should not be combined with antacids or omeprazole.[122] It does not raise the gastric pH (which increases gastric bacterial colonization) and may reduce the incidence of nosocomial pneumonia associated with antacids, omeprazole, or the H_2 blockers.[123] However, a 1998 study from Canada reported that, among critically ill ventilated patients, ranitidine was associated with a lower rate of GI bleeding than sucralfate with no difference in the rate of pneumonia.[124]

    b. Omeprazole (Prilosec) 20 mg qd[125]

    c. Ranitidine 6.25 mg/h as a continuous infusion or 50 mg IV q8h (the continuous infusion is more effective in maintaining a gastric pH greater than 3.5)[124,126,127]

3. **Manifestations.** Drainage of bright red blood through a nasogastric tube or vomiting of blood are signs of upper GI bleeding. Slow bleeding usually produces melena, but very rapid bleeding may produce bloody stools. Attention should be drawn to potential GI bleeding in the critically ill or heparinized patient who has an unexplained fall in hematocrit or progressive tachycardia or hypotension. If GI bleeding cannot be documented, a retroperitoneal bleed should be entertained as a possible diagnosis and evaluated by an abdominal CT scan.

4. **Evaluation and treatment.** Bleeding that persists despite correction of coagulation abnormalities and intensification of a medical regimen requires further evaluation. Bleeding during anticoagulation is commonly associated with some underlying pathology.

a. Omeprazole, but not antacids or H_2 blockers, has been shown to be effective in reducing further bleeding in patients with bleeding ulcers.[128]

b. Upper GI endoscopy should be performed to identify the site of bleeding; it can be used therapeutically with laser bipolar coagulation to control hemorrhage.[129]

c. Because surgery has traditionally been reserved for patients with unremitting hemorrhage, it has been associated with a mortality rate of about 50%. If the patient requires anticoagulation indefinitely following surgery (e.g., for a mechanical prosthetic valve), a definitive procedure must be performed.

F. **Lower GI bleeding** may be manifested by bright red blood per rectum, blood-streaked stool, or melena, and must be differentiated from upper GI bleeding by passage of a nasogastric tube.

1. **Etiology**

a. Mesenteric ischemia or ischemic colitis caused by periods of prolonged hypoperfusion

b. Antibiotic-associated colitis (usually *C. difficile*)

c. Bleeding from colonic lesions (polyps, tumors, diverticular disease) may be precipitated by anticoagulation.

d. Colonic angiodysplasia. This is termed Heyde's syndrome when associated with aortic stenosis. It abates after aortic valve replacement with a tissue valve.[130]

2. **Evaluation.** Once an upper GI source is ruled out, sigmoidoscopy or colonoscopy can be performed. A bleeding scan may identify the bleeding source. Mesenteric arteriography should be considered if bleeding persists.

3. **Treatment** involves correction of any coagulopathy and elimination of precipitating causes. Antibiotics (metronidazole 500 mg PO q8h or vancomycin 500 mg PO q6h) can be used for *C. difficile* colitis. Mesenteric angiography with infusion of vasopressin (0.1–0.4 U/h) or injection of autologous clot or Gelfoam may be considered. Octreotide (Sandostatin) 50 µg over 30 minutes decreases splanchnic blood flow and may be beneficial. Surgical intervention is rarely required for persistent bleeding.

G. **Mesenteric ischemia** is usually noted in elderly patients who have prolonged low cardiac output states requiring pharmacologic or mechanical support.

1. **Etiology.** Nonocclusive mesenteric ischemia resulting from splanchnic hypoperfusion from a low cardiac output state or a long pump run is the most common etiology; atherosclerotic embolism or mesenteric thrombosis occur less commonly.[131]

2. **Presentation.** Typical manifestations are a profound ileus or abdominal pain out of proportion to physical findings. The diagnosis can be very difficult to make in the critically ill patient who is frequently ventilated and heavily sedated. Sepsis, acidosis, re-

spiratory distress, GI bleeding, or diarrhea are often present as well. The diagnosis is typically made about 10 days after surgery.[131]

3. **Diagnosis** can be made by mesenteric arteriography. It can identify or rule out thromboembolic causes and allow for the infusion of mesenteric vasodilators (papaverine).[132] Endoscopy may be helpful in documenting colonic ischemia.

4. **Treatment.** Abdominal exploration is indicated if bowel necrosis is suspected, and it can rule out other intraabdominal pathology. Localized bowel resection can be performed if possible. However, more commonly, there are multiple areas of ischemic bowel that do not allow for extensive bowel resection.

H. **Diarrhea** developing in a patient in the ICU setting is often an ominous sign because it may result from bowel ischemia caused by a low flow state. However, it is frequently caused by treatable problems including:

1. Side effects from medications

   a. Quinidine causes diarrhea in nearly every patient; if persistent, procainamide may be substituted if a type IA antiarrhythmic is indicated.

   b. Antibiotics have been implicated in causing diarrhea from *C. difficile.* Titers should be sent in triplicate and metronidazole 500 mg PO q8h or vancomycin 500 mg PO qid should be given for 7–10 days if titers are high. Rarely a subtotal colectomy is required for severe colitis.

2. Ischemic colitis

3. GI bleeding

4. Intolerance of hyperosmolar tube feedings; dilute with more water and start at a slower infusion rate.

I. **Hepatic dysfunction** manifested by elevation in LFTs, including ALT, AST, bilirubin, and alkaline phosphatase, is fairly common after open-heart surgery. About 20% of patients will develop transient hyperbilirubinemia, but fewer than 1% of patients will have evidence of significant hepatocellular damage that may progress to chronic hepatitis or liver failure.[133–135] The latter is more common in patients with severe underlying liver disease or those who develop multisystem organ failure from prolonged hypoperfusion. The presence of normal preoperative LFTs does not rule out the possibility of significant hepatic dysfunction, and thus is not sensitive enough to identify all patients with an increased susceptibility to perioperative insults. An ominous prognostic sign is evidence of impaired synthetic function (decreased albumin, elevated INR) before surgery.

1. **Etiology**

   a. Hepatocellular necrosis

      i. Low cardiac output states

      ii. Right heart failure or severe tricuspid regurgitation (chronic passive congestion)

      iii. Posttransfusion hepatitis C or cytomegalovirus infection (late)

      iv. Drugs (acetaminophen, quinidine)

    b. Hyperbilirubinemia

       i. Hemolysis (paravalvular leak, long pump run, sepsis, multiple transfusions, drugs)

       ii. Intrahepatic cholestasis (hepatitis, hepatocellular necrosis, benign postoperative cholestasis, parenteral nutrition, bacterial infections, medications)

       iii. Extrahepatic obstruction (biliary tract obstruction)

2. **Manifestations** depend on the specific diagnosis. Jaundice is a common accompaniment of hepatocellular damage or cholestasis. Severe liver failure may result in a coagulopathy, hypoglycemia, or encephalopathy.

3. **Evaluation.** The specific LFT abnormalities usually indicate the nature of the problem. Additional tests may include those that detect hemolysis (LDH, reticulocyte count), assess cardiac and valvular function (echocardiography), identify biliary pathology (right upper quadrant ultrasound or HIDA scan), or detect hepatitis (HBV, HCV serologies).

4. **Treatment**

    a. An elevated bilirubin is usually a benign and self-limited postoperative occurrence. Bilirubin levels will gradually return to normal when hemodynamics improve unless there is evidence of severe underlying liver pathology. In this situation, progressive and irreversible hepatic dysfunction may result, leading to multisystem organ failure and death.

    b. Coagulopathy with "autoanticoagulation" may occur during a period of hepatic dysfunction because of the impaired capacity of the liver to produce clotting factors. In patients requiring anticoagulation, small doses of warfarin should be used to prevent elevation of the prothrombin time to dangerous levels. If this occurs, the patient may develop cardiac tamponade or GI bleeding. In addition, the doses of medications that undergo hepatic metabolism must be altered.

    c. Stress ulcer prophylaxis should be considered using H_2 blockers or omeprazole 20 mg qd.

    d. Hyperammonemia and encephalopathy can be treated with:[136]

       i. Dietary protein restriction

       ii. Lactulose 30 mL qid with sorbitol

       iii. Oral neomycin 6 g qd

       iv. Zinc sulfate 600 mg qd

    e. Blood glucose should be carefully monitored to prevent hypoglycemia.

J. **Hyperamylasemia** is noted in up to 35% of patients following cardiopulmonary bypass, but is associated with clinical pancreatitis in only about 1–3% of patients.[137,138] Isolated hyperamylasemia, not associated with clinical symptoms or an elevated lipase level, is noted in more than half of the patients with an elevated amylase, and probably arises from nonpancreatic sources such as the GI tract. Subclinical pancreatitis is suggested by the presence of mild symptoms (anorexia, nausea, ileus) with elevation of serum lipase levels. A brief period of bowel rest may be beneficial for these patients, but no specific treatment is indicated unless there is clinical evidence of overt pancreatitis or GI tract dysfunction.

K. **Overt pancreatitis** is noted in 1–3% of patients undergoing cardiac surgery, but it is a serious problem associated with a significant mortality rate. Pancreatic necrosis has been noted in 25% of patients dying from multisystem organ failure after cardiac surgery.[137–139]

1. **Etiology.** Pancreatitis usually represents an ischemic, necrotic injury resulting from a low cardiac output state and hypoperfusion. Potential contributing factors during surgery include hypothermia and nonpulsatile perfusion during bypass, systemic emboli, and venous sludging. A persistent low output state requiring vasopressors is usually noted in patients developing overt pancreatitis.

2. **Presentation** is atypical and relatively nonspecific. Fever, elevated WBC, paralytic ileus, and abdominal distention occur first, with abdominal pain, tenderness, and hemodynamic instability representing late manifestations.

3. **Diagnosis** is suggested by the association of abdominal pain with hyperamylasemia. However, in one study, the majority of patients with fulminant pancreatitis did not have elevated amylase levels.[139] Abdominal ultrasound or CT scan may demonstrate a pancreatic phlegmon or abscess.

4. **Treatment** should begin with nasogastric drainage and antibiotics. Exploratory laparotomy with débridement and drainage is usually performed as a desperation measure, but may be the only hope for survival in patients with aggressive necrotizing pancreatitis.

XI. Nutrition

A. Reversal of the catabolic state with adequate nutrition is important during the early phase of postoperative convalescence. The diet must provide enough calories to allow wounds to heal and to maintain immune competence. Although limitations in salt content, fluids, and cholesterol intake are important, overly strict control should be secondary to providing tasty, high caloric foods that stimulate the patient's appetite. Too frequently the combination of anorexia, nausea, and an unpalatable diet prevents the patient from achieving satisfactory nutrition.

B. If caloric intake is not satisfactory but the GI tract is functioning well, a Dobhoff catheter may be placed and tube feedings initiated after confirming the position of the catheter in the stomach, or preferably, in the small bowel. Use of metoclopramide 20 mg IV along with erythromycin 200 mg IV (in 50 mL NS through central line or 200 mL peripherally) to stimulate gastric motility aids in the placement of these catheters. Some of the more popular enteral feedings are listed in Appendices 3 and 4. Those which have specific application to patients with critical illness, respiratory, or renal dysfunction are listed in Appendix 5. If the GI tract cannot be used, total parenteral nutrition (TPN) provided through a central line may be necessary.

C. Most patients who require tracheostomy for prolonged ventilatory support will benefit from the placement of a feeding tube. If there is no evidence of gastroesophageal reflux, a percutaneous gastric feeding tube (PEG) can be placed. If reflux is present, a feeding jejunostomy tube should be placed at the time of the tracheostomy.

D. Total caloric intake should be 25 Kcal/kg/day. General nutritional requirements for adult patients include 1 mL/kg/day of water, 2–5 g/kg/day of glucose, 1.2–1.5 g/kg/day of protein, and 1.2–1.5 g/kg/day of fat, half of which should be omega-6 polyunsaturated fatty acids.[140] Specific considerations in critically ill patients include the following:

1. Multisystem organ failure increases total caloric requirements by about 10–20%. It is associated with protein catabolism and requires an increase in protein intake to 1.5–2.0 g/kg/day. Hyperglycemia may require a reduction in glucose loads and use of intravenous insulin. Triglyceride intolerance often requires a reduction in glucose and fat intake. Increased macro- and micronutrient loss necessitate monitoring and replacement of potassium, zinc, magnesium, calcium, and phosphates, as necessary.

2. Patients with respiratory failure must not be overfed. A respiratory quotient greater than 1 indicates excessive CO_2 production. In this situation, glucose and fat intake should be reduced. Pulmocare is a specially formulated tube feeding with less carbohydrate for use in these patients.

3. Protein intake should be optimized to promote nitrogen retention while avoiding protein overload. Protein should not be restricted in patients with acute renal dysfunction. In patients with chronic renal insufficiency, protein intake should be reduced to 0.5–0.8 g/kg/day. In contrast, protein intake should be increased in patients on dialysis, because peritoneal dialysis removes 40–60 g/day of protein and hemodialysis or hemofiltration removes 3–5 g/h of protein. Nepro is a tube feeding formulated for patients with renal failure that contains high levels of protein and low levels of potassium.

4. Monitoring of visceral protein levels (transferrin and prealbumin) may indicate the adequacy of nutrition, but levels have not been shown to correlate with improved outcomes.

XII. Valve-Associated Problems

A. Careful follow-up is required for all patients who have received a prosthetic valve because of the risk of developing valve-related complications, including thromboembolism, endocarditis, anticoagulant-related hemorrhage, and valve degeneration.[141] It has been aptly stated that the use of a prosthetic valve replaces "one disease with another."

B. **Thromboembolism.** The annual risk of thromboembolism ranges from 1–4% with a slightly higher incidence in patients with mechanical valves taking warfarin than in those with bioprosthetic valves taking only aspirin.

The recommended regimens for tissue and mechanical valves are summarized in Table 12.3.

1. **Valve thrombosis** may occasionally occur with a mechanical valve, even during therapeutic anticoagulation. It is very rare with a bioprosthetic valve. Suspicion of mechanical valve thrombosis is raised by loss of valve clicks and is confirmed by fluoroscopy or two-dimensional echocardiography. Although thrombolytic therapy can be used in selected circumstances, an immediate operation to replace the valve is usually required.[142,143]

2. **Pregnancy** poses a serious problem for the woman with a prosthetic valve. The incidence of fetal wastage is 60% if warfarin is used during the first trimester, and there is a significant incidence of other congenital defects if pregnancy is completed ("coumadin embryopathy"). Porcine valves have been used for women of childbearing age, acknowledging the limited durability of valves in this age group and the need to replace the valve within 10–15 years for valve degeneration. Cryopreserved homograft valves or a pulmonary autograft (Ross procedure) are preferred for patients undergoing aortic valve replacement. One recommended anticoagulation regimen for women with mechanical valves who desire to become pregnant is as follows:[144]

   a. Stop warfarin before conception

   b. Heparin 10,000 U SC q12h throughout pregnancy to achieve a partial thromboplastin time (PTT) of 1.5–2.0 × control (use of low-molecular-weight heparin may be best); consider the use of aspirin 81–100 mg as well. An alternative is to use heparin until the 13th week of pregnancy, then start warfarin to achieve an INR of 2.5–3.0 until the middle of the third trimester, and then reinstitute heparin (often up to 20,000 U SC q12h to achieve a therapeutic PTT 6 h postinjection).

   c. Before delivery, initiate intravenous heparin

   d. With the onset of labor, give heparin 5000 U SC q8h

   e. Resume warfarin after delivery

C. **Anticoagulant-related hemorrhage** is a major source of morbidity in patients receiving warfarin, especially in patients over the age of 65. It is absolutely critical that careful follow-up be arranged for any patient discharged on warfarin. The prothrombin time must remain in the therapeutic range to avoid valve thrombosis or bleeding problems.

D. **Prosthetic valve endocarditis** (PVE) may develop at any time during the life span of a prosthetic valve with an annual risk of approximately 1–2%.[145] Early endocarditis (within 60 days of surgery) usually results from infection with staphylococcal organisms and carries a significantly higher mortality than late PVE. The latter is most commonly caused by *Streptococcus viridans* and *S. epidermidis*. Clinical manifestations may include recurrent fevers, valve dysfunction with regurgitation and heart failure, and most ominously, the development of conduction defects resulting from a periannular abscess. It is critical that the patient understand the need for prophylactic antibiotics when any dental or other surgically invasive procedure is performed. The AHA recommendations detailed on page 399 should be followed.[75]

E. **Hemolysis** usually reflects the development of a paravalvular leak. Subclinical hemolysis is noted by elevation in the LDH and reticulocyte count. The patient may also develop mild jaundice or persistent anemia necessitating transfusion. Valve re-replacement is indicated for severe hemolysis or a significant paravalvular leak.

F. **Valve failure** is defined as a complication necessitating valve replacement. Mechanical valve failure is usually caused by thrombosis, thromboembolism, endocarditis, or anticoagulation-related bleeding, and rarely by structural failure. In contrast, primary tissue failure is the most common cause of bioprosthetic dysfunction necessitating valve replacement. For porcine mitral valves, reoperation is necessary in about 25% of patients at 10 years and 65% at 15 years, but is substantially greater in patients under the age of 35. Structural valve deterioration necessitating reoperation occurs in only about 10% of patients with aortic pericardial valves at 12 years. Nonetheless, earlier failure can occur and constant vigilance and careful follow-up examinations are essential. Fortunately, surgery for bioprosthetic valve failure can usually be performed on an elective basis at low risk in contrast to the high-risk emergency surgery required for catastrophic mechanical valve failure.

XIII. Discharge Planning

A. As the length of hospital stay continues to decrease, appropriate discharge planning is essential to ensure a smooth convalescence after hospital discharge. Patients requiring additional subacute care may be transferred to rehabilitation hospitals or skilled nursing facilities for several days before going home. Even when patients are well enough to be cared for at home, it is not uncommon for separation anxiety to develop, with both patients and family members experiencing difficulty handling minor problems.

B. Appropriate discharge planning should involve the patient, family members, dietitians, nurses, and physicians. Patients must be given explicit instructions as to how they will feel, how fast they should anticipate recovery, what they must do, what they should look for, and when to contact the hospital. Several manuals are available that discuss expectations and the reestablishment of standard routines at home. Phone contact from the doctor's office is very beneficial in allaying patient's fears, answering routine questions, and dealing appropriately with potential problems.

C. Most patients should have an available family member or friend at home for the first week after discharge. This provides reassurance for the patient who may not yet be able to care for him- or herself, and it also provides an objective observer who is able to contact the hospital if serious problems arise.

D. **Medications.** The patient should be provided with a list and schedule of all medications. The reason each medication has been prescribed as well as possible side effects and interactions with other medications should be discussed. If the patient is receiving an anticoagulant such as **warfarin, it** is absolutely imperative that follow-up be arranged for prothrombin times and regulation of drug dosage. The adverse influence of alcohol and other medications on the level of anticoagulation must be emphasized (see Appendix 7, page 457).

E. **Prophylactic antibiotics.** Any patient who has received prosthetic material (valves or grafts) must be aware of the necessity of prophylactic antibiotics if dental work or other surgical procedures are contemplated. Patients should be told to inform their physician or dentist accordingly and follow the AHA guidelines for antibiotic prophylaxis delineated on page 399.[75]

F. **Diet.** Dietitians should meet with patients before discharge to discuss the particular dietary restrictions for their cardiac disease. This entails discussions of the significance of low cholesterol or low salt diets and the provision of appropriate dietary plans. Too few patients with hypercholesterolemia are being treated with HMG CoA reductase agents ("statins") after surgery, despite a plethora of evidence that they can prevent the progression of disease.[146]

G. The patient must participate in self-evaluation at home. A daily assessment of pulse rate, oral temperature, and weight should be performed, and all incisions should be inspected for redness, tenderness, or drainage. Patients should be instructed to contact their physician's office if any abnormalities are noted.

H. Patients should be encouraged to gradually increase their activity as tolerated. For patients with a median sternotomy incision, lifting of objects weighing more than 10 pounds should be discouraged because it puts strain on the healing sternum. Driving should be avoided for 4–6 weeks. In contrast, there are few physical limitations on patients who have small thoracotomy incisions for minimally invasive surgery.

References

1. The Society of Thoracic Surgeons. Data Analyses of The Society of Thoracic Surgeons National Cardiac Surgery Database, January 1996. Summit Medical Systems, 1996. (see also www.STS.org website)
2. Pien FD, Ho PWL, Fergusson DJG. Fever and infection after cardiac operation. Ann Thorac Surg 1982;33:382–4.
3. Curtis JJ, Nawarawong W, Walls JT, et al. Elevated hemidiaphragm after cardiac operations: incidence, prognosis, and relationship to the use of topical ice slush. Ann Thorac Surg 1989;48:764–8.
4. Dimopoulou I, Daganou M, Dafni U, et al. Phrenic nerve dysfunction after cardiac operations. Electrophysiologic evaluation of risk factors. Chest 1998;113:8–14.
5. Yamazaki K, Kato H, Tsujimoto S, Kitamura R. Diabetes mellitus, internal thoracic artery grafting, and the risk of an elevated hemidiaphragm after coronary artery bypass surgery. J Cardiothorac Vasc Anesthesia 1994;8:437–40.
6. Cohen AJ, Katz MG, Katz R, Mayerfeld D, Hauptman E, Schachner A. Phrenic nerve injury after coronary artery grafting; is it always benign? Ann Thorac Surg 1997; 64:148–53.
7. Graham DR, Kaplan D, Evans CC, Hind CRK, Donnelly RJ. Diaphragmatic plication for unilateral diaphragmatic paralysis: a 10-year experience. Ann Thorac Surg 1990;49:248–52.
8. Gullinov AM, Davis EA, Alberg AJ, Rykiel M, Gardner TJ, Cameron DE. Pulmonary embolism in the cardiac surgical patient. Ann Thorac Surg 1992;53:988–91.
9. Hanson EC, Levine FH. Hyperlipoproteinemia as a significant risk factor for pulmonary embolism in patients undergoing coronary artery bypass grafting. Ann Thorac Surg 1982;33:593–8.
10. DeLaria GA, Hunter JA. Deep venous thrombosis. Implications after open heart surgery. Chest 1991;99:284–8.
11. Di Lello F, Werner PH, Kleinman LH, Mullen DC, Flemma RJ. Life-threatening chylothorax after left internal mammary artery dissection: therapeutic considerations. Ann Thorac Surg 1987;44:660–1.
12. Hashimoto K, Ilstrup DM, Schaff HV. Influence of clinical and hemodynamic variables on risk of supraventricular tachycardia after coronary artery bypass. J Thorac Cardiovasc Surg 1991;101:56–65.
13. Rubin DA, Nieminski KE, Reed GE, Herman MV. Predictors, prevention, and long-term prognosis of atrial fibrillation after coronary artery bypass graft operations. J Thorac Cardiovasc Surg 1987;94:331–5.
14. Andrews TC, Reimold SC, Berlin JA, Antman EM. Prevention of supraventricular arrhythmias after coronary artery bypass surgery. A meta-analysis of randomized controlled trials. Circulation 1991;84(suppl 3):III-236–44.
15. Roffman JA, Fieldman A. Digoxin and propranolol in the prophylaxis of supraventricular tachydysrhythmias after coronary artery bypass surgery. Ann Thorac Surg 1981;31:496–501.
16. Fanning WJ, Thomas CS Jr, Roach A, Tomichek R, Alford WC, Stoney WS Jr. Prophylaxis of atrial fibrillation with magnesium sulfate after coronary artery bypass grafting. Ann Thorac Surg 1991;52:529–33.
17. Taylor GJ, Malik SA, Colliver JA, et al. Usefulness of atrial fibrillation as a predictor of stroke after isolated coronary artery bypass grafting. Am J Card 1987;60:905–7.
18. Ellenbogen KA, Dias VC, Plumb VJ, Heywood JT, Mirvis DM. A placebo-controlled trial of continuous intravenous diltiazem infusion for 24-hour heart rate control during atrial fibrillation and atrial flutter: a multicenter study. J Am Coll Cardiol 1991; 18:891–7.

19. Stoddard MF, Dawkins PR, Prince CR, Ammash NM. Left atrial appendage thrombus is not uncommon in patients with acute atrial fibrillation and a recent embolic event: a transesophageal echocardiographic study. J Am Coll Cardiol 1995;25:452–9.

20. Black IW, Fatkin D, Sagar KB, et al. Exclusion of atrial thrombus by transesophageal echocardiography does not preclude embolism after cardioversion of atrial fibrillation. A multicenter study. Circulation 1994;89:2509–13.

21. Harjai KJ, Mobarek SK, Cheirif J, Boulos LM, Murgo JP, Abi-Samra F. Clinical variables affecting recovery of left atrial mechanical function after cardioversion from atrial fibrillation. J Am Coll Cardiol 1997;30:481–6.

22. Rubin DA, Nieminski KE, Monteferrante JC, Magee T, Reed GE, Herman MV. Ventricular arrhythmias after coronary artery bypass graft surgery: incidence, risk factors, and long-term prognosis. J Am Coll Cardiol 1985;6:307–10.

23. Caspi J, Amar R, Elami A, Safadi, T, Merin G. Frequency and significance of complete atrioventricular block after coronary artery bypass grafting. Am J Cardiol 1989;63:526–9.

24. Baerman JM, Kirsh MM, de Buitleir M, et al. Natural history and determinants of conduction defects following coronary artery bypass surgery. Ann Thorac Surg 1987;44:150–3.

25. Stein PD, Dalen JE, Goldman S, Schwartz L, Theroux P, Turpie AGG. Antithrombotic therapy in patients with saphenous vein and internal mammary artery grafts. Chest 1995;108(suppl):425S–30S.

26. Olsen CO, Dunton RF, Maggs PR, Lahey SJ. Review of coronary-subclavian steal following internal mammary artery-coronary artery bypass surgery. Ann Thorac Surg 1988;46:675–8.

27. Kimmelstiel CD, Udelson JE, Salem DN, Bojar R, Rastegar H, Konstam MA. Recurrent angina caused by a left internal mammary artery-to-pulmonary artery fistula. Am Heart J 1993;125:234–6.

28. D'Cruz IA, Overton DH, Pai GM. Pericardial complications of cardiac surgery: emphasis on the diagnostic role of echocardiography. J Cardiac Surg 1992;7:257–68.

29. Pandian NG, Brockway B, Simonetti J, Rosenfield K, Bojar RM, Cleveland RJ. Pericardiocentesis under two-dimensional echocardiographic guidance in loculated pericardial effusion. Ann Thorac Surg 1988;45:99–100.

30. Susini G, Pepi M, Sisillo E, et al. Percutaneous pericardiocentesis versus subxiphoid pericardiotomy in cardiac tamponade due to postoperative pericardial effusion. J Cardiothorac Vasc Anesthesia 1993;7:178–83.

31. Horneffer PJ, Miller RH, Pearson TA, Rykiel MF, Reitz BA, Gardner TJ. The effective treatment of postpericardiotomy syndrome after cardiac operations. A randomized placebo-controlled trial. J Thorac Cardiovasc Surg 1990;100:292–6.

32. Khan AH. The postcardiac surgery syndromes. Clin Cardiol 1992;15:67–72.

33. Cimino JJ, Kogan AD. Constrictive pericarditis after cardiac surgery. Report of three cases and review of the literature. Am Heart J 1989;118:1292–1301.

34. Zerr KJ, Furnary AP, Grunkemeier GL, Bookin S, Kanhere V, Starr A. Glucose control lowers the risk of wound infection in diabetics after open heart operations. Ann Thorac Surg 1997;63:356–61.

35. Del Campo C, Lukman H, Mehta H, McKenzie FN. Iron therapy after cardiac operation: one prescription less? J Thorac Cardiovasc Surg 1982;84:631–3.

36. Waters D, Azar RR. Low-molecular-weight heparins for unstable angina. A better mousetrap? Circulation 1997;96:3–5.

37. Brieger DB, Mak KH, Kottke-Marchant K, Topol EJ. Heparin-induced thrombocytopenia. J Am Coll Cardiol 1998;31:1449–59.

38. Shorten GD, Comunale ME. Heparin-induced thrombocytopenia. J Cardiothorac Vasc Anesthesia 1996;10:521–30.

39. Wall JT, Curtis JJ, Silver D, Boley TM, Schmaltz TA, Naarawong W. Heparin-induced thrombocytopenia in open heart surgical patients: sequelae of late recognition. Ann Thorac Surg 1992;53:787–91.

40. Warkentin TE, Levine MN, Hirsh J, et al. Heparin-induced thrombocytopenia in patients treated with low-molecular-weight heparin or unfractionated heparin. N Engl J Med 1995;332:1330–5.

41. Hirsh J, Raschke R, Warkentin TE, Dalen JE, Deykin D, Poller L. Heparin: mechanism of action, pharmacokinetics, monitoring, efficacy, and safety. Chest 1995;108: 258S–75S.

42. van der Meer J, Brutel A, de la Riviere AB, et al. Effects of low dose aspirin (50 mg/day), low dose aspirin plus dipyridamole, and oral anticoagulant agents after internal mammary artery bypass grafting: patency and clinical outcome at 1 year. J Am Coll Cardiol 1994;24:1181–8.

43. Stein PD, Alpert JS, Dalen JE, Horstkotte D, Turpie AGG. Antithrombotic therapy in patients with mechanical and biological prosthetic heart valves. Chest 1998;114: 602S–610S.

44. Heras M, Chesebro JH, Fuster V, et al. High risk of early thromboemboli after bio-prosthetic cardiac valve replacement. J Am Coll Cardiol 1995;25:1111–9.

45. Blair KL, Hatton AC, White WD, et al. Comparison of anticoagulation regimens after Carpentier-Edwards aortic or mitral valve replacement. Circulation 1994;90(part 2): II-214–9.

46. Orszulak TA, Schaff HV, Mullany CJ, et al. Risk of thromboembolism with the aortic Carpentier-Edwards bioprosthesis. Ann Thorac Surg 1995;59:462–8.

47. Meschengieser SS, Fondevila CG, Frontoth J, Santarelli MT, Lazzari MA. Low-intensity oral anticoagulation plus low-dose aspirin versus high-intensity oral antico-agulation alone: a randomized trial in patients with mechanical heart valves. J Thorac Cardiovasc Surg 1997;113:910–6.

48. Pouleur H, Buyse M. Effects of dipyridamole in combination with anticoagulant therapy on survival and thromboembolic events in patients with prosthetic heart valves. J Thorac Cardiovasc Surg 1995;110:463–72.

49. Turpie AGG, Gent M, Laupacis A, et al. A comparison of aspirin with placebo in patients treated with warfarin after heart-valve replacement. N Engl J Med 1993;329: 524–9.

50. Hirsh J, Dalen JE, Deykin D, Poller L, Bussey H. Oral anticoagulants. Mechanism of action, clinical effectiveness, and optimal therapeutic range. Chest 1995;108(suppl) 231S–46S.

51. Maki DG, Bohn MJ, Stolz SM, et al. Comparative study of cefazolin, cefamandole, and vancomycin for surgical prophylaxis in cardiac and vascular operations. J Thorac Cardiovasc Surg 1992;104:1423–34.

52. Kreter B, Woods M. Antibiotic prophylaxis for cardiothoracic operations. Metaanaly-sis of thirty years of clinical trials. J Thorac Cardiovasc Surg 1992;104:590–9.

53. Niederhäuser U, Vogt M, Vogt P, Genoni M, Künzli A, Turina MI. Cardiac surgery in a high-risk group of patients: is prolonged postoperative antibiotic prophylaxis effec-tive? J Thorac Cardiovasc Surg 1997;114:162–8.

54. Kollef MH, Sharpless L, Vlasnik J, Pasque C, Murphy D, Fraser VJ. The impact of noso-comial infections on patient outcome following cardiac surgery. Chest 1997;112: 666–75.

55. Rebollo MH, Bernal JM, Llorca J, Rabasa JM, Revuelta JM. Nosocomial infections in patients having cardiovascular operations: a multivariate analysis of risk factors. J Thorac Cardiovasc Surg 1996;112:908–13.

56. DeRiso AJ II, Ladowski JS, Dillon TA, Justice JW, Peterson AC. Chlorhexidine gluconate 0.12% oral rinse reduces the incidence of total nosocomial respiratory infection and nonprophylactic systemic antibiotic use in patients undergoing heart surgery. Chest 1996;109:1556–61.

57. Ulicny KS Jr, Hiratzka LF. The risk factors of median sternotomy infection: a current review. J Cardiac Surg 1991;6:338–51.

58. Zacharias A, Habib RH. Factors predisposing to median sternotomy complications. Deep vs superficial infection. Chest 1996;110:1173–8.

59. The Parisian Mediastinitis Study Group. Risk factors for deep sternal infection after sternotomy: a prospective, multicenter study. J Thorac Cardiovasc Surg 1996;111: 1200–7.

60. Loop FD, Lytle BW, Cosgrove DM, et al. Sternal wound complications after isolated coronary artery bypass grafting: early and late mortality, morbidity, and cost of care. Ann Thorac Surg 1990;49:179–87.

61. Newman LS, Szczukowski LC, Bain RP, Perlino CA. Suppurative mediastinitis after open heart surgery. A case control study of risk factors. Chest 1988;94:546–53.

62. Ottino G, De Paulis R, Pansini S, et al. Major sternal wound infection after open-heart surgery: a multivariate analysis of risk factors in 2579 consecutive operative procedures. Ann Thorac Surg 1987;44:173–9.

63. Demmy TL, Park SB, Liebler GA, et al. Recent experience with major sternal wound complications. Ann Thorac Surg 1990;49:458–62.

64. Grossi EA, Culliford AT, Krieger KH, et al. A survey of 77 major infectious complications of median sternotomy: a review of 7949 consecutive operative procedures. Ann Thorac Surg 1985;40:214–23.

65. El Oakley RM, Wright JE. Postoperative mediastinitis: classification and management. Ann Thorac Surg 1996;61:1030–6.

66. Kohman LJ, Coleman MJ, Parker FB Jr. Bacteremia and sternal infection after coronary artery bypass grafting. Ann Thorac Surg 1990;49:454–7.

67. Kay HR, Goodman LR, Teplick SK, Mundth ED. Use of computed tomography to assess mediastinal complications after median sternotomy. Ann Thorac Surg 1983;36: 706–14.

68. Browdie DA, Bernstein RW, Agnew R, Damle A, Fischer M, Balz J. Diagnosis of post-sternotomy infection: comparison of three means of assessment. Ann Thorac Surg 1991;51:290–2.

69. Krabatsch T, Hetzer R. Poststernotomy mediastinitis treated by transposition of the greater omentum. J Card Surg 1995;10:637–43.

70. Jeevanandam V, Smith CR, Rose EA, Malm JA, Hugo NE. Single-stage management of sternal wound infections. J Thorac Cardiovasc Surg 1990;99:256–63.

71. Nahai F, Rand R, Hester R, Bostwick J, Jurkiewicz M. Primary treatment of infected sternotomy wound with muscle flaps: a review of 211 consecutive cases. Plast Reconstr Surg 1989;84:434–41.

72. Cartier R, Diaz OS, Carrier M, Leclerc Y, Castonguay Y, Leung TK. Right ventricular rupture. A complication of postoperative mediastinitis. J Thorac Cardiovasc Surg 1993;106:1036–9.

73. Utley JR, Thomason ME, Wallace DJ, et al. Preoperative correlates of impaired wound healing after saphenous vein excision. J Thorac Cardiovasc Surg 1989;89:147–9.

74. Delaria GA, Hunter JA, Goldin MD, Serry C, Javid H, Najafi H. Leg wound complications associated with coronary revascularization. J Thorac Cardiovasc Surg 1981;81:403–7.

75. Dajani AS, Taubert KA, Wilson W, et al. Prevention of bacterial endocarditis. Recommendations by the American Heart Association. JAMA 1997;277:1794–1801 and Circulation 1997;96:358–66.

76. Mentec H, Vignon P, Terré S, et al. Frequency of bacteremia associated with trans-esophageal echocardiography in intensive care unit patients: a prospective study of 139 patients. Crit Care Med 1995;23:1194–9.

77. McKhann GM, Goldsborough MA, Borowicz LM Jr, et al. Predictors of stroke risk in coronary artery bypass patients. Ann Thorac Surg 1997;63:516–21.

78. Mickelborough LL, Walker PM, Takagi Y, Ohashi M, Ivanov J, Tamariz M. Risk factors for stroke in patients undergoing coronary artery bypass grafting. J Thorac Cardiovasc Surg 1996;112:1250–9.

79. Tuman KJ, McCarthy RJ, Najafi H, Ivankovich AD. Differential effects of advanced age on neurologic and cardiac risks of coronary artery operations. J Thorac Cardiovasc Surg 1992;104:1510–7.

80. Lynn GM, Stefanko K, Reed JF III, Gee W, Nicholas G. Risk factors for stroke after coronary artery bypass. J Thorac Cardiovasc Surg 1992;104:1518–23.

81. Rao V, Christakis GT, Weisel RD, et al. Risk factors for stroke following coronary bypass surgery. J Card Surg 1995;10:468–74.

82. Cernaianu AC, Vassilidze TV, Flum DR, et al. Predictors of stroke after cardiac surgery. J Card Surg 1995;10:334–9.

83. Redmond JM, Greene PS, Goldsborough MA, et al. Neurologic injury in cardiac sur-gical patients with a history of stroke. Ann Thorac Surg 1996;61:42–7.

84. Newman MF, Wolman R, Kanchuger M, et al. Multicenter preoperative stroke risk index for patients undergoing coronary artery bypass graft surgery. Circulation 1996;94(suppl II):II-74–80.

85. Hartman GS, Yao FSF, Bruefach M III, et al. Severity of aortic atheromatous disease diagnosed by transesophageal echocardiography predicts stroke and other outcomes associated with coronary artery surgery: a prospective study. Anesth Analg 1996;83:701–8.

86. Guyton RA, Mellitt RJ, Weintraub WS. A critical assessment of neurological risk during warm heart surgery. J Card Surg 1995;10:488–92.

87. Clark RE, Brillman J, Davis DA, Lovell MR, Price TRP, Magovern GJ. Microemboli during coronary artery bypass grafting. Genesis and effect on outcome. J Thorac Cardiovasc Surg 1995;109:249–58.

88. Shapira OM, Kimmel WA, Lindsey PS, Shahian DM. Anterior ischemic optic neu-ropathy after open heart operations. Ann Thorac Surg 1996;61:660–6.

89. Rizzo RJ, Whittemore AD, Couper GS, et al. Combined carotid and coronary revas-cularization: the preferred approach to the severe vasculopath. Ann Thorac Surg 1992;54:1099–109.

90. Akins CW, Moncure AC, Daggett WM, et al. Safety and efficacy of concomitant carotid and coronary operations. Ann Thorac Surg 1995;60:311–8.

91. Hertzer NR, Loop FD, Beven EG, O'Hara PJ, Krajewski LP. Surgical staging for simul-taneous coronary and carotid disease: a study including prospective randomization. J Vasc Surg 1989;9:455–63.

92. Chang BB, Darling RC III, Shah DM, Paty PSK, Leather RP. Carotid endarterec-tomy can be safely performed with acceptable mortality and morbidity in patients requiring coronary artery bypass grafts. Am J Surg 1994;168:94–101.

93. Daily PO, Freeman RK, Dembitsky WP, et al. Cost reduction by combined carotid endarterectomy and coronary artery bypass grafting. J Thorac Cardiovasc Surg 1996;111:1185–93.

94. Brener BJ, Brief DK, Alpert J, Goldenkranz RJ, Parsonnet V. The risk of stroke in patients with asymptomatic carotid stenosis undergoing cardiac surgery: a follow-up study. J Vasc Surg 1987;5:269–79.

95. D'Agostino RS, Svensson LG, Neuman DJ, Balkhy HH, Williamson WA. Screening

carotid ultrasonography and risk factors for stroke in coronary artery surgery patients. Ann Thorac Surg 1996;62:1714–23.

96. Wareing TH, Davila-Roman VG, Barzilai B, Murphy SF, Kouchoukos NT. Management of the severely atherosclerotic ascending aorta during cardiac operations. A strategy for detection and treatment. J Thorac Cardiovasc Surg 1992;103:453–62.

97. Aranki SR, Sullivan TE, Cohn LH. The effect of the single aortic cross-clamp technique on cardiac and cerebral complications during coronary bypass surgery. J Card Surg 1995;10:498–502.

98. Blauth CI, Smith PL, Arnold JV, Jagoe JR, Wootton R, Taylor KM. Influence of oxygenator type on the prevalence and extent of microembolic retinal ischemia during cardiopulmonary bypass. Assessment by digital image analysis. J Thorac Cardiovasc Surg 1990;99:61–9.

99. Arom KV, Cohen DE, Strobl FT. Effect of intraoperative intervention on neurological outcome based on electroencephalographic monitoring during cardiopulmonary bypass. Ann Thorac Surg 1989;48:476–83.

100. Smith LW, Dimsdale JE. Postcardiotomy delirium: conclusions after 25 years. Am J Psychiatry 1989;146:452–8.

101. Tesar G, Murray G, Cassem NH. Use of high dose intravenous haloperidol in the treatment of agitated cardiac patients. J Clin Psychopharmacol 1983;5:344–7.

102. Breheny FX. Reversal of midazolam sedation with flumazenil. Crit Care Med 1992;20:736–9.

103. McKhann GM, Goldsborough MA, Borowicz LM Jr, et al. Cognitive outcome after coronary artery bypass: a one-year prospective study. Ann Thorac Surg 1997;63: 510–5.

104. Borowicz LM, Goldsborough MA, Selnes OA, McKhann GM. Neuropsychologic change after cardiac surgery: a critical review. J Cardiothorac Vasc Anesthesia 1996;10:105–12.

105. Gill R, Murkin JM. Neuropsychologic dysfunction after cardiac surgery: what is the problem? J Cardiothorac Vasc Anesthesia 1996;10:91–8.

106. Regragui I, Birdi I, Izzat MB, et al. The effects of cardiopulmonary bypass temperature on neuropsychologic outcome after coronary artery operations: a prospective randomized trial. J Thorac Cardiovasc Surg 1996;112:1036–45.

107. Hails KC, Fink PJ. Psychiatric problems after open heart surgery. In: Kotler MN, Alfieri A, eds. Cardiac and noncardiac complications of open heart surgery: prevention, diagnosis, and treatment. Mount Kisco, NY: Futura Publishing, 1992:299–309.

108. Hund EF, Fogel W, Krieger D, DeGeorgia M, Hacke W. Critical illness polyneuropathy: clinical findings and outcomes of a frequent cause of neuromuscular weaning failure. Crit Care Med 1996;24:1328–33.

109. Alhan HC, Cakalagaoglu C, Hanci M, et al. Critical-illness polyneuropathy complicating cardiac operation. Ann Thorac Surg 1996;61:1237–9.

110. Vander Salm TJ, Cereda JM, Cutler BS. Brachial plexus injury following median sternotomy. J Thorac Cardiovasc Surg 1980;80:447–52.

111. Vahl CF, Carl I, Müller-Vahl H, Struck E. Brachial plexus injury after cardiac surgery. The role of internal mammary artery preparation: a prospective study on 1000 consecutive patients. J Thorac Cardiovasc Surg 1991;102:724–9.

112. Phillips TG, Green GE. Left recurrent laryngeal nerve injury following internal mammary artery bypass. Ann Thorac Surg 1987;43:440.

113. Baue AE. The role of the gut in the development of multiple organ dysfunction in cardiothoracic patients. Ann Thorac Surg 1993;55:822–9.

114. Tsiotos GG, Mullany CJ, Zietlow S, van Heerden JA. Abdominal complications following cardiac surgery. Am J Surg 1994;167:553–7.

115. Ott MJ, Buchman TG, Baumgartner WA. Postoperative abdominal complications in

cardiopulmonary bypass patients: a case-controlled study. Ann Thorac Surg 1995;59: 1210–3.

116. Christenson JT, Schmuziger M, Maurice J, Simonet F, Velebit V. Gastrointestinal complications after coronary artery bypass grafting. J Thorac Cardiovasc Surg 1994;108:899–906.

117. Perugini RA, Orr RK, Porter D, Dumas EM, Maini BS. Gastrointestinal complications following cardiac surgery. An analysis of 1477 cardiac surgery patients. Arch Surg 1997;132:352–7.

118. Spotnitz WD, Sanders RP, Hanks JB, et al. General surgical complications can be predicted after cardiopulmonary bypass. Ann Surg 1995;221:489–97.

119. Mercado PD, Farid H, O'Connell TX, Sintek CF, Pfeffer T, Khonsari S. Gastrointestinal complications associated with cardiopulmonary bypass procedures. Am J Surg 1994;60:789–92.

120. Cook DJ, Fuller HD, Guyatt GH, et al. Risk factors for gastrointestinal bleeding in critically ill patients. N Engl J Med 1994;330:377–81.

121. Rosen HR, Vlahakes GJ, Rattner DW. Fulminant peptic ulcer disease in cardiac surgical patients: pathogenesis, prevention, and management. Crit Care Med 1992;20:354–9.

122. Eggleston JM, Pearson RC, Holland J, Tooth JA, Vohra A, Doran BH. Prospective endoscopic study of stress erosions and ulcers in critically ill adult patients treated with sucralfate or placebo. Crit Care Med 1994;22:1949–54.

123. Apte NM, Karnad DR, Medhekar TP, Tilve G, Morye S, Bhave GG. Gastric colonization and pneumonia in intubated critically ill patients receiving stress ulcer prophylaxis: a randomized, controlled trial. Crit Care Med 1992;20:590–3.

124. Cook D, Guyatt G, Marshall J, et al. A comparison of sucralfate and ranitidine for the prevention of upper gastrointestinal bleeding in patients requiring mechanical ventilation. N Engl J Med 1998;338:791–7.

125. Phillips JO, Metzler MH, Palmieri TL, Huckfeldt RE, Dahl NG. A prospective study of simplified omeprazole suspension for the prophylaxis of stress-related mucosal damage. Crit Care Med 1996;24:1793–1800.

126. Rovers JP, Souney PF. A critical review of continuous infusion H_2 receptor therapy. Crit Care Med 1989;17:814–21.

127. Shuman RB, Schuster DP, Zuckerman GR. Prophylactic therapy for stress ulcer bleeding: a reappraisal. Ann Int Med 1987;106:562–7.

128. Khuroo MS, Yattoo GN, Javid G, et al. A comparison of omeprazole and placebo for bleeding peptic ulcer. N Engl J Med 1997;336:1054–8.

129. Laine L. Multipolar electrocoagulation versus injection therapy in the treatment of bleeding peptic ulcers. A prospective, randomized trial. Gastroenterology 1990;99: 1303–6.

130. Cappell MS, Lebwohl O. Cessation of recurrent bleeding from gastrointestinal angiodysplasias after aortic valve replacement. Ann Int Med 1986;105:54–7.

131. Allen KB, Salam AA, Lumsden AB. Acute mesenteric ischemia after cardiopulmonary bypass. J Vasc Surg 1992;16:391–6.

132. Kaleya RN, Sammartano RJ, Boley SJ. Aggressive approach to acute mesenteric ischemia. Surg Clin N Am 1992;72:157–82.

133. Wang MJ, Chao A, Huang CH, et al. Hyperbilirubinemia after cardiac operation. Incidence, risk factors, and clinical significance. J Thorac Cardiovasc Surg 1994;108: 429–36.

134. Collins JD, Ferner R, Murray A, et al. Incidence and prognostic importance of jaundice after cardiopulmonary bypass surgery. Lancet 1983;1:1119–23.

135. Chu CM, Chang CH, Liaw YF, Hsieh MJR. Jaundice after open-heart surgery: a prospective study. Thorax 1984;39:52–6.

136. Riordan SM, Williams R. Treatment of hepatic encephalopathy. N Engl J Med 1997;337:473–9.
137. Rattner DW, Gu ZY, Vlahakes GJ, Warshaw AL. Hyperamylasemia after cardiac surgery. Incidence, significance, and management. Ann Surg 1989;209:279–83.
138. Svensson LG, Decker G, Kinsley RB. A prospective study of hyperamylasemia and pancreatitis after cardiopulmonary bypass. Ann Thorac Surg 1985;39:409–11.
139. Haas GS, Warshaw AL, Daggett WM, Aretz HT. Acute pancreatitis after cardiopulmonary bypass. Am J Surg 1985;149:508–14.
140. Cerra FB, Benitez MR, Blackburn GL, et al. Applied nutrition in ICU patients. A consensus statement of the American College of Chest Physicians. Chest 1997; 111:769–78.
141. Akins CW. Results with mechanical cardiac valvular prosthesis. Ann Thorac Surg 1995;60:1836–44.
142. Deviri E, Sareli P, Wisenbaugh T, Cronje SL. Obstruction of mechanical heart valve prostheses: clinical aspects and surgical management. J Am Coll Cardiol 1991; 17:646–50.
143. Lengyel M, Fuster V, Keltai M, et al. Guidelines for management of left-sided prosthetic valve thrombosis: a role for thrombolytic therapy. J Am Coll Cardiol 1997;30:1521–6.
144. Ginsberg JS, Hirsh J. Use of antithrombotic agents during pregnancy. Chest 1995; 108(suppl):305S–311S.
145. Vlessis AA, Khaki A, Grunkemeier GL, Li HH, Starr A. Risk, diagnosis, and management of prosthetic valve endocarditis: a review. J Heart Valve Dis 1997;6:443–65.
146. The Post Coronary Artery Bypass Graft Trial investigators. The effect of aggressive lowering of low-density lipoprotein cholesterol levels and low-dose anticoagulation on obstructive changes in saphenous-vein coronary-artery bypass grafts. N Engl J Med 1997;336:1153–62.

13 Cardiac Transplantation

13   Cardiac Transplantation

Cardiac transplantation has become a well-accepted therapeutic modality for the patient with end-stage heart disease. Refinement of donor criteria and care, recipient selection, immunosuppressive therapy, diagnosis and treatment of rejection, and an improved understanding of long-term complications have widened the applicability of transplantation and improved long-term results. Current expectations are for an 80% 1-year survival rate with a subsequent mortality rate of 4% per year.[1]

I.   Preoperative Considerations

A. **Indications for surgery**[2] (figure 13.1)

1. Class IV heart failure and poor systolic function (usually EF < 20%) secondary to a dilated or ischemic cardiomyopathy or end-stage valvular disease; these patients have a 1-year life expectancy of less than 50%.

2. Class III heart failure with impairment of exercise tolerance (VO_2 max < 14 mL/kg/min)

3. Intractable angina with nonbypassable coronary artery disease

4. Refractory life-threatening ventricular arrhythmias

B. **Preoperative preparation**

1. Identification of absolute and relative contraindications to transplantation is critical to achieving satisfactory results (table 13.1).[2,3]

2. Preservation of end-organ function is important to minimize the perioperative risk of transplantation. Aggressive use of inotropic medications (milrinone, dobutamine) and even mechanical support with the intraaortic balloon pump (IABP) or circulatory assist devices (usually the HeartMate, Novacor, or Thoratec systems) may be required for prolonged periods of time before a donor heart becomes available. These devices may allow for improvement in organ system function before transplantation. Preservation of hepatic and especially renal function is important before transplantation. Renal function is particularly sensitive to perioperative insults, including cardiopulmonary bypass and the use of cyclosporine A (CyA) for immunosuppression.

3. The severity of pulmonary hypertension is a major determinant of postoperative right ventricular dysfunction and mortality.[4] Reversibility should be assessed with pulmonary vasodilators (prostaglandin, nitric oxide) during right heart catheterization.[5,6] Serial catheterizations may be necessary during the waiting period to determine whether the patient remains a candidate for transplantation. A PVR > 4 Wood units or a transpulmonary gradient (TPG = mean PA pressure minus pulmonary capillary wedge pressure) exceeding 15 mm Hg with poor response to vasodilators raises the surgical risk significantly.

4. The patient's serum is crossmatched against a random panel of lymphocytes (panel-reactive antibody screen or PRA). When a donor heart becomes available, a lymphocytotoxic crossmatch (LXM) of

A

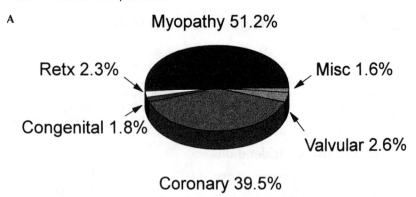

Myopathy 51.2%

Retx 2.3%

Misc 1.6%

Congenital 1.8%

Valvular 2.6%

Coronary 39.5%

B

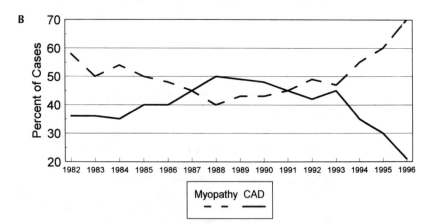

Figure 13.1 (A) Indications for heart transplantation 1982–1996. (B) Cardiomyopathy is currently the most common indication for transplantation. (Reprinted with permission from Hosenspud JD, Bennett LE, Keck BM, Fiol B, Novick RJ. The Registry of the International Society for Heart and Lung Transplantation: Fourteenth Official Report—1997. J Heart Lung Transplant 1997;16:691–712.)

the donor's cells with the patient's serum is performed if the PRA exceeds 20%. Transplantation is generally contraindicated if the LXM is strongly positive, although there is little evidence that a positive LXM is associated with hyperacute rejection. A high PRA and positive LXM are, however, associated with an increased risk of death from acute and chronic rejection.[7]

5. If a donor heart becomes available, any recently acquired contraindication to transplantation, such as infection, must be identified.

C. **Donor considerations**

1. Lack of donor availability is the primary reason for the limited number of cardiac transplants performed (table 13.2). Therefore, it

Table 13.1   *Contraindications to Cardiac Transplantation*

Absolute Contraindications
ABO incompatibility
Fixed pulmonary hypertension with a PVR >6 Wood units
Active systemic infection including positive HIV status and
    hepatitis C
Active malignancy (cured or controlled acceptable)
Systemic disease limiting life expectancy
Irreversible renal or hepatic dysfunction
Severe chronic obstructive pulmonary disease (FEV$_1$ <1 liter)
Diabetes mellitus with end-organ damage
Acute psychiatric illness
Active drug addiction or alcoholism

Relative Contraindications
Age >70 years
Pulmonary hypertension with PVR 3–6 after vasodilators
Moderate chronic obstructive lung disease
Recent pulmonary embolism or infarction
Active peptic ulcer disease
Severe cerebrovascular or peripheral vascular disease
Psychosocial instability
Morbid obesity
Disease likely to recur in graft (amyloid, sarcoid)

is imperative that optimal care be provided to increase the number of "acceptable" donor hearts.[8,9] To accomplish this, some of the traditional contraindications have been relaxed, with acceptance of suboptimal hearts for high status patients. In some cases, valve repair or bypass grafting has been performed on the donor heart.

2. Brain death is accompanied initially by changes in sympathetic tone caused by an increase in intracranial pressure. Transient hypotension is followed by hypertension and tachycardia. Hypothalamic failure leads to diabetes insipidus, causing hypovolemia and electrolyte imbalance. Of much concern is the depletion of high-energy phosphate stores in the myocardium and a depletion of circulating free thyroxine, cortisol, insulin, and vasopressin.

Table 13.2   *Contraindications to Heart Donation*

Major chest trauma
Known cardiac disease
Acute or chronic infection
Prolonged cardiac arrest
HIV positivity or risk factors
Hepatitis B or C positivity
Systemic malignancy

3. Careful monitoring of intravascular pressures is necessary to determine whether fluids, α- or β-agents are indicated to support systemic blood pressure. Use of an "endocrine cocktail" including methylprednisolone (15 μg/kg), insulin (1 U/h), vasopressin (1 U bolus, then 1.5 U/h), and triiodothyronine (4 μg bolus, then 3 μg/h) has been shown to reverse impaired ventricular function to improve donor acceptability.[9,10]

4. Coronary angiography is generally indicated in male donors over age 40 and females over the age of 45. Impaired survival after transplantation is noted with hearts from female donors and those over age 40.[1]

II. Intraoperative Considerations

A. Anesthetic considerations[11]

1. Severely impaired ventricular function is present in nearly all transplant recipients and requires judicious monitoring and pharmacologic management. Narcotic-based anesthesia is used to minimize additional myocardial depression. Most patients have been receiving diuretics, unloading agents, and/or inotropic medications to reduce pulmonary congestion from congestive heart failure. Fluid status is monitored intraoperatively with a central venous pressure (CVP) line, rather than a Swan-Ganz catheter. The central line is inserted through the left internal jugular vein, saving the right side for access for subsequent endomyocardial biopsies.

2. Renal function should be supported during bypass with mannitol, dopamine, and/or furosemide. Cyclosporine is usually withheld until the first or second postoperative day to minimize its impact on renal function.

3. Many recipients are maintained on therapeutic anticoagulation (warfarin) while awaiting transplantation. Aprotinin is routinely used for bleeding prophylaxis. In anticoagulated patients, multiple clotting factor transfusions may be required (fresh frozen plasma, cryoprecipitate) to achieve satisfactory hemostasis at the conclusion of surgery. Cytomegalovirus (CMV) negative recipients must receive packed cells and platelets given through a leukodepletion filter.

4. Preoperative immunosuppressive therapy is not given routinely. Methylprednisolone 500 mg IV and azathioprine 4 mg/kg IV are given after removal of the aortic crossclamp. Giving steroids before bypass may reduce the inflammatory response associated with bypass and might reduce the incidence of rejection.[12] Cyclosporine is started on the first or second postoperative day, orally if possible (8 mg/kg/day in two divided doses). If the patient is still NPO, it is given as a continuous IV infusion of 2 mg/kg/day. If the patient has a creatinine greater than 2.0 mg/dL, OKT3 may be substituted for cyclosporine.

5. Careful coordination between the donor and recipient teams is essential to minimize the ischemic time of the donor heart. Considerations include the number of donor organs being harvested,

the transport time, and the time required for dissection in the recipient, especially when there has been a previous sternotomy incision.

B. **The donor harvest**

1. A preliminary dissection is carried out to inspect the heart for evidence of a cardiac contusion, coronary artery disease, or congenital anomalies such as a left superior vena cava (SVC). Both pleural spaces are opened for inspection of the lungs if lung donation is being considered.

2. During a multiorgan harvest, the abdominal dissection is completed and, after systemic heparinization, the abdominal aorta and inferior vena cava are cannulated.

3. The superior and inferior vena cava (IVC) are clamped, and several beats later, the aorta is crossclamped and cardioplegia is delivered. University of Wisconsin (UW) solution is commonly used and provides excellent preservation.[13] The IVC and inferior pulmonary vein (or the left atrial appendage in cases of bilateral lung harvests) are incised to decompress the heart.

4. The heart is then excised, preserving as much SVC and IVC as possible. The pulmonary veins are divided, preserving a 1 cm cuff of atrium if the lungs are harvested. The aorta is divided just proximal to the crossclamp. The distal main pulmonary artery is divided if the lungs are harvested; otherwise, the individual pulmonary arteries may be divided.

5. The heart is packed in several bags with cold solutions (saline, UW) for transport.

C. **Recipient operation**

1. Once the donor heart is found to be satisfactory, the recipient is placed on cardiopulmonary bypass (CPB) and the diseased heart is excised. A long cuff of SVC and as much low right atrium as possible near the IVC are left with resection of the rest of the right atrium so that bicaval anastomoses can be performed. The great vessels are incised just above the semilunar valves. The left atrium is trimmed to approximate the size of the donor atrium.

2. The traditional technique of orthotopic transplantation involved two atrial suture lines as well as the aortic and pulmonary artery anastomoses. The technique of bicaval anastomoses has supplanted this technique (figure 13.2).[14] An alternative procedure involves two pulmonary venous anastomoses instead of the left atrial one.[15]

III. Early Postoperative Care

A. **Hemodynamic management**

1. The donor heart frequently manifests myocardial dysfunction as the result of a prolonged period of ischemia or reperfusion injury.[16] Right ventricular dysfunction with tricuspid regurgitation is often

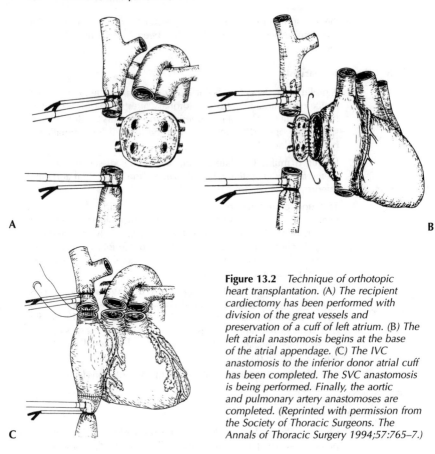

A

B

C

Figure 13.2 *Technique of orthotopic heart transplantation. (A) The recipient cardiectomy has been performed with division of the great vessels and preservation of a cuff of left atrium. (B) The left atrial anastomosis begins at the base of the atrial appendage. (C) The IVC anastomosis to the inferior donor atrial cuff has been completed. The SVC anastomosis is being performed. Finally, the aortic and pulmonary artery anastomoses are completed. (Reprinted with permission from the Society of Thoracic Surgeons. The Annals of Thoracic Surgery 1994;57:765–7.)*

noted in patients with significant pulmonary hypertension or a pre-operative TPG exceeding 12–15 mm Hg. Isoproterenol is started in the operating room to provide inotropy, an increase in heart rate, a reduction in pulmonary vascular resistance (PVR), and an improvement in ventricular diastolic relaxation. If significant pulmonary hypertension is present, inotropes (such as amrinone or milrinone) or pulmonary vasodilators (including nitric oxide, nitroglycerin, and prostaglandin E_1) may be beneficial.[17,18] A Swan-Ganz catheter should be inserted if left or right ventricular dysfunction is present and requires more aggressive management. If inotropic support is inadequate, consideration should be given to use of an IABP or even a circulatory assist device.

2. The use of blood products is a major contributing factor to increased PVR and right ventricular dysfunction, and measures should be taken to minimize intraoperative blood loss (i.e., use of aprotinin).

3. The use of bicaval anastomoses has been associated with preserved atrial systole, lower right atrial pressure, improved cardiac output, less tricuspid regurgitation, and fewer atrial arrhythmias than the standard biatrial procedure.[19–21]

4. Sinus node dysfunction is common after transplantation. The heart rate should be maintained around 100 beats/min after surgery with use of isoproterenol or epicardial pacing wires. The heart does not respond to atropine because of cardiac denervation. Aminophylline or theophylline is frequently beneficial in patients with bradycardia.[22] It may take weeks for the sinus node to resume normal function, and implantation of a permanent pacemaker should generally be delayed for at least 4 weeks.[23]

B. Renal function

1. Perioperative rise in serum creatinine is commonly noted in patients with preoperative renal dysfunction, pulmonary hypertension, or low cardiac output states. Improved myocardial performance from better protection and avoidance of pre- and intraoperative cyclosporine should minimize the renal insult.

2. Use of mannitol, low-dose dopamine, and diuretics is frequently beneficial intraoperatively and in the early postoperative course to maintain urine output and eliminate fluid overload.

3. The initiation of cyclosporine is best deferred until POD #1–2. There is less renal toxicity associated with oral dosing than intravenous infusions. It is preferable to use lower dose CyA than OKT3 when potentially reversible renal dysfunction is noted because of the long-term adverse effects of OKT3. The latter is best reserved for the treatment of severe rejection. If the creatinine rises during CyA therapy and does not respond to lowering of the dose, it may be elected to stop the CyA and use a brief course of OKT3.

4. For patients with significant renal dysfunction, long-term therapy with alternative immunosuppressive drugs such as FK506 (tacrolimus) may be considered.

C. Pulmonary function

1. Patients with significant pulmonary congestion may require several days of mechanical ventilatory support until excess pulmonary extravascular water has been eliminated. The requirement for preoperative ventilatory support increases the operative mortality rate after heart transplantation.[1]

2. Reactive pulmonary hypertension gradually resolves after surgery, but it can, in combination with fluid overload and positive pressure ventilation, exacerbate right ventricular dysfunction. Inotropic support with medications such as amrinone or milrinone, as well as use of potent diuretics, may be required.

D. Immunosuppression

1. Lifelong immunosuppression is required to prevent acute rejection of the transplanted heart. Most protocols include cyclosporine, steroids, and azathioprine ("triple drug therapy"). The protocol

Table 13.3 *Cardiac Transplant Immunosuppression Protocol*

	Cyclosporine	Steroids	Azathioprine
Operation	none	Methylprednisolone 500 mg IV in OR	4 mg/kg IV
POD #1	2 mg/kg/day IV	Methylprednisolone 125 mg IV q8h	2 mg/kg IV qd
POD #2	3 mg/kg PO bid*	Prednisone 0.5 mg/kg PO bid	2 mg/kg PO qd
POD #3		Prednisone 0.5 mg/kg PO bid	
POD #4		Decrease total daily dose by 10 mg	
POD #5		qod until 30 mg qd is reached	
	▼	▼	▼

* Adjusted for blood levels and serum creatinine.

used at New England Medical Center is shown in table 13.3. The most common side effects of the immunosuppressive medications are listed in table 13.4.

2.   **Cyclosporine** may be given initially as a continuous intravenous infusion (2 mg/kg/day). When the patient is taking PO, an oral dose of cyclosporine is given and the IV infusion is stopped immediately. The total daily dose is usually 3 times the IV total daily dose. Cyclosporine dosing is adjusted according to blood levels and renal function. Of the two cyclosporine oral preparations, Neoral (Novartis) results in 24% greater cyclosporine exposure with a similar trough level compared with Sandimmune (Sandoz) and may provide better immunosuppression.[24]

    a.   Measuring a CyA level immediately after a dosing change will not reflect that dose adequately because it takes 2.5 half-lives (more than 2 days) to achieve a steady-state blood

Table 13.4 *Major Side Effects of Immunosuppressive Medications*

Cyclosporine	Steroids	Azathioprine	OKT3
Hypertension	Cushing's syndrome	Bone marrow	Fever and chills
Nephrotoxicity	Glucose intolerance	depression	Dyspnea and
Hepatotoxicity	Osteoporosis	Hepatotoxicity	wheezing
Cholelithiasis	Myopathy	Pancreatitis	Flushing
Neurotoxicity	Cataracts	Cholestatic	Headache
Gingival hyperplasia	Aseptic necrosis	jaundice	GI disturbances
Hirsutism	Hyperlipidemia		Tremors and seizures
Lymphoma	Peptic ulcer		Malaise
	Mental status		Noncardiogenic
	changes		pulmonary edema
			Lymphoma

level. The desirable blood level during the first postoperative month is 320–450 ng/mL.

   b. There are numerous medications that may alter the blood concentration of cyclosporine. Drugs that increase levels are beneficial in that lower doses of CyA can be given, with a significant cost saving. These include diltiazem, ketoconazole,[25] cimetidine, erythromycin, and amphotericin B. In contrast, drugs that decrease CyA levels include phenobarbital and phenytoin (Dilantin).

3. **Prednisone** is usually tapered to a maintenance dose of 20 mg qd after 1 month and to 10 mg qd after 90 days. In some centers, approximately 90% of patients can be weaned completely off steroids within 1 year.

4. **Azathioprine** is given in a dose of 2 mg/kg PO and is monitored by WBC counts. The dosage must be adjusted when the absolute neutrophil count falls below 2000. An alternative to azathioprine is mycophenolate mofetil when the neutrophil count remains low.

5. **OKT3** can be used as an alternative to cyclosporine in the patient with significant renal dysfunction. It is started postoperatively at a dose of 5 mg qd and given for a 7–14 day course, during which time the dose of steroids is lowered significantly. Cyclosporine is initiated and the prednisone dose increased just before terminating OKT3 therapy to ensure adequate immunosuppression.[26] OKT3 is more commonly used for the treatment of rejection refractory to high-dose steroids.

6. **FK506 (tacrolimus)** is a macrolide antibiotic that inhibits T-cell activation. It provides comparable, if not slightly better, immunosuppression than cyclosporine, with fewer rejection episodes and a lower risk of infection. It is diabetogenic and neurotoxic, but is associated with less hypertension and nephrotoxicity. It has been used primarily for patients in whom rejection persists with use of CyA or in whom progressive nephrotoxicity has developed. The usual dose is 0.15–0.3 mg/kg/day in two divided doses.[27–29]

7. **Mycophenolate mofetil** (Cellcept) is a lymphocyte-specific inhibitor of purine synthesis that inhibits T and B lymphocyte proliferation. It may be used as a substitute for azathioprine for chronic immunosuppressive maintenance when neutropenia is present. However, it has other advantages as well. It may reduce vascular rejection and the incidence of allograft coronary artery disease, it is effective in reversing acute rejection, and it may reduce the incidence of B-cell lymphomas because it inhibits EBV-driven lymphocyte proliferation. In patients with CyA-induced nephropathy, it may be substituted for azathioprine and allows for a reduction in CyA dosing.[30] The usual dose is 1 g PO bid.[31,32]

E. **Rejection**

1. Endomyocardial biopsies to screen for acute rejection are performed one week following transplantation, and then weekly or biweekly for the first 2 months, depending on biopsy results. They are then performed at less frequent intervals. Clinical signs of rejec-

tion are infrequent with use of cyclosporine, but the occurrence of persistent bradyarrhythmias or a low output syndrome should prompt an earlier biopsy.[33] Atrial arrhythmias are fairly common after transplantation in the absence of rejection.[34]

2. Histologic grading for acute cardiac rejection

Level	Degree	Description
0	No rejection	Normal
1	Mild	Perivascular lymphocytic infiltrate
2	Mild	Interstitial extension of lymphocytic infiltrate without myocyte necrosis
3	Moderate	Focal interstitial lymphocytic infiltrate with 1–3 foci of myocyte necrosis
4	Moderate-severe	Interstitial lymphocytic infiltrate with necrosis, multifocal or one or more extensive areas
5	Severe	Widespread or diffuse lymphocytic infiltrate with necrosis, and granulocytes (polymorphonuclear leukocytes or eosinophils) and/or vascular injury (edema, hemorrhage or vasculitis)

3. Treatment of rejection
   a. Grade 1 rejection usually does not require treatment.
   b. Grades 2–3 rejection are usually treated on an inpatient basis with methylprednisolone 1 g IV qd × 3 days, then a prednisone taper starting at 1 mg/kg qd. Later development of grades 2–3 rejection may be treated on an outpatient basis with an oral prednisone pulse 100 mg in divided doses PO qd × 3 days, with the dosage decreased by 10 mg/day to a maintenance dose of 30 mg/day.
   c. Grades 4–5 rejection are treated with a course of intravenous steroids as noted. If there are any hemodynamic alterations, a course of OKT3 may also be considered.
   d. Any patient with grades 3–5 rejection should have an assessment of ventricular function.

F. **Infection in the perioperative period**
   1. The patient is most susceptible to infection in the early postoperative period when high-dose immunosuppression is used. Individuals in contact with the patient should wash their hands, but more rigorous isolation procedures are not required. A 48-hour course of perioperative prophylactic antibiotics is used.
   2. The status of the donor and recipient should be reviewed for cytomegalovirus (CMV) and toxoplasmosis (toxo) titers, because these diseases can be transmitted with the donor heart.

3. Cytomegalovirus

   a. Regardless of donor or recipient CMV status, leukodepleted blood is used for all patients.

   b. If the donor is CMV negative and the recipient is CMV negative, no prophylaxis for CMV is required. If **the recipient or the donor is CMV positive**, ganciclovir is given starting immediately after surgery (5 mg/kg IV bid adjusted for renal function) and then converted to 1 g tid when the patient is taking PO, and continued for 100 days.

   c. If the recipient is CMV negative, but the donor is CMV positive, CMV immune globulin intravenous should be given according to the following schedule:

Within 72 hours of transplant	150 mg/kg
2 weeks after transplant	100 mg/kg
4 weeks after transplant	100 mg/kg
6 weeks after transplant	100 mg/kg
8 weeks after transplant	100 mg/kg

4. If the donor is toxoplasmosis positive and the recipient is negative, the recipient should be given pyrimethamine 25 mg qd and folinic acid 6 mg qd for 6 weeks.

5. Nystatin suspension or clotrimazole troches qd are given for 4–6 weeks to prevent oral candidiasis.

6. Sulfamethoxazole-trimethoprim (Bactrim) 1 tablet PO bid 3 times/week × 1 year is used to prevent infection with *Pneumocystis carinii*.

IV. Postoperative Complications

A. Infection

1. The transplant recipient is at greatest risk for infection not only during the early postoperative course, but also during periods of augmented immunosuppression for treatment of rejection. Infections are more common in older patients; in those on ventilatory support or assist devices before transplantation; when OKT3 is used for induction; and when the donor is black, female, or CMV positive.[35] Bacterial and viral infections predominate, although fungal (*Candida*) and protozoan (*P. carinii*, *Toxoplasma gondii*) infections are noted in about 10% of patients. Aggressive evaluation of fevers, rising WBC counts, and abnormal chest x-rays is imperative. Evidence of headaches, mental status changes, and abdominal pain should also prompt investigation for potential infection.

2. Fever, dyspnea, a nonproductive cough, or an infiltrate requires immediate evaluation for suspected pneumonia. Chest x-rays are not routinely obtained unless pneumonia is suspected. However, radiographic changes of pneumonitis may precede clinical symptoms. Other tests may include sputum, transtracheal, transbronchoscopic, or percutaneous aspirates to make the appropriate diagnosis.

3. Cytomegalovirus infection is very common in patients who have undergone cardiac transplantation, and it can produce substantial morbidity. CMV may produce a flu-like syndrome, pneumonitis, enteritis, or hepatitis, and it may also increase the risk of rejection and accelerate the development of allograft coronary disease. Prophylactic therapy as noted above as well as rapid diagnosis with polymerase chain reactions and treatment of clinical syndromes with ganciclovir may reduce the mortality associated with CMV-related disease.

4. Primary Epstein-Barr infections occur in about 5% of seronegative patients receiving seropositive donor hearts, while reactivation of a past infection is noted in 15–20% of seropositive patients. Although mild symptoms are present in nearly half of these patients (sore throat, fever, headache, malaise), some may develop lymphoproliferative diseases and lymphoma (see below).[36]

B. **Rejection.** The risk of acute rejection is greatest during the first 3 months after transplantation, following which there is a low, but constant rate of rejection. Most patients are maintained on cyclosporine and azathioprine with low doses of steroids, but many can be weaned completely off steroids. Risk factors for late recurrent rejection within the first year include younger age, female donor or recipient, positive CMV status, prior infections, and induction with OKT3. After the first year, recurrent rejection is more common in patients with a history of CMV infection or multiple rejections during the first year.[37] Endomyocardial biopsies are performed at increasingly greater intervals during the first year, and are then performed on a yearly basis. Depending on the status of ventricular function, rejection may be treated with intensification of the steroid dosage or use of OKT3 or antithymocyte globulin. FK506, lymphoid irradiation, or methotrexate may be necessary for refractory rejection.[29,38]

C. **Systemic hypertension** develops in about 75% of transplant recipients treated with cyclosporine. It results from altered vascular reactivity caused by cyclosporine as well as by fluid retention from steroids.[39] The calcium-channel blockers and ACE inhibitors are very effective in controlling hypertension and reducing the development of left ventricular hypertrophy. ACE inhibitors must be used cautiously because of the renal dysfunction that generally accompanies the use of cyclosporine. Diltiazem is the preferred oral antihypertensive agent for two reasons: it raises the cyclosporine level so that less CyA can be given, which is cost-effective, and secondly, it has been associated with a lower incidence of allograft coronary artery disease.[40]

D. **Hyperlipidemia** results from the effects of cyclosporine and steroids on hepatic lipoprotein metabolism. It may contribute to allograft coronary artery disease. Reduction in the steroid dosage and use of one of the "statins" will lower lipid levels. These medications have a favorable effect on reducing mortality from allograft coronary artery disease.[41,42]

E. **Allograft coronary artery disease** (CAD) appears to be an inevitable consequence of cardiac transplantation and is felt to be a manifestation of chronic rejection. Approximately 50% of patients will develop graft CAD within 5 years of transplantation. Contributory factors include CMV infection, an increased number of early rejection episodes, older donor age, and possibly elevated lipid levels.[43,44] Because angina does not develop during myocardial ischemia in the denervated heart, patients may present with congestive heart failure from silent myocardial infarctions or they may experience an episode of sudden death. Dobutamine stress echocardiography is very sensitive in diagnosing coronary disease in transplant recipients.[45] As noted above, use of diltiazem as an antihypertensive agent or one of the "statins" may reduce the risk of developing allograft CAD.[40–42] Due to the diffuse nature of allograft CAD, the most effective treatment is retransplantation. Graft vasculopathy is the most common cause of late death following cardiac transplantation.[46]

F. **Nephrotoxicity** is one of the major side effects of cyclosporine and develops on the basis of renovascular ischemia. In patients with a preoperative elevation of serum creatinine (>1.5–2.0 mg/dL), lower doses of CyA should be used. A postoperative rise in creatinine usually responds to a reduction in the cyclosporine dose. OKT3 can be used in the early postoperative period if the creatinine is quite elevated or rises sharply and does not improve with lowering of the cyclosporine dose. A progressive increase in serum creatinine levels may require a lower dose of cyclosporine and augmentation of steroid and azathioprine doses. Alternative immunosupression may involve substitution of FK506 (tacrolimus) for CyA or conversion of azathioprine to mycophenolate mofetil to allow for lowering of the CyA dose.[30]

G. **Malignancies** develop in about 15% of cardiac transplant recipients and are the second most common cause of late death following transplantation.[47] Cutaneous neoplasms are most common, followed by non-Hodgkin's lymphomas and lung cancer. Lymphoproliferative disorders are usually noted in patients who have received high-dose immunosuppression or high doses of OKT3. One study showed that the incidence was higher in patients receiving more than 75 mg of OKT3, and another found it to be higher in patients who were given OKT3 for treatment of rejection, all of whom also received it for 14 days for induction.[48,49] B-cell lymphomas are more common in patients who were seronegative for the Epstein-Barr virus before surgery.[49] Treatment consists of lowering of the immunosuppressive doses and possibly use of acyclovir or ganciclovir.

H. **Dermatologic complications** are very common after transplantation and include skin tumors, viral infections (predominantly herpetic), and drug-related changes, such as striae, acne, and hypertrichosis.

I. **Gastrointestinal problems** develop in 15–20% of transplant recipients and may be associated with significant mortality. Some complications result from the influence of surgical stress on preexisting problems (gastritis, GI tract ulceration and perforation); some are precipitated by the state of immunosuppression (diverticulitis, CMV enteritis or pancreatitis); and some are caused by the immunosuppressive medications (pancreatitis, jaundice, cholelithiasis, GI tract ulceration or bleeding, bowel perforation). Clinical suspicion must be high because the diagnosis may be obscured by the lack of systemic symptoms and local inflammatory signs in patients receiving steroids. In patients with known gallstones or those in whom they develop after surgery, urgent laparoscopic cholecystectomy has been recommended to avoid biliary tract complications.[50]

J. **Osteopenic bone disease** is noted in nearly all patients receiving steroids, although it is most severe in recipients older than age 60. It can be minimized by regular exercise and calcium and vitamin D supplements. Alendronate sodium (Fosamax) 10 mg qd can also be considered.

K. **Muscle deconditioning** is counteracted by physical therapy, frequent ambulation in the hallways, and use of an exercise bicycle.

L. **Psychological problems.** Many patients undergoing transplantation have troubled psychosocial backgrounds and a careful assessment of the ability of the patient and family to cope with the transplant experience is imperative. Many patients experience anxiety, depression, withdrawal, and personality disorders in the early postoperative period that require psychiatric intervention.

References

1. Hosenspud JD, Bennett LE, Keck BM, Fiol B, Novick RJ. The Registry of the International Society for Heart and Lung Transplantation: fourteenth Official Report—1997. J Heart Lung Transplant 1997;16:691–712.

2. Blum A, Aravot D. Heart transplantation—an update. Clin Cardiol 1996;19:930–8.

3. Torre-Amione G, Kapadia S, Short D III, Young JB. Evolving concepts regarding selection of patients for cardiac transplantation. Assessing risks and benefits. Chest 1996;109:223–32.

4. Kormos RL, Thompson M, Hardesty RL, et al. Utility of preoperative right heart catheterization data as a predictor of survival after heart transplantation. J Heart Transplant 1986;5:391–3.

5. Chen JM, Levin HR, Michler RE, Prusmack CJ, Rose EA, Aaronson KD. Reevaluating the significance of pulmonary hypertension before cardiac transplantation: determination of optimal thresholds and quantification of the effect of reversibility on perioperative mortality. J Thorac Cardiovasc Surg 1997;114:627–34.

6. Adatia I, Perry S, Landzberg M, Moore P, Thompson JE, Wessel DL. Inhaled nitric oxide and hemodynamic evaluation of patients with pulmonary hypertension before transplantation. J Am Coll Cardiol 1995;25:1656–64.

7. Loh E, Bergin JD, Couper GS, Mudge GH Jr. Role of panel-reactive antibody cross-reactivity in predicting survival after orthotopic heart transplantation. J Heart Lung Transplant 1994;13:194–201.

8. Hunt SA, Baldwin J, Baumgartner W, et al. Cardiovascular management of a potential heart donor: a statement from the transplantation committee of the American College of Cardiology. Crit Care Med 1996;24:1599–1601.

9. Wheeldon DR, Potter CDO, Oduro A, Wallwork J, Large SR. Transforming the "unacceptable" donor: outcomes from the adoption of a standardized donor management technique. J Heart Lung Transplant 1995;14:734–42.

10. Votapka TV, Canvasser DA, Pennington DG, Koga M, Swartz MT. Effect of triiodothyronine on graft function in a model of heart transplantation. Ann Thorac Surg 1996;62:78–82.

11. Clark NJ, Martin RD. Anesthetic considerations for patients undergoing cardiac transplantation. J Cardiothorac Anesthesia 1988;2:519–42.

12. Wan S, DeSmet JM, Antoine M, Goldman M, Vincent JL, LeClerc JL. Steroid administration in heart and heart-lung transplantation: is the timing adequate? Ann Thorac Surg 1996;61:674–8.

13. Drinkwater DC Jr, Ziv ET, Laks H, et al. Extracellular and standard University of Wisconsin solutions provide equivalent preservation of myocardial function. J Thorac Cardiovasc Surg 1995;110:738–45.

14. Sarsam MAI, Campbell CS, Yonan NA, Deiraniya AK, Rahman AN. An alternative surgical technique in orthotopic cardiac transplantation. J Cardiac Surg 1993; 8:344–9.

15. Blanche C, Valenza M, Czer LSC, et al. Orthotopic heart transplantation with bicaval and pulmonary venous anastomoses. Ann Thorac Surg 1994;58:1505–9.

16. Stein KL, Darby JM, Grenvik A. Intensive care of the cardiac transplant recipient. J Cardiothorac Anesthesia 1988;2:543–53.

17. Auler JOC Jr, Carmona MJC, Bocchi EA, et al. Low doses of inhaled nitric oxide in heart transplant recipients. J Heart Lung Transplant 1996;15:443–50.

18. Kieler-Jensen N, Lundin S, Ricksten SE. Vasodilator therapy after heart transplantation: effects of inhaled nitric oxide and intravenous prostacyclin, prostaglandin E$_1$, and sodium nitroprusside. J Heart Lung Transplant 1995;14:436–43.

19. Deleuze PH, Benvenuti C, Mazzucotelli JP, et al. Orthotopic cardiac transplantation with direct caval anastomosis: is it the optimal procedure? J Thorac Cardiovasc Surg 1995;109:731–7.

20. El Gamel A, Yonan NA, Grant S, et al. Orthotopic cardiac transplantation: a comparison of standard and bicaval Wythenshawe techniques. J Thorac Cardiovasc Surg 1995;109:721–30.

21. El Gamel A, Deiraniya AK, Rahman AN, Campbell CS, Yonan NA. Orthotopic heart transplantation: does atrial preservation improve cardiac output after transplantation? J Heart Lung Transplant 1996;15:564–71.

22. Bertolet BD, Eagle DA, Conti JB, Mills RM Jr., Belardinelli L. Bradycardia after heart transplantation: reversal with theophylline. J Am Coll Cardiol 1996;28:396–9.

23. Scott CD, Dark JH, McComb JM. Sinus node dysfunction after cardiac transplantation. J Am Coll Cardiol 1994;24:1334–41.

24. White M, Pelletier GB, Tan A, Jesina C, Carrier M. Pharmacokinetic, hemodynamic, and metabolic effects of cyclosporine. Sandimmune versus the microemulsion Neoral in heart transplant recipients. J Heart Lung Transplant 1997;16:787–94.

25. Keogh A, Spratt P, McCosker C, Macdonald P, Mundy J, Kaan A. Ketoconazole to reduce the need for cyclosporine after cardiac transplantation. N Engl J Med 1995; 333:628–33.

26. Starnes VA, Oyer PE, Stinson EB, Dein JR, Shumway NE. Prophylactic OKT3 used as induction therapy for heart transplantation. Circulation 1989(suppl 3):III-79–83.

27. Pham SM, Kormos RL, Hattler BG, et al. A prospective trial of tacrolimus (FK506) in clinical heart transplantation: intermediate-term results. J Thorac Cardiovasc Surg 1996;111:764–72.

28. Rinaldi M, Pellegrini C, Martinelli L, et al. FK506 effectiveness in reducing acute rejection after heart transplantation: a prospective randomized study. J Heart Lung Transplant 1997;16:1001–10.

29. Meiser BM, Uberfuhr P, Fuchs A, et al. Tacrolimus: a superior agent to OKT3 for treating cases of persistent rejection after intrathoracic transplantation. J Heart Lung Transplant 1997;16:795–800.

30. Mallinger R, Grimm M, Zuckermann A, et al. Benefit of mycophenolate mofetil (MMF) in cardiac transplant recipients with cyclosporine (CyA) induced nephropathy. J Heart Lung Transplant 1998;17:71.

31. Humiston DJ, Taylor DO, Kfoury AG, Renlund DG. Mycophenolate mofetil: history and introduction into clinical heart transplantation. CVE 1997;2:198–203.

32. Taylor DO, Ensley RD, Olsen SL, Dunn D, Renlund DG. Mycophenolate mofetil (RS-61443): preclinical, clinical, and three-year experience in heart transplantation. J Heart Lung Transplant 1994;13:571–82.

33. Blanche C, Czer LCS, Fishbein MC, Takkenberg JJM, Trento A. Permanent pacemaker for rejection episodes after heart transplantation: a poor prognostic sign. Ann Thorac Surg 1995;60:1263–6.

34. Pavri BB, O'Nunain SS, Newell JB, Ruskin JN, Dec GW. Prevalence and prognostic significance of atrial arrhythmias after orthotopic cardiac transplantation. J Am Coll Cardiol 1995;25:1673–80.

35. Smart FW, Naftel DC, Costanzo MR, et al. Risk factors for early, cumulative, and fatal infections after heart transplantation: a multiinstitutional study. J Heart Lung Transplant 1996;15:329–41.

36. Gray J, Wreghitt TG, Pavel P, et al. Epstein-Barr virus infection in heart and heart-lung transplant recipients: incidence and clinical impact. J Heart Lung Transplant 1995;14: 640–6.

37. Kubo SH, Naftel DC, Mills RM Jr, et al. Risk factors for late recurrent rejection after heart transplantation: a multiinstitutional, multivariable analysis. J Heart Lung Transplant 1995;14:409–18.

38. Ferraro P, Carrier M, White M, Pelletier GB, Pelletier LC. Antithymocyte globulin and methotrexate therapy of severe or persistent cardiac allograft rejection. Ann Thorac Surg 1995;60:372–6.

39. Textor SC, Canzanello VJ, Taler SJ, et al. Cyclosporine-induced hypertension after transplantation. Mayo Clin Proc 1994;69:1182–93.

40. Schroeder JS, Gao SZ, Alderman EL, et al. A preliminary study of diltiazem in the prevention of coronary artery in heart-transplant recipients. N Engl J Med 1993;328: 164–70.

41. Kobashigawa JA, Katznelson S, Laks H, et al. Effect of pravastatin on outcomes after cardiac transplantation. N Engl J Med 1995;333:621–7.

42. Wenke K, Meiser B, Thiery J, et al. Simvastatin reduces graft vessel disease and mortality after heart transplantation. A four-year randomized trial. Circulation 1997;96: 1398–402.

43. McGiffin DC, Savunen T, Kirklin JK, et al. Cardiac transplant coronary artery disease. A multivariable analysis of pretransplantation risk factors for disease development and morbid events. J Thorac Cardiovasc Surg 1995;109:1081–9.

44. Weis M, von Scheidt W. Cardiac allograft vasculopathy. A review. Circulation 1997;96:2069–77.

45. Akosah KO, Mohanty PK. Role of dobutamine stress echocardiography in heart transplant patients. Chest 1998;113:809–15.

46. Gallo P, Agozzino L, Angelini A, et al. Cause of late failure after heart transplantation: a ten-year survey. J Heart Lung Transplant 1997;16:1113–21.

47. Pham SM, Kormos RL, Landreneau RJ, et al. Solid tumors after heart transplantation: lethality of lung cancer. Ann Thorac Surg 1995;60:1623–6.

48. Swinnen LJ, Costanzo-Nordin MR, Fisher SG, et al. Increased incidence of lymphoproliferative disorder after immunosuppression with the monoclonal antibody OKT3 in cardiac-transplant recipients. N Engl J Med 1990;323:1723–8.

49. Walker RC, Paya CV, Marshall WF, et al. Pretransplantation seronegative Epstein-Barr virus status is the primary risk factor for posttransplantation lymphoproliferative disorder in adult heart, lung, and other solid organ transplantations. J Heart Lung Transplant 1995;14:214–21.

50. Peterseim DS, Pappas TN, Meyers CH, Shaeffer GS, Meyers WC, Van Trigt P. Management of biliary complications after heart transplantation. J Heart Lung Transplant 1995;15:623–31.

Part 1 Appendices

Appendix 1   Doses of Parenteral Medications Commonly Used in the ICU and Their Modifications in Renal Failure

Drug Class	Usual Dosage	Route of Elimination[a]	Adjustment in Moderate Renal Failure
Analgesics			
Fentanyl	50–100 µg IV → 50–200 µg/h	H[b]	no change
Ketorolac	30–60 mg IV q6h (×72 hours)	R[c]	reduce
Meperidine	50–100 mg IM q3h	H	use with caution
Morphine	2–10 mg IV/IM q2–4h	H	no change
Antianginals			
Esmolol	0.25–0.5 mg/kg IV → 0.05–0.2 mg/kg/min IV	M[d]	no change
Propranolol	1–5 mg IV q2–4h	H	no change
Metoprolol	5 mg IV q5 min × 3	H	no change
Antiarrhythmics (see also Table 10.13, page 313)			
Bretylium	5 mg/kg IV → 2 mg/min	R	reduce
Digoxin	0.125–0.25 mg IV qd	R	reduce
Lidocaine	1 mg/kg IV → 1–4 mg/min	H	no change
Procainamide	10 mg/kg IV → 1–4 mg/min	R > H	reduce
Antibiotics (prophylactic doses)			
Cefamandole	1 g IV q4–6h	R	reduce
Cefazolin	0.5–1.0 g IV q8h	R	reduce
Ceftriaxone	1 g IV q24h	R	reduce
Vancomycin	1 g IV q8–12h	R	reduce
Antihypertensives (see Table 10.7, page 265)			
Diuretics			
Acetazolamide (Diamox)	250–500 mg IV q6h	R	use with caution
Bumetanide	1–5 mg IV q12h	R > H	use with caution
Chlorothiazide	500 mg IV qd	R	use with caution
Ethacrynic acid	50–100 mg IV q6h	H > R	use with caution
Furosemide	10–500 mg IV q6h	R > H	use with caution
Inotropic Agents (see Table 10.5, page 231)			
Paralytic Agents (see Table 5.2, page 98)			
Atracurium	0.3 mg/kg IV → 0.2–0.4 mg/kg/h	M	no change
Doxacurium	0.06 mg/kg → 0.005 mg/kg q30 min	R	reduce
Pancuronium (Pavulon)	0.1 mg/kg IV → 0.01 mg/kg q1h or 2–4 mg/h	R > H	no change
Vecuronium	0.1 mg/kg IV → 0.01 mg/kg q30–45 min or 2–6 mg/h	H	no change
Psychotropics/Sedatives			
Diazepam (Valium)	2.5–10 mg IV q2–4h	H	no change
Haloperidol (Haldol)	1–5 mg IM/IV q6h	H	no change

continued

Drug Class	Usual Dosage	Route of Elimination[a]	Adjustment in Moderate Renal Failure
Psychotropics/Sedatives (cont.)			
Lorazepam (Ativan)	1–2 mg IV/2–4 mg IM q6h	H	no change
Midazolam (Versed)	2.5–5 mg IV q1–2h	H	no change
Antacids			
Cimetidine (Tagamet)	300 mg IV q6h or 37.5–50 mg/h	R	reduce
Famotidine (Pepcid)	20 mg IV q12h or 2–4 mg/h	R > M	reduce
Ranitidine (Zantac)	50 mg IV q8h or 6.25 mg/h	R	reduce
Other			
Aminophylline	5 mg/kg IV load → 0.2–0.9 mg/kg/h	H	no change
Enoxaparin (Lovenox)	30 mg SC bid		
Flumazenil	0.2 mg over 30 sec, then 0.3 mg, then 0.5 mg up to 3 mg max/h	H	no change
Metoclopramide (Reglan)	10–20 mg IM/IV qid	R > H	reduce
Naloxone	0.4–2 mg IV	H	no change
Ondansetron (Zofran)	4–8 mg IV q4h × 3 doses	H	no change
Prochlorperazine (Compazine)	5–10 mg IM q4h	H	no change

[a] Medications metabolized by the liver do not require reduction in dosage for renal failure; medications metabolized by the kidneys must be adjusted according to the serum creatinine, or more precisely, by the glomerular filtration rate (GFR). The reader should refer to the Physician's Desk Reference for complete prescribing information and to the summary article by Bennett WM, Arnoff FR, Morrison G, et al. Drug prescribing in renal failure: dosing guidelines for adults. Am J Kidney Diseases 1983; 3:155–76 for complete information on drug adjustment at all levels of renal function.
[b] H = hepatic metabolism
[c] R = renal elimination
[d] M = metabolized in the bloodstream

Appendix 2   Doses of Nonparenteral Medications Commonly Used after Heart Surgery and Their Modifications in Renal Failure

Drug Class	Usual Dosage	Route of Elimination[a]	Adjustment in Moderate Renal Failure[b]
Analgesics			
Acetaminophen	650 mg PO q4h	R[d]	reduce
Hydrocodone[c]	5–10 mg q4–6h (40 mg max/d)	H[e]	no change
Ketorolac (Toradol)	20 mg PO → 10 mg q4–6h	R	reduce
Ibuprofen (Motrin)	400–800 mg PO tid	R	reduce
Oxycodone[c]	4.5 mg PO q6h	H	no change
Tramadol (Ultram)	50–100 mg PO q4–6h	R > H	reduce
Antianginals[b]			
β-blockers			
Atenolol	50–100 mg PO qd	R	reduce
Metoprolol	25–100 mg PO bid	H	no change
Propranolol	10–120 mg PO qid	H	no change
Calcium-channel blockers			
Diltiazem	30–60 mg PO tid	H	no change
Nifedipine	10–30 mg PO/SL tid	H	no change
Verapamil	80–160 mg PO tid	H	no change
Nitrates			
Isosorbide dinitrate	5–40 mg PO qid	H	no change
Isosorbide mononitrate	20 mg PO bid (7h apart)	—	no change
Nitropaste	1–3″ q4h	H	no change
Antiarrhythmics (see Table 10.13, page 313)			
Digoxin	0.125–0.25 mg PO qd	R	reduce
Procainamide	Procan SR 500–1000 mg PO q6h Procanbid 500–1000 mg bid	R > H	reduce
Quinidine gluconate	324–486 mg PO q8h	H > R	no change
Antibiotics			
Cephalexin	500 mg PO qid	R	reduce
Ciprofloxacin	500 mg PO bid	R	reduce

continued

Drug Class	Usual Dosage	Route of Elimination[a]	Adjustment in Moderate Renal Failure[b]
Antidiabetic drugs (oral hypoglycemics)			
Chlorpropamide (Diabinese)	250 mg PO qd	R	avoid
Glipizide (Glucotrol)	5 mg PO qAM	H	no change
Glyburide (Micronase, DiaBeta)	2.5–5.0 mg PO qAM	H = R	use with caution
Metformin (Glucophage)	500 mg bid with meals	R	avoid
Antihypertensives			
Angiotensin-converting enzyme (ACE) inhibitors			
Captopril (Capoten)	6.25–50 mg PO bid	R	avoid
Enalapril (Vasotec)	2.5–5 mg PO qd	R	avoid
Lisinopril (Zestril)	10 mg PO qd	R	avoid
Quinapril (Accupril)	10 mg PO qd	R	avoid
β-Blockers (see also antianginals)			
Labetalol (Trandate, Normodyne)	100–400 mg PO qid	H	no change
Calcium-channel blockers (see also antianginal medications)			
Amlodipine	2.5–10 mg PO qd	H	no change
Isradipine	2.5–5 mg PO bid	R	reduce
Nicardipine	20–40 mg PO tid	H	no change
Clonidine (Catapres)	0.1–0.3 mg PO bid	R	reduce
Doxazosin (Cardura)	1–8 mg PO qd	H	no change
Prazosin (Minipress)	1–7.5 mg PO bid	H	no change
Cholesterol-lowering medications			
Atorvastatin (Lipitor)	10 mg PO qd	H	no change
Fluvastatin (Lescol)	20–40 mg PO qd	H	no change
Lovastatin (Mevacor)	20–40 mg PO qd	H	no change
Pravastatin (Pravachol)	10–20 mg PO qd	H	no change
Simvastatin (Zocor)	5–10 mg PO qd	H	no change

continued

Drug Class	Usual Dosage	Route of Elimination[a]	Adjustment in Moderate Renal Failure[b]
Diuretics			
Acetazolamide (Diamox)	250–500 mg PO qid	R	reduce
Furosemide (Lasix)	10–500 mg PO bid	R > H	no change
Hydrochlorothiazide	50–100 mg PO qd	R	no change
Metolazone (Zaroxolyn)	5–20 mg PO qd	R	no change
Psychotropics/Sedatives			
Alprazolam (Xanax)	0.25–0.5 mg PO tid	H, R	reduce
Buspirone (Buspar)	7.5 mg PO bid	M	no change
Chloral hydrate	500 mg PO HS	H	no change
Chlordiazepoxide (Librium)	5–25 mg PO tid	?	no change
Diphenhydramine (Benadryl)	50 mg PO HS	H	no change
Flurazepam (Dalmane)	15–30 mg PO HS	H	no change
Haloperidol (Haldol)	0.5–2.5 mg PO tid	H	no change
Lorazepam (Ativan)	1–2 mg PO bid or HS	H	no change
Temazepam (Restoril)	15–30 mg PO HS	H	no change
Triazolam (Halcion)	0.125–0.25 mg PO HS	H	no change
Antacids/Antireflux Medications			
H₂ blockers			
Cimetidine (Tagamet)	300 mg PO qid	R	reduce
Famotidine (Pepcid)	20–40 mg PO HS	R > M	reduce
Nizatidine (Axid)	150 mg PO bid or 300 mg HS	R	reduce
Ranitidine (Zantac)	150 mg PO bid	R	reduce
Others			
Cisapride (Propulsid)	20 mg PO qid	H	no change
Misoprostol (Cytotec)	200 µg PO qid	R	reduce
Omeprazole (Prilosec)	20 mg PO qd	H	no change
Sucralfate (Carafate)	1 g PO qid	R	reduce

continued

Drug Class	Usual Dosage	Route of Elimination[a]	Adjustment in Moderate Renal Failure[b]
Other			
Amitriptyline (Elavil)	10–20 mg PO qhs or bid	H	no change
Carbamazepine (Tegretol)	200 mg PO bid	H	no change
Metoclopramide	10–15 mg PO qid	R > H	reduce
Theophylline	300 mg PO bid	H	no change

[a] *Medications metabolized by the liver do not require reduction in dosage for renal failure; medications metabolized by the kidneys must be adjusted according to the serum creatinine, or more precisely, by the glomerular filtration rate (GFR). The reader should refer to the Physician's Desk Reference for complete prescribing information and to the summary article by Bennett WM, Arnoff FR, Morrison G, et al. Drug prescribing in renal failure: dosing guidelines for adults. Am J Kidney Diseases 1983; 3:155–76 for complete information on drug adjustment at all levels of renal function.*

[b] *Antianginal medications given 4 times a day (qid) are usually taken 4 hours apart during the daytime. Other medications should generally be taken at equally spaced intervals.*

[c] *Usually given with acetaminophen, 325 mg (Vicodin or Percocet).*

[d] *R = renal elimination*

[e] *H = hepatic metabolism*

[f] *M = metabolized in bloodstream*

Appendix 3   Low Osmolarity Enteral Tube Feedings Commonly Used in ICU Patients

	Osmolite	Osmolite HN	Jevity	Promote
Calories/mL	1.06	1.06	1.06	1.0
Protein (g/L) (% TC)*	37.2 (14.0%)	44.3 (16.7%)	44.4 (16.7%)	62.4 (25%)
Carbohydrate (g/L)	145.4 (54.6%)	143.9 (53.3%)	151.7 (53.3%)	130 (52%)
Fat (g/L)	38.5 (31.4%)	34.7 (30.0%)	36.9 (30.0%)	26 (23%)
Osmolality (mosm/kg H_2O)	300	300	310	350
Sodium (mEq/L)	27.6	40.4	40.4	40.4
Potassium (mEq/L)	25.9	40	40	50.6
Features	low residue	low residue	provides fiber, contains trace elements	high protein

All solutions contain 100% of U.S. RDA for vitamins and minerals in 1400–2000 calories of solution.
* Percent of total calories derived from this constituent.

Appendix 4   Defined (Elemental) Enteral Tube Feedings

	Alitraq	Vital HN	Peptamen VHP
Calories/mL	1.0	1.0	1.0
Protein (g/L) (% TC)*	52.5 (20.8%)	41.7 (16.7%)	62.4 (24.5%)
Carbohydrate (g/L)	165 (65.4%)	185 (74%)	104.4 (40.1%)
Fat (g/L)	15.5 (13.8%)	10.8 (9.7%)	39.2 (34.6%)
Osmolality (mosm/kg H_2O)	575	500	300
Sodium (mEq/L)	43.5	25	22
Potassium (mEq/L)	30.8	36 fortified with glutamine to improve gut mucosal integrity	32 hi protein (peptides) low CHO isotonic 70:30 MCT:LCT

All solutions contain 100% of U.S. RDA for vitamins and minerals in 1400–2000 calories of solution.
* Percent of total calories derived from this constituent.

Appendix 5   Disease-Specific Enteral Tube Feedings

	Nepro (Renal)	Suplena (Renal)	Pulmocare (Pulmonary)	Two Cal HN (Critical Illness)
Calories/mL	2.0	2.0	1.5	2.0
Protein (g/L) (% TC)*	70 (14%)	30 (6%)	62.6 (16.7%)	83.7 (16.6%)
Carbohydrate (g/L)	215 (43%)	255 (51%)	10.7 (28.1%)	217.3 (43%)
Fat (g/L)	96 (43%)	96 (43%)	92.1 (55.2%)	90.9 (40.4%)
Osmolality (mosm/kg H_2O)	635	615	490	690
Sodium (mEq/L)	36	34	57.0	57
Potassium (mEq/L)	27	29	44.3	62.8
Features	High protein For patients on dialysis	Low protein High CHO For renal failure patients not on dialysis	High fat Reduce CO_2 production	High nitrogen/mL Useful if fluid restriction

All solutions contain 100% of U.S. RDA for vitamins and minerals in 1400–2000 calories of solution.
* Percent of total calories derived from this constituent.

Appendix 6   International Normalized Ratio for Reporting of Prothrombin Times

$$INR = (PT\ ratio)^{ISI}$$

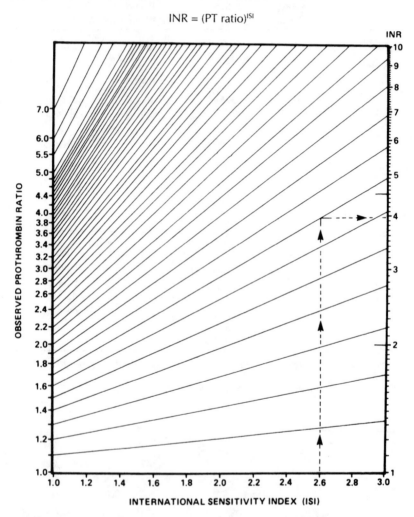

Reproduced with permission from Poller L. A simple nomogram for the derivation of international normalised ratios for the standardisation of prothrombin times. Thromb Haemostasis 1988;60:18–20.

Appendix 7   Commonly Used Drugs That Interact with Warfarin (Coumadin)

Potentiation	Inhibition	No Effect
Acetaminophen	Azathioprine	Alcohol (if no liver disease)
Alcohol (if liver disease)	Barbiturates	Antacids
Amiodarone	Carbamazepine	Atenolol
Anabolic steroids	Chlordiazepoxide	Bumetanide
Chloral hydrate	Cholestyramine	Diltiazem
Cefamandole	Cyclosporine	Famotidine
Cefazolin	Narcillin	Ibuprofen
Cimetidine	Sucralfate	Ketorolac
Clofibrate		Ketoconazole
Erythromycin		Metoprolol
Floxin antibiotics		Nizatidine
Fluconazole		Ranitidine
Isoniazid		Vancomycin
Lovastatin		
Metronidazole		
Omeprazole		
Phenylbutazone		
Phenytoin		
Propranolol		
Quinidine		
Tamoxifen		

Reprinted in part from Hirsh J, Dalen JE, Deykin D, Poller L, Bussey H. Oral anticoagulants. Mechanism of action, clinical effectiveness, and optimal therapeutic range. Chest 1995;108:231S–4S.

Appendix 8   Technique for Tube Thoracostomy

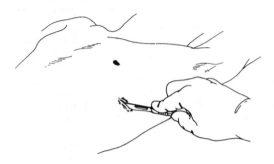

Figure 1   *Skin incision. One percent lidocaine is used for local anesthesia. A subcutaneous wheal is raised over the fifth or sixth intercostal space in the mid-axillary line. The needle is passed to the upper border of the rib and the periosteum is anesthetized. Fluid should be aspirated from an effusion to confirm its location. A 1 cm incision is then made.*

Figure 2   *Pleural entry. The dissection is carried down to and through the intercostal muscles with a Kelly clamp, the parietal pleura is penetrated, and the pleural cavity is entered. Finger dissection should be used only if loculations are known to be present.*

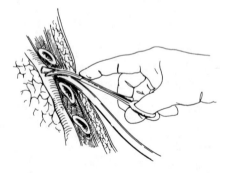

Figure 3   *Chest tube placement. The chest tube is inserted and directed toward the apex for air and posteriorly for fluid. The tube should be clamped during insertion if fluid is being drained. The tube is then secured with a 2-0 silk suture. A trocar can be used as a stent to advance the tube but should never be used to penetrate the pleura.*

Appendix 9   Technique for Insertion of Percutaneous Tracheostomy Tube

This procedure should be performed with the assistance of an individual trained in airway management and bronchoscopy. The diagrams represent an overview of the procedure derived from the package insert for the Ciaglia percutaneous tracheostomy set manufactured by Cook Critical Care. (Reproduced with permission of Cook Critical Care).

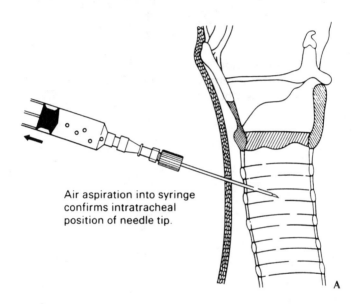

Air aspiration into syringe confirms intratracheal position of needle tip.

A

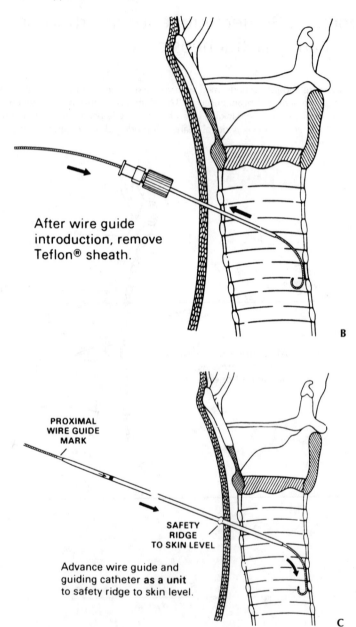

After wire guide introduction, remove Teflon® sheath.

B

PROXIMAL WIRE GUIDE MARK

SAFETY RIDGE TO SKIN LEVEL

Advance wire guide and guiding catheter **as a unit** to safety ridge to skin level.

C

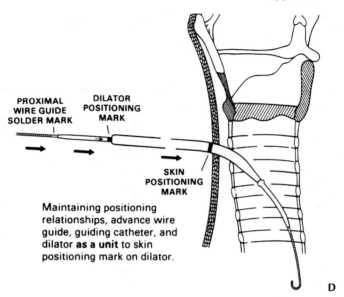

PROXIMAL
WIRE GUIDE
SOLDER MARK

DILATOR
POSITIONING
MARK

SKIN
POSITIONING
MARK

Maintaining positioning
relationships, advance wire
guide, guiding catheter, and
dilator **as a unit** to skin
positioning mark on dilator.

D

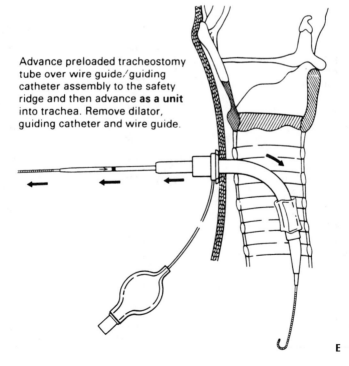

Advance preloaded tracheostomy
tube over wire guide/guiding
catheter assembly to the safety
ridge and then advance **as a unit**
into trachea. Remove dilator,
guiding catheter and wire guide.

E

Appendix 10   Body Surface Area Nomogram for Adults

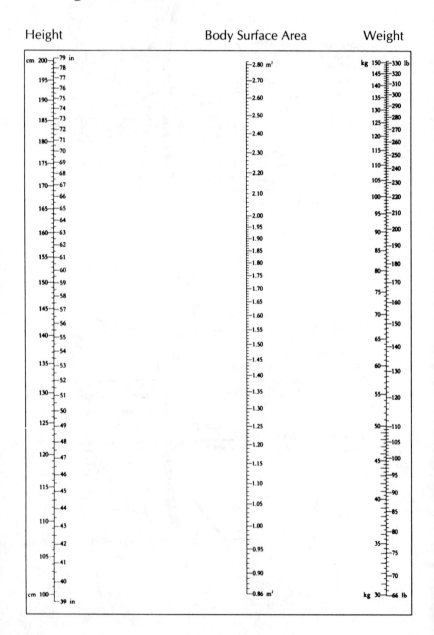

Height   Body Surface Area   Weight

Part 2
Pediatric Cardiac Surgery

14 Synopsis of Congenital Heart Disease

14   Synopsis of Congenital Heart Disease

The surgical management of congenital heart disease presents fascinating and complex challenges to the cardiac surgeon. This chapter briefly summarizes the pathophysiology of the common abnormalities encountered and the operative procedures used for their palliation or correction. This will facilitate the reader's understanding when these abnormalities and procedures are referred to in subsequent chapters. More detailed discussion of these abnormalities can be found in several outstanding textbooks on pediatric cardiac surgery.[1-4] Postoperative management of common defects is presented in Chapter 17.

I.   General Comments

A. The appropriate management of congenital heart disease is predicated on the precise identification of the anatomy and pathophysiology of the patient's abnormality. Arrival at the appropriate diagnosis can usually be achieved by:

1. Clinical assessment: cyanotic or acyanotic, presence of congestive heart failure (CHF)

2. Chest x-ray: assessment of pulmonary blood flow (increased, normal, or decreased)

3. Electrocardiogram: normal vs. left axis deviation, presence of right or left ventricular hypertrophy

4. Echocardiography: anatomy, shunts, valvular lesions, defects

5. Cardiac catheterization: oxygen saturations, shunt calculations, chamber pressures, septal defects, orientation of great vessels

B. Complex congenital heart defects usually involve multiple abnormalities that can influence the clinical presentation. The presence or absence of an atrial septal defect (ASD), ventricular septal defect (VSD), or right- or left-sided obstruction may dictate whether the patient has cyanosis, congestive heart failure, or both. The presence of associated anomalies may determine the natural history of the disease and the necessity or ability to perform a corrective operation.

C. The classification of congenital heart disease is somewhat arbitrary because of the wide spectrum of abnormalities and presentations that may accompany various congenital defects. This is especially true in the complex cyanotic defects associated with extensive intracardiac mixing. Table 14.1 categorizes the more common types of congenital heart disease.

II.   Pure Obstructive Lesions

A. **Pulmonic stenosis**

1. **Pathology and pathophysiology**

a. Pulmonic stenosis (PS) may occur as an isolated defect or may be associated with a variety of complex anomalies. It

---

Table 14.1 *Common Congenital Heart Defects*

I. Pure obstructive lesions
    A. Pulmonic stenosis
    B. Mitral stenosis
    C. Aortic stenosis
    D. Coarctation of the aorta
    E. Interrupted aortic arch

II. Simple left-to-right shunts (acyanotic lesions with increased pulmonary blood flow)
    A. Patent ductus arteriosus
    B. Atrial septal defect
    C. Ventricular septal defect
    D. Endocardial cushion defect (AV canal)
    E. Aortopulmonary window

III. Right-to-left shunts (cyanotic defects with decreased pulmonary blood flow)
    A. Tetralogy of Fallot
    B. Pulmonary atresia with ventricular septal defect
    C. Pulmonary atresia with intact ventricular septum
    D. Tricuspid atresia
    E. Ebstein's anomaly

IV. Complex cyanotic defects ("mixing defects")
    A. Double outlet right ventricle
    B. Univentricular heart
    C. Transposition of the great arteries
    D. Total anomalous pulmonary venous connection
    E. Truncus arteriosus
    F. Hypoplastic left heart syndrome

---

      can result from a dome-shaped or dysplastic valve or commissural fusion of a trileaflet valve. Subpulmonic fixed or dynamic muscular obstruction may occur as a isolated abnormality or in conjunction with valvular PS. Critical PS in neonates is commonly accompanied by right ventricular (RV) hypoplasia.

b. The association of PS with an ASD represents a form of cyanotic heart disease, with the degree of right-to-left shunting determined by the severity of PS. This will lead to right ventricular hypertrophy (RVH) and an elevation in right-sided pressures. Even in the absence of a true ASD, shunting across a patent foramen ovale may eventually occur. Severe stenosis is usually present when the right ventricular/left ventricular pressure ratio exceeds 0.9.[5]

c. The critically ill infant with severe PS is usually cyanotic, with pulmonary blood flow provided by the patent ductus arteriosus (PDA). Prostaglandin E_1 (PGE$_1$) infusion and correction of acidosis followed by urgent intervention is usually required.

d. Children with lesser degrees of PS will gradually develop RVH and right-sided failure, depending on the severity of the outflow tract obstruction.

2. **Indications for surgery.** Urgent intervention is required for critically ill infants to increase pulmonary blood flow and improve cyanosis. Evidence of severe PS or the presence of symptoms warrants surgery in older infants and children.

3. **Surgical procedures**

   a. Balloon valvotomy is the procedure of choice for neonatal critical PS not associated with RV hypoplasia or valve dysplasia.[6] It may also be used in older children.

   b. Pulmonary valvotomy is usually required when balloon techniques are unsuccessful. Surgical valvotomy may be performed via an incision in the main pulmonary artery with or without a brief period of circulatory arrest.

   c. Associated RV outflow tract obstruction is treated with transventricular muscle band resection with or without patch enlargement of the right ventricular outflow tract.

B. **Aortic stenosis**

1. **Pathology and pathophysiology.** Aortic stenosis may occur at the subaortic, valvar, or supravalvar level. Critical stenosis in the infant produces a severe low output state and cyanosis, with systemic flow provided by right-to-left ductal shunting. Older children usually develop symptoms caused by obstruction to left ventricular (LV) outflow and the development of LV hypertrophy (LVH).

   a. Subaortic stenosis results from a discrete fibrous membrane or a diffuse narrowing (tunnel stenosis) of the LV outflow tract.

   b. Valvar stenosis is caused by a unicuspid valve or commissural fusion of a bicuspid valve. Varying degrees of annular hypoplasia may also be present.

   c. Supravalvar stenosis is caused by a discrete fibrous ridge or diffuse hypoplasia of the ascending aorta.

2. **Indications for surgery**

   a. In infants with critical aortic stenosis, intervention is required for severe low output states.[7]

   b. In older children, surgery is indicated for symptoms (angina, heart failure, syncope), an abnormal stress test, LVH on ECG, or a peak gradient exceeding 50 mm Hg. Resection of a subaortic membrane should be considered upon diagnosis to prevent progressive aortic valve insufficiency.

3. **Surgical procedures**

   a. Subaortic stenosis

      i. Stenosis caused by a concentric obstructive membrane can be relieved by resection of the membrane and often by a simultaneous myotomy or myectomy of the hypertrophied ventricular septum.[8]

ii. Tunnel stenosis may occasionally be relieved by aggressive resection of the conal septum through an aortic approach. An aortoventriculoplasty (Konno procedure) is frequently performed in older children. This involves an incision through the aorta, aortic annulus, and ventri-cular septum onto the RV outflow tract. Aortic valve replacement and patching of the septum and outflow tract are then performed.

iii. Subaortic stenosis associated with single ventricle physiology may be repaired by the Damus-Kaye-Stansel procedure (see page 495).[9]

b. Valvar aortic stenosis is usually treated by percutaneous balloon valvotomy. If this is unsuccessful in relieving the gradient, either a direct valvotomy or dilatation through the LV apex is performed using cardiopulmonary bypass (CPB).[10] Valve replacement with either a mechanical prosthesis or a homograft is usually performed in older children. The pulmonary autograft (Ross or the Ross-Konno procedure) with or without resection of obstructive conal septum is an increasingly popular technique used to relieve valvar and/or subvalvar left-sided obstruction in all age groups including neonates.[11]

c. Supravalvar aortic stenosis is repaired by patch augmentation of the ascending aorta.

C. Coarctation of the aorta

1. **Pathology and pathophysiology.** Coarctation of the aorta is a severe stenosis of the aortic isthmus just distal to the left subclavian artery.

a. Coarctation presenting during infancy is often associated with other cardiac defects that reduce intrauterine aortic blood flow, such as a restrictive foramen ovale, hypoplastic left heart syndrome, or mitral/aortic valve abnormalities. A hypoplastic transverse arch is commonly present.

i. The increase in LV afterload will lead to an elevation in left-sided pressures, causing pulmonary vascular congestion and eventually a low cardiac output state.

ii. Right-to-left shunting through the PDA provides perfusion to the lower half of the body and may produce distal cyanosis if the coarctation is severe. When the ductus closes, distal perfusion is compromised, leading to oliguria and metabolic acidosis. Furthermore, ductal closure will promote left-to-right shunting across septal defects, further contributing to CHF.

iii. An intravenous infusion of PGE_1 is essential to maintain ductal patency to alleviate pulmonary vascular congestion and improve systemic flow. Inotropic support and intubation with mechanical ventilation may be necessary. Urgent surgical intervention is then performed.

    b. Adult (postductal) coarctation usually presents later in childhood with upper extremity hypertension, headaches, and decreased femoral pulses. The chest x-ray in older children often reveals rib notching.

2. **Indications for surgery**

    a. Urgent surgery is indicated in infants with severe coarctation and LV failure or ductal dependency, especially in the presence of left-to-right shunts. Repair of the coarctation is performed first, with subsequent VSD closure if the infant has CHF refractory to medical management.

    b. In older children, repair is indicated for resting or exercise-induced hypertension or a gradient exceeding 30 mm Hg across the coarctation.

3. **Surgical procedures.** The operative procedure should be selected so as to minimize the risk of recurrent stenosis (figure 14.1).

    a. Resection of the coarct segment with end-to-end anastomosis is generally performed in children older than 3 months of age.[12] Concerns about recurrent stenosis in young infants with coarctation and a hypoplastic arch have been mitigated by use of an extended end-to-end anastomosis, which augments the arch by anastomosing the descending aorta to the underside of the transverse arch (figure 14.2).[13]

    b. The subclavian flap procedure involves augmenting the narrowed segment with the divided left subclavian artery (figure 14.3). This procedure allows for growth of the aorta, but may potentially lead to left arm ischemia and impaired arm growth.

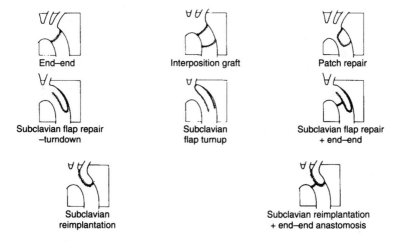

End–end

Interposition graft

Patch repair

Subclavian flap repair –turndown

Subclavian flap turnup

Subclavian flap repair + end–end

Subclavian reimplantation

Subclavian reimplantation + end–end anastomosis

Figure 14.1 *Methods of repairing coarctation of the aorta. The most common types of repair are the subclavian flap and the end-to-end anastomosis. Resection combined with a flap may be used in neonates and young infants to reduce the risk of restenosis. (Reproduced with permission from the Society of Thoracic Surgeons from Amato JJ, Galdieri RJ, Cotroneo JV. Role of extended aortoplasty related to the definition of coarctation of the aorta. Ann Thorac Surg 1991;56:615–20.)*

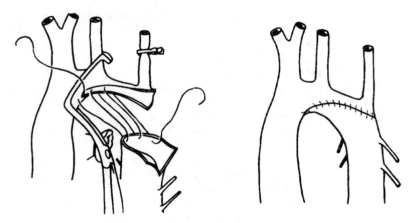

Figure 14.2 *Repair of aortic coarctation by an extended end-to-end anastomosis. The descending aorta is extensively mobilized and an oblique incision is made across the arch. The coarcted segment is resected and the end-to-end anastomosis is performed between the distal arch and the descending aorta. (Reproduced with permission from Lacour-Gayet F, Bruniaux J, Serraf A, et al. Hypoplastic transverse arch and coarctation in neonates. Surgical reconstruction of the aortic arch: a study of sixty-six patients. J Thorac Cardiovasc Surg 1990;100:808–16.)*

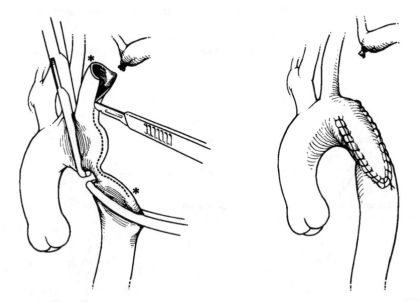

Figure 14.3 *Subclavian flap for repair of coarctation. An incision is made in the aorta and extended into the left subclavian artery. The artery is divided distally and turned down as a flap into the aortic incision. (Reproduced with permission from Cooley DA. Techniques in cardiac surgery, 2nd ed. Philadelphia: WB Saunders, 1984:40.)*

Furthermore, it may leave residual ductal remnants that may contract and cause recoarctation.[14] Improved results in neonates and small infants have been obtained by performing a distal subclavian reimplantation as a patch,[15] or combining a resection with a subclavian flap or distal subclavian reimplantation patch (see figure 14.1).[16]

c. A patch aortoplasty involves a longitudinal incision in the aorta, resection of the coarctation membrane, and placement of an onlay Dacron patch. Because of the significant incidence of aneurysmal formation, most centers have abandoned this technique.[17]

d. In adolescents and adults, the aorta and surrounding connective tissues are less pliable. This may preclude a safe tension-free end-to-end anastomosis and necessitate placement of an interposition Dacron tube graft.

e. The incidence of recurrent stenosis after repair of coarctation in infancy may approach 30%. Recurrent coarctation has been treated by percutaneous balloon dilatation. Surgical treatment can be challenging and may require an interposition tube graft or a bypass graft around the area of stenosis.

D. Interrupted aortic arch

1. Pathology and pathophysiology

a. Unlike coarctation of the aorta, there is true absence of aortic continuity in patients with interrupted aortic arch (IAA). There is usually a considerable distance between the ascending and descending components of the thoracic aorta.

b. IAA is classified according to the location of the interrupted segment. In Type A IAA, the interruption is distal to the left subclavian artery (LSCA). In Type B IAA, the most common type, the interruption is between the LSCA and the left common carotid artery (LCCA). In Type C, the least common type, the interruption is proximal to the LCCA.

c. There is almost always an associated large subaortic VSD.

d. There are often varying degrees of left ventricular outflow tract obstruction, either at the subvalvar or the valvar level.

e. Many patients, particularly those with Type B IAA, have associated DiGeorge syndrome characterized by an absent thymus, deficient parathyroid glands, and hypocalcemia.

f. Systemic flow to the distal aorta is dependent on ductal patency. These neonates often present with evidence of poor organ perfusion and sometimes shock when the PDA closes. Institution of PGE_1 is necessary to restore ductal patency and improve organ perfusion. Patients often require a period of inotropic support and stabilization prior to surgical intervention.

2. **Indications for surgery.** Surgery is performed once the patient is stabilized, usually within the first week of life.

3. **Surgical procedures**

   a. Most centers currently perform a one-stage approach using a median sternotomy and CPB.[18] The descending aorta is anastomosed to the ascending aorta during a short period of circulatory arrest. The VSD is closed with a Dacron patch. Significant subaortic obstruction may be resected.

   b. Less commonly, a two-stage approach is performed. Through a left thoracotomy, either the LCCA or the LSCA can be anastomosed to the descending aorta.[19] A pulmonary artery band is placed. At a second operation, usually before 6 months of age, the band is removed and the VSD is closed via a median sternotomy.

III. Simple Left-to-Right Shunts (Acyanotic Lesions with Increased Pulmonary Blood Flow)

A. **General comments**

1. Left-to-right shunts result from a communication between the right- and left-sided circulations. Flow across these defects is usually from the high resistance circuit (left side) to the low resistance circuit (right side). The amount of pulmonary blood flow (PBF) is determined by the size of the defect and the ratio of the resistances downstream to the defect.

   a. Restrictive shunts are characterized by a significant pressure gradient across the defect. Flow across these small shunts is dictated by the size of the defect.

   b. Nonrestrictive shunts are larger in size and therefore are not associated with a pressure gradient across the defect. Flow is determined principally by the ratio of the pulmonary vascular resistance (PVR) to the systemic vascular resistance (SVR). For example, a high PVR would lessen the degree of left-to-right shunting. Nonrestrictive shunts usually produce excessive PBF, leading to pulmonary vascular congestion.

2. Surgery is generally indicated for symptoms, pulmonary hypertension, cardiomegaly, left ventricular volume overload or strain, or a calculated left-to-right shunt (the ratio of pulmonary to systemic blood flow or $Q_p:Q_s$) of $>1.5:1$. Long-standing shunts may produce pulmonary vascular occlusive disease that leads to shunt reversal and cyanosis (Eisenmenger's syndrome). When the PVR exceeds 8 Wood units and does not fall with oxygen or vasodilators, the patient is considered to be inoperable. Therefore, surgical intervention is indicated in early childhood to prevent the development of pulmonary vascular disease.

B. **Patent ductus arteriosus (PDA)**

1. **Pathology and pathophysiology**

   a. The ductus usually closes within the first 2 weeks of life. If it remains patent, left-to-right shunt flow will increase PBF, producing pulmonary vascular congestion and LV volume overload. In association with the pulmonary disease of prematurity, this will produce pulmonary edema and respiratory distress syndrome in premature infants.

b. Patency of the ductus may be critical to survival in neonates with complex heart disease by providing pulmonary or systemic flow. Left-to-right ductal flow maintains oxygenation when there is severe right-sided obstruction (tricuspid atresia, pulmonary atresia, tetralogy of Fallot). In contrast, right-to-left ductal flow will provide systemic blood flow for left-sided obstructive defects (mitral atresia, hypoplastic LV, critical AS, coarctation).

c. When the child's survival is dependent on ductal patency, PGE_1 should be given to stabilize the patient until urgent surgical repair can be performed. The PDA is ligated at the time of correction of the associated cardiac defects.

2. **Indications for surgery.** A PDA that contributes to respiratory compromise in a premature infant should be ligated, especially if indomethacin fails to achieve closure. A PDA that persists beyond the third month of life should be closed in order to prevent endarteritis and pulmonary vascular disease. Transcatheter closure of a PDA using intravascular coils has recently seen wider application.[20]

3. **Surgical procedures**

a. Simple ligation through a left thoracotomy is usually performed in neonates and can be accomplished safely in the neonatal ICU.[21]

b. Division of the PDA with oversewing of the divided ends may be performed in older children.

C. **Atrial septal defect (ASD)**

1. **Pathology and pathophysiology**

a. An ASD represents a communication between the left and right atrium and may occur at one of several locations in the atrial septum (figure 14.4).

b. When the PVR decreases beyond the neonatal period, an ASD will result in left-to-right shunting with increased PBF, leading to the development of pulmonary vascular congestion or recurrent respiratory infections. The degree of shunting is determined by the size of the defect and the PVR.

2. **Indications for surgery.** An ASD should generally be closed by age 5 when there is echocardiographic evidence of right ventricular volume overload. An uncorrected ASD may eventually lead to atrial arrhythmias, paradoxical systemic embolization, and, eventually, pulmonary hypertension. Thus, ASD closure is indicated in adults with evidence of a left-to-right shunt.

3. **Surgical procedures**

a. **Ostium secundum defects** are caused by a deficiency in the septum primum and are located in the mid-atrium. They are

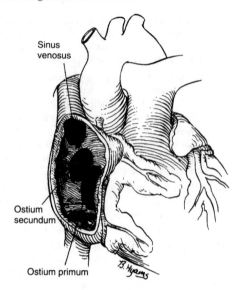

Sinus
venosus

Ostium
secundum

Ostium primum

Figure 14.4   *Location of atrial septal defects. (Reproduced with permission from Cooley DA. Techniques in cardiac surgery, 2nd ed. Philadelphia: WB Saunders, 1984:107.)*

closed by direct suture or with a pericardial or Dacron patch, depending on the size of the defect. These defects have been occluded successfully by transcatheter techniques in the catheterization laboratory.[22]

b. **Ostium primum defects** are located at the lower aspect of the atrial septum and are commonly associated with either partial or complete atrioventricular (AV) canal defects. They are repaired with a patch anchored to the crest of the ventricular septum between the valves. Because the medial border of the defect is the septal leaflet of the tricuspid valve, injury to the AV node may occur with resultant heart block. In two-thirds of patients with an ostium primum ASD, a cleft is present in the anterior leaflet of the mitral valve. This is usually repaired with sutures to either correct or minimize the development of mitral regurgitation.

c. **Sinus venosus defects** are located at the cephalad end of the atrial septum and have no upper septal border. They require patch closure to avoid narrowing of the junction of the superior vena cava (SVC) with the right atrium. These defects are often associated with partial anomalous pulmonary venous drainage of the right upper or middle lobe vein into the SVC. This is baffled into the left atrium through the ASD with a patch.

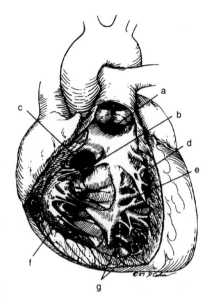

Figure 14.5   *Location of ventricular septal defects. a = outlet (supracristal) defect; b = papillary muscle of conus; c = perimembranous defect; d = marginal muscular defects; e = central muscular defects; f = inlet (AV canal type) defect; g = apical muscular defects. (Reproduced with permission from Adams FH, Emmanouilides GC, Riemenschneider TA, eds. Moss' Heart disease in infants, children, and adolescents, 4th ed. Baltimore: Williams & Wilkins, 1989:191.)*

D. **Ventricular septal defect (VSD)**

1. **Pathology and pathophysiology**

   a. Congenital VSDs may occur in various locations in the ventricular septum. They occur in the membranous portion of the septum in about 80% of patients (figure 14.5). They may be single or multiple, and are often associated with other congenital defects.

   b. Nonrestrictive VSDs produce a left-to-right shunt with increased PBF. The shunt may not be obvious at birth, but will become evident when the PVR falls. The child usually presents with symptoms of pulmonary vascular congestion and recurrent respiratory infections because of the excessive PBF and volume overload.

2. **Indications for surgery.** An untreated VSD with a large shunt ($Q_p:Q_s > 1.5:1$) predisposes to the development of pulmonary vascular disease within the first few years of life. Therefore, repair should be performed by age 1 in all patients with a significant shunt or evidence of left ventricular volume overload. Surgery may be indicated at an earlier age for refractory CHF.

3. **Surgical procedures**

   a. Pulmonary artery (PA) banding to reduce PBF is occasionally performed in severely ill infants or older children with multiple muscular VSDs ("Swiss cheese septum") or other associated complex lesions. A restricting band is placed around the main PA to reduce distal PA pressure to approximately 50% of the right ventricular pressure.

   b. Very small defects can be closed by direct suture, but the majority of VSDs require patch closure.

      i. Perimembranous defects lie in close proximity to the tricuspid valve. They are usually repaired through a right atrial approach, with the posterior row of sutures placed through the septal leaflet of the tricuspid valve. This repair runs the risk of producing heart block.

      ii. Outlet (subpulmonic or supracristal) defects can be repaired either through the pulmonary artery or the right ventricle. They are frequently associated with aortic insufficiency which can be corrected by performing a concomitant aortic valvuloplasty through the aorta.

      iii. The location of muscular defects must be well-defined to select the best approach. This may involve a right atriotomy or a right or left ventriculotomy.[23] Avoidance of a left ventriculotomy is desirable in infants and has led to the development of a transcatheter closure technique for muscular defects.[24]

E. **Endocardial cushion defects (AV canal)**

  1. **Pathology and pathophysiology**

    a. These defects result from deficiency of the atrioventricular septum. They are frequently associated with Trisomy 21 (Down's syndrome).

    b. Partial AV canal is characterized by an ostium primum ASD and a cleft in the anterior leaflet of the mitral valve. Varying degrees of mitral insufficiency may be present.

    c. Complete AV canal is characterized by the presence of a nonrestrictive VSD and an ostium primum ASD, which together produce a large confluent defect in the lower portion of the atrium septum and the inlet portion of the ventricular septum. In addition, there is a single AV valve with varying degrees of right- or left-sided regurgitation. The combination of a large left-to-right shunt and mitral regurgitation produces systemic RV and PA pressures as well as volume overload. This results in significant pulmonary vascular congestion and leads to the early development of pulmonary vascular disease.

  2. **Indications for surgery.** Surgery should be performed by the age of 6 months to prevent the development of pulmonary vascular obstructive disease.

  3. **Surgical procedures**

    a. PA banding to decrease PBF is rarely indicated in the critically ill infant with an AV canal. It may be performed if a primary repair is not considered feasible because of the presence of RV hypoplasia. PA banding should be avoided if significant atrioventricular valvar regurgitation is present.

    b. A balanced defect is present when the common AV valve is centered equally over the two ventricles, which are of equal size. Operative repair entails division of the common AV valve, closure of the ASD and VSD, and resuspension of the right- and left-sided components of the valve to the VSD patch in order to create separate mitral and tricuspid annuli and valves (figure 14.6). Valve repair may be incomplete, leaving residual mitral regurgitation, or it may produce valve stenosis.[25]

   c. An unbalanced defect is present when the common AV valve is preferentially centered over one ventricle (usually the right), while the contralateral ventricle is usually hypoplastic. This may require repair using the Fontan principle (see page 484).

F. **Aortopulmonary window**

  1. **Pathology and pathophysiology**

      a. There is usually a nonrestrictive communication between the posterior aspect of the ascending aorta and either the main pulmonary artery or the right pulmonary artery.[26]

      b. Because the defect is usually large, most patients present in early infancy with significant congestive heart failure.

  2. **Indications for surgery.** Because the defects are usually nonrestrictive, surgery should be performed soon after the diagnosis is made.

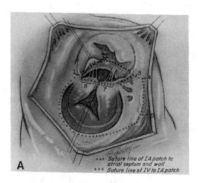

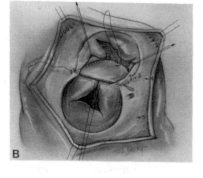

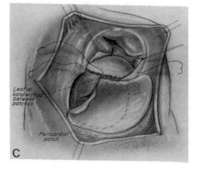

Figure 14.6 *Repair of an AV canal. (A) The defect consists of a large ASD and VSD with a common AV valve. The cleft in the septal leaflet of the mitral valve is closed (7–8). (B) A Dacron patch closes the VSD and is sutured to the crest of the ventricular septum (1–3) and to the edge of the septal leaflets of the mitral and tricuspid valves (6–8). (C) A pericardial patch closes the atrial component of the defect. (Reproduced with permission from Arcinegas E. Pediatric cardiac surgery. Chicago: Year Book Medical Publishers, 1985:162–3.)*

3. **Surgical treatment**

   a. The current approach is to close these defects directly with a patch. The window can be approached either through the aorta or the pulmonary artery.[27,28]

   b. In the past, attempts to close these defects by simple ligation with or without division were hazardous because most aortopulmonary windows do not have a neck.

IV.   Cyanotic Lesions—General Comments

A. Cyanotic congenital heart disease may occur on the basis of one or more mechanisms:

   1. Right-to-left shunting with reduction in the volume of pulmonary blood flow (e.g., tetralogy of Fallot, tricuspid atresia, pulmonary atresia).

   2. Failure of delivery of pulmonary venous blood to the systemic circulation (e.g., transposition of the great arteries [D-TGA], total anomalous pulmonary venous connection [TAPVC]).

   3. Intracardiac mixing of oxygenated and desaturated blood in a chamber proximal to the aorta (e.g., single atrium, single ventricle, double-outlet right ventricle, truncus arteriosus). Mixing provided by an ASD or VSD is essential for survival in nearly all cyanotic defects once the patent ductus closes.

   4. Severe low cardiac output states. These include severe right-sided obstructions (critical pulmonic stenosis/atresia) and left-sided obstructive lesions (critical AS, hypoplastic left heart syndrome).

B. Although most cyanotic lesions are amenable to definitive correction in infancy, temporary surgical palliation may be indicated for severe hypoxia in infancy to allow time for growth of cardiac and pulmonary structures to a size more suitable for definitive correction.

C. In neonates with severe cyanosis, maintenance of ductal patency with PGE$_1$ is invaluable before palliative surgery to maintain PBF and prevent arterial desaturation and acidosis. Because PGE$_1$ is a potent vasodilator, volume infusions may be necessary to support systemic blood pressure. Many patients with severe cyanosis will additionally require intubation and mechanical ventilation, correction of acidosis with bicarbonate, and/or inotropic support while awaiting evaluation by echocardiography and/or cardiac catheterization before an urgent surgical procedure can be performed.

D. **Palliative procedures**[29]

   1. **Procedures to increase pulmonary blood flow**

      a. The creation of a systemic-to-pulmonary artery shunt to increase PBF is useful in patients with right-to-left shunts (tetralogy of Fallot, tricuspid atresia, pulmonary atresia), and other more complex cyanotic lesions. A shunt can provide palliation from a few months to several years before a definitive repair is performed (figure 14.7).

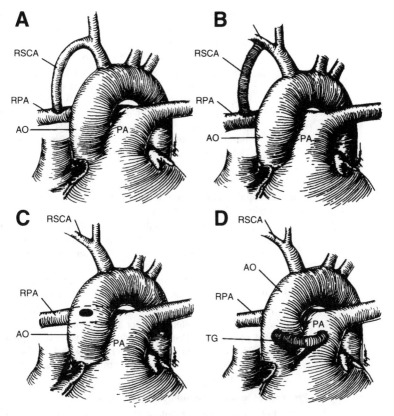

Figure 14.7 *Systemic-to-pulmonary artery shunts. (A) Blalock-Taussig. (B) Modified Blalock-Taussig. (C) Waterston. (D) Central. (Reproduced with permission from Hickey PR, Wessel DL, Reich DL. Anesthesia for treatment of congenital heart disease. In: Kaplan JA, ed. Cardiac anesthesia, 3rd ed. Philadelphia: WB Saunders, 1993:723.)*

  i. A **Blalock-Taussig (BT) shunt** involves an end-to-side anastomosis of the subclavian artery on the side opposite the aortic arch to the ipsilateral pulmonary artery (PA). This shunt and its modifications are commonly used because they are infrequently associated with the development of congestive heart failure or pulmonary vascular disease.

 ii. A **modified Blalock-Taussig shunt (MBTS)** using a 4–5 mm polytetrafluoroethylene (PTFE) tube graft is the shunt of choice in small infants in whom the subclavian artery may be too small to carry sufficient flow. The graft is sewn end-to-side to the subclavian artery near its junction with the innominate artery and to the ipsilateral branch PA. This procedure ensures patency of the subclavian artery and is rarely associated with kinking of the pulmonary artery. Although this shunt provides satisfactory early palliation, it eventually fails to provide sufficient PBF beyond early childhood.[30]

iii. A **"central shunt"** using a short piece of PTFE graft to connect the ascending aorta to the main PA may be employed in small infants. This has replaced the Waterston shunt which entailed an anastomosis of the right posterolateral wall of the aorta to the right pulmonary artery. This procedure provided excessive pulmonary blood flow that led to the development of pulmonary vascular obstructive disease; it also produced distortion of the right pulmonary artery.

b. **Cavopulmonary shunts (Glenn shunt):** see section IV.E on single ventricle physiology.

c. **Pulmonary valvotomy** (balloon or surgical) may be performed for critical pulmonic stenosis or pulmonary atresia, often in association with a shunt. It is beneficial when the right ventricle is of satisfactory size to be used in a subsequent repair. The procedure may be performed directly using inflow occlusion or by transventricular valvotomy.

d. In the presence of a hypoplastic pulmonary valve anulus and small pulmonary arteries, either a **transannular RV outflow tract patch** or an **RV-to-PA conduit** may be used for palliation. The VSD is left open. Antegrade flow through the pulmonary arteries may enhance growth and allow safe closure of the VSD at a later date.[31]

2. **Procedures to decrease pulmonary blood flow**

a. **Pulmonary artery banding** is applicable to patients with excessive PBF caused by complex VSDs (multiple muscular VSDs, associated coarctation), tricuspid atresia, or lesions with single ventricle physiology and excessive PBF. It should generally be reserved for critically ill infants with defects not amenable to early definitive repair.[32]

b. PA banding is usually performed through a left thoracotomy incision. A ligature or band is placed around the main pulmonary artery and tightened. Satisfactory banding is accomplished when the pulmonary pressure is reduced to 30–50% of systemic pressure. Evidence of arterial desaturation by pulse oximetry indicates that the band is too tight.[33]

3. **Procedures to improve intracardiac mixing.** Enlargement of a restrictive ASD can improve the severe cyanosis of defects that require a septal communication to provide mixing of the systemic and pulmonary circulations (D-TGA, TAPVC, tricuspid atresia).

a. A **Rashkind balloon atrial septostomy** should be performed at the time of initial catheterization for D-TGA in anticipation of a neonatal arterial switch operation. In other patients, it may improve hypoxemia for several months prior to a definitive repair.

    b. If cyanosis is not improved by balloon septostomy, a **Blalock-Hanlon atrial septectomy** can be performed. In this procedure, the cavae and aorta are briefly occluded, the right atrium (RA) is entered, and the posterior aspect of the atrial septum is removed.

E. **Treatment of cyanotic defects with "single ventricle" physiology**

1. Several cyanotic congenital heart defects characterized by extensive intracardiac mixing have one functional and one hypoplastic ventricle. When the RV is hypoplastic (tricuspid atresia, pulmonary atresia with intact ventricular septum, most forms of univentricular heart), the LV provides both the systemic and pulmonary flow, usually through a large VSD. When the LV is hypoplastic (hypoplastic left heart syndrome), the RV provides the majority of flow.

2. The degree of cyanosis depends on the amount of PBF and the extent of intracardiac mixing. The greater the degree of pulmonary blood flow relative to the systemic blood flow (i.e., the higher the $Q_p:Q_s$), the greater the arterial saturation. Therefore, alterations in PVR and SVR will determine the $Q_p:Q_s$ ratio and consequently the extent of cyanosis. In addition, the more profound the desaturation of systemic or pulmonary venous blood returning to the site of intracardiac mixing, the greater the degree of hypoxemia and cyanosis.

3. Definitive repair of these defects will require separation of the systemic and pulmonary circulations with the use of the only functional ventricle to provide systemic flow ("the Fontan operation"). This procedure cannot be performed within the first few years of life when the PVR is elevated, because it directs, rather than pumps, systemic venous return into the pulmonary arteries. Therefore, an alternative procedure for increasing pulmonary blood flow must be performed at an earlier age.

4. A systemic-to-pulmonary artery shunt to improve PBF is usually required early in infancy for these lesions. A second shunt is frequently necessary after age 1 to augment PBF. Historically, a Glenn shunt was considered as a secondary procedure in children over 6 months of age to improve oxygenation. This provided a low-pressure system that reduced the volume load on the heart and prevented the development of pulmonary vascular disease.

    a. With this procedure, the SVC was divided at its junction with the RA and anastomosed end-to-side to the right pulmonary artery (RPA), which was detached from the main pulmonary artery.

    b. Drawbacks of the Glenn shunt, which have led to a decrease in its use, include:

- Decreased shunt flow from polycythemia and increased blood viscosity
- Development of venous collaterals from the SVC circuit to the IVC
- $\dot{V}/\dot{Q}$ abnormalities in the right lung secondary to the formation of pulmonary arteriovenous malformations

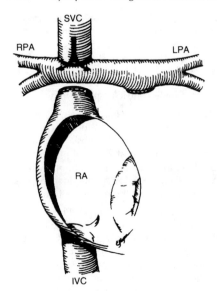

Figure 14.8 *Bidirectional Glenn shunt. The SVC is sewn end-to-side to the right pulmonary artery. The junction of the SVC and right atrium is oversewn. (Reprinted with permission of the American Heart Association, Inc. from Bridges ND, Jonas RA, Mayer JE, Flanagan MF, Kean JF, Castaneda AR. Bidirectional cavopulmonary anastomosis as interim palliation for high-risk Fontan candidates. Early results. Circulation 1990;82(suppl 4): IV-170–6.)*

- Decreased flow to the contralateral lung from closure of the pulmonary outflow tract or VSD
- Difficulty in takedown at reoperation

5. Currently, the **bidirectional Glenn shunt** is the preferred shunt in patients with single ventricle physiology in whom construction of a two-ventricular repair will not be feasible. It entails an anastomosis between the SVC and the right pulmonary artery without division of the RPA, thus providing blood flow to both pulmonary arteries (figure 14.8). This shunt reduces ventricular volume overload, improves ventricular compliance, enhances mixing, and may relieve pulmonary artery distortion.[34] It represents an intermediate stage to the eventual Fontan procedure.

6. The **Fontan operation** is designed to deliver systemic venous blood to the pulmonary artery, eliminate intracardiac mixing, and use the functioning ventricle to provide systemic flow. It has undergone several changes since its original description in 1971. Currently, the two techniques used are the "modified" Fontan and the "lateral tunnel" Fontan.[35–41]

   a. The major prerequisites to performing this operation successfully are adequately-sized pulmonary arteries, PVR < 4 Wood units, mean PA pressure < 20 mm Hg, sinus rhythm, and normal ventricular function. Patients with elevated PVR, increased PA or LV end-diastolic pressures, decreased systolic function, pulmonary artery hypoplasia, or AV valve regurgitation, are considered high-risk candidates for the Fontan procedure.

   b. The "modified" Fontan procedure consists of an anastomosis between the right atrium and pulmonary artery, either

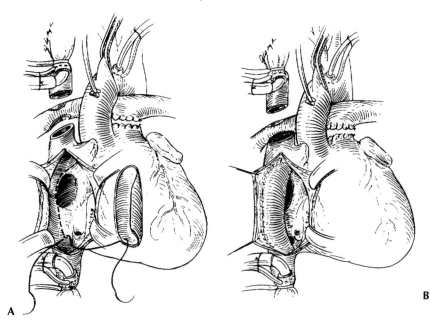

Figure 14.9 *Total cavopulmonary connection achieved with a lateral tunnel Fontan. (A) A patch of PTFE is sewn to the orifices of the cavae to create a tunnel that directs flow from the IVC to the SVC. The pulmonary artery is oversewn and the VSD is divided. (B) The distal SVC is sewn to the undersurface of the right pulmonary artery. The proximal SVC is sewn to the superior aspect of the right pulmonary artery (a bidirectional Glenn). A fenestration may be placed in the roof of the tunnel and in the patch that closes the ASD. (Reproduced with permission from the Society of Thoracic Surgeons from Pearl JM, Laks H, Stein DG, Drinkwater DC, George BL, Williams RG. Total cavopulmonary anastomosis versus conventional modified Fontan procedure. Ann Thorac Surg 1991;52:189–96.)*

directly or with a nonvalved conduit. The main pulmonary artery is transected and oversewn. The ASD is closed, and the tricuspid valve and coronary sinus are covered with a patch to avoid the AV node.

c. The "lateral tunnel" Fontan produces a total cavopulmonary connection. A baffle is used to create a tunnel between the IVC and SVC. The SVC is divided proximal to the cavoatrial junction. The proximal SVC is sewn to the superior aspect of the RPA (the bidirectional Glenn), and the distal SVC is sewn to the inferior surface of the RPA. The main PA is transected and oversewn (figure 14.9).

d. In high-risk patients, improved results have been noted when a small defect is created in the ASD patch and the tunnel to alleviate high right-sided pressures ("fenestrated Fontan"). An adjustable tourniquet can be placed to regulate the size of the defect upon weaning from CPB.[40] The defect can be closed subsequently with a transcatheter device.[41]

V. Right-to-Left Shunts (Cyanotic Defects with Decreased Pulmonary Blood Flow)

A. **Tetralogy of Fallot (TOF)**

1. **Pathology and pathophysiology**

   a. Tetralogy of Fallot is characterized by hypoplasia of the right ventricular infundibulum. This produces the four characteristic features of TOF: a large nonrestrictive anterior malalignment VSD, an "overriding aorta," RV outflow tract (RVOT) obstruction, and right ventricular hypertrophy. The obstruction may be caused by large infundibular muscle bands or pulmonic valvar stenosis. A dynamic component of infundibular "spasm" may also contribute to functional RVOT obstruction. The pulmonary valve annulus and the main PA are often hypoplastic.

   b. The degree of cyanosis is related to the severity of RVOT obstruction, which reduces PBF and increases right-to-left shunting across the VSD. If the RVOT obstruction is minimal, there will be greater PBF and less shunting, producing the so-called "pink tet." In contrast, in patients with significant RVOT obstruction, a transient increase in shunting, triggered by dynamic infundibular spasm from increased oxygen requirements, an increase in PVR, or a decrease in SVR, may precipitate a hypoxic ("tet") spell. This will produce intense cyanosis and can lead to syncope, seizures, and even death.

2. **Indications for surgery** include marked cyanosis, hypoxic "tet" spells, and severe RVOT obstruction. In the absence of symptoms, surgical intervention is usually performed within the first 2 years of life, and frequently in infancy.[42]

3. **Preoperative considerations**

   a. Surgical decision-making requires an assessment of the degree and location of the outflow tract obstruction, the size of the pulmonary arteries, the presence of systemic-to-PA collaterals, the course of the coronary arteries, and the identification of VSDs.

   b. "Tet spells" are more common between the ages of 2 and 3 months, particularly in children with severe cyanosis.

      i. The child develops hyperpnea (increase rate and depth of breathing) and hypoxia, which reduce SVR and increase venous return, leading to increased right-to-left shunting.

      ii. Treatment involves administration of 100% oxygen, placing the child in the knee-chest position ("squatting"), and administering morphine, sodium bicarbonate, or phenylephrine. β-blockers, including propranolol (0.01 μg/kg IV) or esmolol (0.5 mg/kg IV, followed by a continuous infusion) may depress contractility and reduce infundibular spasm.[43,44]

4. **Surgical procedures**

   a. Palliative procedures (systemic-to-PA shunts) are often performed in symptomatic infants with small pulmonary arteries, multiple VSDs, or an anomalous left anterior descending coronary artery crossing the RVOT. The latter makes a ventriculotomy incision very difficult and usually requires repair with an RV-to-PA valved homograft conduit.

   b. In the absence of anatomic contraindications, definitive correction of TOF is performed in infancy in experienced centers. Repair can be performed through a right ventriculotomy or through a right atriotomy with or without a concomitant incision in the main pulmonary artery (trans-atrial-transpulmonary repair).[45]

      i. The VSD is closed with a Dacron patch, and RVOT obstruction is relieved by pulmonary valvotomy and/or division or resection of infundibular muscle bands. The main or branch pulmonary arteries may be augmented with a patch, if necessary.

      ii. When the pulmonary valve annulus is small, an incision is carried across the infundibulum and annulus, and an elliptical pericardial patch is used to close the incision, thus enlarging the RV outflow tract (figure 14.10). Use of a transannular patch renders the pulmonary valve incompetent. Although this is well-tolerated in the absence of distal obstruction or pulmonary hypertension, it may lead to progressive RV volume overload and symptoms of fatigue and exercise intolerance. This problem is treated with a pulmonary valve homograft.[46]

      iii. If an anomalous coronary artery crosses the RV outflow tract, primary repair can be performed at an older age with use of an RV-to-PA valved conduit. This technique may also be used as an alternative to transannular patching when the pulmonary annulus is hypoplastic or the distal pulmonary arteries are very small.[47]

B. **Pulmonary atresia with ventricular septal defect**

   1. **Pathology and pathophysiology**

      a. Pulmonary atresia with VSD represents an extreme form of tetralogy of Fallot in which there is no communication between the RV and the pulmonary artery. The central pulmonary arteries are hypoplastic and there are peripheral arborization abnormalities. However, the RV is of normal size.

      b. Pulmonary blood flow arises from a patent ductus in the neonatal period and from major aortopulmonary collateral arteries (MAPCAs). Right-to-left shunting across the VSD produces mixing of systemic and pulmonary venous blood in the left ventricle. This leads to severe cyanosis at birth.

      c. The nature of the MAPCAs must be defined when contemplating surgical repair. Communicating systemic collaterals

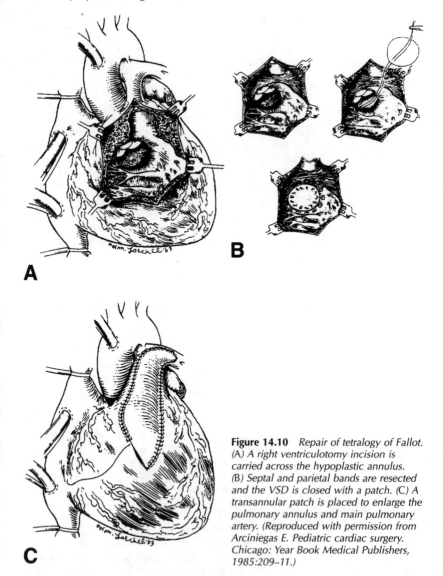

Figure 14.10 *Repair of tetralogy of Fallot. (A) A right ventriculotomy incision is carried across the hypoplastic annulus. (B) Septal and parietal bands are resected and the VSD is closed with a patch. (C) A transannular patch is placed to enlarge the pulmonary annulus and main pulmonary artery. (Reproduced with permission from Arciniegas E. Pediatric cardiac surgery. Chicago: Year Book Medical Publishers, 1985:209–11.)*

connect with the central PAs, whereas noncommunicating collaterals do not. Some MAPCAs become stenotic and contribute to progressive cyanosis. Other MAPCAs, often to the same pulmonary artery segment, provide unrestricted flow that can lead to pulmonary vascular changes.

2. **Indications for surgery.** Palliative surgery is indicated in infancy for severe cyanosis. Subsequent procedures should be directed toward an eventual definitive correction.

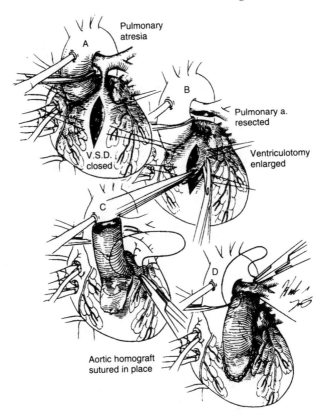

Figure 14.11 *Definitive repair of pulmonary atresia with ventricular septal defect and normal pulmonary arteries. (A) The VSD is closed through a right ventriculotomy. (B) The ventriculotomy is enlarged. (C–D) A homograft valved conduit is placed to reestablish continuity between the RV and PA. (Reproduced with permission from Hallman GL. Surgical treatment of congenital heart disease. Philadelphia: Lea & Febiger, 1975:128.)*

3. **Surgical procedures**

   a. A systemic-to-pulmonary artery shunt may be performed in infancy to improve PBF in severely cyanotic patients. An RVOT patch can also be performed in infancy to increase PBF and encourage growth of hypoplastic central pulmonary arteries.

   b. Definitive correction can be performed when the distal pulmonary arteries have grown to adequate size and there are no arborization abnormalities. The VSD is closed with a Dacron patch, and RV-to-PA continuity is established with a homograft valved conduit (Rastelli-type operation) (figure 14.11).

   c. A staged procedure is required when the central arteries are absent or hypoplastic, or there is inadequate peripheral arborization. A "unifocalization" procedure is performed to improve the arborization pattern of the central arteries. Non-communicating MAPCAs are detached from their origins and anastomosed, either directly or with short grafts, to lobar arteries to restore the confluence between the segmental and lobar arteries. Communicating MAPCAs are interrupted at their origin. The central PAs may be reconstructed. Provided that adequate flow has been established from the central PAs to a sufficient number of bronchopulmonary segments (>10), the definitive correction can be performed. The VSD is closed and a valved homograft conduit is placed between the RVOT and the reconstructed pulmonary arteries.[48–50]

d. In some centers, patients with TOF and pulmonary atresia with MAPCAs are being treated with a single operation, preferably during the first year of life. Through a sternotomy, the MAPCAs are isolated, and central arteries, if present, are augmented by direct anastomoses between the MAPCAs and the central pulmonary arteries. If the mediastinal pulmonary arteries are absent, they are reconstructed with homograft tubes. All patients receive a pulmonary homograft to bridge the RV and the reconstructed pulmonary arteries. The VSD is usually closed provided there is adequate recruitment of MAPCAs and the peripheral pulmonary arteries. The short-term results with this aggressive approach are encouraging.[51,52]

C. **Pulmonary atresia with intact ventricular septum (IVS)**

1. **Pathology and pathophysiology**

   a. This defect produces complete obstruction to RV outflow. The pulmonary arteries are usually normal in size, but the right ventricle and tricuspid valve are commonly hypoplastic.

   b. Severe cyanosis is present at birth, with survival dependent on pulmonary blood flow derived from a PDA and systemic-to-PA collaterals. Right-to-left shunting across an ASD provides complete mixing of the systemic and pulmonary circulations in the left atrium. Pressures in the right ventricle are suprasystemic.

   c. When the RV is severely hypoplastic, RV sinusoids are often present which communicate with the coronary circulation. High RV pressures can provide retrograde perfusion to the myocardium. A surgical procedure that produces RV decompression can precipitate myocardial ischemia by reducing flow through ventriculocoronary connections.[53]

2. **Indications for surgery.** Surgery is indicated in infancy for profound cyanosis.

3. **Surgical procedures.** The surgical approach is dictated by the size of the tricuspid valve annulus and right ventricle.[53–57]

   a. When the right ventricle and tricuspid valve are of adequate size (fewer than 10% of patients), initial palliation is provided by either a balloon or surgical pulmonary valvotomy. An RVOT patch may be required to adequately relieve RVOT obstruction. A supplemental MBTS or central shunt is usually necessary. Provided there is adequate growth of the RV, either transcatheter or surgical closure of the ASD and/or the MBTS may be performed safely at 3–4 years of age. Significant pulmonary regurgitation is sometimes treated with an RV-PA valve homograft.

b. Patients with a severely hypoplastic RV and tricuspid valve are managed initially with an MBTS or central shunt.

    i. If there is no RV infundibulum (pulmonary conus) and the pulmonary arteries are of good size, a Fontan procedure is performed after 2 years of age.

    ii. If an RV infundibulum is present, a simultaneous valvotomy is also performed. If the RV grows to satisfactory size, complete repair with an RVOT patch and ASD closure is performed at 2–4 years of age. If RV growth is borderline, the ASD and shunt are left open. If the RV remains small, a Fontan procedure is performed after 2 years of age.[57]

    iii. An alternative approach when RV growth is marginal is a "one and one-half" ventricle repair.[58] The proximal and distal SVC are connected to the RPA, and RV-to-main PA continuity is established. Thus the pulmonary blood flow is derived from both systemic venous return and RV output.

D. Tricuspid atresia

1. Pathology and pathophysiology

a. Tricuspid atresia is characterized by absence of the tricuspid valve and varying degrees of RV hypoplasia. Because there is no communication between the RA and RV, blood is shunted right-to-left across an ASD to produce complete mixing of the systemic and pulmonary venous blood in the left atrium. The excessive flow into the left heart produces left ventricular volume overload.

b. The classification of tricuspid atresia depends on the orientation of the great vessels (transposed or normal), the size of the VSD, and the degree of pulmonary stenosis (table 14.2). These factors determine the relative amounts of systemic and pulmonary blood flow and the patient's clinical presentation. The spectrum ranges from patients with severe cyanosis (types 1A, 2A) or moderate cyanosis (types 1B, 2B) to those with congestive heart failure (types 1C, 2C).

2. Indications for surgery.
Surgery is indicated for severe cyanosis in infancy or for progressive cyanosis or polycythemia (HCT > 50%) within the first 2 years of life. Children with CHF usually respond to medical therapy, but may require intervention for refractory symptoms.

Table 14.2 *Classification of Tricuspid Atresia*

	Pulmonary Blood Flow	Incidence
Type 1: No TGA		
1A—No VSD, pulmonary atresia	↓	10%
1B—Small VSD, pulmonary stenosis	↓	50%
1C—Large VSD, no pulmonary stenosis	↑	10%
Type 2: D-TGA		
2A—VSD, pulmonary atresia	↓	2%
2B—VSD, pulmonary stenosis	↓	8%
2C—VSD, no pulmonary stenosis	↑↑	20%
Type 3: L-TGA		
3A—VSD, pulmonary stenosis	↓	rare
3B—VSD, subaortic stenosis	↑	rare

TGA, transposition of the great arteries.
Modified with permission from Strafford MA, DiNardo JA. Anesthesia for congenital heart disease. In: DiNardo JA, Schwartz MJ. Anesthesia for cardiac surgery. Norwalk, CT: Appleton & Lange, 1990:148.

3. **Surgical procedures**

   a. A balloon atrial septostomy should be performed in infants with a restrictive ASD. In older children, a blade atrial septostomy or atrial septectomy may be performed.

   b. PA banding is used to reduce PBF in patients with large VSDs and no pulmonary stenosis (types 1C, 2C) to prevent the development of pulmonary vascular disease.

   c. An MBTS is usually required for infants or children with severe cyanosis (types IA, IB, 2A, 2B).

   d. A bidirectional Glenn shunt can be used to improve PBF in children over the age of 6 months in preparation for a subsequent Fontan procedure.

   e. The Fontan operation represents the definitive procedure for patients with tricuspid atresia and is currently performed on children between 2 and 5 years of age.

   f. When significant subaortic obstruction is present with transposition, a Damus-Kaye-Stansel procedure may be performed in conjunction with a bidirectional Glenn shunt or a complete Fontan procedure (Damus-Fontan operation) (figure 14.12).[59]

E. **Ebstein's anomaly**

   1. **Pathology and pathophysiology**

      a. Ebstein's anomaly is a congenital defect of the tricuspid valve in which the septal and posterior leaflets are malformed and displaced into the right ventricle and the anterior leaflet is elongated and "sail-like."

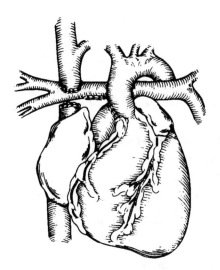

Figure 14.12 *Damus-Kaye-Stansel procedure for single ventricle with transposition and subaortic stenosis. The pulmonary artery is divided and sewn end-to-side to the aorta. A bidirectional Glenn (SVC to RPA anastomosis) is also performed. (Reproduced with permission of the Society of Thoracic Surgeons from Huddleston CB, Canter CE, Spray TL. Damus-Kaye-Stansel with cavopulmonary connection for single ventricle and subaortic obstruction. Ann Thorac Surg 1993;55:339–46.)*

    b.   The portion of the right ventricle that lies above the valve attachments (atrialized right ventricle) is usually thickened and dilated. The portion of the right ventricle that lies below the valve is usually thin-walled and smaller than normal with a decreased amount of muscle fibers. The right atrium is usually enormously enlarged, producing a massive cardiac silhouette on chest x-ray.

    c.   Clinical manifestations depend on the degree of right ventricular dysfunction, tricuspid incompetence, and right-to-left shunting across an interatrial communication, which is usually present.

    d.   Severe cyanosis and right heart failure resulting from severe tricuspid valve incompetence may be noted in the neonatal period. More commonly, progressive cyanosis and CHF with dyspnea and fatigue develop gradually in late childhood or early adulthood. Supraventricular and ventricular arrhythmias are common and cause sudden death in about 20% of patients. Wolff-Parkinson-White syndrome is present in 10% of patients.

  2. **Indications for surgery.** Severe cyanosis with polycythemia, progressive CHF, a left-to-right atrial shunt >2:1, paradoxical emboli, or debilitating arrhythmias from Wolff-Parkinson-White syndrome are indications for a surgical procedure.

  3. **Surgical procedures**

    a.   Surgical options in the newborn are limited. One option is to close the tricuspid valve and place an aortopulmonary shunt. This excludes the right ventricle from the circulation and creates "single ventricle" physiology that is amenable to a subsequent Fontan-like repair. In some centers, cardiac transplantation may be considered.

b. In older children, surgery involves placement of a prosthetic tricuspid valve, closure of the ASD, and occasionally plication of the atrialized right ventricle and excision of redundant right atrial tissue. In selected cases, tricuspid valve repair may be attempted.

c. Patients with concomitant Wolff-Parkinson-White syndrome should have either catheter or surgical ablation of accessory pathways.

VI. Complex Cyanotic Defects ("Mixing Lesions")

A. Double outlet right ventricle (DORV)

1. **Pathology and pathophysiology**

   a. DORV represents a complex spectrum of lesions in which one great artery and more than 50% of the other arise from the right ventricle. Left ventricular outflow to the great arteries must flow through a VSD.

   b. The clinical presentation depends on the orientation of the great vessels, the presence or absence of pulmonic stenosis, the level of PVR, the size and location of the VSD, and the presence of associated anomalies. DORVs are classified by the location of the VSD (subpulmonic, subaortic, doubly committed [lies beneath both valves], or uncommitted).

2. **Indications for surgery.** Surgery is indicated for progressive cyanosis or medically refractory CHF. Palliative procedures can usually delay a definitive correction until the child is at least 6 months of age.

3. **Surgical procedures**

   a. PA banding may be considered for DORV with subpulmonic or uncommitted VSDs and high PBF.

   b. Cyanotic patients may require a systemic-to-pulmonary artery shunt (usually an MBTS). An atrial septostomy or septectomy may be beneficial when there is a subpulmonary VSD.

   c. The technique of repair depends on the spatial relationship of the great arteries to the VSD and requires a thorough understanding of the underlying anatomy.[60,61]

      i. With a subaortic or doubly committed VSD, the VSD is enlarged, and a patch is used to tunnel the left ventricular outflow into the aorta. Resection of muscle bundles, an outflow patch, or an RV-to-PA valved homograft conduit may be required if infundibular obstruction is present.

      ii. When the aortic valve is too remote from the VSD (subpulmonic VSD), the VSD can be patched to tunnel the left ventricular outflow to the pulmonary artery, thus creating transposition of the great arteries. An atrial correction (Mustard, Senning) or arterial switch (Jatene, Damus-Kaye-Stansel) procedure must then be performed to restore a normal circulatory pattern.

        iii. In patients with uncommitted VSDs, it may be possible to tunnel the LV to the PA or the aorta. If this cannot be accomplished, the VSD is closed, an LV-to-PA conduit is placed (creating ventriculoarterial discordance), and an atrial correction procedure is performed. In some cases, a Fontan operation may be required if the intracardiac anatomy precludes a successful LV-to-aorta baffle.

        iv. If one of the ventricles is hypoplastic or there is a "straddling AV valve," a Fontan operation may be indicated.

B. Univentricular heart (single ventricle)

1. Pathology and pathophysiology

    a. Univentricular heart (UVH) refers to a spectrum of anomalies in which the heart has only one effective pumping chamber. The RV is usually hypoplastic while the LV develops normally. The chambers communicate via a large VSD (the bulboventricular foramen). D-TGA is usually present, such that the LV pumps directly into the PA and via the VSD into the aorta. Both AV valves are committed to the dominant chamber, and thus the most common type of UVH is termed a "double inlet left ventricle."

    b. About 40% of patients have pulmonary stenosis and develop cyanosis in early infancy. In its absence, children present with CHF and mild cyanosis from mixing in the single ventricle.

2. Indications for surgery. Palliative procedures may be indicated for progressive cyanosis in infancy or to reduce PBF and prevent pulmonary vascular disease.

3. Surgical procedures

    a. PA banding should be performed to limit excessive PBF to prevent pulmonary vascular disease.

    b. An MBTS should be performed for significant cyanosis resulting from diminished PBF.

    c. One of the modified Fontan procedures is performed after 2 years of age if standard criteria are met (see page 484).[62]

    d. The Damus-Kaye-Stansel procedure, in conjunction with a cavopulmonary anastomosis ("Damus-Fontan" operation), can be used when subaortic stenosis is present (see figure 14.12).[9]

C. Transposition of the great arteries (D-TGA)

1. Pathology and physiology

    a. D-TGA is characterized by the aorta arising anteriorly from the RV (instead of posteriorly from the LV) and the PA arising posteriorly from the LV. Approximately 30% of patients have an associated VSD and 10% also have subpulmonic stenosis.

b. Survival depends on mixing of the two parallel circulations by bidirectional shunting through an ASD, VSD, or PDA. The degree of arterial saturation is determined by the degree of intercirculatory mixing and the amount and saturation of systemic venous blood recirculated into the systemic circulation. Thus, a reduction in PBF caused by a VSD with LV outflow tract obstruction (pulmonic stenosis) or an increase in desaturated blood returning to the heart will produce more hypoxemia despite adequate intercirculatory mixing.

c. Severe cyanosis will be present at birth when the ASD is restrictive or a VSD is absent. This will intensify when the ductus begins to close. Therefore, use of PGE_1 is essential to maintain ductal patency until interventions can be performed.

2. **Indications for surgery.** Most infants have severe cyanosis at birth and require some form of intervention.

3. **Surgical procedures**

a. Initial palliation is obtained by a balloon atrial septostomy to achieve adequate size of the atrial septal communication. Patients with D-TGA, VSD, and PS may require an MBTS to improve pulmonary blood flow.

b. Redirection of flow to establish normal circulatory patterns can be accomplished by a physiologic correction at the atrial level (Mustard or Senning operation), or an anatomic correction at the level of the great arteries (arterial switch).

c. The **Mustard procedure** involves removal of the atrial septum and creation of a pericardial baffle that directs caval blood behind the baffle through the mitral valve into the LV and eventually into the PA. Pulmonary venous blood flows anterior to the baffle to reach the tricuspid valve, the RV, and then the aorta (figure 14.13). Thus the right ventricle continues to function as the systemic ventricle. Although the initial results of this operation were favorable, the late development of RV dysfunction, atrial dysrhythmias, and systemic and pulmonary venous obstruction led to its virtual abandonment.[63]

d. The **Senning operation** uses as much native cardiac tissue as possible for the repair (figure 14.14). It involves mobilizing flaps of the atrial free wall and septum to redirect flow in a manner similar to the Mustard procedure. It is also associated with RV dysfunction and dysrhythmias, and has thus seen limited use in the past few years.[64]

e. The **arterial switch operation** provides a definitive repair of D-TGA by reconnecting the aorta to the left ventricular outflow and the pulmonary artery to the right ventricular outflow. The coronary arteries are then translocated to the new aorta (figure 14.15). This is now considered the operation of choice for D-TGA.[65,66] The success of this procedure

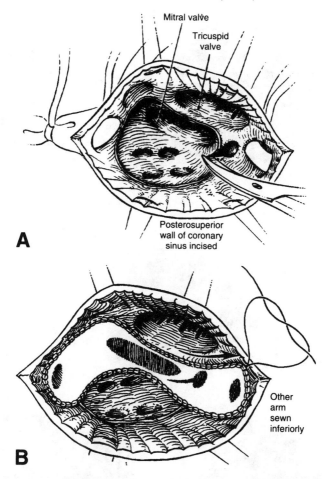

Mitral valve

Tricuspid valve

Posterosuperior wall of coronary sinus incised

A

Other arm sewn inferiorly

B

Figure 14.13 *The Mustard operation for transposition of the great arteries. (A) The atrial septum is excised. (B) A pericardial baffle channels systemic blood through the mitral valve and directs pulmonary venous return through the tricuspid valve. (Reproduced with permission from Hallman GL. Surgical treatment of congenital heart disease. Philadelphia: Lea & Febiger, 1975:163–5.)*

depends on the ability of the left ventricle to pump against systemic vascular resistance.

    i. For patients with D-TGA and intact ventricular septum, an arterial switch is usually performed during the first 2 weeks of life, at which time the left ventricle is thought to be "prepared" to sustain SVR following the operation. If the procedure is not performed at this time, preliminary PA banding (along with construction of an MBTS) may be necessary to prepare the left ventricle to sustain systemic flow.

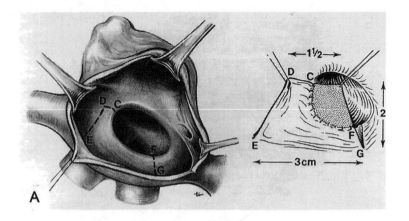

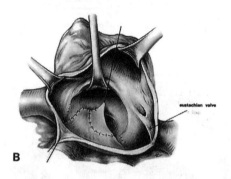

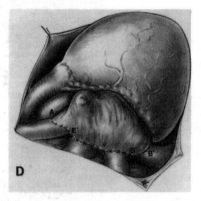

Figure 14.14 *The Senning operation for transposition of the great arteries. (A–B) The atrial septum is incised and sewn to the posterior atrial wall behind the mitral valve. (C) The right atrial free wall is divided longitudinally. The lateral flap is sewn between the mitral and tricuspid annuli to direct systemic venous drainage through the mitral valve. (D) The medial flap is sewn to an incision between the right pulmonary veins to close the neopulmonary venous atrium. (Reproduced with permission from Cohn LH. Modern techniques in surgery, cardiac/thoracic surgery, Mount Kisco, NY: Futura Publishing, 1979:16-5–16-7.)*

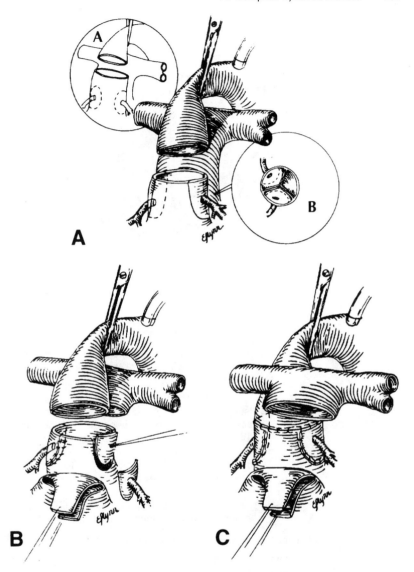

Figure 14.15 *Arterial switch repair for transposition of the great arteries. (A) The anteriorly located aorta is transected and coronary buttons are removed from the native aorta. (B) The pulmonary artery (PA) is transected and the coronary ostial buttons are transferred to the proximal main pulmonary artery (MPA). (C) The distal PA is translocated anterior to the aorta ("Lecompte maneuver") and the distal aorta is then sewn to the proximal MPA. (D) The neopulmonary artery is then reconstructed using pericardial patches to fill in the excised coronary buttons. The distal pulmonary artery is sewn to the old proximal aorta. The VSD is then closed. (Reproduced with permission of the Society of Thoracic Surgeons from Castaneda AR, Norwood WI, Jonas RA, et al. Transposition of the great arteries and intact ventricular septum: anatomical repair in the neonate. Ann Thorac Surg 1984;38:438–43.)*

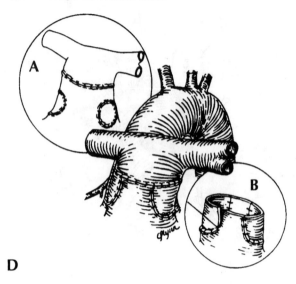

D

Figure 14.15 *Continued*

  ii. Patients with D-TGA with VSD are also candidates for the arterial switch. Even though some centers perform this operation within the first 2 weeks of life, it can often be performed later, because the nonrestrictive VSD ensures systemic LV pressures.

  iii. Patients with D-TGA, VSD, and pulmonic stenosis may develop cyanosis solely on the basis of reduced PBF. A systemic-to-pulmonary artery shunt may be required in infancy. A Rastelli operation is then performed during early childhood. The left ventricular outflow is baffled to the aorta through the VSD with a Dacron patch. The proximal main pulmonary artery is divided, and RV-PA continuity is reestablished with a homograft valved conduit (figure 14.16).[67]

D. **Total anomalous pulmonary venous connection (TAPVC)**

 1. **Pathology and pathophysiology**

  a. TAPVC is present when all of the pulmonary veins empty into the right-sided circulation, rather than draining into the left atrium. This provides complete mixing of pulmonary and systemic venous blood in the right atrium. An ASD must be present to allow blood to shunt right-to-left into the left atrium, then to the LV, and eventually into the systemic circulation.

  b. The extent of cyanosis is related to the adequacy of the ASD and to any obstruction of the pulmonary venous drainage at its connection with the systemic circulation.

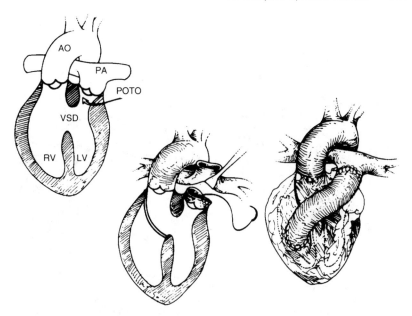

Figure 14.16 *The Rastelli operation for transposition of the great arteries with VSD and LV outflow tract obstruction. A VSD patch is placed to route LV outflow into the anteriorly located aorta. A homograft valved conduit is then placed to reestablish RV-PA continuity. (Reproduced with permission from Vouhe PR, Tamisier D, Leca F, Ouaknine R, Vernant F, Neveux JY. Transposition of the great arteries, ventricular septal defect, and pulmonary outflow tract obstruction. Rastelli or Lecompte procedure? J Thorac Cardiovasc Surg 1992;103:428–36.)*

    i. A restrictive ASD will reduce systemic and increase pulmonary blood flow, resulting in pulmonary vascular congestion. A nonrestrictive ASD will better balance the pulmonary and systemic blood flows.

    ii. Pulmonary venous obstruction is more common when the connecting vein has to travel a longer distance to join the systemic circulation. This will not only produce pulmonary vascular congestion, but will also increase PA pressures and reduce pulmonary blood flow. Consequently, infants with pulmonary venous obstruction will develop cyanosis and hypoxemia from pulmonary edema.

  c. The supracardiac type involves venous drainage directly into the SVC or into a vertical vein which empties into the innominate vein (figure 14.17).

  d. The intracardiac type is characterized by drainage of the common pulmonary vein directly into the coronary sinus or the posterior wall of the RA (figure 14.18). Pulmonary venous obstruction is occasionally observed.

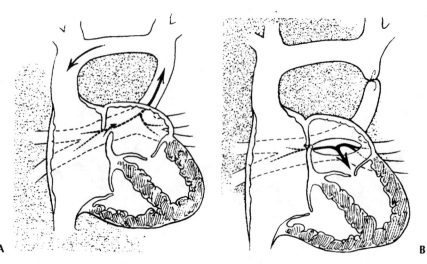

Figure 14.17 *Supracardiac total anomalous pulmonary venous connection. (A) The common pulmonary vein (CPV) connects with a vertical vein which drains into the innominate vein. (B) An anastomosis is made between the CPV and the left atrium. The ASD is then closed. (Reproduced with permission from Cooley DA. Techniques in cardiac surgery, 2nd ed. Philadelphia: WB Saunders, 1984:170.)*

      e. In the infracardiac type, the common pulmonary vein descends inferiorly through the diaphragm to drain into a hepatic vein, the portal vein, or the inferior vena cava (figure 14.19). Pulmonary venous obstruction is very common.

2. **Indications for surgery**

      a. Severe cyanosis or CHF resulting from pulmonary venous obstruction (usually in the infracardiac type) requires urgent intervention soon after birth. Use of PGE_1 for cyanosis is ineffective for this defect.

      b. In the absence of pulmonary venous obstruction, surgery is indicated for CHF or a pulmonary/systemic pressure ratio >0.5. Elective surgery should be performed during infancy.

3. **Surgical procedures**[68–70]

      a. A balloon atrial septostomy may be used for temporary palliation at the time of catheterization if a restrictive ASD is present.

      b. The supracardiac and infracardiac types are repaired by anastomosing the common pulmonary vein to the posterior wall of the left atrium and ligating the connecting vein to the systemic circulation. The ASD is also closed (see figures 14.17 and 14.19).

      c. The intracardiac type is repaired by removing the septum between the foramen ovale and the coronary sinus and placing a baffle over the two orifices to redirect pulmonary venous flow through the ASD into the LA (see figure 14.18).

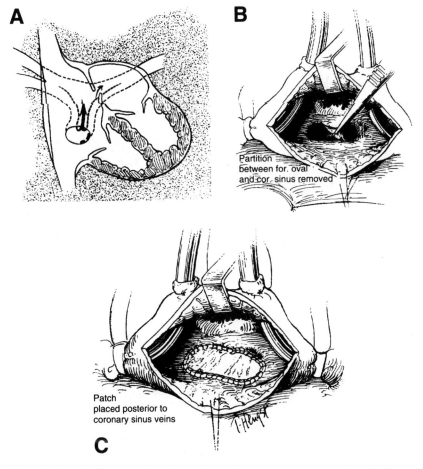

Figure 14.18 *Cardiac type of total anomalous pulmonary venous connection. (A) The common pulmonary vein enters the coronary sinus or posterior wall of the right atrium. (B) The septum between the foramen ovale and coronary sinus is removed. (C) A baffle is placed to redirect the venous return through the ASD into the left atrium. (Reproduced with permission from Cooley DA. Techniques in cardiac surgery, 2nd ed. Philadelphia: WB Saunders, 1984:174.)*

E. **Truncus arteriosus**

1. **Pathology and pathophysiology**

a. Truncus arteriosus is produced by absence of an aorticopulmonary septum. This results in a single great vessel arising from the heart which gives rise to the aorta, pulmonary artery, and coronary arteries. The truncal valve usually has 3–4 cusps and may have varying degrees of regurgitation or stenosis. The valve overlies a large VSD.

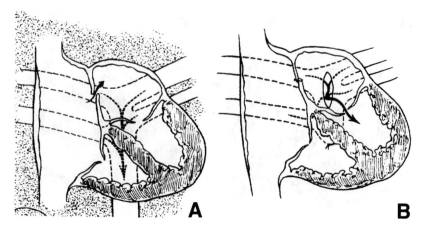

Figure 14.19 *Infracardiac type of total anomalous pulmonary venous connection. (A) The common pulmonary vein (CPV) descends through the diaphragm to enter the systemic venous circulation. (B) An anastomosis is made between the CPV and the left atrium and the vertical vein is ligated. The ASD is then closed. (Reproduced with permission from Cooley DA. Techniques in cardiac surgery, 2nd ed. Philadelphia: WB Saunders, 1984:173.)*

    b. In the most common type, one pulmonary artery arises from the truncus (type I). Less commonly, two separate pulmonary arteries arise side by side (type II). Rarely, the two PAs arise separately from the lateral walls of the truncus (type III).

    c. Most patients with truncus arteriosus manifest both congestive heart failure from excessive PBF and mild cyanosis from complete intracardiac mixing. The degree of CHF may increase when the PVR falls and may be exacerbated by truncal valve regurgitation. The cyanosis is usually mild because of a high $Q_p:Q_s$ ratio. The development of pulmonary vascular obstructive disease, however, will reduce PBF and increase the degree of cyanosis.

  2. **Indications for surgery.** Repair of this defect is recommended within the first 6 months of life to prevent the development of pulmonary vascular disease. Most centers are now performing definitive correction in the neonatal period.[71–73]

  3. **Surgical procedures**

    a. Definitive correction is performed by patch closure of the VSD, separation of the pulmonary artery or arteries from the aorta, closure of the truncal incision, and reestablishment of RV-PA continuity using a homograft valved conduit (figure 14.20). Truncal valve insufficiency may require placement of a mechanical or homograft valve.

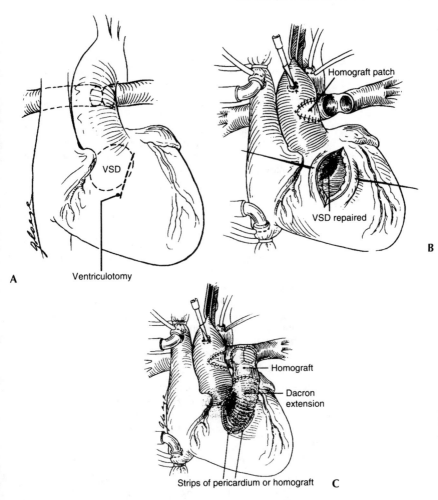

Figure 14.20 *Repair of a type II truncus arteriosus. (A) A right ventriculotomy is made and the VSD is closed. (B) The pulmonary arteries are separated from the truncus and the defect is patched. (C) A valved homograft conduit reestablishes continuity between the right ventricle and the pulmonary artery. (Reproduced with permission of the Society of Thoracic Surgeons from Pearl JL, Laks H, Drinkwater DC Jr, et al. Repair of truncus arteriosus in infancy. Ann Thorac Surg 1991;52:780–6.)*

    b.   Because repair of a truncus arteriosus is performed in a small child using small conduits, at least one additional operation will usually be required in the future for conduit obstruction. Either augmentation of the graft with a Dacron patch (producing pulmonary valve incompetence) or placement of a larger valved homograft conduit is performed.[74]

F. **Hypoplastic left heart syndrome (HLHS)**

1. **Pathology and pathophysiology**

   a. This complex abnormality is characterized by varying degrees of hypoplasia or atresia of the mitral valve, left ventricle, aortic valve, and ascending and transverse aorta.

   b. Blood returning from the lungs encounters a complete obstruction to left atrial outflow. Therefore, it passes left-to-right through an ASD into the right atrium where there is complete mixing of the pulmonary and systemic venous return. The presence of a restrictive ASD will produce pulmonary venous congestion.

   c. Blood then flows through the right ventricle and through the ductus to provide systemic flow. Proximal aortic and coronary blood flow occur retrograde through the hypoplastic ascending aorta. Thus, an infant who is mildly cyanotic at birth will deteriorate acutely when the ductus begins to close. Maintenance of ductal patency with PGE_1 is critical to survival.

   d. This lesion represents a form of single ventricle physiology. The relative amount of pulmonary and systemic blood flow is dictated by the pulmonary and systemic vascular resistances. An increase in PBF may improve oxygenation at the expense of impaired systemic perfusion. Conversely, an increase in systemic flow caused by an increase in PVR will produce hypoxemia.

2. **Indications for surgery.** Urgent surgery is indicated once the diagnosis is made. Until recently, HLHS was considered to be uniformly fatal, and surgical intervention was not advised. However, the Fontan principle can be applied to this defect after several staged procedures.[75–77]

3. **Surgical procedures**

   a. The first stage of repair involves an atrial septectomy to allow adequate mixing of blood, a central systemic-pulmonary artery shunt to provide a regulated amount of pulmonary blood flow, and reconstruction of the aorta to establish satisfactory systemic outflow from the right ventricle (Norwood procedure) (figure 14.21). The latter is accomplished by patch enlargement of the ascending aorta and arch with a homograft or pericardium. The main pulmonary artery is divided at its bifurcation and the proximal MPA is anastomosed to the enlarged neoaorta. The operative mortality for this palliative procedure ranges from 20–50% in most centers.

   b. At approximately 4–8 months of age, a cavopulmonary anastomosis is created between the SVC and the right PA, and the central shunt is ligated. This improves ventricular compliance, reduces volume overload, and encourages growth of the pulmonary arteries.

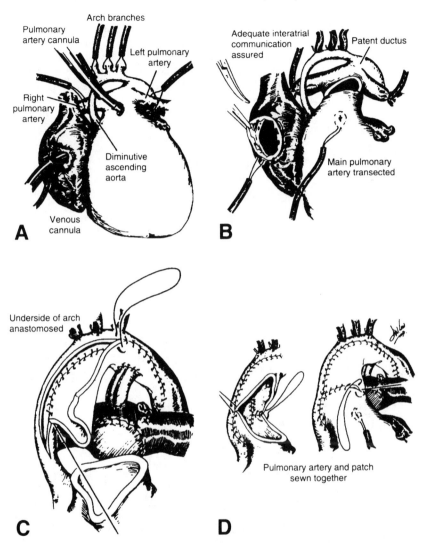

Figure 14.21 *Norwood procedure for hypoplastic left heart syndrome. (A) The basic pathology of this defect. (B) The pulmonary artery is divided, the distal PA is patched, and the ductus is divided. (C) The aorta is augmented with a pulmonary artery homograft gusset and a central shunt is placed to provide PBF. (D) The proximal pulmonary artery stump is then sewn to the reconstructed aorta. (Reproduced with permission from Edmunds LH Jr, Norwood WI, Low DW. Atlas of cardiothoracic surgery. Malvern, PA: Lea & Febiger, 1989.)*

   c. At 2–3 years of age, a modified (lateral tunnel) Fontan pro-
      cedure is performed. An intraatrial baffle is constructed with
      PTFE to channel the IVC flow to the SVC and into the RPA.
      The right ventricle thus serves as the systemic ventricle, and
      pulmonary blood flow is provided directly by systemic
      venous return.

   d. Heart transplantation has been considered a therapeutic
      alternative in infants with HLHS.[78]

References

1. Kirklin JW, Barratt-Boyes BG. Cardiac surgery, 2nd ed. New York: Churchill Livingstone Inc., 1993.
2. Castaneda AR, Jonas RA, Mayer JM, Hanley FL. Pediatric cardiac surgery of the neonate and infant. Philadelphia: WB Saunders, 1994.
3. Stark J, de Leval M. Surgery for congenital heart defects, 2nd ed. Philadelphia: WB Saunders, 1994.
4. Mavroudis C, Backer CL. Pediatric cardiac surgery, 2nd ed. St. Louis: Mosby, 1994.
5. Williams WH. Pulmonary valvar and infundibular stenosis. In: Grillo HC, Austen WG, Wilkins EW Jr, Mathisen DJ, Vlahakes GJ, eds. Current therapy in cardiothoracic surgery. Toronto: BC Decker, 1989:545–7.
6. Caspi J, Coles JG, Benson LN, et al. Management of neonatal critical pulmonic stenosis in the balloon valvotomy era. Ann Thorac Surg 1990;49:273–8.
7. Trusler GA, Williams WG. Congenital aortic stenosis. In: Grillo HC, Austen WG, Wilkins EW Jr, Mathisen DJ, Vlahakes GJ, eds. Current therapy in cardiothoracic surgery. Toronto: BC Decker, 1989:541–5.
8. Lupinetti FM, Pridjian AK, Callow LB, Crowley DC, Beekman RH, Bove EL. Optimum treatment of discrete subaortic stenosis. Ann Thorac Surg 1992;54:467–71.
9. Karl TR, Watterson KG, Sano S, Mee RBB. Operations for subaortic stenosis in univentricular hearts. Ann Thorac Surg 1991;52:420–8.
10. Turley K, Bove EL, Amato JJ, et al. Neonatal aortic stenosis. J Thorac Cardiovasc Surg 1990;99:679–84.
11. Reddy VH, Rajasinghe HA, Teitel DF, Haas GS, Hanley FL. Aortoventriculoplasty with the pulmonary autograft: the "Ross-Konno" procedure. J Thorac Cardiovasc Surg 1996;111:158–67.
12. van Heurn LWE, Wong CC, Spiegelhalter DJ, et al. Surgical treatment of aortic coarctation in infants younger than three months: 1985 to 1990. Success of extended end-to-end arch aortoplasty. J Thorac Cardiovasc Surg 1994;107:74–86.
13. Lacour-Gayet F, Bruniaux J, Serraf A, et al. Hypoplastic transverse arch and coarctation in neonates. Surgical reconstruction of the aortic arch: a study of sixty-six patients. J Thorac Cardiovasc Surg 1990;100:808–16.
14. van Son JAM, Daniels O, Vincent JG, van Lier HJJ, Lacquet LK. Appraisal of resection and end-to-end anastomosis for repair of coarctation of the aorta in infancy: preference for resection. Ann Thorac Surg 1989;48:496–502.
15. Sharma BK, Calderon M, Ott DA. Coarctation repair in neonates with subclavian-sparing advancement flap. Ann Thorac Surg 1992;54:137–41.
16. Dietl CA, Torres AR, Favaloro RG, Fessler CL, Grunkemeier GL. Risk of recoarctation in neonates and infants after repair with patch aortoplasty, subclavian flap, and the combined resection-flap procedure. J Thorac Cardiovasc Surg 1992;103:724–32.
17. Ala-Kulju K, Heikkinen L. Aneurysms after patch graft aortoplasty for coarctation of the aorta: long-term results of surgical management. Ann Thorac Surg 1989;47:853–6.
18. Sell JE, Jonas RA, Mayer JE, Blackstone EH, Kirklin JW, Castaneda AR. The results of a surgical program for interrupted aortic arch. J Thorac Cardiovasc Surg 1988;96:864–77.
19. Hakimi M, Clapp SK, Walters HL, Lyons JM, Morrow WR. Arch growth after staged repair of interrupted aortic arch using carotid artery interposition. Ann Thorac Surg 1997;64:503–7.
20. Hijazi ZM, Geggel RL. Transcatheter device closure of patent ductus arteriosus using coils. Am J Cardiol 1997;79:1279–80.
21. Coster DD, Gorton ME, Grooters RK, Thieman KC, Schneider RF, Soltanzadeh H. Surgical closure of the patent ductus arteriosus in the neonatal intensive care unit. Ann Thorac Surg 1989;48:386–9.

22. Bjornstad PG, Masura J, Thaulow E, et al. Interventional closure of atrial septal defects with the Amplatzer device: first clinical experience. Cardiol Young 1997;7:277–83.

23. McDaniel N, Gutgesell JP, Nolan SP, Kron IL. Repair of large muscular ventricular septal defects in infants employing left ventriculotomy. Ann Thorac Surg 1989;47:593–4.

24. Bridges ND, Perry SB, Kean JF, et al. Preoperative transcatheter closure of congenital muscular ventricular septal defects. N Engl J Med 1991;324:1312–7.

25. Bando K, Turrentine MW, Sun K, et al. Surgical management of complete atrioventricular septal defects. A twenty-year experience. J Thorac Cardiovasc Surg 1995; 110:1543–54.

26. Ho SY, Gerlis LM, Anderson C, Devine WA, Smith A. The morphology of aortopulmonary windows with regard to their classification and morphogenesis. Cardiol Young 1994;4:146–55.

27. Doty DB, Richardson JV, Falkovsky GE, Gordonova MI, Burakovsky VI. Aortopulmonary septal defect: hemodynamics, angiography, and operation. Ann Thorac Surg 1981;32:244–50.

28. Prasad TR, Valiathan MS, Shyamakrishnan KG, Venkitachalam CG. Surgical management of aortopulmonary septal defect. Ann Thorac Surg 1989;47:877–9.

29. de Leval MR. Palliation in congenital heart disease. In: Grillo HC, Austen WG, Wilkins EW Jr, Mathisen DJ, Vlahakes GJ, eds. Current therapy in cardiothoracic surgery. Toronto: BC Decker, 1989:468–71.

30. Tamisier DM, Vouhe PR, Vernant F, Leca F, Massot C, Neveux JY. Modified Blalock-Taussig shunts: results in infants less than 3 months of age. Ann Thorac Surg 1990;49:797–801.

31. Okita Y, Miki S, Kusuhara K, et al. Palliative reconstruction of right ventricular outflow tract in tetralogy with hypoplastic pulmonary arteries. Ann Thorac Surg 1990;49: 775–9.

32. Horowitz MD, Culpepper WS III, Williams LC III, Sundgaard-Riise K, Ochsner JL. Pulmonary artery banding: analysis of a 25-year experience. Ann Thorac Surg 1989;48:444–50.

33. Casthely PA, Redko V, Dluzneski J, et al. Pulse oximetry during pulmonary artery banding. J Cardiothorac Anesthesia 1987;1:297–9.

34. Lamberti JJ, Spicer RL, Waldman JD, et al. The bidirectional cavopulmonary shunt. J Thorac Cardiovasc Surg 1990;100:22–30.

35. Bridges ND, Jonas RA, Mayer JE, Flanagan MF, Keane JF, Castaneda AR. Bidirectional cavopulmonary anastomosis as interim palliation for high-risk Fontan candidates. Early results. Circulation 1990;82(suppl 4):IV-170–6.

36. de Leval MR, Kilner P, Gewillig M, Bull C. Total cavopulmonary connection: a logical alternative to atriopulmonary connection for complex Fontan operations. Experimental studies and early clinical experience. J Thorac Cardiovasc Surg 1988;96:682–95.

37. Giannico S, Corno A, Marino G, et al. Total extracardiac right heart bypass. Circulation 1992;86(suppl 2):II-110–17.

38. Pearl JM, Laks H, Stein DG, Drinkwater DC, George BL, Williams RG. Total cavopulmonary anastomosis versus conventional modified Fontan procedure. Ann Thorac Surg 1991;52:189–96.

39. Mavroudis C, Backer CL, Deal BJ. The total cavopulmonary artery Fontan connection using lateral tunnel and extracardiac techniques. Operative Techniques in Cardiac and Thoracic Surgery 1997;2:180–95.

40. Laks H, Pearl JM, Haas GS, et al. Partial Fontan: advantages of an adjustable interatrial communication. Ann Thorac Surg 1991;52:1084–95.

41. Kopf GS, Kleinman CS, Hijazi ZM, Fahey JT, Dewar ML, Hellenbrand WE. Fenestrated Fontan operation with delayed transcatheter closure of atrial septal defect. Improved results in high-risk patients. J Thorac Cardiovasc Surg 1992;103:1039–48.

42. Abramov D, Barak J, Raanani E, Birk E, Vidne BA. Early definitive repair of tetralogy of Fallot: a review of 74 cases. Cardiol Young 1997;7:254–7.

43. Strafford MA, DiNardo JA. Anesthesia for congenital heart disease. In: DiNardo JA, Schwartz MJ, eds. Anesthesia for cardiac surgery. Norwalk, CT: Appleton & Lange, 1990:117–72.

44. Nussbaum J, Zane EA, Thys DM. Esmolol for treatment of hypercyanotic spells in infants with tetralogy of Fallot. J Cardiothorac Anesthesia 1989;3:200–2.

45. Pacifico AD, Sand ME, Bargeron LM Jr, Colvin EC. Transatrial-transpulmonary repair of tetralogy of Fallot. J Thorac Cardiovasc Surg 1987;93:919–24.

46. Warner KG, Anderson JE, Fulton DR, Payne DD, Geggel RL, Marx GR. Restoration of the pulmonary valve reduces right ventricular volume overload after previous repair of tetralogy of Fallot. Circulation 1993;88(part 2):189–97.

47. Clarke DR, Campbell DN, Pappas G. Pulmonary allograft conduit repair of tetralogy of Fallot. An alternative to transannular patch repair. J Thorac Cardiovasc Surg 1989;98:730–7.

48. Sawatari K, Imai Y, Kurosawa H, Isomatsu Y, Momma K. Staged operation for pulmonary atresia and ventricular septal defect with major aortopulmonary collateral arteries. New technique for complete unifocalization. J Thorac Cardiovasc Surg 1989; 98:738–50.

49. Puga FJ, Leoni FE, Julsrud PR, Mair DD. Complete repair of pulmonary atresia, ventricular septal defect, and severe peripheral arborization abnormalities of the central pulmonary arteries. Experience with preliminary unifocalization procedures in 38 patients. J Thorac Cardiovasc Surg 1989;98:1018–29.

50. Iyer KS, Mee RBB. Staged repair of pulmonary atresia with ventricular septal defect and major systemic to pulmonary artery collaterals. Ann Thorac Surg 1991;51:65–72.

51. Reddy VH, Liddicoat JR, Hanley FL. Midline one-stage complete unifocalization and repair of pulmonary atresia with ventricular septal defect and major aortopulmonary collaterals. J Thorac Cardiovasc Surg 1995;109:832–45.

52. Tchervenkov CJ, Salasidis G, Cecere R, et al. One-stage midline unifocalization and complete repair in infancy versus multiple-stage unifocalization followed by repair for complex heart disease with major aortopulmonary collaterals. J Thorac Cardiovasc Surg 1997;114:727–37.

53. Hanley FL, Sade RM, Blackstone EH, Kirklin JW, Freedom RM, Nanda NC. Outcomes in neonatal pulmonary atresia with intact ventricular septum. A multiinstitutional study. J Thorac Cardiovasc Surg 1993;105:406–27.

54. Hawkins JA, Thorne JK, Boucek MM, et al. Early and late results in pulmonary atresia and intact ventricular septum. J Thorac Cardiovasc Surg 1990;100:492–7.

55. McCaffrey FM, Leatherbury L, Moore HV. Pulmonary atresia and intact ventricular septum. Definitive repair in the neonatal period. J Thorac Cardiovasc Surg 1991;102: 617–23.

56. Pawade A, Mee RBB, Karl T. Right ventricular "overhaul"—an intermediate step in the biventricular repair of pulmonary atresia with intact ventricular septum. Cardiol Young 1995;5:161–5.

57. Mair DD, Julsrud PR, Puga FJ, Danielson GK. The Fontan procedure for pulmonary atresia with intact ventricular septum: operative and late results. J Am Coll Cardiol 1997;29:1359–64.

58. Gentles TL, Keane JF, Jonas RA, Marx GM, Mayer JE. Surgical alternatives to the Fontan procedure incorporating a hypoplastic right ventricle. Circulation 1994;90(part 2): II-1–6.

59. Huddleston CB, Canter CE, Spray TL. Damus-Kaye-Stansel with cavopulmonary connection for single ventricle and subaortic obstruction. Ann Thorac Surg 1993;55: 339–4.

60. Lecompte Y, Batisse A, Di Carlo D. Double-outlet right ventricle: a surgical synthesis. Advances in Cardiac Surgery 1993;4:109–36.
61. Aoki M, Forbess JM, Jonas RA, Mayer JE, Castaneda AR. Result of biventricular repair for double-outlet right ventricle. J Thorac Cardiovasc Surg 1994;107:338–50.
62. Cohen AJ, Cleveland DC, Dyck J, et al. Results of the Fontan operation for patients with univentricular heart. Ann Thorac Surg 1991;52:1266–71.
63. Merlo M, Tommasi MD, Brunelli F, et al. Long-term results after atrial correction of complete transposition of the great arteries. Ann Thorac Surg 1991;51:227–31.
64. Litwin SB, Bhavani SS. The Senning procedure for repair of d-transposition of the great arteries. J Cardiac Surg 1987;2:415–28.
65. Castaneda AR, Jonas RA, Mayer JE, Hanley FL. Cardiac surgery of the neonate and infant. Philadelphia: WB Saunders Co, 1994:420.
66. Mee RBB. The arterial switch operation. In: Stark J, de Leval M, eds. Surgery for congenital heart defects, 2nd ed. Philadelphia: WB Saunders, 1994:483.
67. Vouhe PR, Tamisier D, Leca F, Ouaknine R, Vernant FM, Neveuz JY. Transposition of the great arteries, ventricular septal defect, and pulmonary outflow tract obstruction. Rastelli or Lecompte procedure? J Thorac Cardiovasc Surg 1992;103:428–36.
68. Cobanoglu A, Menashe VD. Total anomalous pulmonary venous connection in neonates and young infants: repair in the current era. Ann Thorac Surg 1993;55:43–9.
69. Wilson WR Jr, Ilbawi MN, DeLeon SY, et al. Technical modifications for improved results in total anomalous pulmonary venous drainage. J Thorac Cardiovasc Surg 1992;103:861–71.
70. Raisher BD, Grant JW, Martin TC, Strauss AW, Spray TL. Complete repair of total anomalous pulmonary venous connection in infancy. J Thorac Cardiovasc Surg 1992; 104:443–8.
71. Turley K. Current method of repair of truncus arteriosus. J Card Surg 1992;7:1–4.
72. Hanley FL, Heinemann MK, Jonas JA, et al. Repair of truncus arteriosus in the neonate. J Thorac Cardiovasc Surg 1993;105:1047–56.
73. Bove EL, Lupinetti FM, Pridjian AK, et al. Results of a policy of primary repair of truncus arteriosus in the neonate. J Thorac Cardiovasc Surg 1993;105:1057–66.
74. Heinemann MK, Hanley FL, Fenton KN, Jonas RA, Mayer JE, Castaneda AR. Fate of small homograft conduits after early repair of truncus arteriosus. Ann Thorac Surg 1993;55:1409–12.
75. Norwood WI Jr. Hypoplastic left heart syndrome. Ann Thorac Surg 1991;52:688–95.
76. Forbess JM, Cook N, Serraf A, Burke RP, Mayer JE, Jonas RC. An institutional experience with second- and third-stage palliative procedures for hypoplastic left heart syndrome: the impact of the bidirectional cavopulmonary shunt. J Am Coll Cardiol 1997;29:665–70.
77. Bove EL, Mosca RS. Surgical repair of hypoplastic left heart syndrome. Progress in Pediatric Cardiol 1996;5:23–35.
78. Razzouk AJ, Chinnock RE, Gundry SR, et al. Transplantation as a primary treatment for hypoplastic left heart syndrome: intermediate-term results. Ann Thorac Surg 1996;62:1–8.

15 Preparation of the Pediatric Patient for Cardiac Surgery

15 Preparation of the Pediatric Patient for Cardiac Surgery

The wide diversity in the ages and sizes of pediatric patients as well as the various presentations of congenital heart disease mandate great attention to detail to optimize perioperative care. Liberal consultation with pediatric cardiologists, pediatricians, and neonatologists should be sought in dealing with the intricate problems unique to the pediatric population.

I. History and Physical Examination

A. The history and examination should seek to identify other congenital abnormalities as well as provide a comprehensive review of the child's health. Specific attention should be directed toward evaluation of cardiac function. This should include any evidence of recent deterioration, such as increasing symptoms of heart failure or cyanosis, change in a cardiac murmur or loss of a shunt murmur, or appearance of a gallop. Any problems that might contraindicate surgery or adversely affect surgical outcome should be identified.

B. Cyanosis is defined as the presence of more than 5 g/dL of reduced hemoglobin. The compensatory response to hypoxia is an increase in hemoglobin concentration (polycythemia), with hematocrits as high as 65%. This response is less efficient in the cyanotic neonate. Anemic children may be more hypoxemic, yet appear less cyanotic, than polycythemic patients despite a similar arterial oxygen saturation because the total amount of reduced hemoglobin is less.

C. Signs and symptoms of cyanosis

1. Tachypnea and tachycardia
2. Clubbing of the nail beds
3. Small for age from poor feeding
4. Fatigue and poor exercise tolerance
5. Mental obtundation

D. Signs and symptoms of congestive heart failure

1. Tachycardia and tachypnea
2. Frequent respiratory infections
3. Wheezing, diffuse rhonchi
4. Feeding difficulties (sweating) and failure to thrive (small for age)
5. Evidence of peripheral vasoconstriction (pale, cool, mottled extremities with poor capillary refill)
6. Hepatomegaly, ascites

II. Considerations in Different Age Groups

A. **Premature infants**

1. Lungs: bronchopulmonary dysplasia, meconium aspiration, pneumothorax

    2. Heart: other associated congenital anomalies

    3. GI tract: malrotation, intestinal atresia, necrotizing enterocolitis

    4. Hematologic: vitamin K deficiency

    5. Metabolic: hypoglycemia, hypocalcemia

B. **Infants (age <1 year)**

    1. Otitis media

    2. Upper respiratory infections: respiratory syncytial virus (RSV) has been associated with postoperative respiratory morbidity and mortality. Any suspicion of RSV should prompt an analysis of nasal washings for viral isolation; a course of ribavirin may be indicated in some patients.[1,2]

C. **Toddlers and children (ages 1 to 11 years)**

    1. Upper respiratory infections (otitis media and tonsillitis) and gastrointestinal infections (including parasites) are the most common problems encountered in these patients.

    2. Parental involvement in daily care and during evaluation of the child (examination and blood drawing) is helpful in allaying the child's fear of separation, and may alleviate parental stress as well.

D. **Teenagers (>11 years of age)**

    1. Viral and bacterial infections and concomitant medical problems (diabetes, asthma, coagulopathy) should be identified. Potential occult conditions—such as venereal or gynecologic disease, pregnancy, or drug dependency—cannot be ignored in this population.

    2. Teenagers are inquisitive with evolving concepts of self-image, and they often require a careful explanation of every procedure and medication. The explanation of the surgical procedure should include both the child and the parents, offering both the opportunity to ask questions.

III.   Preoperative Diagnostic Studies

A. **Hematologic:** CBC, PT, PTT, platelet count (elevated PT and PTT are common in cyanotic children)

B. **Chemistry:** electrolytes, BUN, creatinine, glucose, calcium (in neonates), drug levels (e.g., digoxin)

C. **Urinalysis**

D. **Chest x-ray** allows for the identification of:

    1. Pulmonary infiltrates

    2. Pulmonary vascular congestion (suggesting a left-to-right shunt) or pulmonary hypovascularity (suggesting a right-to-left shunt)

    3. Visceral situs (based on the position of the liver and gastric bubble)

4. Side of the aortic arch (may influence the side of placement of a Blalock-Taussig shunt)

5. Typical appearance of certain abnormalities (i.e., coeur de sabot of tetralogy of Fallot, "egg on side" of D-TGA)

6. Absence of a thymus gland (DiGeorge syndrome): these patients should receive irradiated blood products to destroy lymphocytes and prevent graft-versus-host reaction.

E. **Electrocardiogram**

1. Rate and rhythm

2. Strain patterns (volume overload)

3. Consistency with the preoperative diagnosis (e.g., presence of left axis deviation with an ASD confirms an ostium primum defect)

4. ECG changes or dysrhythmias resulting from previous operations

F. **Two-dimensional echocardiography** is a very sensitive diagnostic tool that has supplanted cardiac catheterization in many centers for the diagnosis of most congenital heart lesions.[3] It should be repeated if there has been a significant change in the child's condition. It can also be used postoperatively to identify residual shunts, persistent septal defects, or assess shunt patency.

G. **Cardiac catheterization** data should be reviewed before surgery to confirm the diagnosis and make operative plans. Specific issues concern:

1. Anatomical abnormalities of the heart, great vessels, and pulmonary arteries; location of septal defects by catheter position and contrast injection

2. Oxygen saturations in the heart chambers

3. Pressures in the heart chambers

4. Systemic/pulmonary flow ratios for shunts

5. Definition of collateral blood flow

6. Gradients across valves or vessels

7. Coronary artery anatomy

IV. Other Preoperative Considerations

A. Therapeutic cardiac catheterization is playing a larger role in the management of children with congenital heart disease.[4] These procedures may improve the patient's condition before surgery, serve as adjuncts to the surgical procedure, or entirely obviate the need for an operation. Procedures include:

1. Balloon atrial septostomy to increase atrial septal mixing and palliate cyanosis

2. Balloon dilatation of pulmonic, mitral, or aortic stenosis

3. Balloon angioplasty of coarctation, systemic venous or branch pulmonary artery stenosis

4. Implantation of devices to occlude collateral vessels (coils), a patent ductus arteriosus (coils), or septal defects, such as a secundum ASD or muscular VSDs.

B. Children with severe cyanosis may be dependent on ductal flow for survival. Prostaglandin E_1 (PGE_1) is given to maintain ductal patency. Because PGE_1 is a potent vasodilator, volume infusions may be necessary to maintain blood pressure and may produce peripheral edema.[5,6] Inotropic support, such as dopamine, may also be necessary to improve hemodynamics. Aggressive correction of acidosis and intubation with mechanical ventilation may also be required to improve the infant's general condition to tolerate an urgent operative procedure. Obstructed total anomalous pulmonary venous connection is the one cyanotic defect that will not improve with PGE_1.

V. Preparation for Surgery

A. Antibiotics

1. Cefazolin 12.5 mg/kg IV before surgical incision
2. Vancomycin 12.5 mg/kg IV before surgical incision if allergic to cephalosporins or anaphylactic reaction to penicillin

B. Blood bank

1. Non-CPB cases
   a. Neonates: 125 mL packed cells (1/2 unit)
   b. Children <10 kg: 250 mL packed cells (1 unit)
   c. Children >10 kg: 500 mL packed cells (2 units)
2. CPB cases
   a. Neonates: 500 mL packed cells (2 units)
   b. Infants and children: 750 mL packed cells (3 units); in addition, 3–6 units of pooled platelets, 2 units of fresh frozen plasma, and 2 units of cryoprecipitate (to be thawed on request) should be available in the blood bank for patients with cyanotic heart disease.
3. Attempts should be made to have fresh whole blood (FWB) available for infants, especially those with cyanotic heart disease. FWB contains platelets and clotting factors and produces superior hemostasis to use of multiple fractionated blood products.

C. Most medications, including digoxin and diuretics, are withheld the morning of surgery.

D. Vitamin K (0.25 mg/kg by slow IV bolus) may be given to infants before open-heart operations to improve their impaired coagulation status.

E. **Premedication** is ordered by the anesthesia service. Avoidance of an increase in pulmonary vascular resistance (PVR) is essential in patients with right-to-left shunts. Premedication is beneficial in reducing the child's baseline oxygen consumption; however, respiratory depression that could produce hypoxia, hypercarbia, or acidosis—factors that increase the PVR—must be avoided. Anesthetic agents that increase SVR (ketamine) or

Table 15.1   *Preoperative Checklist*

Preoperative diagnosis: _____
Planned procedure: _____
Laboratory data:
  Hemoglobin/hematocrit
  White cell count
  PT, PTT, platelet count
  Urinalysis
  Electrolytes, BUN, creatinine, glucose
Catheterization (or echocardiogram) data
Chest x-ray report
ECG in chart with interpretation
Blood product availability: (itemize)
Antibiotics ordered
Anesthetic premedications ordered
Signed informed consent in chart

reduce PVR (fentanyl) are beneficial in cyanotic patients. Patients with CHF may also receive these medications because they produce minimal hemodynamic depression.

F. Most children are kept NPO for solids after midnight. Clear fluids can be given up to about 3–4 hours before surgery in young children and infants to avoid dehydration. This is especially important in cyanotic infants in whom polycythemia is associated with an increase in blood viscosity that can precipitate cerebral or renal thrombosis.[7] Supplemental intravenous fluids should be considered if the child is kept NPO for more than a few hours.

G. Checklist. The evening before surgery, the patient's medical record should be reviewed thoroughly and the patient examined for any contraindications to surgery. Table 15.1 provides a checklist to make sure that important results are not overlooked.

References

1. MacDonald NE, Hall CB, Suffin SC, et al. Respiratory syncytial viral infection in infants with congenital heart disease. N Engl J Med 1982;307:397–400.
2. Sullivan BJ. Respiratory syncytial virus and ribavirin. Pediatr Infect Dis 1986;5:605–6.
3. Gutgesell HP. Echocardiography as an alternative to cardiac catheterization prior to surgery for congenital heart disease. Cardiac surgery : state of the art reviews. Philadelphia: Hanley & Belfus, 1989:279–96.
4. Allen H, Beekman RH III, Garson A Jr, et al. Pediatric therapeutic cardiac catheterization. A statement for health professionals from the council on cardiovascular disease in the young, American Heart Association. Circulation 1998;97:609–35.
5. Freed MD, Heymann MA, Lewis AB, et al. Prostaglandin E_1 in infants with ductus arteriosus-dependent congenital heart disease. Circulation 1981;64:899–905.
6. Lewis AB, Freed MD, Heymann MA, et al. Side effects of therapy with prostaglandin E_1 in infants with critical congenital heart disease. Circulation 1981;64:893–8.
7. Cote GJ. NPO after midnight in children—a reappraisal. Anesthesiology 1990;72:589–92.

16 Postoperative Care in the Pediatric ICU

16 Postoperative Care in the Pediatric ICU

I. Leaving the Operating Room

A. Transfer of the pediatric cardiac surgical patient from the operating room to the ICU is a critical phase when destabilization can occur. Problems such as displacement of the endotracheal tube or intravenous lines, alteration in drug infusion rates, or hypothermia from exposure to ambient temperature may contribute to sudden deterioration.

B. Several measures should be taken to ensure a well-organized transfer from the operating room.

1. The child should be hemodynamically stable before transfer.

2. All catheters and tubes **must be sutured securely** to the skin and reinforced with tape. If a nasotracheal tube is used, it should be secured to the upper lip.

3. Continuous monitoring of ECG and arterial pressure is essential. Pulse oximetry is helpful in assessing oxygen saturation and peripheral perfusion.

4. All medications should be infused using portable infusion control devices whose battery function is ensured before transfer.

5. Equipment for reintubation and management of a cardiac arrest (medications, pacemakers, portable monitor/defibrillator) must be available.

C. The ICU should be aware in advance of the type of ventilatory support that will be required, which intracardiac lines have been placed, and which cardiac medications are being used.

II. Arriving in the ICU

A. A standard acceptance protocol should be followed to ensure a safe transition to the ICU (table 16.1). An individual well-versed in pediatric intensive care who is expert in intubation, line insertion, pharmacologic intervention, and monitoring techniques should supervise the patient's arrival in the ICU.

B. Airway/ventilator

1. Check breath sounds and chest wall movement during manual and then mechanical ventilation.

2. Select initial ventilator settings:

   a. $FIO_2 = 1.0$

   b. Tidal volume $= 10-15$ mL/kg

   c. Peak pressure <25 cm H_2O

   d. PEEP $= 2-5$ cm H_2O

Table 16.1 *Arrival Checklist*

❏ Identify person in charge
❏ Check all vital signs manually
❏ Ventilatory care
  • Check endotracheal tube position and resecure if necessary
  • Transfer patient to ventilator and confirm bilateral breath sounds
❏ Intracardiac and intravenous lines
  • Inspect and check all IVs for patency and resecure if necessary
  • Review all medication drips; check and recalculate infusion doses and rates
❏ Transfer ECG and pressure lines to ICU monitors
❏ Other lines and tubes
  • Aspirate nasogastric tube and place to gravity drainage
  • Connect thoracic drainage system to suction
  • Secure urinary catheter and record initial drainage
❏ Take report
❏ Perform thorough physical examination
❏ Draw blood for laboratory data, including ABGs
❏ Obtain and review portable chest x-ray and note:
  • Endotracheal tube position
  • Bilateral lung expansion
  • Location of intracardiac lines
  • Cardiac silhouette
  • Nasogastric tube location

  e. Respiratory rate for age
      • Newborn: 30–40/min
      • Infant: 20–30/min
      • Older than 1 year: 18–28/min

  f. I/E ratio = 1:2 (use a 1:1 ratio in neonates and young infants, who benefit from a longer inspiratory phase to minimize airway resistance)

C. Vital signs

  1. Confirm rate, rhythm, and ECG morphology on a portable monitor and then connect the leads to the bedside monitor.

  2. Check blood pressure manually by auscultation or Doppler method and check the femoral arterial pulse; if these are satisfactory, connect the arterial line to the calibrated bedside monitor and corroborate the display with manual readings.

  3. Connect intracardiac lines to a calibrated bedside monitor and record readings. Air filters should be considered for both intracardiac and peripheral IV lines in small infants.

  4. Take and record the rectal temperature.

D. Observe the initial amount of chest tube drainage in the collection chamber and examine the amount of blood within the chest tubes.

E. Physical examination

  1. Auscultate for bilateral breath sounds.

  2. Examine extremities for pulses, capillary refill, and temperature.

3. Check all intracardiac lines, chest tubes, and pacing electrodes for security.

F. A comprehensive report should be given by the anesthesia/surgical team to the ICU nursing and physician staff. This should include the patient's history and cardiac pathology, operative procedure and course, current medications, and monitoring lines being used. The location of all lines and tubes should also be diagrammed in the patient's operative note.

G. Postoperative orders should be written (table 16.2), and fluid and drug therapy plans discussed with the nursing service.

1. Confirm all medication drip concentrations and delivery rates.

2. Change over to new medication bottles and intravenous fluid infusions *only after* the patient is settled and hemodynamically stable.

H. A portable supine chest x-ray should be performed once the patient is stabilized to check for:

1. Position of the endotracheal tube (ET) tube, intravascular catheters, and the nasogastric tube

2. Condition of the lung fields (atelectasis, pulmonary vasculature)

3. A pneumothorax or hemothorax (opacification of a hemithorax on a supine film)

4. The width of the cardiac silhouette and the mediastinum

III. Monitoring Techniques in the ICU

The techniques of physiologic monitoring of pediatric patients have advanced greatly during the past few years. Both invasive and noninvasive techniques provide valuable information that should be used in conjunction with patient examination in making management decisions.[1,2]

A. A continuous **ECG** display of heart rate and rhythm permits rapid evaluation of arrhythmias that may herald hemodynamic instability.

B. **Hemodynamics**

1. Continuous **arterial blood pressure** monitoring is accomplished using radial, femoral, or pedal arterial lines which are connected through a transducer to the bedside monitor.[3]

a. Extreme care must be used to maintain the patency of arterial lines and protect them from inadvertent disconnection. A continuous flush device is used to prevent line thrombosis. Forceful manual flushing must be avoided because it can damage the vessel and propel air bubbles and small clots retrograde into the aortic arch and up to the brain. A low pressure alarm should be used to bring attention to disconnection, which could result in exsanguination.

b. These catheters may be a source of sepsis as well as peripheral emboli, which may cause loss of a finger, toe, or even an entire extremity. Attention to distal perfusion is essential. Pulse oximetry may draw attention to impaired peripheral perfusion beyond a catheter.

Table 16.2   *Routine Postoperative Orders*

1. Admit to Intensive Care Unit
2. Procedure: _____
3. Condition: _____
4. Vital signs q15 min until stable, then q30 min
5. Hourly intake and output (I&O)
6. Milk chest tubes and record drainage q15 min for 2 h, then q30 min; notify surgeon for bleeding >5 mL/kg/h
7. NPO
8. Nasogastric tube to gravity drainage
9. Urinary catheter to gravity drainage or patient due to void within 3 hours of arrival in ICU
10. Portable chest x-ray STAT and in morning
11. ECG STAT and in morning
12. Laboratory studies:
    ❑ CBC, PT, PTT, platelet count
    ❑ Electrolytes, glucose, ABGs q3h for 12 h, then q6h for the next 12 h after surgery (include calcium for neonates)
13. Respiratory care:
    ❑ Chest physical therapy q2h and prn
    ❑ Instill saline and suction endotracheal tube q1h and prn while intubated
    ❑ Nasotracheal suction extubated patients q2h prn
14. Ventilator settings:
    FIO_2 = _____
    Wean FIO_2 to 0.40 for PaO_2 > _____ torr
    Respiratory rate = _____/min
    Peak inspiratory pressure _____ cm H_2O (<25 cm H_2O)
    Tidal volume = _____ mL (10–15 mL/kg)
    PEEP = _____ cm H_2O (3–5 cm H_2O)
    Nebulizer temperature at 36°C
15. Pacemaker settings

Medications
16. Dextrose 5% (10% in neonates) in 0.2% normal saline infuse to provide one-half maintenance rate including all drips.
17. Potassium 80 mEq in 250 mL D5W **via central venous line only and via Buretrol up to maximum dose of 0.5 mEq/kg/h** to maintain K^+ between 4.0 and 4.5; check K^+ q2–3h. Or, if no central line available, potassium 2–4 mEq/100 mL maintenance IV fluids
18. Antibiotics (given until chest tubes are removed)
    ❑ Cefazolin 50 mg/kg/24 h IV q8h
      or
    ❑ Vancomycin 40 mg/kg/24 h IV q6h
19. Analgesics and sedatives
    ❑ Morphine sulfate 0.1 mg/kg IV q2h prn (intubated patients only)
    ❑ Fentanyl 2–5 μg/kg/h continuous infusion
    ❑ Midazolam 0.05–0.2 mg/kg q1–2h
20. Acetaminophen suppository 10–15 mg/kg/dose rectally q3h prn pain or temperature >38°C
21. Cardiac medications

c. The direct arterial pressure measurement should be confirmed by a manual technique. The auscultatory method requires use of an occlusive cuff which is 20% wider than the diameter of the limb.

d. A Doppler device (such as the Dinamap system) detects pulsatile flow distal to an occlusive cuff and provides a digital display of both systolic and diastolic blood pressures. This correlates well with direct arterial measurements.

e. An occlusion blood pressure is obtained by inflating the cuff proximal to an arterial line until the arterial waveform disappears on the monitor. As the cuff is deflated, the systolic pressure is noted when the waveform reappears.

2. **Left atrial (LA) catheters** provide valuable information about the status of left ventricular (LV) volume.[4] They are of particular value in patients with potential right ventricular (RV) dysfunction in whom the central venous pressure (CVP) may have little correlation with left-sided filling pressures. These catheters are potentially very dangerous, because they may introduce air or thromboembolism into the cerebral or systemic circulations. Close attention to line patency and waveform is essential.

3. **Right atrial (RA) and central venous lines** may be placed directly into the right atrium during surgery or introduced through the jugular or femoral veins percutaneously or by cutdown. These lines must be flushed carefully because air may enter the systemic circulation in the presence of intracardiac right-to-left shunts. Samples drawn from these lines are fairly representative of a mixed venous oxygen saturation. These lines are also valuable in managing patients with pulmonary hypertension and/or potential RV dysfunction. For example, an increase in CVP without volume infusion may indicate an acute elevation in pulmonary vascular resistance (PVR) causing RV dysfunction.

4. **Pulmonary artery (PA) pressure monitoring lines** placed intraoperatively are useful in the management of patients with pulmonary hypertension (i.e., left-to-right shunts). Several catheters have oximetric capabilities that provide continuous mixed venous O_2 saturation (SvO_2) monitoring. This provides on-line assessment of tissue oxygenation and allows for rapid detection of changes in oxygen supply or demand of the body. The SvO_2 is a nonspecific indicator of low cardiac output, because it also reflects changes in arterial oxygen saturation, hemoglobin level, and tissue metabolism.

5. **Thermodilution cardiac outputs** can be obtained using a pediatric (4–5F) Swan-Ganz catheter or a thermistor placed directly into the pulmonary artery.

6. Intracardiac monitoring lines are generally removed within a few days of surgery, although an RA line may be left for 10–14 days if central access is required for medications or intravenous hyperalimentation. **Mediastinal drainage tubes should be left in place for several hours after removal of all surgically placed intracardiac lines to check for bleeding.**[5]

C. **Respiratory monitoring**

    1. **Respiratory rate** is monitored electronically as well as manually. Mechanical ventilators have rate and pressure alarms that are activated by apneic events. Most bedside monitors calculate respiratory rates through simple skin electrodes. This is extremely useful after extubation.

    2. Measurement of expired volumes confirms that the patient is receiving an adequate tidal volume from the ventilator. However, analysis of arterial blood gases is essential to ensure that oxygenation and ventilation are satisfactory.

    3. Oxygenation is assessed by **ABG analysis** and **pulse oximetry.** The latter provides a continuous on-line assessment of oxygen saturation and correlates closely with saturations measured directly in arterial blood. Pulse oximetry is dependent on peripheral perfusion, so it will be affected by hemodynamic alterations causing peripheral vasoconstriction. Alteration in oxygen saturations may draw attention to changes in intracardiac shunts or cardiac outputs. It is beneficial in both intubated and extubated patients.[6,7]

    4. Ventilation can be monitored by the **end-tidal CO_2**, which is measured by infrared analysis of the concentration of CO_2 in expired gases. Along with pulse oximetry, it provides an excellent evaluation of the patient's ventilatory status. It may also reflect changes in cardiac output and pulmonary blood flow.

D. **Intake and output** (I&O). Precise assessment of fluid balance is critical in children after open-heart surgery. The use of central pressure monitoring lines provides the most important guide to fluid management in the immediate perioperative period; however, they only provide an assessment of intravascular volume. Fluid balance should be determined on an hourly basis for the first 24 hours; thereafter, a careful I&O every 4–8 hours and daily weights are useful guidelines to fluid management.

    1. Input includes an exact quantitation of the amount of fluids, blood products, drug infusions, and flushes, as well as any oral intake. Fluids must be administered in mL/kg or mL/m^2 amounts via "burettes" or controlled infusion pumps.

    2. Output includes drainage from the urinary catheter, the nasogastric tube, and the mediastinal drainage tubes. Because of the length of the connecting tube to the Foley catheter, its entire length should be inspected when assessing urine output. Most infants and small children will void spontaneously every 2–3 hours. A comparison of wet and dry diaper weights gives an excellent assessment of urine volume (1 g = 1 mL). Nasogastric tubes are aspirated upon arrival in the ICU and then placed to gravity drainage. Suction should be avoided.

    3. **Daily weights** should be obtained to confirm fluid balance because they take into account insensible losses and fluid gains from nebulized gases and respirators. Weights must be done in a consistent manner and at the same time that the I&Os are totaled. Temporary pacemakers, IV tubing, dressings, and respirator equipment can add grams to a child's weight, creating distortions in the fluid balance picture.

IV.   Mediastinal Bleeding and Transfusion Therapy

A.   Mediastinal bleeding in the pediatric patient following open-heart surgery can lead to rapid hemodynamic deterioration and must be treated aggressively. Tamponade may occur with as little as 10–20 mL of blood within the mediastinum in the small child. Children at increased risk of mediastinal bleeding include those with:

1.   Cyanotic conditions

2.   Impaired coagulation status (neonates)[8]

3.   Hepatic congestion from RV failure

4.   Use of profound hypothermia with circulatory arrest during surgery

5.   Complicated reoperative procedures

B.   Coagulation studies (PT, PTT, platelet count) should be sent upon arrival in the ICU. The management of mediastinal bleeding should ideally be based on the results of these studies, but empiric therapy is usually required when there is significant bleeding and results are not available.

C.   The postoperative hematocrit should be maintained at 40–45% for patients with continued cyanosis (following palliative procedures with residual shunts or intracardiac mixing) and at 35–40% for all others. Ideally, fresh whole blood should be used, if available, because it contains platelets and clotting factors.

1.   Transfusion of red cells should be based on the most recent hematocrit. If there is ongoing chest tube bleeding, packed red cells, frequently in combination with fresh frozen plasma, may be given in a total volume equal to the previous hour's losses. Autotransfusion systems are available for use in children and are most useful when the child requires volume and red cells, rather than a concentrated red cell transfusion (HCT of a unit of packed RBCs = 70%). Small additional doses of protamine should be given when blood processed with a cell-saving device is administered.

2.   Cold blood should never be transfused; it should be allowed to warm before transfusion or should be administered through a warming device.

3.   The administration of blood products should always be tempered by the potential for transmission of infectious diseases and the possibility of febrile, allergic, or transfusion reactions.

4.   The amount of packed red cells to be given to achieve a specified hematocrit can be determined by the following equation:

mL packed cells transfused

$$= \text{est. blood volume} \times \frac{HCT_{desired} - HCT_{actual}}{HCT_{packed\ cells}}$$

Or more simply:

$$\text{mL packed cells transfused} = \frac{70 \times \text{weight (kg)} \times (\Delta\ HCT)}{70}$$
$$= \text{wt (kg)} \times (\Delta\ HCT)$$

Table 16.3   *Indications for Reoperation for Bleeding*

Time	Percent of Blood Volume Lost	Blood Volume Lost
Any hour	10	8.0 mL/kg
2 consecutive hours	8	6.5 mL/kg
3 consecutive hours	6	5.0 mL/kg

5. Citrate toxicity from massive transfusions is very uncommon; however, if transfusions exceeding one-half of the patient's blood volume are administered (i.e., more than 35 mL/kg), 1 mL of calcium gluconate (10% solution) per 100 mL of transfused blood should be given through a peripheral line.

D. The use of fractionated blood products should be based on the results of the coagulation studies.

1. A prolonged PTT with normal PT suggests heparin excess; give protamine sulfate 0.5–1.0 mg/kg.

2. A prolonged PT and PTT suggests depletion of coagulation factors; give 10 mL/kg of FFP. Cryoprecipitate is rich in factors I and VIII and should be considered if a severe coagulopathy is present. It is given in a dose of 1 U/5 kg.

3. Platelets should be given in a dose of 1 U/5 kg if the platelet count is less than 100,000/µL. This will usually raise the platelet count by about 50,000/µL. A more liberal use of platelets is indicated in cyanotic patients with higher platelet counts because their platelets are usually severely dysfunctional. Platelet transfusions are not indicated in the patient who is not bleeding until the platelet count falls below 30,000/µL.

4. Caution must be used when considering the transfusion of cryoprecipitate and platelets to patients with labile pulmonary hypertension. They can trigger an acute increase in pulmonary vascular resistance.

E. Desmopressin (DDAVP) 0.3 µg/kg IV in 50 mL normal saline over 20 minutes may be beneficial in cases of platelet dysfunction.

F. Bleeding that continues despite normalization of coagulation studies often represents a mechanical source that warrants surgical exploration. Guidelines for reoperation are presented in table 16.3.

V.   Respiratory Management

A. Children undergoing uncomplicated repairs—such as PDA ligation, coarctation repair, or closure of an ASD—may be extubated in the operating room or soon after arrival in the ICU. They should be given supplemental oxygen and observed carefully for signs of respiratory distress. These include tachypnea, tachycardia, intercostal retraction, nasal flaring, grunting, and gasping. Spontaneous respiratory rates will vary according to age (table 16.4).

Table 16.4 *Normal Respiratory Rates in Children*

Age	Respiratory Rate
Newborns	40–60
1 mo–1 yr	30
1–2 yr	26
2–4 yr	24
4–6 yr	22
6–8 yr	21
8–10 yr	20
10–12 yr	19
12–14 yr	18

B. Patients undergoing more complex repairs will require mechanical ventilation for a period of time after returning to the ICU.

C. **Endotracheal tubes**

1. An orotracheal tube may be used if it is anticipated that the duration of intubation will be very short (usually extubation in the operating room). Otherwise, a nasotracheal tube should be placed at the time of intubation for surgery. Oral tubes are subject to repeated movements when the child is agitated and may contribute to subglottic edema. Furthermore, with the use of transesophageal echocardiography during surgery, oral tubes can be easily displaced.

2. Uncuffed endotracheal tubes (ETs) are used exclusively for children less than 8–10 years of age. The appropriate-sized ETs for children are listed in table 16.5. A simple formula for determining ET size in children is:

$$\text{ET tube size (ID mm)} = \frac{\text{age in years} + 16}{4}$$

3. With the use of any uncuffed tube, a leak of more than 10 cm H_2O and less than 35 cm H_2O should be present during mechanical ventilation.

Table 16.5 *Pediatric Endotracheal Tube Sizes*

Age or Weight	Tube Size
<1500 g	2.5–3.0 uncuffed
Newborn–6 mo	3.0–3.5 uncuffed
6–18 mo	4.0 uncuffed
18 mo–3 yr	4.5 uncuffed
3–5 yr	5.0 uncuffed
5–6 yr	5.5 uncuffed
6–10 yr	6.0 uncuffed
10–12 yr	6.5 cuffed
14–16 yr	6.5–7.0 cuffed

Formula: (age + 16)/4 = ET tube size in mm

D. **Mechanical ventilators**[9]

1. **Pressure-limited ventilators** provide an inspiratory volume that is determined by a preset peak airway pressure. They are commonly used for neonates and infants less than 1 year of age who are more susceptible to barotrauma (pneumothorax or pneumomediastinum). This technique may deliver a variable amount of volume and gives no assessment of a change in lung compliance.

2. **Volume-limited ventilators** deliver a preset tidal volume usually at constant flow rates. A peak pressure limit alarm is utilized to prevent the development of excessive pressures which could lead to barotrauma. Alarming may draw attention to changes in ventilatory mechanics (system malfunction, pneumothorax). These ventilators are preferred in older children in whom higher airway pressures are better tolerated and maintenance of a constant tidal volume helps to prevent atelectasis. They can be used as pressure-limited ventilators in younger children by setting a peak pressure to limit the tidal volume.

3. **Time-cycled ventilators** deliver a tidal volume determined by the inspiratory time and flow rate. At preset intermittent intervals, the gas flow is interrupted by a time-cycled expiratory valve. A prolonged inspiratory phase can increase mean airway pressure (similar to a volume-limited system) and improve oxygenation, but it may reduce gas escape during a shorter expiratory phase. These ventilators offer more control over the respiratory cycle, helping the clinician adjust mechanical ventilation to the specific needs of the patient. They are commonly used in infants.

4. Regardless of which type of ventilator is used, vigilant attention to the oxygen flow rates delivered by the ventilator, expiratory volumes, auscultation of bilateral breath sounds, chest wall expansion, arterial blood gas (ABG) analysis, and hemodynamic parameters is essential. Changes in ventilator settings should be based on these assessments.

E. **Management of children during mechanical ventilation**[9,10]

1. All children require sedation during mechanical ventilation. This prevents inadvertent dislodgment of the endotracheal tube, improves the efficiency of gas exchange, and minimizes the development of paroxysmal pulmonary hypertension and arterial desaturation.

2. Opioids and muscle relaxants used during surgery are not reversed, and the child is given additional medications for pain and agitation. Continuous infusions are commonly used in children because they can maintain a more constant level of analgesia with use of less medication. Medications may include the following:

   a. Analgesics and sedatives

      • Morphine, 0.05–0.1 mg/kg q1–2h or 10–40 µg/kg/h continuous infusion

- Fentanyl, 2–5 µg/kg/h continuous infusion; tolerance to this short-acting narcotic may develop, necessitating increasing doses to maintain the same level of analgesia
- Midazolam, 0.05–0.2 mg/kg, then 0.4–1.2 µg/kg/min infusion; this may have a synergistic depressant effect on myocardial function when used with fentanyl[11]

  b. Muscle relaxants
  - Vecuronium, 0.1 mg/kg, then 0.05–0.1 mg/kg/h infusion
  - Pancuronium, 0.1 mg/kg, then 0.05–0.1 mg/kg/h infusion (this increases sympathetic tone and may increase the heart rate)

3. Oxygenation criteria differ depending on the nature of the congenital heart defect and the surgical procedure. Following total anatomic or physiologic correction, a $PO_2 > 80$ torr with an FIO_2 of 0.4 should be expected. However, following palliative procedures for cyanotic defects with continued shunting or intracardiac mixing, an oxygen saturation of 75–85% (PaO_2 of 40–50 torr) is anticipated. In the presence of severe V/Q mismatch or a residual shunt, use of 100% oxygen is incapable of improving oxygenation significantly. The addition of positive end-expiratory pressure (PEEP) (5 cm H_2O) to the ventilatory circuit may be of some benefit in maintaining functional residual capacity and minimizing atelectasis, especially in children with large left-to-right shunts. PEEP should be avoided after a Fontan operation.

4. The FIO_2 is gradually lowered to 0.4 if oxygenation remains satisfactory. This can be assessed continuously by pulse oximetry and confirmed by intermittent ABG analysis.

5. Several physiologic factors unique to the pediatric patient population should be taken into consideration.

   a. The pulmonary vasculature is sensitive to changes in PO_2 and PCO_2. Hypoxia or hypercarbia may produce paroxysmal pulmonary hypertension, which can lead to arterial desaturation and right ventricular decompensation.

   b. Because the endotracheal tubes are so small in children, heated humidification of inspired gases is essential to prevent drying of secretions and the airway mucosa.

   c. Infants depend primarily on the diaphragm to perform the work of breathing. Any impairment of diaphragmatic function (paresis, abdominal distention) can lead to respiratory compromise.

F. **Weaning and extubation**

1. Several days of intubation are beneficial for children with large left-to-right shunts, significant pulmonary hypertension (ratio of PA/systemic pressure greater than 0.75), and young infants undergoing complex cardiac repairs. Weaning is generally accomplished using the intermittent mandatory ventilation (IMV) mode.[1,9]

   a. In infants, the IMV rate is lowered by 2–4 breaths/min and PEEP is decreased to 2–3 cm H_2O. Weaning to continuous positive airway pressure (CPAP) without any positive pressure breaths should be avoided because the endotracheal tube increases airway resistance, the work of breathing, and diaphragmatic fatigue.

b. In older children, the IMV rate is lowered by 2–4 breaths/min to CPAP; PEEP is gradually reduced in 2–3 cm increments to 3–5 cm H_2O. If the duration of intubation is short, extubation can usually be accomplished from 4 breaths/min if the criteria listed below are met.

2. Criteria for weaning and extubation include:

a. Adequate level of consciousness

b. Hemodynamic stability with minimal mediastinal bleeding (<1 mL/kg/h) and adequate peripheral perfusion

c. Normothermia

d. PaO_2 > 80 torr on FIO_2 < 0.4 (40 torr if residual right-to-left shunting)

e. $PaCO_2$ < 50 torr

f. pH 7.35–7.45

g. Vital capacity > 10–15 mL/kg (crying VC > 15 mL/kg in infants)[12]

h. Maximum negative force against an occluded airway > 20–30 cm H_2O (>45 cm H_2O in infants)

3. Humidified oxygen should be given by mask after extubation with rechecking of an ABG within 30 minutes. Subsequently, chest physiotherapy is used to stimulate coughing and mobilize secretions.

4. Children may develop airway obstruction from subglottic edema following extubation. This is usually treated with nebulized racemic epinephrine (0.05 mL/kg diluted to 2 mL of normal saline q2h to a maximum dose of 0.5 mL). If the duration of intubation has been prolonged or there is minimal leak around an uncuffed tube, suggesting the presence of significant subglottic edema, then use of dexamethasone 0.2–0.5 mg/kg IV q4–6h for two doses before extubation may be beneficial.

G. **Acute respiratory failure**

1. The development of acute respiratory failure (inadequate oxygenation or ventilation) in the early postoperative period commonly results from abnormalities that produce $\dot{V}/\dot{Q}$ mismatch and intrapulmonary shunting. A sudden change in ventilatory function is frequently the result of a technical problem.

2. Clinical signs that should draw attention to the possibility of acute respiratory distress include:

a. Cyanosis

b. Hypertension/hypotension

c. Bradycardia/tachycardia

    d. Agitation, tachypnea, subcostal retractions, or nasal flaring in the awake child

    e. Mottled, cool extremities

3. **Etiology** in the intubated patient

    a. Endotracheal tube problems

- Dislodgment or main stem intubation (the trachea is short in children, so the tube must be secured safely; even neck flexion or extension can displace the tube)
- Kinking of the ET or ventilator tubing
- Obstructed ET (dried mucous/clot forming a one-way valve, leading to hyperinflation of the lung and possibly a pneumothorax)

    b. Pain or agitation

    c. Ventilator malfunction

    d. Pleuroparenchymal problems

- Pneumothorax or hemothorax
- Lobar atelectasis
- Pulmonary edema
- Gastric aspiration
- Pneumonia

    e. Phrenic nerve palsy

    f. Cardiac problems

- Acute pulmonary hypertension; its treatment with vasodilators may inhibit hypoxic vasoconstriction, leading to $\dot{V}/\dot{Q}$ mismatch and hypoxemia
- Shunt occlusion
- Low cardiac output states, leading to venous admixture or pulmonary edema

    g. Gastric or abdominal distention

4. **Immediate management**

    a. Disconnect the child from the ventilator and hyperventilate manually with 100% oxygen.

    b. Auscultate for bilateral breath sounds. **Note:** Bilateral breath sounds can be heard with an esophageal intubation in young infants.

    c. Irrigate the endotracheal tube with 1 mL of sterile saline and suction.

    d. If there are suspicions about the patency of the ET or its dislodgment, the tube should be removed and the patient ventilated by mask with an oropharyngeal airway in place. **It is critical that an individual skilled in pediatric airway management be present.** After 5 minutes of satisfactory ventilation, reintubation should be performed.

    e. Obtain a portable chest x-ray to confirm endotracheal tube placement and look for other precipitating causes. A chest tube should be inserted immediately if a pneumothorax is present.

  f. **Note:** Lack of breaths sounds on one side may represent a main stem intubation, not necessarily a pneumothorax.

 5. Subsequent management of hypoxemia or hypercarbia depends on an assessment of hemodynamics, review of the chest x-ray, and identification of contributing factors.

H. Pneumothorax

 1. During positive pressure ventilation, the possibility of a pneumothorax from barotrauma should be suspected when any of the following develops:

  a. Agitation or tachypnea

  b. Cyanosis

  c. Hypoxia or hypercarbia

  d. Hemodynamic decompensation (hypotension, bradycardia, or tachycardia)

  e. Diminished or absent breath sounds

  f. Asymmetrical chest expansion

  g. Tracheal deviation away from the affected side

 2. If the patient is hemodynamically stable, a STAT portable chest x-ray should be obtained and reviewed immediately in the ICU. If the child is unstable, with hypotension and absent breath sounds despite manual ventilation, the following steps should be taken immediately:

  a. Aspirate the pleural space on the suspected side with a 10 mL syringe and 20-gauge needle.

  b. If free air is obtained, remove the syringe and leave the needle in place, open to the atmosphere.

  c. Insert a chest tube.

  d. If improvement does not occur within a few minutes, aspirate the opposite pleural space in a similar manner and insert a chest tube on that side if indicated.

  e. Obtain a portable chest x-ray immediately.

I. Atelectasis

 1. **Etiology**

  a. Malpositioned endotracheal tube (right or left mainstem intubation)

  b. Airway obstruction by blood clot or mucous plug

  c. Insufficient peak airway pressure

  d. Chest wall splinting or hypoventilation

  e. Hemidiaphragm paralysis (in the extubated patient)

 2. **Prevention**

  a. Humidification of inspired gases

  b. Use of PEEP or CPAP during mechanical ventilation

  c. Frequent endotracheal suctioning

d. Chest physiotherapy

e. Pain control

3. **Treatment**

a. Atelectasis can be difficult to distinguish from a pulmonary infiltrate. Secretions should be Gram-stained and cultured. Antibiotics should be considered if fever or an elevated white blood cell count (WBC) is also present.

b. If atelectasis of a lobe or lung is present, intensive tracheal toilet and chest physiotherapy will often reexpand the lung. If endotracheal tube obstruction is suspected, the tube should be removed and replaced. Flexible bronchoscopy can also be used to suction airways and look for obstruction.

c. In the unintubated child, atelectasis may be an indication for short-term endotracheal intubation, vigorous ET suctioning, and positive pressure ventilation with PEEP or CPAP.

J. **Diaphragm paralysis.** Phrenic nerve injury can result in paralysis of a hemidiaphragm, producing hypoventilation and/or atelectasis, and prolonging the need for mechanical ventilatory support. This is particularly problematic in infants in whom the diaphragm provides the majority of the respiratory work. Portable ultrasound examination at the bedside or fluoroscopy can detail diaphragmatic excursion and confirm the diagnosis. Electromyographic studies may be helpful in assessing phrenic nerve function.[13] Inability to wean from mechanical ventilation is an indication for surgical plication of the paralyzed diaphragm.[14]

K. **Chylothorax** can occur after almost any pediatric cardiovascular procedure, but is most common after extrapericardial procedures, such as construction of a Blalock-Taussig shunt or subclavian flap repair for coarctation of the aorta. In these situations, it usually results from injury to the thoracic duct or its tributaries. It may also be seen after open-heart operations, especially a Fontan procedure, which is associated with systemic venous hypertension. A persistent chylothorax may lead to respiratory compromise and malnutrition, caused by the loss of protein, lipids, and fat-soluble vitamins in the chylous fluid.[15]

1. **Diagnosis.** The presence of milky white fluid or clear effusions in the pleural space or pericardium that stain positive for fat with Sudan III, contain chylomicrons, or have a triglyceride level >110 mg/dL confirms the diagnosis.

2. **Treatment.** Conservative therapy with drainage and total parenteral nutrition or a low-fat diet with medium-chain triglycerides should be used. If these measures fail, surgical closure of the leak or interruption of the thoracic duct can be considered.

VI. Cardiovascular Management

The basic concepts of cardiovascular physiology and the management of cardiovascular derangements after surgery have been elucidated in Chapter 10. This section concentrates on the special problems encountered in pediatric patients after cardiac surgery.

A. **Special features of pediatric cardiac management**

1. **Variable pathology.** The nature of the congenital heart defect, the adequacy of the palliative or corrective procedure, and any residual pathophysiologic abnormalities must be taken into consideration when selecting a course of management. Some of these factors include:

   a. The effects of the congenital defect on the ventricles (hypertrophy or dilatation) and on the pulmonary vascular resistance.

   b. Lesions left uncorrected (valve stenosis or insufficiency, small pulmonary arteries, intracardiac shunts).

   c. Surgical trauma (suboptimal myocardial protection, ventriculotomy incisions, heart block).

   d. The possibility of an inadequate or disrupted surgical repair (thrombosed systemic-to-pulmonary shunts, residual intracardiac shunts, persistent valve stenosis or insufficiency after a valve repair).

2. **Compensatory mechanisms** for impaired cardiac function are more effective in children than in adults, but may mask the extent of cardiac dysfunction. Tachycardia is one of the major compensatory mechanisms to maintain cardiac output following surgery. Significant hypovolemia and poor contractility may be present despite a normal blood pressure because of increased systemic resistance. Attention to peripheral signs of circulatory decompensation (impaired perfusion, oliguria, and acidosis) should direct attention toward means of improving cardiac function, because the development of hypotension is a late sign of profound decompensation.

3. **Monitoring limitations** may also prevent the early detection of cardiovascular decompensation. Invasive monitoring to measure cardiac output directly (Swan-Ganz catheter, PA pressure line and thermistors) is cumbersome and hazardous and is generally avoided except in complex cases. Intracardiac monitoring is usually limited to RA and LA lines.[4]

   a. The RA and LA lines provide information on loading conditions of the ventricles; inferences about the status of ventricular function can be made as well, especially after serial volume challenges. Elevated filling pressures suggest the presence of ventricular dysfunction downstream to the measurement.

   b. The arterial pulse pressure is a reflection of left ventricular stroke volume and in small children should exceed 20–25 mm Hg. An arterial pulse pressure of less than 15 mm Hg is a sign of low cardiac output.

   c. A mixed venous oxygen saturation less than 50% (normal = 75%) in the absence of a residual intracardiac shunt reflects either anemia or a low cardiac output. The SvO_2 is ideally measured using a PA catheter, but in its absence, samples drawn from the RA or CVP line are fairly representative.

4. **Assessment of low cardiac output states**

   a. Because of limited monitoring techniques, assessment of cardiac output must involve a careful patient examination, with particular attention paid to peripheral perfusion (skin color, temperature, pedal pulses, capillary refill), and liver size (to assess RA pressure and fluid status).

   b. Urine output is usually a reflection of myocardial function. Evidence of oliguria (<1 mL/kg/h) in a child suggests a low output state.

   c. The development of metabolic acidosis is a reflection of inadequate tissue perfusion. In young infants, it may portend a malignant and sometimes irreversible spiral of cardiac decompensation and must be treated aggressively.

   d. Special care must be paid to normalizing core temperature so that the temperature of the extremities can be used as an index of cardiac function. Measures include use of a heated humidifier in the ventilator circuit, a heating blanket, overhead infrared warmer, and fluid and blood infusion warmers. A core temperature over 39°C reflects a high SVR and inability to conduct heat.

   e. Clinical deterioration should prompt a repeat physical examination. For example, absent bilateral breath sounds may indicate a pneumothorax; loss of a shunt murmur may explain increasing cyanosis; reappearance of a VSD murmur following closure may account for recurrent heart failure.

5. **Special studies.** When cardiac performance is not as expected following corrective surgery and does not respond to standard therapeutic measures, early reinvestigation is indicated.

   a. Echocardiography may detect unsuspected pericardial tamponade, ventricular dysfunction, inadequate or disrupted intracardiac repairs, or malfunctioning prosthetic heart valves.

   b. The intracardiac lines placed during surgery can be used to provide information on pressures, gradients, and shunts. The ratio of pulmonary blood flow to systemic blood flow (Q_p/Q_s) is calculated using the following formula:

   $$Q_p/Q_s = \frac{\text{Aortic } O_2 \text{ sat} - \text{RA } O_2 \text{ sat}}{\text{LA } O_2 \text{ sat} - \text{PA } O_2 \text{ sat}}$$

   A shunt exceeding 2:1 usually requires reoperation, whereas one that is less than 1.5:1 is not hemodynamically significant. Shunts between 1.5:1 and 2:1 require further delineation of cardiac abnormalities and a careful assessment of the patient's clinical status.

   c. Cardiac catheterization may be required to define residual intracardiac lesions, such as a left-to-right shunt with evidence of an oxygen step-up in the right heart chambers. Only early diagnosis of treatable intracardiac pathology will allow reoperation before irreversible cardiac, pulmonary, renal, neurologic, and/or metabolic damage has developed.

Table 16.6 *Normal Blood Pressures for Various Ages*

Ages	Mean Systolic ± 2 SD	Mean Diastolic ± 2 SD
Newborn	80 ± 16	46 ± 16
6 mo–1 yr	90 ± 25	50 ± 20
1–4 yr	95 ± 25	65 ± 25
4–5 yr	100 ± 20	65 ± 15
6–10 yr	105 ± 15	57 ± 8
10–16 yr	115 ± 19	60 ± 10

6. **Acceptable parameters.** Because each child's postoperative cardiac status is unique, initial acceptable parameters for blood pressure, RA and LA pressures, and urine output should be defined by the surgeon/cardiac anesthesiologist for the house staff and nurses at the time the patient arrives in the ICU. In the postoperative patient, there is a variation from normal baseline values for the resting child. Furthermore, there is frequently a change in myocardial performance and peripheral vasomotor tone during the early postoperative period that will require a redefinition of acceptable parameters.

   a. **Systolic blood pressures** for children of various ages are listed in table 16.6.

   b. The usual range of postoperative **RA and LA pressures** is 8–12 mm Hg. However, higher pressures are commonly required to optimize cardiac performance and depend on the specific cardiac lesion and the operative procedure.

   c. **Urine output** should exceed 1 mL/kg/h.

B. **Low cardiac output.** The assessment of low cardiac output states in infants and children requires an integration of clinical and monitoring techniques. In general, children compensate well for a low cardiac output by peripheral vasoconstriction and tachycardia, such that a fall in arterial blood pressure is a late sign of cardiac decompensation.

   1. **Diagnosis**

      a. Suspicion of low cardiac output is raised by evidence of peripheral vasoconstriction (cool, pale extremities, mottling, absent pedal pulses, and capillary refill exceeding 3 seconds), oliguria, metabolic acidosis, and hyperthermia.

      b. A narrow arterial pulse pressure, elevated filling pressures, low RA oxygen saturations, and the development of atrial or ventricular arrhythmias, should also draw attention to a low cardiac output state.

   2. **Treatment**

      a. The treatment of a low cardiac output syndrome requires assessment and manipulation of heart rate and rhythm, volume status, contractility, and afterload. Each of these factors is discussed in the subsequent sections.

Table 16.7 *Average Heart Rates in Children*

Age	Average Heart Rate	
	Mean	Range
Newborn	123	94–154
1–2 days	123	91–159
3–6 days	129	91–166
1–3 wk	148	107–182
1–2 mo	149	121–179
3–5 mo	141	106–186
6–11 mo	134	109–169
1–2 yr	119	89–151
3–4 yr	108	73–137
5–7 yr	100	65–133
8–11 yr	91	62–130
12–15 yr	85	60–119

Adapted by permission from Rowe P, ed. The Harriet Lane Handbook. 11th ed. Chicago: Year Book Medical Publishers, 1987:64.

    b. Additional contributory factors to a low cardiac output state should be identified and treated. These may include:

        i. Cardiac tamponade (assessed by echocardiography)

       ii. Ventilatory problems (chest x-ray to rule out severe pulmonary vascular congestion, atelectasis, pneumothorax, or large hemothorax; ABGs to identify hypoxia or hypercarbia)

      iii. Metabolic problems (acidosis, hypo- or hyperkalemia, hypocalcemia)

C. Heart rate and rhythm

  1. The heart rate and rhythm should be optimized to achieve a regular supraventricular rhythm, if possible. The optimal heart rate is determined by the child's age (table 16.7); the actual pulse rate will usually exceed the resting baseline values because of increased levels of circulating catecholamines and the use of inotropic drugs following surgery. Tachycardia is the most significant compensatory mechanism in children to maintain cardiac output, and may simply reflect hypovolemia that should be treated simultaneously.

  2. Sinus and nodal bradycardias should be treated with atrial pacing.

  3. Complete heart block, which may occur after operations requiring suturing near the AV node (VSD, AV canal), should be treated with AV sequential pacing.[16] It is important to take advantage of the atrial contribution to filling in the early postoperative period.

  4. Supraventricular tachyarrhythmias are more difficult to treat, but usually respond to digoxin, type IA antiarrhythmics, or electrical cardioversion, if necessary. Junctional ectopic tachycardia (JET), a

potentially fatal rhythm associated with subendocardial ischemia and cardiac decompensation, is commonly treated by surface cooling to slow the heart (see page 549).[17]

D. **Volume status**

1. The optimal preload conditions for an individual patient depend on the specific congenital defect, the nature and adequacy of the repair, and the severity of right or left ventricular dysfunction. It is important to document the filling pressures (RA and LA pressures) both at the time of weaning from cardiopulmonary bypass (CPB) and on arrival in the ICU.

   a. It is common to find that higher filling pressures are required 3–6 hours postoperatively, which corresponds to the time of maximal myocardial edema and dysfunction.

   b. An acute change in filling pressures may result from a change in cardiac rhythm.

2. When there is evidence of a low cardiac output syndrome, volume status should be addressed while potential contributing causes are being evaluated. With hypovolemia, the LA pressure will be low (<10 mm Hg) and the arterial pressure tracing will display a narrow waveform reflective of a diminished stroke volume. In addition, the normal respiratory variation in blood pressure noted during positive pressure ventilation will be exaggerated on the arterial display monitor. Careful assessment of the I&O, with particular attention to urine output and chest tube drainage, is also helpful in assessing the degree of hypovolemia.

3. In the absence of an LA line, a low CVP is consistent with hypovolemia. However, a high CVP may indicate RV dysfunction and/or an elevated PVR. In either situation, volume infusion to normalize or increase the CVP may be required to ensure adequate left-sided filling.

4. Hypovolemia should be treated with fluid replacement to expand the intravascular volume. Most centers use either blood or colloid (fresh frozen plasma or 5% albumin) as fluid boluses to maintain adequate preload. The selection of the particular fluid depends on the patient's hematocrit, clotting status, and interval since surgery. Fluids are given in 5–10 mL/kg increments (6–12% of blood volume). Further volume infusion should be based on the hemodynamic response to each fluid bolus. An adequate response should be a rise in filling pressures and blood pressure with a decrease in heart rate and improved peripheral perfusion.

E. **Cardiac contractility and afterload.** When systemic arterial hypotension or signs of low cardiac output persist after restoration of blood volume, then cardiac contractility and/or afterload require manipulation. These two factors must be considered together because of their intrinsic relationship and because most of the relevant pharmacologic agents affect both simultaneously. Virtually all patients undergoing open-heart surgery for congenital heart disease will require some form of inotropic therapy to be weaned from CPB, and these medications are usually continued during the early postoperative period.

Table 16.8 *Doses of Inotropic and Vasopressor Medications in Children*

Drug	Dosage Range
Dopamine	2–20 µg/kg/min
Dobutamine	2–10 µg/kg/min
Amrinone	1 mg/kg load, then 10 µg/kg/min
Milrinone	50 µg/kg load, then 0.375–0.75 µg/kg/min
Epinephrine	0.05–0.5 µg/kg/min
Isoproterenol	0.05–1.0 µg/kg/min
Norepinephrine	0.05–1.0 µg/kg/min
Phenylephrine	0.5–5.0 µg/kg/min

Medication infusions should be mixed using a formula that ensures delivery of X µg/kg/min at a rate of X mL/h:
1. *For dopamine, dobutamine, phenylephrine, and amrinone, place 6 mg/kg in 100 mL (e.g., 5 mL/h = 5 µg/kg/min).*
2. *For epinephrine, isoproterenol, and norepinephrine, place 0.6 mg/kg in 100 mL (e.g., 5 mL/h = 0.5 µg/kg/min).*

1. Contractility refers to the intrinsic strength of myocardial contraction. In congenital heart disease, it is more common to see impairment of RV function, primarily because of preexisting pulmonary hypertension or volume overload.

2. Afterload refers to ventricular wall tension during systole.

    a. LV function may be improved by a reduction in LA pressure and SVR. This is most beneficial in patients with systemic hypertension or residual AV valve regurgitation.

    b. RV function may be improved by a reduction in RV volume and PVR. This is particularly important in neonates and young infants in whom reduction in PVR is essential to maintain RV performance.

F. **Left ventricle and systemic vascular resistance**

1. If a low cardiac output persists after the LA pressure has been raised to 12–15 mm Hg by volume infusion, cardiac contractility is most likely impaired. Further volume infusion to an LA pressure of 15–18 mm Hg may be necessary to obtain more LV output by the Starling mechanism.

2. If high filling pressures are required, an inotropic drug with predominantly β_1 activity should be administered. If the SVR is high, the addition of a vasodilating agent may also be beneficial. The doses of inotropic and vasodilating agents for pediatric patients are noted in tables 16.8 and 16.9.

    a. **Dopamine** increases contractility and heart rate and can be used in doses up to 20 µg/kg/min without compromising renal perfusion.

    b. **Dobutamine** improves contractility and increases heart rate, with less vasoconstrictive effects than dopamine.

Table 16.9   *Doses of Vasodilators in Children*

Drug	Dosage Range
Nitroglycerin	0.5–5 µg/kg/min
Nitroprusside	0.5–5.0 µg/kg/min
Prostaglandin E$_1$	0.05–2.0 µg/kg/min

    c. When profound LV failure is present despite use of these agents, **amrinone** or **milrinone** is very helpful.[18] Their combined inotropic and vasodilating properties enhance both RV and LV output. They are therefore beneficial in patients with either AV valve regurgitation or pulmonary hypertension.

    d. **Epinephrine** in low doses (0.01–0.1 µg/kg/min) is a strong inotrope and chronotrope that is commonly used in neonates undergoing complicated cardiac repairs.

    e. **Isoproterenol** produces primarily an increase in heart rate, but also improves contractility and reduces PVR. Therefore, it is most beneficial for children with RV dysfunction. The tachycardia is well tolerated and often beneficial in small children.

    f. For cardiac failure unresponsive to drug management, intraaortic balloon counterpulsation can be considered in the older pediatric patient.[19] For larger children or adolescents, an LV assist device may be used.[20] Extracorporeal membrane oxygenation (ECMO) can be used for cardiopulmonary failure after bypass.[21–24]

G. **Right ventricle and pulmonary hypertension**

    1. One of the significant differences between adult and pediatric cardiac surgical patients is the common occurrence of reactive pulmonary hypertension in children which may predispose them to episodes of oxygen desaturation and RV failure.

        a. Elevated PVR, whether fixed or dynamic, is often noted in patients with large left-to-right shunts and increased pulmonary blood flow. Coexisting high PVR and an impaired RV is a very dangerous combination. The contribution of an elevated PVR to RV failure is difficult to ascertain unless PA pressures and cardiac outputs can be determined. Nonetheless, the treatment of RV dysfunction usually includes efforts to dilate the pulmonary vascular bed.

        b. The RV may also be predisposed to postoperative failure as a consequence of:

          • Underdevelopment
          • Chronic high pressure loading (hypertrophy)
          • Chronic volume overload (dilatation)
          • Less effective intraoperative myocardial protection
          • Right ventriculotomy incisions

- Interruption of right coronary artery branches
- Residual pulmonary stenosis or insufficiency or tricuspid insufficiency

2. The assessment of RV function depends on clinical signs as well as a comparison of RA and LA pressure measurements.

   a. Clinical signs of RV failure include:

      - Jugular venous distention
      - Hepatomegaly
      - Peripheral edema
      - Ascites
      - Periorbital, flank, and eventually generalized edema
      - Rising BUN

   b. An elevated RA pressure with low LA pressure confirms the diagnosis of RV dysfunction; volume loading to improve cardiac output will raise the RA pressure with proportionately less effect on the LA pressure.

3. **Treatment of RV failure**

   a. Volume loading, often to an RA pressure of 15 mm Hg or greater, may be necessary to ensure adequate left-sided filling.

   b. Use of an inotropic agent that may also produce pulmonary vasodilatation should be selected. These include:

      i. Low-dose dopamine/dobutamine

      ii. Amrinone/milrinone

      iii. Isoproterenol

   c. Right ventricular assist device for older children

4. **Treatment of pulmonary hypertension**

   a. Neonates and infants with chronic large left-to-right shunts (AV canal, VSD, AP window, truncus arteriosus) may have hyperreactive pulmonary vasculature and develop sudden episodes of pulmonary vasospasm after surgery. These episodes are manifested by:

      - Rapid arterial desaturation
      - Agitation
      - Bradycardia/tachycardia
      - Systemic hypotension

   b. An acute increase in PVR may be triggered by hypoxia, hypercarbia, acidosis, or sympathetic stimulation. This is most common during the first 48 hours after surgery. The initial treatment of acute pulmonary hypertension includes:[25,26]

      - Hyperventilation with 100% oxygen to improve oxygenation and induce a respiratory alkalosis (PCO_2 = 30–35 torr, pH > 7.50).
      - Use of sodium bicarbonate to induce a metabolic alkalosis. It should be noted that alkalosis, not hypocarbia, is responsible for reducing PVR.[27]

- Sedation with opioids (fentanyl 2–5 µg/kg/h or morphine 10–40 µg/kg/h) and use of paralytic agents (vecuronium 0.1 mg/kg/h) to suppress the endogenous release of stress hormones and catecholamines.

- To minimize the release of endogenous catecholamines, external stimuli must be avoided. Therefore, endotracheal suctioning, chest physiotherapy, bathing, weighing, and so on should be performed only when necessary.

c. Inotropic agents (amrinone and isoproterenol) may be used to improve RV function by virtue of their ability to reduce PVR.

d. Intravenous pulmonary vasodilators, such as nitroglycerin[28] and prostaglandin (PGE$_1$), are useful in reducing PVR, although their utility may be limited by systemic vasodilatation. PGE$_1$ 0.1 µg/kg/min has been used in adults, but has been used infrequently in children. It must be given into a central vein with infusion of norepinephrine into a left atrial line to support systemic arterial pressure, if necessary.

e. Inhalation of nitric oxide (NO).[29–31] Using a specialized delivery system, administration of 40–80 parts per million of NO has been shown to reduce PVR in neonates in the catheterization lab and following open-heart surgery. Although it still remained an investigational drug in mid-1998, many centers have reported its benefits in reducing PVR after cardiac surgery, particularly in patients who have undergone repair of total anomalous pulmonary venous connection (TAPVC) and anomalies associated with large left-to-right shunts.[32]

H. Arrhythmias

1. Arrhythmias generally arise because of damage to normal pacemaker tissue or conduction pathways or from enhanced automaticity of ectopic foci.

2. Certain rhythm disturbances are associated with specific congenital defects (supraventricular tachycardias in Ebstein's anomaly, complete heart block in corrected transposition of the great arteries [L-TGA]), whereas others may occur after certain surgical procedures. These include:

a. Sinus node dysfunction after a Mustard or Senning operation or repair of a sinus venosus ASD. Abnormalities in intranodal conduction after the Mustard operation may produce atrial flutter and other forms of supraventricular tachycardias.

b. Right bundle branch block (RBBB) after a right ventriculotomy and resection of hypertrophied muscle bundles (tetralogy of Fallot).

Table 16.10 *Doses of Intravenous Antiarrhythmic Medications in Children*

Drug	Dosage
Lidocaine	1 mg/kg bolus, then 20–50 µg/kg/min
Procainamide	2–5 mg/kg bolus over 10 min, then 20–80 µg/kg/min
Bretylium	5–10 mg/kg over 10 min
Propranolol	0.01–0.2 mg/kg over 10 min
Esmolol	0.5 mg/kg over 5 min, then 0.1–0.25 mg/kg/min
Verapamil	0.125–0.25 mg/kg over 5 min
Adenosine	0.05–0.25 mg/kg rapid IV bolus
Amiodarone	5 mg/kg over 5–10 min, then 10–15 mg/kg/day

    c. Complete heart block after operations during which sutures are placed near the AV node or the conduction system, such as closure of a VSD or AV canal.

3. Potential contributing factors should be identified and corrected.

    a. Sympathetic stimulation from pain, anxiety, fear, fever

    b. Hypoxia, hypercarbia, acidosis

    c. Electrolyte abnormalities: hypo- or hyperkalemia, hypocalcemia, hypomagnesemia

    d. Drug effects: catecholamines, digoxin toxicity, proarrhythmic effects of antiarrhythmic medications

    e. Intracardiac monitoring lines

    f. Gastric dilatation

4. Diagnosis should begin with analysis of a surface electrocardiogram. The epicardial pacemaker wires can be used to obtain a simultaneous atrial electrogram, which can differentiate among various supraventricular and ventricular arrhythmias (see Chapter 10).[33] Assessment of ABGs and serum potassium should be performed. Antiarrhythmic doses for children are listed in table 16.10.

5. **Sinus bradycardia** usually results from operative injury to or edema near the sinus node. It is uncommon in children, but its appearance may indicate the presence of hypoxia, hypercarbia, or incipient cardiac decompensation.

    a. Atrial pacing should be instituted while searching for and treating the underlying cause.

    b. In the absence of functioning pacing wires, atropine 0.1 mg/kg IV or a slow bolus of epinephrine 1–2 µg/kg can be used. An infusion of epinephrine or isoproterenol 0.02–1.5 µg/kg/min can also be used to accelerate the heart rate to an acceptable level. Isoproterenol may reduce the systemic blood pressure by reducing SVR.

6. **Sinus tachycardia** is common after pediatric cardiac operations and is generally a sympathetic compensatory response to anemia, hypovolemia, or one of the noncardiac factors listed above.

However, it should always raise the possibility of acute respiratory decompensation (especially an acute pneumothorax) or progressive cardiac dysfunction. If the heart rate exceeds the normal range for the child's age, it should be investigated. In the case of a rapid tachycardia, an atrial electrogram (AEG) will help to distinguish sinus tachycardia from other supraventricular tachycardias. Beyond correction of the underlying cause, further treatment is usually not necessary.

7. **Premature atrial complexes** (PACs) are relatively uncommon in children and are benign, with less likelihood of degenerating into atrial fibrillation than in adults. Digitalis toxicity must be considered. Frequent PACs can be suppressed by atrial pacing, but additional treatment is usually not necessary.

8. **Paroxysmal supraventricular tachycardia** (SVT) at a rate of 150–300 beats/min is one of the most common arrhythmias in the pediatric population, but it is relatively uncommon after surgery. The diagnosis requires an AEG to differentiate it from other tachycardias, especially in the presence of an RBBB.

   a. Adenosine (0.05–0.1 mg/kg) is the treatment of choice for SVT.[34] It induces transient AV block and may interrupt a reentrant rhythm.

   b. Overdrive atrial pacing to disrupt the reentrant rhythm may be effective.

   c. Other medications that may be of benefit in the acute setting include phenylephrine, edrophonium, β-blockers, and verapamil.

   d. Digitalization may be indicated for recurrent or symptomatic episodes.

9. **Atrial fibrillation and flutter** are also uncommon in children. The former is recognized on the surface ECG by its irregularity; the latter may require an AEG to differentiate it from other rapid rhythms.

   a. Synchronized cardioversion with 1–2 J/kg should always be considered first if there is evidence of significant hemodynamic compromise.

   b. Rapid atrial pacing may be successful in terminating atrial flutter.

   c. Intravenous digitalization is used to slow the ventricular rate. If this is not successful, β-blockers (propranolol 0.01–0.1 mg/kg IV) or calcium-channel blockers (verapamil 0.1–0.2 mg/kg IV) may be given slowly and cautiously because of their cardiac depressant effects and the potential for precipitating asystole. Verapamil is not recommended for use in infants <1 year of age. There has been little experience with diltiazem in children, although it has been used commonly in adults.

   d. Following conversion to normal sinus rhythm, maintenance digoxin, often with the addition of a type IA antiarrhythmic drug, may prevent recurrence.

10. **Junctional bradycardia** can result from surgical trauma to the sinus node or interatrial conduction pathways. Its sudden appearance postoperatively, as with any bradycardia, may indicate serious respiratory and/or cardiac problems. It is treated with atrial or AV sequential pacing if there is coexisting heart block.

11. **Junctional ectopic tachycardia (JET)** is one of the most serious supraventricular tachycardias noted after pediatric heart operations. It may develop as a result of AV block and is most common after operations to repair a VSD or tetralogy of Fallot. It has been ascribed to enhanced automaticity in the bundle of His, which explains the failure of this rhythm to respond to rapid atrial pacing or cardioversion. It is often present as a manifestation of advanced cardiac decompensation.

    a. Diagnosis is heralded by a gradually increasing heart rate with AV dissociation. It can be confirmed with an AEG tracing, which will demonstrate a ventricular rate usually between 130–200 beats/min (often faster), without relationship to the atrial complexes. The very rapid ventricular rate and lack of atrial contribution to filling can produce significant hemodynamic compromise.

    b. **Treatment**[17]

        i.   Hypovolemia, anemia, and any metabolic abnormality (hypokalemia, hypocalcemia, hypomagnesemia) should be corrected.

        ii. Digitalization may lower the rate.

        iii. Sophisticated pacing techniques, such as overdrive atrial pacing to induce 2:1 block or paired ventricular pacing, may be effective.

        iv. Induction of hypothermia suppresses automaticity and may slow JET. This entails use of cooling blankets, ice bags, cold gastric lavage, sedation with fentanyl, and muscle relaxation with vecuronium. A decrease in core temperature to 33°–34°C will usually reduce the heart rate to about 150–160.[35]

        v.   Type IA antiarrhythmic agents, particularly intravenous procainamide, have been successful in treating JET.

        vi. Intravenous amiodarone has been used effectively to lower the ventricular response and convert JET to normal sinus rhythm (NSR).[36] It has not been formally approved for this indication, however.

        vii. Other agents that have been used include intravenous propafenone,[37] propranolol, and verapamil. They may slow the rate or produce second-degree AV block, which slows the ventricular response.

        viii. His bundle ablation can be used when JET is refractory to all other measures.

12. **Ventricular arrhythmias** are relatively uncommon after congenital heart surgery. Premature ventricular complexes (PVCs) may result

from hypoxia, hypercarbia, hypokalemia, hypomagnesemia, digoxin toxicity, or excessive doses of β_1 inotropes. Reentrant ventricular tachycardia may develop after a right ventriculotomy, especially after repair of tetralogy of Fallot.

    a. Couplets, multifocal or frequent (>6/min) PVCs, or ventricular tachycardia should be treated with lidocaine 1 mg/kg IV, with a repeat dose in 5–10 minutes if necessary, followed by a maintenance infusion of 20–50 μg/kg/min. **Seizures can occur with excessive dosages.** Drug levels and hepatic function should dictate adjustment of the dosage.

    b. Overdrive atrial pacing may suppress ventricular ectopy.

    c. If ectopy persists, procainamide can be given with a loading dose of 2–5 mg/kg IV over 5 minutes, followed by a maintenance infusion of 20–80 μg/kg/min. For refractory malignant ectopy, bretylium 5–10 mg/kg IV over 10–30 minutes may be considered.

    d. Persistent ventricular tachycardia or ventricular fibrillation requires immediate electrical cardioversion with 1–2 J/kg.

13. **Heart block** may result from suture placement, hemorrhage, edema, or ischemia/infarction in the region of the AV node or His bundle.

    a. **First-degree heart block** may also be a sign of digoxin toxicity. It usually requires no treatment, but digoxin levels should be followed closely.

    b. **Second-degree heart block** with adequate ventricular response does not require treatment. However, connection of the epicardial pacing wires to a backup VVI pacemaker is advisable. The R-wave sensitivity should be tested before initiation of demand pacing.

    c. **Third-degree heart block** with a slow ventricular rate is best treated with AV sequential pacing.[16] Ventricular pacing alone may be inadequate because of the importance of the atrial contribution to ventricular filling in the early postoperative period. AV dissociation with an adequate junctional rate can be managed with a backup demand pacemaker. Third-degree heart block that persists for more than 2 weeks usually requires placement of a permanent pacemaker system.

    d. Intraventricular conduction delays, such as an RBBB, are common after repair of tetralogy of Fallot and AV canal, and are also noted in some patients after repair of a membranous VSD or ostium primum ASD. They are of little significance unless trifascicular block subsequently develops.

I. **Digoxin** is the most common cardiac medication used in children.

  1. **Indications**

    a. Preoperative digoxin therapy

    b. Ventriculotomy

    c. Postoperative atrial tachyarrhythmias

    d. Persistent heart failure

    e. Prolonged suboptimal ventricular performance

2. **Dosage**

    a. Parenteral dosage should be 75% of the preoperative oral dose.

    b. **Digitalizing dose:** 30 µg/kg IV (40 µg/kg PO) with 50% given initially and 25% 8 and 16 hours later.

    c. **Maintenance dose:** 3.5 µg/kg IV q12h (4.5 µg/kg PO q12h).

    d. K^+ should be kept greater than 4.0 mEq/L.

    e. Therapeutic digoxin level is 0.8–2.0 ng/mL (drawn at least 6 hours after last dose). Digoxin levels generally do not reflect digoxin toxicity in children; levels above this range may be required to achieve effect with little evidence of cardiac toxicity.

    f. In renal failure, the maintenance dose is decreased by 50–75%, with the dosage adjusted according to daily blood levels. The dose should be halved when quinidine sulfate is used concomitantly.

J. **Sedation and analgesia** are an integral part of hemodynamic management. They allow for improved gas exchange and safety of intubation during mechanical ventilation, minimize splinting to improve respiratory function after extubation, and can result in improved cardiac performance by reducing both systemic and pulmonary vascular resistance. However, sedation must be used cautiously in the patient with marginal cardiac function because it can induce rapid hemodynamic decompensation.

1. Intubated patients **(always give sedation when using a muscle relaxant!)**

    a. Morphine 0.05–0.1 mg/kg q1–2h or 10–40 µg/kg/h continuous infusion

    b. Fentanyl 2–5 µg/kg/h continuous infusion (watch for increasing tolerance; the dosage may have to be increased to 20 µg/kg/h); if chest wall rigidity develops, a muscle relaxant will be necessary.

    c. Midazolam 0.05–0.2 mg/kg, then 0.4–1.2 µg/kg/min infusion

    d. Vecuronium 0.1 mg/kg, then 0.05–0.1 mg/kg/h infusion

    e. Pancuronium 0.1 mg/kg, then 0.05–0.1 mg/kg/h infusion

2. Extubated patients

    a. Acetaminophen 10–15 mg/kg PO/PR q3–4h

    b. Morphine sulfate 0.05–0.1 mg/kg IV/IM q2–3h for severe pain

    c. Codeine, 0.5–1.0 mg/kg/dose PO q4–6h

    d. Patient-controlled analgesia using morphine is very effective in older children. It provides a more constant blood level of analgesia because it is administered in smaller doses at more frequent intervals.

3. Analgesia selection should be individualized. Acetaminophen may not provide adequate analgesia, even in infants and small children. Use of nonsteroidal antiinflammatory medications such as ibuprofen or ketorolac may be beneficial. Because they are synergistic with the opioids, they can often be used to supplement lower doses of opioids to provide excellent analgesia.

4. **In the event of cardiorespiratory decompensation possibly related to narcotics, naloxone (Narcan), 0.01 mg/kg/dose IV or IM can be given q3min for 3 doses.**

K. **Cardiac arrest**[38,39]

1. Primary cardiac arrest from an arrhythmia is very uncommon in children; most cardiac arrests are secondary to poor cardiac output or respiratory dysfunction with resultant hypoxemia.

2. **Bradycardia** (<80 in an infant or <60 in a child), **asystole,** or **pulseless electrical activity** (EMD) should prompt the following immediate steps:

    a. Secure the airway and manually hyperventilate with 100% O_2

    b. Cardiac massage at 80–100/min if heart rate does not respond to adequate ventilation

    c. Atrial or ventricular pacing if epicardial electrodes are present

    d. Epinephrine 0.01 mg/kg (0.1 mL/kg of a 1 : 10,000 solution = 0.1 mg/mL) or 0.1 mg/kg of a 1 : 1000 solution = 1 mg/mL) via endotracheal tube q3–5 min

    e. Atropine 0.02 mg/kg (0.1 mg/mL solution); maximum dose of 0.5 mg for child and 1.0 mg for adolescent

3. **Ventricular fibrillation/pulseless ventricular tachycardia**

    a. Cardiac massage at 80–100/min

    b. Secure the airway and manually hyperventilate with 100% O_2

    c. Defibrillate with 2 J/kg, then 4 J/kg twice

    d. Epinephrine 0.01 mg/kg IV (1 : 10,000 solution) or 0.1 mg/kg (1 : 1000 solution) via endotracheal tube

    e. Lidocaine 1 mg/kg IV

    f. Repeat defibrillation with 4 J/kg after 60 seconds

    g. If unsuccessful:
      • Epinephrine 0.1 mg/kg IV q3–5 min
      • Lidocaine 1 mg/kg IV
      • Bretylium 5 mg/kg, then 10 mg/kg
      • Defibrillation 4 J/kg after 60 seconds

4. During the resuscitation, precipitating causes should be identified:

    a. Airway obstruction or dislodged endotracheal tube causing hypoxemia

    b. Tension pneumothorax

    c. Cardiac tamponade

    d. Profound hypothermia, acidosis, or hypovolemia

    e. Drug reaction

5. Once a rhythm is restored, other medications may be used to improve blood pressure or maintain cardiac output. Epinephrine, dopamine, and dobutamine are the preferred medications in children.

6. Other medications:

    a. Calcium chloride is recommended only for documented hypocalcemia, hyperkalemia, or hypermagnesemia. It is given in a dose of 20 mg/kg (0.2 mL/kg of a 10% solution).

    b. Use of sodium bicarbonate for a postoperative arrest should be dictated by an understanding of the patient's prearrest status. If there was a period of cardiac decompensation preceding the arrest, or a preexisting abnormality in acid-base status, empiric use of bicarbonate is usually advisable. If the arrest was initiated by a respiratory event, a metabolic acidosis may not be present initially, and use of bicarbonate should be directed by an arterial blood gas or the duration of arrest. The dose of bicarbonate is 1 mEq/kg IV.

L. **Cardiac tamponade** can result from the accumulation of only a small amount of blood in the mediastinum. In an infant, as little as 10–20 mL can restrict venous return and ventricular filling, leading to decreased cardiac output and possible cardiac arrest.

1. Observation of rising filling pressures and a decrease in pulse pressure (decreased systolic and increased diastolic pressure) in the bleeding patient may be early warning signs of tamponade. A widened mediastinum on chest x-ray in the presence of active bleeding should raise suspicion. The following signs may suggest cardiac tamponade.

    a. Hypotension/arrest following mediastinal bleeding that has suddenly stopped

    b. Elevation and equalization of RA (central venous) and LA pressures

    c. Peripheral vasoconstriction

    d. Progressive tachycardia

2. If there is evidence of rapid hemodynamic decompensation, the first step should be stripping of all mediastinal chest tubes to evacuate clot. If there is no improvement, the sternotomy incision should be opened.

    a. A quick preliminary step should be opening of the inferior portion of the sternal incision with placement of a gloved finger below the lower aspect of the sternum. This may reach the pericardium and evacuate blood.

    b. More commonly, the patient manifests extreme hemodynamic instability or a cardiac arrest. In this case, the entire sternal incision should be reopened.

    c.   The sternal wires or sutures are cut and the sternum is retracted laterally.

    d.   Clot is removed from the mediastinum, and gentle internal cardiac massage is begun, if necessary, to restore circulation. Compression of shunt material and conduits should be avoided during massage.

VII. Fluids, Electrolytes, and Renal Failure

A. The use of cardiopulmonary bypass is associated with significant sodium and fluid retention. During the first 24 hours after surgery, fluid management is directed toward optimizing preload and cardiac output based on assessments of RA and/or LA pressures. During this interval, colloid solutions are used to maintain intravascular volume, while maintenance crystalloids are reduced in half. Subsequently, maintenance fluids are based on an assessment of excess extravascular fluid (rales, gallop, hepatomegaly, periorbital or peripheral edema, weight in excess of preoperative weight). Patients with excessive extravascular water commonly have a dilutional hyponatremia and will require diuretics and some restriction in maintenance fluids.

B. **Daily maintenance fluid and electrolyte requirements**

    1.   Fluid volume

        a.   The usual formula for fluid requirements is 4 mL/kg/h for the first 10 kg, 2 mL/kg/h for the next 10 kg, and 1 mg/kg/h for each subsequent kg.

        b.   Intubated patients usually are given two-thirds of this maintenance level because of water gain associated with use of a ventilator.

    2.   Electrolytes

        a.   Sodium: 3 mEq/100 mL/d

        b.   Potassium: 2–3 mEq/100 mL/d

    3.   Five percent dextrose in 0.25% normal saline is used for children >6 months of age.

    4.   Ten percent dextrose in 0.25% normal saline is used for infants <6 months of age because of their greater glucose demands and higher metabolic rates.

    5.   A potassium infusion via a central line (80 mEq/250 mL D5W) may be used to keep the $K^+ > 4.0$ mEq/L. The amount should be based on the patient's weight and adjusted in accordance with frequent electrolyte determinations. **Up to 0.5 mEq/kg/h of KCl** may be given. It should be administered through a Buretrol and a controlled infusion pump to prevent an inadvertent bolus of potassium.

C. **Colloid solutions** are used to expand the intravascular volume without producing interstitial fluid overload.

    1.   In the early postoperative period, either 5% albumin or fresh frozen plasma is usually selected. Packed red cell transfusions are most effective in increasing intravascular volume and should be considered if the hematocrit is less than desired based on the specific

congenital defect (<35% for acyanotic defects, <40% for cyanotic defects). If the patient is not bleeding and has an adequate hematocrit, 5% albumin can be given. The usual fluid bolus in children is 5–10 mL/kg over 10–20 minutes, with subsequent reassessment of filling pressures.

2. The use of 25% albumin can provide a significant oncotic load and is valuable when interstitial volume overload (ascites, pulmonary edema) accompanies intravascular hypovolemia (low LA pressure). It is usually given in 1–2 mL/kg doses over 10 minutes.

D. **Oliguria.** Urine output after cardiac surgery should be maintained at 1–2 mL/kg/h. If the urine output is less than this, attention should be directed initially at optimizing volume status and hemodynamic performance. Subsequently, diuretics may be considered. Early and aggressive treatment of oliguria may prevent the development of acute renal failure.

1. Check patency of the urinary catheter and replace it if necessary.

2. Generally, diuretics are avoided for the first 12 hours after surgery. Beginning on the first postoperative day, a gentle diuresis may be initiated with an initial dose of furosemide 0.5–1 mg/kg IV. This will usually suffice in producing a prompt diuresis. If there is little response, the dose may be increased to a maximum of 3 mg/kg IV for 2 doses, 2–4 hours apart.

3. Use a low-dose dopamine infusion (2–3 µg/kg/min) to improve renal blood flow.

4. Concomitant administration of IV chlorothiazide (Diuril) 10 mg/kg often has a synergistic effect with furosemide in promoting a vigorous diuresis.

5. Patients requiring frequent doses of diuretics may respond favorably to a continuous infusion of furosemide over a 24-hour period. The usual starting dose is 0.1 mg/kg/h.[40] Continuous infusions avoid the fluctuations in hemodynamics commonly seen after bolus doses.

E. **Treatment of established renal failure.**[41] Renal failure usually accompanies low cardiac output states and is more frequent in children undergoing surgery for complex cyanotic heart disease. It may lead to fluid overload, respiratory compromise, or systemic hypertension. In addition, renal failure may lead to hyperkalemia, hypocalcemia, metabolic acidosis, uremic encephalopathy, anemia, and infection.

1. Check electrolytes, BUN, creatinine levels.

2. Reduce fluid intake to measurable and insensible losses.

3. Adjust all medications requiring renal clearance (digoxin, antibiotics, etc.).

4. Nutritional supplements that provide a low-potassium, concentrated caloric mixture should be chosen to avoid fluid overload. Protein intake is limited to 0.5 mg/kg, but is increased to 1–2 g/kg/d for children undergoing dialysis.

5. **Peritoneal dialysis** should be considered in patients with renal failure and hyperkalemia. This requires placement of an intraperi-

toneal catheter and multiple exchanges of dialysate to achieve proper fluid balance and stabilization of electrolytes. It is very effective in young children because of their large peritoneal surface area and is better tolerated during periods of hemodynamic instability than hemodialysis.

6. **Hemodialysis** is very effective in the removal of solute and fluid, but it requires heparinization and hemodynamic stability because it removes a large amount of fluid during a short period of time. Access in infants weighing <10 kg is achieved through the SVC and femoral veins. Access in children weighing >10 kg is provided by a double-lumen catheter placed into the SVC via the subclavian or internal jugular vein.

7. **Ultrafiltration** (continuous AV hemofiltration) can be used to reduce total body water in states of severe fluid overload. It requires placement of both femoral arterial and venous cannulas (5F if <5 kg, 7F for 5–15 kg, and 8F for a child over 15 kg). A systemic blood pressure greater than 80 mm Hg and heparinization are required to keep the lines and filter from clotting. Ultrafiltration is ineffective in correcting hyperkalemia or azotemia.[42–44]

F. **Urgent management of hyperkalemia ($K^+ > 6.0$ mEq/L)**

1. Induce alkalosis by hyperventilation and/or $NaHCO_3$ 1 mEq/kg IV over 20 minutes.

2. Give 25% glucose 1–2 g/kg IV (4–8 mL/kg), followed by regular insulin 0.3 U/kg IV.

3. Give calcium gluconate 20 mg/kg IV over 5 minutes (0.2 mL/kg of a 10% solution with 100 mg/mL).

4. Administer kayexalate (ion exchange resin) 1 g/kg in 70% sorbitol PO or in 30% sorbitol PR q6h.

VIII.   Metabolic Problems

Monitoring of metabolic parameters in newborns and infants is critical in the early postoperative period. Seizures and sudden cardiovascular collapse in this age group can be caused by hypoglycemia and alterations in calcium and magnesium.

A. **Hypoglycemia** (glucose <40 mg/dL in neonates, <60 mg/dL in older infants)

1. Asymptomatic: 0.25 g/kg (1 mL/kg) 25% dextrose IV over 10 minutes, then change maintenance IV to 10% dextrose in 0.25% normal saline.

2. Seizures: 0.25–0.5 g/kg (1–2 mL/kg) 25% dextrose IV (50% dextrose if >10 years old) over 5 minutes; follow blood glucose hourly.

B. **Hypocalcemia.** Almost half of all serum calcium in the body is bound to protein (albumin); approximately 40% is ionized. Clinical disturbances in hypocalcemia result from a decrease in the level of ionized calcium, which must be monitored during the early postbypass period. It is also important to note that acidosis or alkalosis causes a shift in the ratio of ionized-to-bound calcium. Hypocalcemia is present when ionized calcium is <1 mmol/L.

1. Asymptomatic: calcium gluconate (10% solution) 100 mg/kg/d added to maintenance IV fluids.

2. Seizures: calcium gluconate 10 mg/kg (0.1 mL/kg of a 10% solution) IV slowly (can give calcium chloride via a central line); then calcium gluconate 100–200 mg/kg/d by continuous IV infusion.

C. **Hypomagnesemia** (<1.5 mEq/L) is treated with magnesium sulfate (10% solution) in a dose of 1 mL/kg IV (1 mL = 10 mg elemental Mg^{+2}). A dose of 1 mL/kg/day can be added to the maintenance IV.

D. **Metabolic acidosis** may simply reflect mild dehydration in a small child, but it may also indicate progressive subclinical low cardiac output states that may herald hemodynamic collapse. Therefore, the cause should always be investigated and treated aggressively.

1. Particular attention should be paid to:

   a. Peripheral signs of poor tissue perfusion

   b. Urine output

   c. ABGs and serum electrolytes

2. Treatment of metabolic acidosis involves identification and correction of the underlying cause; in the interim, however, correction of acid-base imbalance with sodium bicarbonate must be undertaken. The dose is based on the following equation:

$$mEq\ NaHCO_3 = 0.3 \times weight\ (kg) \times (base\ deficit)$$

Because of their greater extracellular volumes, values of 0.5 for neonates and 0.4 for children under age 6 months should be used in this equation. One-half of the deficit should be replaced initially with subsequent reevaluation of serum electrolytes and ABGs. Dilute $NaHCO_3$ (0.5 mEq/mL) should be used in infants.

E. **Metabolic alkalosis** is uncommon after surgery except in cases of vigorous diuresis or $NaHCO_3$ replacement. It will usually improve with electrolyte replacement (NaCl or KCl) if renal function is normal. If metabolic alkalosis is severe, it can be corrected by administering 0.2 mEq/kg/h of 0.15 N HCl over 16–24 hours via a central venous line.

References

1. Schleien CL, Zahka KG, Rogers MC. Principles of postoperative management in the pediatric intensive care unit. In: Rogers MC, ed. Textbook of pediatric intensive care. Baltimore: Williams & Wilkins, 1987:411–58.
2. Hickey PR, Wessel DL, Reich DL. Anesthesia for treatment of congenital heart disease. In: Kaplan JA, ed. Cardiac anesthesia, 3rd ed. Philadelphia: WB Saunders, 1993: 681–757.
3. Sellden H, Nilsson K, Larsson L, Ekstrom-Jodal B. Radial arterial catheters in children and neonates: a prospective study. Crit Care Med 1987;15:1106–9.
4. Gold JP, Jonas RA, Lang P, Elixson EM, Mayer JE, Castaneda AR. Transthoracic intracardiac monitoring lines in pediatric surgical patients: a ten-year experience. Ann Thorac Surg 1986;42:18–91.
5. Bricker DL, Dalton ML. Cardiac tamponade following dislodgment of a left atrial catheter from coronary artery bypass. J Thorac Cardiovasc Surg 1973;66:636–8.
6. Walsh MC, Noble LM, Carlo WA, Martin RJ. Relationship of pulse oximetry to arterial tension in infants. Crit Care Med 1987;15:1102–5.
7. Mihm FG, Halperin BD. Noninvasive detection of profound arterial desaturations using a pulse oximetry device. Anesthesiology 1985;62:85–7.
8. Kern FH, Morana NJ, Sears JJ, Hickey PR. Coagulation defects in neonates during cardiopulmonary bypass. Ann Thorac Surg 1992;54:541–6.
9. Gioia FR, Stephenson RL, Alterwitz SA. Principles of respiratory support and mechanical ventilation. In: Rogers MC, ed. Textbook of pediatric intensive care. Baltimore: Williams & Wilkins, 1987:113–69.
10. Willson DR. Postoperative respiratory function and its management. In: Lake C, ed. Pediatric cardiac anesthesia. Norwalk, CT: Appleton & Lange, 1988.
11. Silvasi DL, Rosen DA, Rosen KR. Continuous intravenous midazolam infusion for sedation in the pediatric intensive care unit. Anesth Analg 1988;67:286–8.
12. Shimada Y, Yoshiya I, Tanaka K, Yamazaki T, Kumon K. Crying vital capacity and maximal inspiratory pressure as clinical indicators of readiness for weaning of infants less than a year of age. Anesthesiology 1979;51:456–9.
13. Russell RIR, Mulvey D, Laroche C, Shinebourne EA, Green M. Bedside assessment of phrenic nerve function in infants and children. J Thorac Cardiovasc Surg 1991; 101:143–7.
14. Watanabe T, Trusler GA, Williams WG, Edmonds JF, Coles JG, Hosokawa Y. Phrenic nerve paralysis after pediatric cardiac surgery. Retrospective study of 125 cases. J Thorac Cardiovasc Surg 1987;94:383–8.
15. Fairfax AJ, McNabb WR, Spiro SG. Chylothorax: a review of 18 cases. Thorax 1986;41:880–5.
16. Kratz JM, Gillette PC, Crawford FA, Sade RM, Zeigler BL. Atrioventricular pacing in congenital heart disease. Ann Thorac Surg 1992;54:485–9.
17. Braunstein PW Jr, Sade RM, Gillette PC. Life-threatening postoperative junctional ectopic tachycardia. Ann Thorac Surg 1992;53:726–8.
18. Lawless S, Burckart G, Diven W, Thompson A, Siewers R. Amrinone in neonates and infants after cardiac surgery. Crit Care Med 1989;17:751–4.
19. Veasy LG, Blalock RC, Orth JL, Boucek MM. Intra-aortic balloon pumping in infants and children. Circulation 1983;63:1095–1100.
20. Karl TR, Sano S, Horton S, Mee RBB. Centrifugal pump left heart assist in pediatric cardiac operations. Indications, technique, and results. J Thorac Cardiovasc Surg 1991;102:624–30.
21. Rogers AJ, Trento A, Siewers RD, et al. Extracorporeal membrane oxygenation for postcardiotomy cardiogenic shock in children. Ann Thorac Surg 1989;47:903–6.

22. Weinhaus L, Canter C, Noetzel M, McAlister W, Spray TL. Extracorporeal membrane oxygenation for circulatory support after repair of congenital heart defects. Ann Thorac Surg 1989;48:206–12.

23. Ziomek S, Harrell JE Jr, Fasules JW, et al. Extracorporeal membrane oxygenation for cardiac failure after congenital heart operation. Ann Thorac Surg 1992;54: 861–8.

24. Klein MD, Shaheen KW, Whittlesey GC, Pinsky WW, Arciniegas E. Extracorporeal membrane oxygenation for the circulatory support of children after repair of congenital heart disease. J Thorac Cardiovasc Surg 1990;100:498–505.

25. Morray JP, Lynn AM, Mansfield PB. Effect of pH and PCO_2 on pulmonary and systemic hemodynamics after surgery in children with congenital heart disease and pulmonary hypertension. J Pediatr 1988;113:474–9.

26. Hickey PR, Hansen DD, Wessel D, Lang P, Jonas RA, Elixson EM. Blunting of stress responses in the pulmonary circulation of infants by fentanyl. Anesth Analg 1985;64:1137–42.

27. Schreiber MD, Heymann MA, Soifer SJ. Increased arterial pH, not decreased PCO_2, attenuates hypoxia-induced pulmonary vasoconstriction in newborn lambs. Ped Res 1986;20:113–7.

28. Ilbawi MN, Idriss FS, DeLeon SY, Berry TE, Duffy CE, Paul MH. Hemodynamic effects of intravenous nitroglycerin in pediatric patients after heart surgery. Circulation 1985;72(suppl II):II-101–7.

29. Roberts JD Jr, Polaner DM, Todres ID, Lang P, Zapol WM. Inhaled nitric oxide (NO): a selective pulmonary vasodilator for the treatment of persistent pulmonary hypertension of the newborn (PPHN). Circulation 1991;84(suppl II):II-321.

30. Journois D, Pouard P, Mauriat P, Malhere T, Vouhe P, Safran D. Inhaled nitric oxide as a therapy for pulmonary hypertension after operations for congenital heart defects. J Thorac Cardiovasc Surg 1994;107:1129–35.

31. Miller OL, Celermajer DS, Deanfield JE, Macrae DH. Very-low-dose inhaled nitric oxide: a selective pulmonary vasodilator after operations for congenital heart disease. J Thorac Cardiovasc Surg 1994;108:487–94.

32. Goldman AP, Delius DE, Deanfield JE, de Leval MR, Sigston PE, Macrae DJ. Nitric oxide might reduce the need for extracorporeal support in children with critical postoperative pulmonary hypertension. Ann Thorac Surg 1996;62:750–5.

33. Humes RA, Porter CJ, Puga FJ, Schaff HV, Danielson GK. Utility of temporary atrial epicardial electrodes in postoperative pediatric cardiac patients. Mayo Clin Proc 1989;64:516–21.

34. Overholt ED, Rheuban KS, Gutgesell HP, Lerman BB, DiMarco JP. Usefulness of adenosine for arrhythmias in infants and children. Am J Cardiol 1988;61:336–40.

35. Bash SE, Shah JJ, Albers WH, Geiss DM. Hypothermia for the treatment of postsurgical greatly accelerated junctional ectopic tachycardia. J Am Coll Cardiol 1987;10:1095–9.

36. Perry JC, Fenrick AL, Hise JE, Triedman JK, Friedman RA, Lamberti JJ. Pediatric use of intravenous amiodarone: efficacy and safety in critically ill patients from a multicenter protocol. J Am Coll Cardiol 1996;27:1246–50.

37. Paul T, Reimer A, Janousek J, Kallfelz HC. Efficacy and safety of propafenone in congenital junctional ectopic tachycardia. J Am Coll Cardiol 1992;20:911–4.

38. Emergency Cardiac Care Committee and Subcommittees, American Heart Association. Guidelines for cardiopulmonary resuscitation and emergency cardiac care. VI: Pediatric advanced life support. JAMA 1992;268:2262–75.

39. Emergency Cardiac Care Committee and Subcommittees, American Heart Association. Guidelines for cardiopulmonary resuscitation and emergency cardiac care. VII: Neonatal resuscitation. JAMA 1992;268:2276–81.

40. Luciani GB, Nichcani S, Chang AC, Wells WJ, Mewth CJ, Starnes VA. Continuous versus intermittent furosemide infusion in critically ill infants after open heart operations. Ann Thorac Surg 1997;64:1133–9.
41. Maxwell LG, Fivush BA, McLean RH. Renal failure. In: Rogers MC, ed. Textbook of pediatric intensive care. Baltimore: Williams & Wilkins, 1987:1001–55.
42. Zobel G, Stein JI, Kuttnig M, Beitzke A, Metzler H, Rigler B. Continuous extracorporeal fluid removal in children with low cardiac output after cardiac operations. J Thorac Cardiovasc Surg 1991;101:593–7.
43. Paret G, Cohen AJ, Bohn DJ, et al. Continuous arteriovenous hemofiltration after cardiac operations in infants and children. J Thorac Cardiovasc Surg 1992;104: 1225–30.
44. Fleming F, Bohn D, Edwards H, et al. Renal replacement therapy after repair of congenital heart disease in children. A comparison of hemofiltration and peritoneal dialysis. J Thorac Cardiovasc Surg 1995;109:322–31.

17 Common Postoperative Scenarios

17 Common Postoperative Scenarios

Postoperative care of pediatric patients undergoing open-heart surgery is optimized by an understanding of the unique pathophysiologic derangements of various types of congenital heart defects and the impact of surgery on cardiovascular performance. Chapter 14 provided a basic discussion of the pathophysiology of these defects and their surgical correction. This chapter will provide brief descriptions of aspects of postoperative care unique to each of these defects.[1-3]

I. Coarctation of the Aorta

A. Neonates with an associated VSD may experience hemodynamic instability after coarctation repair. Clinical improvement generally occurs because the relief of left ventricular (LV) afterload decreases left-to-right shunting across the VSD. If the infant experiences CHF refractory to medical therapy, closure of the VSD is indicated.

B. After a subclavian flap procedure, pulsatile blood flow will be absent in the left arm. Therefore, blood pressure must be obtained from the right arm. Capillary refill and limb viability should be checked frequently for the first 24 hours.[4]

C. "Paradoxical" hypertension is common in older children.[5] It should be treated initially with sedation and analgesics, but may require aggressive control in extreme cases to minimize bleeding or a neurologic event. Recommended antihypertensives include:

1. Sodium nitroprusside 0.5–5 µg/kg/min often with propranolol 0.01–0.1 mg/kg[6]

2. Esmolol 50–200 µg/kg/min IV

3. Labetalol 0.25 mg/kg IV over 5 minutes, with an infusion 30 minutes later of 0.1–0.2 mg/kg/h[7]

4. Captopril 0.5–3.0 mg/kg/day PO q8h for persistent hypertension[8]

D. The "postcoarctectomy syndrome" is caused by a mesenteric arteritis that may produce abdominal pain, ileus, GI bleeding, or bowel perforation.[9] Nasogastric drainage should routinely be used for at least 24 hours and feeding delayed until gastrointestinal activity has returned. Close observation for these symptoms and use of antihypertensive therapy has decreased the incidence of this severe complication.

E. Paraplegia is a rare complication of coarctation repair, with an incidence of about 0.5%. It is more common in patients with poor collaterals around the coarctation site. A careful neurologic examination is imperative in the early postoperative period.

F. Drainage of a hemo- or pneumothorax with a needle or chest tube must be performed with extreme caution because of the presence of enlarged intercostal arteries.

II.   Patent Ductus Arteriosus

A.   Neonates and premature infants may have associated bronchopulmonary dysplasia or complex heart disease that increases the risk of surgery. Prolonged ventilatory support may be necessary in these situations. Nonetheless, if heart failure persists after PDA ligation, careful examination for a persistent ductus murmur and evaluation by echocardiography are warranted. Most postoperative problems are related to immaturity of other organ systems.

B.   Neonates can experience bleeding if indomethacin was used in an attempt to achieve ductal closure.[10]

C.   Older children usually do not require postoperative intubation or ventilatory support. Aggressive chest physiotherapy and analgesia may be required to minimize chest wall splinting from the thoracotomy incision.

D.   PDA ligation may result in damage to the recurrent laryngeal nerve.

III.   Atrial Septal Defect

A.   Patients undergoing closure of an ASD are usually hemodynamically stable and can be extubated either in the operating room or soon after arrival in the ICU. Prolonged intubation and aggressive hemodynamic management may be indicated in patients with preoperative pulmonary hypertension or congestive heart failure.

B.   Patients should be monitored for the development of arrhythmias and heart block.[11] Atrial fibrillation/flutter and paroxysmal atrial tachycardia are occasionally noted after ASD repairs. A supraventricular rate appropriate for the patient's age should be maintained.

   1.   Sinus node dysfunction is more common after closure of sinus venosus defects, but may be seen after any procedure that involves a right atriotomy incision as a result of direct damage to the SA node or interruption of its blood supply. Atrial or AV pacing may be required if a sinus or junctional bradycardia is too slow for the child's age (see table 16.7).

   2.   Heart block and junctional rhythms may occasionally occur after repair of ostium primum defects, during which suturing is performed close to the AV node.

IV.   Ventricular Septal Defect

A.   Repair of a perimembranous VSD is associated with the development of complete heart block in up to 10% of patients. This results from suturing, edema, or hemorrhage near the AV node, which lies in close proximity to the edge of a membranous VSD.

   1.   Isoproterenol may be helpful in improving AV conduction.

   2.   As with all other postoperative patients, maintenance of a supraventricular mechanism with a heart rate appropriate for the patient's age should be obtained. Atrial or AV pacing may be used, if necessary. Augmentation of cardiac output is obtained primarily by an increase in heart rate in the early postoperative period.

3. Although heart block is frequently transient, it may require place-ment of a permanent pacemaker system if it persists for more than 2 weeks.

B. Children with significant preoperative pulmonary hypertension or hyper-reactive pulmonary vasculature may develop RV failure from increased RV afterload. Performance of a ventriculotomy may also impair RV function.

1. Efforts to reduce pulmonary vascular resistance (PVR) may be nec-essary for several days after surgery. These include sedation, paral-ysis, and ventilatory interventions ($PO_2 > 100$ torr, $PCO_2 < 35$ torr, $pH > 7.50$).[12]

2. Inotropic support of RV function, and occasionally LV function, may be required. Useful medications include dopamine, dobuta-mine, and amrinone.

C. Detection of a new systolic murmur or the development of recurrent heart failure may raise suspicion of a residual VSD or patch dehiscence. This can be evaluated by a comparison of RA and PA O_2 saturations. A $Q_p:Q_s$ greater than $2:1$ generally requires reoperation. A systolic murmur may also indicate tricuspid regurgitation (after a transatrial repair), or ventricu-lar outflow tract obstruction caused by patch placement. A diastolic murmur may indicate the presence of aortic regurgitation related to the VSD.[11]

V. Pulmonary Artery Banding

A. Pulmonary artery banding is a palliative procedure used to reduce pul-monary blood flow (PBF) in patients with multiple muscular VSDs and VSDs associated with complex heart disease not amenable to early repair (see Chapter 14). The band is tightened surgically until the PA pressure distal to the band is one-half of the RV systolic pressure.[13] Inotropic support may be necessary postoperatively because of the increase in RV afterload.

B. A loose band may be associated with persistent symptoms of CHF and difficulty in weaning from the ventilator. If this situation persists despite aggressive medical therapy, reoperation to tighten the band should be considered.

C. Too tight a band is indicated by unacceptable hypoxemia and should be detected by pulse oximetry in the operating room. Band migration may produce distal or proximal pulmonary artery obstruction. This may lead to distortion of the pulmonary arteries, asymmetric distal flow, or right ven-tricular hypertrophy. An excessively tight band may lead to shunt reversal through the VSD and arterial desaturation. Reoperation to loosen the band may be necessary.

VI. Endocardial Cushion Defect (AV Canal)

A. Children with this defect usually come to surgery in suboptimal condition because of chronic CHF and failure to thrive.

B. Hemodynamic problems after repair of a complete AV canal may result from residual left-to-right shunting (ASD or VSD), persistent pulmonary hypertension, or residual mitral valve insufficiency.

1. The use of both LA and RA pressure monitoring is helpful in hemo-dynamic management. A high LA pressure relative to RA pressure may indicate residual left-to-right shunting or mitral regurgitation. Echocardiography or even cardiac catheterization may be neces-sary to define the problem. In contrast, high RA pressure relative to LA pressure may reflect RV dysfunction exacerbated by pul-monary hypertension.

2. Persistent pulmonary hypertension is particularly common after repair of AV canals, especially in children with Down's syndrome. In addition, these children are prone to episodes of transient pul-monary vasospasm.

    a. Aggressive management with sedation, paralysis, and hyper-ventilation with several days of mechanical ventilatory support is commonly required. Use of pulmonary vasodila-tors may occasionally be beneficial.

    b. Inotropic support of RV function is often necessary in patients with elevated PVR. Dopamine, dobutamine, or amrinone is often selected.

3. Mitral valve repair may be incomplete if there is deficient mitral valve tissue. Valve replacement in very young children is usually not feasible, and this problem can be very difficult to manage. Echocardiography can define the degree of residual mitral regur-gitation. Valve repair may also lead to mitral stenosis.

C. Repair of this defect carries the risk of complete heart block, and equip-ment for AV or ventricular pacing should be available.

VII. Palliative Systemic-Pulmonary Shunts[2,14]

A. Palliative shunts are performed to improve pulmonary blood flow and oxygenation in cyanotic defects. They are usually considered to allow for growth of the pulmonary arteries and of the child, in anticipation of subsequent total correction. Thus, they leave the underlying pathology uncorrected.

B. After completion of a shunt, the PaO_2 may approach 100 torr with an FIO_2 of 1.0. As the FIO_2 is weaned, initial O_2 saturations of 90% will gradually decrease to about 75–85% (PO_2 of 40–50 torr). Continuous pulse oxime-try is invaluable in monitoring these patients.

C. After all shunting procedures, it is imperative to listen carefully to the patient for the presence of a shunt murmur. This is frequently difficult to auscultate during the first 24–48 hours after surgery. The chest x-ray will normally show increased vascular markings on the side of the shunt.

1. The development of pulmonary edema is uncommon after the Blalock-Taussig shunts in comparison with central shunts. Evidence of congestive heart failure following the procedure may indicate excessive pulmonary blood flow and the necessity of revising and narrowing the shunt.

2. Maintenance of adequate hydration and systemic blood pressure is essential to promote shunt patency.

3. Rapid cardiovascular decompensation or severe arterial desaturation should raise the suspicion of shunt closure. Emergency echocardiography or cardiac catheterization should be done to confirm the diagnosis before considering reoperation.

D. After a **Blalock-Taussig shunt**, blood pressures must be taken on the arm opposite the shunt. The arm on the involved side should be observed for capillary refill. Pulses are frequently absent for 2–3 days, but will usually return. A chylothorax may rarely develop after this procedure.

E. The **modified Blalock-Taussig shunt** has a higher early patency rate than the traditional BT shunt because of a higher flow rate. It also preserves flow through the subclavian artery and has less influence on subsequent arm growth. Occasionally, leakage of serous fluid through the graft may result in prolonged chest tube drainage or formation of a seroma around the graft. This should be differentiated from a chylothorax, which may also develop after this procedure.

F. **Central shunts** are more prone to provide excessive pulmonary blood flow that leads to congestive heart failure and eventually to pulmonary vascular disease. Careful review of the chest x-ray and the infant's clinical status is essential in assessing the adequacy of the shunt.

G. The **Glenn shunt** represents a low-pressure shunt that should be used only in children over the age of 6 months when there is no evidence of pulmonary vascular disease. It has been associated with multiple complications (see page 483) and has been supplanted by the **bidirectional Glenn**. This procedure has achieved excellent results in appropriately selected patients, but occasionally relief of cyanosis is inadequate because of the presence of venous collaterals.[15,16]

H. Other complications of palliative shunts include phrenic nerve injury, Horner's syndrome, and chylothorax.

VIII. Tetralogy of Fallot/Pulmonary Atresia with VSD

A. The most common problem after repair of tetralogy of Fallot (TOF) is RV dysfunction.[1,2,17] This may occur as a result of:

1. Right ventriculotomy

2. Inadequate myocardial protection

3. Residual RV outflow tract obstruction (infundibular or valvular stenosis, hypoplasia or stenosis of distal pulmonary arteries, RV-PA conduit obstruction in patients with pulmonary atresia)

4. Pulmonary regurgitation caused by placement of a transannular patch

5. Residual VSD

B. Intraoperative echocardiography and measurement of intracardiac pressures at the termination of cardiopulmonary bypass (CPB) may identify several of these problems. For example, a $P_{RV/LV}$ exceeding 0.75 may indicate residual outflow tract obstruction, distal PA stenosis, or a residual VSD. Measurement of simultaneous right ventricular and pulmonary artery pressures, calculation of a shunt from O_2 saturations, and analysis of an echocardiogram can differentiate among these problems.

C. In the ICU, both RA and LA lines can be used to differentiate right from left ventricular failure as the cause of a low cardiac output state.

1. Low RA pressures usually indicate hypovolemia, which may be caused by the increased mediastinal bleeding noted after repair of cyanotic defects.

2. High RA pressures often indicate RV dysfunction that requires inotropic support with dopamine, dobutamine, or amrinone. RA pressures of 15–18 mm Hg may be necessary to ensure left-sided filling and adequate systemic output. Both inotropic support and an increase in heart rate (either pharmacologic or with pacing wires) are usually required to improve cardiac output in these patients.[18]

3. Disproportionate elevation of LA pressure may indicate patch disruption and left-to-right shunting through the VSD, or it may reflect LV failure. Echocardiography can be used to distinguish between these two problems.

D. The occurrence of pulmonary dysfunction following repair of TOF is more common in severely cyanotic infants. Sudden reperfusion of the lungs and the use of cardiopulmonary bypass may produce pulmonary edema on the basis of altered pulmonary capillary permeability.[17] Other contributing factors to respiratory failure include a residual or recurrent VSD and the presence of large systemic-pulmonary collaterals. This is particularly problematic in patients with pulmonary atresia and VSD. Persistent large collaterals may require ligation or coil embolization in the catheterization laboratory.

E. A right bundle branch block is usually seen after a right ventriculotomy incision. The presence of an associated left anterior hemiblock may portend the development of complete heart block. AV pacing should be used in these patients. A permanent pacemaker system may be required if complete heart block persists for more than 1–2 weeks.

F. Late sudden death after TOF repair has been associated with ventricular arrhythmias. This is usually the result of a reentrant ventricular tachycardia arising from the site of the ventriculotomy scar.[19] Patients with ventricular ectopy and residual RV outflow tract (RVOT) obstruction are at greatest risk for developing ventricular tachycardia.

IX.   Pulmonary Atresia with Intact Ventricular Septum

A. Most infants with this problem are ductus-dependent for pulmonary blood flow and are treated preoperatively with prostaglandin E_1 (PGE_1) to maintain ductal patency.

B. If the RV is of normal size or an infundibulum is present, a pulmonary valvotomy and a shunt, or just a shunt, is usually performed. In most of these patients, the PGE_1 can be weaned uneventfully over a 24-hour period after surgery. Inotropic support may be required for a short period of time. Measures to reduce PVR and augment pulmonary blood flow may be beneficial.

C. If only a valvotomy is performed, a low output state and progressive arterial desaturation may develop as PGE$_1$ is weaned. Because the RV is poorly developed and noncompliant, blood continues to shunt right-to-left across the ASD and can exacerbate hypoxemia. This may indicate either pulmonary valve obstruction or dysfunction of the hypoplastic ventricle. Inotropic support and measures to reduce PVR may be necessary. A systemic-to-pulmonary artery shunt should be constructed for persistent hypoxemia.[20]

D. Complications noted after the Fontan correction of this defect are noted in the next section.

X. Fontan Procedure

A. The Fontan procedure is used to treat defects with single ventricle physiology, including tricuspid atresia, pulmonary atresia with intact ventricular septum, univentricular heart, and hypoplastic left heart syndrome.

B. Because the superior vena cava (SVC) is anastomosed to the right pulmonary artery, pulmonary blood flow (PBF) is dependent on the central venous pressure and outflow resistance.[2,3,21]

1. A supranormal central venous pressure (CVP of 15–18 mm Hg) is required to promote PBF and achieve adequate LV filling. The high systemic venous pressure commonly leads to ascites, hepatomegaly, large pleural effusions, and a protein-losing enteropathy. Aggressive therapy with diuretics and pleural drainage is essential to improve pulmonary function and allow weaning from the ventilator. A pleuroperitoneal shunt may be required for persistent chylous effusions.[22]

2. Anatomic or functional obstruction downstream to the SVC-PA anastomosis will reduce flow into the pulmonary circuit. Contributing causes include:

   a. An elevation in PVR. The ventilator settings should be selected to avoid hypoxia, hypercarbia, and acidosis.

   b. Positive pressure ventilation may limit PBF. Large tidal volumes with short inspiratory times to lower airway pressures and avoidance of PEEP are essential during mechanical ventilation. Negative pressure ventilation with a flexible cuirass has been shown to improve cardiac output after the Fontan procedure.[23] High-frequency ventilation has also been shown to be beneficial in the Fontan circulation.[24] However, optimal oxygenation and hemodynamics are obtained after the child is extubated.[25]

   c. LV dysfunction with an increase in diastolic filling (LA) pressures. Use of inotropes to improve contractility or diastolic compliance (amrinone, dobutamine) can therefore improve PBF.

   d. Loss of sinus rhythm will produce atrial-ventricular dyssynchrony and left-sided AV valve regurgitation. This will increase LA pressures and impair PBF. Rhythm problems may be less common with the lateral tunnel Fontan.[26]

3. In high-risk patients (high PA pressures or elevated PVR), a fenestration may be left in the atrial septum. This will allow for a reduction in systemic venous pressure with right-to-left shunting across a small ASD.[27] The defect is small enough not to cause significant arterial desaturation. It may be adjusted in the postoperative period with a snare.[28] Mild cyanosis may also be caused by intrapulmonary shunting.

C. Residual left-to-right shunts may result from aortopulmonary collaterals.

XI.   Double Outlet Right Ventricle

A. The repair of a DORV depends on the relationship of the aorta to the VSD. The simplest repair, used for a subaortic VSD, is an intraventricular patch which routes the LV outflow into the aorta. An RV-to-PA conduit may be placed if there is pulmonic stenosis. Problems noted after this repair include:

1. Heart block that requires AV pacing.

2. Disruption of the VSD patch with left-to-right shunting, producing excessive PBF and pulmonary vascular congestion.

3. Obstruction of RV-to-PA flow by the VSD tunneling patch, producing RV failure and an elevation in RA pressures. Although RV dysfunction may also result from suboptimal myocardial protection, intracavitary obstruction should be ruled out by echocardiography or cardiac catheterization. The patch can also create subaortic stenosis.

B. More complex forms of this anomaly usually involve an arterial switch repair or insertion of an RV-to-PA conduit.

XII.   Transposition of the Great Arteries

A. **Arterial switch operation**

1. An uncomplicated operation should result in a relatively stable patient if the LV was "well prepared" to support the systemic circulation. Poor LV performance from a prolonged operation may necessitate inotropic support. Evaluation of a 12-lead ECG should be performed to rule out myocardial ischemia, which may result from kinking or stretching of the coronary arteries related to their translocations.[29]

2. Inotropic support may be required for several days postoperatively, particularly if the operation is performed in a patient with transposition of the great arteries and intact ventricular septum after 2 weeks of age when the LV may be suboptimally prepared.

3. High left atrial pressures should be avoided since they may lead to ventricular distention which may produce myocardial ischemia. In some centers, vasodilators are routinely used to diminish wall stress.[30]

4. Other late complications, such as supravalvular pulmonary stenosis and semilunar valve insufficiency, are uncommon when the switch operation is performed in neonates.

B. **Mustard and Senning operations**[31]

    1. Supraventricular and junctional arrhythmias may complicate these intraatrial repairs which involve multiple intraatrial suture lines. Damage to the sinus node or its blood supply may lead to sinus bradycardia, junctional escape rhythms, ectopic atrial pacemaker sites, or a sick sinus syndrome.

    2. An atrial correction (especially the Mustard procedure) may be complicated by obstruction of either systemic or pulmonary venous drainage. Obstruction usually develops later during recovery, but it may occasionally be evident in the early postoperative period and require operative revision.

        a. Although a higher CVP is often necessary in the early post-operative period, it may call attention to SVC obstruction. This can be confirmed at catheterization by documenting a gradient exceeding 5 mm Hg between the SVC and the systemic venous atrium. SVC obstruction is frequently asymptomatic because of decompression through the azygous system, but may produce jugular venous distention and periorbital or upper extremity edema. IVC obstruction may be manifest by hepatomegaly and ascites.

        b. Pulmonary venous obstruction will produce pulmonary hypertension, hypoxemia, and pulmonary vascular congestion.

    3. Because the RV is performing a systemic workload, RV dysfunction requiring inotropic support may occur after CPB. At late follow-up, progressive RV dysfunction and tricuspid valve insufficiency develop as a consequence of exposure to systemic pressures.

    4. Residual intraatrial shunts may occur, but arterial desaturation is rarely severe enough to warrant reoperation.

XIII. Total Anomalous Pulmonary Venous Connection

A. Correction of TAPVC associated with pulmonary venous obstruction is usually required on an urgent basis during the neonatal period. The risk is high because of preoperative hypoxemia, acidosis, and a low output state.

B. High LA pressures may be required to ensure LV filling because of the small size of the left atrium and ventricle.

C. RV function may be compromised by preexisting pulmonary vascular disease caused by pulmonary venous obstruction. Furthermore, there may be residual, uncorrected pulmonary venous obstruction after surgery. Therefore, inotropic support with dobutamine or amrinone and measures to reduce PVR should be used to improve RV function. Nitric oxide has proven useful in these circumstances.[32]

XIV. Truncus Arteriosus

A. RV failure may result from pulmonary hypertension or from RV-PA conduit obstruction. In addition, LV dysfunction may occur after CPB as a result of preoperative volume overload from truncal valve insufficiency or a residual VSD.

B. Inotropic support with dopamine, dobutamine, or amrinone can be used to augment myocardial performance while reducing RV afterload. Standard measures to reduce PVR during mechanical ventilation may also be beneficial.[1,2]

XV. Hypoplastic Left Heart Syndrome

A. Children with HLHS are critically ill, with a low cardiac output state and end-organ ischemia. During the prebypass period, the child is susceptible to myocardial ischemia and sudden ventricular fibrillation. In addition, anesthetic agents that reduce PVR may improve oxygenation at the expense of reduced systemic perfusion, leading to cardiovascular collapse.[1]

B. After the Norwood procedure, there remains a delicate balance between systemic and pulmonary blood flows that is dictated by the systemic and pulmonary vascular resistances.[33,34]

   1. In the early postoperative period, an elevated PVR may reduce PBF and produce hypoxemia. Ventilatory settings should be adjusted to maintain a PCO_2 of 20–30 torr and a pH of 7.50–7.60. The FIO_2 must be raised if the PO_2 is less than 30 torr.

   2. When PVR falls, the increase in PBF will improve oxygenation but will reduce systemic cardiac output, producing oliguria, myocardial ischemia, acidosis, and often sudden arrest.

      a. PBF is adequate when the systemic oxygen saturation is 75–82%; higher saturations represent excessive PBF and place the patient at risk of hemodynamic deterioration.

      b. If the PO_2 exceeds 50 torr (O_2 saturation > 85%), measures must be taken to increase PVR to reduce PBF. The FIO_2 should be lowered, and if necessary, carbon dioxide added to the ventilatory circuit to reduce it below 0.21. The PCO_2 should be raised to 40 torr and alkalosis should be avoided.

C. RV dysfunction may result from both volume and pressure overload. This may produce tricuspid regurgitation. The use of inotropes in patients undergoing the Norwood procedure is controversial.[35]

D. Continuous measurement of systemic venous oxygenation may provide an accurate assessment of hemodynamic performance and dictate treatment accordingly.[36,37]

E. Usually the ASD is enlarged at the time of surgery; if it remains restrictive and limits left-to-right atrial shunting, pulmonary venous hypertension may develop.

F. Postoperative care after the Fontan procedure was discussed in section X of this chapter.

XVI. Deep Hypothermia with Circulatory Arrest

A. Deep hypothermia to 20°C with circulatory arrest is commonly used to perform corrective operations in infants weighing less than 10 kg.[38] It provides a quiet, bloodless field, improves myocardial protection, and decreases the metabolic demand of other vital organs. Usually 60 minutes of circulatory arrest can be tolerated at this temperature.

B. Postoperative sequelae may include:

1. CNS complications (seizures, choreoathetosis, neurologic impairment, intellectual dysfunction)[39]

2. Coagulopathy

3. Renal failure

4. Prolonged ventilatory support

References

1. Hickey PR, Wessel DL, Reich DL. Anesthesia for treatment of congenital heart disease. In: Kaplan JA, ed. Cardiac anesthesia, 3rd ed. Philadelphia: WB Saunders, 1993:681–757.

2. Strafford MA, DiNardo JA. Anesthesia for congenital heart disease. In: DiNardo JA, Schwartz MJ. Anesthesia for cardiac surgery. Norwalk, CT: Appleton & Lange, 1990:117–72.

3. Schleien CL, Zahka KG, Rogers MC. Principles of postoperative management in pediatric intensive care unit. In: Rogers MC, ed. Textbook of pediatric intensive care. Baltimore: Williams & Wilkins, 1987:411–58.

4. Todd PJ, Dangerfield PH, Hamilton DI, Wilkinson JL. Late effects on the left upper limb of subclavian flap aortoplasty. J Thorac Cardiovasc Surg 1983;85:678–81.

5. Sealy WC. Paradoxical hypertension after repair of coarctation of the aorta: a review of its causes. Ann Thorac Surg 1990;50:323–9.

6. Will RJ, Walker OM, Traugott RC, Treasure RL. Sodium nitroprusside and propranolol therapy for management of postcoarctectomy hypertension. J Thorac Cardiovasc Surg 1978;75:722–4.

7. Bojar RM, Weiner B, Cleveland RJ. Intravenous labetalol for the control of hypertension following repair of coarctation of the aorta. Clin Cardiol 1988;11:639–41.

8. Casta A, Conti VR, Talabi A, Brouhard BH. Effective use of captopril in postoperative paradoxical hypertension of the aorta. Clin Cardiol 1982;5:551–5.

9. Singleton AO, McGinnis LM, Eason HR. Arteritis following correction of coarctation of the aorta. Surgery 1959;45:665–73.

10. Mahoney L, Carnero V, Brett C, Heymann MA, Clyman RI. Prophylactic indomethacin therapy for patent ductus arteriosus in very-low-birth-weight infants. N Engl J Med 1982;306:506–10.

11. Stewart JR, Bender HW Jr. Management of complications of surgery for septal defects. In: Waldhausen JA, Orringer MB, eds. Complications in cardiothoracic surgery. St. Louis: Mosby Year Book, 1991:168–79.

12. Morray JP, Lynn AM, Mansfield PB. Effect of pH and PCO_2 on pulmonary and systemic hemodynamics after surgery in children with congenital heart disease and pulmonary hypertension. J Pediatr 1988;113:474–9.

13. Horowitz MD, Culpepper WS III, Williams LC III, Sundgaard-Riise K, Ochsner JL. Pulmonary artery banding: analysis of a 25-year experience. Ann Thorac Surg 1989; 48:444–50.

14. Drake DH, Bove EL. Management of complications related to the pulmonary artery. In: Waldhausen JA, Orringer MB, eds. Complications in cardiothoracic surgery. St. Louis: Mosby Year Book, 1991:149–59.

15. Lamberti JJ, Spicer RL, Waldman JD, et al. The bidirectional cavopulmonary shunt. J Thorac Cardiovasc Surg 1990;100:22–30.

16. Hopkins RA, Armstrong BE, Serwer GA, Peterson RJ, Oldham HN Jr. Physiological rationale for a bidirectional cavopulmonary shunt. A versatile complement to the Fontan principle. J Thorac Cardiovasc Surg 1985;89:391–8.

17. Heck HA, Pacifico AD, McConnell ME, Colvin EV, Kirklin JK, Kirklin JW. Management of complications following surgical intervention for tetralogy of Fallot. In: Waldhausen JA, Orringer MB, eds. Complications in cardiothoracic surgery. St. Louis: Mosby Year Book, 1991:180–9.

18. Berner M, Oberhansli I, Rouge JC, Jaccard C, Friedli B. Chronotropic and inotropic supports are both required to increase cardiac output early after corrective operations for tetralogy of Fallot. J Thorac Cardiovasc Surg 1989;97:297–302.

19. Downar E, Harris L, Kimber S, et al. Ventricular tachycardia after surgical repair of tetralogy of Fallot: results of intraoperative mapping studies. J Am Coll Cardiol 1992;20:648–55.

20. Hanley FL, Sade RM, Blackstone EH, Kirklin JW, Freedom RM, Nanda NC. Outcomes in neonatal pulmonary atresia with intact ventricular septum. J Thorac Cardiovasc Surg 1993;105:406–27.

21. de Leval MR, Kilner P, Gewillig M, Bull C. Total cavopulmonary connection: a logical alternative to atriopulmonary connection for complex Fontan operations. Experimental studies and early clinical experience. J Thorac Cardiovasc Surg 1988;96:682–95.

22. Sade RM, Wiles HB. Pleuroperitoneal shunt for persistent pleural drainage after Fontan procedure. J Thorac Cardiovasc Surg 1990;100:621–3.

23. Shekerdemian LS, Shore DF, Lincoln C, Bush A, Redington AN. Negative-pressure ventilation improves cardiac output after right heart surgery. Circulation 1996;94(suppl II):II-49–55

24. Meliones JN, Bove EL, DeKeon MK, et al. High-frequency jet ventilation improves cardiac function after the Fontan procedure. Circulation 1991;84(suppl III):III-364–8.

25. Williams DB, Kiernan PD, Metke MP, Marsh HM, Danielson GK. Hemodynamic response to positive end-expiratory pressure following right atrium-pulmonary artery bypass (Fontan procedure). J Thorac Cardiovasc Surg 1984;87:856–61.

26. Balaji S, Gewillig M, de Leval MR, Deanfield JE. Are post-operative arrhythmias after Fontan operation preventable by the total cavo-pulmonary connection? Circulation 1990;82(suppl III):III-76.

27. Kopf GS, Kleinman CS, Hijazi ZM, Fahey JT, Dewar ML, Hellenbrand WE. Fenestrated Fontan operation with delayed transcatheter closure of atrial septal defect. Improved results in high-risk patients. J Thorac Cardiovasc Surg 1992;103:1039–48.

28. Laks H, Pearl JM, Haas GS, et al. Partial Fontan: advantages of an adjustable interatrial communication. Ann Thorac Surg 1991;52:1084–95.

29. Castaneda AR. Management of complications related to surgery for transposition of the great arteries: arterial switch operation. In: Waldhausen JA, Orringer MB, eds. Complications in cardiothoracic surgery. St. Louis: Mosby Year Book, 1991:195–201.

30. Mee R. The arterial switch operation. In: Stark J and de Leval M, eds. Surgery for congenital heart defects. Philadelphia: WB Saunders, 1994:495.

31. Williams WG, Freedom RM, Trusler GA. Management of complications related to atrial switch procedures for transposition of the great arteries. In: Waldhausen JA, Orringer MB, eds. Complications in cardiothoracic surgery. St. Louis: Mosby Year Book, 1991:190–4.

32. Goldman AP, Deluis RE, Deanfield JE, Macrae DJ. Nitric oxide is superior to prostacyclin for pulmonary hypertension after cardiac operations. Ann Thorac Surg 1995;60:300–6.

33. Mosca RS, Bove EL, Crowley DC, Sandhy SK, Schork MA, Kulik TJ. Hemodynamic characteristics of neonates following first stage palliation for hypoplastic left heart syndrome. Circulation 1995;92(suppl 2):II-267–71.

34. Norwood WI Jr. Hypoplastic left heart syndrome. Ann Thorac Surg 1991;52:688–95.

35. Riordan CJ, Rahdsbaek F, Storey JH, Montgomery WD, Santamore WP, Austin EH. Inotropes in the hypoplastic left heart syndrome: effects in an animal model. Ann Thorac Surg 1996;62:83–90.

36. Riordan RJ, Locher JP, Santamore WP, Villafane J, Austin EH. Monitoring systemic venous saturations in the hypoplastic left heart syndrome. Ann Thorac Surg 1997;63:835–7.

37. Twedell JS, Hoffman GM, Fedderly RT, et al. Phenoxybenzamine improves systemic oxygen delivery following Norwood palliation of hypoplastic left heart syndrome. Pre-

sented at the 34th annual meeting of The Society of Thoracic Surgeons, New Orleans, LA, January 1998.

38. Kirklin JW, Barratt-Boyes BG. Cardiac surgery, 2nd ed. New York: Churchill Livingstone, 1993:61–128.

39. Bellinger DC, Jonas RA, Rappaport LA, et al. Developmental and neurologic status of children after open heart surgery with hypothermic circulatory arrest or low-flow cardiopulmonary bypass. N Engl J Med 1995;332:549–55.

Part 2 Appendices

Appendix 1   Pediatric Drug Doses

Drug Class	Dosage
Analgesics and sedatives	
Acetaminophen	5–15 mg/kg/dose PO/PR q4–6h
Chloral hydrate	30–50 mg/kg/dose PO/PR q8h
Codeine	0.5–1.0 mg/kg/dose PO q4–6h
Diazepam	0.1–0.2 mg/kg/dose IV q2–4h
Fentanyl	2–5 μg/kg/dose IV q1–2h or a continuous infusion of 2–5 μg/kg/h
Meperidine	1 mg/kg/dose IM/IV q2–4h
Midazolam	0.05–0.2 mg/kg IV q1–2h, then a continuous infusion of 0.4–1.2 μg/kg/min
Morphine sulfate	0.05–0.1 mg/kg IV/IM q1–2h or a continuous infusion of 10–40 μg/kg/h
Antiarrhythmics	
Adenosine	0.05–0.25 mg/kg rapid IV bolus
Bretylium	5–10 mg/kg IV over 10 minutes
Esmolol	0.5 mg/kg IV load over 1 minute, then a continuous infusion of 0.1–0.25 mg/kg/min
Lidocaine	1 mg/kg IV, followed by a continuous infusion of 20–50 μg/kg/min
Procainamide	IV: 2–5 mg/kg over 10 minutes, followed by a continuous infusion of 20–80 μg/kg/min
Propranolol	IV: 0.01–0.2 mg/kg over 10 minutes PO: 0.5 mg/kg/day ÷ q6h
Quinidine	Test dose 2 mg/kg PO, then 15–60 mg/kg/d PO ÷ q6h
Verapamil	0.1–0.2 mg/kg/dose IV
Antibiotics	
Cefazolin	25–100 mg/kg/d IV ÷ q8h
Ceftriaxone	50–100 mg/kg/d IV ÷ q12–24h
Cephalexin	25–100 mg/kg/d PO ÷ q6h
Gentamicin	<7 days old: 5 mg/kg/d IV ÷ q12h 7 days–5 years: 7.5 mg/kg/d IV ÷ q8h 5–10 years: 6 mg/kg/d IV ÷ q8h >10 years: 5 mg/kg/d IV ÷ q8h
Vancomycin	<1 week old: 30 mg/kg/d IV ÷ q8h >1 week old: 40–60 mg/kg/d IV ÷ q8h
Anticonvulsants	
Diazepam	0.1–0.3 mg/kg/dose IV slowly
Phenobarbital	10 mg/kg IV load × 1–2 doses; maintenance dose of 3–5 mg/kg/d ÷ q12h
Phenytoin	10 mg/kg IV slowly × 1–2 doses; maintenance dose of 5 mg/kg/d ÷ q12h

continued

Drug Class	Dosage
Antihypertensives	
Captopril	0.5–3.0 mg/kg/d PO ÷ q8h
Esmolol	0.5 mg/kg IV load over 1 minute, then a continuous infusion of 0.1–0.25 mg/kg/min
Hydralazine	IV: 0.1–0.3 mg/kg/dose q4–6h PO: 0.75–3 mg/kg/d ÷ q6–12h
Labetalol	0.25 mg/kg IV load over 5 minutes; 0.1–0.2 mg/kg/min maintenance infusion starting 30 min later
Nitroprusside	0.5–5 µg/kg/min IV
Propranolol	IV: 0.01–0.2 mg/kg over 10 min PO: 0.5 mg/kg/dose q6h
Bronchodilators	
Albuterol	0.25–0.5 mL in 2 mL normal saline q6–8h via nebulizer
Aminophylline	IV: 6 mg/kg IV load over 20 min, followed by an infusion of 0.2–0.9 mg/kg/h (< age 1) or 0.8–1.1 mg/kg/h (ages 1–9)
Isoetharine	0.25–0.5 mL of 1% solution in 2.5 mL normal saline q4h
Racemic epinephrine	0.25–0.5 mL in 2.5 mL normal saline via nebulizer
Terbutaline	0.01 mg/kg SC or 2 µg/kg IV over 5 minutes, followed by a continuous infusion of 0.08 µg/kg/min
Theophylline	3–4 mg/kg/dose q6h
Diuretics	
Acetazolamide	5 mg/kg/dose IV/PO q12h
Chlorothiazide	10 mg/kg/dose PO q12h
Ethacrynic acid	0.5–1.0 mg/kg/dose IV
Furosemide	0.5–3.0 mg/kg/dose IV/PO q6–8h
Hydrochlorothiazide	1–1.5 mg/kg/dose PO q12h
Mannitol	0.25–0.5 g/kg/dose IV over 3–5 min
Inotropes and vasopressors	
Amrinone	1 mg/kg load, then a continuous infusion of 10 µg/kg/min
Dobutamine	2–10 µg/kg/min
Dopamine	2–20 µg/kg/min
Epinephrine	0.05–0.5 µg/kg/min **ARREST:** 0.1–0.3 mL/kg of 1:10,000 solution (0.1 mg/mL)
Isoproterenol	0.05–1.0 µg/kg/min IV
Milrinone	50 µg/kg load, then a continuous infusion of 0.375–0.75 µg/kg/min
Norepinephrine	0.05–1.0 µg/kg/min IV
Phenylephrine	0.5–5.0 µg/kg/min IV bolus: 5–20 µg/kg/dose

continued

Drug Class	Dosage
Muscle relaxants	
Atracurium	0.5 mg/kg/dose IV
Pancuronium	0.1 mg/kg IV q1h, or a continuous infusion of 0.05–0.1 mg/kg IV
Succinylcholine	1.5 mg/kg/dose IV
Vecuronium	0.1 mg/kg IV q1h, or a continuous infusion of 0.05–0.1 mg/kg/h
Pulmonary vasodilators	
Nitroglycerin	0.5–5.0 µg/kg/min
Nitroprusside	0.5–5.0 µg/kg/min
Prostaglandin E_1	0.05–0.2 µg/kg/min
Tolazoline	1–2 mg/kg IV bolus over 10 minutes, then 1–2 mg/kg/h
Other	
Acetaminophen	10–15 mg/kg/dose PR q3h for fever
Atropine	0.01–0.03 mg/kg IV
	ARREST: 0.02 mg/kg (0.1 mg/mL solution) IV/IM/ET tube
Calcium chloride	**ARREST:** 10–20 mg/kg (0.1–0.2 mL/kg of a 10% solution)
Calcium gluconate	100–200 mg/kg/d in IV fluids
Cimetidine	5–10 mg/kg/dose PO/IV q6h
Dexamethasone	0.25–0.5 mg/kg IV q6h
Digoxin	Digitalizing dose: 30 µg/kg IV and 40 µg/kg PO; give 50% initially and 25% 8 and 16 hours later
	Maintenance: 3.5 µg/kg IV q12h or 4.5 µg/kg PO q12h
Naloxone	0.01 mg/kg/dose IV; repeat PRN q3 min
Potassium	0.5 mEq/kg/h maximum infusion rate
Sodium bicarbonate	1 mEq/kg/dose

Appendix 2   Body Surface Nomogram for Children

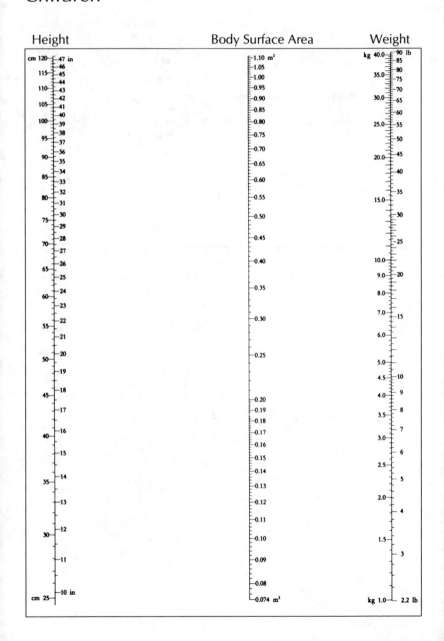

Index

Note: t = table, f = figure, a = appendix